"*Talking Jazz* is rife with all of the stuff th
touching, in particular, those who happen to be
of book that brings a breath of fresh air to an asphyxiating, literary jazz world . . . Mr. Sidran has gone far below the surface of emotions to the very core of our feelings."
—Benny Golson

"Sidran doesn't just ask his guests questions, he interacts with them much in the same way he would if he were accompanying them on a jazz gig, letting the soloist or the singer make a statement, followed by his response to the statement, adding to the overall vocabulary of the tune. This type of interviewing is a godsend to the jazz musicians who have had to put up with years of musically, and often times, racially insensitive questions, cliches and half-truths . . . Sidran's poise, intelligence and ease of delivery puts the most guarded musician at ease, as evidenced by his sensitive interview with the 'Prince of Darkness,' Miles Davis."
—Eugene Holley, Jr., *Quarterly Black Review of Books*

"Ben's knowledge about the music and interest in the music is really inspiring to us as musicians."
—Max Roach

"Ben Sidran's message [is] that we are all fans, in one way or another, and that our job is to be true to the demands of our fandom. If we deal with the music we love on its own terms, speaking to it as honestly and as directly as it has spoken to us, then we have earned the right to call some of its freedom our own."
—*Chicago Tribune*

"[Sidran] covers virtually all stylistic twists since bebop, from cornerstones (Miles and Diz) to Young Turks (Wynton/Branford)—even less obvious choices like Donald Fagen, Charles Brown and Steve Gadd. The conversations are relaxed and illuminating."
—Scott Isler, *Musician*

"Sidran knows a lot about these people and he's excited about their art, so he didn't find it hard to get them to talk. He gives us as much of the atmosphere as he can, preserving the verbal idiosyncrasies. . . . As you read, light bulbs switch on: *that's* what was going on when she recorded that; *now* I can see where he got that sound."
—Greg Burk, *LA Weekly*

"A fascinating kaleidoscopic view of some [of jazz's] major proponents, in their own words."
—*Philadelphia Tribune*

Talking Jazz

An Oral History

EXPANDED EDITION

by Ben Sidran

Photographs by Lee Tanner

DA CAPO PRESS

First Da Capo Press edition 1995

This Da Capo Press paperback edition of *Talking Jazz* is a revised and expanded edition of the one originally published in Petaluma, California in 1992, here supplemented with photographs by Lee Tanner. It is reprinted by arrangement with Ben Sidran.

03 04 05 06 07 - 04 03 02 01 00

Published by Da Capo Press, Inc.
A member of the Perseus Books Group

Manufactured in the United States of America

This book is dedicated to

Judy, Leo and Peaches,

a great rhythm section.

Contents

Introduction to the First Edition

The following talks took place between the summer of 1984 and the spring of 1990. Edited versions of these conversations aired on the National Public Radio series "Sidran On Record," which ultimately amounted to more than one hundred interviews, interspersed with musical demonstrations and recorded examples. While the transcriptions in this book lack these aids, they were taken from original interview tapes, rather than the edited radio shows, and so in some instances are a more complete record of what was said than were the programs.

Of course, we lose a lot going from the living voice to the printed page. Imagine the voice of Miles Davis coming to you across a table on the patio of his Malibu beachhouse, with waves breathing in the background. On the other hand, these interviews read as well as they played on the air, and you can really get a sense of the individual. In editing the text, I've tried to keep as much of the spoken voice as possible, preserving things like syntax, rhythm and idiom. You'll find a fair number of "ahs" and "umms," which give you an idea of favorite "thinking markers," and describe the air in the room. Looking back at the many afternoons and evenings spent talking, an ardent fan was sitting there, whose main objective was to capture the human side of some great artistis. In Phil Woods' phrase, these are America's "warriors," or "samurai," in the language of Abdullah Ibrahim.

As the subtitle says, this is essentially an oral history of a period in American music, as told by a cross-section of people who breathed life into it. And even though trying to capture an oral tradition in writing is like "trying to capture the sea in a fish net," there is always the hope that these interviews, at minimum, show the kinds of things a musician has to deal with on a day-to-day basis, the things they like to talk about. There is also some illumination of the mechanics of making the music, of improvisation and other methods of the art. These interviews, then, can be read on many levels: as anecdotes, instruction, first person *reportage*, reports from the battle front.

Actually, these aren't interviews so much as directed conversations. For the most part, we just hung out and talked about whatever came up, areas of mutual interest. The time spent, usually a few hours, passed very quickly. Of course, I did have favorite topics, and, from time to time, an agenda. I pursued questions like "What is style?" and "How does one find it?" or "What is the impact of technology on jazz?" and "What's the difference between captured music and manufactured music?" I suppose these themes might provide a kind of backbone to the series. But, as so often happens in jazz, what you stumble on is better than what you're looking for. Because, for me, something fascinating is how often these folks revert back to a single generality to explain the heart of their work: the concept of "sound."

It's one of those deceptively simple ideas—what do things *sound* like? —but it comes up so many times that one would be a fool to dismiss it as merely another limitation of the language, or the inability of one language (English) to describe another (Jazz). Whether it was Miles Davis talking, or Gil Evans or McCoy Tyner or Michel Petrucciani, or any number of other people, it was clear that the essence of their work is not in the choice of notes but in the *sound* of those notes. And, as corollary, the sound of those notes (their acoustic shape) is determined by the way in which they arrive. Style, then, is a function of music that arrives right *on time* and in absolutely the "right way." There is a kind of definitiveness about jazz when it's done right, as if it couldn't have happened any other way. Style is the expression of a personal imperative. Miles says, "It's like your sweat."

But again, this was the subtext, and was rarely on our minds when we met, drank coffee, and passed the time in front of a microphone. In fact, one of the greatest pleasures of living the jazz life is just how down to earth it all is. If it doesn't play on the street, it's left on the floor. The old saw still cuts: "It don't mean a thing if it ain't got that swing." Jazz is stuff you can *use*.

I owe these jazz people more than thanks for getting me through so many long days. Often they were like old friends even when we were meeting for the first time, because their music is so generous and so candid. I also owe them a sense of family that I'll always carry with me. And to the friends, and the friends of friends, who through the years turned me on to so much great music, and, later on, to so many of the great people who made it, I owe thanks for giving me a constantly changing way to look at what I carry around inside my head.

—***Ben Sidran***
1992

Introduction to the Da Capo Edition

Since the original publication of *Talking Jazz*, I've had the chance to discuss its themes with many people. The two topics that come up most often are, "Well, how *is* jazz doing these days?" and "What's jazz all about, anyway?" Obviously, these are part of the same question, and therefore the same answer applies:

In many ways, these are the best of times and the worst of times for jazz.

On the one hand, music schools are turning out thousands of thoroughly prepared young players who, at an earlier age, are better versed in the grammar and idioms of jazz than ever before. The recorded evidence speaks eloquently of the "success" of our education system. Again and again, a major record label touts another nineteen- or twenty-year-old musician who is burning up their instrument, playing quotes from the old masters, and leapfrogging through the most difficult chord sequences with the greatest of ease. In the popular press and the trades alike, this is offered up as the promise of a bright jazz future.

On the other hand, most of the new jazz prodigies don't *sound* like anybody. That is, you can't identify their voice on their instrument of choice; you can't pick them out of a crowd. They are just musical faces in a landscape overpopulated with faces. Often dressed in expensive suits and beautifully backlit in photos, they offer up very little in the way of hope or salve for the human condition. In short, they are playing notes rather than feelings.

Why is this? How can one master every aspect of jazz technique and vocabulary but somehow fail to develop one's own voice? Indeed, why does the former sometimes preclude the latter?

There's an old saying that addresses this question: "It ain't what you do, it's the way how you do it." The *way* "how you do it" is *style*. And style is the substance of jazz; it's what jazz is all about.

Perhaps the greatest mystery in the life of a jazz musician is just where this style comes from. Clearly, it's not in the notes, because anybody can play a given sequence of notes. The infinite line of monkeys will eventually come up with the exact composition "'Round Midnight," only it will take a very long time. It's not in the technical mastery, or speed, because often the fastest players are the most boring to listen to.

Why doesn't today's education lead to the development of style?

First of all, we are too often trained to listen without hearing. Not just that we often don't take the time to peer with our ears into the heart of the music and *feel* the relationships between the colors and voices. Or that in attempting to do so we often focus on the literal notes that are being played instead of the larger shadows that are being cast by the movement of great forces. Rather, we are tricked into believing that the information we seek is *literally* there.

Education forces us to categorize what we experience, to define a thing so that we can dispense with it. Jazz students strive to understand that which has practical value to them at the moment: What notes are being played? Is it the raised ninth or the flatted ninth? Yes, the difference is important, but, no, knowing the difference does not necessarily lead to style.

Over and over again, we prove that we can pull the wings off the butterfly to understand the mechanics of its flight and in so doing we end all future possibilities of the same. The notes are the wings; the *sound* is the flight.

While jazz musicians are usually the last to explain *how* they arrive at their sound, they are united and very clear about the fact that it is their *sound* that is the key to their style. The physical sound that they produce, the timbral qualities of their musical voice, rather than the rationality of their note choice, is the heart of the issue. They may talk about their approach to this particular musical puzzle or that specific series of chords, but when you mention their "voice," they just smile and shake their head.

Think of it as a human voice, the sound of a friend calling on the phone. You can distinguish a friend's voice from the first "hello." So too a jazz musician's "sound"; from the first two notes, you know it's Miles or Dizzy or whomever. Their voice, as it emerges through the *act* of making music, can be as recognizable as a friend's. Or, in the case of many of the young "suits," as faceless as the computer down at the telephone company.

The key is that playing jazz is a very physical thing. One spends thousands of hours wrestling with a bit of brass, a few strings or a handful of keys. The "sound" that is produced over years is a product of physical relationships and physical habits, good (i.e. the way Elvin Jones sits on his drum stool prepares him to leap off into the rhythm), bad (i.e. Dizzy Gillespie's huge cheek "pouches" indicate wrong technique but no doubt contributed to his sound) and unique (i.e. Thelonious Monk's straight fingered approach to the keyboard gave his musical lines their distinctive angularity). This physicality in large part determines the quality, the recognizability of the voice.

Indeed, more than a few of the musicians in this collection liken playing music to playing sports, usually basketball. In either occupation, you have to react faster than you can possibly think, rely on motor memory to get you through the ongoing rush of the moment, and trust in the common experience of your fellow players. Yet, ironically, it appears that at the heart of improvisation is a kind of stillness, an active state of readiness, of *not*-doing but allowing the music to be done to and through you. John Coltrane once put it succinctly: "The music doesn't belong to anybody; it passes through us all."

So one's sound really is the sum product of how one physically spends time, both with and without the instrument, both doing and not-doing. Indeed, how one approaches the passage of time itself, and the concept of work, and the act of breathing, and the process of listening, all these are part of the process of hearing and finding your own sound. *How* you stand and wait for the music to arrive determines *what* music will arrive. If one is posing, then what arrives will be the voice of a poseur.

Eventually, the relationship between player and instrument takes on a perverse inversion; the instrument begins to work on the player and ultimately, a jazz musician is not learning to play the music so much as learning to be himself. Learning how to stand. (Miles Davis once said, "You can tell everything about the way I play by watching how I stand"; see his remarks that follow.) How to breathe. How to walk. How to listen. The act of making music transforms the individual, and the jazz musician becomes the product itself, the music just the artifact of this process.

If the musician becomes the product, playing the music becomes the transitory act, a kind of diversion that the musician, over time, uses to transmogrify him or herself into a unique embodiment of the jazz attitude. Historically, this process is forged in the furnace of a brutal commercial marketplace, and, at times, confused by the emergence of new technologies that promise ease of execution but often rob one of the ability to *feel* the process happening. (Using the new digital technology for example, has been described as "making love via television.")

Yet, at the point of success, when a player's "voice" emerges, then whatever comes through the gates of perception and execution, regardless of technology employed or musical idiom favored, has both the spirit of jazz and the signature of style. By extension, then, if Miles Davis ordered a cheeseburger, that was, by definition, a *jazz* cheeseburger.

As usual, musicians sum it up best. Charlie Parker once said, "If you don't live it, it won't come out of your horn." Or again, in the words of John Coltrane, "When I hear a player's *sound*, to me, that is his contribution." Style, then, is the ultimate achievement of a musician, not only the telling of his life's story, but his creation of a living will for future generations.

To compound the difficulty, however, the great jazz players have always demonstrated that what you don't play is often more important than what you do play. The space that is left for others to breathe, the creation of psychic air, the intangible relationships between human voices, these are the things that determine the "sound" of what is happening. Perhaps that is why Thelonious Monk, who has been called "the master of space and time," is mentioned more often than any other musician in the following conversations.

Style, then, can be learned but it can't be taught. If it's in the attitude, in the spaces that are left, in the air between players that can only exist when those players congregate, then obviously it is a cultural occurrence. It is a product of people gathering. Style cannot exist in a vacuum. And so one major subtext of these conversations is whether the economic universe of today's music—the endless round of record companies and their focus on the product, the bad radio formats that pose as the gatekeepers of taste, and the hyper-promotions that pass for real events—whether this business of music is such an extreme cultural vacuum that the jazz life is already gradually dying out, even as the forms of jazz thrive at the University level.

It's not in the *notes*. Although, of course, it is *in* the notes, as they are played by a person with a story to tell.

At the heart of jazz, then, is this terrific contradiction: nothing is what it appears to be, but everything is exactly what it is. There are no secrets, and that, of course, is the secret. It is the art, then, of circumlocution, of learning to approach a truth from many sides. The logic is often not linear. For example, note the way Miles Davis talks around a point or subject, approaching it from different angles, stopping midway, changing tack, coming around; the gesture, the attitude of searching comes through.

The logic is in the effort, not the editing. The message is "being there" or "being in the moment," hearing the "sound" of the composition and playing to that. To hear as well as to listen. "Style" is the act of that struggle; "voice" is the sound that struggle makes.

—***Ben Sidran***
1994

Miles Davis (January, 1986)

The following interview was held on a warm January afternoon on the terrace of Miles Davis' beach house in Malibu, California. I had gone to the house with Miles' record producer, Tommy LiPuma, who had told me that Miles' reputation for being a difficult man to talk to was not necessarily true. From the minute Miles opened the large wooden front door to his house and invited us inside, it was obvious that Tommy was right. In fact, when Tommy introduced us, Miles inexplicably gave me a hug. Throughout the interview, which took place during the afternoon and, informally, continued well into the evening, Miles was gracious, humorous and extremely generous with himself and his time. The interview began with us sitting across from each other at a table, with a bowl of potato chips in-between. Miles had a sketch pad in his lap and was drawing with a large magenta felt-tip pen.

Ben: As we're talking, you're starting to do some drawing. I know that drawing has been a big part of how you've been spending your time for the last several years. Have you always been involved in drawing?

Miles: Yeah, my father taught me and my brother. Actually, I showed my brother how to sketch. My brother can see anything and draw it right off, you know. But he doesn't have any imagination like I have.

Ben: So imagination is . . .

Miles: That's it. In everything. Imagination.

Ben: My impression is that your drawings are related to your playing in some ways, the gestures . . .

Miles: What it is is balance. If you make a drawing on a page, you have to balance it, you know. And that's the way most everything is. Art, music, composition, solos, clothes, you know, when you dress up . . .

Ben: Balance.

Miles: Yeah, a little over *here*, a little *there*, a little *there*.

Ben: I first noticed your sketches on the cover of one of your record albums a few years ago. Is drawing something you've always done, has it always been part of your artistic process, or did you become interested in it again later in life?

Miles: Yeah, you know, I stopped for a while. I really started to sketch again after I married Cicely. Because she takes so long. You know how actresses are. They take so long to get ready for anything, you know. Rather than scream at her, I just started sketching. Especially on planes. After we had a close call going to Peru for the Miss Universe Contest. The plane dropped about 2500 feet and then dropped another 1000 feet. And you know everybody was . . . some people were crying. A lot of celebrities were on that flight. And then I started sketching, you know, cause it really scared me. That's really a trip to do that, to go through that.

So now when I fly from New York to California, sometimes I sketch. Most *all* the time I sketch. If I don't go to sleep, I'm sketching. And I've done sketches that took me five hours, you know, to finish. But it relaxes you, you know?

Ben: Are you spending most of your time in California these days?

Miles: Most of the time I try to. I try to stay here because of my circulation. It's good for my circulation. The cold weather really does a number on my skin in New York, and the air's dirty, the streets are dirty. But that pace in New York, I love that pace. I would never live out here all seasons. Just in the winter time. Either here or the south of France.

Ben: You really are part of the greater art community, not just the music community. You're one of the few American jazz musicians to have made that transition.

Miles: From what to what?

Ben: From being thought of as a *player* to being thought of as an *artist*.

Miles: Oh, yeah. Well you know, if I was thought of any way else than that, I wouldn't want to be here. If I couldn't contribute. You know, I was telling some friends in Sweden if I couldn't do anything to help, even if I was in some other form of art, if I couldn't discover something or help the art, or find a new way to do it, you know, I wouldn't want to be here. I would just want to be dead. If I couldn't create. There would be nothing for me to live for. If I couldn't maybe write a composition that I like. Not somebody else; that *I* would like, and my *friends* would like. And they say "Yeah, Miles, that sounds good." If I couldn't do that, I wouldn't want to be here. It's selfish, I know. But geniuses are selfish. [Laughs.]

Ben: Part of your genius it seems has been to take groups of musicians and put them in challenging situations. Looking back over the output of your recorded work, the "newness" a lot of times stands out as much as anything. You're creating situations that force musicians to rely on their instincts rather than their habits.

Miles: That's right. It's the groups of people that you associate with, you know. It's not all *me*. It's them. People like Herbie Hancock, Chick Corea, those people that I work with. They're talented people. Especially when they get in their creative period. People have creative periods, periods where they [snaps his fingers three times], like that, you know? And then if they could just *wait* on that, or recognize it when it's there. *I* recognize it in other people. I recognized it in Wayne Shorter and Herbie and Chick, Keith Jarrett, Sonny Rollins, different people, you know, Philly Joe, Red Garland. George Duke. He is something else, man. See, I saw that. I heard that. You know, he reminds me so much of Herbie. If Herbie would just slow down a little bit. George has great talent. Have a potato chip.

Ben: Thanks. [Eating sounds.] Again, part of the message of your music seems to be "be yourself," and you use minimalism to achieve this. Like those pretty notes you play, as opposed to a lot of notes.

Miles: Pretty notes! If you play a sound you have to pick out . . . it's like the eye of the hurricane, you know? You have to pick out the most important note that fertilizes the sound. You know what I mean? It makes the sound grow, and then it makes it definite so your other colleagues can hear and *react* to it. You know what I mean? If you play what's already there, *they* know it's there. The thing is to bring it out. It's like putting lemon on fish. Or vegetables. You know, it brings out the flavor. That's what they call pretty notes. Just major notes that *should be* played.

And rhythms. I used to, a lot of times, I would tell Herbie to lay out. He wrote a couple of pieces that were up in tempo, and rather than have him play the sound for me, I played the sound for him to listen to, you know? The sound of the composition he wrote. Because if you have too much background, you can't play an up tempo and really do what the composer tries to give . . . to me. And I try to give to the fans and music lovers.

Ben: You talk about the "sound" of the composition, as if a song has a central "sound" to it, a sound source.

Miles: I try to get *his* sound, whoever is writing the composition. If I'm going to play something against that, I have to get the sound that *he* wants in there, without destroying and blowing over it, so as not to bury it. You know what I mean? So it takes a lot . . . it really takes a long time to do that, you know. But if you're leaning that way, it doesn't. But if you aren't, and somebody tells you?

When I was about fifteen, a drummer I was playing a number with at the Castle Ballroom in Saint Louis . . . we had a ten piece band, three trumpets, four saxophones, you know . . . and he asked me, "Little Davis, why don't you play what you played last night?" I said, "What, what do you mean?" He said, "You don't know what it is?" I said, "No, what is it?" He said, "You were playing something coming out of the middle of the tune, and play it again." I said, "I don't know what I played." He said, "If you don't know what you're playing, then you ain't doing nothing."

Well that hit me. Like *bammm.* So I went and got everything, every book that I could get. To learn about theory. To this day, I know what he's talking about. I know what note he was talking about.

Ben: What note was it?

Miles: It was a raised ninth. I mean a flatted ninth. [Laughs.]

Ben: This conversation about the "sound" of the composition brings to mind the recording *Kind Of Blue.* As you know, *Kind of Blue* is probably the number one jazz record on virtually all the jazz critics' lists.

Miles: Isn't that something.

Ben: Does the success of that record surprise you, Miles? It seems to have been such a simple record in a lot of ways.

Miles: Not back then. Because Bill Evans, his approach to the piano brought that piece out. He used to bring me pieces by Ravel. Like the Concerto for Left Hand and Orchestra. Have you heard that? It's a piece Ravel wrote for his friend who went to the army. He came back, but he was a pianist and he lost his right hand. So Ravel wrote a piece for Left Hand and Orchestra, for piano.

And Bill used to tell me about different modes, which I already knew. And we just agreed on something and that's the way that album *went.* We were just *leaning* toward . . . like Ravel, playing a sound with only the white keys . . . and it just came out. It was like the thing to do. You know what I mean? Like an architect, all of a sudden *all* of the architects in the world start making circles, you know, like Frank Lloyd Wright. All his colleagues are leaning the *same* way at the *same* time, you know?

So it was Bill, and it was *made* for Coltrane, you know, that kind of thing. Because I used to give him a lot of chords. I would give him five chords to play in one chord, and I would tell him he could play either way. He was the only one who could do that. But I got it from Rachmaninov, modulating from key to key. Bill and I used to listen to Bartok and, ah, what's his name, who wrote "The Fire Dance"?

Ben: Khachaturian?

Miles: Yeah, Khachaturian. I would give Coltrane little chords like that to play, you know, against one "sound." You know, instead of saying like "D dominant seventh," or something like that, you could play under the chord, over the chord, or a minor third up from the fifth of the chord, you know?

But is has to be a dramatic player like Trane was, who can just turn you on with the sound of one note, and a group of notes. The only two people I ever heard doing that was Charlie Parker and Coltrane. You know, that's the only two that I ever heard in my life do that.

Ben: You mean the rhythmic freedom in the way they run changes?

Miles: Coltrane didn't start playing like that until . . . A girlfriend of mine in France, one day she said, "Miles, these guys want to talk to you; they want to give you a trumpet or something." So I said, "I don't want to talk to anybody." She said, "They just want to talk to you and maybe you can pick out a couple of trumpets that you want." So I said, "OK." So I also got a soprano sax for Trane. And he never put it down. It was on a tour with Norman Granz. He played soprano sax in the bus, in the hotel, every day, all day, 24 hours a day. And he got that "sound." And then I gave him those chords and he just *went*, you know? Because he wasn't playing like that before. Sometimes a player plays so *loud* that it locks in with the sound that he *left*. You know, like *bammm*. It blocks out everything else. So I gave him all these options. I mean, it sounds technical, but you have to think like that if you're an artist, you know. You have to know how to do different things.

Ben: Hearing you talk about this session, I am struck by the fact that like Duke Ellington you would prepare music for your players, rather than bring music to them and say "play this." Your music really does come out of the people you are hanging out with and recording with.

Miles: Yeah, that's right. Duke is one of my favorite composers. Just lately, I have been hearing in my head "Rain Check," that he wrote.

Ben: You mentioned Coltrane's sound on the soprano saxophone. At one point, Coltrane said that he had been hearing a higher sound in his head, but that it wasn't until he got his hands on the soprano that he was actually able to realize what he had been hearing internally all along.

Miles: Right. See, it takes a long time for guys to develop. You know what I mean?

Ben: How come nobody else can get *your* sound? It's a simple thing, a gesture almost, but it is very difficult.

Miles: I have my own sound, because when I was like this [gestures with his hand low to the floor] my trumpet instructor, I loved the way he sounded. He was black and he used to play with Andy Kirk, and the low register like Harold Baker. And you know, I just leaned toward that cornet sound, you know, like Nat Adderley plays cornet? But it's just a "sound." And it's popular. [Laughs.] You know, like years ago, composers . . . the reason you read about Beethoven was because he was the one they could understand. The other ones, you know, that they couldn't understand, they didn't get mentioned. So my tone must be the easiest for somebody to hear. You know, like Louis Armstrong, that kind of sound.

But you see, your sound is like, it's like your sweat. You know, it's your "sound." Lester Young had his sound. Coleman Hawkins, Clifford Brown, Fats. You know, there's no more "sound" today. Freddie [Hubbard] has a sound but it's . . . during those days when you didn't hear anybody to copy, guys got their *own* sound. But now that you have so many records and cassettes, it's not about sound, you know what I mean? That's the reason they can put the sound in a keyboard [a digital sampling device]. But it's the white sound in the keyboard. It's the white trumpet player's sound in the keyboard.

Ben: You can't put the black sound in a digital sampling keyboard?

Miles: Nobody's done it yet.

Ben: That's an interesting point, that before there was such wide recording distribution, people were forced to develop their own sounds.

Miles: Forced to play without . . . they didn't have anything to listen to, you know? But you *would* watch guys play an instrument and you would like the attitude, the concept, the way it *looks*, they way they hold it, the way they dress. But nowadays, they have . . . I saw maybe three trumpet players in Lionel Hampton's band, and they were white, right? They all sound alike. Wynton [Marsalis]. He doesn't have a distinctive sound. But Freddie almost has. Woody Shaw is a real creative trumpet player. He's like Dizzy. They might do anything. I mean you can still get a good solo out of Dizzy 'cause he's . . . he really turned my brain. And Charlie Parker. You know those guys, they did a number on my head. As far as me learning.

Ben: How did they do it?

Miles: They just opened it up.

Ben: You mean just hearing and watching them?

Miles: See, what they were thinking, it put a stamp on what I was thinking, that it was OK to go like that.

Ben: You mentioned people getting excited just watching a player. I remember you said one time that we could know everything there was to know about your playing by watching how you stand.

Miles: It's a certain way, like when I play, sometimes if I play about that high from the floor [holds his hand out three feet above the floor] it's another sound that you can get . . . there might be one over there [raises his hand higher], may be one up there, but I never go any higher than that. Standing straight up maybe.

But I found out in Julliard that if I stayed any longer, you know, I was going to have to play like a white man. I was going to have to *act* like a white man toward music. The direction, you know what I mean, so I left. Because there was certain things you had to do, or a certain way you had to play to get in there, to be with them. And I didn't come all the way from St. Louis just to be with a white orchestra. You know, I turned down a lot of those.

But I found that I could go my own way. I said to my friend Freddie Webster, I said, "Freddie, I'm going back to St. Louis . . ." And he was one of those who said, "Man, you know if you go to St. Louis, back to St. Louis and them hooges and crackers there, you're going to get mad and blah blah blah . . . you know, you might get killed." So I said, "No, I have to go tell my father that I'm gonna leave Julliard." He said, "Why don't you call him up?" I said, "Uh uh, not my father. I can't call him up and say I'm going with Bird and they do *this* and Dizzy is *this*." You know, my father was a professional man. He was a surgeon. So I caught the train, I went in his office, he looked up and said, "What the fuck are you doing here?" I said, "As soon as you get through." He was working on a patient. He's a dentist. So when he got through I said, "This music is happening, Julliard isn't, and I'm down on the street where everything is happening. I'm learning more down there, what *I* want to do, than at Julliard." My trumpet instructor at Julliard is *still* in the Philharmonic Orchestra, New York. But I couldn't do that, you know? So he said, "OK." So I said, "Save your money." So that was it. But I couldn't stay. I couldn't stay.

[He looks at the sketch he's making.] Damn, am I messing up something right now?

I couldn't phone my father from New York and tell him that. Duke Ellington he knew, but not Dizzy and Bird and Monk and Coleman Hawkins. Although we did have a record of "Body and Soul." And Art Tatum. That's the only records we had in our house.

Ben: Those two records?

Miles: Art Tatum and Duke with Jimmy Blanton. Blanton is from St. Louis, from my home town. Oh yeah, I had Bird with Jay McShann, "Hootie Blues." And Basie. Yeah, we had a few, but that was after I knew what I wanted to hear. Cause those bands, those days, Earl Hines and Jimmy Lunceford . . . Sonny Stitt was with the McKinney Cotton Pickers, and they heard about me in St. Louis and they wanted me to go with them, and my mother wouldn't let me go. And I said, "Ah, shit!"

Ben: You got there by going to Julliard instead.

Miles: Right.

Ben: These days you're talking about seem so far away from today. The times, the way the music was treated by players . . .

Miles: Yeah, I know. Something else gets in your mind, in my head, but those are good memories for me, you know.

Ben: It seems people today, even musicians, do have difficulty keeping interested in the music, when in the past, it was everything.

Miles: You know, it's because they don't take time out to learn different things. They wouldn't take time out to do that. A jazz musician that you call a jazz musician . . . I was reading this damn thing in *The Times* about jazz legends. These legends shouldn't have to call people and ask them, can we play here and stuff like that. I don't do that. I would *never* do that, you know. I didn't get into music just to make money. If I wanted to make money, I know what to do.

Ben: It seems a major thing has happened to all music, not just jazz, and that is it's moved from music that was *captured* in a recording studio to music that was *manufactured* in a recording studio. It's a whole different premise now, the way music is being made. How was recording your latest album, which is done with drum machines and sequencers, different from the way you used to make a record, where you came in with some tunes, did them and left? Do you approach it a lot differently or does it feel the same to you?

Miles: It's easier.

Ben: Really?

Miles: Um hum. Because I show the guys I'm working with what I want. I write it out or play it. And then by the time I get to the studio, it's all on tape. You feed it right into the board. And all I have to do is play over it. It's easier like that. I like to went crazy trying to make *Decoy*. I mean I threw everything out. Now, I just take a studio, we use a drum machine to keep it in, 'cause I tried to put things together in *Decoy*, and they, you know, the ones that didn't have a drum machine, the tempo was doing this and doing that. Musicians feel sad, they have personalities. Like Al Foster, and like some of them want to play and there's no part for them anymore. I can see they don't feel it. But rather than wait for two and three sessions for them to feel like it and learn the composition, they add to the composition, rather than playing over it. Like a lot of guys do, they play too many fucking notes. Like Mike Stern. I tell him all the time, I said, "Mike, you need to go to Notes Anonymous." You know, like Alcoholics Anonymous? I mean, it's much easier now for me.

Because, you know, like a guy like George Duke, he writes a composition, it's all there, all you have to do is play on it, and respect that man's composition. But you have to pick the people that you want.

You see, my voice is changing, because this is very touchy with me. I don't want to fire him, I don't want to fire these guys. But I do want, when a person writes a composition, you have to let that composition *soak in*. You know what I mean? You have to try to *see* or *hear* what the composer wanted, you know, and you have to play that *style*. Not that you're just gonna play *your* style in somebody else's music. If they composed it, they didn't want that kind of thing in there. And you gonna do it on every number?

So we don't need that. Or if you're in the rhythm section and the tempo drops, you get mad 'cause somebody tells you the tempo dropped. We don't need *that*. We have time and it's right there. As long as electricity is *on*, the tempo is like *that*. And you don't have to use an excuse like I can't play with the drum machine, you know, there's no excuse. If you're a musician, if you love music, you would want "Body and Soul" to sound like "Body and Soul."

Ben: Well, what about "Body and Soul," and what about those classic songs?

Miles: Those songs to me don't exist, you know? I'm not gonna play that shit. We don't have time for "Body and Soul," and "I Got Rhythm," you know? Or "So What," or "Kind of Blue." Those things are *there*. They were done in that era, the right hour, the right day, and it happened. It's over, it's on the record. People ask me why don't you play this. Go buy the record. It's still there. What you like is on the record. You don't like *me*, and I don't want you to like me, because of "Kind of Blue." Like me for what we're doing now, you know?

I was put here to play music, and interpret music. That's what I do. No attitude, nothing. That's *all* I want to do. And I do it good. 'Cause my colleagues say "Yeah," you know what I mean, and that's enough for me to keep doing what I do.

I stopped playing the trumpet. Dizzy came over to my house. He said, "What the fuck is wrong with you? Are you crazy or something?" I say "Man, you better get out of here." He said, "No, I'm not either." He's like my brother, you know? But that's it for me. All the rest, people think I do *this*, I do *that*. Yeah, I do *that* and *this*. I might do a lot of things, but the main thing that I *love*, that comes before everything, even breathing, is music. That's it, you know. Nothing. I buy Ferraris, yeah, but music is always there. Right here.

Ben: And that means that you're going to have to keep hanging out with musicians . . .

Miles: That's right.

Ben: And you're going to have to keep your ear tuned to the radio, and you're going to have to plug in all the latest equipment?

Miles: Right.

Ben: Because you can't go back.

Miles: Uh uh. I can't.

Ben: As we've been sitting here talking, you've been drawing. And it's almost been one gesture, drawing and talking . . .

Miles: Right, it's the same thing.

Ben: I got one more question for you. The song "Nardis." How did you happen to name it "Nardis."

Miles: I can't remember. It might have had something to do with nuclear power. I wrote it for Cannonball [Adderley]. I think I just liked the name. What does it mean?

Ben: I don't know, but it's my last name backwards.

Miles: No kidding? No kidding. I don't know, but that's a nice name, man.

* * *

Gil Evans (September, 1986)

At the start of our talk, Gil Evans says, "It's hard to believe," in response to the longevity of his career. What's even harder to believe is how youthful this 75-year-old composer/arranger appeared in person. He arrived at the recording studio wearing blue jeans, running shoes and a polo shirt, and, in part because of his extreme thinness, he exuded the aura of a man at least twenty years younger. It was only after talking to him for a few minutes that one realized the deceptive nature of his appearance. For while he maintained a youthful outlook and the take-it-as-it-comes attitude of a true jazzman, his personal power and his force among younger musicians were precisely tied to the wisdom gained from too many years spent as an outsider to financial success.

Ben: You're a busy man these days. You've written the scores to a couple of films, *Absolute Beginners* and also *The Color of Money*, and you continue to lead a big band on Monday nights here in New York City. But you've been wearing many hats for many decades . . .

Gil: It's hard to believe. Really hard to believe. Of course the only time I know how old I am is when I look in the mirror, right? When I don't look in the mirror, I *never* think of that. But the mirror has to remind me.

Ben: Allow me to also remind you of a time back in the 1930s when you became associated with Claude Thornhill's band.

Gil: Yeah, right, I met Claude Thornhill in Hollywood. I came out there to write some arrangements for this band, Skinny Ennis's band, who was on the Bob Hope show. And I was writing arrangements for that.

Claude had an insurance policy that he was going to cash in, and he couldn't decide whether to go to Tahiti for the rest of his life or go back to New York and start a band. Which he decided to do. So I said to him, "If you ever need an arranger, let me know." So when his chief arranger got drafted, he sent for me. That was in 1941, '42. Then we all got drafted. So when he reorganized back in '46, I was with him again for a while.

But by that time, the scene had changed. The swing band era was over, right? He just missed it by that three or four years in the service. He could have scored, but coming back into it again, pop music had come along and rock and roll, and folk and all that. So he had a hard time booking the band. And the band was big. It was a wonderful workshop for me.

It had three trumpets and two trombones and two french horns and two altos, two tenors, baritone and a separate flute section, right? Three flute players, didn't play anything but flutes. And a tuba. So it was a big nut for him, and he finally had to give it up.

Ben: Was it Claude's idea to include the french horns and the tuba, initially?

Gil: The french horns were his idea, yeah. But the tuba, I got that in there. And the flutes. But the french horns he had quite a while. He had them before the war, too, you know.

He was like a practical joker, in a way. And so a clarinet was out in front of the band playing "Summertime" . . . I don't know if you ever heard of a clarinet player named Fazola?

Ben: Sure, Irving Fazola.

Gil: Beautiful tone, and oh, no one ever had a more beautiful tone than Fazola. So he's out there playing "Summertime," and Claude signaled to these two guys, and they came up from the audience and sat down and started playing these french horns in sustained harmony underneath him. And nobody in the band knew that was going to happen. Faz couldn't believe it. He looked around.

But the band sounded like horns anyway, even before he got them. It was one of the first bands that played without a vibrato, you know. Because the vibrato had been "in" all the time in jazz, ever since, well, Louis Armstrong, you know, that vibrato. But then Claude's band played with no vibrato, and that's what made it compatible with bebop. Because the bebop players were playing with no vibrato. And they were also interested in the impressionistic harmony, you know, that I had used with Claude. The minor ninths and all that.

That's how we got together, really. That's the reason we got together. Because of the fact that there was no vibrato plus the harmonic development. Because up until that time, with the swing bands, mostly the harmony had been from Fletcher Henderson, really. Where you harmonize everything with the major sixth chords and passing tones with a diminished chord, you know. So that was how things changed with bebop.

Ben: Also, the addition of the french horns and the tuba got the arrangements out of the more traditional "sections"—brass section, woodwind section—and made it more of a continuous palette for you.

Gil: Well, when Miles and I got together to do the Capitol record [*Birth of the Cool*] we just had to figure out how few instruments, and which ones, we could use to cover the harmonic needs of Claude Thornhill's band, you know. Naturally, with a big band like that, you have a lot of doubles. But we just trimmed it down to the six horns. Six horns and three rhythm, and those six horns covered all the harmonic needs that we had.

Ben: You mention the Miles session. I'm thinking particularly of the song "Boplicity," with the ensemble that included J.J. Johnson, Lee Konitz, John Lewis, Kenny Clark, John Barber . . .

Gil: Who was on french horn? Gunther Schuller?

Ben: I think it was Sandy Sieglestein . . .

Gil: Sandy, yeah, he played with Claude Thornhill. Great horn player.

Ben: That particular recording very quietly started some sort of revolution in jazz.

Gil: I wasn't even there. You know, I had to go home to see my mother in California, so I wrote that arrangement and gave it to Miles. But we were all so in tune with each other that I didn't have any worries at all. They just played it, and when I heard it, it was as though I had been there.

That's the way it was with all the records I made with Miles, the big band records, too. Because even though the notes were different, and they weren't familiar with the arrangements, they were so familiar with the idiom, you know, that we made those big band records in three three-hour sessions with no rehearsal. Nowadays, that's unheard of, right? You get a hundred hours, now, or more. But we got nine hours to make that thing, with no rehearsals. But the band, the whole band I picked out, they had the idiom under their fingers. So it was possible to do that.

And that's the way it was with the "Boplicity" band too. And Miles, he's the best lead trumpet player I know.

Ben: That band, the "Boplicity" band, came together through a series of informal gatherings at your apartment over a couple of years.

Gil: I rented a room a couple of blocks from 52nd Street, you know. When I got off the train, I got in a cab and I went right to 52nd Street. I didn't have a place to stay. I threw my bag in a check room and I just walked up and down The Street there and met a bunch of my heroes. First night, I met all my heroes! I met Ben [Webster] and Lester [Young], Erroll Garner and Bud Powell, all these people the first night.

So I got a room a couple blocks away, a basement room. Just one big room with a bed and a piano and a record player and a sink. And I left the door open for two years. Just left it open. I never locked it. When I went out, I never locked it. So sometimes I'd come home and I'd meet strangers. And most of the time I met people like Miles and John Lewis and people like that. George Russell.

We talked a lot about harmony. How to get a "sound" out of harmony. Because the harmony has a lot to do with what the music is going to "sound" like. The instruments have their wave form and all that, but the harmony means that you're putting together a group of instruments, and they're going to get their own independent wave form, right? You can't get it any other way except as an ensemble together.

So Miles and I talked about that lots of times. And played chords on the piano. And that's how it happened.

Ben: The "sound" that you did come up with so perfectly suited Miles' sound that it almost seemed like one gesture.

Gil: That's right . . .

Ben: You talk about the extension of the Thornhill sound. You once said about the Thornhill band that "the band was a reduction to inactivity, a stillness . . ."

Gil: Oh, it was. That's right.

Ben: And "the sound would hang like a cloud."

Gil: That's right. Oh yeah.

Ben: Part of what you created, then, in the "Boplicity" session is a new approach to jazz, where even with a small group, it wasn't a separate thing, a rhythm section and a horn section, but rather it was a "sound." Almost a studio form before there were studio forms.

Gil: Yeah, right.

Ben: You mention the *Miles Ahead* big band session. "Boplicity" was recorded in 1949 . . .

Gil: We didn't get together again until '57 . . .

Ben: Miles Ahead was eight years later. What did you do in the interim?

Gil: [Long pause]. Let me see, what did I do. Well, I got married. That was a big thing for me, you know. I was 38 before I got married the first time.

I was really waiting around for Miles, to tell you the truth, during those years. I did a lot of like club date work. A singer would want an arrangement that would sound OK with five men or fifteen men, so I would write some stock arrangement type things for singers. Not the greatest work by any means, but . . .

There was a vocal coach named Sid Shaw, and he had me and a piano player named Jimmy Lyons, and we would go around to these different people's houses, and Sid would pick out the songs that he felt they should sing in their act, and we would write the music for them. So I did quite a bit of that.

Ben: You had started playing piano too, professionally, in that period, hadn't you?

Gil: That's what I did. Yeah, that's right, I went out and played weddings and beer parties, and I played a year downtown at a place called The Nut Club, which is now called Studio One. On Sheridan Square. Well there was a place that had been there since the speakeasy days called

The Nut Club, so I worked there for a year, just to get the practice of playing. And we had drums and tenor, so I would play the bass part. It was a good experience for me. 76 a week.

Ben: 76 a week?

Gil: 76 dollars a week. Incredible.

And then in 1956, I made my first album with Helen Merrill. And then I saw Miles in '56, and we got together in '57.

Ben: Well, back in 1949 the "Boplicity" band had played one little two-week engagement at the Royal Roost club. And outside of the club, for the first time ever, there was a sign that said "arrangements by" Gil Evans. That was the first time an arranger had ever been given public credit like that, in a club. It was unprecedented to promote the arranger, and yet it took eight years for you to finally come around and get some sort of recognition.

Gil: Right, that's true.

Ben: When you finally went in to record *Miles Ahead* in 1957, again the arrangements were "seamless," and they were almost a translation of Miles' "sound" into orchestral terms. At the same time, I remember some little things that you did that were very distinctive. For example, at the end of the song "Miles Ahead," there's an ensemble trumpet figure that's used almost as an acoustic guitar, a Spanish guitar. There were a lot of things like that in your writing that were very unusual, very deceptive.

Gil: Right. People used to think there were strings in those albums. Even somebody as knowledgeable as Gordon Jenkins. Now you know he wrote for strings all the time. He called me up to tell me how he liked it, and he thought there were strings. And I thought, "Gee, that's funny. Imagine him thinking there are strings." Because he wrote for strings, wow, I've seen him. And he had such a feeling for those things. He'd have a big string section, and they'd all be playing an ensemble that he'd write for them with Louis Armstrong in mind, you know?

Ben: You said that in the interim, from 1949 to 1957, you were waiting for Miles . . .

Gil: I was waiting for Miles, basically, I was.

Ben: It's so romantic. It sounds like a love affair when you say that.

Gil: I know.

Ben: Much has been made in the past about how Duke Ellington would write for an individual, as opposed to just bringing different people to his notes. Is this in that tradition?

Gil: You know, I never knew Duke. But one day, he called me, you know. To tell me that I was his favorite jazz orchestrator. It was really nice. It really made me feel good. But we got some very bad reviews on that album too, you know. The *Miles Ahead* album, when it first came out. Wow. They called it the "anti-jazz" album. Stuff like that.

Ben: Well the "Boplicity" session got the same sort of reaction too, didn't it? Critics said it was "devoid of emotion."

Gil: Yeah. We're all victims of the terrible habit of convenience, right? And when you're used to hearing a certain type of music, or a certain "sound" of music, and it changes, and you're not with it, or don't follow it any more, you're home and you stop going out to clubs and all that . . .

Like for example, Coleman Hawkins developed his sound starting in 1924, right? And he was *the* jazz saxophone player for ten years. Well, when Pres came along, people were outraged! Oh, everything you could think of they said about him. You know, "You sound like an alto, why don't you play one." All that kind of thing.

Well a new generation comes along and picks up on it, and then the innovator, if he's still alive, and not a disaster, can get some credit, you know. But a lot of times an innovator can come and go and not have a very good life, you know.

The same thing happened with Coltrane. People were outraged at that sound. "Why would he want to do that when the sound was so good up until now?" You know, that's convenience, right? The world's most prevalent addiction. It's convenience. We all suffer from an overuse of convenience at the expense of passion, right?

Ben: Do jazz critics seem notorious in that regard?

Gil: They're not alone, but they are . . .

Oh, they were terrified of Lester. They used to be so scared of him because of his rhythmic freedom, for one thing. They were used to having somebody play that would take their hand and hold it all the way through, you know what I mean? But with Pres, it was different. You weren't going to get the accents in the usual places, right?

Ben: One of the things I've found fascinating about your arranging is how over the years you've applied it to older forms, older compositions, and really made something new with them. I remember a chart you did for a record in the late 1950s. I think it was for the Pacific Jazz label. It's an arrangement of Don Redman's "Chant of the Weed." [Note: it has been re-released by Blue Note as *Gil Evans: Pacific Standard Time.*]

Gil: I made two albums originally for that company. One with Cannonball. Cannonball played great on that album too. Just the very opening he plays on "Saint Louis Blues," it still gives me chills.

Ben: *Old Wine, New Bottle.*

Gil: Yeah, and on the inside it said *Old Bottle, New Wine*. They couldn't get it straight, so they put one on the cover, one on the inside. So I sent the tapes out to the owner of the company, and he just raised hell with me. Because he said, "What are doing featuring some saxophone player that nobody's heard of? Why didn't you use Bud Shank?" Well, Cannonball became the number one alto player, and so of course the owner of the company didn't hesitate a minute to print "Cannonball Adderley, number one alto player ..." on the cover and go through all that when they reissued it.

That's how it goes.

Ben: That's how it goes.

Gil: But Don Redman was one of my first teachers, you know? Because I lived in a little town in California where nothing like that ever happened. But a man from San Francisco would come up every week to a little record store there and brought the latest releases. So I was really raised on Don Redman, Duke Ellington, the Wolverines, and McKinney's Cotton Pickers. The Casa Loma Band ...

I heard them all. I bought the records. And the radio was a big thing then, in the early thirties. Every day you'd hear a band from New York. At least every day. Duke would be playing from some supper club there, or something like that. And Don Redman had a great band, wow! He had a big band, but they were packed together tight. Did you see that video of them? Three trombones, three or four trumpets, four saxophones, they're all bunched up together.

Don Redman was the original arranger, big band arranger, of jazz. And he used to broadcast from there all the time. He used to sing these songs in his funny little voice. And "Chant of the Weed" was his theme song.

Ben: Like many self-taught musicians, you used the radio and the phonograph as your classroom.

Gil: Yeah, I copied all the records. I had a little crank-up phonograph, you know. And it had a speed regulator on it, which you can't even get now, with all the modern things. You either got to have 33⅓ or 45 or 78. But in those days, it went from 0 to 80. You just have it at any speed you wanted.

So I spent many years of my life copying arrangements off records, you know.

Ben: That's how a lot of guys got Bird's licks. They just slowed it down until they were able to hear it and grab it.

Gil: Yeah. Konitz still does that. When he's on the road, he still plays cassettes of Bird at half time.

Bird still sounds great. There's no thought of him being dated, you know?

Ben: Similarly with your charts, I have to say, they don't sound dated. Whether we hear one that was done in the '40s or one that was done in the '80s, there's a continuity that relates more to the man than to the historical era.

Gil: Yeah. They're all melancholy. That's one of my characteristics.

Ben: Perhaps that's at the heart of your great compatibility with Miles. Miles is the voice of melancholy.

Gil: That's how we got together, basically. Really. The "sound," you know. The "sound" is the thing that put us together immediately, and it's always been like that. It's still the same way today. Even if we don't see each other very often, we're still life-time friends. On account of the "sound."

Because he was a "sound" innovator, and he had his problems too, you know. When he started playing, people were outraged at that. "Why would he want to do that when Louis Armstrong was so great?" He didn't even realize it. One night, he was playing at the Village Vanguard, and we were sitting around during intermission and I said, "Miles, it just occurred to me. I don't know if you ever thought of it or not, but you're the first person to change the tone of the trumpet since Louis Armstrong." Which he was.

Because everybody up until that time came out of Louis Armstrong. Maybe out of somebody else, like Roy Eldridge came out of Louis Armstrong, and then Dizzy came out of Roy. But it was all basically like that.

Miles loved the trumpet, but he didn't like "trumpet" trumpet, you know. And so he had to just start with no tone, no sound whatsoever at first. That first record he made, "Now Is The Time," it's just a skeleton tone that he uses. He gradually filled it in with flesh and blood, from hearing other people that he liked, like Clark Terry, Harry James . . .

Ben: Freddie Webster . . .

Gil: Freddie Webster especially. And it all went into that funnel and came out his sound.

Ben: Speaking about the melancholy aspect of your work, one has to mention the record *Out of the Cool*. The song "Where Flamingos Fly," for example, is terribly sad . . .

Gil: Actually, that's a field song. A man just leaned up against a fence in a field somewhere in Alabama and sang that melody. And Harold Coulander, who was a musicologist among other things, he gathered together, with John Brooks' help, something called *Negro Songs of Alabama*. And "Where Flamingos Fly" is one of those.

I also used some little spice in there that I learned from Flamenco guitar players. So there's always a little spice to the sound. It takes away some of the blandness, you know.

Ben: So the sound doesn't just lay there; it hovers. It has internal motion.

Gil: It gives it a little . . . tortured sound. [Laughs.]

Ben: A tortured sound?

Gil: Something hurting a little bit there.

Actually, I learned how to treat a song and all that from Louis Armstrong. I bought every record of his from 1927. The first one I bought was called "No One Else But You," and it was him and Earl Hines and a band with an arrangement by Don Redman. It's great. Even now. The rhythm section sounds old fashioned but the arrangement is something else.

So anyway, I bought every one of his records from 1927 till around 1936. From then on, he repeated and became more of an entertainer. But for those ten years, he was a great creative artist, you know. Even though he never had any special arrangements for himself. Mostly, he played just stock arrangements. But in every one of those three-minute records, there's a magic moment somewhere. Every one of them.

I really learned how to handle a song from him. I learned how to love music from him. Because he loved music, and he did everything with love and care. So he's my main influence I think.

Ben: Each of your compositions also seems to have a magic moment. Do you remember the song "So Long," from an album you made called *Blues In Orbit* a while ago. That song has some real drama going on.

Gil: You know, "So Long" was written for Coltrane. Because he died just then, he died that week that we made it. And I brought the tape home before I named it. I brought it home and played it and cried bitterly all night long. Because I hadn't really let myself go at the shock of his death. That's how I happened to call it "So Long."

Ben: So it was recorded in 1966?

Gil: I don't know. I'm so old, I don't keep track of years, hardly. [Laughs.]

Ben: There's a little acoustic guitar passage at the end of that composition which reminds me of the trumpet figure we talked about on the end of "Miles Ahead." But for the most part, you had gotten away from traditional writing completely. It's as if you were using "pure sounds," dramatic sounds. Darkness. Light.

Gil: Yeah.

Ben: Was it orchestrated or improvised?

Gil: Either way. Both.

Ben: Your style of orchestration is also reminiscent to me of Charles Mingus' in that so much of it is coached out of great players as opposed to imposed on them. And you did record some of Mingus' compositions. Not long ago, you did "Orange Was The Color of Her Dress," on the *Priestess* album. It featured a long-time Mingus associate, and a man who has played with your band for quite a while, George Adams.

Gil: Yeah, that was originally recorded in England, at Festival Hall. We still play that with the band. We also play Mingus' "Boogie Stop Shuffle." In fact, that's the first number in the movie *Absolute Beginners*. And we played "Better Get It In Your Soul" in the movie, too. We were going to play "Good Bye Pork Pie Hat" in the movie, but as it became more of a pop movie, they had to cut it out.

Ben: Movie work has been good to you lately. As I said at the beginning, you've been busy in general.

Gil: Yeah, I'm working. It's a little different, because I'm so used to living from hand to mouth, you know. [Laughs.] Then all of a sudden this last year I had two concert tours. Italy and France. Then I came home. But even while I was on the road, I had a VCR and a videotape of this movie *The Color of Money*. So I worked on that after the concerts at night. So when I got home, I went right on working.

But it was nice to get a job and work with someone where you both go away with a certified fair share, right? It's so rare, you know. Most all the time, you're either gonna get fucked or you're gonna have to fuck somebody, right? And naturally, you don't want to get fucked. But it's not a pleasant thing to have to do if you don't want to do it, right? But many, many of the business relationships that you have are just on those terms.

So with Robbie Robertson, it was a pleasure to work with him [on *The Color of Money*], because it was "even-Steven."

Ben: I spoke with Mose Allison yesterday. He said he's got it figured out. It always comes down to this: it's somebody's money against somebody else's life. That's all of it. Any situation can be reduced to that.

Gil: That's right.

* * *

Dizzy Gillespie (December, 1985)

Dizzy Gillespie spent his life on the road. In the fifteen years I crossed paths with him, working on television specials, radio broadcasts, jazz conferences and even a live gig or two, he was always just coming from somewhere and on his way to somewhere else. In spite of his incessant traveling, or perhaps because of it, he managed to keep both his marriage to Lorraine and his well-known sense of humor intact. The following conversation took place in the penthouse suite of a large hotel in downtown Chicago. There was a huge television set in the middle of the room with the picture on but no sound (mostly the news channel, but sometimes Diz would use the remote control to flip through some old movies) and from time to time the phone would ring. On two occasions, calls came in from overseas. How did these people in Italy and Japan know where to find Dizzy, let alone manage to time their international calls to catch him at a good hour? Obviously, Dizzy Gillespie was at the heart of some kind of worldwide network. And, as befits a man of his historical importance and cultural understanding, his vision extended far beyond the literal notes he played. A devout member of the Bahai faith, which is opposed to all artificial international borders, and a high priest of bebop, Dizzy Gillespie was dedicated to keeping the channels open and the party rolling.

Ben: Here we are in another hotel, Dizzy, and it's a pretty snappy suite at that.

Dizzy: The reet suite!

Ben: The reet suite on the sweet street . . .

Dizzy: Yeah, what I say!

Ben: How much time each year are you spending out here on the road?

Dizzy: A lot of it. You can tell by my baggage. I carry around everything. If I need anything, I know where to find it in one of my bags, see? It's been . . . oh, man! . . . over thirty-five weeks this year, I guess.

Ben: So knowing how to pack your bags is important?

Dizzy: Yeah, knowing how to have what you need. It's like you're home, so you try to make the road like home. I try to make it like that. And

I succeed, really. I can never remember having needed something on the road and didn't have it somewhere in my bag. Just give me a chance to find it.

Ben: What keeps you traveling so much? Is it the love of playing or is it something else?

Dizzy: Well, it's my life, playing. And my best shot is to be on the road and go to Europe, to go to Japan, go all over the world. Because right now, you see, I'm in a unique position in my profession, where the major contributors to the music that we made in the forties, "bebop," are gone. Most of them. The only ones left now are Sonny Rollins, Jackie McLean, Dexter Gordon, James Moody, Cecil Payne, Gerry Mulligan is from that era . . .

Ben: There's a few of you holding on . . .

Dizzy: Yeah, a few, but man, think about the hundreds of thousands of musicians in the world, and there's only that little core that's left.

Ben: So being a survivor, you feel obligated to keep moving, keep circulating?

Dizzy: Yeah. I think bebop should contribute something. It would be nice to have all the leading figures in bebop to contribute something to world peace. A video or something, for world peace.

Ben: Like the pop videos that have been done for world hunger?

Dizzy: Yeah, but do something for world peace. You know, I was speaking to someone the other day about this idea of Harry Belafonte's, this Aid thing to Africa to feed those people. But if the earth keeps going in the direction it's going without having peace between the nations, all of it, the earth is in jeopardy. Because for the lack of an international law with teeth that can go anywhere and arrest anybody . . . A good example of that happened recently in international espionage, between Israel and the United States. Friends even do it. Your best friend, you're evesdropping on him. You know, and the United States wanted to question some of their officials at the U.N., and they cut out, man, they split! And it was unheard of for them to come back here. So we need some peace.

Ben: Well, you once said that bebop is "the most intelligent form of jazz."

Dizzy: Up to that point.

Ben: Right, up to that point. You may have said it in the '70s but you were referring to the Golden Age during the '40s. Do you feel that the dedication and application of higher intelligence that was going into the music at that point—in the '40s—was more intense than it has been before or since?

Dizzy: Yeah, I think that was one of the most intense areas of jazz as we know it now.

Ben: The community of players, their level of education and world-view?

Dizzy: Yeah, it was great, man. Like a light, shining! It was unbelievable. And Charlie Parker was probably the cause of all this. All this fire that came from that era.

Ben: You would say it was Charlie Parker, as opposed to you *and* Charlie Parker *and* Kenny Clark and a lot of others?

Dizzy: Yeah, well look at it intelligently. Everybody knows that I *am* a contributor to this music. And even to say a "major contributor" to this music. But there are other things in the music that take preference even over my contribution, such as *style*. Charlie Parker, he's the one that created that *style* of playing. And *playing* it. That's what got it, you know? All of us, we had the rhythm. We had the harmony. All of that, before I even met Charlie Parker, I had been a student of harmony. Not a classical trained student, but I learned.

You know, sometimes, I luck-up on something. There's something that I played one time that I lucked-up on, on the piano. And then I heard Ravel, in a spot in one of Ravel's tomes, and I heard the same thing. And I said, "Hey, look-a-there, man, look out! Ravel!" You know what I mean? But Ravel had done that years and years before I was even around.

So that's what happened. That is a very classical way to do jazz, you know. Just from the nub, you know? And now, our young musicians are very well trained. Those people are well trained! And it's good, because they can step anywhere.

Ben: But what about the question of style?

Dizzy: Style will have to come for itself.

Ben: You can't teach it can you?

Dizzy: No. You cannot do that. That's what makes it so great, man. You cannot teach it. You can teach someone to appreciate it. But as far as style, that is the way you play. That's a real personal thing.

Ben: You've had a long career of teaching people to appreciate bebop and the styles that you and Charlie Parker pioneered. And you've always used comedy to do that. In fact, humor has been a big part of your musical personality, as far back as first grade, if I read your autobiography correctly.

Dizzy: Yeah, well I believe in having a good time. You know, I grew up that way. In Miss Wilson's class [his first grade teacher], one day she actually knocked the trumpet out of my mouth. Because she'd be trying to explain something and I'd be fiddling around, and she say, "Stop that, John Birks." And I'd look at her, and then a couple of minutes more, she'd hear it again. And one day she just knocked the trumpet out of my mouth.

Ben: I mentioned that episode because the idea of style seems to be tied in with the idea of personality. And Charlie Parker is quoted somewhere as saying that "if you don't live it, it won't come out of your horn." You have to play from experience.

Dizzy: Oh yes.

Ben: And your personal experience is tied-up with humor and enjoying yourself.

Dizzy: Oh yes, I guess. I like peace. I think I like peace more than anything in the world. I am for peace, I'm a peace-loving man. And anything to formalize peace, I'm for.

Ben: And humor is a way to do this?

Dizzy: Yeah, be happy. People say, "I really identify with that," I guess.

Ben: And it's a good way to get people to open up to what you're going to put on them next?

Dizzy: Yeah, man, yeah, you can work that. I'm getting ready to make another appearance on the Bill Cosby show. I was talking to Cosby down in Cape D'Antibes, and he was talking about Joe Williams coming in as his father-in-law, and he say, "I can hardly wait to see you and that fool together." And with real loose lyrics, you know, let it hang loose a little bit. So I'm going to think of a few little ideas and let him further develop them. You know, he's a genius. Man, he wouldn't even need to perform now. He knows how to tell somebody else to do it. That's great, man, when a guy can do that! Oooo, a teacher, it's a great thing.

Ben: You mention lyrics. You've done some singing in your time. In fact, I remember one occasion backstage at Carnegie Hall when you were trying to teach Jon Hendricks the correct way to sing your song "Ooo Pa Pa Da." And he wasn't singing it quite right, and you kept telling him, "No, man, that's not how it goes."

Dizzy: Well, our music sometimes sounds one way, but it's another way. Look, you say [he starts singing] "Ooo pa pa da . . . blah ba do laaaa . . . blee, b'lue da." See, so now "blee b'lue da" that comes on the beat. *On* the beat. You say, "Ooo pa pa da . . . bleah ba do ahhhh . . . blee b'lue da." [He emphasizes the "blee"]. You know? That "blee b'lue da," that's *on* the beat. It's not off the beat. So here's another one. [Starts singing again.] "Bleah ba do dahhh . . . be blee bop." You know what I mean? That's another one! So it's sort of between the two. It's triplet form. Right in that little part, you jump into triplet form. And you come back out, and that's what it is. Because you can play triplets to make a lazy feeling on a phrase. I guess you would have to write it that way for a classical musician.

Somebody was explaining that to me. Because I've had quite a bit of my compositions done for symphony orchestra. And we play with symphony orchestras, and it's something to hear those guys try to play "bleah ba do ahhh . . . blee b'lee da." One time, I played with an orchestra in Ontario, and I played all the music that I had, and the people kept applauding. So I got this bright idea to let the symphony orchestra sit right there, and I'd give each one a rhythm to play, and then let it build. I had something for everybody, you know? That was my i-dea. So I walked up and I held up my hand, and the people stopped clapping. And I said, "You're out of luck tonight. All the music has been played. I have no more music to play." So I said, "But, I will make up something, as a special deference to you, with the orchestra, out of our heads." Oh, man, you should have seen these guys squirming. The violin players, and the bassoon players, they were wondering, "What the hell is he gonna do?"

So I said, "OK" and I tell them my rhythm to start off. So they start off. [Snaps his fingers to a kind of up-tempo "Charleston" beat.] So I say, "Ok, I want the bassoon to say . . . [sings a part that is reminiscent of the ensemble horn figure that opens 'Night In Tunisia']." And so, they said [sings a very stiff variation of the part]. I said, "No, no, that's not it" [and again sings the correct feeling]. Well this went on, and we were laughing, you know, we were having a good time. But I kept saying "No, no, no, that's not what I'm saying." Then I said, "Oh wait a minute, here's what I want." [He plays sixteenth-note triplets by rubbing his hands together]. You don't miss no beats that way. And they heard it! And they went right into it.

So our music is off-beat. We play a lot of music that is not on a downbeat. Like country-western music is right on the downbeat. [He sings a comic version of country-western music.] You know. When they're singing, the lyrics is right *on* the beat.

Ben: In the furrow.

Dizzy: Yeah, but we differ. We play . . . see our music, it is so contingent on the African looseness of rhythm. That's what makes it. You know, when jazz music becomes classic, it's gonna be . . . yeah, man, it *will* become classic, it'll be one day. I'd just like to be here then and say, "See, I *told you* so." Because it will become classic.

They say that kind of rhythm can't be written, but almost anything you do can be written. Almost. I heard Aretha Franklin do some things that I defy a guy to write out. I mean to write out so that somebody would pick that up a hundred years from now and say, "Aretha sang that." You know, they can't find . . . there's certain people, like Sarah, and Ella, Johnny Hodges, people that have come before us, and are *still* coming on the scene, that can't be duplicated.

Ben: It all gets back to style again. And it sounds to me, listening to your progress through your recordings, that your style of playing is getting more simple, you're using fewer notes.

Dizzy: Well, I guess that's one of the tenures of growing old. Because you come to realize that you don't want to waste any notes. When you're younger, you waste a lot of notes, and some were, ah, really unnecessary, huh? A lot of unnecessary notes have gone by, you know what I mean? So now is the time to try to salvage some of this before you give up completely. So you don't play as many notes. Sometimes, in spurts, you know, in spurts.

Ben: The idea of playing fast has always been very much a part of your style, particularly in the forties.

Dizzy: Yeah, but they play some pretty bad, pretty fast tempos today, too. Yeah, they're way, way up there.

Ben: Yeah, but you used to double-time and triple-time all the time.

Dizzy: Yeah, but now, I don't mean to waste no notes.

Ben: Another unusual part of your style is what has been called "Gillespie Pouches" by a doctor from the National Aironautics and Space Administration, who's studying why your cheeks get so large when you play . . .

Dizzy: I wouldn't advise someone who's trying to go about playing with the technique of your cheeks out there like that, because technically it's wrong. From not being a classically trained musician, with your jaws all in and your erect stature, you know, and you play from your diaphragm, I didn't have that. So I had to hit it the best way I could. So it developed, my jaws gradually developed until this monstrosity now.

Ben: Did you develop this originally to get power and speed going?

Dizzy: I don't know. I don't know. Whatever. I did that to get what I needed, to do what I wanted to do.

Ben: Is it possible for you to play any other way now?

Dizzy: No, with my jaws down? No, no. It's a very pu-pu-puny sound.

Ben: There's a picture of you from the early '50s that's on the cover of the famous *Jazz At Massey Hall* concert [album], taken in Toronto with Bud Powell and Bird and Max Roach and Charles Mingus, and your pouches are there but not nearly so exaggerated.

Dizzy: I had a straight horn then too.

Ben: What about the bent horn . . .

Dizzy: Well, it's fragile. The horn is fragile. If you could grab any trumpet, and grab it by the bell and pull it, and the bell will bend. It will bend up. It's not that strong, you know. Somebody fell over it and it just bent.

Ben: And you picked it up and played it and liked it.

Dizzy: Yeah, this is alright for me.

Ben: It also allows you to put your head down while playing.

Dizzy: That's not the correct way to put your head either. The correct way to put your head is up.

Ben: For breath?

Dizzy: Yeah, for all your organs to be in place, where you need them, instead of scrambled up . . . against some chitlins.

Ben: Well now we've talked about the Gillespie Pouches and the bent horn and playing with your head down, and all these accidents, and you say that these things led you to play incorrectly. And yet they're all a result of your style. And we started out by saying that style is the most important thing.

Dizzy: Yeah, well the legitimate way to play a trumpet is to play like the classical guys do who have good embouchures. Freddie Hubbard has a wonderful embouchure. John Faddis! John Faddis is one of the most phenomenal musicians. He can play the brass part *and* the reed part, right behind it!

Ben: Yes, but even though your technique is not correct—like some people say Thelonious Monk's technique was incorrect, in terms of classically trained musicians, and yet his technique really made up a big part of his style, what he sounded like—isn't that also true in your case?

Dizzy: Yes. It would be true.

Ben: Mentioning the Massey Hall concert, a lot of people would say that was one of the greatest recording sessions of all time. It was done in 1953, several years after you and Bird and Bud Powell had all gone your separate ways. Was that just another jam session to you, or was there something special going on in that particular reunion?

Dizzy: Aw, well we had been playing those arrangements for years. We knew them backwards and forwards. Wake you up in the middle of the night and play those. There were some lapses of memories, though, on some of the endings, but it was so much a part of everybody that they just overcame all of the obstacles that were there.

You know, there's one obstacle on that record, on "Night In Tunisia." Mingus, when we stopped playing, he started playing on the bridge, and then he played that chorus and then he played another chorus. And he played sixteen bars, and I came in on the bridge. He wanted to play one and a half more choruses. So he was sort of "off" about it. So he started to say something to me about it. And I gave him some answer, and that was it.

So years later, I don't remember what I said to him, but it must have been something that was very threatening, or something like that. Well, Mingus had a reputation of like punching musicians. Hit them over the head with his bass. I mean, I'm being extravagant, but anyway, Mingus had a big history of altercations with some of his musicians. So way later on, Mingus called my house. And I hadn't thought of this incident in years. So he called my house and asked Lorraine where was I. And she told him I was out on the road and would be back in a week or so. And he said you can tell him to give me a ring when gets back.

So I came back into town, and there were so many messages and things like that got shuffled around and I didn't call him. So he called back and Lorraine answered the phone. He said, "Lorraine, is Dizzy in?" She said, "Yes." He asked, "How long has Dizzy been home?" She said, "He got in earlier this week." Then he raised his voice. "Didn't you tell him I said call me up?" And so my wife just handed me the phone and said, "It's one of your crazy musicians on the telephone. You better talk to him because he just hollered at me."

So I got on the phone and I said, "Man, what gives you a right to raise your voice at my wife?" He said, "I didn't raise . . . " I said, "Wait a minute. She just passed me the phone. You mean to say that she's a liar?" He said, "No, no, I didn't say that . . . " I said, "Mingus. Wait a minute. You have a reputation. I also have a reputation. And I will come over there and kill you." [Laughs.] And so he said, "Oh, man, don't talk like that. You know I love you and I love Lorraine, and I know you all love me. Although you were going to cut my head off in Toronto, you was going to do it with love in your heart." [Laughs.]

I started laughing! But Mingus was something, man. He was very sick during the time that we went to the White House. And boy, it hurt me to see it. Jimmy Carter came all the way over, walked all the way across the lawn to Mingus, and grabbed him and hugged him. And Mingus started crying. That was very touching. That was the most touching moment in the whole thing.

The next most touching moment was the President shouting "Hey Dizzy! Diz, hey! Play 'Salt Peanuts'!" So we were up on stage, and I had already told Max Roach to have his snare drum ready cause we were going to play a duet. So when the president hollered "Salt Peanuts," I said, "We will play it if you come over here and sing it with us." And that's how it happened, just simultaneously. And it was great, man. And so he came up on stage and we had a lot of fun rehearsing him. And then we went into it, and he sang "Salt Peanuts, Salt Peanuts." And it went world wide.

Ben: The President of the United States sitting in with Dizzy Gillespie.

Dizzy: Singing "Salt Peanuts"!

Ben: Wasn't that your campaign song when you ran for President of the United States back in the sixties? I mean, you got a lot of votes back then, thousands of people wrote your name in on the ballot.

Dizzy: Well, yeah. And they seemed to think it was for real. Ralph Gleason and his wife, Jean, they were my campaign agents on the West Coast. And they devised this whole thing, man, they had everything. Balloons, bumper stickers, petitions. A lot of petitions. Did you sign one?

Ben: I was one of the people who voted for you in the election.

Dizzy: Ahhhh! [Laughs.] Oh, my goodness.

Ben: What's wrong with that? I mean Ronald Reagan was a film actor, and he couldn't improvise at all.

Dizzy: [Laughs.] Well, that was a little thing, you know. See. I belong to . . . my religious faith teaches that there's one world, not one country. So this was a little thing for me to run for President of a country. Because we're thinking in terms of world-wide. And we are not permitted, Bahais are not permitted to run for public office, or ask for votes or anything like that.

Ben: So the Bahais' gain is the United States citizens' loss.

Dizzy: [Laughs.] Well, here I am. Just an ordinary citizen.

Ben: But it sounds like you hope to become more active working for larger issues like world peace.

Dizzy: I imagine I will become very much involved with that. I would like to. It's a primary motive of mine at the moment. It's needed. And you know jazz musicians are just naturally peaceful people.

Ben: That's a little-known fact, I guess.

Dizzy: Yeah, they're very peaceful. Because there's so much on their mind trying to figure this music out that they don't have *time* to be evil. [Laughs.]

Ben: Dizzy, have you thought at all about how you'd like to be remembered?

Dizzy: Just remember how to spell D-I-Z-Z-Y. That's enough.

* * *

Jay McShann (September, 1988)

Pianist Jay McShann is one of those living legends who has survived the winds of fame and the tides of fortune to arrive intact on the rocky beach of today's nightclub scene. Often appearing without much publicity and with a local rhythm section, McShann sings and plays with the same fire and good humor that made him a Kansas City fixture back in the 1930s. His penchant for including contemporary pop and show tunes in his repertoire belies the fact that as a bandleader, he was responsible for introducing a young Charlie Parker to the world. As is often the case with musicians of his era who continue to make the jazz circuit their home, his constant traveling is both a reaffirmation of a way of life and, perhaps, the way to life. For McShann, with his generous smile and comfortable proportions, seems to physically embody the kind of joy that keeps both a person and the music young.

Ben: Jay, I'm glad I caught up with you on the road. You've been kind of hard to catch lately . . . for the last forty or fifty years.

Jay: [Laughs.] How about that.

Ben: Although you've been working and traveling virtually nonstop for more than half a century, you're still most well known as being a part of the local Kansas City music scene in the '30s.

Jay: Yes, that's right.

Ben: Along with Count Basie and a few others, you are one of the most famous band leaders associated with that city and that era. Was the scene really so powerful back then that someone like yourself should spend a lifetime carrying the torch?

Jay: Well, Kansas City in the '30s was a wide-open town. And you know, you take a town when the town is wide open, see, that attracts a lot of people. And it attracts all kinds of people. It attracts musicians, you know, and it attracts gamblers. You know, those gamblers, a wide-open town, that's for them. And it attracts the babes, and the pimps, and so consequently you've got a thing going. And then it attracts just people that's moving around, because they want to find out where, you might say, the action is, what some people say, you know, the way some people describe it. And, Kansas City being a town like that, consequently you had a lot going on, so the town stayed open 24 hours a day. So, if a cat come in and he said, "Man, where's the action," well you said, "Man, just stick around and keep going, you'll find it." Yes.

Ben: The name that you see in the history books as being responsible for this situation is a fellow named Pendergast.

Jay: Yes, well, Pendergast, you know, he was running the town. And he opened it up, and, you know, it helped it economic-wise, as well as a lot of other ways.

Ben: There was no depression in Kansas City?

Jay: No, it wasn't no depression. Everybody was makin' something. [Laughs.]

Ben: How old were you when you came to Kansas City?

Jay: Oh, I don't know. I was in my teens, to pinpoint right off is kind of hard, but it was very early, early teens, you know.

Ben: Did you have your own band at that time?

Jay: Well, I didn't have a band before I came to Kansas City. I never had a group. But I had worked with other groups, you know, like Eddie Hill, I worked with his band. I worked with the Al Dennis band, which was in Tulsa, Oklahoma, you know. And small groups like that I had worked with. Then when I came to Kansas City, there was all this excitement, you know, because of the clubs being open all night. Where I'd been playing, clubs closed at one o'clock. With clubs staying open all night, you know, I could get around and catch a lot of musicians and hear a lot of guys I'd never heard before.

Ben: Back then, you picked up the nickname "Hootie." Where did that come from?

Jay: Ho, Ho! Well, when I first came to Kansas City, you know how guys do, you go around to all the clubs, you know, to meet all the cats. And they, the musicians and the bartenders, you know, they always got something going. So when I'd show up at some of these places, the cats would tell the bartender, say, "Hey, bartender, fix this new cat up a little taste of whatever that stuff you did for us the other night," and then wink at him, you know? The bartender, he says, "OK!" So he'd go back there and he'd bring out that beer and stuff. It'd be in a container and it was so cold you could see the frost on the side of it, you know. But it tasted so good. And they hand it to you, and boom, you didn't know when to put it down. And then they hand it to me the third time and the guy says, "Ok man, we're ready to hit. Come on up and play some." And I tried to get out of my seat, and I couldn't get up. [Laughs.] Then I realized, you know, the joke was on me. Because I realized what they would do, it would be like a 3.2 beer, and then he'd put a certain amount of alcohol in it, you know. And, oh boy, that was really something. It really had a bang to it.

As a result, when they refer to me, they say, "Well, man, you know this cat that came out here the other night?" "Oh, you talkin' 'bout Hootie? The cat that came out here and got Hooted? Yeah! Sure we know, we remember . . ." You know. And it stuck.

Ben: How did you put your first band together?

Jay: Well, it happened that Dave Dexter gave us a write-up in a paper there called the *Journal Post*. He was working there at this public paper at the time, and he came by one night and he saw, I think we had a duo or trio, and we were performing and so he got a kick out of it, so he wrote it up in the Sunday paper. And during that time, you know it wasn't too many . . . very few papers did any write-up on the black musicians. And so a fellow by the name of Walter Bell saw this write-up, so he called down to the union and told them to send me out there, you know, to his house. Because he had some work he wanted me to do, you know. He was a good friend. He and Basie were good friends. And he and Basie used to get together out at the house. He liked to play piano, he was a piano player himself, you know. And he liked to play piano, so he'd bring Basie out. And so Basie had gone East, so then he heard about I was in town, so he sent for me to come out, you know.

So, it was very funny, because I wasn't with the union then, so the union sent somebody else out. The union sent somebody else out and the guy told him, Walter Bell, he says, "Your name McShann?" "No," the guy said, "but the union sent me out." He says, "Well, the union made a mistake. See, I asked for McShann to come out. Go back and tell the union to send McShann out." So, I wasn't a member, so the union got in touch with me and they said, "Listen, you're gonna have to come over here and join the union." They said, "Before we send you out to this guy's house, on any job or anything, you're gonna have to join the union." So, consequently I said OK. And I went out to his house and he had a big grand there, you know, and so we sit down and played tunes and fooled around on the piano, you know, like he and Basie used to do. And, so that was the beginning of it, you know. And whenever Basie would come in town, he would go down to Jenkin's Music and get three pianos. And then we'd just sit up there, all three of us, just sit up there, just enjoy ourselves and just have a ball.

And then Bell told me he had a good friend that had a club in the Plaza there in Kansas City, that's a better part of town. He asked me, he says, "Would you like to go to work there?" I said, "Yeah." He says, "Well, I'll talk to this guy, see if I can get you in there." He says, "Maybe you can take a four, five, six piece group in there." And that's what happened, that was my first job.

Ben: Basie's band at the time was starting to get some national attention, weren't they?

Jay: Yeah, they had gone East. They'd just gone East.

Ben: So that made a little opening for you? [Yes, it did.] Was your band at the time in the style of Basie's band, or did you, as it's been reported, play more blues?

Jay: No, the fact about it, we never . . . we didn't play any blues, up until we got ready to record for Decca. See we were supposed to record for Decca earlier, but we went into Chicago to do the session, and we ran into some complications there with the union because there was no contract sent in, in front. We didn't know anything about you had to send a contract. So when we got there, quite naturally, the union stopped the recording. They told us, "When you all come on back, you all have to do this thing right . . . come back later when you get this business all straightened out." So I guess it must have been two or three years later, before we did record, and this time we had the contract. [Laughs.]

Ben: You weren't a blues player and it wasn't a blues band. What were your influences when you came to Kansas City?

Jay: Well, I had heard Earl Hines, you know, when I was in High School, and I liked Earl's blowin', 'cause at that time, to me, Earl Hines was the rage, you know. Because he used to broadcast from the Grand Terrace. And it didn't cost nothin' to hear him 'cause you could hear him on the radio. So I would tell my folks I was going to stay up and work on my lessons late, these particular nights that Earl Hines would be on the radio. Well, staying up to hear Earl Hines. So they liked that when I say I'm gonna stay up late and get my lessons done. So I'd wait 'til about eleven, eleven-thirty, whatever time he came on, and turn the radio down real low, and sit there and listen to the broadcast. And, it was good to hear the band that was with him. Him, the way they introduced him, and the band and everything. That's what I think really started me to listen to music, you know.

But, I remember, I heard a record, blues record, by I guess must have been Mamie Smith. I heard that record, and I liked it, you know? My dad worked at a furniture store, and, you know, records and things that they got rid of, he would bring' em home. And so I put this on and, well, you know, when they heard what this was, they said, "Boy, don't put that record back on no more." But that was it, I *liked* that record, you know? But, by the time I got to Kansas City, I hadn't played no blues. But I heard all this blues thing going on. Because it was Joe Turner there. There was Walter Brown singing the blues. And other blues singers that, you know, were around town too. So, I gotta chance to hear Joe Turner and Pete [Johnson]. Old Joe'd tell Pete to "roll'em," you know, when Pete'd start playin'. Play about thirty minutes before Joe'd start singing. Then Joe'd sing twenty minutes and Pete would roll a couple more again, and then Joe would sing a couple more and it's out. And, so that's about an hour. That's the first show, one tune an hour.

See, the cats in those days'll work from like eight or nine o'clock at night 'til six in the morning. And so quite natural, you know, the cats just go on and play, sometimes just, they might not have but two or three horns with them, maybe one horn. But Joe and Pete could put it on. And I like to hear old Joe sing them blues and hear Pete roll'em. That was something new that I gotta chance to hear, to listen to, you know.

We started doing the blues later, you know. It was after we got the big band together. Because with the small group, we didn't do any blues. Well, how it happened, us to doing the blues, was: One night I got off the gig, and I came by a club there at 19th and Vine, where Walter Brown and a bunch of musicians were working. And I told them, I says, "Walter," I says, "I'd like you to do that blues over again that you just finished." So, I says, "But I don't have but fifty cents in my pocket." I says, "But here it is." I says, "Do it over again." 'Cause just as I walked into the joint, they were right on their last choruses of this blues. So I heard it the second time, I went back to him and I told him, I says, "Now, tell you what you gotta do. You got to give me twenty-five cents back, because that was my last fifty cents and I wanta get me a chili this morning." I says he had to give me twenty-five cents of that fifty cents back, you know.

And then I explained to him that we might be doing some recording, and I'd want him to come out and rehearse a few tunes with the band. And I told him that we'd probably be recording, maybe in a couple of weeks. Which we did. That's when they called us back for the session. And we didn't wanta do any blues, but I just decided to take him along. I don't know why. I don't get it, but I decided after listening to him do those blues. So, we did. We went to Dallas to record. That was our first recording session. And we had all kinds of numbers like, oh, *Yardbird Suite*, which we used to do with the small group. We did this with the big band, all kinda tunes. And, the guy told us, he says, "Look." He says, "I like those tunes, I like that stuff you guys are doing." He says, "But I just gotta tell ya." He says, "I want something commercial." He says, "What I mean when I say commercial, I want something I can sell." So he says, "Do you know any blues?" "Yeah, maybe." He said, "Do a blues for me." So we did. I think we did *Confessin' the Blues*. And he smiled. He says, "Oh." He says, "Can you do a Boogie-Woogie?" "Yeah." We did *Vine Street Boogie*. So he says, "Tell you what you do." He says, "Do me another blues, and I'll take one of them other old funny tunes you got there." So we did *Hootie Blues*. And then we did *Yardbird Suite*.

Ben: *Hootie Blues* is listed as being co-written by yourself and another band member, a young fellow on alto saxophone, named Charles Parker. And this song turned a lot of musicians around all over the country because after they heard Bird, they never were the same. In fact, several players,

Frank Morgan among them, have told me exactly where they were when they first heard *Hootie Blues*, as if it was a great historical moment. And, of course, it was. Those original Decca sessions were recorded in 1941. Bird had joined the band a few years before that. On and off, I guess he worked with the band for several years . . .

Jay: Yes, that's right . . .

Ben: Tell me how you first came across Charlie Parker.

Jay: Well, during this period when I first came to Kansas City, we were, you know, on 12th Street and they always piped out music into the street. You could hear the bands as you go by. And it was a good thing, because if you heard something you liked, you stop and go in. So I passed by a club called the Barley Duke, and I heard this sound, and I said, "Wait a minute!" I say, "Wonder who is that?" 'Cause as a rule, you hear a guy, you know who it is. I said, "Let's go in and see who this is." We went in, and Bird was up, was blowing, you know. So after he finished blowing, I said, "Hey man, where you from?" He said, "Man," he says, "I'm from Kansas City." I said, "Well, what's your name?" I said, "I've never heard you around here before." He said, "Well, the reason you haven't heard me is because I've been down in the Ozarks with George Lee's band." See it's hard to get musicians to go down in the Ozarks, because there's nothin' happening down there. And he said, "I decided I'm going to do me a little woodsheddin' and so I went down with George . . ." and he says, ". . . I've been down there about three months." Then he says, "It's a good place to woodshed." So I said, "Well, that sounds good." We met and we decided, someday we might get a chance to work together. So I imagine it must not 'a been no more than 'bout two or three months after that that we did get a chance. That's when we were gettin' the small group together.

Ben: This is about 1937?

Jay: '38 . . .

Ben: Did Charlie Parker have his nickname "Bird" then?

Jay: Well, he wasn't called "Bird" until after we had gotten the big group together. He came back with the big group. See they wasn't callin' him Bird then, they was callin' him Charlie Parker. And after we got the big group together, we used to go to different towns, where the colleges and schools, universities were. And we were on our way to Nebraska University to play. And, you know, how you're driving on the highway, the farmer's chickens run out, run along the side of the highway with the cars, and all that. All that used to happen in those days. 'Cause we were using cars for transportation. So they ran over one of the farmer's chickens. So Bird told the kid who was driving, he said, "Man, turn around, back this car back up." Said, "Did you know you hit one of those chickens back there?" So the guy backed it up, Bird got out and got the chicken.

[Laughs.] And put it in the car with him and took it into town. 'Cause those days, we stayed at people's homes. You stayed at homes, and we got rooms like that, after we got in town. So Bird got in town, and the lady's house where he stayed, he asked her would she fix this chicken. He said, "We ran over this chicken." She said, "Sure, I'll be glad to." So she did. So from then on, we called him "Yardbird."

Ben: As I mentioned, that little Charlie Parker solo on the recording of *Hootie Blues* affected a lot of people. Everybody who heard that solo, I think, had the same reaction you did when you were walking down 12th street and you first heard that sound. What effect did Bird have on the band when he joined it? Was his influence as strong back then, even in the beginning?

Jay: Well, everybody liked Bird in the band. But it was a funny thing. There was guys that wanted to be like and play like Bird, and there was guys that wanted to play like Bird, but they wanted to play like Bird their way. But it was no question he had a profound effect on the band, you know what I mean. Most of those guys, I guess they had an idea which way that they wanted to go as well. But it was no question about it, because, when Bird took a solo, he just lifted the band, lifted everybody. And then we used to, on those head tunes, we used to have Bird set all the riffs. J.J., you know, was the first man on all the reading stuff. Bird was on the head stuff.

Ben: J.J., or John Jackson, would play the charts, Bird would set the heads.

Jay: Yeah.

Ben: Basie's band at the time was famous for having these head arrangements too. Not a lot of formalized, written section stuff. How much of your band material was written and how much was "head" arrangements?

Jay: Well, we used both methods. The fact about it, when I enlarged the small group, we went to work playing for what they call a walk-a-thon. You know, you'd have all kinds of entertainment. And you'd have about a twelve, fourteen piece band. And, really, we didn't have any book, when they hired the band. We didn't have any book because I'd only been using that small group. So we got busy from the first night on, you know, gettin' a book together. And so I had Willy Scott writing for the band, making arrangements. And the way we would do it, during the show . . . we played I think it was seven nights a week, you know, and I'd have Willy to take the reeds upstairs, rehearse the guys, rehearse the reeds, and leave the rhythm section and the brass downstairs taking care of the show. Then when the reeds got through rehearsing, then I'd have him take the brass up, and the reeds come down and play with the rhythm section. So we still wasn't cuttin' the music chart in there, see. So we did that night after night, night after night, and this lasted for about, oh, right about four months. So by the time we come outa there in four months, we had a book and didn't even realize it.

We had a heck of a book, you know.

And then, in the meantime, see, while we were there, we were doing heads, head arrangements, you know. And we might wind up doing a new head every other night or something like that. But what amazed me was how these guys could remember those head arrangements. Now they could remember 'em! They just look like, once they hit 'em, they never forgot 'em. And that really amazed me. [Laughs.] So, we got through, we had a heck of a book. Head and music, you know. So the book was there.

Ben: Not long after this period, you did have a little detour into the Army, as most everybody did in the '40s. And when you came out of the Army, I believe you went to Los Angeles. What was that like?

Jay: Well, you know, I still wanted that big band sound. But they told me, they said, "There's no need a-thinkin' about the old days." They says, "Why don't you just go on and get a small group together. And we'll get the same money for a small group that we'd get for a big group for you." I said, "Oh no, man, I wanna hear that sound." You know what I mean. Well not realizing that there's been a lot of changes. See, after you've been in the Army awhile, and you come back out, it's a different thing going. Because they'd made a lot of bowling alleys out of the dance halls, and things like that, and it was gettin' expensive to move a band around. So, it took me about, oh, I guess maybe three or four months to find that out for myself. After I found it out, then I was glad to make a change.

Ben: You tried Hollywood because of the show business that was out there?

Jay: Well, actually I went out there with the big band. And while we were there, on the way out, and all that, doing those one-nighters, is when I suddenly realized, I says, "Well, I'm gonna have to get a smaller group." And so, that's when I sent most of the guys back and just cut the band down to a small group.

Ben: So you sort of got hung up out there. Of course, around that time a lot of people were having this same experience weren't they? Count Basie had to cut his big band down to a small group too, didn't he?

Jay: Yes that's true . . .

Ben: So not long after, you moved back home to Kansas City. Did you find that it was a different city than when you first arrived?

Jay: Yes, it was. Well, you see, I would make these little tours, you know, and come back, and then at the time, I had kids, you know, and I was realizing, I'm gonna have to send these kids to school somewhere. And I was trying to think. I said, "Well I don't want to try Chicago. I wasn't gonna fool with New York. So I figured, well, maybe I'll try in Kansas City." So that's where I finally decided to send them to school. And I just played around Kansas City, for, oh, say about ten years, something like that, before I started getting out again. The kids gettin' ready, they gettin' around to finishing school age and all that. So then I started, you know, going in and out of town a little bit farther, and then by the time they finished High School, well then . . . Yeah, I was on the road again.

Ben: You know, I remember a story, apparently it was true, about a player in Kansas City back in the '30s, he went to a jam session about eight o'clock in the morning and the band was playing *All The Things You Are*, whatever, I don't know. So he went home, he had breakfast, he took a little nap, he took a shower, he changed his clothes, and then he went back to the session. And when he got there, they were still playing *All The Things You Are*. You're laughing. That's true, eh?

Jay: That sounds reasonable. [Laughs.] Yeah.

Ben: Well that scene is a lot different than the one you found when you returned. What happened?

Jay: Well, when you start thinking, it's a lot of things you take under consideration. A lot of places, we don't have as many clubs as we used to have. And then, people try everything for business, you know what I mean. So you find people trying everything, they try this, they try that, they try the other. They don't stay with it. So, consequently, you just don't be surprised at what you run into. You run into many things. Many different things and, you know, we could sit here and talk for a week, you know what I mean. But that's what it amounts to. Everybody's trying to do their thing, everybody's trying to get this on, trying to see how this will work, why that'll work . . . *whatever* works. And they go their own way.

Ben: Another thing perhaps we should remember is that the difference between jazz and dance music wasn't as great back in the '30s as it is today. You could be dancing to jazz all the time back then, so jazz really was popular music.

Jay: That's right. Yes, yes.

Ben: Was that the case in the clubs back in the '30s . . .

Jay: Well, they had dancing, and some people, when they made the difference, they made too much difference between dance music and jazz music. Because it was all the same. To me. To me it's always been the same all these years, and it still is the same. Dance music, jazz music. It depends how far you want to delve into what type of jazz you're playing, or what type of dance music you're playing.

Ben: I guess what I was thinking of was that, you know, back then it would not have been unusual for somebody as modern at the time as Charlie Parker to be playing in a band that was playing dance music. I don't mean lounge music, I mean good time music for people who wanted to get up and dance.

Jay: Well, that's what happened. He was with this group, and we played everything, see. And in playing everything, you know, Charlie could fit anywhere, 'cause Charlie could play anything. And consequently he could fit anywhere. But the funniest thing about it, lot of times, many people didn't realize . . . Sometimes Bird would have a great solo, and play a beautiful solo, and people never would clap or nothing. We had a tenor player come right behind him, a showman, you know, and boom, then the house would just go crazy, you know. And I just never, it was hard for me to understand that, because, as I say, here's a guy who's played everything there is to play, and the people won't even clap. And then turn around, Jimmy Forrest turn right behind him, and, the same tune, you know, and the house would go crazy. But you learn all these things, you know, out there on that road, playing these dates and things. You learn to not let 'em get to you.

Ben: Jimmy Forrest, of course, went on to get a hit record with *Night Train*, and Charlie Parker, of course, went on to change the music.

Jay: That's right.

Ben: Jay, I know a lot of guys at some point say, "I've had it, I've done what I have to do." But you clearly have not done what you have to do. You continue traveling, playing the music and essentially carrying on the tradition you helped start a half century ago. What keeps you going? What are you working toward?

Jay: Well, I'd like to keep on playing. And, you never know, there's probably something you haven't expressed that you still intend to express. Maybe the time hasn't come. So, what you do is continue.

Ben: You've helped educate a lot of young players. You got any advice for young players today?

Jay: Oh yes. If they like it. That's the main thing. If you like playing music, you enjoy it, then go ahead. You know? Because, if you enjoy it—and you know yourself, you don't have to fool yourself, you don't have to go out of the way to fool yourself—you know if you do, and you know if you don't. So it's that easy to find out what you want to do. Whether it's playing music or whatever.

Ben: Of course a lot of students today are studying music in school, and they're learning all the hip chords and the hip notes, but they don't have the experience of playing in front of people a lot. Subsequently, their style isn't as developed as it might be. Have you got advice in terms of how to proceed, how to make your own place in this music?

Jay: Well, I'll tell ya. Lotta times people say try the trial and error method. It might work good with one person, where it probably wouldn't work with another one. But actually, when you sum it up, it all comes to trial and error. Regardless, if you taking on a whole *big* thing or if it's a small thing, it's still trial and error.

Ben: Without the error, there's no trial.

Jay: That's right.

* * *

Red Rodney (October, 1988)

After his life was prominently featured in Clint Eastwood's film Bird, *trumpet player Red Rodney became the subject of a kind of a renaissance. The timing of the film's release was particularly auspicious for him, because his playing, too, was on the rebound. After years of semi-activity due to the physical and emotional complications arising from his involvement with narcotics, Red Rodney came back, leading a series of fiery bands and introducing several new young players to the jazz community, acting as a kind of father figure to the current generation. Red loved his new role as elder statesman, and his attitude and appearance at the time of our conversation belied his rocky past. He was almost boyish and, one felt, as enthusiastic about the music and his future as he had been forty years earlier, when he first met Charlie Parker and decided that the road he would travel was named "bebop." Red Rodney passed away in 1994.*

Ben: Red, it must be strange to see yourself being "played" on the movie screen by an actor. What did it feel like watching "yourself" in Bird.

Red: The young man named Michael Zelniker who portrayed me in the movie did a very good job. I know one thing, he was very conscientious. He followed me around all the time I was in California, and I watched him playing in the picture and he did rather well.

Ben: The movie doesn't suggest what your life was like before you met Charlie Parker. What had you been doing?

Red: Well you know World War II was on when I first came up and all of the good trumpet players were drafted. So the big name band leaders were looking for young kids who weren't old enough or were draft exempt. And I was lucky, I was playing in a house band on the steel pier in Atlantic City, where all the name bands came. Invariably they needed a trumpet, someone had just gotten drafted, so I played with Benny Goodman, I played with Tony Paster and with Les Brown, and I went on the road first with Jerry Wald, who was a big-name band leader in those days. An Artie Shaw clone, and it was a good band.

I wasn't good enough. I came home shortly after and went with a few other local bands, wound up with Jimmy Dorsey, and I *sure* wasn't good enough, and he let me go and I came home and worked with Elliot Lawrence at the radio station in Philadelphia, 1945. That's where I was introduced to the new revolutionary jazz called "bebop." I heard Dizzy Gillespie for the first time in a club called The Downbeat, which I went to work in about three or four weeks afterwards. And I remember my first thought, saying, "He would be great if he didn't play such weird notes." Intellectually, I didn't know what he was doing. Well, three or four weeks later, they didn't sound so weird. Then I knew. And it's strange, because that was my first experience with jazz. Prior to that, I was a Harry James-oriented player and a big band enthusiast. I didn't know anything about jazz. This was it.

So I was very lucky. I came in at the very beginning of the bebop movement. And Dizzy, as he always is, became a mentor. He was always wonderful—and he still is—to young players. And he used to come visit his mother when I was playing at the Downbeat. At this time, I think I'm a full-fledged jazz player. I knew six tunes, maybe, "I Got Rhythm" and the blues and maybe one or two other tunes. [Laughs.] And he'd come and hear, and he'd smile, and say "well, you're getting better." And he said, "Now it's time for you to come to New York and hear my quintet at the Three Deuces."

And that's where I first heard Charlie Parker. And I sat there that first set, in the middle of The Three Deuces, front row table, and I freaked out. When I heard that man, it all came together. I knew exactly what they were doing, and I knew that this was what I wanted to do for the rest of my life. It was like a religious experience. And don't forget, I wasn't 18 yet. And he befriended me. He was so nice to me. In fact, he asked me to loan him ten bucks. That was the first statement he made when we were introduced. If I'd have had a thousand, I would have given it to him. It was wonderful.

So from then on, little by little, I learned and became one of the new players in the bebop movement.

Ben: How close to real life are the movie portrayals of your relationship with Bird? For example, it shows you playing a Hasidic wedding together. I assume that really happened.

Red: Yeah, well it didn't happen exactly like the movie showed it, but it did happen. We went to a Brooklyn place, and we played this Hasidic wedding, and it was hilarious. As the movie portrayed. But we needed the money, and I was doing that kind of work. This happened after I had come to New York and was getting my New York union card together and was working Monday nights at Fifty-Second Street, which would pay all of twenty dollars. So I really made a living playing weddings and Bar Mitzvas, which I knew how to do from back home in Philadelphia. And so when Bird was broke and needed a gig, I said, "Come on, I'll get you a gig."

So that was done. It was rather funny, and they portrayed it rather humorously, in a movie that needed a little humor.

Ben: The movie did seem to leave out a lot of the humor that must have been part of the life back then. I would imagine that humor was what kept a lot of people going during the times when there wasn't much money to be made playing this new music. It had to be a lot more fun than the movie suggested.

Red: Oh, sure. The movie was rather dark and rather sad. I'm so glad that Clint Eastwood made the movie, and of course it's about our greatest hero. And also, it was rather authentic about Charlie Parker and what he did. I would have liked to have seen more about the development of this music, but, of course, I'm not a filmmaker. I would have liked to have seen more of the development of the music and less of the love angle.

Ben: You mention that the movie left out the development of Bird's music. It also ignored significant parts of the man's personality. For example, other people have said that Charlie Parker was an intellectual, that he liked to read and discuss a wide range of topics. There was no suggestion of that in the movie.

Red: Well, when we were on the road together, I never saw him read anything. But he was very knowledgeable about political events and current events and he spoke very well. For a man with no formal education, he spoke like an English professor, when he wanted to. That was his great ear. He was able to emulate people that he admired for their brilliance.

You know, he was so many things to so many people. I had a three-year working relationship as his sideman. I also considered us friends, and we were friends for maybe nine or ten years. And I knew Charlie Parker the way *I* saw him and the way he reacted to me. But there was different Charlie Parkers for different people. When somebody's making a movie, he gets everybody's opinion. I understand that.

Ben: Well, let's put the movie aside for a moment then and talk about the Charlie Parker that you knew.

Red: Well the one I knew was very thoughtful, considerate, kind. He was very humble and modest. And, you know, we are like we play. In most instances you can almost hear a musician's personality by the way he plays. I myself can hear improvement and maturity, over the long run, when I've heard somebody ten years ago, twenty years, and today. Charlie Parker was very much like he played. He was very beautiful. He was so skilled and so proficient that the instrument was like a toy. So he expressed himself easier than anybody else could. And I heard his personality every time.

In fact, he showed me by doing. He never would try to hurt my feelings and tell me what he wanted me to do. He'd do it and do it again. And if I didn't get it by the third or fourth time, he'd look right at me—like he did in one scene of the movie—look right at me, and then I knew that's what he meant. So he always treated me with kid gloves. And I'm sure he did that with everybody else. Except when he got angry. Like any normal person, he would get angry, and he would be a little nasty then. But I thought he was a really beautiful man.

Ben: Why do you think he chose you in 1947 as his sideman?

Red: Well, it's true, I protested for a moment. I said, "I'm really not ready to work with you." And I even mentioned that Fats Navarro was on the scene and he certainly was more ready. Kenny Dorham, who I thought was better. Those are the two names I mentioned. And his reply was "Maybe, but I know a good trumpet player when I hear one and I want you." And I tend to think to this day that he liked me. It was more out of friendship.

And look. He hired Miles when Miles barely could play the instrument well enough to be with Charlie Parker. He, more than anybody, saw this great potential in Miles, and look what happened. Miles became our greatest innovator, more than anybody, more than even Bird. From the point of view of innovation, that is, Miles has to be the leading one we've ever had.

So he may have seen something in me that I couldn't see in myself. Of course I said yes. I was flattered and honored and it was like going to college and graduate school all at once.

Ben: On those early records, like the version of "Swedish Schnapps" that you recorded with Bird and John Lewis and Kenny Clark, you sound pretty confident. Had you been playing the material for a while?

Red: Not that particular recording. In fact those tunes came in that day. I was up in the mountains at Alan Eager's mother's hotel playing a Jewish gig. And I was in the swimming pool and heard over the loudspeaker that I was wanted on the phone. And it was Bird. He said, "Get down here right away, we got a record date for Norman Granz." And so Alan used the staff car and got me down to Manhattan. And I saw the charts and I'm sure John Lewis had written them out. Although Bird composed them, I noticed that John Lewis was writing them down, and I often thought that John had to write it down and notate it because Bird couldn't do it as quickly or as well.

Just like I always felt Bird didn't really play with the knowledge of chord changes. His instinct was so great, and his ear was so great and his ability on his horn was so great that he really didn't have to know. But I caught him a couple of times. I asked him, "Where does this bridge go?" Like on "The Song Is You." And he said, "B flat seventh." And I looked at him, like "what?" And I saw that Al Haig [the pianist] was laughing. And I thought, "Wait a minute, is he putting me on or what?" And it happened two or three more times on different tunes, and it was always "B flat seventh." You know, it might have been F sharp minor seventh or something, and I said, "Oh oh, maybe he *doesn't* know."

I can't tell you to this day, but I always had my suspicions that Bird had very little knowledge of chord changes. Formally. Every time I ever asked him where we were or what this chord was, he'd either say "B flat seventh" or he'd say "wait a minute, wait a minute" and change the subject. Like when you don't know something and don't want to tell anybody you don't know it. And that's what I got from him. But what's the difference? He never played wrong. He always played beautifully.

Ben: Would that also explain what appeared to be his ability to jump up out of a sound sleep on the bandstand and begin soloing at any point in any song?

Red: Well, he wasn't sleeping. His eyes might have been closed and might have looked like he was sleeping. But he was never asleep. He was always right there with you.

He was unique. He was marvelous and it was a great experience.

Ben: Did he actually bill you as blues singer "Albino Red," as portrayed in the movie, so that you could play a segregated gig with him down south?

Red: That's been a big embarrassment for me. It did happen, yes, and of course they've blown it out of proportion. He did it. And you know, he was a practical joker. I think he did it to get me the gig. But you know something, we didn't fool anybody and no one ever said anything. He announced me as "Albino Red," and I hollered a little bit, a couple of blues things. It was funny after you looked at it. Now I can look at it and laugh. But I was very embarrassed by it then. Racial relations were so bad, it horrified me to have to do that and to see what was going on down there. You must admit that it's so much better down there now, things are probably better than they are up here in New York.

Ben: On the movie soundtrack, you play another blues with Bird, the song "Now Is The Time." What's the story on that song? Did Bird get it from "The Huckle Buck" or was it the other way around?

Red: I think the guy that wrote "The Huckle Buck" stole it from Bird. I really think that Bird's came first. I think that "Now Is The Time" came first, then somebody wrote "The Huckle Buck" and that was it. See, Charlie Parker, above all, was primarily a blues player. Everything he played had the feel of the blues in it. And he called the blues, especially down south, he said, "Okay, we're going to play 'rice and beans music.' "

Ben: On that soundtrack recording of "Now Is The Time," you actually replaced the original Miles Davis solo. A lot of the younger players who worked on the film talked about what a thrill it was to record with Bird, even though it was only playing along with his previously recorded work. What was it like for you to get involved in that electronic process after having done the real thing in the past?

Red: This was wonderful. I saw Monte Alexander running down the hall shouting "I played with Bird," and John Faddis was there the same day I was, and he freaked out because he played with Bird. And you know, I felt the same as a lot of the younger guys. Although I had played with him for many many years when we were together, it was just as big a treat to play with him with earphones on. You know, they made an engineering coup, really. It was a miracle that they were able to isolate everything else and bring him up to today's digital standards. It was great fidelity. And I felt lucky to be there and to record it with him. I was thrilled. It was spooky, but I was thrilled.

Ben: It must also be a big thrill for you just to be a survivor of those times—not only a survivor but one in pretty good health—and to be a spokesman for the bebop movement. A lot of people did not survive that time in jazz, and you certainly could have been one of them.

Red: You know, I never thought I would survive it either. There were times when I felt like it was over. I couldn't help myself, everything was futile, I kept getting worse and worse. But somehow, I prevailed.

Ben: Of course, it wasn't the music that almost killed you, it was the heroin.

Red: Oh yeah, many of us emulated our great hero's bad habits, as well as trying to play his great music, and I for one did that. It took me a long time to straighten my life out.

Ben: I assume he told you not to get involved with heroin.

Red: Oh! He threatened to kill me. He threatened to fire me. He was very angry. He hated to see young people doing that. Like a doctor would say, "Don't do as I do, do as I say," he really meant that.

Ben: But you felt that in order to play like Bird you had to shoot heroin like Bird?

Red: Well, imagine a young, immature kid hearing this giant play this great music every night, night after night, and I'm sure I must have thought that if I crossed that line and did what he did maybe I'd be as good, or half as good. Of course it's not true. You have to be healthy to play music. He happened to be a genius. He didn't have to be healthy to play great. But imagine if he were healthy how much better he would have played.

I'm so proud of the young ones today. None of them are using drugs today. I have a young band and I see all their friends and I go to a lot of colleges, and they don't drink, they don't smoke, they're dedicated young men and women playing music, and I love that. It's given us a whole new image. And it's given us the dignity that we deserve. And for those of us . . . and I'm not the only one because anyone who's managed to straighten up deserves to be patted on the back.

And what we do with it, well luck plays a part. Of course we make our own luck. But what matters is what happens to us afterwards. Some people can take adversity and overcome it, and others, adversity knocks down and they can never get up. And I've known a lot of great people like that. I was lucky. I had a new marriage. I started playing again in the jazz idiom and nothing else, no commercial music, no shows, no Las Vegas show bands, no jingles, just jazz. And that helped, of course, because when you're doing it you get better. And I see now, looking back, that between the ages of fifty and sixty I've made my greatest musical improvement.

Ben: You did play a lot of commercial music after leaving New York in the early '50s. What made you leave the jazz scene then, after working and recording with Bird?

Red: Well, I was very messed up. I wanted to go home. You know, hope springs eternal. I tried to straighten my life out. I went back to Philadelphia and I got a little gig in a jazz club, but all the leaders started calling me for the society music, the weddings and Bar Mitzvahs. And I did it to make extra money, and I started doing very well with it. And finally some caterer got me and, bang, he made me a leader, and I had a big business. And I hated it. And of course I didn't straighten out.

So, eventually, I sold the business and ran. First I went to San Francisco. Then I went to Las Vegas, and in Las Vegas you're playing in big showroom orchestras behind the stars, show biz stars. Well, the orchestras are very good, but there's no jazz. And then I went to L.A., and there was very little jazz there, also. You know, I kept running, but you can't run away from yourself. Eventually, you're going to have to meet yourself and find out why you are doing what you're doing and how to correct it. It's like, although I never went, Alcoholics Anonymous. You really have to get help, therapy. You need that.

I wound up in Lexington, which is kind of a U.S. public service hospital. And that was a help. So after that, things started looking up.

Ben: Around this time you also established a musical relationship that contributed to your personal revitalization, and that was your teaming up with Ira Sullivan, a trumpet player who turned to the saxophone.

Red: Well, I first met Ira back in 1951, when I did a three- or four-week engagement with Charlie Ventura's big band in Chicago at the Argyle. I was still with Bird, but Bird was out with the strings, so I went with Charlie Ventura. Ira's father, who was an amateur trumpet player, brought Ira around. Ira sat next to me on the bandstand looking at the music—I didn't know he couldn't read music at the time—and he told me, "I also play saxophone." I said, "Yeah? Great." He said, "I have a little gig around the corner. When you're finished, come by." Which I did. And there he was playing both saxophone and trumpet.

And then when I came back to Chicago in 1955, Joe Segal, the owner of the Jazz Showcase for all these years, was the doorman at the Bee Hive. That was his first little bit of association with a club. And he did the booking too, the host and greeter, I guess you'd call him. He hired me, and Ira Sullivan was there, so it was my group with Norman Simmons and Roy Haynes and Victor Sproles and Ira. And Ira then, as he is now, was a unique player. He could play anything he heard anyone else play. Ira could play four or five different tenor styles and two or three different trumpet styles, like a chameleon. And we did make a lot of records together.

For example, we made a record called *Red Rodney In New York*, which later was called *The Red Arrow*. It was on the Signal label, which is now Onyx, and they're still in court fighting over it. I wish they'd finally rerelease this album, because there we had Philly Joe, Oscar Pettiford and Tommy Flanagan, along with Ira and myself. The next day Philly Joe didn't show up, and he sent a young drummer in whom I didn't know named Elvin Jones. He made the other side of this date. And years later, Elvin told me that this was his very first record date. That was 1957. And you know, that was Tommy Flanagan's first New York record date also.

Ben: That's interesting because for somebody who's best known as a sideman, you've brought some attention to many other important musicians. Ira Sullivan is probably the best example.

Red: Yeah, well Ira and I seem to play very well together. I don't know why. We're very friendly but we've never hung out together. We sort of had a feeling for each other and neither of us could understand it. We just knew when each other was going to breathe. And Ira always makes you play better because he has such great energy, and he's such a magnificent musician, on all of his instruments. He's another great person that I've played with. Today, he's kind of a guru in Florida.

Ben: You worked with him on and off for many years, during the late '50s and '60s. Then during the late '60s and early '70s, that whole period, you were playing in Las Vegas, you were doing commercial music . . .

Red: It was a lost weekend.

Ben: A twenty-year lost weekend?

Red: It really was. I did a lot of very strange things, in music and out of music. But like I said, when you can overcome adversity and learn by all of the terrible things you have done, or that have happened to you, then you become a better person for it. And I'm very lucky that I managed to overcome all that.

Today, I'm a very stable, nested person. But musically, I'm very unnested. I'm always looking for the newer things and the newer young musicians. My youngest son is older than my entire band.

Ben: You did overcome adversity, and it seems that it was the music that led you forward. Is this correct?

Red: That was a big part. You know, I had a lot of terrible dental problems. The will was there, but I certainly had a great disability. So because of that, I sort of lost confidence. And when you lose confidence, it's almost over. I came back to New York with high hopes, and I found a good dentist who supervised a whole program for me which gave me another ten years. And it gave me my best ten years. I've just had another implant operation, and I'm looking to ten more.

Ben: So you're kind of the bionic bebop trumpet player.

Red: [Laughs.]

Ben: It's a surprise, given all your physical problems over the years, that you have retained such a youthful appearance and such an optimistic approach to this life.

Red: Well, I think that it's incumbent upon me as a "proper jazz man"—I'll use the term the British use—to keep growing, to keep taking new forms of music from the young people that come along and adding it to my repertoire. I don't mean some of the "snake charming music" that's out there. I can't identify with that. Maybe I'm not hip enough yet. I do like some of the so-called avant garde music. But I'm still a melody man. If I can't hear that melody and that beauty then I discard it.

Getting back to the youth movement, when Ira left I said, "It's going to be hard to replace him." And it was. He's a phenomenal musician. But a young man named Dick Oats came in, and he had something entirely different. First of all, he's younger, and so he's much more modern. And he's also more of a team player than a person like Ira could be. He brought with him an entirely different thing, and the band gelled immediately. He made it a different band.

So now I'm playing newer music and I'm having a ball, standing up there and playing with these great young musicians.

Ben: You mentioned that maybe you're not "hearing" some of the newer music, the music you call "snake charming music." It brought to mind the time many years ago when you first heard Dizzy Gillespie, and you thought he was great except that he played "too weird." In the back of your mind, do you now wonder if this experience is happening to you all over again and that maybe some of the newer music might one day open a door, as bebop did for you forty years ago? Are you going to give it a second chance?

Red: Of course I am. I'm going to give it a third and fourth chance. You know, throughout the history of any art form, there's always been some people that come in under the guise of the avant garde that have been frauds. I'm not going to name any specific person, but some of the music that's come up with the avant garde sounds to me like snake charming music. I envision a guy sitting there with snakes all around him. To me, that is not pretty.

Now I have been wrong many times in my life and I could be wrong again. If somebody could play this with a pretty melody, I could accept it. But when it's harsh and ugly, I can't accept it.

Ben: Let me be the devil's advocate here. You said before that you suspect Bird wasn't playing from his knowledge of the changes, he was playing from his ear. He was playing what he heard . . .

Red: I said that I suspect he didn't know the changes, formally. He didn't know that B flat minor seventh went to E flat into A flat. He didn't know that. I think. I'm not sure I'm right . . . Yes, I am sure I'm right, because many times I asked him where we were, what chord that was and he always gave me that off-the-wall answer.

Ben: Ok, let's say that Bird didn't know the changes formally but could play the changes. So is there a fine line between that and what you're calling "snake charming music"?

Red: I see what you're getting at. And there probably isn't a fine line. There probably isn't. But as we get older, we become more conservative, politically, socially and even musically. And my ear is attuned to melodic music, melodic jazz. And when I hear some of this what I call "snake charming music" . . . and I say it kiddingly, because I accuse Dick Oats of it all the time. I tease him when he gets way out, but he always knows how to come back in, you see, and he doesn't lose me. And that's okay.

No . . . maybe I should be a little more tolerant. But in my personal likes and dislikes, I don't care how far out you go, or how far away from the changes you go, I still want to hear some beauty.

Ben: Clearly, in your own way, you are passing on to the young players of today the benefit of your many years of experience.

Red: And that's so important. It's one of the great things we do. Now I consider myself an elder statesman of jazz. You know the best thing we can do is give the young people an opportunity to learn the roots and traditions that we have. Of course, I learn from them about the newer forms, but people my age can give them the discipline that's so necessary to be—I'll use the term again—a "proper jazz man." And it takes a long time to become a "proper" jazz player. You just don't do it when you make your first two records. You may be great, like Wynton Marsalis is, of course. His first *one* was great. But he's the first one that says this: It takes a long time to be really a dyed-in-the-wool jazz player. And he's reaching it every time I hear him, more and more he's reaching it. I love him and I have a great deal of respect for his playing, for his interest in playing, for his knowledge of the past, which makes him play better and will make him play better in the future.

And that's important. And we give that to the young people who play with us.

* * *

Frank Morgan (September, 1988)

Alto saxophonist Frank Morgan still answers his telephone "Bebop Lives!" It would be equally appropriate to celebrate the fact that "Frank Morgan lives," because his life's story is a classic encapsulation of the bebop movement, with all the humanity and tragedy that that music has to offer. [In fact, an off-Broadway play, called Prison-Made Tuxedos, *built on Frank's life, was produced in 1987.] Frank became addicted to heroin by age 17, because he thought this would please his friend and hero, Charlie Parker. In his own words, "I tried to be a better junkie than Charlie Parker." His musical star was rising fast in the mid '50s when drug-related offenses caused him to spend the first of what was ultimately to become over 25 years in prison. Upon emerging in 1985, he made a record for the Fantasy label and again, like a wild flower in some deserted field, his career suddenly blossomed. And even though he returned to prison one more time after that, it was to be the end of his long battle with heroin. Released later that year, Frank Morgan found his musical and spiritual feet. Due in part to the revival in the interest in Parker's music and also to the more general reinterpretation of bebop as a "neo-classical" form, Frank has accomplished his long march back to health, proudly carrying the flag of bebop. From the opening notes of the following conversation, it was clear that, like a Frank Morgan ballad, it came straight from the heart.*

Ben: Frank, it's such a pleasure to see you looking so well.

Frank: My pleasure. You know, this is a realization of another dream for me. Because during the years I spent in prison, I used to listen to your radio program all the time. So it was a dream of mine to be free and to meet you and now here we are.

Ben: Of course you've set the stage very dramatically by prefacing anything we say with the fact that you are a free man today but you weren't a free man for quite some time.

Frank: No, I wasn't. And it's a long story but it's an age-old story of one choosing not to be free. And there are many excuses to grab.

Ben: Let's go back to the beginning of the story. Does the story begin when you're seven years old?

Frank: Yes. Around seven, I went to Detroit from Milwaukee, Wisconsin, where I was living, to spend an Easter vacation with my mother and father. My father was Stanley Morgan, a guitarist, and my mother, Geraldine, was on the road with my father. He was working in Detroit with Howard McGhee's band at the time. And he took me to a theater that had stage shows, the Paradise Theater. And Jay McShann's band was featured that week. And like out of a dream, when Charlie Parker stood up and played his alto solo—I later found out it was on the "Hootie Blues"—I heard my voice. And a new life began. You see, I was a guitarist up until that day, pursuant to my father's dream of me being a great guitarist. He had been training me since birth, almost.

Ben: So at age seven you ceased being your father's man and became your own man by way of Charlie Parker?

Frank: Yes. Like I say, I heard my voice. To make it a little more clear, I heard the voice that I would like to be. And I'm still pursuing that, you know?

Ben: That recording of "Hootie Blues," and that single chorus that Charlie Parker played, moved a lot of history. Many musicians have said that when they heard Bird play "Hootie Blues," wherever they were, they stopped and they knew nothing was going to be the same again. Some musicians even packed up and left home upon hearing it, in search of who or whatever it was.

Frank: That's the kind of dramatic effect that a true genius has, if you will—and I think if anyone should wear the title of genius certainly it's fitting for Bird to wear it—it's undeniable. When you hear something like that, it *has* to change your thinking. Or something's wrong with you. You know, whether we realize it or not, these things affect us.

Ben: It certainly must have been overwhelming for a seven-year-old boy. Because you didn't just hear him play at the Paradise Theater. You then went backstage and met Bird.

Frank: Yeah. And, you know, I've never been the same. Thank God I've finally started to recover! [Laughs.] I mean that. I mean, his effect on me was really dramatic. I wanted to do everything that produced this voice, you know. No matter what "no's" I knew not to do, no matter what Bird said, no matter what my father said, no matter what the laws of this fine nation said. I wanted to be a drug addict. Simply because *that voice* experienced this. So I've been that and I am that and I'm the better for it, I think, because thank God I'm still alive and well and able to say that was then and this is now. I feel so fortunate, at 54 years old, every day I'm realizing more dreams. Tomorrow morning I leave for Washington, D.C. to play a week at Blues Alley with McCoy Tyner and his trio. And I'm just going to play some bebop. You know, I'm not going to play any rock and roll.

Ben: You've talked in the past about the nature of bebop and what a spiritual thing it was in the midst of all the drugs and the addict's life. How much of that had to do with the image of Bird? The fact that he was larger than life?

Frank: Yes, we were really in awe of his every move. This fine man was probably one of the most intelligent human beings I've ever encountered. Mysteriously, he seemed to know almost everything. At least something about everything, you know. I mean you wonder how a person could play the horn that well and be a serious abuser of alcohol, drugs and all chemicals and obviously have that kind of information about nuclear physics and chess and religion and whatever else. But he did. I hear some people say that he was obviously from another planet. I don't quite agree with that. I think that he was obviously from and for this planet. I think that there was a great deal that we are still learning from Charlie Parker, Dizzy Gillespie, Mister Monk and Mister Kenny Clarke and Mister John Coltrane, all the people that bring this kind of information to us. And this kind of joy.

Ben: Let's get back to your first meeting with Charlie Parker. What did you say to him at age seven that got you your first horn?

Frank: I just remember very clearly the voice and I remember going backstage with my father and being introduced to Charlie Parker and feeling like I had known him all my life. I think that he and my father decided that they would get together the next day to get the horn for me. And the next day Bird didn't show up but he had sent Wardell Gray and Teddy Edwards, who were both playing alto saxophone at that time, to get me started on clarinet. And I was very let down. I didn't understand the wisdom of starting out on clarinet, Bird's wisdom. As most saxophone players now know, the clarinet is an excellent training instrument for the saxophone because it teaches you to practice control. You have to develop control before you can get the clarinet to stop squeaking.

Ben: You ultimately progressed to alto and then on to California with your family where your father became the owner of a jazz club.

Frank: Yes, it was The Casablanca at 28th and San Pedro in L.A. Bird played there, Diz played there. When I first came to California in 1947, the club was still going on, but Bird wasn't in California at the time. But Dexter Gordon and Hampton Hawes and all those cats were playing there, and it was just an amazing thing to see, all these people I had heard on record playing this wonderful music. Every night. There were so many different saxophone players, Lucky Thompson, you know, Mingus was playing, Buddy Collette, Eric Dolphy, Walter Benton.

There was an alto player, other than the more popular ones from L.A., like Sonny Criss and Eric Dolphy, a gentleman named Gene Cravens that I heard, who was out of sight. I also remember Ornette very early on. We go way back. Another fine alto saxophonist that Billy Higgins can tell you about was George Newman, who Don Cherry and Billy Higgins had a group with before Ornette. George Newman was a fine alto player. All these people influenced me. Benny Carter was my first choice as a teacher in California.

But Charlie Parker was forever embedded in my heart. You know, that *sound*. That soul crying out with each note! I mean, he didn't waste anything.

Ben: Bird also had wide ranging taste and experience. I believe you once went to hear Stravinsky with Bird. What was that like?

Frank: It seems that almost everything I experienced with Bird has a beautiful haze around it today. I went to the Hollywood Bowl and Stravinsky was conducting. And his son, who was a pianist, was playing in the Los Angeles Philharmonic Orchestra. I remember sitting way at the top of the bowl with Bird, and I remember him listening very intently to the music. He seemed to like Stravinsky very much. He liked a lot of classical music. I know he was extremely fond of Bartok. And you heard everything in his playing. You could tell that he listened.

Ben: It's often been said that he was frustrated by not being taken seriously by the classical music establishment. Did you get this sense with him that night?

Frank: No. I don't recall that. You have to understand that at the time I was around Bird I was a teenager. So much went over my head.

I know that he enjoyed very much being showcased with the strings. I know that it hurt him deeply when they were taken away from him. That's the way he described it, that they were taken from him. He once told me, he said, "You know Little Frank," he said, "when I was playing with the strings, I practiced every day and I was always on time and I felt great." He said, "I was there conducting, and I felt like I was really responsible. And then they took them away from me." And it just kind of hung there: "They took them away."

I also know that he was very distressed with the responsibility that he either accepted or felt that went along with people like myself starting to use drugs because we were fond of his music. He didn't feel good about that, like he was leading people into another life because of his behavior. And it was like, "Can't you see what it's doing to me? Why do you want to do that when you see what it's doing to me?"

Ben: Where were you when you started using heroin?

Frank: Oh . . . I would say I was seventeen years old when I started using it. Oddly enough, it was a track star from my school, Jefferson High

School, who had gone on to Los Angeles City College, and at seventeen I was at City College also. And that's when I had my first shot of heroin.

Ben: The story is legend that Bird said over and over again to every young person he met, "Don't do it." I'm sure he told you that.

Frank: Oh yes, in no uncertain terms. But, you know, there's a saying that "I can't hear what you say because what you're doing speaks so loudly." And I think that was the case. I was determined to do what Bird was doing, as I understood it, no matter what he said. That's the nature of that sickness, it goes beyond all reason that anyone can bring to you.

Ben: Is there a part of you that believes that having experienced addiction has made you a better player today then you would have been without that experience?

Frank: Yes and no. I mean I couldn't deny that my use of drugs has happened, and I believe that I am more sensitive because it did happen. I don't want that to be interpreted in any way to mean that I recommend that it happen, or that I give it credit for doing anything for me. I think that one who has experienced cancer knows how deadly cancer is and how fortunate they were to have survived it. So that is the way I mean it. I think I am much more sensitive to human degradation and to the loss of freedom just as I am more sensitive to *freedom* and the desire to be free, because my use of drugs took me to some places and took me to some depths in living that I know I don't want to go back to. So I am more sensitive to being free, because I know what it is to not be free.

Ben: Is it true, as you were once quoted as saying, that you did some of your best playing in prison?

Frank: Yes, I did some of my best playing there.

Ben: You've also said that you felt more secure when you were in prison than out on the streets. How can that be?

Frank: Well, my thinking found that acceptable, to be a big fish in a little pond. I guess due to my insecurity or whatever. For what reasons, I don't know, but somehow I have to accept the fact that I seem to find it comfortable in prison. Because I kept going back. I mean the band wasn't that good. Now that the truth be known. I mean, I've been quoted as saying that the best band I ever played with was in San Quentin. No, that's not the truth. I played with Hank Jones at Lincoln Center the other night, you know. [Laughs.] The whole band in prison wasn't that good!

Ben: You spent more than 25 years in and out of prisons, including San Quentin, but were freed in 1985, when you recorded with Cedar Walton, Billy Higgins and Tony Dumas for Fantasy records. The title of that record was *Easy Living*. A truly ironic title, don't you think, for your first come-back record?

Frank: I didn't understand that at the time. At the time I recorded "Easy Living," I didn't know it was going to be the title track of the album. It was just a tune I wanted to play. At that time, "easy living" was not happening. In fact, at the time, I was a fugitive. The parole department had a warrant out for my arrest. When I finished that recording, I turned myself back in to my parole officer and went back to prison for four months. I was released in 1985, two weeks after the album was released.

I thought it was pretty weird that Fantasy would call the album *Easy Living* because I was in prison per se at the time it was released. Then two weeks later, I was released.

And now I understand. It was a projected view. Because living *is* easy. I mean, it's beautiful now. Because I'm free and I'm intending to be free for the rest of my life. I mean really free to play the music to the best of my ability.

Ben: The critical reaction to your re-emergence on the music scene the past four years has been unanimous. In these few short years you've made a half dozen great albums. Does it bother you then that you are still living in the shadow of Charlie Parker and that you are constantly being talked about in the context of Bird?

Frank: Well, it's quite an honor, believe me. It's no longer really frightening. It used to frighten me to be compared with Charlie Parker, and now I simply consider it an honor to be mentioned in the same breath. Simply that. And I understand that Charlie Parker is Charlie Parker and I'm Frank Morgan. I cannot be Charlie Parker. I won't even try any more.

I'm just really grateful to be here. I've seen so many fine artists perish.

Ben: It's seems that now your future is so bright that you're able to see your past in a new light.

Frank: Yes. For example, I finally got to play in Paris. And it was awesome, I mean to play five nights, and each night was sold out prior to the performances.

I mean bebop does live and living is easy. I couldn't ask for a better chance, and I intend to seize the time. I enjoy practicing many hours a day and I intend to practice many more hours. And it's all about love. I mean, it's a lovely world.

Ben: You're describing something many musicians have said, which is when you work on your horn you're really working on yourself.

Frank: Yes, exactly, it's my therapy.

Ben: And it seems your playing is growing too. For example, your later recordings feel like you are expanding your horizons and growing beyond the influence of Bird. I hear some Johnny Hodges in your recent stuff.

Frank: Oh, Johnny Hodges! That's one of the things that I'm trying to bring out of me now is the tender side of my playing. And lately I've been looking more into the way Johnny Hodges has influenced me and the way he plays ballads. I think he influenced Bird and everyone. Of course Bird influenced Johnny Hodges too. Such is life. The life of a person who is in pursuit of new information all the time, we draw upon every source.

But I was thinking about the way Johnny Hodges just paints such a beautiful picture when he plays those Billy Strayhorn ballads. I've been dealing a little bit with "A Flower Is A Lovesome Thing" and how Johnny would influence the way that I would play it.

Ben: They talk about Bird's sound as being such a "human" sound, and the same term has often been used to describe Johnny Hodges' sound.

Frank: I think it's been said that we should seek to make our instrument an extension of us. Well Bird had to be doing this for the love to leap out of his horn and make me hear my voice and change my life so dramatically.

Ben: Is that "human thing" something only time can teach?

Frank: Yes. You know that life is so instructive. You can't imagine how much better it feels to be sitting here with you in a recording studio doing beautiful things when I've been in many studios in my other life figuring what to steal. Like these Neuman U87 microphones, or the 67's or the 47's.

Ben: It's so good to be free of that.

Frank: Yeah, just to get right down there with it. You know, I have to come from gut level just to state it on base terms. I mean, I'm really grateful that I could go to Paris and be given the choice of brand new horns. The welcome mat was really laid out for me. Because I know what it is to steal Selmer saxophones and not even have the means to keep one for myself. Or the care to keep one, you know? I mean, I had a fifteen-hundred-dollar-a-day habit.

But that only indicates how big a damn fool I was. So I'm really grateful. I feel so much better today.

Ben: It's amazing that you managed to keep your music together through that long night.

Frank: It's God, man. God did it. I mean I did everything I could not to be here. Truth. I mean I tried not to be here. It just didn't work. It must be a greater purpose.

I mean look at the immense amount of publicity I've had. I know I don't play that well. I'm not crazy. I know there's a bigger blessing. So I take it seriously. I have trouble now with maybe having too much enthusiasm for some of the older musicians. You know, they say, "Slow down, man, everything's going to be alright. We just got to float around . . ." No, no. We don't just have to float, we've got to work hard at this music. We've got to do the *best* we can. If we're not doing our *best* every time we hit the bandstand then we're not . . . I mean, I've got a burning desire to do my best and to try and infuse that spirit into everyone.

Because so many of us, we don't realize what a blessing it is to be able to work and make a living and feed our family and live a nice lifestyle playing the music that you want to play. With who you want to play it with, you know, and just meeting gorgeous people all over the world. And to spread the love.

I mean I take this seriously. No matter how frightening it gets. And it does get frightening. It is very frightening for a 54-year-old person to deal with success when you've never dealt with anything but failure before. I worked *hard* at failure. I mean, I worked hard at it. I gave it my best. So I'm trying to learn how to give success my best now. It's not easy. [Laughs.] It's frightening.

You think it ain't frightening to go play a week with McCoy Tyner? He's going to have all week long to listen to me. Not just a little time at the studio. [Laughs.] Man, this cat is bashing! But I like that high energy. The higher energy the better. And he doesn't lighten up. He just does not let up.

I mean, I'm very happy. It's a good time for me.

Ben: It's particularly good timing in that drugs, in terms of society, used to be "their" problem, referring to musicians or whatever. Now the drug problem in this country has spread to all levels, to lawyers and the business community, for example. So it turns out that musicians really were like the canaries in the coal mine, who sang at the first sign of danger.

Frank: Yes. See, I really believe that it's up to us to save the world, before we blow it up.

Ben: With a horn instead of a bomb.

Frank: Sure, I'm happy to be the pied piper. You know, thank God for people like Wynton Marsalis, who are able to show the younger people by example, by choice, just how beautiful this music is. And people are starting to really identify with the music. Because your thinking improves when you do.

So this is what we have to do now. We have to take it to the schools. We have to do what we can to be more accessible to the younger people. I think that we have to make sure we're doing all that we can. Because, well it keeps me cool. I mean I understand myself a little better. I'm either real constructive or real destructive. So I'm putting it all into the constructive energy side.

Ben: It also sounds like you feel it's too late in the day to be bitter about what wasn't.

Frank: Right. What was, was. I mean, I got a chance, man. Major changes.

Ben: Do you feel that in some ways you got the chance on behalf of a lot of guys who didn't survive?

Frank: Sure. I have a tremendous responsibility. Tremendous responsibility. And I love it, you know? I'm trying to be up to the task. That's why I got to practice hard.

Ben: It makes you feel lucky you stuck to your guns, right?

Frank: Yeah, bebop lives!

* * *

Jon Hendricks (November, 1985)

Nobody has done a better job of translating the vocabulary of bebop into standard English than Jon Hendricks. As a founding member of the landmark vocal group Lambert, Hendricks & Ross, he pioneered the field of "vocalese," which took the tradition of "scat singing," or singing nonsense syllables, one step further, by actually writing a verbal narrative to go with well known jazz solos. He has, over the years, become one of the music's foremost historians, creating and starring in the stage production The Evolution of the Blues, *which traced in music and verse the African-American experience and the power of its oral tradition. I first met Jon in the mid-seventies, when I produced a record with him and learned, first hand, that "in jazz there are no mistakes, only opportunities." Or, as Jon likes to say, "The mistakes are sometimes the only part that's jazz." Jon Hendricks continues today to be a father figure to literally dozens of vocal improvisors and devotes his time and talent to the nurturing of the art form, working primarily with Jon Hendricks & Co., a vocal quartet that includes his wife and daughters.*

Ben: Jon, we're sitting here talking about Shakespeare and Francis Bacon, and the controversy over who really wrote those plays. First of all, what's the real lowdown ?

Jon: Well, there is no real lowdown. As I was saying to you, and I don't like to offend a lot of tender sensibilities, but I can sum up by rephrasing what Mark Twain said about the whole Shakespeare-Bacon controversy. You know, he said, "Anyone who thinks Shakespeare wrote those plays is a damn fool." I agree with Mark.

Ben: OK, that's the literary perspective from the "Godfather of Vocalese." Actually, I brought that up because you are the most literary jazz face I know. I don't know anybody who is deeper into the literary tradition, and I think that really has a bearing on your work.

Jon: Well, it's because I lead . . .

Ben: Three lives?

Jon: No, two. You know, I came from a very straight-laced, staid family. My father was a minister in the African-Methodist-Episcopal church, and he was the cultural and the moral foundation of our entire neighborhood, you know, in my home town. And so, we, all his children, had to exemplify all the things for which he stood. So I had a very straight life, never engaged in any gambling. We never used any profane language anywhere near the house. There was no alcohol in the house, no smoking. We had to, when we got up in the morning, we had to pray, before we went to sleep at night we prayed. We learned, very early, that we are children of a living God and that we bow our heads to God, but to no man. So we were what might now be called militant even then, but not against any other man. We were just militant in our self-respect and all that. So, that's the way I grew up.

So then, when I started singing jazz, and I had to consort [laughs] with these musicians, you know? I had to maintain two vocabularies. Like, I couldn't come to the gig, you know, which I did every night while I was going to the University—I was working on a gig at that time playing drums—but I couldn't come to the gig and say, "My wife and I went to a cinema today." Which would be the way I would normally speak, if I was in the University. I would say, "Me and my bed-buddy took in a flick." You know. [Laughs.] So I had to maintain these two vocabularies starting very early. So it gave me a much more broad spectrum of life and outlook on life. And to this day, I think that the language of the American jazz musician is the most functional and, in its way of expressing itself, the most beautiful of all languages. It's the greatest way to speak, ever.

Ben: Well, you have been one of the foremost translators from one language into the other, from jazz into English and back again. On the liner notes for a King Pleasure record, you once wrote: "Man must have made his first musical instruments in imitation of his own voice. The song mother nature sang, and the wind through the trees, and the thunder and the sound of waves against the shore, and the sound of beast and the sound of bird, and more, was his only other choice." What a nice scan. It almost sounds like an instrument playing, right there.

Jon: Yeah, that's right. That's what I always try for. I always try to swing, whatever I do. I think that's what I got most from singing with good jazz musicians. You don't just have to swing on the bandstand. Everything you do can swing. The way you relate to your fellow man, you know, that can swing. The way you pick up your little child, and bounce him, there's a swing to that. Everything can swing. I think everything in nature does swing.

Ben: Your lyrics are grounded in philosophy and metaphysics and in history, am I right? Those are your areas. And when you approach a lyric, even if it's a boy-girl lyric, somehow you've always got some greater vista you're painting.

Jon: Well, there've been some great boys and some great girls in love. [Laughs.]

Ben: And you're still writing the love songs . . .

Jon: Yeah . . .

Ben: Let's go back and get some personal information. You make reference to growing up in a very straight family. And that was in Toledo, Ohio, right?

Jon: Right.

Ben: And you went to college as an English literature major?

Jon: After I came out of the war, which nearly destroyed my sanity, World War II that is, I went to college in self-defense. Because at that time, if you were reasonably alert, reasonably intelligent, society had aligned itself against you unless you were to approach it from the inside. For example, if you were a young 26-year-old Negro, your future was to work, unless you did something to raise your status from that of a potential worker to, say, a lawyer or a doctor. I applied first to medical school at the University of Rochester, and they said, "I'm sorry, we have filled our quota." And in my naivete I thought they meant their quota of doctors. [Laughs.] Because I must say, I never, well, I think I got this from my father, I never looked at mankind as one separate from another. I had to *learn* that there was such a thing as racism. Which I learned in the Army.

Before I went into the Army, I didn't even know I was colored, 'cause I acted and behaved and did anything I wanted to. It was only when I went into the Army. And then I got into a segregated Army. That I couldn't believe. What are we going to Europe to fight Nazism for, with two Armies? That incensed me. That really upset me quite a bit, and put me at war with the United States Army, which war has never ended, as far as I'm concerned. I never will get over it. That was the depth of stupidity, you know? And then I talked to people who went to Vietnam, and they say the same thing. When they went on pass, there was a part of town that was for the Blacks, and a part of the town that was for the Whites. The stupidity that these people continue to perpetrate on each other, to me is so monumental that I don't even take part in it. I refuse to take any part in anything in which anybody is going to separate the children of God into groups to suit their own madness, you know? I'll never have anything to do with that.

Ben: So you say in self-defense, or for reasons of self-preservation, you went into the University?

Jon: That's right. I was gonna become a lawyer, you know, so I could defend myself. [Laughs.]

Ben: Right, you'd figured out by then what were the real weapons in this life. Did you graduate?

Jon: I didn't, my G.I. Bill ran out. My G.I. Bill ran out 18 months short of a law degree, and I remember, about six months before that happened, I had sung with Bird. He played a one-nighter in Toledo with Max Roach and Tommy Potter, Kenny Dorham and Al Haig on piano. And I got up and scatted with him. And when I got through scatting, Kenny Dorham went up to the microphone to play, so there was a vacant chair. So when I started off the bandstand, Bird literally reached out and took hold of my coat. I mean, he pulled my coat. You've heard the expression, that he "pulled my coat"? Well he literally pulled mine, you know. He waved me over and I went and I sat down next to him, and we had this hectic, nine-minute bandstand conversation in the midst of Max and Tommy and Al, and everything going on. And Bird says, "Hey man, you sing your ass off," you know? And I said, "Thanks." He says, "Whadaya do?" I said, "I'm a law student." He said, "What?" I said, "I'm a law student at the University of Toledo." And he said, "Aw, man, you ain't no lawyer." I said, "Whadaya mean?" He says, "You ain't no lawyer, man, you're a jazz singer." I said, "Well, what'll I do about that?" Being a little facetious, you know? I'm gonna put this cat on. He said, "Well, you gotta come to New York." I said, "I don't know anybody in New York." And I'm thinking eight million people at that time. With a million passing through every day. He said, "Well, you know *me*." I said, "Well, where will I find you?" He said, "Just ask anybody." [Laughs.]

And I thought, "What an egotistical cat this is." And I really looked at him as if to say, "Well, you really think you're something else." And he's sitting there with a smile on his face. He didn't change expression. And, about six months after that, I decided to move out of Toledo to Toronto. And I got in my Chevy with my wife and my son and my set of drums; went to the Canadian boarder, outside Buffalo. And they asked me did I have 2000 dollars. And I said, "No." They said, "Then you cannot move into Canada." I said, "Whadaya mean?" They said, "You have to have at least 2000 dollars to start your family out, so you will not be dependent on the Canadian government." You know, so I said, "Well, what do I do?" He says, "Well, you'll have to go someplace else." So we were crushed, because I had intended to start a new life up in Canada, and where can we go, where can we go?

And I remembered this mad bandstand conversation with this strange self-possessed man. [Laughs.] And I remember the whole thing. He said, "Just ask anybody." So I said, "OK, we're going to New York." So, on the way to New York, the Chevy broke down. Took most of the money I had to try to fix it, and it could not be fixed. So, we left it and got a Greyhound bus. Arrived in New York at the bus station with a wife, a son, and about 27 dollars.

Ben: And a set of drums . . .

Jon: And a set of drums. I went into the phone booth and called Joe Carroll, who is an old friend of mine. He took my place with Dizzy. I was supposed to be the vocalist with Dizzy, but when he came to Rochester looking for me, I had moved back to Toledo, at which time he hired Joe Carroll.

I missed that gig. So, I called up Joe. I said, "Hey Joe, I'm in town." He says, "Oh, beautiful, man." Really lovely guy. I said, "What can I do?" He said, "Well, go on 116th street and Comden Avenue. Hotel called the Hotel Clairmont, right across the street from Columbia University." I said, "Okay, where can I find Bird?" He said, "The Apollo bar, 125th Street and 7th Ave." I couldn't believe it . . .

Ben: Third stool from the left . . .

Jon: I couldn't believe it. It was incredible. Can you imagine that? It's incredible. I said, "OK." So I check into the hotel. I got somebody to sit with my baby. I got myself reasonably unpacked. I took my wife. We went over to the Apollo bar. Now, I had met this man on a bandstand on a one-nighter in Toledo. For a period of about eleven minutes. And I was wondering, what are you gonna do if he doesn't recognize you? So I walk in the club and he's playing "The Song Is You." And he's blowing, man. He's got Roy Haynes on drums, Bud is on piano. What's the bass player from Kansas City? His original bass player?

Ben: Curly Russell . . .

Jon: Curly Russell, was on bass. And Gerry Mulligan was on tenor saxophone, with blood red hair and a blood red beard, and raggedy as a bowlyyacka. Man! [Laughs.] So I walk past the bandstand, and Bird is . . . [Jon sings a melodic line] . . . "Hey, Jon, how ya doin' man, wanna sing some'm?" [sings on another second or two]. I couldn't, that was it, I thought I was goin' crazy. Say what kinda cat is that, man. This had been almost a year, then. I couldn't get my mind together, my knees were shaking. I sit down at the table, and I look at him, he's smiling. He remembered. He remembered me.

So I figured, and I been figuring this thing out for about 25 years, and the nearest I can figure, I must have sung pretty good. I must have done something for him to remember me, you know? And after that, he came off the bandstand, asked me where I was living, what I wanted to do. "Well, I want a gig, you know." All doors opened for me after that. I had no real struggle in New York.

Ben: Did you work with Bird after that?

Jon: Only once, only once. And I just walked right into every gig. People called me that I never heard of. "Yeah, man, we heard about you from Bird, you know." I met Miles that way. Miles says [using gravelly voice], "Yeah, man, I heard about ya." . . .

Ben: This must have been around 1951, an interesting time for a jazz singer . . .

Jon: Mr. B [Billy Eckstine] was it.

Ben: Mr. B was it, but there was also Dave Lambert, Buddy Stewart, and, just on the other side of the horizon, there was Eddie Jefferson.

Jon: Yeah, Eddie Jefferson was on the way with his "Mood For Love." But Dave and Buddy, I was listening to them in Toledo. In fact I was doing "A Cent And A Half" at that time. I loved that. I loved what they did. Of course we were late getting those records. We didn't get 'em right away. Had to wait a little while.

Ben: The group, of course, that stands out as the monumental group, and you're smiling, nodding your head, 'cause we're gonna talk about Lambert, Hendricks and Ross.

Jon: Well, you know, when you say "the group," that always makes me laugh, you know, because, we never had any idea to have a group. [Laughs.]

Ben: Is that right?

Jon: Never! We never intended to have a group. Dave and I were starving, and I mean starving. I had divorced my first wife, and my children were with my sister in Toledo. I was in New York on my own, and I was paying rent in the Cecil Hotel, in the Village. And spending all my days over at Dave's apartment, because we had done a record called "Four Brothers" on some little obscure label. And it was a bomb, but it attracted the attention of some people, including Milt Gabler at Decca, who gave us a gig to do it over again. On the Decca label, backed by a song called "Cloudburst," which I had heard on an album on MGM with Claude Cloud and His Thunderclaps, whom I knew to be Leroy Kirkland, the ex-guitar player with Jimmy Lunceford's Orchestra. Leroy had been looking for a hit for twenty years, you know. Walking around the Brill Building, peddling his songs like all of us. And he finally gets this opportunity to record, so he gets this band together and he hires saxophone player Sam "The Man" Taylor. And records this one tune "Cloudburst," and turns Sam loose. And Sam could play. Sam played this brilliant solo. Low and behold, the record is a hit. But nobody to this day still knows Leroy Kirkland. [Laughs.] So this man died in obscurity and the big chance he had for his name to be known, he had changed it to "Claude Cloud and His Thunderclaps." That's very, very ironic.

So anyway, we did this and it was a flop in America. But in England, a trombonist named Don Langhorn listened to "Cloudburst," and he dug it. And he recorded it, and he changed his name to Don Lang, and it went number one. So here were Dave and I, with the number one song in England and France, and we didn't know what else to do. We had no record company. We didn't know, how can we follow this thing up? You know, the little company for which we'd done our original thing had gone out of business. Milt Gabler wasn't interested in doing anything else with us because the "Four Brothers" record that he'd made had been a flop in America. At that time they only judged by America. They weren't judging by all the other markets, like they do now.

Ben: Point of interest. Was this the same song "Cloudburst" that we all know now from the Lambert, Hendricks and Ross album that became such a hit in the late Fifties?

Jon: Oh, yes, this is the one . . .

Ben: Same lyric?

Jon: Same lyric . . .

Ben: And what year was this?

Jon: This is late '55, early '56. So, here were Dave and I, hits in England and France, and Belgium and Holland and Denmark and Germany, and nobody knew us. And we were starving. And when I say starving, I mean, we got up most mornings, and there was maybe enough instant coffee to make two cups. And maybe there was eleven cents. And we'd go around the corner and buy two day-old rolls. And that would be our breakfast. Then we would start out and walk around the village and see who we knew and who we'd meet. And who would wanna buy us a cup of coffee or maybe invite us to dinner that evening. And that, we were actually, actively, engaged in starving. So Dave came up with this idea. He says, "Look, as long as we're starving," he says, "Before we die, why don't we . . ." You know Dave Lambert. He's the most beautiful man I ever met. He says, "Why don't we create a work of art, so we can leave, so they'll know who we were." Instead of just being two dead men, you know. [Laughs.]

And he was so funny, but at the same time he was so serious that I said, "Yeah, whadaya got in mind?" He said, "Well, I always liked Basie, you always liked Basie. Why don't you put lyrics to some tunes of Basie. I'll arrange them, and we'll sing 'em." And I looked at this man, you know, this pixie. I looked at this little pixie, and he's sittin' there across from me, and I thought, "This guy is out of his mind." 'Cause I thought what it had taken to write for "Four Brothers." All the time and the detail, you know . . .

Ben: Every horn part . . .

Jon: Not only that, you have to weave . . . first you have to tell a story. You have to construct a beginning, a middle and an end plot, from the title. And you have to build all these . . . It's like putting meat on a skeleton until you have the living, breathing person, you know?

Ben: You're saying the song title is the subject, the first thirty-two bars become the plot, and the horns become the characters.

Jon: Yeah, that's right. And this, you know, this takes a lot out of you. And I'm thinking, "Ten of these things." So I told Dave, I says, "Man you're out of your mind." He says, "Whadaya mean?" I said, "That's a lotta work." He said, "So what else you got to do?" I said, "Yeah, well, that's right." He says, "Come on, let's go." So I said, "Okay." So he dragged me kicking and screaming into stardom. [Laughs.]

Because we started this thing, and we wrote four of the songs. Actually we wrote six, but we took four to show. And we didn't have money to ride the bus or the subway. We lived on Cornelia Street, which is a one block street behind Sixth Avenue, off West Fourth to Bleecker. It runs West Fourth to Bleecker. It's where the gangsters used to drop the bodies. They'd drive down Sixth Avenue, turn right on West Fourth into Cornelia, dump the bodies, down to Bleecker, around, back up Sixth Avenue. [Laughs.] So this is where we lived. And we'd have to walk from there. It was, you know when I look back on it, it was really quite beautiful. I was so busy being drugged by it, you know, both Dave and I, that we didn't realize what a picturesque life we were living. And what a wonderful life we had. 'Cause it was beautiful. Everybody loved us. The whole Village loved Dave and Jon, you know, 'cause we were always on the scene, we were always ready to perform, we gave everybody our art and what we had to offer, freely, at all times. You know, advice to other poets and writers.

So we'd walk uptown to the Fifties, every day, all the way up, and all the way back, and we'd visit the record companies. And these people would all say the same thing, "Well, you'll have to make a demo." You know, you have to make us a demo, and bring us a demo. And Dave would always point out, "It's 20 dollars per side per hour for voices. If we had 1,500 dollars to make a demo, we wouldn't need to come to you. We can't make the demo, we don't have the money." So they'd say, "Well, I'm sorry, unless I get a demo I can take into my board, there's nothing I can do to help you." 'Cause, you know, they were afraid for their jobs, they were not real artists, you know, creative artists, who would take hold of the reins of things and go on and do something. They were just little functionaries who wanted to collect their weekly pay. We understood who they were, because that was the kind of life we had assiduously dodged all our lives, so we knew about them.

So finally, we went to a record company called ABC Paramount. And there was a young man there named Creed Taylor. Very straight-laced, very unsmiling, and very, if you looked at him you'd think he was cold . . . and very square. Boy, was he square. He still is to this day, you know? I mean, you know Creed, that's just the way he is. But, behind that facade of squareness, there's a mind there, working like a steel trap. And a very creative mind, too. So he heard us, he says, "I think this is really very good." [Laughs.] So Dave and I look at each other, "What does that mean?" You know? And he said, "Well, I suppose if you had the money to make a demo, you would already have done so by now." Very intelligent man.

Ben: The first sign of life here.

Jon: Yeah, right. That's true. So he said, "Well, I'll have to go into my board and see if I can get them to accept this idea without a demo." He's the first one that said that. So we said, "Okay, we'll go home and wait for your call." We walked back down and we waited. Two, three days went by. Finally the fourth day, the phone rang. Creed says, "Okay, they'll let us have one date to see how it turns out. If it's gonna turn out okay, they'll give the money to go ahead for the whole album."

Ben: Now this is the album that eventually became *Sing A Song of Basie*, based on vocal arrangements of Count Basie's music with singers doing the big band charts.

Jon: Yeah, that's right. It's the first time anything like that had ever been done, in the history of the recording business. So Dave and I danced around the room, because it meant we would have 500 dollars apiece in our pockets. 'Cause he said as soon as they accepted us, we could get an advance of a thousand dollars. So we were gonna be able to pay the rent. We were gonna be able to buy some food. We were gonna be able to even maybe, you know, go and have a bowl and get high. Maybe. Do *something*, you know. And so we were very happy. And, you know, we made a business arrangement, as near to business as we ever came. Dave and I would be "Dave Lambert and His Singers, John Hendricks and His Lyrics, Sing a Song of Basie." And we said, "Okay, that's fair, that's good." And the reason Dave's name was first is because he had been in show-business longer than me, and he was older than me. [Laughs.] And that was fair too. See, I mean, we did everything straight down the line, fair. Dave Lambert was one of the fairest people I ever met in my life. This was a fair man. He would never do an unfair thing.

So we went into the studio, and Dave had these thirteen singers. And we had the Count Basie rhythm section, which was then Freddie Green, guitar; Eddie Jones, bass; Sonny Payne, drums, and Nat Pierce, piano. And these thirteen Dave Lambert singers, whom Dave had used for various other things, you know, backing up Jo Stafford, doing "Hawaiian War Chant" on Capital. These were great singers. They could come in and read a score. I saw one guy read the score upside down, you know, standing in front of the music stand, looking over the score reading it. They were monsters. But they couldn't swing. They couldn't swing Basie. Instead, well take a song like "Blues Backstage," they would go [sings corny and straight]. You know. Now that sounds okay, right? But Basie did it [sings hip Basie style]. You see, there's all the difference in the world in those two examples, but to tell someone what that difference is, even though you have the superb English language, is impossible . . .

Ben: And impractical . . .

Jon: It's impractical, you don't have the time, it . . . As the cat said, it can't be did. [Laughs.] So there we were, man . . .

Ben: With thirteen folks and a record date to do and the clock running.

Jon: Two and a half hours of studio time had elapsed. We were trying. I mean, the rhythm section even got down and walked amongst them. Eddie Jones would go over to the girls and the men and say, "No, you don't *slow down*, you *lay back,*" you know. Telling them these things, but they're not *of* or *in* the culture. So these words didn't mean anything to them, you know? Because "laying back" to a person who doesn't know the subtlety of laying back *is* slowing down. But the way it becomes "laying back in lieu of slowing down" is that what you lose on the three beats, you catch up on the fourth one . . .

Ben: Or the seventh one . . .

Jon: Or the seventh one, or ninth one, exactly. So, it was impossible. So we . . . so there we were. So Creed Taylor looked very shocked. Very shocked, because it was 1,500 dollars down the drain. And ABC Paramount was not about to stand for that, not out of a new young executive in its department. And he knew he was finished. His job, he was done, that was it, that was gonna be the end of his career. So, this is when I learned what I love about Creed Taylor. He, his job was on the line. I'm sure he had, if not a wife and family, then he probably had a girl he wanted to marry. But, he never put his worry on us. He never started shaking, or saying, "What are we gonna do, what are we gonna do?" And nothing like that. He says, "Well, what do you suggest?" So Dave said, "Well, we'll multi-track."

I looked at Creed, and Creed looked at me. And we both looked at Dave. And we both said, "We'll what?" And Dave says, "We'll multi-track." We said, "What in the world is that?" And Dave says, "Aw, that's, you know, you take a tape, you know what tape is?" He says, "Tape, you know, you can do anything with tape," he says. And this was in the age of the two track machine. That's all they had. They didn't have four- track, eight-track, sixteen-track. Dave said, "You take the tape and you record something on it. And then you take that tape off and you put another one on and you record something on that. And then you run the tapes together, and you get both things." So we knew that could be done with two tapes. So we figured, "Yeah, but we gotta do twelve voices." He said, "Well then, we do it four times."

So we both naturally thought this man was nuts. So Creed, he was so desperate, you know, he said, "Well." He said, "About how long would this take?" Dave says, "Well, Annie Ross does it good." You know. I said, "Yeah, that girl is pretty hip." I had heard of Annie's things on the Prestige label. And so we both decided, "Yeah, that girl can work along with us on this. And we can do three voices at a time. And we only have to do it four times." So Creed says, "Well how long you think it will take?" Dave says, "Well, it take us a month." Creed says, "Well how am I gonna keep that secret from the people upstairs?" And Dave says, "We'll do it at night." You know, it was their studio, and all they had to do was see that the engineer got paid, which he figured out a way he could finagle from the petty cash. So, we began to work on this project at midnight, every night, when everybody had gone home. At that time, they didn't record all night like they do now. And when everybody went home, we'd come in, and we started on this monumental thing. And low and behold, we finished it. And on the day we finished it, I staggered out of the studio into a taxi and went to Bellevue. I had to have a benevolent cyst removed on my right side. I was just overtired, overexerted, overstimulated, you know.

Ben: Jon, let's get this in perspective, because *Sing A Song of Basie* was a tremendous undertaking, and, as you say, a musical and technological breakthrough. But there had been some "vocalese" success before this, particularly King Pleasure's version of "Moody's Mood For Love," which was recorded in 1952. In the liner notes to the reissued version of that record, you mentioned the impact of hearing "Moody's Mood For Love" for the first time. Had you ever considered writing lyrics to jazz solos before you heard that song?

Jon: I never had that idea. When I heard "Moody's Mood for Love," it opened a door in my mind, as big as the whole universe. It just was like a revelation to me. Because I had been writing 32-bar songs. I had had a hit song, actually, with "I Want You To Be My Baby," by Lillian Briggs, which I had written, incidentally, for Louie Jordan. I was writing for Louie. And I had the number one rhythm and blues song of 1957, "I'll Die Happy," which I wrote for Louie Jordan.

So, I was used to writing 32 bars, but the ideas that I had were always more in quantity than there were bars in the song. So that when I would finish the song of 32 bars, I'd always feel, "Doggone, I wish there was more I could say," you know? It never occurred to me to write other verses. This is what Johnny Mercer used to do. And all the old mainstream composers. They would feel the same way, but they'd write more verses. That never occurred to me. Once the song was finished, it was finished, 'cause I always was writing on a deadline or something, anyway. And also, I didn't get any money until I turned it in. So I wasn't subsidized like they were, you know, by the movie industry. So as soon as I got 32 bars out of the way, I'd say, "Gimme the money." So, when I heard this song ["Moody's Mood For Love"], I said, "Whew! Good heavens. I don't have to stop at the first chorus anymore. Boy, look what I can do."

Ben: Not only that, but the melody was given to you. It's a solo that you've been listening to and loving for years, and suddenly it becomes something you could write lyrics to.

Jon: That's right. It was a gift.

It opened up the most beautiful world to me. And then, what else it did, was it gave me my little niche in the world, my little cultural contribution, if you will. Because nobody had tried it with orchestral things. Both Eddie Jefferson, who wrote the lyrics to "Moody's Mood For Love," and King Pleasure had stuck to the small format, the saxophone, trumpet, piano and rhythm section thing.

Well, the first thing I thought was, "Now I can put words to what I've been singing in my head all the time." And one of the things I'd been singing in my head was Woody Herman's "Four Brothers." Boy, I loved that. I used to sing that while I was at work, typing bills for this newspaper firm. I used to sing music in my head. I'm sure all musicians do that. You do that. You just sit still, people think your ruminating and cogitating, and you're playing Lord knows who in your head. Coleman Hawkins is blowing, you know? And you can hear all this, you know, that's the beauty of the mind. I mean, the mind is the most wonderful creation of all. 'Cause you can hear anything in your mind. You can hear Shostakovitch conducted by Dmitri Metropolis, you know, and no one needs to know about it. You just sit there and enjoy it. And I heard this song, I loved this song. I heard all the solos, you know. I learned them all. And here at last, I could do something about that. I could write words for "Four Brothers."

Ben: A natural.

Jon: I sat right down and did it. I did it on a park bench in Washington Square Park. From memory, cause I didn't have any tapes like they have today. They have these Walkman tapes that you can use, but we didn't have anything like that. I just sat down and did it from memory.

Ben: You once told me that the way you write lyrics, I remember specifically what you said, you said you "internalize the music to the point where you let the music talk." . . .

Jon: Exactly, exactly . . .

Ben: You don't have to "write" the lyrics. The music talks.

Jon: Yeah, it just comes out. It just speaks. It speaks out, you know. For example, there is one sound in John Coltrane's solo on "All Blue" where he says, what to me, is a word generally considered vulgar, and probably is, you know. But it's so clear that I don't know how I'm going to write that lyric without saying that word. [Laughs.]

Ben: You say you let the line speak to you. Are you, when you're writing a line like that, literally listening to the intonation of the notes and hearing vowel sounds and everything? Do you hear the language, literally?

Jon: Oh yeah, yeah, yeah. I always, I hear it in total. You know, and it's instantaneous. That's what . . . it even knocks me out. I'm the most surprised person of all, 'cause it just, bam, you know?

Ben: Well that's funny, you know, because I get the feeling sometimes, listening to bebop, specifically bebop, that it's the closest thing to verbal expression that music has come up with.

Jon: That's right. I say it in a different way, but I say of all the world's art forms, music is the oldest. Of all the world's art forms, jazz is the youngest. And the highest that the young art form of jazz has risen is bebop.

Ben: Do you think maybe it has to do with the fact that, by the time the '40s came along, the musicians who made this music, and who pioneered the idiom of bebop, had become, not just masters of their instruments, but intellectuals as well—had turned to literature, and that was reflected in the playing?

Jon: You read my mind. They had not only done that, but you can even see the reasons that they had done that, because, from World War One up to that time, there was a struggle, economically, just to stay alive. So you had no time to address the intellect. There was no time. But as the style of life got better, the people had more time to give to their minds, or to the intellect, and a result of a little extra time given to the intellect is bebop. 'Cause it's a very intellectual music.

Ben: And it left a lot of people in the dust at one time because of that.

Jon: Exactly, exactly. I mean, look here, I can't figure this out, so it must be nothing, you know.

Ben: You talk about your meeting with Charley Parker. One of the things that I was surprised to learn about Bird, in talking to Pepper Adams, was what a voracious reader Bird was, and what a great intellect he was. You never hear about that.

Jon: Oh, no. But he could discuss anything.

Ben: And that kind of intellectual concern comes across in the playing, to the extent where these lines start to speak to you.

Jon: Well, you can hear it, in his solos, you know. Because the way he gets from one chordal passage to the other, you can literally hear this intelligent mind at work. 'Cause it's done with such grace, charm, creativity and humor. The cat is funny. You know?

Ben: You've written lyrics to dozens, probably hundreds, of jazz classics.

Jon: Oh yeah. I don't even know how many anymore.

Ben: One of my favorite sets of lyrics that you've come up with is on the Manhattan Transfer record called *Vocalese*. Your lyrics to the Sonny Rollins composition "Airegin" are a delight, and if people take the time to see what you've written, well it's quite a story. Tell me the story of these lyrics.

Jon: Well, years ago, I originally lyricized just the tune. You know, just the outside. And then Zoot Sims played a chorus, and Dave Lambert scatted a chorus. Then Russ Freeman played a chorus, then I scatted a chorus. And then we sang it out. Well, the Manhattan Transfer had the idea to do the Lambert, Hendricks and Ross version, but they asked me to lyricize Zoot Sims' tenor chorus, Dave Lambert's scat chorus, Russ Freeman's piano chorus, and my own scat chorus, which was the hardest thing I ever had to do in my whole life.

Ben: Is that right? Writing lyrics to your own scatting.

Jon: Well, first you have to learn what you did. It's when you have to do a thing like that, you come face to face with the fact that when you are improvising, it's no mind on the earth at work. Because when you approach that with your earthly mind, you don't even know what that is. You have no idea. You keep saying, "What the fuck is that?" [Laughs.]

Ben: Well, you started your narrative from the title, as you say you do. "Airegin" is Nigeria spelled backwards. And the front of your lyric is "Wait'll you dig it on the map. Airegin spelled backwards, really closin' up the gap. Airegin."

Jon: "Gone factwords . . ."

Ben: Gone "factwords"?

Jon: Well, that means they're learning, you know?

Ben: Let me continue reading from the lyrics. "Back a long time ago they saw a ghost, ghost made a boast, soon the ghost was host." And off it goes. Then the story that you're writing dovetails into the cradle of civilization and, I mean, it's difficult the first time you hear it to get into the narrative. Matter of fact, that's one of the charming things of the Lambert, Hendricks, and Ross records. They printed the lyrics, and people would follow these amazing stories and were able to learn it and memorize them. It was a whole new oral tradition in the making. But continue, what did you go through trying to write lyrics to a scat solo you had done years before.

Jon: Well, I had to learn what I had done. I had no idea what I had done. It was just something that I did, you know. And I can see when you speak to jazz musicians about solos that they've done, you know, how they'd be apt to say, "What solo, when?" Because, it's not *they* who did it. It's whatever muse speaks through them that has done all solos. [Laughs.] And they are perhaps the last person you should ask about that. And that's when I found out that when I approached myself, I myself was the last authority on what I had done. Because I had no idea. I had to relearn what I had done, and I felt stupid.

Ben: Do you remember the solo now?

Jon: No . . .

Ben: Now that's interesting. You probably have hundreds of solos in your head, and yet you're not retaining your own.

Jon: Your own is further away from you than anything. Have you ever had a dream, and you're slowly waking up, and, as you awaken, you wanna remember this dream? And as you realize you wanna remember it, it's fading. And then when you're fully awake, it's totally gone. Has that ever happened to you?

Ben: Oh, yes . . .

Jon: That's what it is. Whatever that is, that's what it is.

* * *

Max Roach (January, 1986)

Max Roach was the first of the new breed of jazz drummers to emerge during the late '40s and early '50s. Schooled in the traditional jazz techniques of the late '30s big band era, when musicians often played in large vaudeville theaters and tap dancers were known to trade "fours" with the rhythm section, he went on to become the perfect foil for Charlie Parker's new rhythmic conception. He carried forward the styles of Baby Dodds, Big Sid Catlett, Chick Webb and Kenny Clarke and reinvented the role of the drum kit, making it a melodic instrument on a par with other front line soloists. Max was in very good spirits when we met at a recording studio in Manhattan. His ears are always open to new sounds and environmental influences to add to his drum technique, and, clearly, he felt that today's music is a fertile field in which to grow. He has recorded more during the past few years—with his various large and small ensembles—than ever before. Although we had not met previously, he made me feel like an old friend, complimenting me on some of my own past recordings and including me in the great body of ongoing jazz works. Perhaps more than anything, this is his current mission: to keep the long revolution marching forward to a new beat.

Ben: Max, you've been in the studio a lot recently recording with your various ensembles. Let's talk about some of these recordings. For example, the quartet album called *In The Light* that came out on the Soul Note label; I'm particularly interested in the song "The Henry Street Blues" because it has such a dramatic feel to it. Is there a story behind that piece?

Max: It's a piece from a play that I did by a very fine poet/writer, Larry Neil. It was called *The Monster in the Bell of the Horn*, and it was produced out here at the Henry Street Theater. Hence the title "The Henry Street Blues." It was a story about Philadelphia, and the leading character was a composite of Charlie Parker and Clifford Brown.

Ben: A composite in which way? Those are two very different personalities, aren't they?

Max: Right. Well, it takes place in Philadelphia, and this person, who is a great musician, has a tragic end. But the way Larry dealt with the character was he took these two great, seminal figures and the hero was a saxophone player, like Bird, but he was killed in an automobile accident, as Clifford was. So "Henry Street Blues" was part of the music that I did for that particular play.

Ben: One of the things that stood out to me when I heard that piece of music was the way the drums were used. They were used as a lead instrument and also as a comping instrument.

Max: Yeah, well I got away from the ride cymbal on that one and used the snare, which was doing a marching beat. It comes out of the traditional drumming of Baby Dodds and that crowd, only we updated it for today. But it was mainly just snare and bass drum and maybe a little high-hat once in a while. But it had that kind of feeling behind the whole piece.

And as you know, Henry Street is a busy street down here on the East Side of New York City, with a lot of shops and street vendors, and it has that kind of feeling to it also.

Ben: There's one point in the song where it breaks down to just the bass and the drums, and the interaction between these two instruments is traditional, but in some ways the playing isn't.

Max: No, it's very contemporary, but it comes out of a traditional mode, when drummers didn't deal as much with the ride cymbal and they swung the band on the snare and bass drum. So I was thinking like that to get away from the ride, which has become almost rule-of-thumb today. Although now, with the way that percussionists and set drummers are playing, they're using just about everything. It's really very advanced.

Ben: Of course, you've used a piano-less group for quite some time. And when I refer back to a song like this, that has no piano, it strikes me that the piano is really another percussion instrument. And that's kind of a come-back for the drums, because the drums are not just a percussion instrument. They can play a melody as well. So not having a piano on this track allows you to comp more, as a piano might.

Max: Well you know jazz grew out of piano-less groups. It came out of marching bands. The old New Orleans bands, there was no pianos on the streets. Piano really became popular during the ragtime period, and then it just took over, it took over totally, during Scott Joplin and all those great rag creators. And it became *the* instrument.

And out of that the instrumentalists, horns and drums, had to take a complete back seat when the ragtime period flourished. But the piano, using it in the band, is still kind of touchy. Many of the musicians, the great soloists, they love pianists like Count Basie . . .

Ben: Who leaves a lot of space . . .

Max: Right, because the harmony and the melody and the rhythm are all implied in all the other instruments. You know, when you listen to an orchestra, unless it's a piano concerto, the piano is not there, basically. Although the way we use the piano, the way Basie or Thelonious Monk would use the piano, it's just wonderful. So comping is an art all unto itself.

But piano was used as a solo instrument, and of course the innovative pianists started, as far as American music is concerned, with the ragtime pianists. I mean when they *really* started innovating, you know, stride and all that counterpoint, and out of that evolved people like Tatum and so forth. But ragtime was the very beginning of what we might call American piano virtuosity.

But in some of the other groups, as you know, Ben, I do use piano. It's just that in the quartet, I find I like this particular instrumental format, with two horns and bass and drums, because it affords me a lot of space and there are two lean lines. It's almost like Japanese painting. The lines are lean and very transparent. It doesn't have that chordal thickness that a piano gives to it. But I do use pianos, like if I record with a chorus. For example, I did some things with a gospel choir. Things like that.

Ben: You mentioned Clifford Brown before. Of course it would be remiss not to remember the group that you co-led with Clifford Brown. That seems to have been the last period when you used a piano player no matter what the composition. Of course the piano player in that group was Richie Powell. This was during the late fifties. Was there some reason you felt that after that group ended you had to move on and get away from the piano?

Max: Well, you know when Clifford and Richie were taken away from us in that awful accident, that unfortunate accident that happened, you know, the group still traveled. We had been booked beyond that, so I honored some of those jobs, as much as I could. Of course, it was a traumatic and emotional experience for me. I mean, I was really in never-never land for quite a while.

So Sonny Rollins and George Morrow and myself, as a trio, honored some of the things that had been committed, without Brownie and Richard. And I guess that might have been the beginning of what I began to hear. Out of that tragedy, as we worked these trio things—and it was almost like a memorial to these two very wonderful musicians—as we played these few jobs we had committed ourselves to without them, Sonny and myself, we both began to adapt to just that sound. And we tried to compensate for the fact that the piano wasn't there. And I began to hear something else. And so did Sonny. And out of that, of course, Sonny did his first "Freedom Suite" with Oscar Pettiford and myself.

You know, it wasn't a new thing on the scene, because Mulligan and Baker were doing it out on the West Coast. But I got involved in it by way of the tragedy.

Ben: I understand. Speak for a moment about how you approach tuning your drums.

Max: Well the way I deal with the set is I treat it as an instrument of indeterminate pitch. I say the largest drum, that's the bottom. I usually tune to the size. I don't tune for fifths or fourths or thirds or anything like that. I recognize the fact that the instrument itself is of indeterminate pitch.

The best drummers know how to beat the instrument into the key that the music is being played in at the particular time. And one person who especially stands out is Art Blakey. Art Blakey gets on the stand with anybody's drum set. If you're in F, G, B flat, E flat, the drums sound like they're in that key. So it's a way that your ear and your familiarity with the kit, and the cymbals and all that, seem to serve. You just go right to it. But of course these are seasoned people who've been dealing with it for quite some time.

And also, many of the drummers who can do that are excellent musicians. Art Blakey was originally a pianist, as I was. And you'll find Elvin Jones is a good guitar player, and Tony Williams, people like that, they're composers as well. But most drummers do it anyway. I hear drummers and they're right there.

The instrument allows it. You know, the drum set is perhaps the only instrument that came out of the United States of America's experience. They grew out of that. It's the only one. When you look at percussion, across the world, Africa, Europe, The Middle East, the Far East, South America, the drummers don't play with their feet. You see, the USA drummer, we are like one-man percussion ensembles. And that instrument is really home-grown USA, the drum set itself. Trumpets and saxophones and violins and pianos and congas, all the other instruments come out of another part of the world. But that instrument really is a USA instrument. It's probably the only original instrument that came out of the USA's experience.

Ben: The gathering of the various elements, some came out of the parades, some came from the necessity to get a back-beat going on a high-hat cymbal, whatever . . .

Max: Right, it kind of evolved. And then, of course, there's the sociological make-up of the people, you know. We use the cymbals, which are Middle Eastern. We use tom-toms that resemble the tom-toms from Africa and also from the American Indian. Of course you have the snares and bass drums that come out of the European experience.

You know, when you look at a symphony orchestra, you see maybe four or five people in a percussion ensemble, who serve to play the lower parts of the instrument and all the other things, triangles and cymbals. You look at the African percussion ensembles, they have the daddy, mama and kinto, smaller drums, and you have four or five players in drum ensembles there as well. But here, the drummer is a one-man band.

It's amazing. Recently, Mongo Santa-Maria and Tito Puente and myself, we did a fund-raising concert at the University of Massachusetts. I went on stage and just played some solos by myself, unaccompanied. Because it was Mongo's band and Tito and I were guests. So we eventually all played together, and played with Mongo's band. But to start off the program, we all did little solos individually. So when I played my section and came off stage, Tito was going on after me, I said "What are you gonna do, Tito?" He said, "I'm gonna play with the band," he said, "because you got a whole orchestra there with the kit." Of course, he's an unbelievable musician, because he's a composer and the king of timbales. But it was funny the way he said it. He said, "That's a one-man band you have there." And that's what the drum set actually is. It's a percussion ensemble unto itself that one player deals with.

Ben: Your mentioning the drummer having to use his feet brings to mind the influence of the great tap dancers on jazz drumming. It's my understanding that tap dancers had a definite impact on the styles of bebop drumming.

Max: Well you're absolutely right. In fact, the earlier drummers, like Papa Jo Jones, Buddy Rich, these guys were tap dancers. And good tap dancers. Philly Joe is a good tap dancer. I do a little rattle and roll myself. You almost had to deal with it. And it was good for your feet. But J.C. Heard, these people were *dancers*, and then drummers. And great dancers. They danced on the theater circuit, in the variety shows that we had.

You know, like the four-stroke ruffs [sings one], they are things that tap dancers used. The sound of the paradiddle, the double paradiddle and the triple paradiddle, well also the feet do that. [Sings them all.] And cramps were like ruffs. [Sings them as well.]

And of course, when I was growing up during the forties, there was a lot of theater—this was all over the country—and they had variety shows. So you not only played with the band, but you also played with dancers and you played with singers and chorus girls and all these things. So tap dancers were headliners. Especially when Bill "BoJangles" Robinson was alive. Tap dancers would sometimes head a show. If Bill Robinson was on a show with Duke Ellington, he'd get top billing. So dance was *big*. It was like a pop singer is today. So dancers were always on the streets. You could go on the street corner and you'd find dancers of all persuasions, just rattling and rattling and rattling. Ground Hog, Baby Lawrence.

And there's a great dancer who's still performing in New York, Chuck Green. I recently did a show with him in Europe called "Cotton Club At The Ritz."

And the drummers and dancers would do duets. We'd play duets together. They'd do some unbelievable things, and we'd try to imitate or catch them, and they would try to imitate or catch the things that we were doing. So tap dancing is great, because it's a rhythmic thing.

Ben: That's a wonderful example of how rhythm is kind of a universal feeling, and it's carried in different parts of the body. I mean, it might come up from the feet and be carried in the hands on the drums and then go back to the feet...

Max: Absolutely.

Ben: But the rhythm is there.

Max: It always exists. See, what we started doing was, alright, you have the snare. If you had, say, a four-stroke ruff on the snare [sings an example], the tap dancer would answer it. Now we had all four limbs so we had the bass drum and the snare drum and side drums, so we had all kinds of ways of doing it, and the dancers would kind of cock their ear at us. But most of these folks were just wonderful. When you listen to a solo by people like Papa Jo Jones, or Buddy Rich, you hear a lot of dance steps. Because they are dancers. Good dancers.

Ben: We should point out that the tradition is very much alive today. One of the best modern drummers, Steve Gadd, started out as a tap dancer.

Max: There you go. It's still alive.

Ben: The discussion of the orchestral use of the drums leads me to your recordings with the "double quartet," which features a string quartet and a traditional jazz ensemble. You recorded a composition called "Bird Says," which is interesting in part because of the way the drums and the string quartet interact. In fact, it may be revolutionary.

Max: Well, It had always been a desire of mine to do something with drums and strings. A trap set and strings that is. You know, because strings were always used in a lush, very romantic way, and I wanted to use them in a lush and romantic way also. For example, on the *Survivors* album, one side is just strings and drum solos. To me, that's a drummer's ballad. You get a chance to deal with the total percussion kit and do all the techniques that are involved with that, and you have string accompaniment, which is sharp and hitting.

On "Bird Says," which was a tribute to Charlie Parker, of course, what we did to my knowledge had never been done before. We got the strings to play those intricate and unique phrases of Charlie Parker's. The song is based on a Charlie Parker harmonic theme "Confirmation." What Cecil [Bridgewater] did was take quotes from Bird and deal with it through a string ensemble. Now, strings had never, excepting the earlier string players, Stuff Smith and Eddie South—they approached jazz playing more like the horn players of the day—but the string players mostly, they've always been kind of legato on the instrument. It was either legato or staccato playing, but jazz is unique in that nothing is ever *on it* that much. Things are always legato *and* staccato. [Sings a bebop line illustrating this.]

Now that's a funny feeling altogether. It's not like saying [sings strict eight notes] or [sings a wide legato phrase]. It's all of this combined. It's using the same thing, you know, like blues is both major and minor. It's never this or that. It's usually a combination of everything together, to create some kind of feeling. Like a major chord sounds bluesy if you put a minor in it. So dealing with this music, one of the very special qualities about it, is how it kind of fuses everything together.

It's like the USA. All these people are here, we got to live together. So we *do* live together. You see people borrowing from everybody. You find white guys curling their hair and black guys straightening their hair, you know, it's just . . . you see, the music is just a reflection of this.

To me, I always like to say the music is very democratic. For example, with us, everybody gets an opportunity to speak. You have a quartet, a quintet, even in the "Bird Says" piece, you know we all are free to deal with what we have to deal with. Everybody gets a chance to say his solo and everybody is free to express in his own way what goes on, and to accompany another person. It isn't just laid down for you. You get a chance to think. And to be creative as you think.

But I think the unique thing about this double quartet album was it was a breakthrough to hear a string quartet phrase like that. And I knew it could, even though the string players, even though these kids grew up studying at places like Oberlin and Julliard, and they were well-versed with the classics, they could do it, because every day of their lives they've heard the Charlie Parkers and Louis Armstrongs, and they hear all the contemporary music as well.

So it was a matter of them *singing* the phrases. We would have them *sing* a Charlie Parker lick, and then figure out a way it should be fingered on the instrument. Because there's nowhere in the string literature that they have [sings a Charlie Parker line]. You don't have that in string literature. So they had to create a way of fingering it and bowing it, which they did.

Ben: That's a wonderful example of the oral tradition in the music, the importance of the human voice and the importance of rhythm in forming the oral tradition.

Max: Right.

Ben: It's not *just* vocalized tone, but it's vocalized tone that comes from a rhythmic attitude, being translated all the way to the bastion of the classical Western tradition. To get string players to play with some jazz feeling, it immediately stands out when you hear it because you almost never hear it.

Max: And you know we experimented with a classical string quartet in Europe, the Swedenbourg String Quartet.

These young players had never played anything. They played "Bird Says," and they were really industrious. They heard it, they saw the music, and they wanted to play it, because it was a challenge. And they played it. And it was amazing how fast they got to it. But they learned how to deal with it, as you say, by the oral tradition. They sang it first.

We'd say, "We call this in America a 'ghost note.'" They'd say, "A ghost note?" We'd say, "You have a string of eighth notes which would ordinarily be played strictly. Well, we would play it with a swing feel." [He sings a demonstration.] Well, that note that you hardly can hear, that's a ghost note. It's played and it's heard but not as loud as the others. Now they had a term for it in the classical literature and it was pretty close. And we found that by talking about it and singing it that we could communicate and work it out. And it was wonderful.

Ben: Historically, looking back at your work, you seem to be very much a group-oriented person. You appear to develop very close relationships with the musicians you use, and you tend to use the same players consistently. For example, when you're playing so strong behind trumpet player Cecil Bridgewater on the front of "Bird Says," it reminds me of the great duets that Elvin Jones played with Coltrane. And that's only possible after years of playing together, isn't it?

Max: Yes it is. I've heard that same attitude that you talk about between Elvin and John with Charlie Parker and Dizzy. And I've heard it also with Sidney Bechet and Louis Armstrong, when they worked with Baby Dodds and that group. It does come from working together. But the wonderful thing about the music is that it's based on the personalities within the group.

For example, when Clifford Brown and Richie were killed in that awful automobile accident, I felt that the people, when they booked Max Roach, they'd expect him to play some of the things he did with Clifford. Well, it was impossible to do, because there was only one Clifford. So therefore, I had to find a trumpet player and a repertoire that was not that familiar. It took me a long while before I went back to that repertoire. For many reasons, of course.

You know, in the recording industry, you can only survive if you come up with new product. You can't do what you did before, anyway. You know they'll tell you in a minute you have to come back. They ask, "What you want to do, Max?" and if I say "Well I want to record 'Dahoud' and 'Joy Spring' and all the wonderful things I did with Brownie," they'd say, "Well, you already recorded that. You'll have to come up with something new." One of the ways of doing that is to change the personnel and try to find the people who do not sound like the people who were with you prior to that period. In the case of Brownie, you'll never find another one.

So what I looked for were people like Kenny Dorham or Booker Little. They're different. Because otherwise, I would always sound like I'm back in that period. That's one of the things. So what I'm basically saying is that groups change with the personnel if the leader of the group allows that to happen. Even Duke Ellington, when Ben Webster was with the band, it sounded totally different than when Paul Gonsalves was with the band. You deal with the musical personalities.

My band today is different than the one last year. Attitude, personality. And you try to use as much of each person that's individual to them as possible.

Ben: I remember the group you put together with Kenny Dorham on trumpet, Sonny Rollins on tenor and Ray Bryant on piano back in 1956. You did a song called "Mr. X." I always wondered who Mr. X was. Was it you? Or was it perhaps Billy Eckstine?

Max: Actually, "Mr. X" was dedicated to Malcolm X. He was very young at that time and just about to get on the scene. Very few people knew about him then. But we knew him and we knew how dynamic he was, you know, and what a wonderful human being he was. And he saw, at that young age, all the things that we saw happening to black folks around the United States of America, the racism that had been in existence for years. So we would hear him talk. So the piece is really dedicated to a young Malcolm. That was way before anybody was really aware of what was happening.

But I guess it also was a part of me, growing up in the United States of America, and being black, of course, to be conscious of all those things. There's no way you can not be conscious of all that. And I was born in the deep South, in North Carolina, and so you're always conscious of things. And whenever a voice comes up to speak, like a Paul Robeson or a Malcolm or a Martin Luther King . . . incidentally, I just finished a television show dedicated to Martin Luther King. It's called "A Dream And A Drum." It was based on something I did for CBS, that "Chatahoochie Red" album, where I played solo underneath Martin Luther King's "I Have A Dream" speech. Do you know that old record?

Ben: Yes, I do. Let's talk for a moment then about the economic exploitation, not just of black musicians but of all musicians, in the process of reissued records. There's some element of reissues that people don't talk about. Of course, there's a wonderful aspect in that it makes great music available for a longer period of time. And I particularly like the fact that a record that meant a lot twenty years ago means even more today. Not just as much, but even more. But there's a dark side of it, isn't there?

Max: Yes, there is. But firstly, musicians, and this is unfortunate, any musicians who deal in the world of jazz, it's rough. It's always tough. It's rough in music for the artist generally, but when we're dealing with this music, jazz has to *fight* to get on the radio, on the airwaves. If it weren't for people like you, it would be dead city for us. The pop scene, it's like fast food, you know. They get these young artists, make a hit record, throw them away and get the next one. Whereas jazz is something that twenty years from now you can reissue.

Now that's good. Educationally it gives a new audience to what we have been about and what things are about. But the people who suffer are the sidemen on these dates. You know, the leader doesn't get a new fee, but he gets artist royalties. But the men who helped make that record—and as I said earlier, jazz is a democratic form—they suffer.

Usually, when we're booked on concerts, in Europe and every place else, they want to know who your personnel is. They say, "Okay, I got Gerry Mulligan, but who's playing with him? I got Max Roach but who's in the band? Who's with Miles now," or this and that. They buy according to who the drummer and everybody else is in the band. Because that's the way this music is.

Ben: And the music is totally different with a different band. It is different music.

Max: Right. So then when you listen to these great records, say the records we made with Charlie Parker that are being reissued. You know, we got paid the minimum back in those days. It was a period when there was a record ban on. You know, that early stuff that we did with Charlie Parker, if it hadn't been for the "bodaciousness," I guess you might say, of the producers at that time and we as musicians, we would have never made those records. We had to clandestinely sneak into studios after hours, because the union was checking on all the recording studios. At that time, the musician's union was afraid that the recording industry was going to hurt live music. And it was "patronize live music" in the '40s. In England, Canada, all over the world, the international musician's union put a ban on recording. And so we recorded anyway during that period. Because that was one way we could augment our income.

And now, we'll be listening to these records and they've become classics. The union doesn't say anything, because of course you do still pay what they call union dues for each one of these sessions. But the tragedy of it today is that for the record companies, the costs are minimal. They don't have studio costs, they don't have musicians' costs, they don't have arrangers' costs, they don't have art costs for the cover, etc. And so right from the very beginning, it's all gravy.

So my thing is I think that the sidemen should be paid. And a lot of the stuff that's coming out now today, of course I was a sideman on. The things with Charlie Parker and Coleman Hawkins and those wonderful people I had a chance to work with. And of course on the records of my things that are coming out now, I think about Richie Powell's family and about George Morrow, Harold Land and Booker Little, and all these folks. They should at least get paid the current union scale.

Ben: We should point out also that many of these records were made at a time when leaders often didn't get royalties, only a flat fee, and so the record companies today, in some cases, pay no money to musicians at all.

Max: Yeah, back then if you were a writer, sometimes you even sold your rights. In the case of Charlie Parker, he sold a lot of his material to different record companies and publishing companies. Bud Powell. Even Duke. A lot of people got caught in that, you know? Musicians of every persuasion. I'm just talking about guys I knew, but everybody got caught up in that. And that still exists today with some of these young rock people. When you look at the recording and you check out who the publisher is, you'll find more than likely that publishers are not the people who write the music.

Ben: We've been talking about the importance of the individual members to any group, and one of the most interesting groups you've been recording with is your percussion ensemble M'Boom, which includes guys like Roy Brooks and Freddie Waits. We also talked a little about street dancing before, and there's a song with that name on the M'Boom record. It has a great groove that comes mostly from the bass drum. The importance of the bass drum on that track reminds me of stories I've heard about a drummer in New Orleans long ago named Black Benny. It was reported that he could swing an entire parade down the street with just the one bass drum.

Max: The bass drum is so important. You know, when we formed M'Boom, it grew out of the fact that drummers were always the second line. The front line was the front line. So here were all these great drummers, they all can write, Roy Brooks is a fine composer, Joe Chambers is a great orchestrator/composer, Warren Smith, Freddie Waits, all piano players. So we decided to get together. We said the total percussion family, from bells down to bass marimbas and timpani, they have the entire musical spectrum, melodically and harmonically.

And this is old hat, of course, because there have been percussion ensembles from the beginning of time, I imagine. But we decided to form one that we felt would best express the feeling we have in America, the USA that is, and design it around what we all are about: jazz. Bird and Duke Ellington. As an ensemble, that has written aspects along with a lot of improvisation aspects, and just democratic input from everybody.

So I'll bring in a theme, like "Street Dance," and I'll say, "OK, Brooks, you play the saw on this, and Kenyatay, you play traps, and Waits, you do this." And everybody hears the flavor of the piece and goes right into it. You know, you direct just the flavor. Each piece is like that. So some of it's written, and a large part of it is just, OK, you know what the character of the piece is. It's a street dance and a march, so get into it like that.

So now we had all these wonderful percussionists who people know as drummers, as jazz drummers. But they also play mallet instruments and timpani and all these other wonderful instruments that belong to the percussion family. And we're continuing to record the group. But the thing is we're on imports, and so the record collector has to really search for them because it isn't domestic and it costs a bit more. But I find that in Europe, the producers are a bit more adventurous when it comes to sound. Everything isn't "Okay, it's got to sell a million records." So our label Soul Note is really a case in point, where Mr. Bonandrini, who's the producer there, it's almost like a one family thing, he loves the music.

I know the first time I played the tape of the duet with Cecil Taylor and myself for him, he cried. He said, "This is real music," you know. And that's very hard to get to, because that album is very difficult to listen to. I mean, the energy is so high in the LP itself, 'till I put on one side at a time, and I have to take a breath. 'Cause it's very exciting. But he sat and listened to the whole tape before he bought it. And he was crying.

They have that fervor. And of course, they listen with a different ear. Mr. Bonandrini has been a musician, he's been a teacher, and he's retired and has decided to deal with this music. So naturally, he does a lot of adventurous things. I dare say a lot of it isn't really, as far as our country is concerned, very commercial.

Ben: It would probably never be recorded, in fact.

Max: It's difficult to play. I know we did a radio show in England, and the interviewer wanted to play a bit of the Cecil Taylor thing. So I said, "Just put the needle down anyplace, fade up on it, and then after two minutes, fade out." Anyplace you put it down, it's gonna work.

Ben: You mention the *sound* of the M'Boom record. I first heard a tape of the group when you did a concert with the World Saxophone Quartet. It was recorded in a cathedral. And the *sound* of that tape, not unlike the sound of the record, was very unusual. Not just what was being played, but the care that was given to the recording and the acoustic space that was created was very special.

Max: Thank you.

Ben: Which leads me to the subject of contemporary drums which include Lynn drums and electronic drums. These are drums that are plugged directly from a microchip into a tape recorder. There is no acoustic space involved, and yet their sound is part of today's musical reality. It's the other end of the spectrum from the acoustics of M'Boom, but we are all dealing with it. Are you dealing with Lynn drums as well?

Max: Yes, I've had a chance to do something with the Lynn, and it was at an experimental rap thing at a theater here in New York. It was a great learning experience. What I found was the whole rap-grafitti-breakdance thing grew out of the communities in our country where art, music and dance were taken out of the educational system. Like in certain areas of the big cities, like Harlem, the South Bronx, Bed-Sty in Brooklyn, areas like that around the country. The urban areas. So now these kids say. "Okay, I can't study music," so they create a way to create sounds with turntables. These are the DJ's, right? And then, "Okay, I can't study rhetoric or poetry," the schools are so bad, so they created a way of dealing with poetry.

Ben: Street poetry.

Max: They're street poets, that's what they are. Then they said, "Okay, they don't have dance classes, and they don't have movement," so there's breakdancing. It all kind of works together. Graffiti came out because there were no art classes. And to me, it was almost like a phoenix, out of all this came . . . a culture.

This is what I learned. I was first introduced to it by a young producer out of Minneapolis, Tim Carr. He said, "You like to experiment with things, Max. What about doing something with some breakdancers and rap groups." I said, "I have to think about it." And he said, "Well, you know, I met a young man who is the son of somebody you grew up with in Brooklyn. His name is Freddie Braithwaite." Avid Bird, Lester Young, I mean a dyed-in-the-wool guy. And I knew his son. Fab-Five-Fred. He said, "It would make a nice story, since you came from Brooklyn and you grew up with Freddie, and all of a sudden, you're working with his son." Well how can I refuse that. Here's one of my best friends saying, "Here's my son, Max."

So, Okay, he's got the hook in me. Tim knew what he was doing, right? So then I went to see Freddie, and he began to take me around. He took me to his DJ's house and showed me how he dealt with the records, which to me, the co-ordination was unbelievable. Like how he changed records and made sounds and kept it in sync, rhythmically. Then some breakdancers from the Bronx, they came down. And of course Fab-Five is the rap man. And so I was hooked.

So they said, "Okay, now we'll program the Lynn drum to keep everything together, like with that pulse, and you just play off of that." And that's just what I did. They programmed the Lynn, and I just played. And what I did with the breakdancers was similar to what I would do with Baby Lawrence and the tap dancers. I would catch things that they did, spins and all kinds of things, and come back to the rhythm. So it was a lot of fun. We did two performances. And after the first night, the breakdancers, who are about fifteen or sixteen—and they're famous now, because some of them performed for the President at the White House when they honored Katherine Dunham—one of the young guys came back, and he said, "Hey, man, what's your name?" I told him my name. He said, "You're alright!"

So, to me, it was like I made it with them, in a sense. We had a lot of fun. But I've learned so much about it and how it really is a viable art form.

Ben: And the drum machine is part of the new arsenal of electronic technology that originally threatened a lot of jazz players. But more and more players are seeing it as a tool you can use.

Max: It frees you. I think it helps to free you to do other things.

Ben: It will put the pulse down for you. The pulse won't breathe, however.

Max: It won't breathe, no, but you can use it for effects. And it can work, you know, 'cause then *you* breathe. It's like having a rhythm section. Because, it's a funny thing. I found that many times the drummer was just required to keep the time, you know. So now they developed it to the extent where you can almost make the drum machine sound just a wee-bit ahead of the beat, like Philly Joe. Or you can make it lag, like, you know, Art Blakey. Or you could almost program these sounds in where it does sound elastic. It won't breathe, but it can wave. So you can use it like that.

And of course they're using it in the studios, and it's a threat to the percussion players, because they have to learn how to deal with that.

Ben: One of my favorite stories is told by Ralph Ellison, where he tells about a trip he once took to Africa many years ago. And he describes a situation where there's a gasoline engine running, you know, backfiring and popping. And the tribe, in the village, was dancing to the rhythm of the gasoline engine.

Max: I'll bet.

Ben: So machinery can be musical.

Max: Yeah. I know when I was traveling back and forth from Brooklyn to the Manhattan School of Music, and riding the subways, a lot of ideas came out of the rattles of those wheels on those trains. I mean, it's unbelievable the rhythms that the subway creates. When you're interested in percussion, you know. I'd sit down and close my eyes and just swoon.

Ben: You know, it's almost as if the music that you're playing now has achieved a kind of timeless quality. You're covering the history of the drums, from before there was a trap set, up through tap dancing and on into today, when machines are part of the groove.

Max: You know recently I did something with Sam Shepard. Some music for three of his plays in repertoire. All three were totally different. All three required different kinds of music. And Sam Shepard was a drummer. His father was also a drummer. And of course when you look at Shepard, he deals with country-western flavored things. He deals with avant-garde stuff. He deals with the jazz world. Well that's the drummer's life.

And I began to understand he was a drummer when we did the three plays in repertoire up here at the La Mama Theater. It was amazing, because one play, "Back Bar Beach Bait" was Cajun. And the music required was Cajun. So I had to really get into that whole culture, records and everything. The other one was "Angel City," about Hollywood, and who can make the most horrible picture. He must have gone to Hollywood and tried to write and all they wanted was horror films. The music he wants in that is real abstract. I mean abstract, spooky. And then he did one called "Suicide In B Flat," and that's about the jazz world. It's amazing how close he was to it. It's almost a story of Charlie Parker. How society crucifies the artist is what it was. But he used the jazz world to deal with it. So that was right at home, you know, the sounds were right in the pocket.

But see, a drummer has to be able to play, the way I grew up in New York City, from Bar Mitzvas to marching bands to traditional New Orleans Dixieland. You have to be prepared to deal with any kind of situation. Play timpani in a local symphony orchestra at the Brooklyn Museum. Just everything, so you're prepared, you're not confined to do this or that. I played with Louis Jordan and he was the shuffle king at that time, and I'd have to come back the next night and play with Bird and Diz.

So when you say the variety of things that happen, if you come out of the rhythm section, you are exposed to all kinds of things. Whereas you may not be if you say, "I'm a soloist and a specialist." You may not be privy to all the other little things that would give you the kind of scope that lets you say, "Okay, I'll have an M'Boom percussion ensemble, I'll try something with a string quartet, I'll do a duet with Cecil Taylor, or I'll try something with the drum machine." It's all part of just being a drummer.

Ben: It's kind of the good news for drummers out there, isn't it? It's a wide open world.

Max: Yeah, it is. It's really uncharted territory.

* * *

Willie Ruff (January, 1988)

Willie Ruff is a rare individual in many ways. For one thing, not many musicians excel at both the bass and the French horn. Nor are many masters of the blues also professors at Ivy League institutions. Willie's combination of down-home wisdom and intellectual fervor, which comes across in his playing as well as his conversation, and his absolute commitment to carrying forward the torch of this music, are as much a part of who he is as his old partner, pianist Dwike Mitchell. The duo of Willie and Dwike has actually been together longer than any other group in jazz (including the MJQ). Their story was sketched in William Zinsser's fine book Willie and Dwike, *which chronicles their travels throughout the United States, Europe and China. This conversation took place in the music building on the campus of Yale University.*

Ben: Willie, what is your official academic title these days?

Willie: Well, I am a music professor at the Yale School of Music and I am the founding director of the Duke Ellington Fellowship Program at Yale.

Ben: In the book that was written about you and your partner, Dwike Mitchell, by William Zinsser, he starts with a description of a trip that you and Dwike took to China, and then he finally got around to the roots of your story. Let's do it the other way. Let's start at the beginning, in rural Alabama.

Willie: Absolutely. The little town I come from in Alabama, Ben, is called Sheffield, and it's in the heart of the Tennessee Valley. It's called the Muscle Shoals area of Alabama, and it is distinguished by the fact that both W. C. Handy and Helen Keller come from there. Helen Keller comes from the south side of the river, and W. C. Handy from the north side. And these were two large figures looming in the lives of everybody in the Muscle Shoals area when I grew up.

Ben: Zinsser refers to the fact that Helen Keller made it real tough on all the kids, because every time you got a little lazy, they'd say, "Well look at what that little Helen Keller girl can do."

***Willie:* That's right. Said that, said, "Boy, what's your excuse? Why you so lazy. That little Helen Keller girl just rub on them little dots 'til her fingers just bleed, lookin' for knowledge."**

Ben: Yeah. And your neighborhood also placed you in a fortuitous spot. In your backyard was a Sanctified Church, in your front yard was a friend who was a drummer . . .

Willie: Right . . .

Ben: Talk a little bit about those influences.

Willie: Well, in the backyard was this black Sanctified Church, where I was a teacher, Ben. I started teaching in the Sanctified Church when I was five years old, because I could read. And what I could read were simple things. But my students could not. And they were very old people, old in age, some of them in their nineties, who had the spirit and vitality of very young people. And they were people who—we're talking about the mid 1930s—people who had been born into slavery. And, for that reason, had not had access to reading. And I, as the youngest member in the congregation who could read, was sort of admonished to share that with my elders. And I would stand up in front of a class of, oh, maybe seven or eight people in their eighties and nineties, and read from my little Sunday school cards, something as simple as "God is Love." And they would say, "Whoo! Listen at 'im go! Ain't he a scholar. Can 'ee getta job?" [Laughs.] So then I knew that teaching would be a big part of my life.

But in my front yard, across the street from us, was a very kind older white boy, who is about ten years older than I am. And he played the drums like a demon. And he had a fabulous set of drums, and Gene Krupa was his man. And I would go across the street and watch him practice, and stick around on his drums. I'd get so close to him, to the sticks, he was afraid he'd knock my eyes out, so he gave me my own. You know, took off the snare and gave it to me, and taught me how to read music. I learned how to read music about the time I learned how to read writin'. And he and I had our favorites, as drummers. Miss Nance was the bass drummer in the Sanctified Church. And we used to go and sit out on the grass every night and listen to the sanctified meeting, and Miss Nance played the bass drum with a wooden mixin' spoon, wrapped in a boot sock. She didn't have one of those fancy beaters that you see the drum majors use. And with that wooden spoon wrapped in that boot sock she could get more out of a single bass drum than most people can out of a whole set. She could make it talk.

Ben: She could make it talk, and we're not talkin' metaphorically . . .

Willie: No, no, no, no. I mean, it spoke words. It could say, "Hallelu-jah," "Thank you Je-sus," "Yee-aaa-esss." [laughs] Yeah. She used to play with both hands, with the spoon and the flat of her left palm, on two heads. Miss Nance could get it.

Ben: Very soon thereafter, you joined the army. You joined the army when you were fourteen years old, I believe, you snuck in there.

Willie: Yeah. That's right. My mother had died when I was thirteen, and living with my father was not what it had been livin' with Momma. You know, every child learns sooner or later that Momma and Daddy are different, even though they both do the best they can. And it was clear that after a year, about a year after my mother had died, that the place for me was in something I'd heard about. Heard about the army, the musical activities in the army.

You see, something that has never been properly credited is, with the black musicians, even before this century, if there was an interest in having a professional career in music, the only place for a viable, professional, non-jazz career has been in the U.S. military. And black soldiers have been pursuing professional careers there for well over a hundred years now, and develop a kind of invisible conservatory. A kind of conservatory without walls. Where one could go and make music among one's betters, one's elders and much betters, and it was pretty common knowledge among my crowd, in my part of the world, that if you were good enough to find your way into that, then that was a beginning.

And I mercifully did find my way into that, and learned how to play the French horn. Started at about age fifteen. And in the army there, I found others who were there for this invisible conservatory. Among them was the man I play with now, Dwike Mitchell. Elvin Jones was also a part of the band, and another young saxophonist named John Gilmore. But we were all out-classed. We were the youngsters of the group, and on the receiving end of the whole learning process there. And our musical beginnings were there.

Ben: You also mentioned another woman from the church, a Miss Appleton.

Willie: Right, Miss Ceelie Appleton . . .

Ben: Miss Ceelie Appleton, whose voice so closely resembled a French horn, and that that's why you got to the instrument . . .

Willie: That's right . . .

Ben: The French horn was kind of a curious instrument for you to pick. Had you played some bass before that?

Willie: Not really. No . . .

Ben: Well how in the world did you get into a music division with no instrument?

Willie: I played the drums. And I could read. McCord, this white boy who lived there across the street from me in Alabama, taught me. When he left, going to the army himself, he gave me his whole set of drums. So I got in a band, in Wyoming, as a drummer. But, as I said, my world of drumming had been peopled by Gene Krupa and Cozy Cole, who were men who played for swing bands, for the most part. And I found myself really at odds with the new higher mathematics of bebop drumming in the army. And I was unable to give up the driving four-beat foot pedal. That's the way you learn. You start playing, and first thing that goes is your foot. And you keep the "boom, boom, boom" in, you know, and all the older guys were saying, "This is the atomic age, kid. Give that bass drum time to breathe." You know. And, so the higher mathematics of drumming were too complex for me, or for my grasp at that point, and I was displaced as a drummer. And I decided I would choose an instrument that I was not likely to be so easily displaced from, and also one that spoke especially to me because when I'd heard other people who could play it, it sounded very close to what Miss Ceelie Appleton used to be. And Miss Ceelie was a real contralto. She had that rich sound that Marian Anderson and a few others had.

Ben: Still very much a young boy, really, fresh out of Alabama, finding yourself among some very serious musicians, I would assume. People who had spent their entire professional careers in the army and the band. How did you earn your stripes?

Willie: I earned my stripes playing the French horn. I was a Sergeant when I was 15. Because they were quick to reward you for progress. And so I was able then to, not only be helped by the older men who were far, far better musicians with a horn like that, but I was tutored privately in academic subjects. Because I'd only been in the ninth grade. And with the help of these men, I was able to finish high school in the army, through an army correspondence course. And they prepared me to leave there and come to Yale as a freshman, when I was 17, with the G.I. bill and three and a half years of military service.

Ben: And so you left Alabama very young, although you still go home from time to time, don't you? But you did leave that life behind as a very young man to discover the world.

Willie: I did, but I always kept a small part of it, or I should say, a big part of it in my small heart.

Ben: And the Lionel Hampton band played a part in your discovering the world.

Willie: It did. It did. I would say the army and Lionel Hampton, or the experience in Lionel Hampton's band together, would have characterized, really, the hottest part of the learning experience of the music world for me.

Ben: And of course, they both share a common thread in your partner, pianist Dwike Mitchell.

Willie: Right. Well, Mitchell had taught me to play the bass in the army, because the bass player that he had worked with before I'd joined that band had just gotten discharged, and he hated playing alone. So he came to a practice room one day where I was practicing the horn, and he watched me pat my feet. And he saw that I kept pretty good time with my feet while I played. And he said, "Hey, you wanna learn how to play the bass?" Now he might have already seen me holding a bass. I used to fool around with it. I pick up anything if the owner was not there looking at it. I try to play anything that was lying around. So he'd probably seen me fool around with the bass, because I've always loved the sound of the bass too. And he agreed to teach me, and he says, "OK, I'll start teaching you after chow tonight and, incidentally, we're playing on the radio tomorrow afternoon. 'Body and Soul.' "

Ben: Really? . . .

Willie: Yes. I almost got killed, because I played a wrong note in the bridge, a wrong chord in the bridge that next afternoon, and at the last chord, he jumped up from the piano and started choking me. So this was the style of my lessons all during that period. Needless to say, I learned pretty quickly.

Ben: That's kind of Pavlovian, though, isn't it?

Willie: That's right. You wanna keep breathing, you play a tune. So, we had talked about making a duo when we got out of the service. All guys in the service say, "Hey, we gotta stay in touch." Well, you never do. And I got out and he got out of the service in 1949. We were stationed out at this all-black air force base in Columbus, Ohio. Lockborn Air Force Base. With Elvin and the others. And I had come to Yale, and he had gone to Philadelphia Musical Academy. And we'd lost track of one another. And one night . . . I had tried for some symphony orchestra jobs in America, at that time, after having graduated from Yale. But, as I knew, before I came to Yale to prepare for a career in classical music, orchestras, the major symphony orchestras in the country, were accepting no black players. So I couldn't even get auditions to play for orchestras in America. And I accepted a position in Israel, in Tel Aviv, in the Tel Aviv Philharmonic Orchestra.

And just before flying off to Israel, I happened to turn on the Ed Sullivan show in the apartment. And there was Lionel Hampton's band, and the camera panned over to the piano, and there was Mitchell. And I went to the phone, called CBS, and told them I wanted back stage, wherever the Ed Sullivan show was. And they connected me, and I said I wanted to speak to the piano player. And they, "Oh, fine, just hold on a minute there, they're ending their set right now." And when they ended, he came over and, man it was, you know, laughter mostly, on the phone. Silly, and like that. And he said, "Well, you know, what are you doing?" I said, "I'm about to leave for Israel next Thursday." He says, "Don't you dare." He says, "I been, you know, wondering where you were." Says, "We're gonna play near you in Bridgeport tomorrow. Come and bring your horn and we'll see if we can't get you in this band." So I went to the Ritz Ballroom in Bridgeport and sat in. There were no horn parts. I just had to transpose and make up stuff as we went. And Gates liked it, and I got in the band, and the plan was for us to stay there until we got our duo together. Which we did in 1955.

Ben: This was after you had studied with Paul Hindemith?

Willie: Yes, I'd been out of school a year.

Ben: Talk about how you came to study with Paul Hindemith. I believe you saw an article that quoted Charlie Parker as saying if he could, he would study with this composer at Yale named Paul Hindemith. Why was that?

Willie: Paul Hindemith was a master of the craft of composition. And there was something about his music, as it was true in the case of the music of Stravinsky, that was modern and constructed along the lines that the practitioners of the progressive jazz strived for. And Charlie Parker could see the excellence of Hindemith's musical thinking, particularly in pieces of his like "The Symphonic Metamorphoses on Themes of Weber." And I think Bird had heard this on a radio performance some place. He also knew about the books on theory that Hindemith was writing. Hindemith was a character that was a total enigma. He never finished high-school, and he wasn't troubled by the truant officers about going to school, because he played the violin so beautifully. And he creamed everything he touched, although he didn't graduate from high-school. He taught medieval Latin and mathematics at the Hauptschule in Berlin, and knew several languages. Was able to write and produce music at an extremely high level. And he was very selective with his education. He stayed away from school houses. Was a man who totally took his education à la carte.

He chose the things that he thought were important. And somehow, this notion caught Charlie Parker's fancy. And Parker said, "Look, if I could find the wherewithal to do with my life what I would like to in the next several years, I'd go sit at this cat's feet and learn me some music." And when I read that article, even though I'd never heard of Paul Hindemith before, or knew what his music was like, if that was good enough for Charlie Parker, in that little school that he taught in up there in Connecticut, it was certainly good enough for me. So I proceeded to get myself out of the army and into Yale.

Ben: It sounds like you had more in common with Paul Hindemith than merely a musical basis. I mean, the way you came to higher learning was not unlike the way he came to higher learning.

Willie: Yes, that's true. But I didn't know that at the time, though. You know, I didn't know about our similarities then.

Ben: Talking about how you came to team up as a duo with pianist Dwike Mitchell. I mean, your story is so elaborate, we can't really do it justice here in the few minutes that we have. But when you did finally form your duo with Mitchell, you were able then to work in many clubs across the States, and to become part of the extended family of jazz players.

Willie: Right, right. And there were some good reasons for that, Ben. It was, and I'm not being modest, but it, it was so, fortuitous that here was this group of two young musicians. As a group, the irreducible minimum, and we were cheap. Scale for the most part. And it meant that we got teamed up, so that we could balance club owners' budgets, whenever they hired the most expensive names in jazz. Which turned out to be wonderful for us, because our real musical training as a duo came when we asked for, and got, the very liberal criticism of artists like Joe Williams and Count Basie.

Basie was fabulous for us. We would go on . . . I remember the first time we played Birdland opposite the Basie band. Was just in 1955, when "Every Day" was a hit. You know, it was the hottest record of all time. And once we had agreed to take the job, we had second thoughts about it, and said, "This has to have been a mistake. What are two guys gonna do on a band stand, when Basie's band gets off and Joe Williams has just sung 'Every Day'?" And so the band played and the audience was there, that first night. And the lights went off, and Pee Wee Marquette went up and announced that these two kids were gonna come up and play. And we started to play, and the band was sort of filtering out into the audience. And Basie did something that was fabulous. He stood at the table where his wife and his guests were and he wouldn't sit. He let it be made obvious that he was listening. And that drew the attention of that audience to us. Our only strategy was, the louder Basie plays, the softer we're gonna play. And he made this effort to listen, and the room quietened. And immediately, the last cadence, he led the applause.

Now, he didn't have to do that, and had he not, I shudder to try to imagine the death we would have died on that stage. And when it was over, and the audience had treated us very warmly, Mitchell and I left the stage, you know, and I said, "You know, that's one example of the nobility of a musician." And Mitchell says, "Well, you can call it nobility if you want it, I call it his religion." [Laughs.] So it was nobly religious.

Ben: Not long after that event, you subsequently took the religion across the ocean, by becoming the first jazz group to go to Russia, in 1959. Your story, you know, Willie, it sounds almost like an animated saga . . .

Willie: It's crazy, isn't it? . . .

Ben: It is crazy. Well, briefly, you were the first group to go to Russia. And, you mentioned Hindemith speaking many languages. But the story goes that you taught yourself to speak Russian, so that you could present the music properly when you arrived there.

Willie: Yes. The Russians so much appreciated having somebody stand up there and struggle through bad Russian, to try to tell them the story of this music. And I'll never forget, in Moscow, we played at the large hall in the Tchaikovsky Conservatory. And this little Russian woman with this shriveled up old face, and babushka tied under her chin. At some point, after I'd given this long talk about how this music had sprung from the breast of people in America, this woman raised her hand and stood up and says to me, "[speaks long Russian phrase]." Translated as: "Please, please, sing or play some of that sad, sad, Negro music." And we laid it on her, you know. And she wept buckets. It was something. We sang a spiritual, and Mitchell played a blues that'd make an alligator cry. Yeah, we got right on it. It was fabulous.

Ben: Well now, some time ago, you also mentioned to me something that you learned from hearing Paul Robeson, about the way African music came to Europe. Could you briefly sketch that story?

Willie: Well, Robeson was the ultimate music scholar, Ben. He not only sang brilliantly, but he learned all of these folk songs of the world. I think he could sing in something like 14 or 15 different languages, and do it beautifully. Russian, his Russian was so poetic it'd make you weep. Even songs that I don't understand, just his delivery of them, it just kills me every time. But on a record that he made in Carnegie Hall, he sang some African chants, melodies from East Africa, and then he sang some Czech plain-chants. And they were almost the same melodies. Just different words. And then he sang some of the plain-chants that found their way into the Gregorian religious ceremony, the Catholic service. And you could almost, I mean, you couldn't tell the difference in the melodies of both of these, coming from widespread areas of the world, this common way of expressing feeling that people have had, particularly in their religious music. And the fact that the Eastern Church of the Sudan, and the invasion of the Byzantine filtering through Europe, and through that whole trade route that was Venice, just had made East and West come together in a way that had surprised me. And to see that this similarity in our music lived, made a profound impression on me.

Ben: You actually made in a recording in St. Mark's cathedral when you visited Venice, not too long ago. It was a solo French horn performance, including the spiritual "Go Down Moses." Almost as a kind of a sidelight to your whole career, you've been very sensitive, I think, to the environment, when you play music, and where you play music. Very aware of jazz in a natural context, almost as if you don't want to uproot a plant in order to display its beauty. You want the beauty to be a living beauty. Hence the natural acoustics of where you play are very important...

Willie: Right. They are indeed...

Ben: When we think of the African roots of our music, we think of rhythm automatically. We automatically trace that as the mother source, and we think of the harmony as the European contribution. When we talk about how rhythm is carried forward, however, it's not always in the drums. Sometimes it's carried forward through the original instrument, the human being, right?

Willie: That's right. And, the human and the drum made one intriguing combination. I am always still in awe when I think about the power that drumming has in it. It was one of the reasons, I'm sure, I was attracted to it early in life, and that it was my first instrument. But I fear the drum. It is . . . one of the reasons I was, I was glad to give it up, when I got run off of it in the army, it's too hot for me. And one thing that parents should be mindful of, when they give a young kid a set of drums, is a responsibility that goes with that. Because it is harder to make a judicious decision about what to do with those things than it is to play a melodic instrument, or one that you can use ten fingers on. Your chances of being too loud are great. And it's one of the hardest things to know, how to accompany this.

Ben: Too much freedom almost . . .

Willie: Too much, too much freedom, and you're really not familiar . . . it takes years and years to get familiar with the technique of really doing it judiciously, and doing it right. It's a big, big choice.

Ben: What's the hambone?

Willie: The hambone is one of the many drum substitutes that we have. See, when the drum was outlawed, the people who had their drum taken away, because it was thought to be an instrument of insurrection. The slave owners didn't want the slaves talking in a language they [the owners] couldn't understand on a drum, because they could easily revolt that way. So one of the first laws governing slave behavior in America was to outlaw the drum. And to equally make inaccessible reading and writing that way, also by law at a similar time. So that people who have their drum taken away do things that people who keep their drums don't do. And since Americans, American slaves were unique in having their drum taken away, they did some unique things in the absence of the drum. Like tap dancing. That's uniquely ours. Hambone is uniquely ours. Spirituals are uniquely ours. The blues, uniquely ours. Ragtime uniquely ours. Bebop uniquely ours.

Ben: All different ways to carry the drum.

Willie: All different ways, that's right, to carry the drum. Boogie-woogie is another of the drum substitutes, you know? People who got the drums don't need to invent like that. And growing up in the south, as I did in Alabama, I got pretty good on this drum substitute that uses the body, the thigh [hitting hand rhythmically on those areas], and the chest, called the hambone. I like the tempo a little bit faster than that. But you can do it with two hands. I'm just doing it with one now. And you can even cross your legs, or go across, but you aren't just restricted to the chest and the thighs. You have other parts of your body that are ever so musical. Like the puckered lips. [Makes lip popping sounds and hand on body rhythms for a minute.] That's a hambone.

Ben: I mentioned before that you're somebody who loves the context of music, not just the notes themselves, but where the notes are played. And I love the context of a distinguished professor of music at Yale University —and we're, actually, talking here on the campus at Yale— demonstrating the hambone. This is part of the higher mathematics of the music, as I see it. But, the reason I mentioned your love for the context is that, in all the recordings that you do, and many of them tend to be live recordings, you're very conscientious about recording the ambience as well as the instruments. Almost as if it's important for us to know *where* this music is being played, not just *that* it's being played.

And when I hear you play, I always hear the inner environment. Willie, I'm kind of hitting that theme because I want to talk about perhaps one of the most unusual recording projects that has ever been done . . .

Willie: [laughing] Yes . . .

Ben: You talked earlier about how your were scared off playing drums because of the higher mathematics of bebop. However, years later, to add to the many ironies of your experience, you became involved in the higher mathematics, not just of bebop, but of the universe. I'm talking about a recording that you made which was a representation of Kepler's "Harmony Of The Spheres." What is this record?

Willie: This record, Ben, is something again that has its beginnings in the Charlie Parker legend. Because Charlie Parker's fascination with Paul Hindemith led me to Yale as a student, and, to my great disgust, Hindemith didn't wanna talk about modern music. He insisted on going back to the very beginnings. He taught a course called the "History Of The Theory Of Music," and he was very much taken with those great scientists during all of history who had not only been outstanding in their own fields, but who had also written extensively on the subject of music theory. Ptolemy, the great Greek astronomer. Euclid, the geometer. And Kepler, the astronomer, mathematician. Hindemith posited that, had it not been for Kepler's grounding in music theory, he might not have discovered the three laws of planetary motion, which are three of the landmark laws in the whole history of science.

And Kepler was able to see musical relationships in the proportions that the planets had in their movement, one to the other, in their march around the sun. And he said that, during his lifetime, he challenged the musicians of his time to make a sacred setting. That is, to give a sacred text to this music of the heavens, which he described as one continuous song, in which there are clausulas, in which there are cadences, in which there are all of the musical devices that man, in his feeble attempt with imperfect instruments here below, tries to pull together in making a musical performance. And Kepler's notion was that, in the elliptical paths that the planets assumed, that each planet individually slows down and speeds up as it approaches the sun, or as it goes around that way. And that taken all together, they would make a construct that has some very consonant moments and some very dissonant moments. So they move in and out of this very strange harmonic construct. And in that harmonic construct are all of the musical relationships that we could ever think up. I mean, these harmonies just go all over the place, and they're not all pleasant. He describes it as being, at times, as harmonious as an organ chord in church, and at other times it would be dissonance that is visceral shaking.

Ben: So he was clearly hearing "in his inner ear" what he was talking about.

Willie: That's right. Absolutely. And he was clear to describe this as a music for the intellect, not for the ear, for some very practical reasons. Number one, there is no atmosphere out there for these planets to vibrate in. They move too slowly. Thirty years it takes for Saturn just to make one orbit. We don't have that kind of time to sit around and listen. He said, however, that if the musicians of his time would set this stuff to a sacred text, he would show them where these moments are in astronomical time. Well, in the 375 years or so from the time he died until the time I heard about this, nobody'd ever picked up his challenge. And for good reason. We didn't have the instruments of precision needed to do that.

But by the time I came back to Yale to teach, in the '70s, the computer was here, and the tone generator was here. So we could at last pick up Kepler's challenge, and put it on tape and make this aural planetarium. This planetarium for the ear rather than the eye, that he had imagined all his life and worked so hard toward. And I, having heard this from my old music professor, Hindemith, I found myself with technology in my lap, and time on my side, and I could do nothing but find the collaborator who did have the better higher math in astronomy, and this is what we got on the tape and it is what Kepler promised.

Ben: And the earth sings the blues. It's a minor second interval . . .

Willie: That's right . . .

Ben: Starting on a dirt road in Sheffield, Alabama, and winding up making available the music of outer space here at Yale. Willie, what's next?

Willie: I don't know Ben. When I grow up, I wanna be a musician. [Laughs.]

You know, the other day in New York, a photographer for the *Times* was taking some pictures that went out in a *Times* story about the theater. And she was trying to move people around the stage, you know, getting people out of the way and all, and she says, "Now, Mr. Choreographer, would you have the musician walk up." And I said, "Oh lady, please say it again. It just sounds so nice . . ." I said, "God, my Momma always wanted a musician in our family."

* * *

Art Blakey (January, 1985)

Art Blakey led the charge on the jazz scene for four decades, and his group, The Jazz Messengers, formed back in the '50s with pianist Horace Silver and continuing on in various guises, remained one of the hottest bands until Blakey's passing in 1990. Blakey's spirit, both behind the drum kit and out in the world at large, was so formidable that musicians always turned to him as a natural leader. The way he chose his musicians and how he formed his philosophy of leadership was of great interest to me as we sat down to talk in New York. The list of musicians he discovered and brought along over the years staggers the imagination; even a partial list of just the trumpet players is mind-boggling and would have to include Lee Morgan, Donald Byrd, Freddie Hubbard, and Wynton Marsalis. Before the formal part of our conversation began, we talked a little bit about his growing family. In his late sixties, he was both a grandfather and the father of an infant. Then we got down to his role as one of the great practical jazz educators, as well as a drummer of unparalleled energy and style.

Ben: Art, you've been called a one-man University for young jazz players because you seem to always find the best new players and turn them into leaders. This has been going on for years. What do you look for in a young player? How do you find them and how do you bring them along?

Art: Well, I think one begets another. One musician brings in another. And what we do is I meet them and the musicians talk about them and I get to hear them, and you hear the potential. A lot of musicians I hear I'd like to have in the band but they won't fit. Their personalities won't fit. You have to find out about their backgrounds and their dislikes to bring about cohesion in the band and in the music, you know? Because if it's up there and it's a dislike among the different personalities on the bandstand, it certainly comes through the music.

I teach musicians to look at it this way. You are, in fact, you're in the nude. You're in your birthday suit. People can see clean through you. Your music, your actions, and your vibes that you bring forth to the audience come out and you cannot hide that. It's got to be right. It's got to be cohesion, it's got to be love, and then the band begins to come together in a matter of a few months. Playing together every night, you begin to know each other, trust each other. The band begins to come together. Otherwise, it just can't make it.

And I know many bands have gotten together with some of the finest musicians in the world, they got together and they play, but they can't come across the floodlights. You've got to come past the floodlights to the people. Because that's the main thing about playing jazz is the contact with your audience. You know, it's one of the most wonderful things in the world, because they [the musicians] don't know what they're going to play. It's from the Creator to the artist to the audience. And then from the audience back to the artist and so on.

It's a rapport between the audience and the music. That's what makes jazz jazz. And they [the musicians] don't know what they're gonna do. You can change in a split second and play something else. And the only way you know is you begin to know a person so well and like him so well that you look. And the eyes are the windows of the soul, you see. And when we look at each other, they know just what to do. If I look at them in a certain way, they know just what to do, in a split second. They say "Oh, he's gonna change this way," or I'll make a cue on the drums, say "Ok, we're gonna change this."

Because at no time are all the tunes set at exactly the same tempo. I may change the tempo one night to see how this tune works at a new tempo. We might be playing it too fast. Because we like to keep it at a tempo where the public can pat their feet. You see, and enjoy it. And if it gets so they can't pat their feet, it gets to be a time that you make the public feel that they have to be educated—they didn't come here to get educated! Because the music is supposed to wash away the dust of everyday life. So they're supposed to come in there and enjoy themselves. So if they start feeling like they need to be educated, then it's not interesting anymore.

Ben: One of the things you mentioned was the little gestures you might do to conduct the band. It's very interesting because not that many drummers are leaders, and you're conducting from behind the drum kit. I know one of the things you do is use a press roll to signal to a player that he has to get his solo into the next gear, or maybe that it's time to give it to the next player.

Art: I think the father of that, and where I learned that from, where it comes from, is Chick Webb. You see, it used to be, to me, before the advent of Chick Webb, I think the drummer was just a time keeper. It was like fourteen musicians and a drummer. In a jazz orchestra. And after the advent of Chick Webb it became fifteen musicians. He brought the drummer from in the back out to the front.

Ben: I notice when you're playing behind a soloist, first of all you're giving them some momentum from the cross rhythms. You'll keep the time up on the cymbals but you're gonna give them some momentum with the left hand. And you'll also, at the right point in the solo, give them that press roll.

Art: Well the idea of that is this. I try to teach drummers, I tell musicians that the idea of this . . . I'm the leader, this is true. Now I don't have to make this known. If we're playing and you're coming out, you're having dinner or you want to enjoy yourself, how many drum solos can you listen to? It becomes noise to you. People don't give a damn how many paradiddles or ratamacues you make. All they know is what they *feel*. Once again, they did not come to be educated. They come to enjoy themselves.

The drum is an instrument of accompaniment. He's back there in the rhythm section. He's supposed to play with the bass, the guitar, the piano, whatever you have. He's supposed to play *with* them to accompany the soloist so he won't feel lost when he's out there. You're supposed to make him feel good. Maybe he had a hard time that day. Maybe his old lady gave him a bad time. When he hits that bandstand, he's got to learn to leave his worldly problems off. Because to me the bandstand is hallowed ground. You come up here, you're supposed to play. A musician is supposed to play, if he gets up off his deathbed he's supposed to get up and play.

This is the way you're supposed to love what you're doing. Because how many people are given that much talent to do that? So he *must* do it. Because talent is like to be on loan. It doesn't belong to the artists, the musicians or whoever has it. It belongs to the people. No matter how great the painter is. No matter how great the musician is. If nobody comes there to listen to him and what he has done, he's lost. So you have to give it to the people. So if you don't, you're moved out of the way and somebody comes and takes your place. You're always, you need that, you're not above it.

So this is the whole thing. You learn to sit back there and make that man *play*. It's just like putting a soloist, a man, anybody, out in the ice cold water without his boots on, rubber boots. And you get him out there, you make him feel good and make him play, and stay *behind* him. And try to make him build up. And each chorus you just keep building up and keep building up. And a guy goes a certain distance, I make a roll. They know when I make that roll, they got a certain distance. They say, well, I got three choruses to play. After that roll, I know I got to play now.

And this is it. And by the time he ends up, you're in high pitch. You don't overplay him. Or get in competition with him. You accompany him. And make him feel good. And usually, in the times I worked in other bands, Duke Ellington, Count Basie, all the big bands, I worked with everybody, but the first thing I do I go in and introduce myself to all the individual musicians, and the soloists. And I ask them is there anything I can do to make them sound better or make them feel good. That's the most important thing. The important thing isn't to get up on the bandstand and come into Count Basie's orchestra or Duke Ellington's orchestra, anyone's orchestra, you don't come in and play Art Blakey. You come in and play whoever you're working for. And I always said to myself, "Well, you have to make the punishment fit the crime." So whatever you're in, you play at.

And when I'm in my group, I play Art Blakey. And I have a good time doing it.

Ben: Well you do, and that comes across as well as the mutual respect you're talking about. I've seen several incarnations of your band and there's another theme that runs through them. You've referred to the bandstand as "hallowed ground," and when you're on the stand you seem to treat each other in a very formal way. You're having fun but you're very serious about it.

Art: Yeah. It's better that way. Always, I do that. And what I appreciate most is not being, not trying to push myself ahead. Well, I tell you what. When I was with Billy Eckstine. Now we had all the stars in the country at that time. There was Sarah Vaughan, Lady Day was working with us on this show, and we had Charlie Parker, Dexter Gordon, Lucky Thompson, Fats Navarro, Dizzy Gillespie. Oh, you just name them, every star in the country came out. And that was bebop coming out at that time. And Earl Hines' band was the cradle of it, because most of Earl Hines' band left him for Billy Eckstine. And here I'm sitting there now, there's no room on the marquee for me, so I'm not going to sit back there and pound drums or twirl those sticks in the air and try to get attention. I want to play the arrangements and play with the musicians.

And I didn't care what they said, just as long as they said *something*. And a young lady came and interviewed the band in California, at the theater. And I was playing my heart out. So she wrote in the paper, "Gene Ammons looked like a big black snortin' bull, and fire coming from his nostrils." And she said, "The drummer, Billy Eckstine just bought him a brand new set of drums, and he looks like a little black pygmy sitting back there saying 'we're gonna eat the white man tonight'." So everybody said, "Man, you should get mad."

And I said, "No. She spelled my name right. That's the most important thing." So the people come to see the little black pygmy. And they make the decision for themselves. It doesn't matter. In the business, if they don't say something about you, you're lost.

Ben: Well, as I said before, people usually say that you are one of the finest developers of talent in the world of jazz. You've had a string of amazing trumpet players and saxophone players come through the band. Tell me a little about the formation of the band you have right now. How did the current lineup come about?

Art: Well, the band is just a continuation from the other band, the one with Wynton Marsalis. And the next band will be a continuation from this, because we always have understudies. When Wynton was in the band, Terrance Blanchard was the understudy, because they were good friends. So Wynton sent him tapes and he learned the music. And he had practiced the music and listened to the tapes and how it was supposed to go, so when Wynton got ready to leave, it was just a smooth transition. And there's another trumpet player in-between called Wallace Roney who's still around.

There's always trumpet players and saxophone players that know the whole book. And there's other musicians, we have a big band we take on concerts. A bunch of youngsters, they know all the music. They come and we rehearse that day and play a concert that night. I just can't believe it, it sounds so good. Because the musicians now they're younger, they can read, all of them can read, they've got a good sound, and they know how it goes, and it makes it so much easier for me. You don't have to teach them because they've got the idea how it's supposed to go. And they've got the idea what I like, and I don't have to tell them what to do or what to wear or anything.

They know what I like. You come on the bandstand, look professional, be sharp. They see you before they hear you and don't come up there looking like something that jumped out of the garbage can, or like you're gonna give somebody a grease job. Because I don't go for that. I think that they must learn to have more respect for the audience.

So most of the musicians who come out of the band, that's what we train them for. They become leaders. All of them won't. 'Cause all of them don't have that quality. A lot of them do, and they have to be developed. They come in and they find out how to do it. Some don't become leaders. They know how to get out if they get a gig, and how to make the gig, make the gig on time, they know. But all of them can't be leaders because that's not supposed to be. But most of them come out of there can lead the band. They know just what it's about.

Ben: This sounds like the curriculum at the University of Art Blakey. You've been doing it for so long. Can you even keep track of all the players and recordings?

Art: Well, according to the count out there, counting the bootleg records and everything, we have 475 albums.

Ben: You've made a lot of live recordings, more than most artists. Why is that? Do you like making a live record better than a studio date?

Art: Well, I'll tell you, it was an idea. We were the first to make a live record. And that happened on *A Night At Birdland* for Blue Note. It was just an idea of mine. And I went to Blue Note and asked them. They thought I was crazy. I said "Let's try it. Let's do it. Right there with the live audience." I don't know if we were the first ones to ever make a live recording, but I think in jazz we were the first to make a live record with the audience. Because I wanted that *feeling*. So we did it at Birdland and, do you know, it came off. The musicians didn't even know we were recording. And it just came off. It happened. They were very relaxed, they got out of the idea of being tense.

And sometimes, like records they make now, like most music, especially in rock music, they make the records in the jazz music too, the studio sounds so clinical. It really sounds too clinical. And when people hear it, it ain't like that. The engineers have doctored it up so, you know what I mean, and that's very bad. It's bad for the musician. He should know, and hear his mistakes loud so he can correct them. So they end up never developing musicians too much.

It's like in a big band. I love big bands, I love the sound of them, but I can't handle them because there's not enough blowing room for the individual musician to develop. If he sits in the back in a big band and plays sixteen or twelve bars a night, he ain't going to make it. He's got to play. He's got to be playing all the time. So therefore, I always went back to the combo idea. Because in a combo, every tub has got to sit on its own bottom.

You know, there's a spiritual part to the music. And there's more to it than making loud sounds and everything. People are supposed to sit there and they can't keep their feet still, you know. Just forget about their problems out there. They can pick them up when they come out of the place after they hear you play. But that's your job.

Ben: When you take your band into the recording studio, how do you maintain this feeling you're talking about?

Art: In a studio? Well, we just record in a studio, but I don't let it happen too much. They always say, "Okay, let's make another take, make another take." Well, you wear the musicians out. They give us only five hours to make a whole album. And those same people will turn around and give a rock group six weeks to make an album. You see, that's your superiority of the musicians. That shows what's happening. So they come in and they said, "Do it again, another take," and I said, "No, you can't do that. Because we have to play this thing over and over and it gets monotonous. The first take is your take. That's it. You ain't going to get a better one." Not that day. Tomorrow he may come back and play it different. It will feel different. But you're not going to get the same thing in jazz. And if you do, it sounds clinical.

We did a record one time and Benny Golson wrote it, and it goes into different tempos. Benny even wrote out the drum solo and I played it exactly as he wrote it out. Sounds horrible. Sounds like Joe Doaks and His Salt Shakers. Yes, it was in tune. Yes, we were playing the notes right. But it was terrible. You can't do things like that. It doesn't happen like that in jazz. I play a solo one way one time, I'll turn that thing around because it gets monotonous to me. If I'm not having fun up there it becomes a job, I don't want to do it.

I just like to change everything. You make a mistake, you're supposed to be so professional and know your instrument, master your instrument so well, that you go back and you make that same mistake the same way and make something out of it. See, that's how jazz was born. Somebody goofed.

You stop doing that and start getting clinical you don't play jazz any more.

Ben: Do you follow the recording careers of musicians once they've left your band?

Art: No. I don't even listen to my own records. I listened to it when I made it and that's enough for me. No, I don't listen to them because of this reason. It's got nothing to do with ego or anything. I don't listen to other guy's records because I always wanted to be an innovator. I like to search for other things. Now, my ears are so big, musically, if I listen to a record and hear a drummer doing something, it will stick in my head. And when I'm playing somewhere, automatically, I'll play it. And that would cut off my creativity.

I'm an innovator. That's what I am. I like to find new things on the drums. I like to hear drummers playing things that I tried out fifteen, twenty, thirty years ago. I like to hear drummers now doing it. Because all that can be played on that instrument has not been played. And it's a bastard instrument. And I think I must help to try and get it back to where it belongs.

Sometime the drummers, they run me out of there. And they can play, but they play too goddamned loud. And I wear a hearing aid and I don't want to hear all that. I want to hear a drummer play the drum, not beat the drum. Because I think the instrument should be played right, and they should think about it. And they should know how to handle the snare drum and how to roll. And I try and tell them everything.

You know, when I first met Kenny Clarke, all he had was a snare drum, a bass drum and one cymbal. That's all he had. The high hat hadn't even been invented. He was with Edgar Hayes and the Mills Blue Rhythm Orchestra and their records are there to prove it, what he did. Because most of them, they don't do it. And they won't play brushes. And that annoys me.

So I feel that I have to keep searching and find something to make them really want to get into it. So I have to keep going in and finding new things and new ways and letting the drummers know that this is something different. The bass drum is there for some things. It's not there just for accents. It's there to be played at all times, and make your accents too. But I find that they'll be jiving, because the bass drum is the bottom of the group. That's the bottom of the group. That's why, because guys didn't play the bass drums, acoustic music, they have to push it out. They had to bring in electric bass. To keep that bottom.

See, you got four extremities, you got left hand, right hand, left foot, right foot. You ain't supposed to let your right hand know what your left hand is doing, your left foot know what your right foot is doing. Everything is supposed to go in a different direction and still keep the swing. You can play loud when you play loud and you can play soft, but don't lose the intensity of the beat. Once you lose the intensity, all is lost.

Ben: A lot of groups today don't stay together long enough to develop a group sound, or to learn things like how to play soft without losing that intensity.

Art: Well, I think they need managing, booking and all that kind of stuff, which I hope in the near future to try and do. To help groups out like that. To book them, to manage them and get them going. Once you get them going, it will be alright. But somebody's got to be out there to help get them going. Take care of the business end. Because musicians, I'm one myself, you know, they're sad businessmen. The secular part of the thing, they don't want to be bothered with. You can't blame them for that. Because it's ridiculous to try to handle the secular part and to handle the musical part too. That's really hard. Somehow I do it, because I have to do it. I have to do it now.

I used to do it with my manager, Jack Whitamore. And when he passed, I just took it up and kept going. Because I was doing it before he passed, you know, and he taught me a lot about the booking business. And my wife was his secretary. And he told her where the body was buried, and we just went straight ahead. Now we're trying to get our organization together so she can go on and book other artists and handle them. And get them out there where they can play.

That's what's happening to jazz today. We need other people to come in. Not musicians. We need other people to come in and work at this thing. But a lot of them, it's hard, because the best brains now, it's big money out there handling rock and handling other things, you know. And these guys come in and they're looking for some pie in the sky, and you tell them, "Man, it's hard work. This is an art form, and you're going to have to work at it." You know, it will pay off, if you work at it and you believe in it. But that's what we need. Young minds who believe in this thing and just go forward with it. Young people.

Ben: It seems there are more young people working on the business side of jazz. But it isn't getting any easier to get good bookings.

Art: Well, mostly the agencies, they don't know what they're selling. They don't know what they got. Some of them never come and hear the groups that they're booking. They just get on the telephone and just, you know. They never come down and see the impact this group is bringing upon the audience that they play for. They don't know what they're selling. They're not interested. Because all they're interested in is the cash register. They're not interested in the art form.

It's like when I was with Billy Eckstine. That great band with all them great stars, they never recorded them guys. Every record we made, if Billy wasn't on it singing or doing something, or playing a trumpet or trombone, which he wasn't a trumpet player. He had the greatest trumpets in the world, he didn't need to play no trumpet. But it had to be on there. You see, they weren't interested in the band. And all that other went lacking. They weren't interested in Sarah Vaughan, Charlie Parker, Dizzy. You know what I mean? This is the way they are. Because this is the great art form, so that's what happened.

We need to get young people in there to handle business who are really interested in the music and understand about it as well as the young Europeans, or the young Japanese. They understand it. And it's a shame. Of all the records I told you we made, we could go to all the record stores in this country and you can't even find those records. You go to Japan, you can find every one of them. Even back to King Oliver, you can find them in Japan, but not here.

Ben: A lot of classic jazz is definitely coming back to us from Japan and Europe. It seems that bebop is more popular there now than ever before.

Art: You want to know a frightening thing? We played London, we played Ronnie Scott's, and I noticed in the audience there were a lot of punk rock kids there. I was shocked. But they were communicating with my guys on the stage, because they're young. After we finished playing Ronnie Scott's, we had to go to the punk rock disco and sign autographs, because "Ping Pong," the thing we made about thirty years ago, is now the big hit over there. The thing Wayne Shorter wrote. Now they're playing albums we did thirty years ago in the disco.

Ben: Did you ever think you would be the king of the disco?

Art: [Laughs.] Well the kids like it because of the way it starts out. You know, the simple rhythm, you know, the "bop bop . . ." [He sings the opening from "Ping Pong."] And the kids can dance on it.

You know, I'm very much encouraged with the music now. Everybody's crying about this and about that. About the music going down. But we never had no problem. We just work. You know, it gets bad here, we leave and go to the Continent, it get's bad there, we go somewhere else. You know, we've been to Japan 47 times.

Ben: So the University of Art Blakey remains on the road and open for business.

Art: Yeah!

* * *

Betty Carter (January, 1988)

A fiercely independent woman, Betty Carter has been a jazz singer's jazz singer since her emergence in the 1940s with the Lionel Hampton band. She has continued since then to find young jazz musicians and to train them in the finer points of their craft, expanding the boundaries of her own performances even as she maintained a rigorous traveling and performance schedule. Recently, her recordings have become prominent on the jazz charts in the United States, but for years before this turnaround in 1988, she worked the clubs and, occasionally, concerts without much visibility or the recognition that she so obviously deserved. The reasons for this sad omission included her obvious commitment to the highest artistic standards (her refusal to change her presentation to satisfy anybody else's idea of commercial music) and the fact that her style of interpreting popular songs has always been a challenge for the average listener to absorb. The following conversation was held just as her business fortunes were beginning to change for the better.

Ben: You finally have a record deal with a major American label and they are about to reissue a lot of the great music that you recorded and released yourself over the years for your own label. As we speak, you also have records doing well on the American jazz charts. So these seem to be pretty good times for Betty Carter. But I know the ride has not been easy for you and that you've traveled a long way since you were a teenager back in Detroit during the '40s. It's a road that very few women have traveled in jazz.

Betty: Well you have to start somewhere, you know. And I did start with the Lionel Hampton band about 1948. So it's been about forty years. But before then I had some experience living in Detroit, which was the place where I learned all about the music, swing and bebop. When bebop came in, I was right on it. And so was the West side of Detroit. It was really strange how the West side of Detroit was more for the bebop than the East side of Detroit. I lived on the West side, so in my high school, we were turned on to the music, which enlightened us a lot.

Ben: That period has always seemed to be one of the most vibrant periods for jazz. Is that your impression also?

Betty: That was the most creative period in jazz. We had a lot of individuals begin to surface, and musicians knew from the very beginning that they had to be themselves, even though they had the role models of Charlie Parker and Dizzy there. They still knew that they had to be themselves in order to be successful.

And that is the period where we developed a lot of individualists. And that's the reason that we have so many records out there today to reissue. During that period record companies really were recording "potential" artists, artists who had not found themselves. But they [the record companies] could see or hear in that artist the potential of him, or her, becoming a great musician one day. And the record companies took a chance on them when they were very young, growing up in the business.

Ben: Today the business seems more directed toward whatever the latest fad happens to be, rather than the process you describe, which is directed toward what is new or innovative.

Betty: Well, the environment was different. We never even thought about it like that. You think about it like that today because of the environment that's here. It's overwhelming now. The music business is very electronic and very technical these days. They don't really need you in the recording studio to make a record. But in those days, you didn't think about that like we think about it now. It was about learning the music and having a lot of fun. It wasn't about money. Just how to learn our craft and become individuals. So that one day we *would* earn some money. That's what I mean.

Ben: Hearing you talk about learning your craft brings to mind the way you met Charlie Parker. You've said that the first time it was "on you," but the second time it was "on him." What did you mean by that?

Betty: Well you know, you want your ego stroked when you perform. I don't know how I got on that stage, but I did. It was Miles Davis and Tommy Potter and Duke Jordan and Max Roach, that band, and Charlie Parker. And I happened to strike up a conversation with Charlie Parker during rehearsal. I told him that I sang and I was trying to get in the business. So he asked me to sing. So I got up there did my little diddly-daddly, you know. But the next time I showed up, I'm standing close to the band, I'm hoping now that I would have turned him on the night before enough for him to ask me. That's what I mean you need your ego stroked by somebody like that. You want them to ask you, "Do you want to sing?" And that's good for the ego. It keeps you in the business. So it happened to me. Twice. With Charlie Parker and with Dizzy. Dizzy did the same thing.

Ben: You became a big band singer shortly after that rather than a small group singer. Why did you join a large outfit like the Lionel Hampton band rather than a bebop group which was your obvious love?

Betty: The opportunity came for me to get some experience. I'm fresh out of high school. What do I know? I'm young and everybody young thinks they know everything. But they find out they don't know anything at all. Here was an organization that wanted me, the Lionel Hampton organization. So why not go for the experience? I wanted to go, I wanted to do things, so I did.

I was there for two and a half years. What did I learn? I learned how to write. I was taught by Bobby Plater how to score arrangements. I learned the keys musicians played in. I learned about fast tempos and slow tempos and mistakes and out of tune and all that stuff. And I saw a lot. I traveled all over the country. And the band was run by Miss Gladys Hampton, who really was my first role model, in a sense, because she was a black woman that was the head of an organization and was literally telling the people how she wanted it to go. And it was successful. *She* was successful. And I had her to look up to in my beginnings.

So I got something out of it, there's no doubt about it. Maybe I wanted to be with Dizzy Gillespie's band, but that was impossible. As I look back now, the Lionel Hampton band was the best band I could have been with at the time because of its stability. It was run very well and was very well organized. I was with the band that I should have been with at the time. Now it was up to me to develop my own thing. Lionel Hampton shouldn't have affected what I did with my music. All he offered me was an experience.

But what I learned affected my music. I didn't realize it then. Sure I wanted to sing love songs and things like that, and all he had me do was improvising. I didn't realize at that time how valuable that kind of ear training was. Until twenty years later, you know. Now I do it at the drop of a hat. Back then, my biggest complaint was I wanted to sing about love, and songs with melodies.

Ben: And he just wanted you to scat sing?

Betty: All I did was improvise with the band. That's all I ever did. He had other singers who did the big ballads. And I wanted to sing the ballads. But I never realized until years later that the ear training I got from being told to just sit in here and sit in there and sit in over there, you know, taught me an awful lot about what I'm doing today.

Ben: That's interesting because very shortly after leaving Lionel Hampton's band you recorded a solo album and it was an album full of beautiful ballads. And at the time, the way you gloried in the sound of the lyrics of those ballads set you apart from any other singer. It was as if all that improvisation came home to roost in those first solo recordings, and you were able to make so much more out of mundane material.

Betty: Well if I was going to sustain myself in this business, I was going to have to do something like that. I couldn't go around improvising all the time.

But I left the band and decided I was going to start working on my own, doing some songs I wanted to do. And I wanted to be a person that communicated to the audience. That was the most important thing.

Ben: How important were these things like theatrics and dramatic narrative to you at that time?

Betty: When you were brought up like I was in the business, when you play the Apollo Theater as often as I did—even when I was with Lionel Hampton I played there four or five times, and after that at least once a year until it closed—you had to communicate. There was no other way that you could deal on that stage. In fact, that is what you're supposed to do when you get up there. Communicate and *entertain*. That's the only way that you're going to survive. You've got to entertain.

Ben: Your vocal style, even then, was highly distinctive. I realize that is the goal, that is the message of this music. But it was almost unprecedented in the degree to which you pushed the boundaries of popular songs. Yet surely you had models. Talk about some of the singers or instrumentalists that helped shape your narrative style, the way you deliver a lyric.

Betty: First, you concentrate on the lyric. You read the lyric. You're an actor actually. You've got to make that audience *understand* that lyric. I mean, you can't just say the words and expect the audience to feel it. You've got to really believe them at the moment, and believe in what you're singing about. Just like the actor does on the stage, you know? He has to believe his lines when he says them to be effective. And that's the same thing I have to do to be an effective singer.

And I could not, in those days, think about any other singers. I was *not* influenced by singers. The opportunity that the singers gave me to do what I'm doing now came about, naturally, when Sarah Vaughan took those melodies and did something else with them. So she opened the door to do anything you wanted to do with a melody. And it wasn't applauded by everyone because a lot of composers really want their melodies sung the way they wrote them, you know. And there are lots of singers that accommodate these composers, and give them the melody the way they wrote it. In fact, 99 percent of the singers do the standard melodies the way they're written.

So I knew that I had to develop Betty Carter. That meant that I had to think for Betty Carter and not be influenced by other singers, because the jazz world was not going to allow a duplicate. See, that's the one thing in black jazz, there are no duplicates. It's only one of a kind. So

I had to be me. I had to get away from the songs that Sarah sang. I couldn't sing "You're Blasé" or "The Nearness of You" or "Tenderly" or any of that stuff, because it would remind the people of Sarah Vaughan. And I could not sing Ella Fitzgerald's popular hits either, or Billie Holiday's. So I just tried to find songs that nobody ever thought of singing before. I used to come up with songs that they didn't touch so that I could create my own identity. So that when the audience left the club or the concert hall they'd have no one on their mind but Betty Carter.

That's the only way I could have gotten this far. If I sang like any one of those other ladies, I'd still be in my home town singing just like they do, right?

Ben: Perhaps you're being overly modest by saying that the material you chose was the determining factor in separating you from the others. Part of what distinguished you wasn't the different songs or the different notes that you would sing, but the impact you would breathe into the syllables, beyond the meaning of the words. In fact, I think it's possible to listen to your singing and not understand the English language and still get a lot out of it.

Betty: [Laughs.] Boy, that's really saying something.

Ben: What about the influence of instrumentalists? For example, sometimes I think I can hear the influence of Miles Davis in your singing, particularly in your choice of notes, your timing and your use of space. I know you spent time with Miles. Was that an influence at all?

Betty: I don't think so. You know, I don't sit around listening to jazz or to horn players all day. And the reason for that is because I want to be *free* of what they're doing. I don't want them to influence me. I want to appreciate what they do. I want to love what they do and know what they do. But I don't want to *do* what they do. I want to do what *I* do. So in order to do what I do, I can't sit and listen to them do what they do. Those pretty notes that Miles Davis does, see, that's Miles Davis' notes. The notes that I pick are *my* notes.

Space is something I've always liked. I think space gives you a chance to think about what you're getting ready to say to somebody. That's one reason why I probably do this now. Because I do want to talk to the audience. It's about communication. You give the audience a chance to relax and absorb what you just said. Before you give them that other line. And they'll expect the line to come in another place anyway. They're way ahead of you. Especially if they know the tune, they're way ahead of you. In their mind, they're singing the melody. Now how are *you* going to do it?

You know, if I could have foreseen what I was going to do, I would know how to describe it to you. But the way I've evolved, it just *happened*, on the job. And it happens every night on the job. It still hasn't stopped happening. And I've allowed myself to be that free. I didn't realize I could be that free until I really found that I *could be*. That's the only way I can describe it to you. I can't even describe how it happened. Because there was no set plan for me to do this with a song or do that with a song. I would sit down and arrange a song and tell my musicians how I wanted this arrangement to go. But how my concept was going to deal with this arrangement . . . Because sometimes these arrangements would be very challenging even to me.

You know, I have to do things that even I don't think I can do. In fact, there's a song now I'm trying to put back into the book that I recorded about 1964. I changed the keys on the break and for the life of me, I can't seem to do that today. I can change the key but not the same way I did it then. Or with the clearness that I did it then. I am singing better than I was singing years ago, but, still, my approach to this tune is really driving me crazy. I sit and ask myself what did I do at that point in my life, in the mid '60s? It was just a break and a change of key, you know?

Ben: Further proof that in jazz it's not important whether you step in the same stream twice but whether you can step in it once. Hearing you say that if you knew what you were doing you'd be able to tell me how you were doing it brings to mind a song you wrote years ago called "I Can't Help It (That's The Way I Am)." The message of that song is quite clear: be yourself.

Betty: Well that song was back in '57 or '58. I was still in that "be yourself" groove in '58.

Ben: There's a couplet in that song, "Have you considered what it does to your soul, you sell it when you play some other's role," that seems to be a rule you've lived by.

Betty: Yeah. Most people who try to benefit off of somebody else's success sell their soul and eventually wind up not accomplishing anything.

Ben: Around the time you wrote this song, you were doing club work, opening shows for Miles and other great players, but even though you were gaining success, you were also encountering new problems in the business. Somehow you developed a reputation for being difficult to work with and it seemed that the major record companies didn't want to record you for a while. Why was that?

Betty: Well, the record business became a money-making business, a *real* money-making business. It happened in 1964. Because that's when the whole thing changed. But in the meantime, I had recorded with ABC Paramount, with Atco, with Ray Charles on United Artists. So it wasn't that I had a reputation of being hard to get along with. That wasn't it. Because I really didn't give anybody any static. Because everybody came to me, I didn't go to them. Every record company I recorded for came to me. So if they came to me, then they already must have decided some time ago that they liked what I was doing. Now if I go to them with my project in hand and say "Record me" then I'm obligated to do what *they* say. But this didn't happen. They came to me and said, "We want you to record for our company." So I said "Okay." There are about four albums I did from 1957, one on Peacock, two on ABC Paramount, then one on Atco which was out there for a minute. And then one on United Artists, which is called "Inside Betty Carter." And Alan Douglas, who did this record, he and I were very good friends. So it wasn't about me not getting along with anybody. I don't know how that got out at all.

I did what I had to do when I started my own record company, because it was a sign of the times. Anybody with any brains could see what was happening in 1964. Jazz was going down the tubes as far as record companies were concerned. They could make more money off of that other stuff.

Ben: It was a critical period wasn't it?

Betty: It was a critical period for the whole business. Because The Beatles came on the scene. Motown came on the scene. The "avant garde" came on the scene. The whole scene was changing.

The Beatles opened up the doors for the white people to start dealing with black music out in the open, by saying that they [The Beatles] had been inspired by black artists. It freed them [white people] up. Motown was in Detroit, developing its own black world. If it had not been for Motown, being where it was at the time, we probably would have lost a lot of black artists that we have today in the commercial field. Because the white market was much larger and they were overwhelming the business. They were calling this "rock and roll" music theirs. They did their research on the rhythm and blues of the black old-timers. They drug them up from the grave and searched them out to teach what was happening with black music. Then the avant garde came in, with musicians getting frustrated and the music becoming mundane, and vamped, and long long long solos, and no rhythm. And that was a problem. Record companies were no longer interested in recording jazz because they could make more money off of rhythm and blues or rock and roll. So why record jazz?

So anybody with any sense would seem to say, "Well, where's my future? I'm a jazz artist. Either I switch over and join them or I do it myself." The record business was still there. Technology had come into play. So there were things to be done about that period. Civil rights was coming in. There was a lot of emotion going on in the mid-sixties. And it got crazy.

Ben: You say that anybody with any sense would have gone into the record business for themselves, but really, very few musicians, notably yourself and Charles Mingus, made a real commitment to try it.

Betty: Yeah. Well, I don't think they really believed that they could do it. I didn't either. It came to me like out of the blue, for me to start my own record company. It was a lady who owned a pressing plant in New Jersey who's another one of my role models. She said, "Do it yourself." I said, "What do mean do it yourself?" She said, "You can do it yourself. We're a pressing plant. We press for anybody. So do it yourself." So you start thinking about it. You know about tapes. You know about studios. She said, "Hire a truck, record yourself, make a master." And that's literally how it happened.

Ben: What was your first recording session for your own Bet-Car label?

Betty: It was at the Vanguard, I did it live. I created a birthday party. Hired a truck. Had Norman Simmons, Lyle Atkinson and Al Harewood, three fine musicians, and we had been working together, so we knew our material and everything. We just went there and recorded that afternoon. And then we listened back to see what we had to do. Then I went to the RCA man to do my master of the tape. And you know, he's been doing my mastering ever since then. And that's really how it started. And the pressing plant, they pressed the record, got the jackets together. They pointed me in the right direction. All you have to do is get on the telephone. That's all you have to do. There are people who do these services. All you have to do is just call them up.

Today we got a CD market and the CD prices are coming down to the point where a lot of independent companies are going to be able to afford having the music on CDs. Because to do a record costs about 65 cents and now you can do a CD for about a dollar. So here we are, we're down to the point where an independent can join the CD field.

Ben: I think it's always good to remind people that one of the most important instruments in the music business—just as in any business—is the telephone. Okay, so now you're in the record business. How did you get the records out of your garage and into the marketplace?

Betty: Well, I had a little clout at that particular time. I was doing quite well. The name "Betty Carter" wasn't exactly unknown in the New York area, you know, because like I said, I worked the Apollo all the time, I did the album with Ray Charles. And I was consistent whenever I worked. So I went to a distributor and asked them to carry my records on consignment. I did just what everybody else does when you start something. You say, "Look, I'll give you some records on consignment."

I've never sold records on my job. That's the one thing that I said no to. I wasn't going to have a box of them out on my job and sell them after the job is all over. You know, I didn't do that, and I'm very glad

I didn't do that. I sent them through distributors, and they got in the stores, believe it or not. And people bought them.

Also there were a lot of independent distributors coming on the scene then to handle independent labels. So that side of the market was growing. I just happened to be there kind of early. But we could see that this was going to happen.

Ben: All along, you developed not only your own marketing system, but you also developed the young talent you came across. As a matter of fact, your reputation for finding young musicians and rehearsing them—a lot—is legend in the business.

Betty: Oh, I didn't know that. But I do rehearse a lot. I feel that young musicians should rehearse a lot. I think they should practice. I think they should take lessons as long as they possibly can. I do believe that. I want them to become good musicians. I want them to know what they're doing when they get on the stage. I want them to be secure on their instruments, and the only way they're going to feel secure is for them to rehearse and rehearse and practice and practice and practice and practice. And I do. I'm not sorry I do that. I'm very proud of that. Because I think that's very necessary.

One thing I don't do, though, I don't take advantage of musicians because they work with me and rehearse them just for nothing. It's a gig, so they get paid. I'm not using them, you know. When I call a musician in to rehearse with me, I'm going to pay him for that rehearsal so that he won't have to deal with me or get angry, saying "I'm coming to a rehearsal again and again and again and getting no money for it." That's not the way I do it.

So I love to rehearse, but I pay for it.

Ben: And along the way you've found a lot of great young players to rehearse with. Just in terms of drummers, you found a young drummer in Chicago named Jack DeJohnette, and you discovered other young drummers like Kenny Washington and Billy Hart. How do you find these players? Do they come to you?

Betty: Now it's usually when I get the word out that I want to change musicians, since musicians know that I will deal with young musicians if they have some ability. I will try them out. So usually they come.

But it's a shame that I and Art Blakey are the only two people that will really take that shot with the young twenty and twenty-one year-olds, when there are so many musicians, my contemporaries, who have not yet made this sacrifice to educate young players. We need more people like me and Art Blakey who will give these young musicians a job. They don't have big bands anymore, like they used to have, where they can get that kind of training. And if you've been in the business as long as I've been in the business, there's a lot you can teach a young man or young woman.

So I think that it's really not speaking too well about the jazz community that the older ones are not always going out of their way to find young musicians and to train them. A lot of them don't want to spend the time practicing and rehearsing these guys, you see. That's the hard part you know. A lot of people want to hurry up and get it over with. They don't want to spend time going over things. But we need the musicians that will take this chance to give more musicians a job. Because I'm sure that a lot of musicians out there don't want to play for a singer. And a lot of them may not want to even play for Art Blakey. I mean, there's a lot of drummers out there who *can't* play with Art Blakey.

See, I'm practically the only gig that a lot of the young drummers can get and keep for a long time. They get some long-term experience in all kinds of tempos and meters. I try to do that to educate them and to educate myself. Sometimes, I stretch out on that meter bit because I want to keep them from being bored, but also to teach them. And also it teaches me. It teaches me to sing in 5/4 and it teaches me to sing in 7/4. It teaches me to stop and start in different kinds of tempos and create surprises for the audience so that they won't get dull. This all educates me too, when I try to deliver the kind of education that I want for these young musicians.

So I think a lot of us older musicians must do this, if we care at all about the music. A lot of us say we do. A lot of us are on a soapbox and ready to criticize what the people in the music business are *not* doing for the music. But, listen, you have to work for that, you know. If we're going to maintain a future for the business and for these musicians, we've got to train the young ones. We've got to give them some encouragement to want to *stay* in the business and not go over there and do that "track music."

I say that only because once you get over, getting back on the other side is not as easy as they think it is. You know, in the beginning, I used to get that thing, "Why don't you get a hit record and then you can do anything you want to do." It's not that easy. I think a lot of people who defected from jazz to go to get the hit record find it's not easy coming back. Something happens. You lose something.

Ben: Clearly, you're not thinking about commercial airplay when you record. In the first place, most of the songs on your albums are quite long.

Betty: They're live. And so when you do it live, you tend to stretch it a little bit. But I've only done two albums in the recording studio, the recent one ["Look What I Got"] and the second album. Everything else is live. So that's the reason.

Ben: Were economics the reason? I know that it's usually less expensive to record live.

Betty: Well, you know, for a long time I didn't like to go into the studios and deal with the separation and the non-communication with your musicians. I mean, having musicians in a booth and one of them over in that corner and the other one over in that corner and you got to put earphones on and stuff. And you're trying to get the same feeling that you get on the stage. It's not there.

I'm getting used to it now. I did my last album in the studio and I'm more satisfied with the way that I sound, also. You say that after all these years I should have been satisfied a long time ago? No, I was never really satisfied. So now I'm satisfied. [Laughs.] So I don't care about going into the studio as much as I used to.

Ben: Are you satisfied because you've changed or because you've accepted yourself?

Betty: I've just realized that I'm a better singer than I thought I was.

Ben: That's probably hard for most people to grasp, that a singer like yourself could have trouble accepting herself.

Betty: Well, after forty years, it's good that I finally did. I have a lot more confidence in myself now than I had, say, ten years ago. Because now people are accepting me for what I am. Now I can sing a Sarah Vaughan song, you dig? Now I can sing a Billie Holiday song and no one will think about Sarah Vaughan or Billie Holiday. It may be for a fleeting minute, but my concept, they *expect* me to do something else with these songs. They don't expect for me to sing these songs like anybody else has. They *know* that I'm going to it differently. You know, that gives you a lot of confidence then, when the audience is aware of your work and you can go out there on that stage and change that song around the way you want to sing it and the audience expects for you to do that.

I met a guy one time in Washington, D.C. And I think I've wanted to hear this statement from someone for years but no one has ever said it to me but this guy one time. He said, "You know, I've been watching you for sixteen years and I've never caught you the same way twice." And I just loved that. Here's a guy that's been dealing with me for sixteen years. That, to me, is what I've wanted to do, to accomplish. An audience can come back and come back and come back and it just won't be like it was the last time.

So now I've developed where I've got the confidence in what I'm doing. Musically, I know now where I'm coming from. I've challenged myself quite a bit now, and now I know what I can do musically. So I really feel good about my work. So now I don't mind going into a studio.

Ben: Obviously, this is a good time for Betty Carter. Do you feel it's a good time in the larger sense for jazz?

Betty: I think it's a good time. Whether we take advantage of it or not is another thing. You know, 'cause we're still out there telling people what jazz is by some of the musicians that come along with hit records and things like that. And they've told the audience, "This is a jazz player." A lot of the audience, and musicians, and disc jockeys don't even know what jazz *is*. But this is really, right now, a good time if we know what to do with it.

Ben: How can we screw it up?

Betty: By not taking advantage of what's happening now. By not encouraging these young players to continue. By the record companies not taking advantage of this youth and recording this youth. And let them be the creative part of it. And stop dealing with producers telling them what to do.

I want to be a producer, but I don't want to tell my musicians what to do. I want to help it. I know that I can be of assistance to a young group, because the environment is different, they don't get a chance to work as hard as I did in the '50s to develop their concept. So I know about concept. I know about audience appeal. I know what can happen to music. So that I can give to a musician. But I can't tell him what to do with his style, how to play or anything like that. That should be his. And this young musicians should be allowed to do.

I think that Wynton Marsalis has had a great impact on the business also, even though he's young and a lot of people say, "He's young and he's cocky." Well so is everybody young and cocky. I was young and cocky too, you know. But he has said some valid things. And he's put his mouth . . .

Ben: Where his money is?

Betty: [Laughs.] Right. Where his money is. He's supported it. He has done what is necessary and a lot of young musicians, he's their role model. And I'm really really proud to see that and I'm very very glad he's on the scene to do what he's doing and to say what he's saying at this point in his young life.

Ben: A good case in point, because Wynton is not only focussed on jazz education, but he's also an employer of young musicians. He makes it a point to use his band as a training group for other young players, and along the way he's developing stylists in the classic tradition.

Betty: Well, you have to work in order to develop your style. You have to do some live work. And there's not a lot of that out there for young players. There's not a lot of work out there for young players unless people like me, who've been around in the business for a long time, give a young player a job. So they can get their name out there. That's the only way we're going to develop young players and teach them that just playing like somebody else isn't the way to go. We can talk about it all day long, but if we don't provide room and a job for them to practice in—go through trial and error like we did in the '50s—we're not going to see the development.

We're going to see them, in the beginning, try to imitate Coltrane. Now we're getting to see some more influence from Charlie Parker again, in the young players. They've found him again, which is quite different also. And a lot of piano players would like to imitate Thelonious Monk. So here we are now with these young kids loving that kind of music and wanting to learn that kind of music. They should be encouraged to develop off of that kind of music by giving them work. With no work, they can't develop. They can only practice in their room and that's it. They've got to have on-the-job training. That's how we learn in this business.

But education, to me, is also very very important. Because everybody can't be leaders. Everybody can't be a star. Some horn players should be writers or composers. Or arrangers. And some of them should be section men. But out there now everybody wants to be a leader. We've had a whole two decades of musicians who come up who want to be a leader. And everybody can't be. But how do you know you're not a leader until you get a job to find out that you really can't lead anything, you know?

Like Quincy Jones was a trumpet player. He played in a section with Lionel Hampton. He knew he wasn't a soloist, he didn't have nothing going for him. But he could *write*. But he found that out through experience, that he was a better writer than he is a soloist. So what is he doing? He's writing. A lot of the musicians should face it, with what they do. But the opportunities for them to write is not there either, there's no big bands to write for.

It's not easy for the young players today. Believe me. It's a lot of hard work. Much harder. I don't know what I would have done if I had started in this business, say, twenty years ago and decided I wanted to be a jazz singer. Look, I have no idea what I'd be doing today. Would I be influenced by the whole stuff that's around me? How would I be thinking? I'm only thinking this way because of what I've gone through. But if I was young like a lot of young singers are today, who have to live in this time and are told that money is the way to go and you gotta get money and you gotta make money and that's it, money is it! And musicians hear the same thing, it's all about money.

So how do we expect to develop anybody that really wants to stick with an art form that you may not make any money in at all . . . for years. It's very difficult to ask somebody to hang around here and wait. Develop yourself for the next fifteen years and don't do anything crazy now, don't form a rock band or anything like that. When the opportunity comes and some record company says, "I'll give you ten thousand dollars," how are you going to tell them to turn down ten thousand or twenty thousand dollars? Don't take the money, how are you going to say that to a young kid?

I mean the value of the music, it isn't as valuable to them as it is to me. You see? It's a different period. The only way it's going to become valuable to them is if they see it and they fall *in love*. They have to fall *in* love. They just can't be one of those millions of people who say "I love jazz." I hear millions of people say that all the time, "I love jazz." They probably never heard any before, but they all say that, you know.

So it's very difficult out here for young players. Very very difficult.

Ben: These are not romantic times.

Betty: No, not for the music. Especially in a world that feeds on money. The way this world is, everyone feeds on it. So that's the name of the game. So it's very difficult now for young players to make that decision.

Take the money and run, that's what it's all about.

Ben: As you say, you don't know what you would have done because you didn't have to make that decision.

Betty: No, I came up not thinking about the money. Just learning our craft and developing, that's all we wanted. To get on the stage and do our thing. The applause meant more to us than anything else. You know, that's how I was brought up. Oh, you made the money, sure, but the applause, oh, wow, that was it.

* * *

Jackie McLean (October, 1987)

Alto saxophonist Jackie McLean and I first met on the telephone many years ago, and we have kept up our long-distance friendship ever since. But even though we had talked often, our first face-to-face conversation took place at a recording studio in New York City for the purpose of recording this interview. We had to reschedule the interview several times, mostly because of his busy teaching schedule in Hartford, Connecticut, where he now lives, and, the last time, because of a spill he had taken on a motorbike which put him on crutches. Jackie has survived what he calls the heroin plague and has been a leading stylist on the jazz scene for four decades. His is one of the more important careers, spanning as it does a role in the bebop revolution of the '40s and '50s, the avant-garde movement of the '50s and '60s and the great exodus (to teaching and other activities) from the New York jazz life during the '70s and '80s. And yet, except among fans and folks "in the know," Jackie has been relatively unheralded during the latter two decades. This interview is one of the few he had done at the time.

Ben: Jackie, you look like you've recovered nicely from that little motorbike fall. How are you feeling?

Jackie: I feel good, and I'm practicing as much as I can and trying to keep my saxophone well used.

Ben: Keeping the instrument warm.

Jackie: Yeah, keeping the reed wet.

Ben: Well, we are finally able to meet here in New York City, which is particularly appropriate, I think, because if there's one musician who typifies the New York sound and attitude in jazz, it's yourself. You grew up not too far from where we are now sitting.

Jackie: Right, I was born at Flower Hospital right at Fifth Avenue around 107th Street. At that time my family lived on 135th Street, between Seventh and Lenox Avenue, and so those are the earliest years I remember, along 135th Street. And then my mother moved to various places downtown, further, to 200 West 111th Street. We lived at 1855 Seventh Avenue. And then my mother remarried to my stepfather, Jimmy Briggs, and we moved up on what was called Sugar Hill at that time. At that time, I lived at 158th Street and Saint Nicholas. And it was quite a neighborhood.

Ben: Yes it was. I've spoken with some of your childhood friends from that neighborhood about it. One of them, Sonny Rollins, has told me it was an amazing musical environment.

Jackie: It was. And looking back, it's even more astonishing, because there were so many incredible musicians around at that time that I wasn't familiar with. I knew about Duke Ellington, but Don Redman was somebody that I saw a lot in that neighborhood, and I had no idea who he was. I didn't find out until maybe twenty years ago who he is, you know. And of course Nat Cole and Andy Kirk and Arnett Cobb and a lot of guys from Lunceford's band, [Jimmy] Crawford, the drummer and Joe Thomas the tenor saxophone player and Earle Warren, I think, lived there at that time. So there were many musicians in that neighborhood.

Ben: And right around the corner was Bud Powell, who you spent some time with when you were just a kid.

Jackie: Right. I met Bud because my stepfather opened up a record shop on Eighth Avenue at 141st Street, and Bud lived at 140th and Saint Nicholas. Through a dispute with Richard Powell, at the time, who came in to the record shop one Sunday. I was playing some Bud for a customer on a record, and when I said "Bud Powell" to the customer, Richard said "That's my brother." And I said, "Well, do you play piano?" And so he said "No," and I told him I didn't believe that was his brother. You know, right out, flat. And he told me, "Well I'll come back and get you next week and introduce you to my brother. I'll prove it to you."

So one week later, I had forgotten about it, he came into the record shop one Sunday and took me out of the record shop. I closed the shop, grabbed my horn and went around the corner and went up to this apartment and met this guy. Now I had never seen Bud in my life, so I didn't know if it was Bud or not. So Richard told Bud that I didn't believe that they were brothers. And I said, "Well, I don't know." And he said, "Well, do you think I'm Bud Powell?" And he went over to the piano and played, and I said, "I *know* you're Bud Powell." And that's how I met him, you know.

And of course he said, "Well what do you do?" And I said, "Well, I play the saxophone." And he said, "Well take it out, let me hear you play." And I played "Buzzy" with him, in B flat, which was all I could play at that time. I must have been about sixteen. And that was how our friendship began.

Ben: You once told me a funny story about how you got that saxophone, and how you thought it was something other than what it was.

Jackie: Right. The very first horn I owned was a soprano. It was a straight silver soprano that my godfather gave me. He used to play saxophone in the Abyssinian Baptist Choir Orchestra. And I was interested in playing it, so he gave me the horn when I was fourteen and gave me some lessons on it. But I told my mother I wanted a curved gold saxophone. At that time, I didn't know the difference between alto and tenor. So my mother went down to the New York School of Music on 125th Street and bought me a second-hand alto and brought it home. And on my fifteenth birthday I got this horn. And then when I tried to play from the recordings of Lester Young and Ben Webster, I couldn't match the sound. And it was my stepfather who told me I had the wrong horn. So that's why in my earliest years I tried to play everything like a tenor, and I didn't relate much to the alto players until I heard Charlie Parker.

Ben: I've heard similar stories from other players, that they wanted to play tenor but were given an alto. Johnny Griffin, for example, started out on alto and later, by accident, found his way to the tenor. But in your case, your big "tenor sound" on the alto turned out to be what you became famous for.

Jackie: Right. It's strange.

Ben: Did you have that sound back when you played "Buzzy" with Bud Powell? Did you always have that sound?

Jackie: I think I always had a sound that was leaning towards a tenor sound, even from the beginning, because I already had a mindset when I got my horn. I wanted to play like Pres. That was the sound I wanted. Then I heard Ben Webster, and I liked him very much. Then I heard Dexter and Gene Ammons. The recording was "Blowing The Blues Away," Billy Eckstine's Big Band, and it was all tenors, you know. Then, a year later, I think it was 1946, the first time I heard Charlie Parker, and it was what I had been waiting for.

Ben: Did you immediately go out and try to find Bird?

Jackie: Well, I was too young to get into the clubs on 52nd Street, so I used to just see him in front of the club and speak to him and then get on the subway and go back home. We used to run down there on Friday nights and Saturday nights and hang around the clubs just to see the musicians go in and out. So it took me about a year or two before I could actually see him play in person. But the recordings were coming very fast then. "Koko" and "Billy's Bounce" and all those early recordings. Then I discovered Sonny Stitt.

But an interesting thing is that I couldn't pick off Charlie Parker or Sonny Stitt's things. But there was an alto player named Rudy Williams, he played with the Savoy Sultans. He made a recording with Babs' Three Bips and a Bop. Babs Gonzales, on Blue Note. He was the alto player that I liked a lot that I could play his ideas, because they were simpler than Bird's. And he was like a stepping stone to Charlie Parker.

Ben: In time, you became very close with Bird. I know that wasn't always an easy thing for you. You told me about one event where he asked you to kick him that sounded especially distressing.

Jackie: Oh man, yeah. It was a strange evening. My wife Dolly and I were home that evening, and we went out to take a walk and we ran into Bird in the street. And Bird used to like to go into different clubs and take a drink, a beer. At this time he was living down on Avenue B and he was frequenting the clubs in the Village quite a bit. So Bird said, "Let's go someplace where we can play." So I went home and got my horn and came back and met them on the corner.

We started walking towards the Village. Well, we went to the Open Door; they wouldn't let us in there. Then we ran into Hank Mobley in the streets, so there was like three or four of us then. And we went to a club named Arthur's, it's still there in the Village, up around Seventh or Eighth Street, right off of Eighth Avenue. We went in there, and there was a piano and bass all set up, and drums. So Al Levitt sat down on the drums, I don't know who played piano, I don't know who played bass, and I gave Bird my horn and he went up and played.

He'd start a tune and play, and then I'd go up and play some and take it out. Then he'd start another tune and play. And it went like that. So during the break I went outside with him and we were talking. And he said to me, "You know, you're getting ready to have a child." He said, "Your wife is pregnant." He said, "You know, you're not going nowhere if you try to live the life that I lived. You ought to try and be healthy and clean like Horace Silver." He said, "I feel real guilty for a lot of people that are doing this stupid thing, using drugs. It's not right." And then he bent over and said, "Come on, go ahead, kick me." So I said, "For what?" And he said, "Kick me." And it was funny, you know. There was my idol all bent over. And the last thing I ever would want to do would be to kick him. So just to get him out of that position, because he had been drinking, I just went up and kind of kneed him on the butt a little bit.

So that was it. That was how that happened.

Ben: Obviously a lot of misery has come from drugs. Is there another side to it? For example, did heroin have an impact on the development of bebop as a musical form?

Jackie: Well, I think it would have developed anyway, because the precursors had already set the style in motion, and by precursors I'm talking about Pres and Jimmy Blanton and Charlie Christian and Slam Stewart, of course. They were already playing some lines that were changing the language and the concept a little bit. I don't think heroin itself had so much to do with the music, making the music. It was just a terrible drug that was unleashed on the public by the powers that be.

Because I still feel that way about drugs. I feel that if this government that can protect the Persian Gulf and be down in Nicaragua and do all these things, they certainly can stop heroin and cocaine from coming into this country. So somebody's making some money. And a lot of people are suffering because of it. And a lot of times people try to say, "Well, don't you think Billie Holiday and Charlie Parker were the cause of you folks taking that step?" And I always say, "No, I wouldn't blame them. I'd blame the people that allowed those narcotics to come into the communities." And that's what happened.

Ben: It's one of those things that has become part of the myth, and, unfortunately, it's also becoming more of the reality again these days. This myth has been the subject for works of art. One of them was a movie that you participated in called *The Connection*. Everybody these days knows about the movie *Round Midnight* with Dexter Gordon, but most people don't realize that you participated along with Freddie Redd in Jack Gelber's play and the movie of that play that was released more than twenty years ago. For those people who haven't seen the movie, we should say that it appears to be a very realistic event. Four or five musicians are sitting around their apartment waiting for their connection to come, and they're playing music and talking about the life they lead. How improvised was *The Connection*?

Jackie: Well, it was certainly a step in a new direction for theater, period. Because there was audience participation in the theater. When we performed live on stage, there were actors set up in the audience to say things to get a reaction from the stage and then from other people in the audience. So that was a new idea. And then also it was one of the first plays where musicians were allowed to improvise freely within the context of the story, to play music. You know, we'd play a whole tune, full improvisation, melody, solos, melody out and then into the next part of the play.

There were things you could do, there were some liberties you could take, but it mostly was written. It was Jack Gelber's play that was written just as you see it. When we did it on stage, I could walk off stage and get a drink of water any time that I wanted to, as long as I didn't have any lines or any music to play. So it was free like that, to move around, but it had some discipline to it.

Ben: There was a recording of the music from *The Connection* issued on Blue Note under the leadership of Freddie Redd. And even though you were a sideman on it, I always thought that your sound and your conception were so strong that, even though you weren't the leader, you really shaped the finished product. That was also true on some other records you made as a sideman, particularly the Sonny Clark dates for Blue Note.

Jackie: Oh, Sonny was also a very fabulous musician. I was very fortunate and every day when I pray I thank The Creator for giving me the experience that I had, allowing me to perform with such a variety of great musicians.

As far as my sound is concerned, I think the person that influenced me the most about how to use my sound was Miles. Because I felt the same way about him that you just described my playing. I used to listen to Miles on all the sideman things that he was on, even with Bird, and he would always emerge with something of his very own. You know, that haunting kind of sitting alone in Alaska kind of sound that Miles gets. It's a very lonely and mournful sound that he gets. And even though I can't emulate that on the alto, I certainly can parallel it in some ways. And my years that I worked with Miles, well he had a great influence on me. About sound, the *sound* of the instrument.

Ben: He once talked to me about his sound in terms of seasoning. He said it was like putting lemon on fish, it brought out the flavor of the composition.

Jackie: Yeah, most definitely. And at a time in the music which was so fast and furious, the way Bird played, the way Bud played, the way Clifford Brown played, here was Miles, holding on to notes over the bar line. He could hold one note for two or three beats, and it had more meaning to it than fifty notes that somebody else could play.

Ben: Another interesting aspect of your recording career is how during the '50s and '60s you played on so many dates, as a leader and a sideman, with many of the same musicians. Sonny Clark, Philly Joe Jones, Paul Chambers. You must have done hundreds of sessions together.

Jackie: Right. Well it was like a little group of musicians that the people at Blue Note were choosing from, Arthur Taylor, Paul Chambers, Philly Joe, Cedar Walton, a young Herbie Hancock when he first came on the scene. Of course, there were the musicians that I brought to Blue Note, like Tony Williams and Bobby Hutcherson.

Ben: You actually had to convince Tony's parents to let him leave Boston and come to New York with you, because he was under age, didn't you?

Jackie: Well, I didn't see his dad, but I went and saw his mom and told her that I would bring him to my house and treat him as one of my children, you know. Because he was sixteen then, and I must have been about thirty-something. It was Christmas Eve of that year, 1963 I think it was. I brought Tony into my house and kept him there until he was ready to move out on his own.

Which wasn't long. In fact he only stayed at my house a couple of months, and then he moved into an apartment in the Village. And of course I called his mother to find out if that would be OK. And he was very mature for a sixteen-year-old. Certainly he played the drums like somebody that had been here before, you know.

Ben: Just before this period, your music went through an interesting evolution. You were pushing for a way to get out of some of the standard bebop formulas.

Jackie: Even before that, it was apparent in my writing. When I wrote "Dr. Jackyl," that was around the time I wrote "Minor March" and "Little Melonae," and all those were written between 1953 and 1955. And certainly on the lines, like, of "Dr. Jackyl," it's not a regular blues line. And "Little Melonae" gets into the modal bag way back then, you know, the way the chords were structured. And I recorded, in 1957, before the whole avant garde, Ornette Coleman thing came, in '57 I wrote some tunes that had no chord changes to them. One of them is on Prestige. It's called "Ending," and it has no chord changes on the melody, but when we got to the solo section, we played some "I Got Rhythm," just to play over it.

But I was already thinking about trying to find a way to get away from just the bebop style. And, of course, when I went with Mingus, in 1957, he really helped me formulate that kind of concept. Because he was years ahead of his time. He and Cecil Taylor, who I heard around New York. And there was a guy named Valdo Williams that was playing like Cecil was playing, but he was doing it back in 1948. I don't know where Valdo is today. I've heard that he's in Canada, but he was the very first avant garde musician that I heard. He was playing totally free back then, in '48. Sonny Rollins knew about him. He knew him and played with him.

Ben: When you got together with musicians back in 1956, was there a real desire to do away with chord changes as early as then, or was this something that just a few people were working on?

Jackie: I don't think a lot of people. I know Cecil was, because Cecil came to my house and wanted to do some rehearsing. It was during the time that I was working with Donald Byrd in George Wallington's band, with Arthur Taylor and Paul Chambers at the Bohemia. That was another point where I was trying to think of some other way to play, some other way to express.

No, I found it difficult trying to convince musicians that we should try some things like this. It wasn't until I went with Mingus that I found a place that . . . in fact, Mingus was going much further than I wanted to go. He used to tell me to just forget chords altogether and just let it go. And I had spent so many years trying to learn how to play in the style of Bud Powell and Charlie Parker and Monk and Dizzy that I had invested too much to just throw it away, you know. And I was looking for a middle road somewhere.

Ben: I remember one example that might have been that middle road on a Blue Note record you made back in 1962. The album was called *Jackie's Bag* and the song was "Quadrangle." "Quadrangle" definitely sounded like a departure for you at the time.

Jackie: Ben, you know "Quadrangle" is another title for the piece I was telling you about. "Quadrangle" is, in fact, the piece "Ending" that we did on Prestige in '56. But, you're right, the song has no chord changes and the melody is kind of free. So there are two recordings of it.

Ben: Again, it didn't seem to matter what you were playing, whether it was with chord changes or free form, as long as it was you that was playing it. I think one of the lessons of Jackie McLean to young players today might be the importance of an identifiable sound. A personal sound really cuts through all idioms. How do you feel about that? On the other hand . . . people keep focussing on your sound. Does it bug you because it's just something you found naturally?

Jackie: You know what? I had a funny experience. Somebody said "Jackie, I can tell your sound anywhere." So one night I was riding home from a concert with my wife and I said, "You know, I'm beginning to wonder if that's a compliment. Maybe I'm out so far, my sound is so bad, that everybody can tell it. And that it's not something so pleasant." I don't know. And it still bothers me sometime. I wonder if people love it, and like it because it's something special, or is it something that you want to throw your fingers up to your ears. I mean, I wouldn't ask you, Ben, because I know that you like the sound. But I still don't know.

Ben: Well, you're right about that. I guess part of what I see today is many gifted young players who don't have access to their own sound. And I think that maybe we're getting away from something that has been very valuable.

Jackie: I agree. Because all the alto players today, and tenor players in the commercial field, are all playing out of that King Curtis style and David Sanborn style. Which is fine, but I just think there are so many other ways to express the music. You're right. I think we're getting hung up in kind of drones, you know?

Ben: You've been involved with the education system for a long time.

Jackie: 17 years. I moved up to Hartford and started out teaching one day a week at the University of Hartford, doing a class in History, music from 1945 to the present. And one class in improvisation. And over the seventeen years, that has grown into a degree program. We offer a degree in African-American music at the Hart School of Music. I'm chairman of the department and founder of the department. And we have a nice little tight program with about forty students, very talented saxophone players, trumpet players, trombone players, guitar, piano, bass and drums. I'm very excited. It's very rewarding.

I'm not saying that I wouldn't prefer to be out playing music full time. But I don't feel that I've wasted my time, seventeen years. I might have suffered in terms of not spending that time playing the saxophone, but I did another thing that I'm very proud of. I founded a cultural program in Hartford called The Artist's Collective. That too is fifteen years old, and it's a cultural center for the inner city kids; it teaches them drama, dance, music and the visual arts. And thousands of kids have gone through that program, and I'm very happy to say that we're doing very positive things in Hartford.

And right now we're getting ready to put up a five-million-dollar building in that town. It will be the first cultural center put up by inner city folk. And my wife Dolly and I are in the process of this capital campaign, and we're doing very well.

Ben: So this program that you're running is not just a music program.

Jackie: It's become one of the major institutions in Connecticut. We've been funded by the Arts Council in Hartford for more than twelve years, and just recently the National Endowment for the Arts has given us their blessing and a nice grant of $175,000 towards our new building.

Ben: Has your experience as an improviser helped you to function in this world?

Jackie: Yeah, improvise! It's been great. A lot of people that know Robert's Rules of Order and sit in those board meetings, our board meetings have to follow those rules and regulations, but I find that most of the strides that Dolly and I have made have been shooting from the hip and keeping our dream in front of us and not wavering from it. It's been very helpful, improvising, right.

Ben: How about being involved with kids? Did working with your own son, Renee, and his musical career lead you toward working with kids?

Jackie: Well, I had always worked with kids. Even back in the days when I had the trouble of drug addiction, I still had drum and bugle corps on the lower East Side. I worked for Adventure Corps, which was mobilization for youth, which was a program started by Robert Kennedy. I worked there for four or five years, and Renee worked there with me. I've always kind of worked with young people and kids, because I felt that I could have avoided all of the trouble, the eighteen years of addiction that I had from 1949 until 1965. I felt that that could have been avoided if somebody had been in charge at the time to sit down and help kids to miss that fork in the road. If somebody had been there directing the traffic.

Ben: Directing the traffic. That's an ironic way to put it, isn't it?

Jackie: Right, the drugs go this way and the kids go the other way. If drugs are going to be here, and certainly it's here. America had a period where there wasn't a lot of heroin. Prior to 1946, heroin wasn't a big problem in the United States. It was right at the end of World War II that all this heroin began to come into the poorer communities across the country.

So I feel like I'm doing what I'm supposed to do, to try and do all that I can to help kids. And I'm sure Bird must be very happy up in the big music room upstairs to see that I'm doing things that will alleviate some of the guilt that he might have felt the day that he asked me to kick him.

Because kids are starting to use drugs and make babies much earlier today. And we're dealing with all of that. We're dealing with unwed mothers up in Hartford and young kids and all the new phenomena, diseases and new plagues like herpes and AIDS. So we're confronted with a lot of different things today that we weren't confronted with in the past.

Ben: How is jazz music integrated into this greater program?

Jackie: Because I'm at the center of the program, the music is always there in the wake. The music is always there. We have named the rooms up there and we keep changing the names of the rooms. Like we have the Max Roach Vibration Chamber. So when we take the kids in there, we explain to them who Max is, show them a picture of Max and let them hear the music so they'll know. We have the Paul Robeson Room, and we introduce the kids to Paul Robeson. So it's just a wider range of artists that we try and introduce young people to today, so that all they know about isn't Michael Jackson and Prince and the people that are currently the stars of commercial music. And we try and help them see that there have been great people before, and you'd be surprised how much those kids appreciate that too.

Ben: This multicultural approach must be particularly rewarding for somebody like yourself who was interested in the visual arts as well as the musical arts as a young man. I know that as a young man you applied to the High School of Music and Art in New York City as a music student but were turned down . . .

Jackie: Right, and then I reapplied as an art student and was accepted. And I was crushed. And instead of going to Music and Art, I went to Benjamin Franklin High School on 116th Street. And the reason that I went there was because Sonny Rollins, who was about two years ahead of me in school, had gone to Benjamin Franklin. So I wanted to go. He was in his senior year, and I came in my freshman year, and I stayed there exactly one year, until he graduated. Then I went all the way to the Bronx. Another saxophone player, a friend of mine who was in school in the Bronx, his name is Andy Kirk Jr. I left and went up to that school, 'cause he was there. So it seems that High School to me was about following some great saxophone player.

Ben: Both you and Sonny Rollins play all too rarely these days. I know you're busy with other things. But I wonder if it also isn't because the scene has changed so drastically, and the kinds of opportunities that might have been there for you in the past just aren't there now.

Jackie: Well yeah, and you know, there are a lot of young players out there today. And a lot of young great players out there today. I just think that there's plenty of room for everybody to play. I don't agree, when I look at the scene. I pick up a paper and look through the *Village Voice* or I look through the *Post* or the *Times* and see who's playing in town, and it's always the same people coming back and back, over and over again. And there are a lot of people available that can play, you know.

Yeah, it's a changing scene. And it's, you know, it's like more of the same. All the time.

Ben: I remember reading an interview done with an older musician sometime in the '40s. And he was complaining that the young beboppers at the time—which might have been yourself and your peers—seemed to want the old guys to move on. He said it felt like they wanted him to just die out. Is that what you're talking about today, that the youth keeps coming up and now you're feeling "Hey man, I'm not done yet . . . "

Jackie: Well, no, you know, I don't feel that way, because I'm helping to develop some of these people who are going to step into my shoes. And so I realize when I'm doing that. I just think that there's enough room and enough of an audience out there to hear everybody. To hear Buddy Tate and Sonny Rollins and Kenny Garrett and Branford Marsalis and Wallace Roney and Nat Reeves and Mulgrew Miller. I mean all these guys are my friends. It's not that I'm separated from them. But, I just think that we're not using our resources as good as we could.

Ben: Listening to your latest records and listening to your early records, what do you hear?

Jackie: Well it's hard. I'm still trying to get better. A lot of people may think if a guy's been playing the saxophone for as many years as somebody like myself—I've been playing now since 1946, it's a long time—it would seem as though all of your problems should be ironed out. But it's not.

I'm always dealing with something else and trying to polish my style a little better. And what I hear on my earlier records is I just wish that I had the knowledge then that I have now. And I wish I had the energy now that I had then. I just hope that I can keep my music interesting enough and keep some fire in my playing enough that it will keep an audience happy.

Ben: There's an old saying that a man is truly fulfilled when he has raised a child, planted a tree and written a book. I know you must have planted some trees and you raised a child. What about the book?

Jackie: The *books*. I've got several books in my head that I want to do. I want to do an autobiography of my life. And I also want to do a book on some of the musicians that I feel were bypassed and that there needs to be more information on them. Like Rudy Williams, the alto player that was with the Savoy Sultans. Like Kenny Dorham. Most people know Kenny, but Kenny during his whole life time never got the accolades and never got the roses that he should have received for all that he gave us. And also Andy Kirk Jr., even though he's not recorded, I'd like to let people know more about him. And there's several other musicians. Grachan Moncur, who is still in Newark today and still playing. He just played this summer in Japan, but we don't hear from Grachan hardly anymore. And another guy that I mentioned earlier, Valdo Williams, the pianist that was playing freeform style in 1948. So I want to do a book like that. Then I want to do another book on the history of the music. So there are several books that I want to put together. Then I'll be fulfilled.

Ben: If you were to do your autobiography, what might the title be?

Jackie: Oh man, wow, I don't know. Well, let's see. It might be called *The Soul Bandits*. I thought of *The Soul Bandits*, because the exploitation in the music business is so awesome. I know I've lived through all these decades of writing and recording music, and I have a lot of sour grapes that I could mash, but I don't want to do that. I want to do something very positive when I write a book.

But there are so many people, you know, Ben, for instance like one of the people that I really love dearly, one of the great musicians, a vocalist that's around, a guy named Little Jimmy Scott. I'm sure you know who Jimmy is. He is so great, so wonderful that it's just ridiculous that we don't get a chance to experience his gift. And of course there's Earl Coleman, he's still around singing beautiful.

So I don't know, man, it's just like we live in a throw-away society. The only place these guys get a chance to play is if they go off to Europe, go to Japan. They're not getting any kind of exposure here in the States. And there are so many clubs. There are always new ones coming on the scene. And I just want to put down on paper my feelings about some of these people and their plight. I think it would be interesting reading.

Ben: It almost sounds like by writing the story of these people who didn't get the accolades and roses they should have gotten, you are, in a way, writing an extension of your own autobiography.

Jackie: Right. It could be. It could be.

* * *

Horace Silver (November, 1985)

The success of pianist Horace Silver's recordings for the Blue Note label during the '50s and '60s, both with The Jazz Messengers featuring Art Blakey and with his various quintets, not only set a style and a sound for other Blue Note albums but helped the whole jazz scene reach a much greater audience as well. The epitome of "hard bop" and "soul jazz," these recordings captured key moments in the evolution of jazz and made Horace Silver a top attraction on the jazz circuit. To this day, jazz players "quote" his writing and playing, and many of the young lions, those emerging jazz musicians who are so celebrated in the popular press, try their best to imitate his compositional devices and to reinvent the Horace Silver sound. Horace himself is an extremely gentle, even self-effacing individual. Whereas his playing is forceful and direct, he is almost shy when talking about celebrity and the great historical importance of his music. He becomes animated, however, when talking about his latest projects, the "self-help, holistic, metaphysical music" that has become his life's work. It is significant to note that when this interview was first broadcast on National Public Radio, we received an extraordinary amount of interest from people all around the country interested in the possibility that music had, quite literally, healing qualities. It's clear that Horace Silver has once again tapped into a deep well of highly emotional public longing, which in the final analysis is perhaps his greatest talent. He is truly a "people's jazz musician." We spoke one spring day in Los Angeles, not far from his home near the Pacific ocean, but many miles and several musical lifetimes away from his early days as a Jazz Messenger.

Ben: So much of what happens in jazz is a result of fortunate accidents. The story goes that your first record as a leader, a trio date, was initially a Lou Donaldson session for Blue Note and Lou didn't make it. Subsequently it became a Horace Silver trio date and it went real well. And then you got together with Alfred Lion of Blue Note and you decided you wanted horns on the next record. And you added Kenny Dorham and Hank Mobley and that developed into a quintet sound. And that went so well that the quintet became a permanent quintet called the Jazz Messengers with Art Blakey . . .

Horace: That's right, yeah . . .

Ben: And Art Blakey has said, forgive me for these quotes but I want to get it correct with you, "At that time, a guy would just call a bunch of musicians and they'd just show up and play some standards and it got boring, and people got tired of jamming. So we decided to put something together and make a presentation for the people. And this helped the clubs and the whole scene, because other guys would form *real* bands and start working." You had put a little repertoire together, and you had made this record and it became very successful. And because you had made a more "formal presentation" than other people were doing at the time, this was a start of the Blue Note "group sound." Is that the case?

Horace: Well, I'll tell you how I got together with Art Blakey. First of all, Stan Getz discovered me in Hartford Connecticut, and I worked with him for about a year, you know. And then, after I finished working with him, I settled in New York City, and was living in the Bronx. And I was working on weekends out in Carteret, New Jersey, playing a little bar out there on Friday, Saturday and Sundays. We were playing for floor shows and for dancing, you know. And the tenor saxophone player in the band, his name was Bo McCain, he was working with Art Blakey's semi-big band. At that time, Art had a band consisting of about nine pieces, I believe it was. Let's see, he had trumpet, trombone, alto sax, tenor sax, baritone sax, piano, bass, drums, and congas. Right. And it was kind of a dance band. Like, you know, playing around Harlem and in the Bronx and all over Manhattan for different dance functions, you know, club affairs and things like that. And anyway, Bo McCain was working with that band. They weren't working very regular, but he was working with them.

But he also played this weekend job out in Carteret, New Jersey, that I worked on. And Art's piano player at that time was goofin' off and wasn't making the rehearsals, or wasn't showing up sometime for the gigs, something where he'd be late or something, and they wanted a new piano player. So Bo recommended me and he brought me by to a rehearsal one day, and I, you know, sat down, and I was able to read the music okay. I read music pretty good and they hired me, you know, for the gig. That's how I got that gig, that's how I first met Art Blakey and started working with him, with that nine-piece band.

And, as I said before, that didn't last very long because we could only get maybe one night a week at a dance gig or something, you know. That fizzled out after a while, but later on, when I lucked up on this trio session, you know, which was the result of Lou Donaldson not being able to make a session that I was supposed to do with him, that went well and we did another trio session, and then came the session with horns and I said to

Alfred I wanted to use, you know, Art Blakey and I wanted to use Kenny Dorham and Hank Mobley and Doug Watkins. That's how all that came about.

But the thing that Art said was true. You know, most of the time, most of the records that were made then were "jammed" records. But, you know, we had some little arrangements on a lot of the tunes. But I would say Rudy Van Gelder, the engineer, had a great deal to do with the Blue Note sound. As every engineer has a great deal to do with the sound of every record. But I mean, Rudy is such a great engineer. And Alfred Lyon, the owner at that time of Blue Note Records, also had a great deal to do with the Blue Note sound. Alfred was not a musician, but Alfred was a jazz fan, and had been a jazz fan since he was a little kid, you know. And he had a certain sound in his head that he liked and that he wanted to hear, and he used to tell Rudy, you know, how he'd like the bass drum to sound, and how he'd like different things to sound, and him and Rudy would work together, you know. So I think a lot of it comes from the engineer Rudy Van Gelder, and from Alfred Lyon, getting their heads together to get the Blue Note sound.

Now the rest of it comes from the musicians of course, you know. You know, like my things I had like small band arrangements, on the tunes, and things I did with Art Blakey, we did pretty much small combo arrangements on most of those tunes.

Ben: You've always had a sympathy with horn players. Were you a horn player originally?

Horace: No, I played tenor saxophone in ninth grade in junior high school and all through high school. I also played baritone saxophone in high school. But piano was my original instrument. I started on piano and continued on piano throughout. Just that, when I got into public school, 'cause I went to Catholic school up until eighth grade, then I went into junior high ninth grade. And I found out in public school I could get the use of a horn free and get free lessons and be in the band and orchestra. You know, and get extra points to graduate too, so I said, "Yeah, that's for me." Yeah, 'cause I loved Lester Young and I used to try to play like Prez, you know. And so I took up the tenor in junior high and also, first year of high-school, I played tenor. Then the second year of high-school, they took the tenor away from me and stuck a baritone sax in my mouth, because the baritone sax player had graduated. So I had to go out and buy my own tenor then, you know. But I continued to play the baritone in high-school band.

Ben: So much has been written about the so-called "cool school" of jazz in the '50s and how it was so cerebral, and then suddenly along came this band with Horace Silver and Art Blakey. Today they might call it "fusion music," or dance music, but back then they called it "soul music," or funk. Were you consciously trying to carve that area out, were you reacting to the "cool school," or did it just happen?

Horace: No, it just happened. Just happened, yeah . . .

Ben: And the whole cast of characters that you wound up developing as a composer, that kind of fit in with that "soul" theme, "The Preacher," and "Juicy Lucy," and "Sister Sadie" . . .

Horace: . . . and "Filthy McNasty . . ."

Ben: Yeah, well, that was a little later when "Filthy McNasty" came along, but were those based on real characters or were you creating this imaginary scene?

Horace: They were imaginative, imaginative characters. Not real people. It was just a point in my life I guess, where I was . . . well, I'm a Virgo, which means I'm a kinda basic type person anyway . . . but I was, you know, just wantin' to get to the nitty-gritty at that time, you know. And I came up with these characters, just figments of my imagination, actually.

Ben: When you say you wanted to "get to the nitty-gritty" at the time, your style, even today, is very direct. When you're sittin' at the keyboard, there's very little wasted effort. I mean, you get right to the point. Most pianists during the fifties were very much under the wing of Bud Powell and other players who tended to play "busier." How did you develop your style out of that tradition?

Horace: Well Bud Powell is one of my main mentors, you know. Bud Powell and Thelonious Monk are my two main piano mentors. Of that era. Of course, I had two other mentors before them, which were Teddy Wilson and Art Tatum. And even before that, I was into blues and boogie-woogie type of piano playing, you know. Before I heard Art Tatum and Teddy Wilson, I was into playing boogie-woogie and blues and checking out all those boogie-woogie blues piano players. But then when I heard Tatum and Teddy Wilson, I got involved in that. And of course Tatum was too swift for me to try to copy off the record. Teddy Wilson I copied a little of his stuff. I could copy some of his stuff off the record. I couldn't catch all of it. I had pretty good ears, but I bought a couple of Teddy Wilson piano folios and tried to practice out of them, you know. Art Tatum piano folios were impossible for me to read. I couldn't get through 'em, there were so many thirty-second notes, sixty-fourth notes, it looked like somebody took some ink and just threw it at the paper, you know.

But anyway, those are, you know, my formative mentors. And then came Bud Powell and Thelonious Monk. And I was heavily into Bud Powell, before I even knew about Monk. And when I first heard Monk, I actually thought he was puttin' everybody on at first, when I first heard 'im, because it sounded so foreign to me and so kinda way out, so abstract, that I didn't think he was serious, you know. I thought he was kinda joshing around on the piano, or trying to put people on, you know. And when

I found out he was *serious*, I started listening more intently, and I realized, "God, this man has something very unique here and something very beautiful. You know, let me check him out." And I got more heavily into Monk.

And then I came to a point in my career, somewhere I guess in my early twenties or mid-twenties, or something there, where I said to myself, "Well, I'm gonna find myself, you know. There's something in my playing that's original." Because, you know, when I made my first records with Stan Getz, I could hear a lot of Bud Powell in them. After, when the records came out and I listened back, I could hear a lot of Bud Powell in there. But, then, the second set of records I made was with Lou Donaldson. Those were the records that really made me realize that I had something of my own going, you know, because when I heard those records back, I said, "Hey, wait a minute now, I can hear some Bud in there, but there's something else in there that ain't Bud. That's me, you know. Lemme, lemme play that over and over and check out what that is, and then try to embellish upon that, you know?" That's when I decided to take all my Bud Powell collection and my Monk records, and all the records and put 'em in the closet, and lock the door, and just work on trying to develop what I heard in those Lou Donaldson records that was Horace Silver. That part of the solo playing that I felt was not Bud but was *me*.

Ben: And you simplified it. You got closer to that.

Horace: Well, you know, I can't tell you verbatim what I did, because I don't really know what I did. But I just had it very deeply impressed in my mind that I was going to practice hard everyday, for long hours, and try to bring out whatever that was that I heard in there that was me, you know.

Ben: One of the things that you have in your playing is a gesture with your left hand. I noticed it the first time I heard you on record. It's very percussive, almost the way a stride piano might throw the left hand down there, but more as a rhythm accent than a harmonic gesture. Am I hearing that correctly? Is that what you are doing?

Horace: Well, you know, that's very strange what I do with my left hand, because what I do with my left hand is completely subconscious, you know. I know what you're talking about and other people have commented on that, you know, but it's not something that I ever tried to develop or strived to do. It's something that I wasn't aware of even doing it, you know? People kind of call my attention to it later on, you know, and I said, "Oh, yeah." But it's just something that just happens. I don't think about it. It's just something that comes out of me. I don't know where it comes from or how it happens.

Ben: You say working with Lou Donaldson started to bring out something in your piano playing that was uniquely yours. As you began to lead your own bands, how did that affect your playing, and, by extension, your compositions?

Horace: Well, you know, if you have a vehicle to write for, you become much more interested in writing, and much more involved in it, and you do more of it, because somebody's gonna play it. Now when I was with Art, he would play all the music the guys in the band would write, so naturally I was at the piano all the time, trying to write something. And 'course then when I got my own band, naturally I could go crazy and write whatever I wanted and play all of my stuff, you know.

But, again, I'm a Virgo and that sign believes in perfection. And I've always believed in a well rehearsed group, you know. I've always believed if you're gonna do something, do it right, don't do it haphazardly, you know. And if you gonna present a group, have it well rehearsed and have it well written. I wanna have plenty open space for blowing. I wanna have a lot of freedom within the band. Freedom, but within an organized context. You know, there's got to be organization in my bands. There's got to be organization there. But freedom *within* that organization. Not just total chaos or total, you know, looseness where you can do completely everything you want to. There has to be certain guidelines and things you must follow. But within that, there's plenty of freedom to do your thing.

Ben: You also developed some techniques I think that are still used today, such as the way you used interludes to set up the solos and the melody and the way you used themes that really set your writing aside from a lot of the blowing dates that were going on in the '50s.

Horace: Well, I was trying to do something a little bit different I guess, you know, to make our band sound uncommon. 'Cause most of the groups, they came in, they played the head and soloed and played the head on out and that was it, you know? Whereas I thought to color it up a little bit and make the whole presentation more uplifting and desirable for people to listen to. You know, with an introduction and a few little interludes here and there. Maybe a shout chorus or a tag ending or whatever, you know. Embellish upon it a little bit. Not overarrange, but, you know, just something to make it a little more interesting, and more unique. More original.

Ben: One of your original records, *Blowin' The Blues Away*, has been re-released on CD by the Blue Note label. It's a classic in that it has all the things you just mentioned. The use of the interlude and the variation on the theme and the shout chorus; complex for the time. And some great playing by Blue Mitchell on trumpet and Junior Cook on tenor. I once asked Blue Mitchell, after I found that he wasn't a good reader,

"How in the world did you get all those Horace Silver arrangements together if you couldn't read the charts?" And he said, "Well, Horace was very patient with me. And we would play the songs on gigs and learn them, and then when we got into the studio, it was our tune." I thought that was very interesting. That you would choose a guy for his sound and his playing rather than for his mechanics or his technique.

Horace: Well, I used to tell the guys to take the music to the hotel with them. You know, we played these weekly gigs at clubs where lot of times the club was downstairs from the hotel or something, you know, maybe the club was down the block from the hotel. But I'd say, "Look, take the music back to the hotel with you and shed on it." Or, if we were in New York City, you know, which was home for us, I'd say, "Take the music home with you, you know, practice it, woodshed on it. You know, keep going over it 'til you get it right." I wouldn't just say, "Here, we rehearsed the tune, and give me the music back, you know, next time you come in, we'll rehearse it again." I let 'em take the music on with 'em. And they would, they'd work on it. Come back in and have it together.

Ben: I think maybe having the band made the music. I don't think it was a case of having the music made the band.

Horace: Well, we had a lot of fun in that band, you know. The cats used to complain sometimes because I used to rehearse them to death. You know, they used to say, "Another rehearsal. Wow." But after awhile I think they appreciated it. They enjoyed it, you know. You know, sometimes they'd complain, "Well, my chops, I won't have no chops for tonight." You know, we were rehearsing too much. But, you know I was a stickler for really getting the arrangements down right, and I was also a stickler for making sure the cats knew the chord changes, and all of that. And I think, after the band got to sounding so good, as a result of the rehearsals, you know, and the people was commenting on how good the band sounds, I think they really appreciated the rehearsals.

Ben: The simplicity of what you were doing back then, I think, made it possible. Everything, down to the last three notes of a song like "Blowin' The Blues Away," was definitive and simple and right *on* it. There was no question about what you were doing or what your musical intentions were.

Horace: Well, you know, I think it takes a composer a while to learn simplicity. Some of the early things that I've written were too notey, you know. I wrote a lot of bebop lines in the early days that had a lot of notes to it, you know, that were difficult to play and not much space for the horns to catch their breath in between phrases and all that kind of stuff. But as I got a little older and learned a little more, I began to realize that all that wasn't necessary, you know. You can cut out all of those notes and it can still be great, and might even be greater, because more people can understand it. And it still can be profound, you know, and beautiful. Beautiful, profound harmonies and beautiful, profound simple melody . . . simplicity is very difficult, you know.

Now, in my opinion, you gotta be very careful with simplicity because, if you're not careful, you can write a simple melody that can be very trite and non-meaningful, you know. But it's most difficult to write a simple melody that is profound and deep. That is a very difficult thing to do. Find some beautiful harmonies that are not too complex, but yet beautiful, different, moving in different directions, interesting, you know, stimulating to the mind, for a player. But not too complex, so that it makes it hard to play. And a simple melody that's not complex to play either, but yet it's beautiful and has some depth and some beauty and some meaning to it, you know. Because if you're not careful, when you're trying to be simple, it can be very corny or trite, you know. That's the hard part about simplicity. But once you get it, you really got something.

Ben: You've written a lot of songs that fit that description—simple but elegant—songs like "The Preacher" or "Juicy Lucy," or even "Silver's Serenade" or "Nica's Dream." Generally, did you have to work a long time to make them sound simple?

Horace: No, no, they just came, just came that way, yeah. Most of the songs I write, they just come, you know, they don't take a long time. I mean, I've written a few tunes throughout my career that I've labored over, you know. Might taken several days, or maybe a week or two with something to write. And usually those are the tunes that, not to say that they're bad tunes, but they were tunes that never really got off the ground, or got any recognition or went anywhere, you know, because I took too long to write 'em. I had to labor over 'em, you know. But most of them have come fairly quickly and easily. Usually when a song comes into my mind, I hear it all at one time. Lot of times, you know, I'll hear a melody, and harmony and rhythm. They all seem to flow in at the same time, you know. You seated at the piano there, and you're fooling around, and all of a sudden . . . It doesn't always come in the same order. Sometimes you get a rhythmic concept first. You get a beat, and then you put some chords to it, or you get a melody first and then you harmonize it, and you put the rhythm to it, or it can come in any different way, one segment at a time. And then sometimes it comes in all together, you know, simultaneously. You feel it and hear it all together, you know. And it comes in and you get it.

Ben: The reason I'm so interested in the way your band developed in parallel with your music is because it seems that these days there are very few people playing with a common purpose. They get together for a recording session, perhaps, and then they go off in different ways. We're gettin' a lot of interesting records, but very few bands.

Horace: Well, as I say, I was looking to be unique and do something different than the other bands were doing, you know. 'Course I always loved the writing of Tad Dameron, as well as Duke Ellington, of course, you know, and many other writers too. And Tad used those devices too, you know, interludes and tag endings and, well, you know, I didn't wanna have the kind of a band that was too overly arranged, but yet I didn't want it under-arranged either. I didn't want it to sound like a jam session band, you know. I want it to sound like a well-organized band. And the arrangements to be different than and have something unique about them.

Ben: What I find interesting is that, these days, we gotta advertise for guys to get together. In the old days, you couldn't keep them apart, you know?

Horace: That's true. Well, New York was such a melting pot in the old days. You know, all the guys from all over the country, various guys, they'd migrate to New York to try to make it in jazz, and just so many great young players around on the scene, you know. Whole bunch of cats.

Ben: When you go to New York these days, how does it feel for you?

Horace: It's still happening in New York. I must say, yeah. Maybe not quite as much as it was back in those days, but it's still happening. More so than any other part of the country, I feel, you know. When I go to New York, there's still a lot a clubs that are flourishing, and a lot of good jazz being played around. And you'd be surprised by some of the good jazz you hear on the street corner in New York, you know. Guys just blowin' on the street, be cookin', you know. I heard several guys on the street, they were burnin', you know. Really good, good players.

Ben: You've had a lot of great bands. Did you have a favorite?

Horace: Not really, although, you know, I must say that the group that had Blue Mitchell, Junior Cook and Gene Taylor and Louis Hayes, who was replaced later by Roy Brooks, that group, you know, has a special place in my heart, I guess, because we were together for about seven years or so, which is a long time for some guys to stick together. And we produced a lot of good music together. We had several records that were pretty popular and sold very well, you know. But I've had a lot of good bands, you know. The band with Joe Henderson and Woody Shaw was a hell of a fine band. And the one with Art Farmer and Clifford Jordan was a nice band. The one with Randy Brecker and Mike Brecker, that was a nice band, you know. Tom Harrell and Bob Berg, that was a hell of a band, you know. So, I've been fortunate to have some good guys, you know.

Ben: How do you find them?

Horace: Well, it's getting increasingly harder these days to find them. I'll tell you the truth, it was a little bit easier in those days to find them. There were more of them around. But today, it's a little difficult to find 'em. You have to search high and low, you know. They're out there somewhere if you can just dig 'em out of the woodwork, you know. It's kinda difficult to find 'em though today.

Ben: The simplicity you describe in song writing contrasts dramatically with the complexity of the music business today. Especially because, after twenty years of being with Blue Note, in fact, after being one of the most identifiable Blue Note artists, you left to start your own record label, Silvetto Records. And I know this label is tied directly into your interest in the spiritual aspect of the music. Of course, many people feel that your music has always had a spiritual, even sanctified quality to it.

Horace: Well, I've had Silvetto Records now for almost four years. And we call the music we're producing on Silvetto, we call it "self-help, holistic, metaphysical music." "Self-help" because we're trying to produce the kind of music on Silvetto that'll help people to help themselves. "Holistic" because we're trying to put in the lyrics to the various compositions the type of philosophies and psychologies, and sometimes even physiologies, that will help people. And "metaphysical" because we're trying to help them to get to the spiritual side of themselves, as the mental and physical. You know, most people today are involved in the physical and mental aspects of themselves, but a very small segment of people take time to investigate the spiritual side of themselves. You know, because man is really a trilogy, consisting of spirit, mind and body. And you're really only working two-thirds of the way on yourself if you're just mostly engrossed in your physical self and the physical world and your mental self, you know, in the mental world. You have to get into the spiritual part of yourself too. Investigate it, you know, 'cause there's a lot to learn about that.

Ben: You're a record executive. How much time do you put in to running a record company?

Horace: As much time as I can. It's a full-time job.

Ben: Is it something that you get rewards from? I mean, obviously there's, hopefully, financial rewards, but is it contributing anything else to you, or is it something you'd like to get out from under?

Horace: Well, yeah, it's, it's doin' a lot for me. I mean, the financial rewards are not that great so far. You know, it's growing, you know, slowly it's growing. Every year when I do my income tax, I find that we've sold a little bit more this year than we did last year, which is encouraging, you know. I'd like to see a lot more sold, naturally. But it's, you know, every business has to grow. So the financial rewards are not that great so far. But I'm being rewarded in other ways, because this is something that I've kinda yearned to do for years, you know. I've been thinking about music for healing, music for healing, and what can I do, how can I study and learn more about it, and how can I use my music in that direction, you know. And I got into it with Blue Note, little bit, you know. I didn't wanna go too far with it, 'cause I didn't wanna turn the record company off. 'Cause it was a new concept. Well actually, I did have some confrontation with them about it, because they couldn't understand exactly where I was comin' from with it, and where I was goin' with it, and where I was trying to go with it. And, but now that I'm runnin' the show myself, I have no one to answer to, you know. I can do my thing. And it's something that I've wanted to do for a long time, you know. I feel very strongly about helping people who are ill, you know. I've had several illnesses in my life and I know what it is to suffer with sicknesses and whatnot, and I've seen a lot of my family members suffer with sickness, and it's not anything very pleasant. And I'd like to be able to use my music to help in that direction, you know. And I feel that the music can. You know, I'm learning more about it every day and what I learn will be injected into the music and, as it grows, I'm sure the music will be that much more beneficial to help people.

Ben: When you play in front of the average nightclub audience, do they pick up on this holistic aspect of the music?

Horace: Well, I think the song titles give them some idea where we're comin' from, with the spiritual part of the music. 'Cause the song titles will kinda give them some clue of where we're comin' from with all of that, you know. And then, you know, I believe in talking to the people when we're performing in the club, you know, between the tunes. I explain about the various tunes we're playing, what they represent. Sometimes I might explain why I wrote a particular tune, you know, the purpose behind a tune or whatever, or what the meaning of the tune is, you know, and things like that. So they get kind of an idea where we're comin' from there, with the new music on the Silvetto label.

You know, the Silvetto label is the only record company I know of, so far, that has a prayer group affiliated with it. We have a prayer group called the Silvetto Prayer Group. And we have eighty-some odd members in the group right now. And we pray for sick people. Because, you know, we hope that these Silvetto records will gain acceptance from the medical profession eventually, and that they will use them in conjunction with their treatments. Because we feel that the material that we record on the Silvetto label will help people to help themselves, and help people to open up so that the doctor's treatment can be more effective. So we're hoping that the medical profession eventually will zero in on our recordings and recommend them or even prescribe them for some of their patients, you know. In conjunction with their treatments.

Ben: Well, I personally would have no problem prescribing your music to heal many things. But I would also say that's true about your early music as well.

Horace: Well Ben, you know, I feel that all music has healing potential, you know. All good music has healing potential. I felt the music we did in the past, before this Silvetto music, had healing potential, to a degree, you know. But I feel that the music we're doing now has a *greater* healing potential, because the intent behind this music is for healing, you know. I mean, the intent behind the music we did in the earlier part of our career was to bring happiness, joy, you know, so you can dance to it, you can, you know, pat your foot to it and to uplift the spirits. Which was good, and to make people happy, and all of that, fine, you know. And that is still our intent, even with the new music, it is still our intent to bring about all those things. But, we go beyond that now, and we're trying to uplift peoples' thinking. You know, we're not a religious organization. We don't belong to any religious group. We're just trying to tout here, through the lyrics, a few spiritual principles that everybody needs to get in tune with. And a few psychological things that everybody needs to get in tune with. You know, we're trying to promote positive thinking in a sense, and get people to think positive rather than negative. And open up more. And, I feel in doing this it'll make whatever treatments they're getting more effective.

Ben: How did you become interested in physical healing through music?

Horace: Well, quite some time ago I read some things about the subject, and I got very interested in it. And I tried to go out and buy books on musical therapy. And I only found one book on musical therapy and it didn't satisfy me, 'cause it didn't seem to go as deep as I would like to get into it, you know. And then I found in London, one time, I was looking for books on musical therapy, and I found a book on some Sufi teachings, you know. And I bought that book and I read it and something in that book turned me on to approaching my music the way I'm approaching it now. You know, for healing.

Ben: Do you think, for example, there are some chord voicings that are more constructive or some melodies or some keys that are more positive . . .

Horace: Definitely, definitely! But, you know, I haven't got into it. I'm hopin' to, but, you know, there's no place where you can study this. You have to just grope for it yourself. Maybe if I grope long enough and learn enough about it, maybe I can start some school and start to teach it. But I wish there was some place where you could study this type of thing. But I really do feel that music, there's a science to this. You know, there are certain chords that I feel can, you know, have a healing effect. Or certain key signatures for certain people. You know, you might require a certain key at a certain time, it may be major or it may be minor. You might require an augmented chord, or something, or, whatever, you know. But we don't know the science of this yet. But I feel it's *there*. You know, it is there. Most definitely there. It's for us to figure out.

* * *

Abdullah Ibrahim (November, 1985)

Pianist Abdullah Ibrahim, a.k.a. Dollar Brand, has an aura about him that recalls the mystical, and his speech is hypnotic to listen to and metaphorical in content. Yet his explanation, for example, of music theory in terms of the relationships between the father, the mother and the child was not only unexpected but also so simple that one could immediately grasp why some popular songs succeed (or, indeed, become the basis for jazz standards) while others fail; there are, perhaps, some basic, internal themes that cultures carry with them (possibly related to what Ibrahim calls the "silent music") and when these themes are articulated, like chords strummed on some great cosmic harp, the general population quite naturally responds. In any case, this all seems plausible when sitting across the piano from a man who carries in him both the joy of South African Township music and the despair of the apartheid system, with unbending dignity and a kind of offhand predisposition to laugh at the ridiculousness of Western theory.

Ben: Your career is long and varied, not only in time, but in distance. You are still a citizen of South Africa?

Abdullah: I always will be. Until the day when we effect our liberation and get rid of the fascist in South Africa, and institute a just society where we will all be able to return. But we still regard ourselves as South African citizens.

Ben: Let's talk a little bit about your early days growing up in South Africa. I've read that in the '40s one of your musical influences was music that you heard on the streets, the music that came out of ice cream trucks. And they would play the music of Louis Jordan and other American blues and jazz musicians. Is this true?

Abdullah: Yes, I think maybe we should update that into the '50s. The '50s, in the townships of South Africa, the first music, so called jazz music, that we were exposed to was, like you say, from ice cream vans, who played Louis Jordan, Erskine Hawkins, Andy Kirk. And the music was very popular. It was a very close affinity to Afro-American experience, our experience of South Africa. On all levels, politically, economically, socially.

My grandmother, for example, was the founding member of the A.M.E. church, in Kensington, which is a suburb about seven miles from the heart of Capetown. The A.M.E. church, as you well know, was formed here in the United States, in Philadelphia to be exact. The African and Methodist Episcopal church, which was founded by Richard Allen, who had moved from the South with his family, and on a Sunday went to worship in a Philadelphia church. Of course, being all white, they refused him entry, and he went to form the African Methodist Episcopal church, which is very, very strong in this country. And in South Africa, it is quite understandable why it has attained a lot of followers and also is a very, very, very, very strong social force. And that's where I learned some of the Afro-American experience, like the spirituals and the hymns.

Ben: The music you played commercially was related to the jump music and the jazz that we spoke about, the Louis Jordan type of music, but weren't you also involved in a vocal group too, before you took up the piano? I've read you were once part of a street-corner singing group.

Abdullah: No. In Africa, there is a very, very strong oral tradition. Because, firstly, it's not just a question of having to play the music, it's the *purpose* for playing the music. Basically it's because we, in Africa, in some areas, we're still going through the throws of industrial revolution. So we still have an agricultural community, where the music is still functional. So that your oral tradition, or the injection of words into the music, is very important, because it relates directly to an event that is occuring at that moment.

Ben: When you did become a professional musician, what sort of places did you play? Were the clubs integrated?

Abdullah: We never really played the music originally for white people. This is . . . the music is the music of the community. We played dances in the community. We played the carnival, the annual carnival. And occasionally there would be a job to play for white people. Possibly for a dance or some event. The idea of playing actual concerts was started, and that first came about, in the '50s. I remember playing the first concert in Capetown, so called jazz concert, which was to a sitting audience. And that, of course, was more or less integrated. But, basically, we played the music first in the community.

Ben: In this country, obviously, many white musicians were involved in the evolution of jazz music. Throughout all periods, but particularly during the '40s, during the bebop era, a lot of white musicians went to where the black musicians were. Was that the case in South Africa as well?

Abdullah: Well, see, when we are talking about the social connotations of the music, we first have to understand, when we start playing the music, you see, music is nothing else but pure spirit. It is . . . you start the music in church, with a question. As Muslim, there is *thikr*, or remembrance of Allah. There is the *Qasidah*, where the name of Allah is repeated and mentioned through song. When you say "to play the music commercially," there was never really that hard distinction.

What motivates and dynamos the individual is "what is the heart's deepest wish?" See, and with musical, or any so-called art form, it's not a question of whether someone is white or someone is black. It is what motivates the heart. In fact, that's with everything. What is the heart's deepest wish? When we started playing the music, even now, the heart's deepest wish is that we might become better human beings and serve our . . . and praise our creator by whatever name we know him by.

Ben: The apocryphal event that's mentioned in your personal history more often than not is a chance meeting with Duke Ellington in Switzerland during the '60s. It was after you'd left South Africa, clearly for political reasons, cultural reasons. And, through Duke Ellington's auspices, you came to the United States and became involved in what was then the so-called avant-garde jazz movement. What did coming here represent to you at that time? Was it coming toward a musical home of some kind? Or was it a . . .

Abdullah: . . . confirmation. Wherever we are in the world, wherever we go, whatever we seek, there's only confirmation. And there are those who have trodden the same path, or who are treading the same path, or on the verge of coming to tread that path. We don't think it's by chance that we meet. It is the heart's deepest wish. And when we do, when we do meet, there is absolutely nothing to say. It's like, there's nothing to say but, "Ah, praise Allah," or "Praise be to the Almighty." This is how our meeting was with Duke. And with Monk, and with Coltrane. Though it was not necessary to talk about music—and people always write, with Monk, always told us that Monk was very difficult—and when we met, I met him the first time, we said, "Thank you for all the inspiration." We told him who we were, and he said, "You know, you are the first piano player to tell me that." Which was confirmation.

It was really, you know, with Coltrane, it was the same. We met with Coltrane, with John Coltrane, in Zurich. And we sat down. There was, there was nothing, there was nothing musical to talk about. It was a meeting of the hearts and soul and long lost friends. And, in South Africa, we never regard them as "American" musicians. Ellington for us was just wise. He's the wise old man. You know, in the global village, there was consensus that Ellington was, he was the master, whether he was in South Africa, whether he was in the United States. No, it is just that extended family, that he is wherever those of the same intention in the heart are.

Ben: At the time of your meeting with Ellington, you had not yet converted to the Muslim faith, and were known by the name of Dollar Brand. Dollar was a nickname, I assume?

Abdullah: Yeah. It's a nickname, because we . . . Capetown being a sea port, it was of course a strong shipping port. And when I was teenager, [I] worked with a company called the Africa Line, there, for cargo vessels. I remember the African Star, the African Moon. And they were manned by Afro-American seamen. And we used to meet them. Go down into the docks and bring them home. Because, invariably, there would be musicians on board. And record collectors. And this is how I got the name, the nickname, Dollar, from hanging out with these long lost extended family.

Ben: When you met Duke, or at that period in your life, clearly, you defined the world in spiritual terms. Did you see the world in those terms even as a child?

Abdullah: Oh yes. This is what I try to say. We always, we always do. Doesn't matter where we are in the world. Those the creator endows with a special gift of what we call making music, it's always a spiritual experience.

Ben: Even before you had the words or the reference?

Abdullah: Even before. You cannot, perhaps you cannot articulate it, see. You, yourself, cannot articulate it. And the society around you cannot articulate it. And that is why the so-called musician, artist, unquote, has so many problems. Because the society does not really accommodate that inclination. In traditional society it was there. 'Cause, if at an early age, you showed any musical ability, you were immediately drafted into medicine. Because medicine was still the same, in African medicine, the medicine and music goes together. You were drafted into, into the secrets of music. What we call the silent music, which is music that any but the initiate will not hear. The silent music, and then into medicine. And in Africa, you'll be drafted, and study medicine for forty years. And after forty years you would be initiated and become a medicine man. But the music and the healing was never separated. You would . . . you then became the keeper of the keys of the mysteries. [Laughs.]

Ben: You laugh. Is it the words "the mysteries" that you laugh at?

Abdullah: Yes, because there are no mysteries, there are only basics. And it's only a question of having enough determination and having enough conditioning to, to stay with the basics. Because, the secrets, there are no secrets. It's there, in the basics. The question is whether we do have enough commitment to exercise the basics. Which of course means that one has to become so . . . become humble in heart, in order to realize that there are secrets in the basics. Otherwise we will have all these lofty ideals and look for supernatural answers.

Ben: I notice, of course, that you generally use the reference "we" instead of the word "I." When I hear you say that, I think perhaps it is related to the humility you're speaking of. Is that correct?

Abdullah: Well. That even is a trap, you see, to answer. [Laughs.] That's, we [laughing], where we deal, where we deal with having to become better human beings. You see, it's a lesson in the *Qur'an*, Satan, or the devil, is an open enemy to you. So treat him like one. And his job is to let you experience the lower self, and keep you there. That's his job. To become better human beings is that we must not devour, at least annihilate him. We have to get him under control. Because unless we know the low, we will never know the high. So when we even talk about humility, see, and then he whispers and says, "You are very humble." That is the trap, the constant, constant battle, we recognize in training.

Ben: You talk about ". . . there's no mystery, there are only basics." Would it be possible to look at your music and try to understand what the basic elements of that music are? At a piano keyboard? . . .

Abdullah: Absolutely. Okay. Well, basically, this keyboard and these twelve tones, was devised for us by Pythagoras . . . [laughs]. Okay, if you take the scale of C for example . . . [plays scale] . . . which is like . . . [plays and counts] one, two, three, four, five, six, seven—and then eight of course is the same tone, except an octave higher. So what we are dealing with is, really, is arithmetic. Algebra, geometry. Everything is time, space, the community. Everything is within that, and then of course you have your passing tones . . . [plays chromatic scale] . . . which will make it twelve, right? Seven plus five. So you're using seven plus five. Seven, five, three. These are the basic numbers that are the keys to the mysteries. Three, five, and seven.

What the western world conceives as zero, in their interpretation of the symbol, they say it means nothing. For us, the symbol, what they call zero, to us means everything. This is why in Africa, we have the symbol of the snake with a tail in its mouth. The time consuming everything. This is your first unit. The first unit is not a zero, the first unit is "the everything."

Okay. Now, the basic unit is not one. The basic unit is three. Three in one. This is how the Christians interpret the father, son and holy ghost, it is true. But we have to see it in its broader context: plus, neutral, minus. These three make one. Because nothing can exist without the other. This is the basis of electricity. If you have two similar poles, you will not have light. You must have plus and minus. And a neutrality, and you create light.

Which is the sun, and the moon. And the sun represents plus, strongness, and does not change. And it's hot. And the moon is cool, and it changes. And between it, there's the light, because there is no such thing as moonlight. It is sunlight that is reflected, deflected. So it is only an illusion that it changes, that the moon changes. Because that's why the man is represented by the sun, and the woman is represented by the moon. That's why a woman gets menstruation, menstrual changes, with the changing of the phases of the moon. And this is the basic unit, the ying and the yang. It's like the Japanese say, "Ten-yi, Chi-yi, Jin-yi." Ten-yi is the sky, with the dragon, Chi-yi is the earth, or the tiger, and Jin-yi, the people. In this heaven, earth. And the human body, and the human spirit, the human creates one.

And I remember we sat and spoke to Duke about this. I was sharing with Ellington once about this, the very basic principle of the first unit. And Duke said that he had written a ballet with this principle. And he interpreted it as the stillness of the lake, the meander of the river, and the sea. One drop of water in three conditions. But the stillness of the lake, and the movement of the water in the sea is only an illusion, because it's only a wave that passes through it. The same principle then is man, woman, and love of the child, that flows through. There's your basic unit of three in one. The next . . .

Ben: I'm still somehow trying to relate this philosophy to the piano keyboard . . .

Abdullah: Okay, here we come . . . So, you have [playing] one, two, three, four, five, six, seven. Right? The next unit is five. You see. It's everything, or zero, then three. The next unit is five. Five represents the five elements, and the five elements represent the earth; the physical manifestation of the spirit is five. Then you have, the next unit is seven. Seven represents change. When a child is seven, it goes to school. Fourteen, what is the word? Puberty.

Now when you apply this to music, you see what Pythagoras has done. When you talk about harmonies, one, three, five. [Plays chord.] Father, child, mother. Right? Boy [major chord], [minor chord] girl. Now this is your basic unit as a chord. Now, what they call the so-called dominant fifth triad, which means [plays scale to seventh note, then resolves to "1" chord]. Right? The moment you play a triad [plays] on the dominant, which is your fifth, that seventh note is in there. This is what you call your cycle of fifths, right? [Plays a cycle of fifths.] And every time you hit a dominant chord, it's five, with the seventh in it, and you must come back to one, which is the father. So there you see your father [plays chord], here's the mother [plays chord], right? And now, you find that what makes the mother so unique from the father is that seventh is in there. And that seventh chord represents the child. Right? Now, it's like the mother being pregnant with the child. And both of them relate to the father. So you have one, the father [plays root note], [plays the fourth up from root] four, the child [plays one step higher], five, the mother [plays chordal passage, gospel style].

Africans worked with this through millions of years, and finally pared it down to the basics. Now, you can identify other people's society by just listening to the music. You'll find, for example, that if there is a male-dominated society [plays short chordal and melodic passage] it stays on number one. Number one is the dominant, dominant key, doesn't move anywhere. It's a male-dominated society. Then you find in [another chordal melodic sequence], right? There's only adult music, right? You can listen to it, you see, one and five. Can you see? There's only adults, there's no room for children. When you look at the society, you'll find that it's like that. Right?

Everything is incorporated in there. The basic family structure, which is the father, the child, and the mother, one, four, and five [plays notes]. And four and five, because the child is much closer to the mother than to the father. Then you have the related chords [plays chords], which could be the grandfather.

And everything, everything, everything in music is based on these principles.

Ben: Later, perhaps, we can talk a little bit about Horace Silver, who's very much involved with similar holistic powers of music. Do you speak with Horace?

Abdullah: Oh, we know each other a long time. We first met in Switzerland, when we first came out of South Africa in the '60s, when he was there with . . . who was with him?

Ben: Blue Mitchell, Junior Cook . . .

Abdullah: Blue Mitchell. We made an album with Blue Mitchell when he was in South Africa, you know. He was there some years ago before he passed on. Yeah.

Ben: How does this whole process of musical relationships you have been describing affect how you organize your band and your recordings? For example, I know that you don't rehearse your band, in the formal sense that is.

Abdullah: Hmm. How does it come together . . . See, it's like, when, for example, Strayhorn and Duke, when they took the pencil and the manuscript, the composition was finished. The arrangement was finished. So it was just a matter of recording it now, you see, of putting it down on paper. That was a matter of recording it. But the concept was complete. We are samurai . . .

Ben: Samurai? . . .

Abdullah: Samurai. I've been studying martial arts now for about twenty years. And we have many teachers. The so-called improvisation means that you must be a samurai. Miamotu Musashi, a very famous Japanese swordsman, said, "Under the sword lifted high, there is hell to make you tremble. But go ahead anyway and you will find bliss." And this is the concept that you have to have when you play this music. You have to lay your life on the line, because you don't know what the outcome is going to be. You only make your intentions. It's very well to go over there and play music, from a written music. Everybody is safe. And everybody knows what's going to happen, even the audience.

We're living in that kind of age. Ever since we are being inundated by machines, you know? That, that indomitable human spirit . . . Duke always said that he would rather play with an unschooled musician, because the chances of that unschooled musician finding something beautiful is much more than a schooled one. So the samurai, what we do, is we try to surround ourselves by samurai. Each one being a master in his own craft. In this country, for example, there are so many unsung samurai, musicians. It's incredible.

Well, it's like a matter of casting. I only see myself, not even as a director, as casting. Wherever, play or other situation, we cast, and our work is only to try to bring great conditions, so that will bring the best out in the other human beings. So, the song itself is only a formula to allow the person to delve into the depths of the soul that he would not normally dare to go, and feel comfortable that he has community within, at that particular moment, when he starts, starts to take off.

Ben: The process you describe, and your music on record, reminds me of what I understand to have been Charles Mingus's process. I asked one of his musicians to describe the recording of "Goodbye Pork Pie Hat" [on the album *Mingus Ah Um*]. This musician had played a very highly regarded solo on this particular recording. He told me, "Well, we didn't have any chord changes. And the melody was not written out either . . ."

Abdullah: Exactly . . .

Ben: I said, "Well, if you were to replay that song now, what would you write out for chord changes?" He said, "Oh, I supposed I could write out some changes for you. But in the studio, Mingus didn't give us changes. As a matter of fact, he withheld changes . . ."

Abdullah: Right . . .

Ben: He *withheld* them . . . intentionally. Making the musicians fly blind.

Abdullah: Exactly . . .

Ben: This is similar to your process?

Abdullah: Similar. Because the music is not only music. It is not on paper, the music is in your heart, wherever it is, but it's definitely not on that paper. [Laughs.]

Ben: Charles Mingus, like yourself, developed bands with repertory companies, using the same common group of players. How important is the same group of players to you?

Abdullah: In any home there's the formula for any group of people, whether it's a family, whether it's a orchestra, whether it's a football team, or basketball team, or just this planet. The formula is that some come, some stay, and some go.

Ben: I would like to play you a Mingus composition for your comment. [Plays the composition "Reincarnation of A Lovebird."] Would you comment a bit on the Mingus piece that you just heard?

Abdullah: Oh, I never listen to music, you know. This is the first time I've heard a record in, I don't know. I don't listen to music. Even with this group. We recorded a few weeks ago, and we have to edit the tape, and it's difficult for me to sit down. I have my wife, Satima, who is also beautiful musician, to help. I let her get the stuff out and listen. Records, I used to listen to records much. I don't listen to it anymore. Well, when you, when you are on the path, the music is only a means to an end. We don't really have to listen to the actual, actual sounds, right? We are so busy formulating our own remedies, for a specific purpose. Mingus is a medical practitioner. And so are the Ellingtons, and the Coltranes. Those unsung teachers that we have. And when we get together, we never discuss music. And we never discuss about what solo somebody took. We never discuss our opinion, because there is no opinion, there is only consensus.

Ben: Well, Mingus, for example, was known to be very opinionated and if a musician played one wrong chord, there are many stories and observations of Mingus saying, "Stop, stop! No."

Abdullah: Yeah, well, this is, this is within his, within his own compound.

Ben: Having not listened to music for a long time, and then hearing a piece of music like this, is it like a cool drink of water on a dry day, or . . .

Abdullah: Well, what is the purpose of it? You know. What is the purpose? What is the purpose for the music, for the piece? I don't know. I don't know what he, what Mingus had intended his "Reincarnation Of A Love Bird." I . . . it's a title. I can't comment on it.

See, somebody asked me that one time. I was in a studio. It was here in New York, and I was on this talk show, and this man said to me, "You're a South Africa pianist, and we have another piano player here." So he had that piano player play, and then he asked me, "What do you think of it?" I said, "Why? Why do you want to know?" I couldn't understand the question. He asked me, "What do you think of him?" I said, "What do you think of him? What does anybody think of it? What is? I don't understand the rationality of asking me." What do I think of it? Because everybody has their own opinion, their own way that they move. This is a, a personal gift. Once you receive it, it's your personal gift. This is what you have received. It's like dispensing with medicine, or dispensing with food. There are certain things that are spiritually *you*, that are, that are.

You remember when Jesus healed a man. He said, "Man, I'll heal you but one condition. You won't tell anybody." Don't go and tell anybody. Same thing we feel about that. I think we, the music has never been in the realm where we have to discuss. Whether music is set out there, the purpose of the music, how the music has touched you, for what you personally need, and how it has touched me, is very, very personal. And for us, that is where, that is where it stops.

* * *

Mose Allison **(September, 1986)**

Mose Allison has been called "the William Faulkner of jazz," in part because of the literary nature of his lyrics, in part because his work so poignantly embodies the Southern experience, and, in no small part, because he is a great writer masquerading as just-plain-folks. He is a "road warrior" in the classic jazz tradition, working the clubs and concerts from coast to coast, month to month. He believes he has "over-recorded" and has little or no faith in the ability of the machinery of the music industry, specifically the record business, to deliver or care for his message. And his message, itself, is somewhat hard to pin down because it moves as Mose does, from town to town, year to year. It grows with him and is fleshed out by the dozens of characters that have appeared in his writing, from the "Wild man on the loose" to the father wondering "How much truth can a man stand, looking at his teenage daughter, just another lamb for slaughter . . . " He has honed the fine art of masquerade by presenting the truth; he says his songs are not about him, but nobody else can deliver them so simply and make the listener feel that something so profound has happened. Perhaps his style is best summed up by a blurb from one of his middle-period recordings: "More words of wisdom," it read, "from the jazz sage." He hates that blurb.

Ben: Your lyrics have a lot of different elements to them. There's something so personable about what you're doing, I'm sure when you go around the country a lot of people want to talk to you about your songs.

Mose: Yeah. I sort of have to rely on the comments I get from perceptive listeners and on the gig, you know, as to how well they're gettin' through. And sometimes when I do a song, I notice that people are sort of puzzled for like two or three years. Then all of a sudden, they'll start responding to it. So either I'm learning how to put it over better, or else there's something is happening in the interim that made them understand the song. But that's happened with several songs, and some of the newer numbers I'm doing now, I got that same reaction when I first started doing 'em and now they're beginning to get across, you know.

Ben: Such as "Ever Since the World Ended I Don't Get Out as Much," for example?

Mose: Well, "What's Your Movie," for instance, you know. First few times I did that on the job, people sort of looked puzzled, you know. But now they're beginning to pick up on it. People used to ask me about the idioms in my tunes, whether they would be hard to transfer to foreign languages. They asked me if there's any problem playing in foreign places, and I always responded that "it took ten years before they started pickin' up on 'em here." You know. 'Cause I can remember, I had been playing all over the country for years, maybe ten years, and then I played a job at Berkeley, California. And for the first time in my life I noticed that people were singing along. So that was the first I ever had the feeling that it was coming through and people were picking up on it and they were gettin' this stuff, you know.

Ben: That's not unlike what Monk said when he was asked why he didn't write more tunes. He said something like, "Well, they still haven't learned the old ones."

Mose: Yeah, right, that's it, man. I have a lot of stuff, you know, that I felt like it's never has really gotten through the way I meant for it to, you know. Especially some of the poetic things . . .

Ben: You mention the "poetic" things as opposed to some of the others. How would you characterize the different types of songs you write?

Mose: Well, the slapstick, you know. I usually categorize a song "slapstick," "social comment," or "personal crisis."

Ben: Those are your three main areas?

Mose: Yeah, and sometimes all three of those elements wind up in a tune. And that's good, and I've covered the whole thing. But some of them are strictly slapstick, and so forth.

Ben: Your personal biography is pretty well known. You came from rural Mississippi, the city of Tippo to be exact, and arrived in New York City in the mid '50s, where you played piano with Stan Getz. And I know, in talking to Dave Frishberg, you also played trumpet. He told me the first time he saw you at a session in New York, back in the '50s, you were playing trumpet, not piano.

Mose: Yeah, right, yeah. I was playing trumpet when I first came here, yeah.

Ben: And aspiring to be a trumpet player? Or not necessarily?

Mose: Well, I always liked playing trumpet, but you know, I never did have the confidence. And it's because I didn't get a very good foundation as a trumpet player. I learned how to play trumpet from a saxophone player in high-school band, you know, and he just said, "Well, you just put it up there and blow." So I developed, over the years. The trumpet players that I liked at that time were like Dizzy and people like that, and they all had these tremendous chops and everything. So I developed some bad habits, of trying to force notes and things. So I never did get very consistent on trumpet. At times, I would be able to play well, and at other times, I would have problems. And, so, I always relied on my piano playing to work and for my survival. When I first started working, I started working as a piano player. I never did much work as a trumpet player, actually.

Ben: Were you a songwriter also? Were you always writing tunes?

Mose: I wrote songs in high school and grade school. I had a hit in high school, man, called the "Fourteen Day Palmolive Plan." It was about radio commercials. I used to sing that thing, you know, at parties. It got to be real popular around Tallahatchie county. It was sort of a Louis Jordan type thing about how you turn the radio on, trying to get some music, you know, and somebody comes up, starts talking about the "fourteen day Palmolive plan." That was the idea.

Ben: So you always did a little bit of singing.

Mose: Yeah, it was, well, you know, "I woke up this morning feelin' low," that kind of thing. Louis Jordan bounce.

Ben: You did get a degree in English literature as well?

Mose: Yeah, from LSU.

Ben: Was it your love for literature that kept you there?

Mose: Well, you know, I wasted so much time in college, taking things that I wasn't interested in. I started out in chemical engineering. I took a year of chemical engineering and those six-hour labs were getting to me or something. But then I went to the Army. And then, when I came out of the Army, I didn't know what I wanted to study, and I just sort of studied whatever was handy, like economics, whatever. So when I got back, I got married and went to LSU, and I was a little more serious by then. And I decided that I wanted to get a degree, and I wanted to get into something I liked. So I took English and Philosophy. Had some real good courses in esthetics and metaphysics and so forth, and literature, and I really enjoyed it. And, I gave some thought to trying to write, and I figured that if I couldn't do anything else, I might be able to teach.

But graduation day, I got a job in a honky-tonk in Jackson, Mississippi, so I missed the graduation and went to work at Bill Bennett's club on the outskirts of Jackson. And, actually, B.B. King was there. And I remember, Percy Mayfield was in town there one time. So, that was right after gettin' out of college, and I just stayed with it ever since, more or less, except for a couple of times when I went back to Mississippi for two months rest or something, if things got slow.

Ben: But initially, it was just a gig that happened instead of graduation. Then another gig, and then another gig.

Mose: Yeah, right, and then I started, I had some pals that liked to play. And when one gig would run out, we'd go to a different town, try to get another gig.

Ben: Eventually, you came to New York City.

Mose: Yup. Finally, the jazz boom started jumpin' off in the late '50s, and I started reading these stories about these jazz musicians that were makin' money. So, I decided, you know, I'm gonna come on up and see what I could do.

Ben: And this is in '56, '57?

Mose: Yeah, I came here in '56. Just to stay. I had been here before. I'd been here in the summer of '51. But it was a little overwhelming for me at that time, and also, that was during the period when there wasn't much happening. And a lot of jazz stars were out on the corner trying to borrow five dollars, and so the whole scene sort of sent me back to Louisiana.

Ben: But you did come here . . .

Mose: Yeah, well, Al Cohn was the first guy to do anything for me. I had met his wife at the time, the wife he had at the time, Marilyn Moore. I met her in Galveston and played behind her at a jam session one night. And she told me if I came to New York to get in touch with them.

Ben: How did that lead to your first record session as a leader?

Mose: Well, Al Cohn gave me my first record date, actually. A date with Bobby Brookmeyer, Teddy Kotick, and Nick Stabulas. And then, a few months later, George Wallington helped me to get the date at Prestige. The contract there . . .

Ben: Really? And that lead to your album *Back Country Suite*?

Mose: Yeah, I had been playing little excerpts from the "Back Country Suite" around at various places, and I played some of it for George and his wife Billie. And so George took me up to Prestige, and I had a tape of the "Back Country Suite."

Ben: Telescoping time, of course, that led to the situation at Columbia, where they thought you were going to be a popular artist there for a while.

Mose: Yeah, right, yeah. Well, you know, they spent a little money, and the irony is that the promotion that Columbia did didn't help them, because they had *The Transfiguration of Hiram Brown*, which didn't make it commercially. But Prestige put out a re-issue of all the vocals on Prestige, and that thing sold a lot. I'll never know how much that sold. It's called *Mose Allison Sings*. That's probably the biggest record I ever had.

Ben: And that record included all the vocal hits, including "Parchman Farm."

Mose: It also had some of the tunes that were slightly romantic, you know, like "Baby Let Me Hold Your Hand," and "Gotta Right To Cry," and "Hadn't Anyone 'Til You." Things like that. Which I realized a few years ago, you've got to have if you want a popular record. I mean, if you want the record to sell, it's got to have that element of crotch fever in there somewhere.

Ben: Your kind of humor has been linked to the fact that you grew up in the South, so you had a unique perspective on the New York scene when you arrived. "The Transfiguration of Hiram Brown Suite," for example, seems based on that.

Mose: Oh, yeah, sure is. Detribalism . . .

Ben: Detribalism? The end of regionalism?

Mose: Yeah, right, yeah . . .

Ben: On the notes to one of your records, it talks about the theme of "Transfiguration of Hiram Brown Suite," and it says, "The following young man comes from the country, goes to the city, is overwhelmed and disillusioned. Longs for his youth. Finds that too is an illusion. Despairs. Goes through a crisis and is transfigured . . ."

Mose: Yeah, right . . .

Ben: In retrospect now, after the many years since you've written that, does our hero get transfigured at that point? Is that the end of it, or what happens next?

Mose: Well, you just keep gettin' more transfigured. If you're lucky. You know, you keep goin' through all sorts of phases. But I mean, that was meant to give an impression of, as I say, this detribalization process which is taking place all over the world, and all kinds of people are going through it. Going from agrarian society into the urban society. That's one of the main themes of this century I see, I guess. And, so I just felt like I had been through that, and that was what it was all about . . .

Ben: And it just keeps going . . .

Mose: Yeah, there's no end to it. I mean, you don't get from one thing to another and just stop, you know. Then, after you get into the urban thing, there's all sorts of ways you can go from there. And what I think what everything is headed at is some sort of synthesis. You take the best aspects of all these different modes of living and try to put together a new way to live that will allow us to survive.

Ben: Reminiscent of another one of your lines. "Mixing up the Boogie with the Doe-See-Doe."

Mose: Oh, yeah, right, I feel like I've always been doing that.

Ben: I think that's a real good definition of your piano style, too, the country element in there is something that suggests your roots. You grew up listening to more rural musicians like Sonny Boy Williamson and John Lee Hooker. And I've heard, in passages where you stretch, pianistically, I hear your technique sort of goes forward and backward at the same time. Outside jazz meets rural blues . . .

Mose: Oh yeah, well, you know, I've been saying that I'm trying to unite New Orleans and Vienna. I mean, so much of modern jazz has become more European, you know, it's closer to Schoenberg than it is to Louis Armstrong. I feel like there's elements in my playing that are strictly New

Orleans, basic New Orleans shuffle, and then there's other elements that get into the Schoenberg and the Ives and that sort of thing. And along the way, I also feel like I'm still doing some Kansas City swing and some bebop and some other stuff. So I feel like these elements are all part of what I'm doing.

Ben: What happened at that one point in the late '60s or early '70s, whenever it was, when your piano style changed dramatically? You kind of "turned left" and started adopting a lot of two-handed parallel runs, some chromatics, you even got into suspending the time and the bar lines. Did something happen?

Mose: Well, I just got kinda bored with the one-note, single-note style, and with the comping with the left hand. I mean, everybody was doing it, and it just seemed to me that it was getting kinda boring. I mean, you followed the guy's right hand, and, you know, the left hand was just negligible practically. And I felt like, for me, it was becoming boring. Although, I mean, there's still great players that can do it. It's a legitimate approach, you know, I'm not knocking it as an approach.

But, I started listening to piano sonatas and things, and I started seeing the way in which composers work the two hands together, and played off one line against another. And when they did one thing with the right thing, they did something else with the left, and I saw how they were developing those sorts of techniques. And I decided to see if I could pick up on a few of those things and just improvise with it, you know. And I'm still in the early stages. And, you know, it's a big order to try to improvise with both hands. There've been a few people who can do it, I'm sure, but I was never a real accomplished technician, anyhow. And my style has been pretty much just self-taught, primitive type. So I had to develop facility with my left hand. And that's a hard job, you know. Even real technical wizards on the piano will tell you that you have to work to keep that left hand up and keep it sharp and everything. So, ideally speaking, what I try to get into is to be able to have freedom to be able to use both hands in the improvising. And, you play 'em against each other and there's a lot of different ways to do it, you know. Sometimes you play parallel lines, or sometimes you play octaves in one hand and harmonies in the other, there's all sorts of things. But you can find all the techniques in classical composers, you know. A lot of it's in Bach, a lot of counterpoint and all that.

Ben: Talking about your getting away from the single-note style of bebop phrasing, you once mentioned to me that you like to go into what you call "the Italian section."

Mose: Yeah, I have a little thing that I work in every night that I consider sort of an interlude. I put it in at a place that I feel is effective, and this interlude, I sometime refer to it as the Italian section, or sort of like a

European blues, or something. And I try to use certain harmonies, you know, close harmonies that I've worked out that enable me to improvise loosely, certain melodies and counter-melodies between the right and left hand. And I feel like it's just a little alternative to this heavy rhythmical thing that goes on before and afterward. So, I just feel like it's a little respite.

Ben: Did you develop this in response to having to put your set together night after night . . .

Mose: Yeah, right. You know, I look at a set as an hour of music, you know. And I try to get everything that I'm interested in doing into that hour, or hour and ten minutes. And this is one of the things, from listening a lot to classical music and then picking up on odd harmonies and odd voicings, I just came to the conclusion that it would be nice to utilize those things as sort of a momentary respite from the pressure of swinging hard. And as a little countermeasure, it gives you a little alternate feeling. And not have any time. It's out of time, and it's improvised within certain limits. I mean, I have freedom to go different ways with it, you know. But I notice that I go through stages. I'll play some of the same melodies every night, you know. And then sometimes I'll change it up. Sometimes I'll change it up drastically. And it came from listening just to all kinds of music. And most music you hear, composed music, there's always that second section, you know. There'll be a furious first section and then there'll be the second section will sort of remind you of ". . . meanwhile back on the ranch" or " . . . back on the levee."

Ben: For the technically minded, what you're doing is, you're stacking thirds in a way. Taking one triad and putting the adjacent intervals on top of it.

Mose: Yeah, right, well that's always in there. The minor versus the major. That's always in there.

Ben: The minor versus the major. A lot of piano players will do that sort of thing in fourths, using stacked fourths. I think what's different here is that you're doing it in thirds, and it's got more of a blues or a country feel to it, doin' it that way.

Mose: Yeah, as I say, it reminds of sort of a European blues, you know? Some of the things you hear in European composers, there, it is a blues tonality. It has a blues mood.

Ben: We're talkin' in a very intellectual way about something which I'm sure you approach very emotionally. But your songs lead one to talk that way. The themes are intellectual themes, sometimes cleverly disguised as just little tunes.

Mose: Yeah, well, I like to catch a phrase or something that sounds simple on the surface but has some underlying meanings, you know. That's one of the things I've always looked for.

Ben: Is that how you tend to write lyrics? You back into a good phrase?

Mose: Pretty much, yeah. Start out with a very simple idea that most people are familiar with, and then try to work it in ways that you can get some deeper meanings out of.

Ben: I know that no two songs get written the same way. But are there some songs that you can point to as, perhaps, songs that you still wonder how you wrote?

Mose: Well, you know, I don't know how I wrote any of my songs, really. I mean, I know how I'm writing the ones I'm writing now. But, you know, people ask me "what inspired you to do this," or what instance, and sometime I'm not sure. You know, some things I can trace back to the perceptions, or that intuition, where you got this spark for this song. I can remember I was inspired to write "Hello Universe" when I was riding a motorcycle down the wet Pacific Coast Highway one night, during the full moon. So, I can remember some instances like that, you know. But, as you say, the idea and the way it's developed dictates the form of the song, you know. Like, "Your mind is on vacation, your mouth's working overtime." That just sort of dictates a straight forward blues presentation. Whereas something like "How Much Truth Can A Man Stand." That's a completely different song form.

Ben: What are some of your precedents in terms of musical construction? I don't mean piano players who sing a little bit, but song writers, or just writers perhaps.

Mose: Well, if you listen to a lot of different types of music, and when I was coming up the jazz players always told me, "What you do is, you listen a little here, you listen a little there, and you put your own little stuff that you figured out in there with it, and you come up with a style." And that was the way I always approached it. Funny thing about it is, when you get a style, then somebody says, "Oh, he sounds the same way all the time." So, you know, it's like you're damned if you do and you're damned if you don't. But I think if a person's got any talent for it, or any capacity for doing it, he puts things together in a way that gives an illusion of originality. In fact, sometimes when people ask me what I am, I say I'm an illusionist. You know, because I create an illusion of originality, by putting things together in a way that they haven't been done exactly that way before.

Ben: To me, one original aspect of what you're doing is the fact that it's not just entertainment, it's not just fun for the night. The audience can walk out of the experience with more than they came in with.

Mose: Yeah, well, I've always admired the phrase "to instruct and entertain." You know, and I feel like there's so much out there in the pop music business that's completely superficial. Why waste your time doing something else unless that's your game, and that's where you wanna play, you know? But I always had these people ask me if I'm a romantic. I say, "Man, sure I'm a romantic." Anybody who goes out and plays as much as I do, and has got no better sense than to believe that it matters whether he plays well or not, has got to be a romantic. And, so, like I feel like I'm trying to do the best I can with what I've got, and I'm trying to make it mean something, you know, without being pompous about it. But, I like to think that if you analyze my songs and everything, you'll get something out of it, other than just a circus swing, or whatever it is, you know. And a lot of people approach me and tell me that they got something out of it. A lot of people imply that there is a therapeutic quality to some of the songs or something, it helps them get through bad times. And that's what they been for me too, so that's good.

Ben: So it is an autobiographical form and an exorcism.

Mose: Oh, sure. It's all autobiographical, but it's reshuffled around. It's repackaged so that it's not complete, it's not straight autobiography, you know, it's translated. To start with, the song has to apply to me. I think if it doesn't apply to me, well I don't figure it's gonna apply to anybody else. But then I don't want the song to apply only to me. So, like you look for reinforcement and the experience of others, or to the newspaper or TV set, or whatever, to try to help you universalize your own experience.

Ben: The experience you describe is not unlike what an author goes through. You take all your experience and you create a character. And somebody says that's me, or that's him, and the author says, "No it's not, I made that up. I mean, he might have your ears, and he might have your belt on, but that's not you, that's something I put together." Which brings me back to the whole English literature aspect of your work. You do seem to be writing almost in the sense of a literary person, as well as a piano player and a song stylist.

Mose: Well, I think so. You know, somebody told me that they were studying some of my songs in college now someplace. That's flattering and, you know, you want your stuff to have an effect. I mean, you don't want it to go off everybody like water off a duck's back. You feel you want to try to do something meaningful. But I think everybody wants to do that. They want to try to do something meaningful. And I spent a lot of time, you know, trying to get the right word and the right phrase, and this instead of that, and all that. And I'm sure all the writers go through that as well as musicians and composers, and all sorts of people who are trying to invent something.

Ben: I'm sure you have thought of the irony of doing these tunes in the context of the nightclub, where people are hustling and do whatever they're doing, and you're singing about "everybody's crying mercy and they don't know the meaning of the word..."

Mose: You know, that whole thing appeals to me. I once heard the phrase "an irony hang-up." Well, you know, I don't know that I've got an irony hang-up or not, but irony has followed me like the albatross or something. I can find so many situations that are just completely ironical in my life. And that's part of my movie, you know. The playing in nightclubs. I'm not trying to write poems straight out, you know, that you go around and read in literary teas or whatever. That whole thing doesn't appeal to me. I still dig the boogie-woogie and the feeling, you know, the swing, the rhythmic thing, and I think that's all a part of it. That's the reason I'm always surprised when people accuse me of being cynical. Because, like the time, the rhythm and everything, the context that I'm working with is, you know, that's a life force. A very positive force. You know, the rhythm of jazz and blues or whatever. That whole thing is like a positive force, you know.

Ben: Forgive me for throwing quotes back at you all the time, but you once said, "I'm not cynical, John Denver is cynical. I'm the antidote to John Denver."

Mose: Yeah, right, and to me, the most cynical musical experience of this century is when you get four self-indulgent young millionaires together and they tell everybody that all they need is love. That's the epitome of cynicism, I think.

Ben: We're really talking about the evolution of the record business, and you've lived through it. When you started, it was still kind of a causal thing that you got involved in, you played a little trumpet, played a little piano, played some gigs. Now it's a real big business, and, ironically, even you are part of that end of it; you've been out from time to time touring with Van Morrison.

Mose: Yeah. Well that's a different game, that's a completely different league, playing with Van. You know, Van fills up these places, man, fifteen thousand people, with no problem at all. And I really admire Van. He writes good songs. And he does it from a musician's approach. I mean, there's no show biz, there's no outrageous acts or uniforms or costumes. And there are no antics on the stage. He strictly just goes out and plays, and he has a real good band, and I think Van is, like, he is not the usual music business success, you know. Like, I mean, he's a success in spite of the music business. His songs just reached enough people to make him that strong, you know, to be able to fill big halls and everything. And he doesn't have any of the mannerisms that you would associate with some of the more outrageous musical acts that are doing real good in the music business.

Ben: It's obviously, physically, a much easier gig for you to play.

Mose: Spend all day gettin' there, and play forty-five minutes, and then it's all over.

Ben: Do you feel cheated as a performer when you do it?

Mose: Not really. You know, it's just a different category. It's a different category of job, and you have to try to concentrate more, and try to get it all in in 45 minutes. You just, the intensity is up a little. You don't have the luxury of being able to work into that second or that third set, or whatever, and stretch it out a little. You have to like try to hit it right on the head and get it really going, and try to get as much as you can into that 45 minutes. And it's hard too, because of the sound. You know, the sound's always different. You're playing on big stages, and sometimes big open-air situations. And you can't hear. You're completely dependent upon monitors and stuff like that to be able to hear well. So that's another thing that can be a problem. But, it's a challenge. And it's just another venue, you know, and I'm up for it. I enjoy it.

Ben: You came in the door today saying that you've played something like 60 out of the last 90 days?

Mose: Oh, about 75 days out of the last 90 days or 80 days.

Ben: 75 out of 90. That's a lot of days. But that's not unusual for you. I see your name everywhere. You're constantly traveling.

Mose: Yeah, I been playing, I think I been playing 220, 230 nights a year, something like that. For the last five, six years, maybe more.

Ben: How long can you keep this up?

Mose: Well, you know, like, I've got some time off this next month. I'm not working that much so I'll get myself together and get settled down. It was beginning to get to me this summer, you know. One thing is the heat. Like, when we were playing the dates with Van, a lot of the dates we played, it was like 100 degrees out, and in fact, I've been in that sort of heat all summer. I started out in Texas, and it was 95 every day there, and that's the sort of story of how it went up until I got to San Francisco and I froze there. But for some reason, the summer, which used to be sort of a slack period, has gotten to be the busiest time of the year. And, I just got real busy. But the weather, we went through a lot of hot, humid weather, and it was beginning to wear me out.

Ben: Is there anything you wanna do, other than what you're doing?

Mose: Not really. You know, I just I look forward to playing. I once said that the main thing I like about what I'm trying to do is that I know that it's impossible. Because, you know, to play real first rate jazz piano and sing and write your own material and make it all happen, and carry the load, night after night, it's a pretty big order. And I used to say, if anybody thinks it's easy, you know, try it sometime.

Ben: What about a long-form project? I'm sure that people have approached you with the idea of doing a suite, or a musical, or an opera . . .

Mose: Yeah, well, there's been a lot of talk of that, but I'm not geared for that sort of thing. You know, I've done a little arranging, but I don't enjoy it that much. And, as I said before, the main attraction for me is getting up every night and trying to make it happen. And trying to get a couple of good players and, hopefully, get an audience and try to make it happen. That's the ultimate to me, and if and when I can't do that, then I'll start thinking about these alternate projects. But as long as I can keep up the pace of performing, that's what I prefer to do.

You know, I recently had the thought that I could probably do an interview and just quote myself. Just quote from songs. I could probably cover pretty much anything anybody wants to ask me about myself. And, so it'll count for something. One of the days I'm gonna try that, just by quoting myself, answering all the questions.

Ben: That's actually a testament to the proliferation of your music. I mean, you've managed to cover in depth a lot of these themes. You started out by saying there are three categories . . .

Mose: The social comment, personal crisis, and slapstick.

Ben: That kind of covers it all . . .

Mose: Yup . . .

* * *

Sonny Rollins (January, 1986)

Sonny Rollins is an extremely soft-spoken gentleman whose career in the jazz world has covered a tremendous amount of history. Because he is tall with a dramatic look, and because his contributions to the music loom so large in the historiography, he is often approached as a "giant" both by his fans and critics. This has made him leery of public encounters. Subsequently, he has done relatively few interviews over the years. I met him on a cold winter afternoon at a recording studio in New York City. We talked briefly about some mutual friends, and then got right to the heart of the interview. Throughout the day he proved to be a most generous man and quite willing to share his history and his personal feelings. It is hard not to be impressed by his gentleness and modesty. The following is a document of some of that conversation.

Ben: Back when you first came on the scene, you were hailed as a "saxophone colossus," and you were quoted as saying that it bothered you to be thought of this way—as an influence—because you felt you still had an awful lot of work to do. How do you feel today?

Sonny: Well, in a way I still feel that way, because I had the opportunity of coming up with some of the really great people—Thelonious Monk and Bud Powell and you know, all of the really greats—so I was always a little younger than they were, and to me it's always been a learning thing.

I sort of came into music later than a lot of people. Although I started early, I decided that music should be my life a little later. So I've always sort of been learning as I've gone along. I kind of think that I'm still learning. At least I hope I am, because you know music is endless, you can always learn something.

Ben: I know you're a native of New York City, and you grew up in the neighborhood with a lot of wonderful players.

Sonny: Yeah. Bud Powell lived not too far from us. And, as a matter of fact, Ben, the area I grew up in, which was called Sugar Hill, at that time was sort of the place where most of the black artists—who were able to—lived. It was sort of the nicest part. So Duke Ellington actually lived on our block. This was when I was really a kid. And all of the great guys lived there. Andy Kirk lived there. Coleman Hawkins lived around the corner. We used to see guys like Sid Catlett, John Kirby, all of these guys we saw every day almost, because they all lived in the neighborhood. So it was a beautiful place to grow up. Because we all wanted to be musicians, really.

Ben: You began as a piano player and an alto player and eventually found your way to the tenor saxophone. Your sound on the tenor is such an archetypical tenor sound that one might assume that you always wanted to play it. But that wasn't the case.

Sonny: Well, I did want to play it actually. But first, I liked this guy Louis Jordan. I used to have all of his records, you know, the original Timpani Five Band. There used to be a little short guy who played piano, and a trumpet player that used to play with the mutes and sounded a lot like Miles started to sound later, you know, the muted style. So I really loved that band, and I loved Louis. And he played a lot of alto at that time, although he did play some tenor. So I liked the alto.

But when I heard [Coleman] Hawkins, and really got into Hawkins, I sort of knew that this was my instrument, this is where I wanted to go. So I used to play the alto with the tenor reed. Which made it sound more like a tenor. At least I thought it did, you know. It probably did give it a little bit of a heavier sound. But I began to want to really play the tenor when I began listening to Hawkins and, you know, the big bands. And I always recognized the tenor player. So I kind of felt this was my voice, this was what I wanted to do.

Ben: You say you delayed becoming a professional musician. Why was that?

Sonny: Well, when I got out of high school, I used to be very much interested in art. I used to love to do cartooning. And at that time, that was sort of my first love. And I sort of felt that this was what I would like to do.

But I guess the main thing that I should say is that I didn't have a lot of confidence that I was good enough to really make it, you know. So even though we had our little bands and everything during high school, I never really thought I was good enough to play with some of these guys and make this music, you know. That confidence came after I played a while, and the big guys wanted me to play with them.

You know, Bud put me on that album, and Fats Navarro wanted me to join his band. And J.J. [Johnson] wanted me to play, and used some of my tunes on some of his early records I did with him. And Miles, you know, asked me to join his band and all that. So then I realized, "OK, I must have something that's okay, and I better try and work on it and develop it."

But also, I felt insecure because I never really studied music in school. And so my training was not formal, although I had a brother that was formally trained—a violinist, he's really great. And my sister played a lot and sort of had more of a formal music training than I did. So this is why I had some reservations that I would actually really get into it, you know.

Ben: Were you surprised, then, when you became so highly regarded so quickly, and, in fact, became an influence on other musicians at such a young age?

Sonny: Well, when I began making my first records I guess around 1948 or 1949, I had begun to get a reputation around the block, among my peers at the time. People began knowing I was good. This was all teenagers, you know. So, you know, the bug was beginning to hit me pretty strong, and of course the competitive thing is always there, and I had to actually blow with other horn players, you know. In those days, it was always a battle of the saxes. It was almost like a boxing match. You had to battle another guy who's supposed to be good. So I had to go through a lot of those wars with other guys coming up, so my confidence was beginning to assert itself at that time.

Ben: Was the development of a big sound on the saxophone part of your way to survive in those battles?

Sonny: Yeah, yeah, because guys would tell me . . . in fact, the way I've learned a lot has been through people telling me, guys that I've looked up to, telling me what to do and how to sound. So in a way I was self-taught, but I got a lot of help along the way from a lot of senior guys. But, you know, I found out that I had to have a big sound. You know, you *had* to have a big sound in those days to make it. A big sound was more "in." Plus a lot of the clubs didn't have the mike setups like they do now. So I had to develop a big sound.

Of course, my idols were Hawkins, and I liked [Ben] Webster a lot too. Guys who had big sounds. Byas, too, of course. Don Byas. So I kind of liked that big sound.

Ben: Were there any specific technical things that other guys gave you early on to help you develop your music facility?

Sonny: No, I think I learned a lot by listening and being around guys. In those days we listened to records a lot. And we used to get all the latest records, take them home and try to copy the solos from the records, you know. And I kind of learned like that. It was difficult because I had to keep a posture of being good enough to be there, so I didn't want to kind of say, "Well, man, how do you do that?" you know. So I tried to learn without asking, so to speak.

Ben: A lot of what makes a soloist successful seems to be magic to those who are striving to get there, or are outside of the circle. I'm struck by something you once said regarding Charlie Parker. You said that as soon as he starts to play, he "creates a complete mood." Being able to create a complete mood seems to be exactly what you do as well.

Sonny: I don't remember the quote, but I probably did say it, because Charlie Parker was one of my big idols. I put him up there with Hawkins, too. And of course I loved anything that he did. We used to follow Bird around, you know, we were a bunch of kids bothering him. He came off of his sets down on 52nd Street, and actually he was really good to us, you know, he treated us like sons. But I loved his work, and of course when Bird played, we were agape, with mouths open and everything, just checking him out. He was really great, in so many ways . . . musically, and he was also sort of a social leader. And a spiritual leader, I guess I should say.

Ben: Your name appears on so many classic recordings, it's difficult to pick out one of them to talk about. But I'm most curious about the album *Sonny Rollins Volume Two* on Blue Note, because it contains that remarkable version of Monk's "Misterioso." I'm talking about the version featuring both Horace Silver and Thelonious Monk on piano. That session also had kind of a magical feel to it. What are your memories of that particular recording session, and how did two pianists turn up on the same song?

Sonny: Well, I remember that Monk was originally supposed to be there and Horace also came by or was there or was invited or something. But in those days, it was a tremendous feeling of comradery among those that were playing and doing the recordings, so everything worked out beautifully. There were no problems, no ego problems.

Ben: Perhaps that's the magic. The feeling was so open that two different piano players could make their statement in the course of one single tune. Of course, your work with Monk, I think, is among the most important, historically, that you've done. How do you see that period of history?

Sonny: Well, first I'd have to say that Monk's music is difficult. It's difficult music. As Coltrane said one time, if you miss a change with Monk's music, it's like stepping into an elevator shaft when it's empty. The music is difficult. I was always fortunate. Monk liked my work, you know, Monk really liked me. I mean, you know, I was younger than Monk, much younger actually than Thelonious, but this was also a great source of strength for me, the fact that Monk really dug what I was doing. He liked my work all the way along.

Even when I began rehearsing with his band when I was still in high school. We used to go down to Monk's house there on 63rd Street. And the whole band would be in Monk's small apartment, rehearsing, you know, and Monk would have what seemed to be way-out stuff at the time, and all the guys would look at it and say "Monk, we can't play this stuff . . . we can't make this on the trumpet," and then it would end up that everybody would be playing it by the end of the rehearsal, you know.

It was a beautiful experience, hanging out with Monk and everything. It was hard music. I'm not sure that I was able to capture everything that I wanted to, playing with Monk and playing his stuff. I was not sure about it, but as I said, Monk seemed to feel that I was doing OK, and he encouraged me. And I found out that he really liked my work, so I did it. But I'm not sure that I got out of Monk's music everything that I could have gotten out of it.

Ben: Of course one of the major messages of Monk's music is "be yourself," the individualism that's stressed in Monk's music . . .

Sonny: Yeah, that says it all, because he really wanted me to be myself . . .

Ben: And it seems, looking back, that one of the reasons that people pointed to you as such a strong force in the music was that you were unlike most of the other players at the time. There was a sense that you were an individual, not a follower of fashion.

Sonny: Yeah, I would say that's probably true. [Laughs.]

Ben: You laugh about that. Is it in retrospect now something that became blown up out of proportion, something that was just sort of happening at the time, or were you really trying to do that, to be different?

Sonny: No, I think, as I said, I was learning all the way along, so the fact that people would want to play like me is something that never entered my mind. I mean, it just may have been very recently that I even considered the fact that there might be enough in my playing that someone else could actually get something out of it, another horn player.

As I said, I was always thinking of getting better, you know. So this was where I was at. I mean, it wasn't a big thing about trying to be a unique player. I was just at that particular point in my development. This was just what I could do at that time.

Ben: Soon after this period we're talking about, you worked with the Max Roach/Clifford Brown ensemble. That lasted a couple of years and then you "dropped out" of the jazz scene. Clearly, you kept playing, because you kept improving. But what was that period like for you, when you left the scene?

Sonny: Well, again, that's all part of the self-improvement thing. Although I had dropped out before, for other reasons, my first real disappearance came around 1959. And, you know, things were going on in the music, and I was getting . . .

Actually, what was happening was this, Ben. I was getting a lot of play from people. Every place I went it was "Sonny Rollins," and you know, "Oh boy, he's the cat to see." Which was good, except that I didn't have the feeling within myself that I was really able to put out what they expected from me. And I remember one particular job that I had in Baltimore. Elvin Jones was playing with me around that time. And my playing . . . I felt that I disappointed the people, you know. A lot of fans were there, and they all, you know, "Oh, Sonny, Sonny," you know, but it didn't come out right. And I felt that this was because I didn't really have all my stuff together. And this was really beginning to take me out. I was really upset about it, you know.

So I realized, "Well, look, man; either you're going to stay out here and go around and face nights like this, or you're going to try to get yourself together." Brush up on this, learn that, get this together, different things like that. So that's what I did. I said, "Okay, I'm not going to appear anymore. I'm going to lay off the scene, go back in the woodshed and get these things together." And that's basically what that thing on the bridge was all about.

Ben: That's also an archetypical story for jazz fans, the image of you practicing on a bridge. You went there, because, acoustically, the properties were such that you liked the sound, or because people wouldn't bother you?

Sonny: Right.

Ben: Which bridge did you favor?

Sonny: I did play on the Brooklyn Bridge, but the bridge that I found was best was the Williamsburg Bridge, because it had the wider expanse. And actually, the pedestrian walk had much more place to play. So I tried the Brooklyn Bridge also, I was on the Manhattan Bridge, too. That didn't work out. The pedestrian walk was much smaller and noisier. So the one that worked out the best was the Williamsburg Bridge.

Ben: You'd go out there in the evenings mostly?

Sonny: I'd go out there anytime. Anytime I'd want to. I'd go there at night, I'd go there in the daytime. And there would be some cats that would come up there with me at different times. I used to bring Steve Lacy, Jackie McLean would come up there with me. And it was beautiful, because you were playing against the air, you know, the sky, and it was just a beautiful place to practice a horn. And I could play as loud as I wanted to and just go through anything I wanted to do, so it really proved an excellent spot for me.

Ben: The bridge became a metaphor too for a transition from the music of the '50s to the music of the '60s. Were you trying to work through specific musical and artistic barriers up there as well?

Sonny: Yeah, I guess so. Basically, it was myself. It wasn't so much . . . I mean, I've heard a lot of people say "Well, Sonny was trying to get into or compete with what Ornette was doing, or Coltrane was doing," and all that. Basically, I was trying to get myself together. I mean there was a lot of things in my own playing that I wanted to kind of improve on and get a handle on. So I was sort of working against myself, rather than against what was going on in the business, or what was going on outside, you know.

Ben: Technically, one of the things that you've developed is the idea of "double breathing" or "circular breathing." What is circular breathing?

Sonny: Actually, I first heard it done when I used to go to the Apollo Theater. Every week we used to go and catch all the bands that came to New York. We used to catch everybody. We'd be there every week and stay all day. Because I think that they had four shows at that time. So if it was a good band that we liked . . . usually, any band we liked, all the bands . . . but if it was a specific great band, we'd stay there all day, you know. And we'd have to watch the movie over and over again, you know. They'd have some of these "B" movies. But anyway, it was great, because after the movie, then would come the theme song, you know . . . [he sings the theme song] . . . then the stage show would start.

So anyway, I saw John Kirby's band and a very fine player named Buster Bailey, a clarinet player. And I saw Buster do it. I remember the song was "Saint Louis Blues," and he held this note, you know. The band kept playing and he just held it and held it. So it was amazing. And it seemed impossible, of course, to do. But that was the first time that I had heard it done.

Then in later years, I actually learned to do it from a sax player named Kermit Scott, who used to play with Dizzy and Monk at Mintons. And he used to play with Earl Hines, I think; that's where he might have met those guys. But he's a very fine horn player—he's living in San Francisco now—so Scotty did it a lot. So I was friends with Scotty, and I asked him "Would you show me this?" Because actually, this is one of these things that would be a secret, that you don't actually want to give to your competitors, you know. You see what I mean? But he was a beautiful guy, and he said, "Sure," he'd show me how to do it.

So the idea, of course, is to keep the sound going through your instrument. And the basic principle involves breathing through the nose while you keeping the breath going through your chops, through the mouth. And you can practice it without your horn. You can practice the principle of it by just holding your finger up to your mouth and just blowing and . . . [demonstrates] . . . and at that point where you run out of breath, you breathe through your nose, right at that point, and you let the air right out of your cheeks. Then you're back, you get some breathe and you're back again for your next cycle. So that you can keep on indefinitely.

Actually, it's something that's done a lot in the East, a lot of these guys do it. When I was in India, the snake charming guys did it. And then guys like Bismira Kahn, he had a beautiful group, they used to keep the drone going with the shinais, just going all the time, and one guy would play lead but the guys in the background would keep the circular thing going. So it's an accepted thing that's probably old as anything.

But anyway, I practiced this a lot, and got to use it, and it's really invaluable. I don't want to call it a gimmick, because it's not a gimmick, but when you use it people go, "Wow, how do you keep that going?" It does kind of bring people out; it's good for a performance, you know. It's nothing cheap about it. It's a trick, I could say, that keeps the audience involved in what you're doing. And it's helped me over a lot of nights when maybe ideas weren't coming to me like I wanted them to. So I'd do that for a while . . .

Ben: Keep the energy up . . .

Sonny: Right, keep the energy up and wake up the crowd a little bit, yeah. So it's been invaluable to me. And it's a good technique I think for any wind player to work with, actually.

Ben: There are other things you do from time to time, almost as a way of tipping your hat to the crowd. One of them is using a lot of quotes from popular songs. Some people call that being "corny." Do you think of it as "corny"?

Sonny: No, I don't think it's corny. I'll tell you why. Because it's difficult to really use quotes. I think it's ingenious. I'm not the first guy to do it, you know, but I think it's really difficult to bring another song into what you're doing and make it fit. Harmonically it's tricky. You can't put any song just anywhere. And there are degrees of doing it. I mean you can always quote something simple. At any place in a blues or something like that. But if you're playing a more involved harmonic structured song, it involves a certain amount of deftness to actually place the right quote in the right place and make the chords come out right.

I get a lot of kick out of doing it. I mean, if people don't like it or think it's corny, I'll forgo that, because it knocks me out. It's like a puzzle. For myself, I get a lot of pleasure out of fitting different songs into other songs. It's something I enjoy doing. And I think it's difficult to do.

Ben: Of course, Charlie Parker was a master at it.

Sonny: Charlie Parker did it a lot. And it's not easy to do, especially when it's harmonically difficult changes, to fit it all together.

Ben: I'm also struck by how easy to "hear" a lot of your compositions are, and I think that's one of the reasons they've been lasting compositions. "Doxy" is one of them; "St. Thomas" is another. Apparently very simple tunes, but when you play them, like Monk's tunes, they keep giving something back to you over and over again.

Sonny: Yeah, I like more or less simple songs. I think the thing about my playing is the development. The development of a simple idea and to take it through difficult waters and to maintain this basic simplicity. And carry it through a lot of things and then bring it back. Of course, it's always there, the basic chords are always there. So I think that's the thing about my playing that distinguishes me in some way, you know.

Ben: It's the mystery of the journey, not the complexity of the map?

Sonny: Yeah, that's where I'm at, yeah. And it's not necessarily better than some other guy that makes a complex map, you know. I mean, I would be the last one to even suggest that, but it's my way of doing it.

Ben: The composition "St. Thomas" was heralded at the time because of its Caribbean premise. You've had an obvious interest in Caribbean flavored music all along. Recently you put out a record, *Sunny Days, Starry Nights*, with a song called "Mava Mava" on it, which also has this same foundation. You really seem to favor this idiom.

Sonny: Yeah, well my mother came from St. Thomas, and when I was really young, she used to take me to some of these dances, so I got some of that influence, you know. And it's probably a part of my playing, in a way. I didn't really get a chance to accentuate it until later in my career, when I had gone through a lot of the other things that were happening. In other words, I had to prove myself playing whatever else was out there. I couldn't begin by being a guy that played a lot of Caribbean rhythms. But it's a part of my playing, and I think I play it easily. You can feel it's not forced. So I enjoy doing it. And I've got to get *some* enjoyment out of my playing. [Laughs.]

Ben: You've got to get something back...

Sonny: Right, for me, you know. I'm hard on myself, man, so I've got to get something I like...

Ben: You *are* hard on yourself. Your reputation is somebody who's an absolute perfectionist.

Sonny: Yeah, it's a drag at times, you know. So things like the quotes, and some of these Caribbean type things, these are the things that kind of give me a little bit of it back, you know.

Ben: Lately, the last ten years or so, you've been working more or less when you want to work. Other musicians have told me, however, that the work just isn't there anymore like it used to be. These days, if you can work six or seven nights a month, that's doing well. As opposed to six nights a week, which was reasonable several generations ago. You're a perfectionist. How do you stay in shape?

Sonny: I find, actually, Ben, that I put so much out when I do a job that it works best for me to take some time in between so that I kind of recharge myself. I find that if I play every night, I get wired up too much. So at my age now, the best thing for me to do is to just play on special jobs.

Fortunately, I'm able to, like you say, just pick the things I do, so I'm not out there all the time. I don't do really grueling things, you know, and I kind of make my schedule easier on myself. The reason is that I put out a lot when I play. So that I kind of keep myself together by doing that.

When I'm not actually playing, I practice, of course, every day. You have to practice every day. A horn player has to keep his lips in shape. So I practice every day as much as I'm able to. And I'm thinking music all the time anyway. Music is such a part of my life that I'm never really far from it, even though I'm not out on the bandstand. I mean it's going around up there constantly, anyway.

I don't listen to a lot of records, because I'm constantly writing my own stuff or practicing. So usually when I'm not playing, I don't listen to a lot of records, you know. People send me records of people I should hear, new guys, so on and so forth, but I don't listen to a lot of records, I really don't. Occasionally, I'll listen to something, but as a steady diet, I don't listen to many records.

Ben: When you practice, do you practice scales, do you practice songs, do you practice improvisation? How do you approach a practice session?

Sonny: Well, I practice some scales. There's a very good book out now by my good friend Yusef Lateef, and I practice some out of that book. It has a lot of scales and different patterns. Ancient scales and so on. So at times I practice out of some books. And sometimes I practice just free form, just as if I was playing. You know, I just let whatever come into my head. Just basically to keep my chops up. I don't really think a lot about what I do. It's like when I'm on the stand, I really want to reach a point where I don't have to think about what I'm playing.

You know, my best work comes when I'm not really thinking about what I'm doing; when it just starts to come by itself. So I try to prepare myself by keeping my chops in shape, going over some chords I might need to have under my fingers, and then letting it happen by itself. Because that's really where it's at, you know. Letting the music come through me, instead of my trying to constantly create it myself.

Ben: Is that what happened at the Sculpture Garden of the Museum of Modern Art in July of 1985, when you walked out on the stage all alone? [Note: the concert was recorded and released by Landmark Records as *Soloscope.*]

Sonny: Well, that's what I wanted to happen, you know. And, in fact, I had nobody playing with me, so I had to kind of let it happen like that. So I did. It was a completely free-form performance. I did have some motifs that I had prepared there that I might use, depending on how the evening went. I had several "modus operandi" that I was going to try. But it worked out better that I just do it free form, so I didn't get into the prepared stuff. There were so many people there, and it was so jammed, you know, there was just no way for me really to do the other thing ... to play the motifs and develop them. So I just did a completely free form thing.

Ben: There's a picture of you standing in this sculpture garden. And there's a sense—if you know the area—of the traffic going by just on the other side of the wall. And I'm sure the traffic made itself known to you from time to time.

Sonny: Yeah, it was difficult because of the car horns and everything. And, as I said, that particular night, it was really an event. There were so many people there. It was gratifying to me, you know, I'm really happy about it. But the sounds of the city did intrude at times, and I had to really block it out. So it was a really mental thing, too, because there were a lot of things that could distract me. And for moments they did. I had to overcome it, you know. In fact, there was an alarm, a car alarm that went off there for a while. It went on and on and on. It kept going for a long time.

So there were some distractions. However, I guess it all just added to the document that night. It's just the way it happened that night, and that's what we put on the record.

Ben: Jazz, of course, has traditionally been collective improvisation. But when you're by yourself, you don't have anyone else to rely on. Is this experience substantially different than group playing? Did you have to change your approach?

Sonny: Collectively, everybody in the band does contribute. And this is a little different. But basically, I don't want to think of it as being completely divorced from playing with other people, because I'm still trying to do the same things.

I'm still trying to create, I'm still trying to be innovative, I'm still trying to make sense, I'm still trying to play with drive, I'm still trying to play with meaning, I'm still trying to transcend . . . The same things I'm doing with the group, I'm doing by myself. So in many ways, it's the same.

Ben: Almost a more pure form, in some sense.

Sonny: Maybe, yeah, you could say that. Yeah, in some ways it's a more pure form. In some ways, it's easier for me to do that [play solo]. Except, it's a long long trip. Like on this album, in fact we had to leave out some of the things we did. There wasn't enough time on one album. So in a way it's physically exhausting to play that long, but it's rewarding in other ways.

And I like playing by myself, anyway. Even when I'm playing with a band I try to play some a cappella things during a show.

Ben: You mentioned that in the past, some of the things that you got out of the music was the humor, and the quotes, and the references to the Caribbean. Looking back at this extraordinary experience, what are your favorite moments?

Sonny: Well, again the thing that really struck me was, as I was preparing to do the concert, up on the second or third floor of the museum, on the 53rd Street side, I looked over the balcony, and I saw the crowds lined up from Fifth Avenue all the way down to Sixth Avenue, and that meant they were lined up on Fifth Avenue down 53rd Street. And it was great. It was touching, you know.

I mean, I'm never so big, I'm never so sure of myself, that I take it for granted that people are going to come to see me. I mean, I've been in this business too long to expect that, hey, man, everybody's going to be here and love me. I mean, I've seen the lean times enough times to know that they can happen any time. So that was beautiful that people were there. And the whole thing was a very moving evening from that point of view.

I'm never completely happy with my work. So, you know, I could have done better. In fact, I might do it again sometime because I think I can improve on that performance. But the whole evening was pretty special in those other ways.

Ben: You said to me earlier, when we were talking about your recorded work, that all the records fall short of the mark as far as you're concerned. What's the most important work for you that remains to be done?

Sonny: Well, the most important thing I really want to do, Ben, is to just get to the point where my level is constantly higher. I know that I'll never satisfy myself every night. I mean, I know that that's perhaps beyond reach. But I'm trying to get my level up higher. You know, always that my level should be higher than it is now. So that even on bad nights, it's always good enough that at last I'm not completely wiped out by what happened. You know, I feel good about what I'm doing, up to a point. I know it's not going to be perfect, but I want to feel good at least that it happened up to perhaps a six or a seven rather than a four or a five.

And that's about it. Just to keep playing. Keep improving. Because as you know, music is something which you never . . . it's a magical thing. You know, the keys are there on the piano, but you can do so many different things with them that it's magic. It's the same keys but what you do with them Tuesday night is going to be different than anything you could have thought about on Sunday. So this is the magic of it, and it's a beautiful life. I mean, I'm really happy to be playing, because this is what I love doing.

Ben: It sounds like it keeps getting better as you get older.

Sonny: Well, my appreciation of it does, and as long as I can keep my physical side up, then it's great.

* * *

Phil Woods (February, 1985)

For many years, Phil Woods has been called the "king of the alto saxophone." While jazz writers have felt they were flattering him by offering him the crown after Charlie Parker's death, Phil himself has never let this praise sway him from his quest for personal satisfaction and control of his musical expression. ("Better living through bebop," as he might say.) His sound is characterized by intense passion, as if his soul is literally trying to burst through his horn. During his long career, he has employed this intensity, along with flawless technique, to conquer virtually every summit of jazz and several commercial ones as well (it was Phil's unmistakable saxophone that graced Billy Joel's hit song "Just The Way You Are"). His ability to endure the shifting tides of the jazz life have made him a legend within the community of players the world over. True to form, when his home was destroyed by a fire recently, taking with it most of his personal momentos as well as his record collection, Phil managed to grab his horn as he fled the burning building and didn't miss a beat getting his group, which he has kept intact for more than a decade, to the next gig. In his own words, he has become the ultimate "jazz warrior."

Ben: Phil, you're known for the wide range of expression in your playing. It has such a "human" quality to it. Is there some secret to your approach to the saxophone?

Phil: I'm a lucky guy. My kid, I have a son, my only male heir, he's in his twenties, you know, and about a year ago he came over to the house and we were partying one night. And we had a good talk. And he said, "Pop, how do you keep your passion?" 'Cause he wanted to have some, too.

But I was passionately involved with music when I was twelve years old. I mean, when I found music, when I discovered the whole world of jazz, that was it. I was passionately involved, and that's never changed for me. I'm more passionate now about music, and I think I'm better equipped to express the passion. But when he asked me how do you keep it going, that I don't know. I think that's the hard part. You gotta be a little hard-headed to stay passionate in a . . . I don't dare use the word industry, but in a business that sort of ignores real feelings. If it can't be packaged, it ain't cool, you know?

Ben: That's a good point. Because we are in this business, and it seems that people who really succeed in it get further and further removed from that passion which drew them to the business in the first place.

Phil: I think you've got to be a passionate player. I think most of the cats are passionate. I mean, I appreciate what you're saying, but that's the great tradition of making music from the voice. It's got to mean something. Some of the cats, they forget the thrill they had the first time they sounded good. For whatever reason, maybe they've been sitting in the pit too long. I mean this can happen to a musician. It can happen to any way of life.

You see, I have the quintet, and I play jazz, and I have good friends like you who are supporting the music, and my kids are all grown, I've got no heavy nut. I got a lady who loves me and life is mellow. So now I can really get passionate. These little buns are not for sale as much as they used to be.

Ben: You once told me a funny thing, back when you were working with a quartet. You said, "Well, I've kept this quartet together for many years. And times are getting tough. So what we're going to do is go to a quintet." And then you said, "If times get really tough, we're going to a big band."

Phil: [Laughs.] Expand! Expand! It's the American way. Yeah, sure, why not?

No, it was an investment. I was quite aware of what I was doing. Because the quartet had been around for nine years or so. And we have a nice audience out there, contrary to what a lot of record companies might think. There is a very healthy audience out there of young people who love jazz. And they've been listening to us a long time. I thought it might be nice to expand. And originally I added Tom Harrell, because I think he is one of the finest talents in the world today. He's probably one of the finest musicians I've ever worked with, and I've worked with them all. This guy is quite special. Dizzy sat on stage through our whole concert in Germany—he never heard Tom before—and loved it. So I thought the audience was due for a treat.

Plus it gave the quartet new impetus. You know, new blood. I wasn't looking for a trumpet. I was looking for a musician of this caliber. Because I know I'm good. I have no false humility about being good. I have a certain standard to maintain, and this guy makes me do my homework, that's what I'm looking for. I'm not looking for a cat I can play better than. I'm looking for a cat who can blow *me* away so that I can maintain the challenge. A good healthy competitiveness. You can get complacent with a quartet, you're the only voice, you know. Now we're a band.

Ben: It's also a classic format, the two horns up front. The sound is well-established.

Phil: Yeah, it's classic. I'm going to bring the clarinet in a little more, too, so we're getting into more color areas. Once you have a double front line, you have a real band. A quartet is one thing, but five, with two horns, becomes more of an ensemble.

Ben: I guess that's the passionate approach to solving the problem.

Phil: Well, the music has still got to thrill me. I mean, I've got to be thrilled with my profession. I mean this. I love to go to work. I love coming into town to do this with you. Anything to do with music. I'm not too full of fire unless I'm involved with music. It's my hobby, my profession, it's what I do. Except build model airplanes and watch football.

Ben: You have also been involved in an interesting array of recordings recently. For example, not long ago you and the group worked with synthesizer expert Chris Swanson.

Phil: Yes, he's an old friend. A pure spirit. He probably utilizes the synthesizer better than anybody I know.

Ben: That record was also nominated for a Grammy in the category "best group" recording.

Phil: Which was interesting, because the record was done piecemeal. Everybody did their part one at a time. [Laughs.] We made the record with scotch tape, you know. So to come off sounding that cohesive speaks well about the arranger and the musicians involved, which was Hal Galper, Bill Goodwin and Steve Gilmore.

Ben: Now you have a reputation for being a totally acoustic player. You've avoided technology at all costs.

Phil: Yeah, I even record without microphones. [Laughs.]

Ben: [Laughs.] Oh, I didn't know that.

Phil: Yeah, it's zen, baby.

Ben: That gives new meaning to the idea of "direct to disc."

Phil: No, but that's kind of a bum rap, cats say, "Oh, man, you're so old fashioned." I mean, I had the first Veritone that Selmer came out with. It weighed about eighty pounds. I had the first one in Europe. Eddie Harris had the first one in the States. This goes back fifteen or sixteen years. Gordon Beck had the Hohner, and we were experimenting. I had the first Oberheim Ring Modulator. So I have done my homework, and I don't mean to imply with the present acoustic group that it's not music. It's a tool and I'm interested in it. As far as the music that the quintet plays, that's something else.

Ben: Many people see it as a confrontation between the old and the new, but really it's about the development of tools to further the music. It's all music and you've got to use what's there for you.

Phil: Well, it's bloody hard to play without microphones, I must say. It really is a challenge. The more you do it, and we've been doing it for eight or nine years . . .

Ben: We should explain that you often literally do without microphones when you perform live.

Phil: Whenever we work a club or a hall up to the size of fifteen hundred people—in Japan and Europe up to three thousand people in a good opera hall—we do it without any amplification whatsoever. Except for a bass amp for Mr. Gilmore. You need some sensitive souls to carry it off. It's different, and a lot of cats are starting to jump on it. Because you don't need a lot of microphones, especially in a club. If I can't get my sound from here to the bar, I'm in the wrong business, man. Back to selling storm windows, you know?

Ben: It's almost a question of having to educate the audience as well, because many people don't know how to listen to a piano that's not equal in volume to the drums.

Phil: Yeah, but they've all been in a spot somewhere, at a Christmas party, sitting around the piano, all singing acoustically. And having a good time. And the best music I ever heard was in Zoot's living room. You know, it was born in a brothel. It's not meant to play Yankee Stadium.

I think the cats are abusing the amplification thing. You know, the bass player's too loud. It used to be it was the drummer that was a drag, now it's the bass player. So now the drummer's got to be a drag to keep up with the drag bass player. And the piano player, he needs *two* microphones. And then you put a couple of horns on top of that and you have something fairly loud. And you call it an acoustic jazz group. It's very strange.

Ben: Getting back to this synthesizer record you did with Chris Swanson called *Piper at the Gates.* How did you put it together so that it was done in parts but sounded like a group effort?

Phil: The process was rather strange. What we did was, we did the initial tracks for this in Straudsberg [Pennsylvania]. We sat down and said, "We'll do a 'Rhythm' tune, we'll do this kind of tune," mostly standards, and we just played. I mean I just jammed. Not even a melody in some cases. And Chris took that back to his house and put all the horns on. Then he brought that back to us, the finished horns, and then we put the rhythm section back on. Because by then, what we'd done had been wiped out by layering and all that. So to get the quartet back up front of the big band, you've got to put the quartet back on. The first guy to go was Gilmore on bass. He did the whole album, all the tunes, bass parts. Then Bill on drums, then Galper. And then after me sitting around for two and a half days, I got a chance to go on top. It was kind of wild.

Ben: You said before that it was interesting this record was nominated for a Grammy as a group recording, because it was done in layers, but having heard you describe it, it seems that it was possible only because you are a functioning group and able to anticipate what the next guy is going to do.

Phil: We know each other so well that we can work that way, instinctively. I mean, the rhythm section was comping, and they hadn't heard my solo. But never the less, I know what they're doing there. I can feel it. The hardest thing to do was to not go with the machine. I insisted that the machine go with me.

Ben: Even though it was there first?

Phil: Well, you can't, because it won't budge. The rhythm is locked in. You just go over the top of it. I learned a lot about rhythm and stuff like that. The machine won't budge, but you can swing it. Just don't try to do what it does.

Ben: Don't try to push *it*.

Phil: Yeah, don't try to be mechanical with it, but play against it.

Ben: You know, the first time I heard the Billy Joel hit "Just The Way You Are," I said, "That's Phil Woods on saxophone, but I wonder who the singer is." The sound of your horn is so distinctive that it rivals some of the most well known singers for recognition.

Phil: You know, I've been playing this thing for so long. But it's nice to have a voice. I think I do have a voice. I think that's sort of a gift, too. I could always get a good tone. That's nature's gift. I have a natural embouchure and it has nothing to do with your music-making ability. Instrumentally, I think I was built to play the saxophone.

Now playing it well, that's something else. I always think of the great voices, like Bud Johnson and Zoot and Al and Clifford and Pres and Bird and Pete Brown, Sonny Stitt, I could always spot those guys. Or Bud Powell or Barry Harris. You can tell Tommy Flanagan from Hank Jones. I mean, if you really know the music you can say "that's him." But that doesn't happen when they first leave Detroit or Massachusetts or wherever. It takes a long time to develop that stuff. So I think style is really a tribute to survivability more than anything else.

In the old days when [Gene] Quill and I would do big band dates, we couldn't tell who was playing lead or not. There was a whole school of alto players who had a more or less similar approach. I just happen to be the only one left. [Laughs.] Not really, but you'd be surprised, the rate of attrition, for one reason or another, in the music business. A lot of guys don't stay at it for forty years. It's true.

Ben: But there is still something very special about your personal voice on the instrument. It's so expressive . . .

Phil: Yeah, well, when you play "Harlem Nocturne" five times a night at the Nut Club, where they pass out hammers as you come in, you gotta sing, baby, or those strippers will kill you. You gotta be cool. [Laughs.]

But expressiveness, yeah, I know nothing but expressiveness. I don't understand, I mean, there are some cold fish out there who think they're musicians. I mean, there are some Berklee graduates, or North Texas graduates, fill in your own school, who are very fine players, whether it be legit or jazz. But play me a whole note. Play me two whole notes. Play me the first bar of "The Man I Love" or "I Can't Get Started." Just play me the pickups. They don't know what you're talking about. I mean they may play the notes or whatever, but they got no idea...

First you have to know the literature. America has such a rich ballad tradition. My dream is to know all of Gershwin and Porter and Arlen and Harry Warren. Johnny Mercer and Hoagy Carmichael. Well, you know, Ben...

Ben: When you talk about knowing the literature, you're not limiting yourself to knowing the lyrics...

Phil: No. Like listen to Hodges play. I listen to Benny Carter and I listen to Cannonball, and Louis Armstrong. Without Louis we wouldn't have any expressiveness at all. Jazz expressiveness. You know what I'm saying, when to bend, when to growl. You know, the whole jazz vocabulary, which most modern American composers are ignoring. Thank you very much, fellows. They're writing saxophone sonatas and they don't use anything of what Coltrane left us and what Bird left us. Saxophonic type of things. All the little devices, the harmonic things, or slap-tongue.

The first cat I saw, when I really felt I wanted to be on the road with a band, it was at the Broadway Theater in Springfield, with Duke Ellington's band, the lights went down, all blue, and Johnny Hodges stepped out and he played I think it was "Mood To Be Wooed," and man, I said "That's for me." I still go to Rabbit if you want to talk about alto passion. Bird used to call him the Lily Pons of the alto. A lot of people thought that Bird was putting Rabbit down. But it was au contraire. Bird loved Lily Pons. He just meant it was so beautiful.

Ben: You mentioned Cannonball, who really was a great ballad player, as well as a man who could burn. He had that passion.

Phil: Yes indeed. I remember the night he came to town. He sat in at the Bohemia with Oscar Pettiford's group. I was working at the Nut Club, that strip joint in the Village at the time, and Jackie McLean was working around the corner somewhere. I was on my break and Jackie said, "Come here a minute." And, you know, Bird had just died and Jackie and I were sort of with the same label and kind of thinking now we're gonna get all the glory and the bread and the broads, you know. And he looked a little dejected. He said, "Phil, come here." And he took me over to the

Bohemia where Cannonball was sitting in. We just sat there, listened to a couple of tunes. Then we went outside, and he looked at me and I looked at him and we just said, "Oh shit." [Laughs.] Cause he was the baddest thing we'd ever heard.

Nobody does Cannonball. It's a funny kind of rhythmical approach. It's riveting, it's intense kind of eighth notes. It's not choppy, but it's very highly articulated. And the cats do not try to do that. It's too hard.

But I wish the cats would pick up a little bit of that. A little of Rabbit, a little bit of Benny Carter. And mix it all up. Whatever. Take the gifts, make them all into your package.

Ben: Well, no matter how hard they try, they're never going to come out sounding like Phil Woods are they?

Phil: I got a lot of licks to steal yet. I'm not through stealing. [Laughs.]

Ben: I initiated this discussion wondering if I would discover the inner secrets of the Phil Woods sound. But what I'm discovering is that the inner secrets of the Phil Woods sound is what came before Phil Woods.

Phil: Oh yes. Oh yes.

Ben: So there is no secret here.

Phil: No. Just a lot of hard work. And copying. I mean that seriously, copying. I'm still working on that Hodges gliss, where he goes from the top F all the way down, without breaking. It will take me a while, but I'll get it. I'm coming late to that type of vocabulary, but it's there to be absorbed and I did all my bebop studies, now I want to get into that lyric thing that the older cats have. They understood the space of a melody. And the young cats, you can't blame the teachers, either, if the young cats ain't listening right. Just listen to Ben Webster, on a slow one, or Gene Ammons play a ballad. Or Louis Armstrong, I mean goodness gracious, such passion.

Ben: You yourself have had a long, colorful recording career . . .

Phil: A bizarre career.

Ben: A colorful career . . .

Phil: I mean, I am so bored; people always say "I can't find your records." And every time we go somewhere, you can always find the old bad ones, a few that I'd rather they can't find, they're always there.

Ben: It sounds like you're angry about this.

Phil: I'm bugged, I'm real bugged about it. It's like with RCA . . . well, it's not totally RCA's fault. They're so big they don't know what's happening. A man I really have respect for is Bruce Lundvall, who said if you don't keep the jazz thing, I'm gone. And split. You don't have many guys like that. A lot of these guys are summer soldiers. They talk a mean ballgame, but if the boss says, "Hey, you got to drop the jazz line," they'll drop it. I think you've got to say, if you're into the jazz business, you drop my line, you drop me. I'm gonna stand for something.

We've won Grammy's for companies. They say "Jazz doesn't sell." So the *Show Boat* album we did for RCA won a Grammy that year. And six months later, it's off the market, withdrawn, cut out. They wouldn't do that to any other form of music. They wouldn't do it to pop and they certainly wouldn't do it to classical. But they do it to jazz.

But I understand. They're talking mega-bucks, and I'm trying to fill a club with a hundred people.

Ben: Mose Allison told me that putting out a record is like putting out an expensive calling card. You have to have one in order to work.

Phil: And you can't compete with these *Guinness Book of Records* groups. You can't compete with The Stones and these cats who can do three shows in Yankee Stadium. And we're sort of asked to compete with them.

Ben: We're all in the same business.

Phil: We're in the same business, exactly. And it ain't fair.

Ben: Our tapes go to the same place, they stamp out the same plastic, they put it in the same cardboard, they ship to the same distributors, they're bought in the same outlets . . .

Phil: And we've probably reached the peak, I think, as far as my little band is concerned. A club can only pay so much. My band is probably making as much as any band. That's all they can pay. Otherwise the kids can't afford it. So where do you go? I mean, it ain't just more, more, more money. Some people think it is. But I'd like to just keep it going, you know.

Ben: Jazz musicians, generally, they're trying to make a living, not a killing.

Phil: Yeah, but I'm not going to produce any more records with my own bread. I'll never get my kitchen finished that way. [Laughs.]

Ben: How have you been approaching your recent studio recordings? How do you keep the "liveness"?

Phil: Well, we approach it like a live set. We do five tunes, take a break, come back and do five more. Over a two-day period, then pick the best stuff. It's so much fun for me to have another horn. Musically, it's challenging to match up intonation and phrasing and all these musical values as well as the jazz part. But ensemble-wise, you really have to work. Pitch is a bitch. When it's right, there's nothing like it. You know, most jazz groups are not really in tune. And being perfectly in tune, you get a great cutting. So a lot of the charts have evolved from just messing about on the bandstand.

Ben: It seems that most of what you do on records has its roots in live performance. These days, the opposite is usually the case. Most musicians learn the music in the studio and then try to reproduce it live. Actually, there was an interesting twist on this on a Dave Sanborn record not long ago, where he brought an audience into a studio and then did "live" versions of previous studio material. The album was called *Straight to the Heart*. Do you know it?

Phil: I don't understand the live part of that date.

I mean, I was lucky, I was perched historically when the LP came out. I was a studio man in the late '50s and '60s, when music was music and machines were rather new, and a splice was a big deal. Now the whole studio scene is so different, I wouldn't even know it.

It's an old idea though. Didn't Tom Waits do that on one of his albums? Set the studio up like a club and invite people in. But I don't know. With that kind of music [Sanborn] it's hard to tell the difference. I bet he would play it the same way whether the audience was there or not. And he's a very passionate player. But there's no real dialogue. I don't think the audience is such an integral part of the performance. Everybody just listens, but you don't follow the improv or the development. I mean it's rather packaged and nice to listen to, but, you know. In fact, with that kind of music, if *I* was at the record date, I'd talk through it. And drink, carry on, make a little noise.

Ben: I guess the difference might be that when you make a live version of a studio concept, everybody has parts to play.

Phil: It's a different kind of music. But I do like the idea of having an audience in the studio, even if it's just a few people. Because recording, for me, I mean the red light still makes us all cowards. I've never gotten over that. I always know when I'm recording, and I've been doing it for years. I don't know of anybody . . . it's like if you don't get a little nervous about going on stage, you know, you wanna do good, you gotta get up for it. Same way when that red light's on. It's very rare when you can just hit that completely relaxed groove, you know. And then you're probably so relaxed you sound rotten. Maintaining the discipline and the excitement, that's tough. Once you know that thing is on, it's hard to divide yourself. That's why I like *live*. Because you never think about recording when you're live.

Ben: One of my favorite recent albums, and one that was nominated for a Grammy, was the one that Pepper Adams recorded live at Fat Tuesday's in New York.

Phil: Yeah, Pepper is a bebopper to his socks.

Ben: Recording that one live at Fat Tuesday's must have been a real challenge, because the stage there is so narrow. There's not much depth, so the band has to line up in a row . . .

Phil: It's like recording in a bowling alley. [Laughs]

Ben: I get a sense of this listening to Pepper's record, too. The rhythm section sounds a little disjointed. How much does the physical set-up of the band affect the live recording?

Phil: I don't really know too much about that stuff. I like the notes. I mean, I just listen to the notes. I'm not that much of a fussbudget. I remember carrying around my 78's and my windup record player, you know what I mean. I'm just delighted when both speakers work. I think you can overdo that stuff.

Nevertheless, with compact discs and all the new digital stuff coming, this is where it's going to be at. Because the equipment will be able to tell a real record from a phony record. The best sounding stuff will be a live recording. An acoustically sound recording, not something that's been messed with.

Ben: Captured rather than manufactured music?

Phil: Yeah, and that will be the standard by which people buy records. Which means only the cats who can play from the intro to the coda will get the work. Well . . . I have a lot of dreams. But the equipment could help. I mean, look at cable. Eventually, there'll be a channel for everybody's needs. If there's a dollar in it, somebody's gonna sell it to you. Or buying records through your home computer. That way, you can bypass the accountants who say it's not selling. This eliminates distribution problems, you don't have to sell a lot in order to keep it in the catalog. It could be a positive thing.

Ben: Pepper Adams had the same problem you've mentioned. He often complained about his records getting cut out. And he never got the critical acclaim he deserved. He was such a passionate player, but his playing also had what I think of as a "literary" quality. He sounded well-read, you know what I mean?

Phil: He was. He spoke several languages. He knew wine. He was a warrior. He never compromised. He always played full out. Pepper would never skate. He always had that intense passion from his big horn. You don't hear too many people trying to do a Pepper Adams. Or Harry Carney. You know, when you get real good, you get the big sax.

Ben: When I asked Pepper about this literary aspect of his playing, he said "Well of course it sounds that way. I read. We all read." He said, a lot of people never knew that Charlie Parker was interested in politics and interested in art, and in the greater culture . . .

Phil: Sure, he painted, he wrote poetry . . .

Ben: People just assumed that Bird was only interested in getting high, eating and women.

Phil: I remember reading when I was a kid, before I left home, that Charlie Parker loved Schoenberg. So I went to the library and got the album and went to my den and put this stuff on. My parents thought I had really gone off the deep end. Because that's a heavy twelve-tone number. I must say, I was a bit confused. You know, Bird likes this? But when somebody you admire says something like that, and you dig where he's at, you follow through.

And there's been a great intellectual movement, a lot of information in this jazz community. I mean, Dave Tough was a brilliant guy. And Eddie Condon was a pretty good writer. These guys were smart cookies. You have to be fairly intelligent to survive in this weird business, where the brightest guy in the room, except for the musicians, is the club owner.

Ben: Who was smart enough to hire the band.

Phil: Well, I mean this guy ain't smart enough to be a hip criminal. He can't be ripping off the Rolling Stones, so he's got to mess with us jazzers, you know, nickle-dime stuff. A failed con guy. The guys who buy and sell us are not the great people, I find. Let's face it. They can afford Picassos. They just don't know what they are.

Ben: But for the musicians, if you want to play this music, you must let your mind range into all sorts of areas. It's not just a question of focussing on what a hit record is today.

Phil: Right, but if you want to work, you've got to get along with these other dummies who don't read. But thank God, on the bandstand most of the cats are pretty bright. I mean, in my band, Goodwin is a voracious reader. We can't carry enough books for my band. And I don't think we're that special. And sitting on a bus long enough, reading is about the only way to pass the time if you want to survive.

Ben: That's right. In days past, when riding the bus was a big part of playing jazz, it was literature and humor that got you through, and not necessarily in that order.

Phil: My first real bus—except for The McGuire Sisters and a few strange ones, you know, like Dick Hayman, the harmonica player—was the Birdland Allstar tour of '56. It was Basie's band, Sarah Vaughan, Al Hibbler, Bud Powell, Lester Young. I was with a group with Al Cohn, Conte Candoli, Kenny Dorham. I mean, you got on a bus with these guys, and you learned so much. These cats, they knew how to laugh to pass the time. There was never this agonizing artist stuff, you know, like, "God, what a rotten President," "Oh, life is terrible . . . check the stock reports." You know what I mean? They had a passion about the life. No phony bitching. And everybody knew what was happening. But within the confines of the bus. You'd leave that stuff off the bandstand, man.

You know, I don't like politicized music, message music. There are project albums and all that stuff, but generally, that's a failed form. I mean, just look at the Polonaise by Chopin. Rotten. [Laughs]. But whenever musicians try to . . . except Beethoven, he could get away with it . . . but generally, we should just play our horns and let the music speak. I mean, Bird wasn't even trying to be a revolutionary. Not in the term of the barricades and stuff. But he changed the world with his music. And he changed every musician he touched. He certainly changed my life. Just reading about him in *Down Beat*.

I wonder what the kids are getting from *Down Beat* now? I haven't seen Schoenberg mentioned in years. For whatever reason, it seems to be a rather intellectual desert out there. They go to college, but they still don't read. I did a poll in my house with teenagers. I said, "What are they teaching you in school?" And they knew nothing. And these are my kids, they're supposed to be hip. So it's hard for me to indict society or indict the schools. You've got to do it yourself. You got to read certain people. When I started reading, I read everything by Thomas Wolfe. I loved Wolfe, so I read everything of his. I loved Hemingway, so I read everything of his. I loved F. Scott Fitzgerald, so I read everything of his.

You don't just pick up a book occasionally. You know, again, it's passion. Passion.

Ben: Yes. Even kids today who read science fiction think the book *Dune* is a treatment of a movie. There's no sense of permanent history. History is whatever was a top-forty record last week.

Phil: Well, I mean, at best they only go back as far as Coltrane in their jazz history. But isn't that the wonderful part? Through all of this being ignored, to produce such a strong, vital music that the world has taken note. I mean, everybody in the world would like to sound like Americans. I don't mean just jazz. I mean American musicians are considered now to be the best.

And you can't get a pearl without some sand. You know, we got a lot of sand. I'm wondering if we were more culturally aware, and we were so fair . . . well, if we were so fair, we wouldn't have brought all those people out of Africa, you know what I mean?

* * *

Johnny Griffin (April, 1988)

Tenor saxophonist Johnny Griffin is known as the "Little Giant" because, for a man of small physical stature, he casts an enormous shadow over the jazz firmament. His style, technique and attitude place him among that select group of players who emerged during the heyday of bebop, carrying the flame of Parker, Gillespie, et. al., and he remains a vibrant practitioner and spiritual guru of the idiom today. A "jazz warrior" who has managed to keep the fire in his playing through years of constant global traveling, it is a sad fact that his music receives scant attention in today's media. However, it is easy to predict that as his work, both present and past, with such legends as Thelonious Monk, continues to spread the word, Johnny Griffin will ultimately be recognized as one of the music's true giants.

Ben: One of my favorite lines, and I've used it too many times, I'm embarrassed to say, comes from a man I refer to as a great philosopher of jazz, Mr. Johnny Griffin. The line is, "Jazz is music made by and for people who have chosen to feel good *in spite of* conditions."

Johnny: Yeah, that's it. It's pretty much the way I see it.

Ben: It was a line that I heard you say at a gig when a lot of people were shouting at you to hurry up and go over here and go over there and do this and do that, and you were totally relaxed and in control of the space, and you got up on stage and that's what you said. It was great. Is that the philosophy you live by?

Johnny: Yes. Well, to me, that's the basis of the magnetism that makes this music so accepted in all quarters of this planet, all places. Because, you know, jazz music actually is an international language, so you find people enjoying this music, say, in diverse places like Japan, even in India and wherever—places where people have no ideas or contact with what's happening here in America, only what they have read or seen in music or things like that. But yet still they can feel the magnetism of this music, possibly because they have the same feelings in their own countries, wherever they are.

Ben: Your personal story is fascinating in that you began here in Chicago and have traveled and lived throughout the world, an ambassador of jazz.

You got your start at a very famous music program, run by Captain Walter Diet, when you attended Du Sable High School. Many musicians came out of his program, including, to name a couple, Nat King Cole and Richard Davis. What was that program about?

Johnny: Well, I think that program was about Captain Diet. The man himself, having the talent, even being the strict disciplinarian, because he could take these kids off the street and mold them into young people with dignity. Because he was like a surrogate father to these young kids whose families may be at the lower end of the economic scale, from poor to middle class, like that, at the time I went to school. And he had a unique, well, maybe not unique, but a different way of approaching music, because he really made you learn the foundations of classical music to begin with, or just learn music from the basics, in a class, whereas usually to have that kind of training you have to normally have private instruction. For instance, when I started at Du Sable High School, I wanted to play tenor saxophone. The first thing he informed me was that tenor saxophone was too large an instrument for me to play, as I was only about 4′6″ or something. The damn thing weighed about 70 pounds. And in the second place he informed me that if I wanted to be in the school band, or to have him as an instructor, I would have to learn clarinet, which I didn't want to play clarinet.

Ben: Absolutely not.

Johnny: I mean, I had no desire to be another Benny Goodman, or Artie Shaw, or whatever, you know, but he let me know that the clarinet was actually the father of the reed instruments, and if I wanted to play in the school band I would have to learn clarinet first. Then as I advanced, he *might* allow me to play saxophone, alto saxophone, in the booster band, which was the school dance orchestra, *if* I had advanced enough on clarinet over a certain period of years.

Ben: Years, eh?

Johnny: Years! So, you know, actually, we started the classes; he made sure that everyone could read music. I mean, he used to walk around the floor counting and sub-dividing time, and before we were allowed to play our instruments, we had to buzz the mouthpieces. Now actually, he never sat down to teach us, because he had helpers. Like, there was a young lady by the name of Geraldine Springs who actually taught me clarinet. But she had been his student earlier. So that was like a beginners' band, which would have maybe upwards of 130 students, which would last for, say, four or five months. And if you were advanced enough, you were allowed to play in the second concert band, very light stuff, but then that band was about 100, say about 120 pieces. Then after that year was out, if you were advanced enough, then you could play in the main concert band, which was around 115 students. And which went into heavier music. Classical music.

Ben: You obviously got your hands on an alto before it was done.

Johnny: Yeah, well what happened, I remember I had a newspaper route, and I bought this old Wurlitzer . . . "Gee, dad, it's a Wurlitzer!" . . . I bought this old Wurlitzer, and meanwhile I was learning the clarinet very well. He'd start me on like third clarinet, and after I got in the concert band, I worked up to solo clarinet, but just when I thought he was going to allow me to play saxophone, the oboist graduated, and he wanted to do a program with some Ravel in it. Especially he wanted to do "Bolero," which the oboe and English horn plays a prominent part. So I had to learn those instruments. I didn't even know what an oboe was, you know, which actually saved my life later on in the Military, when they . . . well, that's another story. Anyway, but I got my hands on this old alto . . .

Ben: Now I want to hear that story! How did the oboe save your life?

Johnny: Well, I got drafted in 1951 during the Korean War. I got drafted in Chicago, with seven other black kids on the South Side. I was actually trying to evade the draft, 'cause I had registered in New York, only when they called in New York, I ran to Chicago. And they called me and they weren't going to let me off. And finally, I wound up back in Chicago, and they sent a representative of the establishment [laugh] . . . told me that if I didn't report by Tuesday, they were going to incarcerate me.

Ben: Give you a different kind of time.

Johnny: Yeah! Very . . . Yeah! No swinging in *that* time. Anyway, I got drafted, and first they wanted to send me to Ft. Chaffe, Arkansas, on the train, which I'd had some experience in the South that I didn't want to have repeated. Because I didn't agree with the Southern philosophy from Blacks and Whites. So I and the six other cats from Chicago decided we weren't going South. So we told the Lieutenant in charge of us that we refused to go to Camp Chaffe, Arkansas, and that was that. In which we caused a couple of riots down in Ft. Sheridan, right out of Chicago, here.

So the Captain looked up our MOS's and everything, saying: "Well, we find that you qualify to go and train in Hawaii." In Hawaii, you know, everybody sees Hawaii, Wow! All these Hula girls and paradise and the Pacific and lovely weather, Waikiki Beach and I'm thinking: Yeah! Eight weeks of basic training. Eight weeks B.T.U., Band Training Unit, for the musicians. Yeah, I've got it figured out fantastic. I'm gonna have a ball. Not knowing they didn't have a band training unit in Hawaii. Hawaii was the fodder: F-O-D-D-E-R. That's fodder, Cannon Fodder, for Korea. The 45th Regimental Combat Team trained there, and it was sustaining a casualty rate of 75 percent killed and wounded. But I didn't know this at the time. So we volunteered for Hawaii, so I had eight weeks Basic Training, eight weeks Advanced Infantry Training, and a couple of weeks with some light artillery stuff and demolition. And when my battalion graduated, my orders were cut to go to FECOM, which is the Far Eastern Command, to Japan, to Korea.

Well, it so happened that when the battalion was graduated, on the bulletin board in the orderly room they put up a notice that if you had any talent or you wanted to participate in the entertainment program at the Officers Club for the Officers of the graduating battalion, you could sign up and be on the program. So I knew some of the musicians in the battalion. I got 'em together, we rehearsed a few little arrangements, and proceeded to go on the program and blow the Army dance-band off the stage. 'Cause these cats were like a bunch of refugees anyways . . . sad! The Colonel got drunk, and jumped up and said, "Alright, put that boy, that boy, and that boy in the band, that boy, that boy." But first they had to go and look and see who qualified, through our records, you know, because you had to read music. You know, you couldn't just play by ear, 'cause at least then you had to read. So they saw my MOS, where I had played oboe, and this was exactly what the bandmaster wanted, an oboist. So he put me in the band.

Meanwhile, the other six gentlemen that went with me, went to Korea, and they were writing me, and they all got killed. This was in the time when MacArthur was talking about home for Christmas, and a million Chinese came across the Yallu River, and chased the Americans all the way back down to the bottom of South Korea. And those boys got killed, every one of them.

Ben: "In spite of conditions . . ."

Johnny: Yes indeed.

Ben: Well, you got your hands on an alto, and my favorite story, actually, which I've read about, but I've never heard you tell it, was the story of joining Hamp's band and showing up with an alto and finding out that's not what you were supposed to be playing.

Johnny: Yeah, well that happened, because in my graduating year at Du Sable, possibly in February or March, Hamp came through town, and he picked up Jay Peters, the late Jay Peters, who was a very wonderful tenor saxophonist from Chicago. But anyway, when Hamp passed through town, he came by Du Sable H.S. and sat in with some members of the school band, which I happened to be one of. Herbie Fields was there, Milt Buckner was there, who else? Anyway, we had a little jam session in the school auditorium.

And when Hamp came back in June, at the end of the June, to play the Regal Theater, Jay Peters had been drafted into the service. But I didn't know this. My class graduated, I think, June 25 or 27, I can't remember right now. But anyway, we took off, three friends, and we went up in the state of Michigan to a cabin, and we were partying, like over the weekend. And the band starts at the Regal, like, on a Thursday, I think, yeah. Then when I came back home Sunday, my mother was all . . . 'cause nobody knew where we were, we'd just slipped off, terrible kids, really . . . my mother told me, "Say, Lionel Hampton's been lookin' for you." I said, "What? You know, what's happening?" She rushed me and displayed me out and sent me to the Regal Theater. So I showed up with my alto saxophone, of course, 'cause that's what I was playing. And Hamp just threw me out in the stage with Arnett Cobb, who played "Flyin' Home" or whatever, you know.

So I finished the week and they hired me to come with the band. Well, nobody said anything to me, you know, they just hired me with the band, so I packed up and left the next Thursday or Friday to go play the RKO Theater in Toledo, Ohio. Well that Friday when the band was opening up I was walking out to the stage with my alto, you know, and Gladys Hampton met me and said, "Johnny, where you going with that alto?" I said, "Well, I'm gettin' ready to go play!" "Yeah, but you're playing tenor saxophone in this band." Which was a big surprise to me. I mean, it was the first I'd heard of it. But I was playing alto more or less like a tenor anyway, because I was growlin' on it like a Ben Webster, and kinda sounded like Prez, or whatever, at that time, you know. So I immediately left, 'cause there was nothing to be found in Toledo, Ohio, this being the year 1945, and the war was going on, you know, 'cause nobody was making instruments, all those factories were making weapons. And so I left for Chicago and found an old Conn and rejoined the band like two days later. And that was the start of me playing tenor.

Ben: And you never looked back!

Johnny: No! 'Cause this was the instrument I wanted to play.

Ben: The first recording that I know of you being on, I suspect there might be earlier ones, was a record that was reissued on Atlantic recently, and it's an anthology. It's called *Atlantic Honkers*. I don't think they're talking about you personally, but it's a Rhythm and Blues collection, and it's got a cut on there that features yourself and Joe Morris. It's called "Low Groovin'."

Johnny: "Low Groovin'," yeah, I think that's George Freeman's tune, the guitarist, who also went to high school with me.

Ben: It was recorded in 1947. You must have been about nineteen years old. The record sounds like a bunch of kids from Chicago, out on the road, having a good time.

Johnny: Exactly!

Ben: Was that the philosophy? I mean I've heard you talk about the spirit of that time, that you carried with you.

Johnny: It was strictly a party. Strictly a party. That band and . . . Well, see Joe Morris was a trumpet player with Lionel Hampton's band, and, actually, I quit the band twice, trying to get him out to Hampton's band, 'cause I joined Hamp's band, like I said, in June '45, and I left the band in December of '46. And they enticed me back into the band, because Arnett Cobb left, I think it was March 1947. Arnett Cobb left the band, and then I took his chair, and a saxophone player, I think he was from Milwaukee, around there someplace, a young big white boy, what's his name? Kenny Mann, took my seat that I had. And anyway, I stayed with the band from March 'til May. They signed me to a seven year contract. And I lasted exactly March 'til May. [Laughs.] I couldn't stand it anymore.

Ben: Like being back in the Army?

Johnny: No, no, you know, but Hamp, Hamp had a fabulous library, I mean, because everybody wrote for him. But we would only rehearse the tunes and never play them. Because we'd always wind up playing "Hamp's Boogie-Woogie," "Hey Bob-a-Re-Bop," and "Flyin' Home." We must of had 60,000 arrangements of "Flyin' Home," and every time we played it, we'd play it different. But it's the same thing, you know, and at this time I was very enthusiastic about this new music I'd been hearing from Bird and Dizzy and Fats and, you know, and the cats. This was what I wanted to play. And all the time Hamp was telling me, "You're the greatest, you're the greatest!" But I knew what was happening with me, you know.

So he had me with this seven year contract. I said, "This is impossible. I'm not, I can't . . . for seven years, I'm finished." So I stayed two months and quit. And Hamp tried to get me put out of the union, you know, and I was writing rebuttals to the union. You know, he was talking about his contract, which he did have a contract. But they slipped up. They was supposed to give me some publicity in certain places, which was in the contract, and I didn't get this publicity, so I called back, and said I was automatically cancelled out, you know, blah, blah, blah, so finally they just cut me loose. Finally.

Ben: So you and Joe Morris had this band, but it sounded like you weren't playing a whole lot of bebop. Mostly R&B.

Johnny: Well actually, when the band started, the tunes that we were playing were bebop. But what you hear, like this, from Atlantic Records, was really the blues. We had made other records that were never released, something on Aladdin which was never released, and maybe some other company, maybe, I can't remember. OK Records or something. At any rate, this is a date done, like you said, for Atlantic Records.

I would like to say that we started Atlantic Records. Herb Abramson and Marian Abramson and Ahmet Ertegun, who were the original owners, and none of them had any money. Ahmet had just been working in a record shop in Washington D.C. Nesuhi was still in Turkey somewhere, and we had to pay their hotel rent. And now you know how big Atlantic is!

Ben: The band paid their rent?

Johnny: We paid their rent. They didn't have anything. Yeah.

Ben: Well, you must have thousands and thousands of shares of Warner Brothers stock today, then, I suppose.

Johnny: [Laughs.] Yeah, you better believe it, you see how rich I'm lookin'.

Ben: You look great. [More laughter.]

Johnny: I have nothing. These guys are multi-millionaires. They own all kind of sports teams and whatever. But that's the way it goes.

But anyway, they insisted for these dates to be on a rhythm and blues thing, and finally, in the end, I left Joe Morris because of this. Because he wanted to make some money, which, okay, is good. He discovered some singer, like Fay Adams or something, on the tours in the South, and he did make some hit records. But I had gone. But the Chicago band only lasted one year, 'cause we went back to New York and reorganized, and finally wound up with, like, Philly Joe Jones and Percy Heath and Nelson Boyd, you know. And then we had Leo Parker, Lucky Thompson would be in the band, not to stay in the band, but to sit in. And we began playing arrangements of Monk's tunes and Bud's stuff, and Elmo's stuff, which was very fast at that time.

Ben: Actually your association with Monk, from that fateful stint in 1958 at the Five Spot in New York, is how most people came across Johnny Griffin. Everybody talks about the '57, '58 period when Monk was at the Five Spot, and that period really changed not only the way people looked at Monk but the way people looked at music.

Johnny: Yeah, 'cause that's like when they really discovered him. Because at first, in '57, he had Coltrane, Wilbur Ware and Shadow Wilson in the band. That was the year I was playing with the Jazz Messengers, with Art Blakey. And the next year I played with Monk, with Roy Haynes on drums and Ahmad Abdul Mallack on bass.

Ben: The album *Thelonious In Action*, which was recorded in 1958 at The Five Spot, is still a good seller on Riverside Records. Your playing on that album was still close to the blues. Really, everybody who plays with Monk says something or other about the blues tradition, when you work with him. Or at least, which is almost the same sort of thing, about being left to your own devices.

Johnny: Oh, you're very much left to your own devices, you know, playing Monk's music with Monk accompanying, it's something else. Now you can play Monk's music with other musicians, and it's fantastic, of course, 'cause all of his music is completely different than the norm for compositions are concerned. Monk is more or less in the style of playing like Billy Strayhorn's music. Similar to that in scope; resolutions or harmonic colors, the same. But playing with Monk, playing his music, with himself playing the piano, that is an *experience*.

I found it difficult at times, I mean, DIFFICULT. I enjoying playing with him, enjoying playing music, but when I'm playing my solos, for instance, the way his comping is so strong, playing his own music, that it's almost like you're in a padded cell. I mean, trying to express yourself, because his music, with him comping, is so overwhelming, like it's almost like you're trying to break out of a room made of marshmallows. [Laughs.] What I mean...

Ben: The more you fight it the more you get caught?

Johnny: You said it... Yeah! You know, it's like when they said the Japanese invaded China, they could only get so far because so many millions of people and so much space, they could never, you know, really conquer this place. So, like, what I would do is call "strollers," and Monk would immediately stop playing the piano and go to the bar and bring us both a drink. And I'm just playing with Ahmad and Roy Haynes. And he'd come on back in when it's time for his solo, or maybe he might start playing near the end of my solo, something like that. But I mean, it was really difficult for me, because, I mean, I had certain things that I wanted to express, and playing Monk's music, some of his tunes, especially like "Comin' on the Hudson," some of his other tunes that you must play exactly the color that he's putting down, laying down on the piano. Any deviation, one note off, and you sound like you're playing another tune, or you're not paying attention to what's going on. And it's so evident. At least that's the way I felt. There's no space. And his sense of rhythm is something else too.

Ben: That's really ironic, to hear how boxed-in you felt, in that he leaves you so much space on the surface, a lot of open areas for improvisation.

Johnny: Yes, but then it seems like he put his hands right down just where you least expect it. Or if you're really sensitive to what's going on around you, and if you're pretty strong in your own way, it seems like it can cause, not friction, but it can cause a little... you know, you need some elbow space. Like you're sitting on an airplane riding in the tourist class and the cat sittin' next to you is kinda fat, and there's a fat one on the other side of you, and when they start eating, you ain't got no space to put your own elbows. But I must say, it is one of the greatest experiences I've ever had in my life, to play with Thelonious. Not only that he's my favorite musician, his personality, his humor, especially, 'cause I knew him, like I said, in the '40s.

In fact, after meeting Elmo Hope, I met Bud and Monk, and these three guys hung out together. I mean, those three, they're all pianists of course, and they allowed me to run with them all the time. In fact, they'd be comin' and pick me up and take me with them. I don't know why, 'cause it just happened that I happened to know a little bit about the piano and I was always trying to see what they were doing. I didn't want to play like the other saxophonists, so I'd spend my time with the keyboard, with the pianists and the trumpet players, like Fats Navarro, Kenny Durham, or Dizzy when I had the chance. And I suppose I played with Joe Morris and Benny Harris, you know, so that the main thing for me was the music, and I figured I could learn much more by looking at the piano, which I had a little training in when I was a kid. And I could see everything like that. To me the piano was the whole orchestra, and everything was there. So being around Thelonious, and being amazed at his concept, of his composing and his sense of rhythm, and then being overwhelmed by the fire that Bud Powell could play with. And Elmo, which is a different way, but Elmo and Bud were like twins. Really. But Bud, I called Bud a thumper because he'd thump the keys very strongly. Elmo played in a lighter way. But to me, that was like my higher education in music, being with those three pianists.

Ben: That maybe explains a little bit the speed that you approach the instrument with.

Johnny: Oh, I'm just nervous. [Laughs.]

Ben: But it was a time when saxophone players, it seems . . . well of course, Bird was playing a lot of notes. But there was a whole other tradition of playing the saxophone, which I've heard you do as well, where you're "soft and warm and furry," whatever you call it, you have a song title like that . . .

Johnny: Well, yeah! Soft and warm and furry? What are you talking about? That's part of my pornographic suite.

Ben: Your pornographic suite?

Johnny: "Soft and Furry."

Ben: That's it.

Johnny: Yeah, yeah! No, that comes from, you see my first masters were actually Johnny Hodges, Ben Webster. Although I was playing alto saxophone, I tried to emulate Ben Webster. Because if I played a ballad, I tried to do lip slurs like Johnny Hodges, when I was a kid, you know, and Ben Webster was doing the same thing with tenor saxophone.

Actually, Johnny Hodges and Ben Webster were one in their conception of playing. Really, I didn't realize it then, 'til later on I spent some time with Ben, when Ben came to live in Europe, after a lot of time, and he was at my house, and I was speaking with him about Kansas City and the old days. And he'd told me. Ben was a real story teller. Now he could really tell you a story, you know. Be about when he grew up, he learned his music through Mr. Young, Lester Young's father, and he was staying at the house, and that's where he learned how to play. And how Prez used to take him on his gigs, and he liked the way Ben comped on the piano. And all these things. It's a pity I didn't have a working tape machine at the time, 'cause those stories about Kansas City, and the things that Don Byas told me, too, because he came from Oklahoma into Kansas City all the time. I mean, such fantastic things to have learned, to be around these masters, you know.

Because these cats were really my masters; to me, the greatest sounds ever. Like Don Byas, he was like Art Tatum on saxophone. The way that he used his harmonic intelligence, so to speak, you know, and the beauty of his smoothness, how fast he could play, and so smooth, like velvet. And Ben's big sound, although Don Byas had a big sound too, but Ben's sound was so warm and enveloping and, you know, Ben could play one note, and you could play one hundred notes, and he'd get more effect out of one note than you'd get out of one hundred.

Ben: Like Monk...

Johnny: Like Monk!

Ben: Let's talk a little bit about the record you made after you left Monk's band, which came out on Riverside and was called *Johnny Griffin and the Big Soul Band*. I remember getting it when it was a new record, when it came out in 1960. I loved the version of "Wade In The Water" that combined gospel and jazz in a big band. It was a different thing.

Johnny: Well, it was an idea to do some Negro spirituals, and at the time we were bending the idea around, and I'd see Orrin Keepnews over at Riverside, and he'd say, okay, it was a good idea to them, too. You know, and I had Norman Simmons from Chicago, a piano player and arranger, a very good arranger. And I knew Norman, and how his feelings were musically, the way that he would write, and of course then I had access to many musicians because I was there in New York. So I had, if I can remember correctly, Clark Terry and I think I had Julian Priester.

Ben: And you had Bobby Timmons on piano.

Johnny: Yeah, in fact we did some of his tunes on the date too. Yeah.

Ben: When you say you were interested in doing these spirituals, or Gospel music, was it strictly a musical interest, was it a philosophical interest, was it an emotional interest?

Johnny: I think it was a bit of all of that. Mainly musical, because the music itself had a certain, ah, feeling of philosophical content. And the way that Norman arranged it with the little big band, 'cause his arrangements weren't anything difficult to play, so to speak, but the way he put it together, the balance between the three or four saxophones and the four brass, you know, made for a very spiritual feeling. I mean, the musicians that were chosen for the date had this Baptist feeling, so you know, they were able to project this good feeling, good soul, Church gathering feeling in the studio.

Ben: That record kind of capped off the so-called "soul jazz" movement in a way, because even though Art Blakey and Horace Silver had done records that were being talked about as "soul jazz" before that...

Johnny: Aw, then it really started. Well then Ramsey Lewis came out with "Wade In The Water," and it was a big hit actually. Yeah.

Ben: Well, a lot of jazz players were using the gospel approach but weren't playing the actual gospel tunes. I think this is one of the first examples where you went to the songs themselves.

Johnny: Yeah, straight to the source.

Ben: You left the source soon after this. You went to Europe.

Johnny: Yeah. Well I went to Europe the first time in December, 1962, more or less on a publicity thing for Riverside Records. Although I played in Paris for a month at the Blue Note there. And then in January, I went to Stockholm for a month at the Golden Circle. And came back for another week at the Blue Note, then I went to Ronnie Scott's in London for a month. And then I wound up playing for a week in Holland. I came back in March 1963, and stayed until May 1963, which is like two months, and then Babs Gonsalves and I caught the Rotterdam and went to Holland in May, and ah . . .

Ben: You crossed the ocean with Babs on the Rotterdam?

Johnny: Oh my God! Oh yeah! [Laughs.] We had a ball, though. We had a ball. We stayed in Holland for about two weeks, and then I went to the Blue Note in Paris. And I stayed there, stayed in Europe fifteen years. But actually I was escaping from some problems I had, family problems, and IRS problems.

And I was in total disagreement with the major disc-jockeys of that time, the so-called jazz critics of the day, who were proclaiming a new noise that they called music, which turned out to be avant garde, and free jazz, and I thought it was all rubbish. Which it has proved to have been, all rubbish, a bad joke on music, which I think really helped to destroy the jazz scene as such here in America in the '60s and early '70s, almost completely, from what I found out later on.

Ben: And I believe the avant garde scene continues in Europe to this day. I mean, there's still a greater interest there in free jazz than anywhere else.

Johnny: Yeah, well the Europeans, ah, they don't call it "free jazz" so much anymore. They used to call it "improvisational music," you know, which I prefer. They should call it something else, because "jazz" got such a name that's been bastardized so much that, to me, what they call jazz, even in America, sounds strange, with all electronics and all that mess. But I mean, it's just the way that the modern ears have been trained to listen to all this plugged-in music, plugged-in noise. So, man, I can only speak for myself. But, actually, I don't even know what's happening when, as soon as I hear it, I turn it off.

Ben: Fifteen years in Europe. Did it go by fast?

Johnny: Yes, 'cause I was enjoying myself.

Ben: In spite of conditions?

Johnny: In spite of conditions. I had a good time over there, you see, because the Europeans, really, the philosophy for living their lives over there, is to me much more different than here, especially living in France. The French, 'cause they . . . I really learned how to relax. I never knew how to relax in America. You know? When I first got to Paris, I want something, I want it done quick, you know. I just left New York running like on a tread mill, you know, from the club to the record company back to the booking agency, back to the club, so I was blam, bam bam. Every day going no place. Complete dead end street. Hustlin' my distributors, radio stations, going no place. All I was doing was gettin' stoned, you know, and in a rush all the time; everything's in a rush. If I walked down the street, I'm running. Never taking my time. And I do that now when I go to New York. And I still go down the street in New York, I find myself flying down the street, going no place.

But in France, everybody's coolin' it, you know. For instance, I remember staying in this hotel in Paris, and I pick up the phone, trying to make a call, and it must have been 11:30 or something, so, the guy told me at the desk, "Line's busy." So, OK, I said, "I'll call again." And the guy said, "Well, I'll try in a few minutes." And, half an hour, nothing. I pick up the phone, nobody answers the phone. So I go downstairs and the guys gone to lunch. And so when he comes back I say, "Man, I'm trying to get this call," you know, "blah, blah, blah." And he's a Frenchman, you know, "Mais Monsieur . . . ," like you know, "what's the big rush?" Is it life and death, you know? I'm going crazy, I want the telephone call right now. So they teach you how to wait a minute. Take your time, take your time, have a good glass of some good Bordeaux and relax. You know? I'm coming from New York, man, where everybody's running like crazy, man. France, everybody have lunch for two-and-one-half to three hours, you know, just gettin' to the third course of the meal. You know, just changin' wines, "taste this wine, taste that wine." My first meals over there, man, there's so much food, I ate so much for the first course not realizing they got about four more courses. The third course comes, I'm full up to my ears. You know, they're takin' their time, conversing and changing wines. You know, the graciousness of living.

Ben: How has this affected your music? Are you taking your time more?

Johnny: Oh yes, I'm taking my time more, though some people may not think so. [Laughs.]

Ben: Well, I remember when you returned from Europe in 1978. I saw you on that return tour. Boy, you were playing great. And not long after that you made a couple more records for Orrin Keepnews again. The one you made in 1983, *Call It Whachawana,* really showed this new relaxed attitude you're talking about, as well as reflecting what I think sounds like the spirit of Thelonious. Your original writing even seems to be taking on a Monkish quality. I don't know if that's intentional on your part, but I hear it.

Johnny: I hadn't realized how much Thelonious affected me until years later. Actually, when I'm bangin' on the piano or something, when I'm amusing myself, so to speak, 'cause I'm not a pianist, but when I hear certain dissonances, seconds and minors and clusters and things, it all goes back, actually, to Monk. Of course I listen to classical music, too, so a lot of it is there too. But Thelonious, I mean, Thelonious was a master of space, you know, like Prez. Lester Young was a master of space. That's why Miles, I'm sure this is why Miles Davis learned his mastery of playing in space, from Prez. But Thelonious really took that to another degree, that spacing, man, the way he could just play one note now and then, and be so effective. But you see, people didn't realize how much a master of humor Thelonious was, and still is. Not only his music, but to have known him, you know, if you could ever have seen behind his facade that he had, always, and this mask that he always carried around with him, looking like Jomo Kenyatta or something. People were afraid to speak to him. But behind that man was a master of humor. Thelonious.

Ben: What kind of humor? You mean like joke humor?

Johnny: Oh yeah, joke humor. Anything to cause some innocent fun. For instance, when I was working in the Five Spot, we'd finished a set, and we're coming off the stage. I told Monk, I said, "Monk, ah, why don't you tell your drummer, tell him that when I'm playing . . ." And we're talking about Roy Haynes now, who's a master drummer . . . "Tell your drummer that when I'm playing my solo, just give me a little dinga-ling-ling-dinga-ling-ling. Hey, stop pitty-pattin' all over the drums, just give me a little swing, you know?" Monk said, "Hmm, you tell him yourself!" So I said, okay, 'cause Hagnus and I—I call Roy Haynes "Hagnus"—Hagnus and I are friends. I mean, I don't know why you'd say anything to Monk anyway, he's gonna tell you somethin' smart. So anyway, after the set, we would usually go back in the kitchen, 'cause the cats were back there cookin' hamburgers, and behind the kitchen was a little yard, where we would go out and puff the fresh air. So anyway, when we got over the set, I called Roy, I called Hagnus, "I wanta speak to you for a minute." "Yeah, okay, Johnny." So we went out in the back yard, I said, "Listen, don't get mad with me now, but I have somethin' to tell you." "So go ahead, go ahead tell me," he says. "Well, you know," I said, "Listen, when I'm playin my solo, you know, just give me a little dinga-ling-ding-ding-ding, ding-dinka-ding, ding-dinka-ding, you know, that's much better . . ." And he blew up. "Oh, I played with Charlie Parker, Sarah Vaughan . . ." I said, "See, I told you not to get angry with me . . ." I say, "Okay, excuse me a moment."

Anyway, that didn't last but a few minutes. It was nothing. 'Cause Roy and I are friends, always. So maybe two days later, in the kitchen after one of the sets, now see, Thelonious is the type of guy, he'll walk around and talk around with that big mouth and tellin' lies or whatever, havin' fun joking. Thelonious would just usually walk around stroking his little van dyke or his little beard, you know, and just listening, pacing the floor a little, like a wild beast. But like he's not listening to anything. I don't know what we were talkin' about at this particular time, but after some space happened, nobody said anything, so out of the blue Monk said, "Hmm, Johnny Griffin ain't scared of Roy Haynes." [Laughs.] "Johnny Griffin ain't scared of Roy Haynes," you know? Broke everybody up. I mean, Roy and I, we just fell out over the floor.

He did that to me the year before. I came in the club, Art Blakey and I. I was with the Jazz Messengers. We arrived in New York, and I was staying at Bu's [Blakey's] house. Anyway, I went down to Birdland and met Nica down there, the Baroness. And she said, "Johnny, come on over with me, I'm going down to the Five Spot before it's closed, you know, to see Thelonious. And I want to drive you down in my new car." She had bought a new Bentley convertible to race with Art Blakey, 'cause she had been trying to race with him before in her Rolls Royce but she couldn't keep up with him. But, you know, I'm a fool. I get in this Bentley with her and she pulls out in traffic, and she doesn't stop from Broadway, going diagonally across New York, all the way down, she doesn't stop for a red light or nothing. And I'm hiding. She's flying in this car. I say, "I know I'm going to die." She goes all the way downtown as fast as this Bentley would take her, and anyway, we got there late. The band had just stopped. When we walked in the door, they're gettin' off the bandstand. And when I walk in the door, Monk looked up and said: "Hmm, Johnny Griffin ain't scared of John Coltrane." [Laughs.] And the people look around like what's going on, you know? See, Monk was just devilish like that. You know, he'd agitate us to see what was going to happen, what kind of reaction he was going to get out of people. But then he may not say anything for an hour.

Ben: Hearing you talk about the old days, when you were a kid hanging out on the scene, you seem so happy. Now you got kids, young players hanging out around you, probably saving up their Johnny Griffin stories to tell on you later on.

Johnny: They take very good care of the old man.

Ben: Do they look after you?

Johnny: Yeah, they look after me. Yeah. They draw lines for me. They tell me I better not cross them. But these young men are all serious, and they know this form, they know jazz music, they know the history, and they all have enough technical competence to express themselves very well. Very well. And to hear them is to believe . . . really.

* * *

Pepper Adams (January, 1986)

Baritone saxophone player Pepper Adams is, in Phil Woods' expression, "a bebopper down to his socks." Pepper played with literally hundreds of key bebop musicians over the course of his career and provided a very strong alternative to the style of baritone saxophone playing that was most popular at the time, that of Gerry Mulligan. His sense of "swing," or forward progress, in his improvisation was extraordinary, and his choice of notes always seemed to be the most intelligent alternative given the harmonic possibilities of the moment. Perhaps it was the somewhat odd nature of his instrument (the baritone can look a bit awkward around the neck of stringy guy like Pepper) that kept him relatively obscure, even through the heydays of the bebop movement. Also, as he candidly remembered while we spoke, there was the issue of having to please the jazz critics. He never did try too hard to do that, and the repercussions of their negative reviews stayed with him until the end. Pepper died of brain cancer several weeks after our talk.

Ben: I consider you to be one of the most literate of jazz musicians, not necessarily because you're so well read, although you may be, but because your playing strikes me as being so intelligent. I'm not embarrassed to say that we first met several years ago when I ran up to you in a hotel and said, "Pepper, do you remember the solo you played on Thelonious Monk's 'Little Rootie-Tootie,' from the *Town Hall Concert?*" And you stopped and said, "Yes, I think I remember that."

Pepper: You know, I could hardly deny it.

Ben: And I know I went on about how literate I thought that particular solo was, that it struck me as being almost verbal in nature, and I asked you, "Does that make any sense to you?" At the time you said "Yes," but of course you were under duress from this mad fan. But does that make any sense to you today, that your solo should be seen as almost verbal?

Pepper: Oh, certainly. Yeah. I can certainly see that.

Ben: How can a saxophone solo be like the written word? In what ways?

Pepper: Well, if it flows in a logical sequence, with an occasional surprise here and there, that's almost a form of verbalization. I'd like to get conversation going about the same rate. Probably time-feeling has something to do with it, too, I would imagine.

Ben: And intonation contouring, I suppose, the way the lines move up and down, and the way the breaths are taken...

Pepper: Umhm. Yeah, certainly...

Ben: I think also what I heard, and what I hear in the best of jazz recordings, is a room full of people that are very comfortable with one another and aren't very self-conscious of what they are doing. They're not trying too hard. On that recording, you don't sound like you're trying too hard.

But let's change directions and come around through the back door on this. Let's find out some personal history, so that your musical style has a context. You're associated with the Detroit school of jazz players. You spent your formative years in Detroit, Michigan...

Pepper: Primarily so, yes...

Ben: There's an apocryphal story that I read which places you in an instrument repair shop back in Detroit. You were a tenor player at the time. And you came across this baritone saxophone and rescued it from the junk heap and made it your own.

Pepper: Well, that is apocryphal. It is not the way it actually happened. How I did fall into playing baritone, more or less, is by accident. And a repair shop enters into it. Would you like me to tell the true story for the record?...

Ben: Absolutely, we're interested in the truth...

Pepper: Well, I was only about sixteen, and at Christmas I was just hired on as extra help in the record department of a large music store, which was called Grinnells. It had branches throughout the state of Michigan. But their main shop was in Detroit, right downtown. And I was a Christmas extra. Right next door was their repair department, and a baritone saxophone that they had taken in trade passed through their repair department. I had become friendly with the repair man by this point, and so he suggested that I try it out. I did, and I enjoyed playing it. So, using my employee's discount, and I think my friend Mark Degreder made me a loan to begin with, I purchased that instrument, and played it about six weeks. By then, I decided that I enjoyed the baritone so much I really wanted a good one, and was able to get a brand new Selmer on hire-purchase. That's not an American phrase, is it?

Ben: Right, it's British, and it refers to the act of lease-renting, right?...

Pepper: Yeah, something like that...

Ben: The importance of your choice of instrument is made more significant, I think, by the fact that there are so few baritone players. There are tenor players who play baritone, and there are other people who play the instrument casually, but you're a baritone saxophone player.

Pepper: Yeah, it's becoming rather more common now than it was in earlier times. But it is still a relative rarity.

Ben: One thinks of Gerry Mulligan, of course, in the '50s, as having a real influence on the instrument, and your emergence on the jazz scene, as a countertheme to the way he approached the instrument, was noteworthy. You put the muscle back in the instrument through more aggressive playing. If his approach was typically "West Coast," you were clearly from the East.

Pepper: Yeah, I've always felt there was no real competition between Gerry and myself, since we approach the instrument so differently. I really enjoy listening to him play. It's just a different approach than I would feel comfortable with for myself.

Ben: I'm also reminded of something John Coltrane said about why he took up the soprano saxophone after playing tenor for so long. He said he'd been hearing a higher sound in his head for years and years, and it wasn't until he got the soprano in his hands that he realized, "This is what I've been hearing." Did you have a similar feeling? Had you heard a lower voice in your head as you were playing other horns, and when you got the baritone, you said, "Yeah, this is what I hear inside"?

Pepper: There probably is something to that, yes, since I played soprano when I was young, and I played some alto. And I don't think I could anymore. I don't think I can hear intonation up that high anymore.

Ben: So you were hearing it lower.

Pepper: And a number of people have pointed out that, in terms of natural form of expression, the baritone seems to fit with my speaking voice.

Ben: True enough. Traditionally, people, because it's played in the lower register, would think of it as being a slower instrument to get around on. You've disproved that. Did you have to go to great lengths to disprove that?

Pepper: Actually, baritone tends to sound logy a lot, and a lot of baritone players always seem to be behind the beat, just struggling to catch up. Which, I think, can come from two basic reasons. One being just a sheer lack of technical expertise. And the other is that, if you play everything legato, and don't use the tongue, and don't outline where the note is gonna hit, everything tends to run together. Because it is lower-pitched. And this has no rhythmic impact, or impulse behind it. So I've tried to use a legato tongue so that there is differentiation between the notes. And I try to do a lot with articulation, because that has a lot to do with what the time feeling is going to be. And if you fail to articulate on a baritone, or any lower pitched instrument, it is gonna be just one constant rumble after a while.

Ben: Is it a technique you specifically had to find for yourself, or did you apply a broader tenor technique to it?

Pepper: You know, I really don't know. I think I kinda stumbled into it. As a way of trying to make the instrument seem like it was actually playing in time with the rest of the band. When I was first playing the baritone, well, Harry Carney was of course my favorite player, and still is, as far as his ability with the instrument overall, and everything he could do with the instrument. I guess you'd have to say that the popular baritone player among the young musicians of that time, or the only one that they really heard very much, would have been Serge Chaloff. And I didn't care for his playing at all, for one thing. He always sounded like he was behind and struggling to catch up. And so I guess it was the fact that people were listening to him, gave me the idea of listening to him, and finding out what I didn't like, and then working from there.

Ben: Could be a good technical guidepost for young players: as well as finding people you do like, find out people you don't like.

But early on, you also found some aggressive players to hang out with in Detroit, world class players, that kept you playing strong to keep up with them. I'm thinking specifically of Tommy Flanagan and Barry Harris and the Jones brothers, Elvin, Hank and Thad.

Pepper: Well, I think that Detroit, historically, has always had a great jazz scene. I remember people like Rex Stewart and Quentin Jackson talking about having been there with McKinney's Cotton Pickers in 1930. And, I think that throughout the '30s and '40s and '50s, there was a high level of musical consciousness in the city, so that there were indeed a lot of fine local musicians. And one factor I've mentioned before is that there was such a high overall level of musicianship in Detroit that if you were a young musician and really aspired to work and make money playing your instrument, you *had* to get awful doggone good to be on a level to compete at all. And I didn't realize how true this was until I left Detroit and went to the Army. Get out in the rest of the world and found out the standards elsewhere were not nearly as high.

Ben: Barry Harris has mentioned the same thing. The level of achievement in Detroit was very high. Were you aware of a Detroit sound? or were you aware of doing it a particular way in Detroit?

Pepper: I think as time went on, indeed I was, yeah. I think basically it was the time feeling. More than anything else, the kind of loose swing with no doubt of where the time lay. I found it difficult to listen to people with floundering time feels. And I liked to play with the time. I like to play tricks with it, of course, but always knowing where I am and being able to come back to where the time is in such a secure manner as to make the listener wonder if I had ever really left.

Ben: Kind of The Pepper Adams Theory of Relativity there. You and many of the Detroit players, of course, wound up in New York City eventually. Was it difficult initially to get work as a baritone saxophone player in New York City? Was the instrument any problem, in terms of getting employment?

Pepper: I suppose, to some extent, it would be with a club owner who'd never had a baritone player in the front line before, just wondering, "What is that thing?" And thinking that maybe this isn't the way he should go. So perhaps to some extent, but I think, in a sense, it helped me in that I came to New York pretty well-equipped already as a musician. I was no kid. I was 25 or 26 when I came here, I think. And in Detroit, I worked practically all the time, from the time I returned from the Army, for the next three years. When I stayed in Detroit, I was working six nights a week, pretty much steadily, and I had never had any trouble reading anything, so I was equipped for a variety of work.

Ben: What's the first job you got when you got to the city?

Pepper: Wow, I'm not really positive. I had a number of friends here, when I moved here. One of them being Oscar Pettiford. I think Oscar got me the first gig, and that was out at a place, long gone now, that was called the Cork and Bib, in Westbury, Long Island. I remember being new to New York, and not knowing very much about the city. I knew Manhattan a little bit, but the environs, I knew nothing. But when I went to the Cork and Bib, in Westbury, and discovered an outfitters shop for polo ponies next door, I figured, "I think I must be in a fairly affluent part of Long Island."

Ben: Circle the wagons boys, we're here. Well, it's a far cry from what the rest of the employment must have been like, 'cause I know that the club scene in the city was of a different order.

Pepper: Yeah. Let's see, I worked out my union card transfer. And again, Oscar Pettiford kind of forced me onto Stan Kenton's band. Forced both of us. Forced me to do it, because I was never very much of a fan of that band. And talked Kenton into hiring me, sight unseen. And, there's a very long story that we could insert here, but that can go elsewhere. So actually, I worked out part of my transfer time while on the road with Kenton's band.

Ben: Well, we've kind of arrived full circle to the recording I mentioned at the beginning, the one that you made in February of 1959, at Town Hall in New York City. It was released originally on Riverside Records. It's the album *Thelonious Monk Orchestra at Town Hall*, featuring Monk, of course, on piano, Donald Byrd on trumpet, Phil Woods on alto saxophone, Charlie Rouse, on tenor, Sam Jones on bass, Art Taylor, drums, and yourself on baritone saxophone.

Pepper: Don't forget Jay McAllister on tuba. I got Jay McAllister on the gig. He'd been in Kenton's band with me.

Ben: A very high point in the history of jazz, from the fans' point of view. It's a record that's traded and highly praised all over. One wonders why this particular format of Monk's music, the big little band, didn't go on beyond this one concert. Was this like a one-shot thing?

Pepper: That wasn't the intention. When we were rehearsing for the concert, there was talk, in fact, it was supposed to be definite, that a concert tour of about three weeks had been set up for the group, that was to begin something like four weeks after the concert. So we had that, were to do the Town Hall concert, have three or four weeks, add some more pieces to the repertoire, have further rehearsals, paid for, and then go on this tour of concerts, primarily in colleges, I believe. And that was the whole theory. And that in fact was part of the package that I was approached with initially, when I was asked to play in this band for Town Hall.

Ben: In other words, to take out a month and devote yourself to this project.

Pepper: Yeah. Which sounded fine. It was certainly enjoyable, the rehearsals were just great. We had a lot of fun. But we went on, played the concert, and the immediate reviews that we received were so bad that all of the rest of the concerts were cancelled.

Ben: I can't believe it. How bad could they have been, and what in fact did they say?

Pepper: Actually, my basic memory of the situation was, that it was a case of the immediate reaction being bad. That is, in New York daily press, or weekly press, such as the *Village Voice*, which I believe would have been Nat Hentoff in those days. And, recently somebody gave me a review of the concert from the *New York Times*, for Monday, March 2nd, '59 . . .

I've mentioned a number of times before about how this was supposed to have been a continuing working band, and how the reviewers just put it away so badly that we never got another gig. Actually, we had one about a year later. One festival. And there's been a lot of disbelief around, since this record is held in such high esteem these days. But the fact is that the daily and weekly press put us away so bad, and I can quote now from the review in the *New York Times*. There is mention of some of the titles that the ten piece band played, one of them incorrectly. We did not play "Crepuscule with Nellie." And then it says that ". . . Mr. Monk's determination to impose his musical personality on his musicians and the surging, sweaty efforts of the musicians to wrestle with Mr. Monk's music, give the disks a raw excitement." He's speaking of previous Monk recordings with a smaller group. "But none of this could be found in the bland, workaday performances of the large group, with which Mr. Monk played Saturday evening. The arrangements smoothed out the characteristically Monkian lumps and bumps, diluted his tartness and robbed the works of their zest. It was a pipe-and-slippers version of music that is naturally querulous."

Ben: And, why don't we, since we've listed the soloist of the day, why don't we also list the writer of this review as well.

Pepper: Well, the reviewer? John S. Wilson.

Ben: John S. Wilson, the *New York Times*. So his opinions, which have clearly been proven wrong in the light of history, were a big part of the reason why promoters cancelled the tour of the Monk big band. The fact of the matter, then, is the press has a lot to do with our jobs out here. Wilson's review stopped that tour, right?

Pepper: Yeah, certainly. Put an end to that band.

Ben: A moment of silence here for what might have been. And for all critics and would-be critics to examine their consciences.

You mentioned that the rehearsals with Monk were fun. Hall Overton, of course, came in with charts, and he had orchestrated some Monk piano solos.

Pepper: Oh, yeah, and they were terrific. He had done a beautiful job. And the rehearsals were held in Hall Overton's loft, which was in the flower district here, like the 20s and Sixth Avenue. And we had great fun. As you know, there's some pretty tough music in there, so there were some things to wrestle with, and it was a lot of fun. Demanding and enjoyable.

Ben: You talk about the tonguing being important, to get the rhythmic feel. Well, Monk's lines are just skipping all over the place rhythmically. And the ensemble work is tight without being rigid. I mean, you seem to be skipping, but together. When you get through playing those lines behind the rhythm section, is your solo at all influenced then by the ensemble work, or do you just step out front and play what you will?

Pepper: That's interesting. Sometimes a solo can grow out of what has preceded it. Or act as a commentary on the surroundings in some way. Other times, it just doesn't seem to work out. But it's nice when it does, when you're in a big band setting. So many of the solos in Ellington's band were like that. Where they were almost an indispensable part of the arrangement after a while.

Ben: Ellington was reputed to have written the arrangement sometimes to make the other side of it happen, to make the solos happen.

Pepper: I wouldn't be at all surprised.

Ben: I'm struck, Pepper, by the amount of live recording you've done. This Monk at Town Hall is an exception only in the sense that it's not a Pepper Adams date. But there are some serious Pepper Adams live dates out there. I think the first record you made as a leader was the album *Ten to Four at the Five Spot*, with Donald Byrd on trumpet, Doug Watkins, bass, Elvin Jones on drums and Bobby Timmons on piano. Do you remember how out of tune that piano was on that date? It was outrageous. You know, it speaks about the conditions under which this particular art form is practiced daily. How do you put a piano like that out of your mind and execute a lovely ballad like you did on that record?

Pepper: Ho, ho, ho. I tell you, it's excruciating, really. Because I completely lose track of where the core of the intonation is, if indeed there is one. And so, very quickly, instead of just competing with an out-of-tune piano, I have lost all track of intonation within myself. So I'm not even sure to what extent my intonation on my own instrument is. To use the Irish expression, "Something like that'd make your face hurt." It's tough and was probably made even worse by the fact that everything on that album was taken from the very last set of the night.

Ben: Really? How did that happen?

Pepper: I think we did three or four sets in there, this was when stereo was first coming in, if you noticed by the date there. And it was Riverside's first attempt at recording stereo on a live date. So we completed the earlier part of the evening and I think Ray Fowler was the engineer, if I'm remembering correctly, and Orrin Keepnews was there, of course, overseeing things. And he says, "Well, I think we've got a lot of great music there. I think we can even start packing up now." And, Orrin had Elvin and myself go to the bar for a drink, and Ray Fowler comes running up and says, "One of our microphone leads has been out all night. Nothing is in stereo." And that was part of the whole point, this is their first live stereo recording. So we quickly had to do one more set, and that's the entire album.

Ben: April 15, 1958, at the Five Spot Cafe in New York. You are there.

Pepper: And Elvin Jones had a black eye. Not from any disagreement. He had had a wisdom tooth removed a couple of days earlier, and the roots had gone back so far that its removal caused the blood vessels to burst inside, giving him a rather spectacular black eye. If you've never seen Elvin with a black eye, you're really missing something there.

Ben: When you hear the small handful of people clapping at the end of that record, the four or five people left in the club, again you're reminded of the number of brilliant recordings that have been made in front of a few dedicated, or oblivious, people who just happened to be in the joint, and who probably don't even realize what's just happened in front of them. And it's only because there's a document that anybody says years later, "Wow, that music was great! Were you really there that night?" Important history often feels pretty ordinary when you're right in the middle of it. But I bring up the subject of live recordings with you, because captured music, versus manufactured music, seems to be important to what you're all about, Pepper. Do you have any feelings about live recordings versus studio recordings?

Pepper: No, not really. I think that the feeling within the group is the primary thing. And there's been a lot of things written about the inspiration that an audience can give. Well, the sort of audience you mentioned, you know, it sounds like the end of *Laugh-In* . . .

Ben: Yeah, the sound of one hand clapping . . .

Pepper: Now that's a dubious inspiration right there.

Ben: But you know, sometimes I think that when you hear somebody playing great, in the face of adversity, maybe with instruments that are out of tune, an audience that's somehow indifferent, it brings even more greatness to the music. I know it's perverse to say that.

Pepper: Well, I can see the poignancy of it. I've made some live recordings of which I'm quite fond. But also some studio recordings. I can't say that I played better in one context then the other, necessarily.

Ben: Well, perhaps ironically then, after many years of recordings, live and in-studio, you finally got some critical recognition recently when you were nominated for a Grammy, and it was for a live album . . . The album was called *Pepper Adams Live at Fat Tuesdays* and, again, featured some of your old Detroit pals, like Hank Jones and Louis Hayes. So you're still hangin' out with some of those same Detroit guys, I see.

Pepper: Oh yeah. Certainly. Actually, there's a large number of musicians and people who are our friends from Detroit, and we have continued to be good friends for thirty years or so. And that's nice, that's really nice to have. Like I could sit and name forty or fifty people that I've maintained friendships with consistently for over at least a thirty-year span. And I doubt if there are many people in other walks of life could do that.

Ben: Why do you think that is? Because parts of the jazz world do seem like a big family at times.

Pepper: I think it's a basic closeness and mutual respect that we share. And just a strong liking. There are a lot of the musicians, some that you started naming before, that came from Detroit and became internationally known. There are an awful lot of really nice fellows among 'em too. Wouldn't want to meet anybody nicer than Tommy Flanagan. Or Barry Harris, or Kenny Burrell. Any number of others. Roland Hanna, Louis Hayes, and it just goes on and on. And there a number of musicians that never left Detroit, that we all know, us Detroit musicians. They're just not known to the general public, because they never received the exposure. For one reason or another.

Ben: It's like the famous Steinberg map of the United States as seen from the New York City perspective. There's New York City and then there's Japan, and everything in between is just a wasteland. That's the way the New York press often perceives it, anyway.

You know, Phil Woods refers to you as one of the warriors of this music. You bring that up with Phil, if you like. But I think the image is apt. There's a clear dedication in your playing to some of the pure values of the music that first drew you to it.

Pepper: You know, I don't wanna take much credit for that, because I try to play as well as I can, as an improvising jazz artist, as much of the time as I can. I'm capable of sitting in a section and playing perfectly well, because that's part of the craft. But I try as much as I can to work as a soloist, and try to play, just try to swing for one thing, and the various other ways that I try to approach playing. But I'm doing that not so much because of any kind of altruistic thing; it's because that's what I feel I do best. So if I have any shot at survival at all out here, I better stick to what I do best, even though it sometimes seems to be overlooked or downgraded in the press. Musicians seem to iike it. And the public seems to like it. The class that I don't seem to satisfy are the critics. The *Live at Fat Tuesday's* album, which as you mentioned was nominated for a Grammy, only received two and a half stars in *Down Beat*. I mean, you've got to make a pretty bad album to get two and a half stars.

Ben: Yeah. Especially when times are such that they give four and five stars to some rock and roll records.

Pepper: Yeah. That was one of the problems with *Live at Fat Tuesday's*, of course; no synthesizers on it.

Ben: Well, the concept of a warrior, then, I think is apt.

Pepper: Yeah, but I don't wanna take credit for it, because if I wanted to make a crossover record, or something like that, I wouldn't know the first thing about it. Freddie Hubbard said he sold out and it wasn't worth it, because he didn't make enough money. Well, I would feel, you know, I don't know anything about the criteria for judging any of that other stuff. All I know about is jazz. And so I figure I better stick to that, because I just don't know the esthetics of the jazz-rock or pop-rock.

Ben: Years ago, when we first talked about your solo on Monk's "Little Rootie-Tootie," and I said to you, "It sounds so verbal, so literate, do you think there's any connection between the bebop style of playing and the highly literate times, the bohemian era of the forties and fifties?" And I remember you said to me, "Oh, absolutely. You know, Charlie Parker was a great reader." But nobody knows that about Charlie Parker. Nobody thinks of that. What you hear about Charlie Parker is his life of excess, things that the press can play up and sell issues, you know. And they dispense with the man, almost, by trivializing the depth of the work . . .

Pepper: Um, hm, very true . . .

Ben: So back to the point: I hear in your playing a very literate sensibility. Are you a great reader? Are you a somebody who spends time with books?

Pepper: Oh yes. Very definitely. Always have been, yeah.

Ben: Who are some of your favorite writers?

Pepper: Currently? William Trevor. Josef Skvorecky. Right now I'm reading Ludwig Bemelmans, which is going back to the '30s and '40s. It is very funny. Let's see. Among people writing right now, Keith Waterhouse is a terrific writer, who is hardly known in the United States. He wrote the novel *Billy Liar*, from which came the film. But he's written eight, ten other novels in a variety of styles, and several of them with considerable humor. And he's an awful lot of fun.

Ben: The element of humor being a big part of jazz too.

Pepper: I think so. I love it and I think sometimes mine might go almost a little overboard, into the slapstick thing. But so does Thad's. I love playing with Thad [Jones], because sometimes the slapstick kind of humor starts flowing . . .

Ben: Physical or musical humor?

Pepper: Musical. But so broad as to approach farce.

Ben: Referring perhaps to quotes, musical quotes, the way you approach that.

Pepper: Yeah. Or making fun of a style that we don't care for by exaggerated vibrato. Taking a well-known phrase from something and distorting it. Or particularly playing it in another key. And creating the tensions that occur when you play something that is totally recognizable as a melody, except that the whole rest of the band is in an entirely different key. I like that. One of my favorite classical composers is Arthur Honegger. And I love, particularly, the way he mixes keys. He'll have a beautiful melody going, and with a very strong accompaniment, but they could be, not the easy intervals, not necessarily the tri-tone interval or something like that, but be a minor third apart, or a second apart. It really gets fascinating.

Ben: Do you use any of that sort of abstraction when you play? Are you thinking consciously of that? Or are you talking as you talk to me now?

Pepper: Well, I'm not sure how conscious it is. I do often try to play in another key, sometimes. For various effects. It can be for a drama, it can be for humor, poignancy. All these effects can occur with a bitonal approach. And a lot of that has to do with how you resolve it at the end, too. You can either leave it hanging, or you can bring it back in.

But, to me, just improvising more or less straight-ahead jazz on a rhythmic basis, and over a regulated set of chord changes, is endlessly fascinating. Where did I see that quote? Oh, Stanley Dance, who is a very nice man, and a very good friend. But he doesn't care much for music since '45 or so, refers to the harmonic cul-de-sac of bebop. I would have to argue with Stanley about that one, because there is much, much more that can be done with the harmonies. And melodies.

I don't really necessarily think of myself as a bebop player. I don't know about that. I'm suspicious of all labels. And particularly that one, because when I was young and in Detroit, the bebop players really denigrated my playing, because they told me I wasn't doing it right. And I wasn't trying to do it right. I was not imitating Charlie Parker in the sense of playing his phrases, as most of the youngsters, younger players at that time would try to do. To be hip, you played a phrase of his. I never tried that. I never memorized solos or studied solos in particular at all. What I would do, certainly, was pay attention to his harmonic usages, and his melodic usages, and try to learn from them, and then do it in a way that was comfortable to me. So based on that, I really don't think of myself as particularly a bebopper at all. And the label "hard bop," I don't know where that came from. That's kind of a handy term of denigration that writers like Martin Williams or Whitney Balliet seemed to use with reckless abandon, grouping together people that don't play alike at all. But, since they disapprove of this style, they can apply it to anyone whom they don't care for.

Ben: There's an intellectual tradition, where you define a thing in order to dispense with it.

Pepper: Yeah, oh yeah, certainly. Very good. Um, hm.

Ben: Well, have we left out any critics? Is there anybody we didn't take to task here?

Pepper: "Whom have we not yet offended," in Mort Sahl's phrase.

Ben: You come here very much a man at the top of his career, somebody who's mastered his craft. Is there something that you would say to a younger player today, faced with the adversity of this business, and the randomness of critical acclaim, and the difficulty of developing a style? Any advice to a young player?

Pepper: I think I would tell just about any young player, "Enjoy what you do, but don't really count on making a living at doing this," because if it's something you approach cold-bloodedly, as if you're gonna become a star, I don't think it can be worthwhile for you. It can be worthwhile only if you love the music and derive enough enjoyment from the music and the people you're involved with in the music to compensate for what is quite likely to be a life below the poverty line. I think those are just about the facts. I mean, there are young players coming to New York, who are making out fine. A few. But for the vast majority, it's tremendously difficult, much more so than when I came here, 25, 30 years ago. And I don't really know how they get along. And I hear fine young players all the time. Our educational system is turning out fine young players. Jerry Dodgion asks, "But what are they gonna do with all this expertise?" Only so many can work with Woody Herman at one given time, you know?

* * *

les Davis (top), Max Roach (bottom)

Dizzy Gillespie

rank Morgan

Art Blakey (top), Horace Silver (bottom)

ckie McLean

Abdullah Ibrahim

Mose Allison

Sonny Rollins

Phil Woods (top), Tony Williams (bottom)

Johnny Griffin

rchie Shepp

George Benson

. John

Jack DeJohnette

arla Bley

Bobby McFerrin (with Jon Hendricks)

Michel Petrucciani (September, 1988)

The first time you meet Michel Petrucciani, it can be rather daunting. His person is smaller than you can imagine, even from pictures, perhaps not even three feet in height, but his presence is enormous, all laughter and energy and musician's street talk, "Hey brother, what's happening?" with a combination of New York hustle and French elan. Fortunately, our getting together for this conversation was not the first time I had met Michel. The first time was at a small club in Brussels, where I was playing, and suddenly Michel showed up with drummer Roy Haynes. They settled into a table directly behind the piano where they proceeded to order drinks, party and call out requests. (I remember distinctly Michel requesting "that song about all the Piano Players" in a way that left no room to suggest that it had already been played in the first set.) Often, when such renowned musicians arrive in a jazz club, the band can become rattled. But Michel's presence only made us enjoy ourselves more. Michel is very aware of the temporary nature of life, that being here is a gift, and he is intent on sharing his gift with all, and at all deliberate speed.

Ben: You've been a resident of New York City for some time, but your journey here is a long one and, I think, the story of how you came to live in New York tells a lot of the power of the music that you play. You started in France. Tell us a little bit about your boyhood, or the environment.

Michel: Okay. Well, I was, like, some lucky kids that grew up in a jazz music environment. My father's a guitar player, and my two brothers also play music, jazz music. And I think that the first sound I ever heard, as a baby, I would imagine was jazz. And so I always wanted to play jazz music, but I studied classical music, because I was in France, and my parents wanted me to have some kind of formal education. So I studied classical music for about, I would say, eight to ten years. You know, eight years solid and then the last couple of years, a little shaky, because I didn't wanna play classical music anymore. And after that, I played jazz with my father. We had a little band, you know, called the Petrucciani Trio, and it was my father on guitar, and my brother Louie on bass. And myself. We didn't have any drummer. And we play all the old Tal Farlow, you know, Red Norvo kind of style, things like that. Wes Montgomery's tunes, arrangements. I would pick it up from albums, you know, and just copy the arrangement, write the chords down, like that.

Ben: What, what kind of city were you living in?

Michel: Oh, I was born in Orange, France, and we toured, you know, like in the periphery of, I don't know, a hundred miles. That's it, around that town. That's the further we ever went. Paris once for a radio show. It was like a big event. The family was getting excited. You know, it was great and like that. I'm talking, I was very young then. I mean, I was like, 10, 11, 12, 13, 14, like that. And then, when I turned 16, I met Aldo Romano, and he's very well known in Europe, and also in the states. But especially in Europe. And he was the one, you know, he heard me play and he said, "Look, I have to play with that kid. I wanna be given the possibility to do his first album," and like that. So he came and talked to my father for days. It was like a marriage. You know, my father was asking him all kind of questions. Because my father didn't want me to leave the house. He was scared of the music business and all that kind of stuff. He was afraid of what was gonna happen to his kid. You know, going out there by myself. We're dudes and what people think of jazz sometimes it's a little crazy.

Anyway, he talked him into it, and I went to Paris and I did this album with Aldo on drums and J. F. Jenny Clark on bass. And, that was for Owl record company in France. And when the album came out, it was like really the beginning, because somehow, a lot of people bought it and it was like a big success right away. Really. It was phenomenal. It was one of those magic moments. You know, you do something and all of a sudden you sell a lot, without anybody knowing you or anything like that. Not even special publicity or advertisement or anything. It was just, boom, it was just out there and it sold.

Ben: On the cover of that album is a photo of you wearing this rather dapper hat. And if you look at the photo, it's hard to tell how old you are. You could be in your early twenties perhaps. There's no sense that you're seventeen years old at the time. You were seventeen years old when you made that record. Listening to your playing at that time, obviously it's very mature for a seventeen-year-old. Your style is a very searching style. Kind of reminiscent of, well people have mentioned Bill Evans. I hear also other parallels, perhaps Lennie Tristano or any number of players.

Michel: Yeah. Also Oscar Peterson. I was listening to him a lot that time.

Ben: Really? Who else at that point was an inspiration for you musically?

Michel: Well, always has been Wes Montgomery. A lot, a lot. Like in fact, I think I know more Wes Montgomery solos by heart than any other musicians that you could mention. I know like maybe 10, 15, 20 solos of Wes Montgomery, that he has recorded on albums. I could tell you the cover of the album, everything. So he's been like really more influenceable for me, than other musicians.

Bill Evans was a different thing. I discovered Bill Evans in 1970...

Ben: You were eight years old...

Michel: Yeah. And I didn't like it. My brother came up. We used to have a music store, and, you know, my brother would pick up the jazz record and bring it upstairs to the house. And he'd say, "Check this out." He'd say, "This is great." My brother Louie was already much more advanced than I was as far as the years. I was more middle jazz, you know, like into Erroll Garner. You know, like Bill Evans was too progressive for me. I didn't understand it. And he played me the album on the little machine, you know, really funky thing and I said, "Now that, I don't like that. This guy doesn't know how to play." I said, "This guy can't play." That really that was my first reaction on Bill Evans. And, he said, "No, no. You're wrong, you're wrong. You don't know what you talkin' about." He was right, of course.

And I listened because I was open, you know, I was open-minded. So I said, "Okay, well, if you say I'm wrong, I'm gonna really check it out." And I listened, and listened, and listened. The more I listen, I said, "He's right." And I came and apologized to him. You know, but way later. It was like, I listened to Bill for months before I could even understand what he was doing. It was like, so foreign to me, so... I couldn't understand anything. I thought he was just playing, I don't know what, but it didn't sound right. It didn't touch my ears. I couldn't understand the chord, the progressions, the tempos. It was the first time I ever heard a waltz, for instance, when he played very early in that album. It was *Montreux 1970* and he played with Eddie Gomez and Marty Morell on drums. And later, little by little, he became like a major influence on me. Because I realized what he was doing. But ironically I didn't like Bill at first.

Ben: It's astounding to me that an eight-year-old child would be presumptuous enough to say, "He's not playing. Bill Evans is not playing."

Michel: I don't know. It's just that I was arrogant. Always, I mean, little guys, you know. Little people, short people. They're arrogant little creeps, you know? And I admit that I have that kind of energy sometimes. I say, "I don't like that." You know, "Raaa." But then, I come back to it and listen. I'm not close-minded, but it come off that way sometimes. But it's not true. It's not really me. I'm not like that. But, yes, I was like that, especially with my brothers, you know, my older brothers. I like to kick butt a little bit, sometimes.

Ben: You mentioned your size. In fact, you're about three feet tall. You were born with what is called "glass bones"...

Michel: The technical term is osteogenesis imperfecta.

Ben: Was there a time when you were growing up that you said, "This is no longer a problem?"

Michel: It was never a problem . . .

Ben: It was never a problem?

Michel: No. Because I was born with it. When you're born with something, you don't know how it feels like to be somebody else. So, you know, it was not a problem. Never, in fact. I was really lucky to be raised like a normal kid, like my two other brothers. There was no problem like that. I was punished when I did things that I wasn't supposed to do, and I was rewarded when I did nice things. Just, you know, the same. Nobody pampered me. You know, I'm really grateful for that.

Ben: Obviously, it was probably part of your father's concern, your going off to Paris now with Aldo Romano. Because Aldo physically carried you into the jazz scene in Paris. There are some famous photos of him holding you. What did it feel like to arrive in Paris at that point?

Michel: Well, it was interesting because I was afraid. It was like a new adventure. People talked different there. You know, I'm from the south. They have a different kind of way of joking and thinking, and like that, so I kinda lay back and watch and look and learn. And, I have to say that, I don't wanna be pretentious but, I think that when I want to learn something, I can do it very fast. Because I take the time to listen. I let myself open. And I say, "Okay, I'm gonna check this out. See where I could, you know, learn out of that." And that's what I did when I arrived in Paris. I shut my mouth a lot, you know? I was just listening to other people. Listen to the musician, what they were talking about and, you know, I just put my nose everywhere. But without even saying anything. And, tell you the truth, there was a lot of things that I like. There's a lot of things that I didn't like, about the jazz scene in France.

In fact, later on, I said, "You know, the French people invented blasé." "Blasé" is French, and, you know, only the French people could feel a certain way. So they say, "I feel a certain way. How can we call the way I feel. Let's call it blasé. Put it in the dictionary." You know what I mean? And that's exactly like, you say, you don't get motivated too easy. It's gotta be like very strongly intellectualized or whatever. Is that kind of thing. And I got tired of that very quick. You know, I say, "Wake up! Get up!" You know, like "Smile. Hmm?" I got a little tired of that.

Ben: Your playing is very emotional playing. I mean, I could see where it wasn't just cultural, it was also musical. You're not just an idea player, you're a heart player.

Michel: I think you play like you are. I mean, you're a musician and, probably, you feel the same way. You know, you could really define somebody's personality by his music. Sometime I hear somebody play and I could almost tell how he's gonna be. In life.

Ben: The passion in your playing no doubt is what, allegedly, motivated Charles Lloyd to come out of retirement and go back to active performing.

Michel: Should I keep going? And tell my life story? . . .

Ben: [Laughs.] You bet . . .

Michel: Okay. So, I was eighteen, and I was kind of tired of Europe, especially France, and the scene over there. It was a little boring for me, and I wanted to see something else. And I had this friend of mine that I knew from France, but moved back to California. And he used to call me and write me and said, "You have to come here one day. It's great." You know. So that's when I came to California. Okay, so, eighteen, and I go, and I go visit this friend of mine. And, he was living at Charles Lloyd's house.

Ben: Charles was retired at this point, I assume.

Michel: Right, and I didn't even know who Charles was. I think I told you that. I didn't even know, and Charles says, "Do you know 'Forest Flower?' " And I said, "What?" He said, "Come on." He said, "People would stop me on the street to make me sing that song." I mean, he exaggerated a little bit, but of course he was very famous in the '60s. But I didn't know that because it was after my time. I was born in '62, so when he stopped . . . I think he finish playing, what year was it? I mean, you should know that better than me.

Ben: Well, he really became famous after the Monterey Pop period in the late '60s. By about the early '70s, he was pretty much retired.

Michel: Right, and I was eight, you know. So I didn't know really who he was. And, again, his music was very progressive to the kind of music I was raised with. Because we were talking of Tal Farlow, Wes, Erroll Garner. You know, no way we could find a Charles Lloyd album in the house. No way. He was way too avant-garde for my father's taste. Because I was listening to what my father was listening. I had no choice. I didn't go in the store and buy my own albums.

So when I met Charles, I didn't know who he was. And I stayed at his house for about a month. There was a piano, like in the studio, there was a piano there. But I have a rule. I never touch other people's instrument unless they ask me to. This is a thing. And I don't like when people do that in my house. If you come to my house and sit on the piano and don't ask me, I'm not gonna say anything, but I'm gonna say, "Okay, no class." Because it's like a thing that I've learned. You know, you say, "Please, can I? Is that okay if I sit down?" And I didn't wanna say that to him, because I didn't want to play, you know. And one day he said, "What do you do?" I say, "Well, I play the piano." He said,

"Well, sit down and play. Would you play something for me?" And I say, "Okay," and by that time it was a month without playing. I was dying to touch the ivories, you know? And, so I did. And I was playing. I was so much into what I was doing that I look up and he was gone.

And I say, "Oh, my god, he really didn't like what I did. I chased him away." And I turn around and he was right behind me with a saxophone in my ear. He was going "Bwooop!" You know, and we start playing. And we play until like four or five in the morning. That day. Then we went to sleep. And I went to sleep in the trailer. I had a little trailer that Charles had provided for me with a little bed in it and a little fridge, you know. And it was like camping. It was fun, you know. I had a great time. I slept for about two hours, and he came with the horn. Obviously, he didn't sleep at all. And he said "Come on man! Get up! Let's go!" You know. We go doing it again. And we play like that for like three days. Like non-stop, with like little intermission of two or three hours of sleep, taking a little nap, you know, getting up, just playing, sleep again, you know, like that.

And it was crazy, it was great. And then he said, "Okay, you want to stay here?" And I said, "Well, I don't know." Because he was very, you know, abrupt? You say that? And he said, "Yeah, I want you to stay here. I want to play again. Would you like to be in my band?" I say, "Great." And that's . . . then I started, you know, touring the states. And I lived in California in Big Sur for four and a half years . . .

Ben: A magic place . . .

Michel: Yes. Different. Is very different. Wow. I took my lady there, for the first time. And she's from California. She's from L.A. And I took her to Big Sur. She freaked. She went, "My God, where are we? What is this?" Yeah, this is amazing. At first it's like really different.

Ben: Of course, once Charles Lloyd and you began touring, you immediately got the attention of the world. And very soon thereafter, the recording business entered your life in a real way. At one point, George Wein decided to start his own label, featuring new talent. And you were one of the first artists he decided to feature. The record that you made on George Wein's private label was called *A Hundred Hearts*. There's a song on the album, "Three Forgotten Magic Words," and on the jacket, there's a hint about the title, that it came in a dream to your wife?

Michel: No, it was my ex-wife at the time that dreamed it. One morning she said, "I dreamt that somebody was telling me three magic words. But," she say, "I forgot them." And, you know, it sounded good. I say, "That's neat." I just liked the idea. But the music has nothing to do with the title.

Ben: It's a great title though.

Michel: Yeah, it's cute. I like it too.

Ben: And the playing has a certain dream-like quality to it. Almost an impressionistic quality.

That record started to bring quite a lot of notoriety to you in the United States. Did your life change at all at that point?

Michel: I don't know. It became more complicated. I think it's more complicated now then it was before. But there are good things. You know, it's interesting to see that I come from like a very little town in the south of France. Okay. It's like the smallest town in Ohio, something, you know, like, there's nothing happening there. And, sometime, like I'm on the stage now with people like Roy Haynes or Freddie Hubbard and, even today, I still pinch myself and say, "Wow, I'm really playing with these people. These people used to be my heros." You know, they're the people I listened to when I was a kid, and you know, I say "Wow!"

I'm blabbering here. I can't really get to what I wanna say. What I wanna say is that I never thought I would be who I am now. If somebody, when I was in France, said, "You know, you gonna play with Freddie Hubbard. You're gonna record with Roy Haynes. You're gonna play with Lee Konitz and Charles Lloyd, and . . ." If people were to tell me that, I would say, "No, you crazy." You know, "No way. It's not gonna happen to me." And it *did* happen. And, to this day, I'm still happy about it and shocked. You know, I go, "Man, I'm like, I'm joking around, I'm making fun of Roy Haynes now." I mean, not fun, but you know, we make fun on the bus or laughing or telling jokes and stuff like that. And like, you know, for a minute, it goes by in a flash, and I say, "Man, I'm doing this with Roy Haynes. This guy's a legend." You know, there's not a lot of kids my age that could say they worked with Roy Haynes four months, you know, in the band, and playing my compositions and stuff like that. It's like a great experience and a great honor for me.

But things go so slow in a band, you know how it is. It get so slow that you don't see yourself progressing, even in the music. I mean, like, if I hear myself, like I hear the last album I did, and I don't like it. I mean, I like it, but I say, "Aw, why did I do that for?" You know, and so I hope that the mistake I made on that one I won't make it the next one. Because I always try to be better, to do better, because I don't like what I do. I mean, I like what I do, but I have a lot to learn. And, in fact, I'm very happy about that, because I think if somebody said, "That's it, I know it all," then the best would be to quit and change business. Do something else, become a painter or something. You know, if you knew you were the greatest of what you do, that there could be nobody better than you, I think it would be sad, in a way. That would be probably when death started come.

Ben: They say, "If you're not busy being born, you're busy dying."

Michel: Right. Exactly. And that's how I feel. I mean, I try to go slow but surely to where I want to be. Which I don't even know where I want to be. Sometime I know, like I'm practicing something on the instrument and I say, "Okay, I have to define something." You know, I get to a door and I say, "Okay, that door. Okay." So now I open this door and the work that is there behind that door is unbelievable. I go, "Oh, my God." You know? "I got it for another ten years." And then eventually I get through that, cleaning that up, whatever, like an airplane garage or something. So when you finish cleaning that up, you open another door and there's something even bigger than that. And it never, never ends. And it's, sometime it's depressing. But I find it very encouraging and really lifelike, you know, and that's the beauty of it.

Ben: I love the fact that you describe it as such a physical thing, like having to clean up an airplane hanger. It's not cerebral, it's very physical.

Michel: Yeah. It is. I feel like that on the piano, too. Piano is a very physical instrument, don't you think?

Ben: Absolutely. When you project your music . . . and I know that you probably don't look ahead any more than you look behind; you look where you are and you do the work that is directly in front of you . . . but when you do look ahead, where do you want to go and what sorts of things are you working on to get there?

Michel: Whew. I don't know. I really don't know. I have the feeling that I'm getting more and more a personality, like my own personality. I don't really know how to describe, because I mean I still have the same mind. I still think of Bill Evans and Wes and Miles and Coltrane and all these people, and other people that I've played with. And things on the radio. Classical music. I mean, just the big massive, you know, big salad of all that. But somehow, the more I listen to my music, which I don't do very often, but when I do an album, I listen to it a lot . . . after it's done, you know, because I wanna criticize and like that . . . but I realize that I'm getting more and more to be myself. If that means anything, you know, to anybody. But it's getting more and more Michel Petrucciani's sound and not Michel Petrucciani quote Bill Evans quote McCoy Tyner quote, Keith Jarrett quote, you know, everybody in town *except* me, you know?

So now it's becoming more me. And I'm not looking for that. Because, if you look for that, then it's wrong. You'll never get it because it comes naturally, I think. So that's what I'm looking for in my music. I wanna play stronger, better, and sound more like myself. If that means anything. Because it really doesn't. Because I think that the musicians, we all a big tree. It's like a family tree. We all, we're born, we all have a father or a mother, you know. It's like, I come from a somebody and, you know, eventually, one of these days, somebody will come out of me. It's a big tree. You got Art Tatum and Oscar and, you know, Bud, Monk, like that.

Ben: Do you agree, as many people have suggested, that becoming more like yourself often means simplifying, playing less rather than more?

Michel: Yeah, these are cliches. I mean, of course, less is more, you know.

I think what I'm looking for, right now, is the *sound*. I'm looking after the sound of the piano. Because I think that if you have the sound, if the sound is right, and strong enough, it could . . . you know, the sound is like . . . Picture a sound like a Swiss watch. If it's on time, if you play on time, you gonna get the sound. And if you play on time you gonna get the sound, then you don't need to play anything else but that. OK. And it's like a very hard thing to do, because, I find myself now, when I think of playing like that, I get lost sometimes. Because the chord changes go by and the tempo is here, and, you know, like I'm trying to play, "Okay, now play the sound." Meanwhile, you know, fifteen bars went by in front of my eyes and I didn't see it. You know? And I go, "Hiya, where are we now?" But I'm working on that. You know?

But I think that the sound is the most important thing. Because if you got that and the timing, then everything will come. It's like if you get that, you don't, you don't play anymore, somebody else plays for you. You see what I mean? You don't need to play. It'll come, it'll come, just like, "Whew!" You know, and you could play three hours and say, "Wow, I just started!" Okay, because time, if it's right, it fools you like that. Anyway, that's what I'm working on.

Ben: That's beautiful. When you say the sound is driven by the time, you mean, literally by a time sense?

Michel: Yeah, by the time sense, yes. And especially the frequency of the sound. When you stop playing a note, and it's on time, that means it'll be time for you to play another one. Okay. So you have to find out where that high peak goes. Okay, you go from zero to thiry and back to zero. So when that thing goes to thirty, then it's time to stop, or fade, or play something else, or start again. You know, but you have to find out where is the *peak* of the sound. You know, I'm saying thirty, it's like an imaginary number. But where it hits thirty is really what you have to look for, and if you don't bring the sound to the climax, you don't play. It's just, that's not it, you know? That's not enough.

Ben: Just wonderful. It's a kind of a technical explanation for something that's almost metaphysical, which is, how to birth the music. How to give birth to the music. How to let the music play you.

Michel: Right, exactly.

* * *

McCoy Tyner (September, 1985)

Pianist McCoy Tyner had developed his own sound on the instrument while still a teenager, but it wasn't until he joined John Coltrane's quartet as a young man in his twenties that his playing reached full blossom. As an integral part of that group from 1960 through 1965, his fondness for modes, what Coltrane called "McCoy's . . . well developed sense of form," and his ability to "take anything, no matter how weird, and make it sound beautiful" had a profound effect not only on the direction of the quartet but on practically every pianist who followed. He has always been a man of great humility and dedication. I was first introduced to him back in the early '60s, and at that time I told him it was "an honor to meet him." He looked at me kind of sadly and said, "Oh man, don't do that to me." Since that time, he's covered more road than virtually any other piano player, leaving a brilliant trail of solo, trio, small and big band recordings as evidence, yet he still insists that "keeping it light" is what it's all about.

Ben: I noticed when I looked at the calendar this morning, today is September 23rd, which is the anniversary of John Coltrane's birthday.

McCoy: Yeah, that's right. That's very true.

Ben: It's a complete coincidence. I mean, I wasn't aware of it when we set this up. He's been gone a long time, but he's certainly still very much with us, musically. And I'm sure people continue to associate you with your stay in his quartet.

McCoy: Right. Yeah, I understand that. Of course that was a major period in my life. My association with John, I mean, some people, whenever they hear me they think of John immediately, you know. Although there's a younger generation now that don't have that reference so what they do is they accept me for what I am today. Basically, I'm very proud of my association with the Coltrane quartet. But, you know, right now I'm involved in . . . we have to continue, you know?

Ben: I remember first hearing you with the Jazztet . . .

McCoy: Right, exactly . . .

Ben: You were a very young man then, obviously. What, nineteen years old?

McCoy: Yeah, something like that. I think bordering on twenty.

Ben: But even then, you had an identifiable style that didn't sound like all the other piano players at that time. You had tremendous technical facility, obviously, but there was something about the intervals you played, I suppose, that just jumped out. How did you develop that intervallic sense at such an early age? What did you do?

McCoy: Well, it's really funny, because I was hearing different harmonically, when I was very young. It's really funny, you know. I can't really explain it because I was drawn to different types of composers. For instance, I liked Debussy and I liked Stravinsky's music and a lot of Ravel. Different types of music. I think that before I had a chance to really allow this sound to come out, I just liked hearing different intervals and different voicings. And I think this maybe contributed to the fact that, you know, that my sound was able to be nurtured within me, and then eventually, being with John, it was allowed to come out.

Ben: But what sort of conscious process did you go through to bring out what became a very recognizable style, perhaps the most recognizable piano style in jazz today?

McCoy: Well, I was very fortunate, I had the pleasure of meeting and hanging out with Bud Powell. I was so young, but we used to follow him around and try to get him to play, you know. Quite a few times, because he moved around the corner from me. Him and Richie Powell, his brother. And we used to follow Bud around, you know. We had a place where musicians used to hang out and we'd have dances on the weekend. But the musicians could live in this place. It was called Rittenhouse Hall. It doesn't exist anymore, but, you know, that was dedicated to musicians and you could go there and jam and rehearse, do whatever you wanted to do. And we used to try to get Bud to come up and play. This is before he went to Paris.

Ben: Were you also friends with Richie? . . .

McCoy: Well, I met Richie, but we weren't really friends. I think he was out on the road with Max Roach at that time, and I didn't really get a chance to meet him that much. But anyway, Bud of course, I did get a chance to meet Bud, and he played my piano. That was really a thrill, because he didn't have a piano. It's ironic, as I think they just moved, Bud and Richard, and I don't think they had a piano in their apartment, so I had one, and you know, I got Bud to come on and play it. I'll never forgot that. He initiated my piano. And I saw him later on in Paris and I said, "Remember when you came to my house and played my piano and I offered you a sandwich." He said, "Yeah, I remember that."

Ben: He say what kind of sandwich it was?

McCoy: He didn't accept it, so I don't know, maybe he wasn't hungry. But anyway, he was a great man, and, you know, I'm really thrilled to have been in his presence. And he really helped me a lot, just the way he approached the instrument.

Ben: You know, that's interesting, because often, it isn't copying somebody's notes that's important, but simply being in their presence. You can pick up a lot that way.

McCoy: He was a very dynamic person on the instrument, and I liked that, the way he approached it, you know. So I was inspired a lot by Bud.

But I try to tell young musicians that the sound is *within* you. You have to develop what's you. You have an identification, in terms of sound, within yourself, you know. It's just a matter of finding it. I think that that's what it is. And, of course, some people happen to find it at a young age and it's very visible.

I don't know, I think the fact that being with John, and him allowing you to be yourself, I mean, he wasn't the type of person that, you know, would be categorized as a dictator. He allowed you to develop your own inner feelings. In other words, he really allowed you the freedom to do what you wanted to do.

And I think that that's it. And I've adopted that same thing. I feel the same way about guys who are working with me. Young musicians, and whatever age the person is, develop in their own way, you know.

Ben: The other thing too, of course, is that you would play long with John Coltrane. I heard Elvin tell a story about a matinee that the band played. The band played one song for a three hour matinee. And, if you're playing that long, you're gonna have to dig deep and develop your ability to identify and sustain your style.

McCoy: Yeah. I think what happened is that the standard that was set in that band, you had to meet. The thing is, at first, I sort of resented sitting up there and strolling, what we call strolling, which is allowing John and Elvin, or John and Jimmy, you know, to do whatever they had to do to develop something. To just sit there and, you know, play for a while, a few choruses and then allow them to have it . . .

When John suggested that one time, I said, "Well, why should I sit there and do nothing?" But then, I realized it was a blessing in a way, because, I mean, it didn't make sense for me to play for two hours, you know, comping. It wasn't necessary. And it really gave it a lot of contrast dynamically by me restraining for a while, you know.

Ben: We've been talking about how you get your own sound on the piano. A lot of people think, "Well, there's only 88 keys and every piano player plays the same 88 keys, so there probably isn't that much difference in the way one piano player would sound on the same instrument." That's not true. Every piano player will make the same piano sound different.

McCoy: I mean, that's the thing, you know. Your sound is within you. I think it has a lot to do with touch, but then it's a little bit more than that. I mean, it's just like when John used to pick up a horn, a saxophone, you know, whatever it was. You could say, "Oh, that's still John." The sound is identifiable. It's *the person*. And I think that whatever instrument you play, if you have a definite sound, or one that can be recognized immediately, you know, even if the instrument is not in correct working order, you can still say, "Well, that's so and so."

Ben: Could you define the characteristics of your piano style?

McCoy: I think that one of the characteristics of my style is I can take a dominant chord and do a lot of different things with it, and utilizing suspensions and moving around that particular sound. Really, just developing it, you know. And my composing, like "The Greeting," has sort of a modal sound to it, you know. But you can go in so many different directions with it, and that's what I like. Most of my compositions, the melody is usually very simple. But I think the harmonic movement is what makes it interesting. You know, the fact that underneath it all, everything's happening.

What it is, I think, it's just your approach to the scale. I think that's what you're dealing with, you know. It's hard for me to define, really, what I would do, because the circumstance has a lot to do with what's going on too. The type of feeling I have will determine what direction I'll go into.

Ben: What about using fourths on what is normally a chord structure based on thirds, and getting a different extension than a lot of other players did get in the past?

McCoy: Right. Yeah, right, well, that's true. Yeah, I think we all have some sort of an identifying characteristic about what we do. It's a sort of a musical vocabulary that's pretty recognizable. I think that that's important, you know. It's like when you're talking, you know. You have a sound like, how do you say, "Well maybe I might hear you later." I'll say, that's Ben talking, you know. It may not be what the words you used, and then again, it may be. Or it may be just your *sound*, you know?

See, the thing is, sometimes to define the difference between a B flat minor and B flat seventh, sometimes it doesn't really make that much difference. It all depends on what it is. I find out, like when you're playing a blues it doesn't matter if you play a B flat seven or a B flat minor, you know? It's the *scale* that counts. You know, you're really playing off of a *sound*, rather than just defining what notes they are. I think that *sound* has become more important to me over the years than the actual notes, that you're dealing with. I think that what's important is the type of sound that you get, you know, rather than dealing with individual notes. Some people say, "Well, how can you think of all those notes, you know, in one tune." I mean, you don't think of it like that. You're thinking more or less of sound. And sometimes you're not even thinking about what chord you're playing. I mean, because the chord is just a symbol. The chord signatures are just symbols of a particular *sound*, you know?

Ben: Do you then ultimately approach the keyboard as just one big chord?

McCoy: Yeah, yeah, well more or less that way. Because it's how you resolve things that matters. It's how you resolve them. It's just like having a conversation, you know? I mean, you have your exclamation marks, your question marks, your periods. All those things make up a good sentence. I mean you just don't keep running on. You put periods, you put question marks, you know? And that's the same thing with music, you have to punctuate. And that's what makes sense, that's what makes it music, when you punctuate correctly and you make what you say a reasonable resolution, according to what's happening at the time.

Ben: The point you're making about the *sound* of the chord being more important than the actual notes is a good one, because that's a key, that's a way to get in there, to understand the difference between having a sense of direction and a road map.

McCoy: I think the reason why I may have used fourths, or began to use them more and more as time went on, or developed my style on that, is that, actually, it's more than fourths. There are a lot of different things. You're allowing yourself to do a lot of things with sound when you leave your voicings open. You see, a long time ago, a lot of the piano players used to lock, close everything up, you know. Play all the notes in the chord. They left no space. But I'm finding a space, and the spaces between the intervals are just as important—or more important sometimes—than filling the chords up.

Ben: That's wonderful. Time and time again, talking to players, I hear that: what you don't play is just as important as what you do . . .

McCoy: Yeah, and like when you hear Duke and Basie, you know, like, what they left out was very important. The fact that they left this out of here. Thelonious too, you know? I mean, very, very beautiful.

Ben: On a recent trio recording, you dedicated a composition to Basie. And it really captured his spirit.

McCoy: Yeah, well, it's funny. I'd never met Basie before. And I met him about six years ago. And I was really thrilled to meet him, you know. I mean, I been around a long time, on various occasions, and actually I heard the band live, but I just never met him. So I wanted to write something. Well, of course, after he passed, I decided to write something that would express how I thought about him as a musician, you know. As a great musician.

I believe in honoring my predecessors, you know, and I've written some music, like, for instance, I dedicated some music to Duke and this is for

Basie, and then for Coltrane, Thelonious, you know. So I try to honor those who went before me.

Ben: As a player, you do seem particularly sensitive to this sort of thing. For example, you sound completely different on that trio date than on the album you made with John Faddis and Jackie McLean. I mean, it's still you, your sound, but . . .

McCoy: Yeah. [Laughs.] . . .

Ben: What's goin' on here?

McCoy: No, it's, I'm not trying to confuse anybody. It's just, it's funny, but I play according to the personalities around me, the musical personalities that are surrounding me. And that's something that I think is very important, that you play within context, you know. I think that different people inspire me different ways, and I think that's good. I mean, people can still identify who I am by my playing, but, by the same token . . . I tell you what. I don't like to approach every recording the same. Yeah, I think that that's the reason why maybe I might sound different from the trio record.

Ben: And maybe that's another good reason for young musicians to go out and play with the best musicians they can find. When you put yourself in an experience like that, you can't help but become a different person.

McCoy: Yeah. Exactly, 'cause that's how I learned when I was coming up. I played with the musicians who I thought could teach me something, you know. And I surrounded myself with them as much as possible, as well as some people who were my generation. But most of the guys were older than me.

Ben: This brings to mind the Blue Note Night at Town Hall that happened early in 1985. It was an historical reunion with a lot of well known Blue Note players, yourself, of course, included, and a lot of younger players got to mix it up with the previous generation. Only this time, you were part of the establishment, and younger guys, like Michel Petrucciani, were there to pick up on the tradition. Kind of passing on the baton.

McCoy: He's an amazing guy. Michel. I mean, as a person as well as a musician. He's always laughing. I mean, not all the time. He's not *always* laughing, but he has a bit of that in his personality. He's great, you know.

Ben: His playing has a lot of humor in it also . . .

McCoy: Yeah, yeah. Well that's the way Michel is, I think as a person. I mean, he's a very serious pianist, you know. We've played on occasion opposite each other. And I admire him in a lot of ways. He sounds like himself, and that's what's important. That's what I try to emphasize. His technical facility is definitely happening. But what I like about his playing is the fact that he he's not hung up in cliches. I mean, he's playing things that he feels. I think we all have a musical vocabulary that we sort of rely on, you know, and I think that it's good to be able to work around that. And I feel as though he's just playing himself, you know. He's expressing himself.

Ben: He's clearly got that kind of light attitude about a very serious subject, music. I can't imagine, for example, that when you were working with John Coltrane's quartet that you were unaware of the historical importance of what you were doing. But, at the same time, I also can't imagine that you were concerned about it either.

McCoy: Well, it was, it was an experience that I can't even describe. I mean, on a day-to-day or night-to-night basis, it's really hard to find words to define the type of effect that it had on me. Yeah, because it was on such a creative, high creative level. The dedication there, the fact that there weren't any assertion of egos at all. It was just basically the music was what was important. And, of course, John's a very, very dedicated musician and to have him in the forefront, and under his leadership, I think was really great. So I didn't think about it. I knew it was great, but when you are a part of that whole flow, it's hard to really say, "Well, what am I involved with?" I mean, you know it's great, but by the same token, you don't really know until you look back in retrospect and say, "Wow, that was really amazing."

Ben: So you step out of it and you realize that the rest of the earth is not moving quite at that speed...

McCoy: That's true.

Ben: We're talking about how you can't take history too seriously when you're in the middle of it, or it can make you freeze up. You've got to tread lightly...

McCoy: You got to, Ben. You've got to have a humorous attitude about life to a degree. I mean, even though we are involved in an art form, I think that's one of the things that I'd like to see more emphasis on. I know in my playing, especially, I like to not only, you know, give people experience musically, but I like to make them feel good and walk out with a smile, or whatever. There are many ways to approach it. I think that in the early days, jazz was definitely viewed that way, as a music to really make people feel good and walk out with a smile. Those things are very important, you know.

***

Max Gordon (December, 1986)

Interviewing Max Gordon was like talking to a combination of Mel Brooks' 2000-year-old man and Yoda. He was beyond elderly at the time of our talk, about four foot ten, thinning white hair, a face shaped by cigars, virtually tottering. In a business where nightclubs come and go with the seasons, Max successfully ran the Village Vanguard in the same location for more than five decades. Five decades of great artists—writers, painters (like Stuart Davis), and musicians—spent many a night surrounded by the artifacts that Max collected. The cluttered walls, the piano, the atmosphere—everything became definitive of what a jazz club should be. In fact, there's an apocryphal story about a Japanese aficionado who once offered him a million dollars to buy the club so that he could take it apart, brick by brick, and reassemble it in Tokyo. It was said the stage was haunted, and many musicians claimed that music never sounded better than when it was being played from that dark little corner, behind the pillars. Max wasn't a romantic about the business. When asked about the good old days Max let you know that they never were. As he said, "It's about the same. The same problems. Find the band and find the money to pay 'em." Yet he talked about the "sound" of the room almost the way musicians talk about their own personal sound or the sound that makes one player different from another. Night after night, Max held court at the Vanguard, mostly running the place from his "office" in the kitchen (a table and chair shoved into one corner). For him, it was about feel. *Feel for a music, a scene, an environment. Till the end (he died not long after our talk), he marveled at his success, saying to me, kind of slyly, "And the people seemed to like it . . ."*

Ben: I don't think anybody has had more years in this music than you have. The Vanguard has been operating for how many years?

Max: Well, we opened up our present, in our present location, in 1935. That's 50 years; our 51st year comin' up. And now we always had, have the big jazz shows. We had singers, poets, artists, and like that, at the beginning. But then we changed about the middle '50s to a full jazz policy. And we've been at it ever since.

Ben: Strictly jazz since the '50s.

Max: Strictly jazz. No rock, no fusion, no, you know, tough electric jazz. Just acoustic jazz, mostly acoustic jazz.

Ben: When you started, there was a lot of poetry there. A lot of...

Max: Yes, we had poetry, and we had discussion groups and we had little shows. We had little reviews, that we, I used to bring down from the Catskills. Well, my, the original review I had, the one that set me off in a big way, was the one they called The Reviewers, in which Judy Holiday was a member. There were five young people, and they're just all outa school and writing their own material, doing their stuff, writing their own music, and performing it. And they did, and they worked every night there for one year, doing that.

Ben: And jazz was part of this whole milieu?

Max: And then, yes, jazz was just part of it, you know, there's your pianists, trios, duos, and like that. And we had comedians comin' in, which, and singers, and... but now we have, we have singers occasionally. If they're good, if the group itself brings in a singer, then we have a singer. But we don't go out and hire a singer.

Ben: This is part of your policy, obviously.

Max: Yes, that's the policy, yeah.

Ben: I gotta ask you. The jazz clubs all around the country are closing and opening and closing for years. Except for The Vanguard. You're the only one that's been there through it all. What's the secret, Max? How come you can run a club for fifty years in one location, and everybody else is closing?

Max: Well... this... just... there's no secret about it, really. You know, the New York dramatic scene calls us the greatest jazz club in the world. I don't call it that, but they do. And, what makes us the greatest? I don't know.

I mean, I think, I have an idea, that, when I look around, and I see the Vanguard in operation, I say, well, I think one of the things is we don't... we don't get tough with our customers. We allow our customers a lot of leeway and a lot of freedom. They pay, but we don't pressure them and we don't annoy them, you know? I think that's one reason why we have lasted so long and why people have fallen in love with the Vanguard, really. I mean, every day somebody comes up and tells me, "Well I used to... I've been comin' here for thirty years, or twenty years, eleven years." And, "Every time I come to New York...," their travels, they're living outside of the city, maybe, and "I never fail to come to the Vanguard." Well, you know, I hear this, and I begin to feel that maybe there is something to the place. And that the people that call it the greatest, maybe know what they're talkin' about.

Ben: You never fail to come to the Vanguard either. They know that when they come to the club, you'll be there.

Max: Yes, they always find me there. I'm usually hanging out there. Not as much as I used to, and not as late as I used to. But I'm there. I had some people come up last night, for instance. I was there. We had a wonderful group, there, the Arthur Blythe group, with John Hicks at the piano, playing there. And the people seemed to like it very much. And a fellow came up to me, two Japanese men, came over to me there. I get a lot of Japanese, by the way. And they wanted to buy a book. And wanted me to sign the book, which I did, of course. And this goes on every night, more or less. I've sold, I've probably sold a couple of thousand copies of my book *Live at the Village Vanguard*, over the last three, four years.

Ben: This book, by the way, it's available in book stores around the country, yes?

Max: Yes, I hope they are. I know that people sometimes have trouble finding it. So they come to the Vanguard. They know they can get one there.

Ben: They come to the Vanguard. The book tells the story of the Vanguard. And in the book it tells how you came from Portland, Oregon.

Max: Portland, Oregon. Yeah, that's where I grew up. I went there, grammar school, high school, and I went to Reed college, graduated Reed college and came to New York.

Ben: Came to New York, pretending to be a law student.

Max: Well, yes, my mother wanted me to be a lawyer, but I didn't want to be a lawyer, and I didn't know. I didn't wanna open exactly a nightclub. I didn't know what nightclubs were. I'd never been to one. I sorta stumbled into it. Some gal that was working one of the joints called Paul's. And she was a waitress there, and she, she sold me on the idea. She hated Paul so much, she hated the place, that she said, "Max, why don't you open a decent place." What she meant by decent is, I hardly know. But I had an idea. And that's what the Vanguard is. I think it's a decent place. That's maybe why it's as, you know, as popular as it is, to some people.

Ben: There are a lot of wonderful stories in your book. One of my favorites is how a plumber named the club for you . . .

Max: A plumber? . . .

Ben: Harry the plumber?

Max: Oh, Harry the plumber, yeah. Well Harry, you know, was one of the men hangin' on in the kitchen. He was a plumber. He did plumbing work all around. That's how he lived, that's how he made a living. And he could also build things, fix things. And without him, I could never have opened up the original place. Which was not on the present location, but on One Charles Street basement. And that's where he helped me get goin'. I paid him, I don't know, here and there, over the years. He took it out in trade, I think . . .

Ben: And the book tells the story of how you agreed at one point to name the club the Vanguard, which is a name that he came up with. And he agreed . . .

Max: Yeah, he helped me name the place . . .

Ben: He agreed to defer the payment if you called it the Vanguard.

Max: Yes. So I made it the Village Vanguard. Yes . . .

Ben: Why The Village Vanguard? . . .

Max: He was a radical gentleman. You know, he was politically radical, you know. And "vanguard" was, for him, a word that expressed the future of the world, the future of the workers of the world. That was really . . . and I sort of embraced the name. I liked the name. And so a lot of people seemed to like it too.

Ben: When you first started, you say you had no intention of opening up a nightclub. You didn't know what a nightclub was . . .

Max: That's true . . . Well I tried to find something to do with my life, you know. I got out of college. I took liberal arts. I had no profession. I didn't go on with law, become a lawyer. I didn't wanna become a lawyer. I didn't have the money to go to Columbia. Oh, I matriculated there. I got out fast, because I knew I couldn't keep it up, you know, and I knew that I had to go out and go to work and earn, earn my way. My poor . . . I come from a poor family. My mother, father, you know, couldn't send me any money. When I was in Portland, I used to work. I used to work when I went to school. I used to bring the money home to pay the rent. Help pay the rent. So I certainly couldn't expect them to send me money to New York. So I had to do something. And this girl gave, put the idea in my head. This, this waitress, who was working for Paul's, whom she hated, by the way. And she hated Paul and she hated the place, although she kept working there. And she's the one kept saying to me, "Max, why don't you open up a decent place in New York."

Ben: But she only lasted six weeks at your place, and you're still there . . .

Max: Well, she didn't stay very long. But once she opened up, she was my hostess. And she was supposed to get all the poets in there, which she did, you know. And they all came in and they left Paul and came to me. That's what happened.

Ben: Have you always been a night person?

Max: Not really. I just worked at night, which made me a night person. But I was, I don't, I don't know exactly what a night person is. A man who stays up late? And likes to stay up late? And hang out late? And all that? I wouldn't particularly do that. The only reason I've done it is because it's . . . my work called for it. My doing it, otherwise I'd be sort of out . . . I'd be home, wondering about what's happening down at the place. And besides, I didn't have the help. I needed, I depended upon myself to do everything.

Ben: I know you've had a lot of various types of entertainment in there, with poets, and so forth. But I'm particularly interested in how you became the premiere jazz club. How did you develop a jazz policy?

Max: Well, I listened to a lot of jazz, you know, and I listened to a lot of records. I always did, you know, even when I was, even when I wasn't operating a jazz club, I was listening to jazz. I listened to jazz radio, I listened to jazz, buy jazz records. And I used to hang out, and I used to go into a jazz place, I couldn't afford to buy the, buy the records. But they, in those days, they used to allow you to go in there and listen, before you bought a record. They don't do that anymore. And I used to hang out there for hours, listening to records. And that way, I got acquainted with jazz, got acquainted with people who played jazz. And naturally, they came, they started coming around to me. I said, "My goodness, I used to listen to him. He was great."

Ben: Who were some of the first musicians to start coming?

Max: Well, I've had all kinds . . . I had like John Coltrane, Miles Davis of course, with me for years. Mingus. Bill Evans, Zoot Sims, all of 'em. I've, I've had 'em all, all, all those years, you know.

Bill Evans once reminded me that when he, when he first worked at the Vanguard, he worked at it as a soloist. He didn't have his trio together, so he worked opposite the Modern Jazz Quartet. And I, I'd forgotten about it. The middle '50s. And I used to get some pretty good, some pretty groups in there. In those days I could afford 'em. Well, when I had Modern Jazz Quartet, I couldn't afford a Modern Jazz Quartet today. But I, I paid pretty good prices to some, some groups. But, I couldn't, for instance, when the xylophone player, what's his name, that plays for the Modern Jazz Quartet . . .

Ben: Milt Jackson?

Max: Milt Jackson. When, when the, see the Modern Jazz Quartet had broken up for a while. So Milt Jackson put a quartet together. Well, I put him to work. I could afford him. And, as a matter of fact, I'm lookin' forward to putting him back in the next two weeks or so. But unfortunately, they're together again. They come together and then they separate, and they come together again. And this goes on and on.

Ben: Was it easier in the '50s to have a jazz policy than it is today?

Max: Well, not really. You know, I didn't know if it was easier or harder. I had less money to pay, so it was a little harder. Now I have a little more money to pay, and I'm able to hire some of the people that I really want, you know. So I would say it's about, about the same. The same problem. Find the band, and find the money to pay 'em.

Ben: Well, you found a lot of great ones, obviously, and many great artists have chosen to record at the Vanguard. I think there are probably more "Live From the Village Vanguard" records than any other live "from" records.

Max: Yes, I lost count of 'em. The only people who know the exact are the Japanese. And they once published it in their magazine, *The Swing [Journal]*. They had a magazine that I get every month from Tokyo. And I forgot now exactly the amount. But we did a record last week, and then two weeks ago we did another one. And then we're gonna do another one, maybe next week.

Ben: Everybody wants to record live at the Vanguard.

Max: Live at the Vanguard. Yes, it seems to sell records.

Ben: There are so many great records recorded at the Village Vanguard, real landmark recordings. Like the one recorded in June of 1961, the famous recording of Bill Evans, Scott LaFaro and Paul Motian.

Max: Yes. Bill did a lot of records down there. He was one of my real favorites. And I used to use him a lot. I could afford him. And I got to know him very well. Got to be very good friends of his. Not every musician, you know, is going to become a friend. I don't see them that much, you know. They, they stay a week, and then they leave. Then maybe I don't see 'em for a year or so. But Bill used to come back often. I went to his house for dinner, for instance. I met his wife, his children. I say his children—his child. He had one son. Yes. That's been my . . . it's been my history in a way. Some of them I got to know well, and some I just simply got to know for the moment, while they're working the place. And then I never used to see 'em maybe for a year, or two years, or three years sometimes.

Ben: Which musicians stand out in your memory?

Max: Well, we talked about Bill. One man that I got to know pretty well is Miles Davis. Miles used to work there quite often. For a while. He doesn't work here—there—anymore. But, Mingus, Mingus was one of my favorites. He gave me a lot of . . . he used to be a little trouble. But he was worth the trouble. He was a great musician. And, well, I liked Zoot Sims very much. Zoot was one of my favorites. I could go on, you know, and name a lot of musicians that I enjoyed. And I don't know. I mean, I liked . . . well, I mean, for instance, I liked Al Grey. And they're comin' in, Al Grey and Buddy Tate. They're comin' in next week with a quintet. Roland Hanna. Roland Hanna played for me once for eighteen weeks straight. That was in the '50s. And he used to play for some of the singers that I had there. Used to accompany. He played with a trio and he used to play his music, and then he would accompany the singers that I used to hire at the time. Like Dinah Washington and some others that I can't remember, tell you the truth.

Dinah was a great girl. She worked there quite a bit. Dinah came out in a blond wig one time, and it was a real . . . Well we, we didn't, we didn't laugh, and we didn't remark about it. We just sort of looked at it, and wondered about it. Wanted to know what happened to her. And Dinah was a great gal. Once, once she caught cold, but she, that didn't stop her from comin' down and doing her gig, you know, because she needed the money. But, she brought down another singer with her. What is the name of that girl she brought down? . . .

Ben: I think in your book you mentioned Gloria Lynn.

Max: Gloria Lynn, yes, and she killed 'em out, and she and Gloria Lynn would do the show. And when, during the nights when she felt bad, she would start the show, and then let Gloria Lynn finish it. Then at the end, she'd come out and take a bow.

Ben: Gloria would finish the show and then Dinah would take a bow? . . .

Max: That's right . . .

Ben: Did you ever find yourself in the position of having to give musicians a little fatherly advice, that might have affected their music?

Max: Not too much. No, I never used to discuss much. I'd just tell 'em to be on time and stay the set, and don't be late, that's all . . .

Ben: That's all you wanted? . . .

Max: Take it easy. Well I mean, I never used to tell 'em much on how to play their music. That was, they knew more about it than I did and I, I used to just sort of, you know, listen. If I liked some of their music, I used to tell 'em, of course. We used to talk about it, you know. But I wouldn't advise them, and criticize them . . .

Ben: Have you "discovered" a lot of jazz musicians, or mostly do people get well known and then come to you?

Max: Well, we, in order to book a group, a man in the Vanguard, he has to be, has to have some sort of a name. Has to have some sort of a notoriety in the jazz world. So the people will come to hear him. I can't just simply take an unknown, even though he may be very good. Although I've taken chances on some people. They were not, who hadn't, you know, achieved a great notoriety. And I put 'em to work, you know. And I helped make it, I helped make them a name. Yes.

Ben: And sometimes, the club itself is almost the star of the shows. For example, I've seen maybe fifty different drawings, photos, of the Village Vanguard on album covers. I notice, you haven't done a whole lot to update it, have you, Max?

Max: Well, the Vanguard is the Vanguard. It's the same Vanguard it was from the very beginning, although of course we have done . . . we've given it a little more style, a little more class. A little. But we mustn't disturb it too much, because the Vanguard "sound" is there, and we don't wanna set up, put in anything that might, in any way, disturb that sound. I don't know how we ever got that sound. Just the walls, the ceiling, the floor, it's there, and we just leave it alone. We change a few pictures and all that. But the Vanguard is not highly decorated at all, and it's just a simple place.

Ben: For people who haven't been in, you go down a long, rather steep flight of stairs...

Max: Yes, it's in the basement and some people love basements. I love a basement.

Ben: And it's a small room. How many people does it hold?

Max: It holds about 125 people.

Ben: It's crowded if 125...

Max: And sometimes we have as many as 150. Come to last night, we had people standing up, and had people waiting on the stairs to come in for the second show. We're gettin' a lot of that. The Vanguard's a crowded place. It has been doing well this last few months, more so than before. It's grown a little bit.

Ben: Why do you suppose that is?

Max: I don't know. I think the people are beginning to find the Vanguard. Especially the Japanese. They come in in great numbers. And we have tours, from Europe, making a point of coming to the Vanguard. They hear, they hear of the Vanguard. This a place they wanna come to when they come to New York. Seems that way anyway, to me.

Ben: You say it's not highly decorated, but there are a lot of photographs and drawings on the wall that have become synonymous with the Vanguard. Often, on live records from the Vanguard, you see that interior, and that interior has become kind of famous.

Max: That's true. I know, we do put up pictures. And like all the walls are full of pictures and it sort of, it gives you a history of the Vanguard there. Musical history. Peoples' faces, of men that played in the place, men who have made their careers in the place and all that. There they are.

Ben: One of the reasons that the many tourists come to the Vanguard from overseas is because of the reputation it has as a spiritual home for the music. But there's also talk among musicians of spirits living in the Vanguard. Musicians' spirits.

Max: Yeah, well I've had musicians say to me, "Max, this is a place I wanna work." Even last night, you know, one of the musicians that plays around, and he's really quite a great musician, and he's made a reputation for himself, and told me that this is the place he'd rather work than any other place. Why? The sound is right for him. He seems to, you know, welcome the sound that he can get in the place. Which he doesn't seem to be able to get anywhere else, he says.

Ben: It's very curious, isn't it...

Max: Wynton Marsalis told me that. That's quite a, quite a compliment to the Vanguard.

Ben: It's also quoted on the back of another record that was recorded here, called *Saturday Night In The Cosmos* by the George Adams and Don Pullen Quartet. This is a record recorded in August of 1983. But on the back of the record, there's a long quote from George Adams, who says, "Musicians of course always play their best when they play the Vanguard, because the club has so much to do with jazz music." And then Don Pullen is quoted as saying, "Danny Richmond [Mingus' drummer] always said if the sound isn't right, it's not like the Vanguard. The Vanguard's got the best sound." But what's curious is, you don't have much of a sound system down there, at all. You don't have a lot of speakers, not a lot of mics . . .

Max: Well, we have a sound system, but . . .

Ben: It's not a big deal . . .

Max: . . . it's not a big deal. In fact I think we have one group that comes in that doesn't wanna use the sound. I don't remember his name now. He lives in Delaware Gap . . .

Ben: Phil Woods . . .

Max: Phil Woods. Phil Woods will not use the sound system. And he sounds great.

Ben: Do you, like so many people in jazz, miss the old days, miss the '50s and '60s?

Max: No I don't. No. I mean, I miss some of the men that used to play in those days, you know. I miss some of the people. You lose, you know, jazzmen don't live long, unfortunately. They die young. And this year for instance, we lost quite a few people, like Thad Jones, Zoot Sims, and a few others like that, and I miss them, of course. But the music goes on. There are always new people, new men, taking over. And thank God for that.

Ben: Would you say there's any difference between the way players comport themselves today as opposed to the way they did in the '50s and '60s? Do we have a different kind of jazz player these days?

Max: Not really. Not so much different, you know. There's always some difference between people, but not a difference between one area and another. Or one year and another. It's still, they still come a little late [laughs], for their gigs. But I must say, they're improving, some of them are improving. That's one thing I just talk to them about. Like, for instance, John Hicks. Well, John is on time now. He used to be, he used to be in the habit of coming late all the time. But he was there last week and he was there on time every night.

Ben: So you think you're makin' some progress here?

Max: I think he's makin' a little progress there. As a piano player, he's the same. Good.

Ben: They used to say about Miles Davis, he'd show up late, but he'd still be way ahead of everybody else.

Max: Miles Davis had a bad habit, a few bad habits. We know he had some of those, now. Miles Davis would walk off on the third set, sometimes, because some girl called up. She was in another club drunk, and, his girl, and he'd just walk out. He'd walk out. Then he'd leave his quintet or sextet playing, Herbie Hancock at the piano, leading the band. It's happened, not often, but it's happened several times. Miles is tough. He was the toughest to handle that I had, that I can remember.

Ben: Did you ever try to renegotiate the price if he left the club?

Max: No, I wouldn't even think of it. He had no chance for that at all. He was always ahead anyway, you know. He always drew ahead. You couldn't possibly get him to reimburse you. That was out of the question.

Ben: You mentioned John Coltrane earlier . . .

Max: Oh, Coltrane, of course, was a great man. One of the outstanding jazzmen. He came with his quartet. I never got to know him too well. You know, Coltrane never talked very much. He's a very shy man. I used to talk to his wife more than I talked to him. And he died soon after he appeared the last time in the place. Coltrane was great, there's no doubt about it. He was one of the outstanding men. He, he was a giant.

Ben: Made outstanding records at your club as well.

Max: Yes, he did. He made several records.

Ben: The first one, *Live From The Village Vanguard,* was recorded in November, 1961, with McCoy Tyner, Elvin Jones, Jimmy Garrison, Eric Dolphy . . .

Max: '61 he recorded that, huh? . . .

Ben: It's 25 years ago . . . He recorded a song called "Spiritual" on that record. Were the nights when Coltrane played at the Vanguard special in that way? Were the people who came to hear him a particular kind of audience?

Max: No. They were just people. They were just people, just people who liked jazz. I didn't notice particular there were any certain type of person. I didn't, you know, examine them that carefully. What I worry about is the size of the audience. And whether they paid, and whether buy another drink or something. That was my problem.

Ben: So the makeup of the crowd isn't that important to you. You are interested in, are they buyin' drinks . . .

Max: Yeah . . .

Ben: . . . are they behavin' themselves?

Max: That's right. And listening to the music. They came to hear the music, and that's what they're doing. You see, that's what I've learned about the Vanguard. On a Saturday night, you know, when the music starts, the place just goes quiet like Town Hall. And it's, it's amazing, you know, 'cause, that's why you have to keep the music good, to make people wanna hear it. Make it worthwhile hearing, you know. And, people "shush" each other too, you know. Sometimes, I'll be "shushed."

Ben: They tell you to be quiet.

Max: To quiet myself. Yes. Say, "Hey." And that's what it is about—the music. The music is the thing. That's what brings 'em all. We don't serve food. We only serve drinks. And we have a small minimum, small and very reasonable. I think that the Vanguard is very reasonable. And that's the way it goes. You know. We keep the music as the most important part of the place. And the people come to hear it especially, and they wanna hear it. They're paying their way in, they're paying admission to hear the music, and they wanna hear it.

Ben: Have you had times where business was so bad you thought about getting out of jazz and getting into something else?

Max: Well, not really. We've had bad times, don't get me wrong. But we always kept hoping that it would improve, and it did improve, you know. The '60s were tough. Yeah. And we were able to navigate. Were able to pay our way. We didn't make much money, maybe, but we didn't lose much either, you know. And, times, we had our ups and downs. Like every business. But we have been able to establish a place now, and now we're doin' pretty well. I must say.

Ben: The Vanguard is a family business too, isn't it?

Max: Well, I have my wife now, joining me, in operating the place, and it's a good thing for me, because I'm gettin' kind of tired. Sometimes my age is creeping up on me. And she's able to give it a little help. A little of this, which it needs. And it's good to have her. I mean, I'm enjoying having her.

Ben: Do you still make all the decisions about who plays there?

Max: I do, yes, I do. But I'm willing to listen to reason. [Laughs.] I don't mind having someone suggest something to me, and I listen to it. And I don't feel perfect, that I'm perfect in my judgement about jazz. Some people can teach me things, too. And some listeners especially, you know, I listen to them. I get all kinds of ideas. I mean, and sometimes, I have, an agent will call me and he'll give me an idea. And my wife will sometimes give me an idea. I don't mind listening to her.

Ben: You've listened to more jazz than most people ever could listen to, because it's been right there in front of you night after night. Do any great moments stand out?

Max: Well, there are moments of course, but they come and go, you know. There was, even last week, I got Arthur Blythe. You know Arthur Blythe? Some of his numbers I don't care for, but some that I thought were great.

I just love 'em. And I had a remark about that to a man in the kitchen that works for me, Jed. And he says, oh, it's the same with him, you know. You hear 'em one night, you hear 'em another night, just a little different.

Ben: Your club has played a big part in the re-emergence of a lot of players. Frank Morgan obviously is one . . .

Max: Yeah, that's right . . .

Ben: Back in 1967, it was very important in the re-emergence of Dexter Gordon also.

Max: Yeah, Dexter Gordon, yeah, I think it was a girl who called me up and said, from London, and asked me if I wanted her to bring Dexter in, and give'm a job for a few weeks. And I said I certainly would. And I hope to use him again. Now that he's become, of course, now that he's become a great movie star, I don't know if I can get him so easily. But I hope he'll be playing again, and playing at the Vanguard. He owes me some time. Yes.

Ben: Many musicians, I'm sure, owe you some time.

Max: Owe me some time, and some of them a little money too. [Laughs.]

* * *

Archie Shepp (December, 1985)

Archie Shepp has long been a leading spokesperson for the black experience in America. During the '60s, his recordings on the Impulse label embodied a rare fusion of the so-called "free" music of John Coltrane and the soul music of James Brown. His inclusion of long tone poems on his albums anticipated the rise of jazz poets, such as Gil Scott-Heron, and indicated the range and depth of his cultural thinking. Today, he is a full professor at the University of Massachusetts at Amherst and carries himself with all the dignity that title bestows. On the other hand, he is also the quintessential street musician, with an ear for the rhythms of ghetto life and an eye toward its ironies. He is a rare individual whose experience as an actor in the legitimate theater, a musical protégé of John Coltrane, and an educator at a leading American University gives him a particularly broad overview of the jazz scene. The following conversation took place in New York City, where we met one winter afternoon, Archie driving the three hours from Amherst and myself flying in from Chicago. We briefly renewed old acquaintances (Archie and I had last seen each other in 1984 when we played a concert together) and then rolled the tape.

Ben: You've been at Amherst a long time now.

Archie: It's been about fifteen years now.

Ben: It's quite a different world today than it was fifteen years ago, both in the academic community and in the music community.

Archie: Yes, it's changed profoundly, in ways that I'm sure none of us could have predicted. [Laughs.]

Ben: Describe to me what motivated you to leave the avant-garde New York performing scene of fifteen years ago and move to Amherst.

Archie: Well mostly it was my family, my immediate family, meaning my wife and children. And then my mother, who's now deceased, encouraged me to get out of the city and try to own something, some property. So I did. I live on a farm. I suppose most of us ghetto guys opt for farms when we get out of the city.

Ben: The wide open.

Archie: Yeah, the wide open spaces.

Ben: You say you're a city boy. Where did you spend your early years?

Archie: Well I was born in Fort Lauderdale, Florida, and raised there for the first seven years or so. I grew up in Philadelphia and spent my formative years there. So I do count myself an urban person. Even Fort Lauderdale wasn't the sticks. So I perhaps have more of a nostalgic attitude about my rural-ness than actually being a part of my growing up. I grew up pretty much in the city, and the city's a tough place. Especially for, I think, minority people.

I grew up in a place that's known as the "brickyard." In fact, it had been a brickyard when the Irish lived there originally. And then they moved out and the Italians moved in. And then black folks started moving in during the forties, which is about the time we came along. And it still carries the name today. In fact, it's not called "the brickyard." It's called simply "brickyard," without the article. As its name implies, it was a very stoic, a very Spartan upbringing.

I was fortunate that I was raised pretty much as an only child. My brothers and sisters didn't come until later. In fact, I'm fifteen years older than my oldest sister. So perhaps that's one of the reasons I was able to enjoy some of the benefits of simply growing up. I mean the piano lessons, the music lessons. And I was a good reader all through school, because my aunt and my grandmother spent a lot of time teaching me my alphabet, and reading. So from an academic standpoint and a cultural standpoint, perhaps I enjoyed things that many of my peers did not. And even my sisters and brothers after me, I think, found it a bit tougher.

But the "ghetto life" was important to me because it taught me the elements of survival. And it taught me a certain . . . it deepened my sensitivity and compassion. Many of my friends are dead, and I feel as though I've come through a war, although I never went to Vietnam.

Ben: At what point did music, and specifically the saxophone, become your ally and a weapon with which to deal with this war?

Archie: Well, I started out on piano at a very early age. I think I was about ten years old. And then I studied the clarinet from about the age of thirteen. When I was fifteen, my grandmother and my aunt purchased a saxophone for me, and I probably studied the saxophone less formally than I studied the piano, in a way. So the bulk of my lessons were on clarinet and piano. As I say, I was very fortunate to have that training. And without my grandparents, it probably wouldn't have been possible.

Ben: I, of course, like so many people, became aware of you through your recorded work. The first record album I remember was called *Four For Trane*. There's a picture on that album of you sitting on some stairs, smoking your pipe, and behind you, looking down at you, is John Coltrane. That album revealed you as an artist with an original approach, as well as something of an academic. How did that session, and that photograph, come about?

Archie: I should say first that I was very fortunate to have met John Coltrane as a young man, and I was among a number of young people in whom he took an active interest. And he was perhaps essential to my making the first recording I did for Impulse records. I must say that Bob Thiele, who later became quite an aficionado of this kind of music, really couldn't stand it when he first heard it. And he was very suspicious of my motives. I used to call him every day on the phone. And his secretary used to tell me either "Bob is out to lunch" or "He's at a meeting," you know. This went on for a few months.

I was on welfare. I used to take ten dimes out of my welfare check a day—I was in a fifth floor walk-up in New York—and I'd run down to the telephone at the drug store on the corner and I'd call ten times each day. I put aside a dollar a day to call Bob Theil. And for over a month, I would get this answer, "Bob just left" or "He's out to lunch" or "He's in a meeting." So Bill Dixon suggested to me that I ask John directly to intercede. And I was very humble about that kind of thing. I didn't want to put myself on John or take advantage of what was an acquaintance. I can't really say that it was a friendship in that sense, because I didn't really know him perhaps as well as he might have known me at the time. I think that always accrues in a relationship between an older and a younger person. Because I found out later that he probably thought a lot more of me than I thought he did.

So I did, I asked him. And, in fact, he was working that night down at the Half Note when I asked him, down on Spring Street, and it was on the intermission. And I hemmed and hawed. I didn't quite know how to get it out. I wanted him to intercede for me at this record date. So finally he said, "Well what are you trying to say, Shepp?" So I said, "Well, John, I want you to ask Bob Theil to give me a record date." So he looked at me very hard, you know. And I thought, "Oh God, I've done it." And then he said, "You know, people are always taking advantage of me, because they think I'm easy." And he looked at me very hard. And then he said, "Well, I'll see what I can do."

And he did. The next day, I called Bob, and low and behold, I spoke to him. And he said, "Yeah, John told me about it." He said, "The only problem is . . . " And this is the way he used to brush off all the young guys, the avant garde players, because Coltrane had interceded before for other people. This is the way Bob usually got them off his back. He'd say "You can't record your own music. You'll have to record all of Coltrane's music." Well, I knew about this little gimmick, and I had been actively rehearsing my band. In fact, I had arranged the songs already, so I said "Great!" So this is how we did the "Four For Trane" date, because four of the compositions were John's.

Bob was really upset at the record date, because I think he felt that John had forced him into something he really didn't want to do. And he was smoking his pipe like a chimney in the corner, at Rudy Van Gelder's studio. He didn't even turn around to look at us as we were warming up. But after the first song, he got on the phone and he called John out on Long Island. He said, "Trane, this stuff is great! You got to come out here." It's eleven o'clock at night. So John, being the gracious man he was, came out, without even his socks on. In fact, in the photo on the album, you'll see he has no socks on. And he sort of oversaw my first recording for Impulse.

And after we finished the fourth song, there was one left, the original piece I had written called "Rufus (Swung His Back at Last to the Wind and Then His Neck Snapped)." Of course this was one of the songs that Bob thought we should never include in the album. He wanted John to hear this, because it was just enough to fill out the album. We needed that much time, and it wasn't a very long piece. And it was the only, you might say, piece from the album that fit the avant garde description—certainly the one that I was later to be titled with. So he said, "John, listen to this piece. I don't like it very much, so tell me what you think."

So Trane listened to "Rufus" very attentively, and after the piece was over he said, "Well, I like it, Bob. I think you ought to leave it in." So Bob said, "You really like it?"

So because of John, that one piece was left in. And I think it was important, too, because that was an original piece by myself, and it served to underscore some of my own originality. Once again, and I say it very humbly, without Mr. Coltrane, this would not have been possible at all. And I think of him, even today, as a person who is very responsible for the integrity and the authenticity of whatever we have left of this kind of music. Because, as you know, more and more we are deluged by commercial pop music, rock and roll, cross-over music, and so on. These are important forms, but I think the kind of music that was played then is important, too.

Ben: This track, you mentioned, "Rufus," was important also in that it included a vocal as well. And it was from the lyrical content that listeners were able to infer your academic or intellectual identity. I suspect it was from that part of the presentation that we were able to realize there was something new operating here. Not just musically, but conceptually. Here was a young jazz musician who had a larger agenda to get across.

Archie: Yes, and we were talking earlier about vocalized tone. Certainly a piece like "Rufus" had, for me, many implications. I think Jimmy Baldwin, in one of his books—*The Fire Next Time* or *Blues for Mister Charlie*—has a hero whose name is Rufus. And this is where I might have gleaned the title. Because I made, even at that time, certain literary analogies in my music, specifically in the titles of my music, because I have felt that in order to get something across to people, sometimes musical notes are not enough. Sometimes, we have to say these things in words.

And I think it's been born out by the kind of music we hear today, which is more and more vocal music, and less and less instrumental. There is that need, I think, especially on the part of our two-thousand-and-year-one audience to have that verbal communication. The vernacular.

Ben: And that holds true today for your own music. You've been doing vocals over a kind of dance rhythm for many years. I remember years ago an album you made called "Mama Too Tight." And recently you made a record called "Down Home New York" that is both an inside and outside approach to vocal jazz. James Brown meets John Coltrane.

Archie: I'm glad you mentioned that name [James Brown]. I think he's a really important person, regardless of style or type of music. I think he's changed the way soul music is played today, especially the backgrounds, double-timing the figures against the drum beat, and so on. He and Ray Charles are very important. Ray brought in the gospel element, and Brown reinforced that element, and also introduced a rhythmic element. You know, one of my fantasies is to have heard James Brown and John Coltrane together.

Ben: Mine also.

Archie: Because I think we would have found a nexus there that hadn't quite been forced yet.

Ben: I can hear that you, in your music, have been going toward that nexus from time to time.

Archie: Oh yes.

Ben: And it was refreshingly pure, in contrast to the rather polite ways other jazz musicians were trying to incorporate popular dance beats into their music, when you did it in the '60s. Your music seemed to illustrate that critical point where the primitive meets the avant-garde.

Archie: I think so. And I must say that I was very influenced by Lee Morgan's recording of "The Sidewinder." Lee was very influential to me growing up. I'm just a year older than he was. And he was quite a mentor to me during those few years. I used to comp piano backgrounds for him when he was growing up, as a youngster. Usually because he couldn't find a real piano player. But it helped me a lot. It helped me to learn to play the piano.

Ben: Really? This was back in Philadelphia, of course.

Archie: Yes. On Saturday afternoons I used to go to his mother's house and very often I would either bring some music or play some music he had. Things like "Sippin At Bells" or "Tempus Fugit," where I'd play the chords just straight up, you know, root up. And eventually I learned to voice chords that way. And Lee was very helpful to me on the saxophone. He led me to identify solos and to learn how to play, you might say, notes against the chords.

Piano players are very fortunate in that when they look at the piano they can see what they're doing. But horn players have to do all that from their mind. They have to envisage what they're actually playing. So by learning to back up horn players on the piano, I eventually began to get a concept on the saxophone. You might say it's a piano concept. Much more so than a saxophonic one.

Ben: You mean in your choice of notes, specifically?

Archie: Oh definitely. I see the saxophone keyboard much like I would see a piano keyboard. Because I can visualize it. I think that's an advantage to me, in a way. It can be a disadvantage, because you play too many notes sometimes. And so that's a thing I've been getting into, as Miles says, learning to edit myself. But it's because sometimes I see perhaps too much, and it's a question of distilling. But it's been very helpful to me, my knowledge of the piano, over the years, and it's profoundly influenced my concept on the saxophone.

Ben: One reason why that surprises me is that you play with such a highly vocalized tone. I have assumed that you approached the saxophone from the human voice point of view and were finding ways to turn it loose. And yet you say that the way you chose was more traditional, through the keyboard.

Archie: Yes, indeed. I don't think that you're altogether wrong about that, though, because before I began to meld these two concepts, I certainly went through a period where my approach to the saxophone was certainly more melodic than harmonic. It was after my meeting with Coltrane and because of his influence—and others, Golson, Lucky Thompson—that I began to think of different ways to play chords, so that I could get to as many notes as possible. Now, I'm on the reverse side of that. I'm trying to play as few notes as possible. But that certainly was helpful to my technique.

Ben: Speaking of your mature work, I particularly like your more recent recordings where you are reintegrating some of the more traditional jazz repertoire. I'm thinking particularly of the Horace Silver tribute you did called *Tray of Silver*, where you even used Roy Brooks on drums, who used to record with Horace.

Archie: Much of the Blue Note catalog was very influential to me, as I'm sure it was to many musicians. And it's interesting that the entire Blue Note series was made available in Japan after it was out of print here. When I researched that album, *Tray of Silver*, I had been very enamored of Horace's compositions for quite a while—I think he's one of the important composers out of that period—and I couldn't find several of his records. And I didn't find them until I went to Japan.

Ben: Do you get the feeling that we're being colonized with our own culture?

Archie: [Laughs.] Yeah, how about that. It serves us right. Admiral Perry and all those guys notwithstanding.

Ben: Did learning the music of Horace Silver, which is almost classical in terms of jazz today, help breathe new life into your own current playing? Is that one of the reasons for returning to the well, so to speak?

Archie: I think most musicians have in the back of their mind some guy that they always wanted to play with. And Horace is one of those guys, one of those bands that I always wanted to be in, in the fifties and the sixties. Back when a lot of his important things were coming out, like "Senior Blues." Gee, I envied the hell out of Junior Cook and those guys for the fact that they were able to be there. Not that they weren't, certainly at that time, much more ready to be there.

I had just come out of college, and though I knew my changes, as they say, I didn't have the experience. I learned that from the sessions at Basie's. I used to be at the sessions with Richard Williams and John Handy and Freddie and all those guys, before they joined the bands. And they were a little ahead of me then, because, you know, as a college boy, I just couldn't put all the time into my horn that I wanted to. And those guys were playing the music pretty much twenty-four hours a day.

So when I'd come home in the summers, I'd stay with my aunt. I used to go up to the sessions at Basie's, and I'd go home many a night discouraged, you know, because those guys were playing so much music. So, once again, when I did put together that album with Roy Brooks and those guys, I was especially happy. Roy is really one of the formidable percussionists in the field.

Ben: We started this discussion with you positioned at the very edge of the avant-garde—that's how you were portrayed during the sixties—only to discover your long-standing association with mainstream jazz. Were you upset during the sixties to find yourself being saddled with the avant-garde label?

Archie: Well, you know any label confuses people. When we start saying "jazz," "soul," "bebop," "blues," it can sound like gobbledygook. I was reading recently where Dizzy Gillespie had been warned by Ellington not to let the critics call his music "bebop," because if you name it, you date it. I think that's a very profound insight. It implies something of your work, the book *Black Talk*, in which you point out that language means so much, even in the way we categorize phenomena. So that given all the other problems that Negro music faces here in the United States, that's just another problem heaped on to it, when you label it, and it's labeled something that nobody understands.

For instance, "jazz" itself, as I often tell my classes, has as many social meanings as cultural and musical ones. It's not like when we say "Baroque" or "Renaissance" or "Classical." Those things have very specific and definite meanings. But when we describe the phenomena that attempts to portray the cultural perceptions of minority people, especially Negroes, it seems that our language goes haywire. And when we try to put that in an academic context, I mean, for example when you want to teach people what it is . . . forget it.

Recently, I gave my students an assignment to do a paper on gospel music or jazz music or soul music, they could chose what they wanted. And I was just amazed by their confusion when it comes to describing what this music really is. Except for a very few people, who usually are musicians themselves. It's very difficult for the lay person to articulate what it is they're listening to.

For example, I went out to Chicago to do a performance recently. And the cab driver was talking about how much he liked Herbie Hancock. And so finally, he said, "He's a jazz player, isn't he?" So I said, "Well, today it's difficult to know." Those labels don't mean what they used to mean.

You know, I think part of our problem is in defining ourselves.

Ben: That reminds me of something that H. Rap Brown said during the sixties. He said that the first task of the revolutionary is to define the space you occupy. Never let somebody else define your terms.

Archie: Exactly.

Ben: You talk about the interrelationship between all the various black idioms—gospel, soul, blues and jazz. And one of the things that these idioms have in common is what we call highly vocalized tone. Anybody listening to your playing must be struck by this aspect of your work. Lately, however, you've even begun singing standards as well. You recently recorded the saloon song "The Good Life" as a vocal, dedicating the performance to the memory of Sonny Stitt.

Archie: Yeah. Once again, I was doing a performance in Chicago, two or three years ago, before Sonny died. And I happened to see Von Freeman, the father of Chico Freeman, who's a very fine saxophonist. And he said "You know, Sonny Stitt was just out here. And Sonny was playing 'The Good Life.' " And he laughed, in a very wry way.

And I'm such a fan of Sonny Stitt's, and I've listening to so many of his recordings, that I could almost hear him playing the song. And Sonny, like Billie Holiday, had very good taste in the material he chose to play. Speaking of the vocality of these things, he often chose songs that had vocal implication. Some people might consider "The Good Life" a very banal melody, sung by Tony Bennet. But it has a tremendous message, if you listen to the inside of it. And I could just hear Sonny playing it, with all the depth and imagination and technique that he could bring to it.

And so I thought about playing it myself. And I said, "Well, gee, maybe I'll never rise to that occasion. Maybe I should sing it. This is my chance to sing." So I decided to sing it and dedicate it to Sonny, whom I never heard play it, but in my mind's heart, I think I heard him play it. Of course, I didn't sing it with all the finesse that he played it, but maybe if I keep getting to record my voice I'll come up to that level.

Ben: Again, it reminds me that jazz music, even in its abstract and historical context, is essentially popular music. When it's at its best.

Archie: Oh yes. I think Duke's old adage, "It don't mean a thing if it ain't got that swing," is very important. It's one of the reasons I began to try to fit my material more to popular taste, and by popular taste I mean I wanted to attract a wider audience. Because I feel audiences should have some alternative to rock and roll. I think musicians, especially those who come from my kind of a background, should think twice, and more than that, when they play for people. That today's audience is not as sophisticated as the audiences of the sixties, at least from a listening point of view.

They couldn't possible be, because they don't hear the same things. When we grew up, radio was perhaps the overriding medium. You didn't see what you heard, so your mind's eye had to fashion that picture. And your ears were bigger. The things we heard were more complicated. In other words, Kate Smith would never have made it today. Not because she couldn't sing in tune, but because she was fat!

You know, jazz musicians didn't have to look good. Rock and roll musicians . . . I tell my kids this, probably the thing that militates mostly against my becoming a rock musician is my image. I'm getting too old for it. Guys like me, and I even say that about people like Miles . . . I find it embarrassing at times that sixty-year-old men have to act like twenty-year-old boys. It's a tragedy that such a gifted musician can't live out his life on his own merits and on his own terms. That suddenly, in order to be successful, whatever that means, or to make millions of dollars, whatever that means, you have to become something else. Put on high-heeled shoes or loosen your tie, or whatever.

Some of these things seem so superficial when we look at them, but the world has changed so dramatically from the time that I first heard Coltrane, with Miles, to the time, say, I heard Branford Marsalis with Miles. The influences are the same, in a way, but the medium has changed. I think McLuhan, and you mention this in your book, was really right on it. It's the global village now. When the kids turn on their television sets, they want to see a Michael Jackson. And if it's a Miles Davis, he damn well better look something like a Michael Jackson.

Ben: Perhaps the technology has come home to roost.

Archie: Yes, hasn't it, Ben!

Ben: Technology really determines what music sounds like, in a very basic way. So the human scale is becoming obscured. Coltrane played magnificent music on a human scale. It wasn't about technology so much as it was about a great human spirit.

Archie: Of course, and I think one thing that underscores that is I remember hearing John here at the East Village Inn, which later became the Fillmore East when Bill Graham took it over. I used to live right around the corner. So I went there one evening to hear Coltrane, and John had what they call the young Turks, all the young players who were really hammering out the music. And I was sitting right up front. And I could see Trane bending and blowing. But I could hardly hear anything. Of course, I knew his music and I could feel the vibe.

And I remember coming back a few weeks later when Bill Graham took over the place, and he completely installed a new sound system. I went to hear Charles Lloyd. The night I went to John with his group, the place was almost empty. But this night, the place was packed! And I stood at the back of the auditorium—you know it was one of the old Lowes theaters, so it's a huge place that held two or three thousand people—I was standing in the back of the theater. Charles was playing a flute solo, which was coming clear as a bell. And the bass player was louder than he was! And I thought back to when I heard Coltrane with those seven or eight young players, blowing their guts out, and you couldn't hear them in the first row.

So getting back to the technology of it all, yes, times have changed.

Ben: I think that might have been a pivotal moment you witnessed.

Archie: Indeed it was. And it's frustrating, because it's those kinds of things that, as you say, are not only pivotal but part of the whole transition that we've been into, how technology can make a person imitating another person sound better than the original.

Ben: Well, technology will never be able to surpass or recreate the great voices. Like Ben Webster, for example, or Dinah Washington.

Archie: Oh Dinah, I miss that voice. It's a sound from the past, you might say, that can never really be recreated. I hear some of her in Aretha Franklin, who's a really great voice, too. Today, voices are much more specialized. A singer has to be, like Donna Summers, who has a very fine voice, but she has to be a rock and roll singer. A few years ago, in Dinah's time, a singer like Donna Summers or Aretha Franklin would have had to do it all.

Ben: They would have been jazz singers?

Archie: Yes, they would have been jazz singers. That's a peculiar part of today's definition, today's organization. We've gotten so far away from the use of the term jazz, for lack of a better word, but so much of what we hear actually falls into that category. And a few years ago, back in the thirties and forties and going all the way back to race records, jazz just happened to be one of the many ways of describing a number of different types of musical events that took place in the community. And a horn player or a singer had to do it all. I mean, you could walk into a bar and buy a beer and maybe hear Coltrane playing "How High The Moon," followed by Ruth Jones doing a blues. The audiences were much more demanding at that time.

Again, the audience was a much more sophisticated audience due to their ear training and the kind of music they listened to. Today, we're much more visually oriented. I think of my presentations as partly dramatic, today, and my acting training and all that comes in very handy for me. Because as a vocalist who used to work with me, Bozzy Grey, said, "In the old days, people used to come into the Five Spot to hear the musicians." I was putting my reed on the mouthpiece at the time, and he was watching a woman in the audience watching me so attentively, just mesmerized by what I was doing. And he said, "Today, the people don't come to hear, they come to see."

And you know, I've added that to my performance. I spend as much time with visual events, from the way I dress, from the way my behavior is on stage, as with musical ones. Because, of course, musical practice takes place at home anyway. But the audience today is much more demanding, they demand a visual experience just as well as a musical performance.

Ben: I mentioned Ben Webster also because what he does with sound is similar to what Coltrane achieved with technique. And, of course, your sound has been compared to his from time to time.

Archie: Well, my sound has been compared with Webster and I feel more and more humble every day about that because I think he has one of the most sophisticated and perfected voices on the instrument that I've heard. And then Webster seems to have added a dimension. Prez is very important from the point of view of sound, but his emphasis wasn't sound. Even Hawkins, who was gifted with perhaps the generic saxophone sound, it wasn't something he concentrated on so much as something he had. But Ben seems to have understood, the way Coltrane did later, the implications of what the saxophone could do. That these trick notes, as they call them, really weren't trick notes but were, in fact, another way of vocalizing sound.

Ben: A point of departure for yourself, no doubt.

Archie: Right, that was where I took off from. From Ben and Coltrane. They were my two biggest influences. And Eddie Davis. I shouldn't leave out Jaws.

Ben: Let's return briefly to the subject of your teaching. That too has been a point of departure for you. What are your plans in that regard?

Archie: Well, I think that African American music can be better understood if we approach it not only from the point of view of performance, but from an academic standpoint, discussing its history, going all the way back to Africa, and so on. And I think the implications of teaching are vast, in the sense that not only do I have a musical presence at the University—my presence is felt as a musician—but also, from the larger cultural point of view, I'm able to make the statement that jazz musicians, especially black jazz musicians, do something other than blow saxophones and get high or whatever we're stereotyped as doing. That we're also capable of expressing ideas, that we're sensible and that we're capable of sensitivity.

And that we have a history. Our music has a history, which is important to tell people about. And I think it's important to impress this upon the younger musicians, that not only are we performers, but we are people who live out our lives on an intellectual and cultural basis as well as a performance one.

Ben: I think that's an important point. In jazz, the artist is the treasure. The recording industry would have us believe it's the other way around, that it's the plastic artifact that is most valuable. Again, we have to keep our eye on the human scale, not the technology.

Archie: Precisely.

* * *

Herbie Hancock (January, 1987)

It's impossible not to notice the unusual circumstances surrounding the career of Herbie Hancock, and so, of course, we began by talking about his phenomenal success in the record business. Our conversation took place not long after the release of the movie 'Round Midnight, *in which he and saxophonist Dexter Gordon had received very positive reviews for their acting roles. Interestingly, and perhaps somewhat ironically, Dexter Gordon was also a participant in Herbie's first great commercial success, the recording of his hit song "Watermelon Man." Herbie and I spoke in a hotel room in downtown Manhattan, just one of the many stops on his endless rounds of the world's jazz capitals. Herbie is truly a contemporary jazz entrepreneur, as well as one of the finest living practitioners of the art of the keyboard.*

Ben: You've had a very unusual history in the record business, if for no other reason than you've sold a ton of records. Most jazz artists don't even dream of the kind of success that you've had, even from the beginning of your career. For example, your first record as a leader, which was released on Blue Note back in 1962, contained a "hit" song, "Watermelon Man." Of course you had played on a few earlier Blue Note sessions, on some Donald Byrd recordings. But your first record as a leader was a big success.

Herbie: Yeah, it did real well. Much to my surprise and the record company's surprise. Actually, it was in the top 100 of the pop charts. They only had pop charts at that time.

Ben: Right, there were no jazz charts back in the '60s.

Herbie: Right, there were no jazz charts, there weren't any R&B charts, I don't think there were even any Country charts. That I don't remember for sure. I only remember it was just the pop charts. They didn't have it all sub-divided into different things. And, I think, it got as high as 80 or 76, or something like that. And then Mongo Santamaria recorded it and his went through the roof. His version got to be number ten, I think. Nine or ten, it was in the top ten.

Ben: Your version was a jazz hit, but his version was a serious hit.

Herbie: Yeah, well I had originally just conceived it as a kinda funky jazz tune. That's all. But, either just before the record was released or just after I got a gig with Mongo Santamaria. I played with him one weekend. And I'd never played Latin music before. Never played with a Latin band. And he was between piano players. One guy was quitting, and a guy named Roger Scrant was coming to replace him. Who was a guy I knew, too. Roger lived in my building in the Bronx. He lived downstairs on the second floor, I think. Donald Byrd and I lived on the fifth floor. Walk up. No elevator. Hey, it was in "those" days. So, anyway, I knew Roger was coming in, and I replaced some piano player. I didn't find out 'til about maybe six or seven years ago who the piano player was that I replaced. Now this incident happened in 1963 I guess. Yeah, '63.

Ben: Less than a year after your version was released...

Herbie: Yeah, during the year it was released. Anyway, so I played this gig with Mongo, actually there were three gigs I played, three nights I played with Mongo. One night we played in the Bronx, where Donald Byrd and I lived. Donald Byrd was my roommate, see. So we lived in the Bronx. And Donald came by to hear. Donald was like my older brother, you know. And, he used to laugh at me a lot. 'Cause I was kind of young and green to New York, you know. But he kinda watched over me. So he came by the gig and between shows, he and Mongo got into this very serious conversation about the relationship between Afro-Cuban music and Afro-American music. Slave ships went to both places, you know. Where's that link between the two? And Mongo had never found it. So I sort of half listened to the conversation. It was a little too heavy for me.

And Donald finally says, "Herbie, why don't you play 'Watermelon Man' for Mongo." I said, "What?" He said, "Play 'Watermelon Man' for Mongo." I said, "What's that got to do with what you're talking about?" He said, "Play it." So I said "Okay." 'Cause see, I conceived of it as a kinda funky jazz tune. So I went and started playing it. Mongo gets up, says, "Keep playin' it." He walks over to his congas. As soon as he start playing the congas, it fit like a hand in a glove. Just perfectly. And little by little, his band members joined in. The bass player start watching the notes I was playing in my left hand. Checking out the form. So he picked up the bass line. And then the horn players picked up the melody line and somebody starts soloing and, little by little, the people... It was a supper club. So, you know, people would dance. So little by little, people got up from the tables, and started getting on the floor. Pretty soon, everybody was dancing. And screaming and hollering, because they loved the tune.

And then Mongo, after that he said, "This is a Juajita." You know, which is a type of country song they sing in the mountains. And I said,

"A what?" I had no idea, you know, about any of this. And so he said, "Can I record it?" I says, "Sure." So, we recorded it, and, you know what was interesting? One week after he recorded it, Xavier Cugat came out with the same arrangement of "Watermelon Man." I don't know where he got it, how he heard it, or what, but he got it, for his big band. But it just didn't have that feeling, you know. Was a little stiff.

Ben: That almost sounds like a scene from a movie, the scene you just described in the club, with Mongo and everybody, and it fallin' together.

Herbie: Yeah. It was. It was blowin' my mind. It reminded me of, you know, of these very romantic ideas about stardom or something like that. You know, movies like *Marjorie Morningstar*, it reminded me of that. But it actually happened like that. I mean, people on the dance floor, they were actually screaming. And women were hugging me and saying, "It's a hit." And saying things like that. It was phenomenal, you know?

Ben: That's amazing, because so much of your story, personally, is out of the normal realm of what a jazz player would experience in a lifetime.

Herbie: Right. Exactly. I know that. And it completely blew my mind. And I loved that experience. But, of course, I didn't sit there and think, "Okay, I got a hit on my hands." You can't go around thinking that. I mean, nobody knows the secret to that. But when they recorded it, the thing came out, and it was a hit. That was unusual anyway. It's always been unusual that an instrumental would be a hit. But for some reason, I've been able to make hits with instrumentals. Not often. I mean it's like every ten years I come out with something. That happened in '63. The *Headhunters* hit was '73. And the *Future Shock* album with "Rockit" was '83.

Ben: So, what we're hearing now is, by 1993 you're gonna have another instrumental hit for us, there's no doubt about it.

Herbie: In the meantime, I'll starve. [Laughs.]

Ben: Let's not get too far ahead of ourselves, because after this first hit happened for you, you became involved in another series of records that in terms of the jazz world was in many ways more monumental than the success of "Watermelon Man." "Watermelon Man" was nice. It was a jazz record that did real well, and when a jazz record does well, it's good for all jazz players. But the records that you made, particularly starting with the *Maiden Voyage* period, seemed to really mark something else for jazz players, too. It was a period where the chord changes, in the traditional way, suddenly fell aside, and more of a mood, or a group spirit started to happen.

Herbie: Yeah. A lot of that happened. Well, first of all, the same year that "Watermelon Man" became a hit, that was the year I joined Miles Davis's band. And that was a very, very important step in my own musical development. Because of Miles and because of all the other guys in the band, Ron Carter on bass, Tony Williams, drums, first George Coleman and then Wayne Shorter on saxophone. And I was 23 in 1963, so those years with Miles, five and a half years with Miles, were my formative years. But I had my own record contract. With Blue Note records. Incidentally, when I did "Watermelon Man," that was a one-shot deal . . .

Ben: Really? . . .

Herbie: Yeah. It was just for one record. But that record did well, so they asked me to sign a full contract with them.

Ben: That was a good position to negotiate from.

Herbie: Yeah, yeah, yeah. It was very good. So, anyway, I had my own recordings that I did under my own name, and I also recorded with Miles Davis's band. And, a phenomenon that a lot of people may not realize is that if you play as a sideman with somebody else's band, but you also record on your own, quite often the songs that you record on your own, for your own solo albums, never get to be played live. Because you're playing with somebody else's band. So you record that stuff, and you never get to play it anymore. Unless the guy whose band you're playing with is also playing some of your music, and somehow some of it might be included. But most of the songs that I did on all those albums I did for Blue Note, while I was with Miles, I never got to play them. Unless I got a trio gig somewhere, which was not that often. Sometimes when I was in New York, and Miles wasn't working, I'd get the chance to work for a week at the Village Vanguard or something. And then I might get a chance to play "Speak Like A Child" and "Maiden Voyage" and a few other of my tunes. But normally I would never play "Maiden Voyage." 'Cause we didn't play it with Miles's band.

Ben: That clears up something for me, because not long ago I spoke with Michael Cuscuna, and he told me about a show in Japan that he recently produced with you, and he said he had asked you to play one of your earlier songs, but you told him that he better have the changes, because you never played it. I wondered at the time if you simply didn't like the composition any more.

Herbie: Exactly, exactly. Yeah, I remember. I can't remember which song it was that he asked me for. Well, see, what happened, actually, after I quit Miles's band, I got my own band. Then I got to play my songs. So, that's when I really learned to play "Speak Like A Child" and learned really to play "Maiden Voyage." That's when I began to develop.

Ben: There's one song that was on both the *Maiden Voyage* album you made and the Miles Davis *ESP* record. That's the song "Little One."

Herbie: Right, that's one of the few.

Ben: That album *ESP* was a real watershed album for Miles, too, I think, and for yourself as well. Jazz turned a corner at that point, it seemed.

Herbie: I remember, before we recorded the album *ESP*, I remember we worked one time in Detroit. This was before Wayne [Shorter] was in the band. George Coleman was still playing tenor saxophone with Miles. And Tony Williams, Ron [Carter] and I would play differently behind George than we would behind Miles. Behind Miles, we would play in a way that was more reminiscent of what we were accustomed to hearing behind Miles. You know, I would be thinking more in terms of Wynton Kelly and Bill Evans, you know, that kind of thing. Tony was thinking more in terms of Philly Joe and Jimmy Cobb, and Ron, more in terms of Paul Chambers. Although Ron's approach reminds me in many ways of Paul Chambers, but further developed. On the other hand, Paul was a great genius of the bass. He was incredible, you know. Some of the things he did weren't really touched by anybody. Just things that he could do, nobody really knew what it was he was doing. He was fantastic, but, anyway, this one gig we're playing in Detroit, and behind George we would really open up. Sometimes not even play the time. We'd play all kinds of figures and things, rhythmic figures behind George, do things that were considered more toward the avant-garde. Things that were maybe more expected of a sound that you'd hear behind John Coltrane . . .

Ben: That was the era . . .

Herbie: Yeah, exactly. See, those were the two bands. 'Trane's band and Miles's band . . .

Ben: . . . and at that point, when you were with Miles's band, you were playing a lot of the old standard tunes, just at blazing tempos. You were trying to push them, it seemed, like trying to get through some sort of barrier or something.

Herbie: Yeah, yeah. We still played Miles's repertoire, "If I Were A Bell" and "Autumn Leaves" and all of those things. And so, actually what was happening, we were playing freer behind George Coleman than we were behind Miles. And one day Miles said, "Why don't you play behind me the way you play behind George?" And I looked at Tony, Tony said, "Really?" We said, "Okay." So we started doing that stuff. I mean, playing with the rhythms and doing all kinds of wild things behind Miles. Things that we never heard on Miles's records before. And in the beginning, I remember, Miles started bobbing and weaving and trying to find a place in that stuff. He was kinda starting and stopping, and he was really being thrown by it. And the second day we just continued to do it. He wanted it, so we continued. Next day, there was less bobbing and weaving, you know. He was finding some stuff. By the third day, not only was he not bobbing and weaving, I was the one bobbing and weaving, and trying to find my place, 'cause Miles had it then. He found a way to play in that context that had me trying to figure out what *he* was doing. And right after we played that set, that third night, Miles said, "I don't wanna play any chords anymore." So, Okay, you know. And the next album was the *ESP* date.

Ben: And there were no more chords after that . . .

Herbie: Um hm . . .

Ben: Yeah. Again, your career seems to be the stuff movies are made of, not only because of the success, but also because you've really been at the right moment at the right time.

Herbie: Yeah, that's happened a lot to me.

Ben: It has. You mentioned the *Headhunters* album. The *Headhunters* album is another example of right place/right time, and it's also an example of actively not using chords in the traditional way, and at the same time, using a lot of the newer technology and studio techniques that, at the time, was foreign to most jazz players.

I remember when the album came out in '73 it was a stunning success, I think the biggest selling jazz record of all time. And I spoke at that time with David Rubinson, who produced the album with you on it, about how the record came to be. And he said, "We did everything possible to make that record. If there was a trick in the studio, we used it . . ." Cutting up takes, doing overdubs, whatever it took.

Herbie: Yeah, yeah. We did a lot of different kinds of things with effects and using the technology that was available at that time. Which normally was not applied to jazz records.

See David Rubinson was my manager and my record producer at that time, and the reason he was suggested to me as the producer of my records was because I had moved from Blue Note Records to Warner Brothers Records. And I did an album called *Fat Albert Rotunda*, which was a re-recording of music I did for the first "Fat Albert Animated Special" that Bill Cosby did back in 1969 or early 1970, I don't know exactly when. But the record didn't do so well. It actually sold about as well as *Maiden Voyage* did. But this was not Blue Note Records anymore, this was Warner Brothers. That's the big time. The big guys. Those kind of sales are not good enough for them. And so they thought that maybe if they got me a record producer that had a broad enough taste and broad enough understanding of music and a broad enough commitment to music to be able to relate to what I'm doing, that I could relate to him. But at the same time they thought maybe he could pull me over to doing some more commercial stuff, right?

The funny thing was, after I met Dave Rubinson, I did the least commercial stuff that I ever did. 'Cause the next album, the first one that David Rubinson produced for me, was *Mwandishi.* That was a whole lot less commercial than *Fat Albert Rotunda.* But what happened in the meantime was David Rubinson heard my sextet, and we were playing a very avant-garde music that completely captured him, captivated him. And then he became a champion of our cause, instead of him being a champion of the record company's cause. But at the same time, his problem was he really wanted to stand up for what we were doing, because he thought it was valuable, but he's thinking, "How can we make this music as palatable as it can be, without changing the music?" So we were always trying to think of things to do.

That was one reason we got into electronics, because electronics was associated with rock and roll at the time. The synthesizers, you know, just the sound of the stuff. And so, we felt like if we could do anything that could link us somehow with a wider audience, as weird as that music was, it could possibly help sales. You never know what can happen. Sometimes you take someone who knows nothing about the kind of music you're doing, the hearing can sometimes be so pure that it can just go right to their heart, and they can just really love it without having any kind of intellectual understanding of it. And that kind of music, even though a lot of intellect went into the playing of it, the purpose of it was really non-intellectual. It was purely emotional.

Ben: I think a good example and a distinction between where you came from and where you were heading is the version of "Watermelon Man" that you rerecorded on the *Headhunters* album, as opposed to that little funky twist groove of the original. Instead of going back to the changes you normally played, you used some newer harmonies. And even just the "sound" of the newer version, in the way the electronics were used, the way it was recorded, even the use of bottles for the rhythm track. Were those real bottles or a synthesizer?

Herbie: Yeah, that was a beer bottle, and Bill Summers playing a style of music that was related to Pygmy music from Africa. Authentic kind of sound. It started off that way, you know. That was the intro, with Bill doing that. And it became the signature for the tune. And it did very well. It did *very* well. And that was, again, ten years after it had been a radio hit before. And that tune, I don't know, somehow it's still, it still gets a reaction out of people, you know. Even people who've never heard it.

Ben: Talk about the connection between that kind of approach to music, the conception that created *Headhunters,* and the approach you were doing at the same time when you played with more straight-ahead bands. I mean, are they two different directions, or are they really the same direction re-examined?

Herbie: Well, when I did "Maiden Voyage," one type of approach to rhythm really was close to my heart and still is. It's integrated with the harmonic approach, having to do with a floating feeling, kind of a putting aside of the traditional harmonies of jazz and makin' it kind of a mood. A lot of that harmony could be related to a technical word in music, which is "modal" music. You know, having to do with modes. And that started, in jazz, with Miles. As a formal approach in jazz, it started with Miles's album *Kind of Blue*. And that album had a big effect on me too. Because I loved that sound, you know?

But now, "Maiden Voyage," when I did "Maiden Voyage," here's how I'll tie this in with "Watermelon Man." When I did "Maiden Voyage," I was looking for a way to have a pop tune that didn't have a backbeat on the second and the fourth beat. I was looking for a backbeat on other beats. That's what I was looking for. But in the meantime, I found something that didn't really fulfill that requirement. But, see, I was putting, I was playing around with puttin' beats on different parts of the musical phrase, right? And that's how I did the rhythm of "Maiden Voyage"; was just [sings the rhythmic phrase of the opening of the song]. I was thinking maybe I could use that as a backbeat. But I put chords to that. When I put chords to that, I heard it in a very different way. But what I heard, I liked, so I said, "Okay, I'll forget about trying to find a backbeat, let me do this. This is something to work with," you know? So I worked with the song as it was, and it wound up being "Maiden Voyage." But I was really trying to find a rhythm that would revolutionize what we call a backbeat, which is the beat that you normally clap your hands on, two and four.

And the other thing that related it to a song like "Watermelon Man" is that it contains what we call "even eighth notes." Where as in jazz, traditional jazz, the swing beat goes [sings: dinka din, dinka din, etc.] and when you say "even eighth notes," it would be [sings: deh, denka deh, etc.] instead of [sings swing eighth notes again]. So that "even eighth note" sound links together a song like "Maiden Voyage" or "Speak Like a Child" or "Watermelon Man" or "Rocket" or "Canteloupe Island," which I did on an earlier album. So, somehow, on every album, I had at least one song that had those "even eighth notes."

Ben: So that all through your career, there's been this thread, this "even eighth note" thread that stitched together the major successes you had.

Herbie: Right.

Ben: After the success of *Headhunters*, your ability to work, and the ways you worked and the types of gigs you played changed dramatically. I mean, when you sell a million records, you're not playing the bebop clubs anymore.

Herbie: Yeah, a lot of things changed. I remember one of the first concerts that I did after I did *Headhunters*. We were working opposite a couple of other groups, I think in Philly. And I walked in there, and one of the opening acts was on, and I looked at the audience. I said, "Wow, that's a lot of people here. Who's the headliner?" I thought I was one of the opening acts. I said, "Who's headlining this show?" And David Rubinson says, "Don't you know what's happening here? You're headlining this show." He said, "All those people came to see you." I said, "Come on, you're kidding." 'Cause it was a concert. We used to play in clubs, with like two hundred people at the most. This was like thousands of people, and they're comin' to see me? He said, "You have a hit record. Don't you know this?" It was so foreign to me, I just didn't understand it. And I'd never played for that many . . . well, I had played for that many people at the Newport Festival and some other festivals in Chicago, but this was a whole different ballgame. I was the headliner of this.

And after that, my club work almost completely disappeared. I didn't do any clubs after that. Well, in the beginning I did some, a few, but they were very large clubs. And what I wound up doing mostly is concerts. And, at the same time, the scene began to change for jazz too. 'Cause other jazz musicians began playing mostly concerts. Miles was already playing concerts. He was already playing his electric music, at the time. Chick Corea was playing his electric music. Weather Report was, maybe hadn't quite gotten formed yet, but they were in the process of gettin' formed. So the type of music that became known as jazz fusion was born.

Ben: And so we entered an era in the '70s where people thought that acoustic jazz was in the past and many people looked toward the future of the music with a lot of trepidation, being afraid that the future would be totally devoid of the values of acoustic playing and improvisation and chord changes.

Herbie: Yeah, the only people that thought that were the people who weren't still going to the clubs. But anybody who was on the jazz scene knew that that wasn't true, because the music was still going on. It just wasn't getting the recognition. In other words, the traditional form of jazz wasn't getting the recognition that this new form was getting, because the new form related a little more easily to the most popular form of music at that time, which was rock and roll.

Ben: And, almost as a reaction to this fear, some years later we saw a tremendous serge of publicity for, and interest in, the so-called return of straight-ahead jazz, which was theoretically signaled by the success of players like Wynton Marsalis and, specifically, in your case, the formation of V.S.O.P., a band that played a lot of festivals throughout the world and featured yourself and Ron Carter and Tony Williams, the old Miles Davis rhythm section, but also included Wynton Marsalis replacing Miles. And that group put a tremendous amount of life back into the image of acoustic playing.

Herbie: Actually, what happened was George Wein, who runs the Newport Festival and several festivals in Europe, called my manager and was talking to him about me participating in the Newport Festival in New York. And my manager, who was not so concerned about me participating in a jazz festival at that time, because I was still riding the waves of a hit pop record, which *Headhunters* was considered to be, he asked for something that he thought George would never do. He said, "Yeah, Herbie'll do it if you do like a retrospective of Herbie's music." You know, thinking, "George ain't gonna do that, he hasn't done a retrospective on Miles's music yet." Or Duke. Why would he do Herbie Hancock, you know, I was Miles's sideman? So George came back to him and said, "I think it's a great idea, let's do it."

So what wound up happening was we had a retrospective of my music at Town Hall in 1976, which was the year of the bicentennial. And I had three groups there. I kinda had an unusual situation. I had three different kinds of groups that were really part of my career. One was Miles, the Miles Davis group. But at the same time of course, I did a lot of things with Ron Carter and Tony Williams. We were the rhythm section. And many times Wayne Shorter was added to that. I recorded on a lot of Wayne's albums, and we played a lot of gigs as a quartet with Wayne. And Freddie Hubbard was instrumental in my career at key places. He was on my very first album. I'd been on many of his albums. And we were all part of this kind of hot team of young musicians on the Blue Note record label. And so Freddie was part of that particular group at Town Hall. And that was one phase of what I had been into.

Then there was the sextet, the group that had done albums called *Mwandishi* and *Crossings* and *Sextant*. That had Eddie Henderson on trumpet and flugelhorn, Benny Maupin on reeds, Julian Priester on trombone and Billy Hart on drums, Buster Williams on bass. That was my sextet, you know, after I had left Miles. That had a completely different sound then the sound I'd had during my time with Miles. Okay, then there was the *Headhunters* band. Paul Jackson on bass, you know, Bill Summers, percussion, Harvey Mason on drums. Harvey recorded the album, but he didn't play many live gigs with us because he really wanted to continue his career as a studio musician in L.A. And by that time, Mike Clark was playing.

So we did an album called *V.S.O.P.* with the three different groups. It was the album made up of the live performance of that concert. Anyway, the final band was myself, Ron Carter, Tony Williams, Wayne Shorter and Freddie Hubbard. It was like a dream band because it contained a great part of the character of Miles's band from the '60s. And this was in 1976, and many people hadn't heard music in that direction since 1968, you know, or '69.

Ben: Of course people have come to call that style of jazz playing "classic" jazz, which is kind of ironic when you consider that originally the bebop and post-bop idioms were developed in part as a reaction against some of the more traditional forms that came before them, as much as they were a flowering of past traditions. But anyway, this brings us, I guess inevitably, to the the film *'Round Midnight*, in which you acted and worked as the music director. It was a very romantic vision of jazz that they said couldn't be made, because it was about real people making real music and it didn't have a happy ending. There was no duck that came down and gave anybody a million dollars in that movie. What was it like to make that movie? Was it tedious and hard work, as movies usually are, or was it inspirational, 'cause you were part of this tribute that was being made?

Herbie: It was everything that you said. It was tedious, it was hard, it was exciting, it was inspiring, all of those things. The one thing that dominated everything is sincerity. Everybody that participated in this film, whether they were musicians or not, whether they were actors, whether they knew about jazz or not, really put their hearts into it. Everybody felt the significance of the music that we call jazz, and the dedication of the participants throughout the years. And they were all moved, they were all touched and excited, and the camaraderie was so great, so strong, during the filming of that movie that many of the actors who had completed their part for the film would show up the next week, or a few days later, just to be on the set and hang out. Just to be a part of it. Nobody wanted to leave, you know? They all wanted to stay there.

Ben: It's one of the few movies where the music isn't tacked on. It's at the heart of it. It's actually being played in the middle of the film.

Herbie: Right, exactly. Bertrand Tavernier, the director, wanted to capture the spirit of improvised jazz. And I think he did it in many, many ways in the film. One of them is, Bertrand listened to everything that the musicians said on and off the set. He revised the script constantly, according to many suggestions that we made. Dexter made certain suggestions, major ones, you know, that made the points in the film stronger. There's one scene in the film where Dexter, the Dale Turner character, the first time he goes over to François's house, and Dale Turner says to François, he says, "François, is there water in this wine?" In the script, François says "no." But, before we shot that scene, Dexter had a conversation with Bertrand, and Dexter said, "Bertrand, if Dale Turner says to François, did you put water in the wine, if François lies the first time he asks him a serious question like that, Dale would never trust him again. François has to say yes for it to be real." Bertrand says, "Of course, you're absolutely right." And he changed it. So he says "yes" in the film. And it makes the rest of it make sense. So he never lies to him. People that never lie to you, you can trust them. You know, and that's how they got to be great friends. So, anyway, little things like that.

There were other things also that we changed. But, for example, one time we were out to dinner, and Wayne Shorter was having dinner with us along with Bertrand and a bunch of people. Wayne starts talking about *The Red Shoes*. Giving excerpts, you know. He knows it line for line. He's seen it 76 times. It's his favorite movie of all times. And so Bertrand, who's also a great movie buff, he's of course the director of *'Round Midnight*, he was laughing like crazy at what Wayne was doing. Wayne was so funny that night. Bertrand says, "I'm using it in the film." And you know, he did. There's a part in the film where we were in a recording studio, just to show the kind of relaxed atmosphere in a recording studio. Guys are talking between songs and so forth, and Wayne is talking about *The Red Shoes*, which has nothing to do with the music, you know. But he's describing it. But that way you get to see what musicians do in a recording studio. That's what they do. And so Bertrand had this sense to take heed of how musicians really are.

And some other things I discovered from reading a review that were not apparent to me at first. Maybe this was an analysis that this review made that Bertrand was not conscious of. 'Cause sometimes it happens. Sometimes, if something is right, you can analyze it afterwards and see things in it that you never saw before. They mentioned about the pacing of the film. It's a very slow-paced film. But Dexter Gordon is very slow-paced. The way he speaks is slow-paced. And a lot of things are understated, because he does a lot of things with gestures. That's part of the rhythm of the film too. The way Bertrand shot it. A lot of scenes have a certain improvisatory quality to them. There's a party scene, and almost all of that is improvised. In other words, what I'm saying is there's a real synchronicity between the mechanical elements of the film and the spirit of the music and the musicians themselves.

Ben: It has the ring of reality about it. But is it simply a past reality, or is there some future to this reality as well? I mean, this vision of jazz musicians hanging out and being relaxed and playing in clubs. Is it gone?

Herbie: I don't think it's gone. It's hard to say. The club scene, I wouldn't bet too heavily on that. I can't make a firm speculation about the life of the club scene. But I can tell you this, see, because many things have changed. Now, many musicians are also educators. You know, they teach in schools. I think it's very good.

Ben: More than the club scene, though. The way guys used to learn music. The way jazz was passed on from sideman to sideman, or whatever.

Herbie: That is different. That is different. We used to have jam sessions. That doesn't exist anymore.

Ben: People learn music from records now . . .

Herbie: Now they learn from records, and it's not the same. But what's amazing, what is amazing, is that somehow it still works. Because how do you think Wynton Marsalis and Branford Marsalis learned? They learned from records.

The funny thing is that many times records have a perfection that is not representative of the average playing or average performance of musicians, or even the type of music. It has its good points and has its bad points. You can give a performance in front of an audience that is far greater than what you can do on a record which is recorded in a studio. That's not abnormal. Anytime you have this extreme inspiration, of course, that's gonna be rare, but it's more easily captured live. It's more easily performed live, too, you know, because of this relationship that you feel as a musician with the audience. And that kind of stimulation, that feedback you get from the audience. In the studio, there's no feedback except for the other musicians. But still, there's a kind of professionalism in recording that doesn't represent the average kind of playing. You know, somebody told me a story about Art Tatum, that because he was blind, he had heard some piano rolls that were recorded by two pianists, four hands, and he thought that there was only one guy playing all that stuff. So he wound up playing piano with two hands as though they were four. And maybe this is why Wynton and Branford, at such a young age, play so well, because they've heard records that didn't have a lot of the mistakes that musicians might make in a normal, average performing situation. I may be completely off my rocker about this, but it's just something to look at anyway.

Ben: That's interesting; where the good news could be the bad news, in a way.

Herbie: See, because I couldn't play like that when I was that age. I don't know anybody that could. I mean, the younger players are coming up now that play better at a younger age than the previous generations could at that age.

Ben: On the other hand, jazz musicians have said for years that the mistakes are the only part that's jazz. Or at least that what appears to be a mistake to one person could be part of another person's style.

Herbie: That's funny. The funny thing is the depth of the playing, the part that really moves you, is not something that is directly related to the technical perfection of the playing. And there's nothing that replaces experience. The young players know that, they know that. They may know that they have a facility that the older players developed at a later age. And many times these older players don't have the same facility anymore, because they've gotten older. But not one of those young guys that I know is ignorant of this element that they know they need to get to. Which is the thing that only comes from experience. That depth. And I'm including Wynton Marsalis because, although he says a lot of things in print which I hate, I don't think it comes from the deepest part of him. I think it's his reaction, somehow. He has some kind of hangup, evidently, and it makes a lot of things come out of his mouth. I think he gets caught up in the words tripping out of his mouth or something. I don't think he believes a lot of what he says, not deep down in his heart, because when he played with me, when I've been around him, he has a great respect for the very people who he talks about in print, you know. In truth, he knows better.

Ben: Your point about the young players having respect for experience and the value of experience, it sounds to me like, regardless of whether the club scene is with us or not, it really doesn't affect the bottom line in getting a sound. For a young player to have a sound, they have to have some real experience. There's no alternative. No amount of recording studio work or school work is going to take the place of this.

Herbie: Yeah, absolutely, absolutely . . .

* * *

Tony Williams **(September, 1985)**

Tony Williams is the stuff that jazz legends are made of. As a very young man—some would say as a boy—he became one of the most influential jazz musicians in the world,working with one of the premier jazz bands, the Miles Davis Quintet. At the same time that he exhibited this maturity as a performer, he also established himself as a composer of note on his own seminal Blue Note recordings. Yet, despite the unusual circumstances of his story and the vast amounts of publicity that he has generated over the years, Tony has remained something of an enigma in jazz. And he has done little to dispel that image. He currently lives outside of San Francisco, as far as possible from his roots in the East Coast jazz scene while remaining in the continental United States. Because he is a "musician's musician," his isolation from the jazz capitol and his peers only seems to enhance his image as an innovator and an enfant terrible. Our conversation took place in a recording studio in New York City where Tony had just completed a recent recording project. Almost ten years before, we had worked on several record projects together, and had not seen much of each other since then.

Ben: A lot of people haven't run into you in a while. What I mean is you have a kind of reclusive image. Do you think of yourself that way at all?

Tony: Well, I really like staying home. I live north of San Francisco about forty minutes, and I very rarely get into San Francisco. Yeah, I stay home quite a bit. I like my house and my little environment that I have.

Ben: You once told me that students come to you for lessons, and when you ask them about Max Roach or some of the great drummers that you listened to as a young man, they often don't know what you're talking about. Students today might not share your sense of history. I suspect they many of them might not know your own history either.

Let's talk a little about your career. It's been very unusual. You appeared to burst full-blown onto the scene at seventeen years old with Miles Davis's band. Before that, of course, you played with Jackie McLean.

Tony: Yeah. Jackie McLean was the first big break I got. I met Jackie in Boston, and he liked the way I played, and he asked me to come to New York. So I was fortunate to come to New York with a job.

Ben: One of the distinctive elements of your playing back then was the sound you got on the ride cymbal. Everybody was wondering how you got that distinctive sound on the ride. You told me something funny about that. You said "Oh that old cymbal. As soon as I got some money I threw it away."

Tony: [Laughs.]

Ben: Is that true? Or were you just putting me on.

Tony: I don't even remember that. I don't remember *that*. [Laughs.] No, that sound that I had, the cymbal I got, that was given to me by Max Roach.

Ben: Is that right?

Tony: Yeah, that original cymbal on all those records I did early on, on Blue Note and Columbia. That cymbal was given to me by Max.

Ben: Do you still have it?

Tony: I have it, but I can't play it. Years ago, it became broken and repaired and broken again, so I have it in my "safe" at home.

Ben: In any case, you really established a reputation early on with Miles, and as a composer yourself. You made some solo records for Blue Note. And your compositions on those records were highly regarded. Was that something you had studied?

Tony: I studied a little bit at the time, and continued off and on. And then six years ago, I really started to intensively pursue composition classes with one of the faculty at University of California at Berkeley. So I've been doing that for almost seven years now, really studying all the forms of composition. I did a year and a half just writing fugues. Then writing all sorts of forms, like minuet and trio or theme and variations. All the large forms for orchestra writing, studying composers and having to write models off of Beethoven. Things like that. So that's been really exciting for me.

Ben: Does that affect your drumming?

Tony: No, not at all.

Ben: It doesn't cross over to your playing?

Tony: No.

Ben: After Miles' group, you went on to lead a group called "The Lifetime." Various incarnations of that included Larry Young and John McLaughlin. It was one of the first real high energy bands that might be called "fusion" now.

Tony: Yeah. When we started they called it "jazz rock." I like that term more than I do "fusion." Later, after we broke up, they started calling other bands "fusion."

Ben: When you were growing up, I know you were interested in all sorts of music. People assumed that anybody who accomplished as much as you did, and as fast as you did, had to be completely given over to just one way of playing. But that wasn't that case, was it?

Tony: [Laughs.] No, it wasn't. You know, I was listening to a lot to Indian music in the early '60s. Before it became fashionable in the late '60s. And when I was with Miles and playing all that bebop, I had already been listening to a lot of rock and roll. I was a big fan of The Beatles just before they first came over here.

Ben: 1963?

Tony: Yeah. Or '64. And being in Boston, being around that intellectual atmosphere, I had always been exposed to a lot of classical music, orchestra music. So one of my goals, from then to now, is to be involved with orchestra music. To be able to write something and have thirty pieces playing it. Standing there conducting it. I'm even going to be taking some classes in conducting.

Ben: So there are many streams passing through your experience: rock and roll, Indian music, bebop music. It's not just a desire on your part, for example, to "cop" the rock and roll attitude, but rather it's a real part of your whole musical universe, since your formative years.

Tony: Yeah. It was. Because when I was a child, I had the opportunity to play at night a lot of times with my dad, because he was a musician. That's how I got into music. And at night, I'd be living this one life, as a child eleven or twelve years old playing with men in their thirties and forties—and I'm in these nightclubs at night—and in the daytime, after school, I'm hanging out with my friends from the sixth grade and we're going home and watching *American Bandstand*. This was in 1957 and 1958, you know. So I was living two lives all the time. That had a big influence on me.

Ben: Did you feel thoroughly at home on the stand, hanging out with the adults?

Tony: Oh yeah. I felt more comfortable doing that than I felt at any other time. So I've taken time out to learn about that and make my personal life a lot more comfortable now than it had been fifteen years ago.

Ben: Getting us back to the fact that you tend to be reclusive these days.

Tony: Yeah. That's why I tend to stay home now.

Ben: Making up for lost time?

Tony: Yeah. Because I missed a lot of things, I think. So it's taking me a while to catch up.

Ben: You've been watching those reruns on TV?

Tony: [Laughs.]

Ben: Back when you were a kid, you were also a student of Alan Dawson in Boston.

Tony: Yeah. He was my first and only teacher. I studied with him for about a year, on and off.

Ben: The similarity between your styles was striking in part because of his use of the four-four on the high-hat cymbal, even at fast tempos. At the time, he was doing a lot of recording and the fact that he would play four on the high-hat cymbal became very influential. It seemed to be something unique to his playing, almost a trademark, until you began recording.

Tony: Yeah, well he got that from me.

Ben: Really?

Tony: Right. He never did that before I did it. And he was not . . . well, that's all I can tell you about that. It was something nobody had been doing before a certain time. And I know I didn't get it from him.

Ben: Well that certainly casts a new light on that little corner of musical history.

Tony: [Laughs.] Good.

Ben: Okay. Let's come back to the present. Not long ago, you returned to the Blue Note label after many years. Your first "comeback" album, *Foreign Intrigue*, featured several new original compositions. One that I find particularly interesting from a compositional point of view is "My Michelle." How did that composition come together?

Tony: It was originally composed on a couple of synthesizers I have at home. And it was originally thought of in a different vein. But I realized I was making a "Blue Note" record, so I sort of fit this other rhythm into it. So the rhythm you hear the drums playing is something that just fell into place. It was like putting a collage together. I sort of mashed the melody onto this drum rhythm.

Ben: Well, I had that feeling. It is kind of like a collage. What was the original feeling of the song?

Tony: It was composed in a very romantic vein. When I wrote the song, I had this person, Michelle, in mind.

Ben: When you came into the studio, did you have exact charts made out or was it an idea that grew there?

Tony: Oh, it was all done, formally written out, the copyist had done the parts, so all the musicians had to do was "play the ink."

Ben: You didn't just "play the ink," though. You really turned it loose.

Tony: Well, I didn't write out a drum part. [Laughs.]

Ben: And that drum part really has your personal stamp. It has your "signature" four-four on the high-hat. But it also has some exotic cross rhythms.

Tony: Well, the bass drum is playing a kind of Samba feel. And then, when you add the hands, many embellishments are possible.

Ben: Your style of drumming is often hard to capture in the recording studio. It's very open; there are a lot of harmonics floating around. For example, you tend to leave that high-hat open so it rings out, and this creates a constant layer of upper harmonics for the microphone to deal with. It's becoming more unusual in these days, when most drummers are padding their drums down in the studio.

Tony: Yeah. I like the drums to sound like a drum set instead of something else. Most of the drum sounds you hear on records, those are not drummer's sounds. They're producer's sounds. And engineer's sounds. You know, people who sit in the booth need to hear a certain thing. And it ends up not being what a drummer needs to hear. So I really like to hear drum sounds. You know, I don't want to hear "boxes" and "cans" and things like that. And that's the way most drums sound.

I know that I'll listen to drummers sometimes, and when I close my eyes, I can't tell what drum they're playing, what type of tom-tom they're playing. You see some drummers and they've got ten drums on stage, and every drum sounds the same. There's no definition between any of them. So that is disturbing. So I try to get the drums to sound really distinct in themselves.

Ben: Your approach to the drums, then, is the opposite from that of a "studio" or session drummer.

Tony: Yeah. Exactly.

Ben: I notice, however, that you do use the Simmons electronic tom-tom on this album.

Tony: Yeah. I play the Simmons electronic drums and an Oberheim drum machine on this album. And what I wanted to do was to introduce those devices into what's called a "straight ahead" jazz context. Because everyone kind of thinks of those devices as only being used in pop music. And I'm convinced that you can use them any way you like. I'm convinced that this is a good outlet for me, so I put those in, the drum machine and the electronic drums.

Ben: Both Jack DeJohnette and Max Roach have used drum machines recently. However, it seems that nobody has yet come up with the ultimate format to incorporate the silicone chip into the acoustic world.

Tony: Well, they're all just tools and musical devices.

Ben: One of the things we're talking around is the problem of being a leader as well as a drummer, and developing a solo career as well as being a member of a rhythm section. Do you think it's harder for a drummer to do that?

Tony: Yeah, because you're in the back all the time, at the back of the stage, and you've got all these drums and people can't see you sometimes. There's a whole aura around all the instruments. So the guys out front are always thought of as leaders, whether it's the guitar player or the saxophone player or the keyboard player. And it's hard for audiences to relate to drummers as the leader. And it's also hard for other musicians to. So you have an uphill battle.

And drummers, in the past, have also been thought of as the least intelligent, or the low man on the totem pole, or you get paid the least. There's all sorts of areas where you're less than equal with the other members of the group. So it's an uphill battle all the way.

Ben: The image is "here, take these sticks and go hit those drums."

Tony: Yeah, you know, the drummer is just kind of a wild and crazy guy, and a savage. And he just beats on the drums, that's all he can do. You know, give him a piece of raw meat.

Ben: Many drummers in the past have fought that image. I'm thinking for example of the late Philly Joe Jones, who was accused of playing "too loud" or too aggressively, but in fact was a complete musician, a fine keyboard player.

Tony: Well Philly Joe's forte was really his swinging ability. He could swing the band and play hard, and that's what made him an influence.

Ben: Perhaps that also made it more difficult for him to establish himself as a leader, as he tried to do with Dameronia and his own solo albums. People thought of him as back there in the rhythm section.

Tony: And it's always hard, too, for someone who is a player, and doesn't write music, and doesn't present a vision of their own, to establish themselves as a leader. I mean, whether you're a piano player or a bass player or whatever, if you don't write music, it's harder to do.

Certain drummers have been leaders, like Art Blakey. But that has a lot to do with his force of personality and his sound as a drummer, and the fact that the original band that he had was with Horace Silver and Donald Byrd, and the music that they played made such an impact on the post-bebop scene.

Ben: It's really tough, then, if what you're selling is a "groove" and not a harmonic or lyric approach. A "groove" is such an ephemeral thing.

Tony: Yeah, it really is.

Ben: Another drummer who has made headway recently as a leader is Ronald Shannon Jackson. Have you heard his record *Decode Yourself*? It was produced by Bill Laswell, a dance music producer in New York.

Tony: Yeah, I like some of that stuff. Bill Laswell is a producer that I'm working with also. As I said earlier, I'm pursuing different streams of music, and I have an interest in more dance-oriented music.

Ben: One interesting aspect about the *Decode Yourself* sound is that they use a lot of space and then amplify the groove with many small rhythmic ideas and interventions.

Tony: Yeah, but what makes it really interesting for me is just the "sound" of some of that music. The sound of all the instruments and the way they are recorded, rather than . . . well what they play is also important, but the sound of it sometimes takes over and creates that hypnotic feeling. More so than what the guy plays sometimes. The sound of it makes it special.

Ben: That's just what people said years ago when they first heard the Miles Davis *In a Silent Way* album. That repetitive high-hat figure you played was hypnotic and led people through the music.

Tony: Yeah, that's true.

Ben: Following the theme of drummers searching for ways to exert their musical influence, I'm reminded of a cut on a recent Billy Higgins record called "East Side Stomp." He doesn't even solo on the song, but because it's divided into several musical sections, he sort of orchestrates or conducts the group through the composition. This is another subtle but interesting way to put the drummer out front.

Tony: I don't know the song, but Billy's always been one of my favorite drummers. He's very relaxed, and his feeling is great. His approach to the cymbals, his ride cymbal, is unique. His way of playing time is unusual, and Billy doesn't do a lot of crashing. It's a very smooth kind of sound. You know, it frames everything else, almost a kind of background sound.

Ben: You've been part of so many classic recording sessions. To pick one is hard, but let's talk about the Eric Dolphy *Out To Lunch* date. Blue Note recently released it on CD. Along with Dolphy and yourself, it featured Freddie Hubbard, Bobby Hutcherson and Richard Davis. Do you remember anything in particular about that date?

Tony: Yeah. I remember that at the time we made that record, all those players had been working together in different little bands. There was a club in Brooklyn, I forget the name of it, but everybody would work there. One night we'd work in Birdland, the next night it would be the Five Spot or something like that, the next night might be out in Brooklyn. So there was a lot of experimenting going on. And I had just been in New York a couple of years, so I was really into it and really intent on experimenting with different sounds on the drums and with different ways of playing things.

So what you hear on the record and on those sessions, especially because it was Eric's session and everyone really loved Eric because he was such a sweet person, he had a real good heart, and that alone made everyone want to do their best for Eric. Not just because we were making a record, but because Eric was there and everyone liked him. So that's what you're hearing when you hear that music. A lot of different things going on at once.

Ben: I think of your playing on that date as a series of duets. First you're playing with Eric, then with Richard, then Bobby. You seem to be shifting your focus throughout, teaming up with various players during the course of the songs.

Tony: That's the way I like to play. Whenever someone plays, I play with them, and then when the next person plays, I have to shift the focus, because everyone plays different. So when you go from a trumpet player to a saxophone player, there's a different dynamic. You can't keep doing one thing. I mean, if you're like a brick wall, it's not the same thing. You have to make adjustments. And on that date, *everyone* was doing that. For example, Richard Davis is a bass player who has a unique style, and he contributed a lot.

Ben: In 1985, many of the same musicians tried to re-create this session, and it was recorded live at Town Hall by Blue Note. And it was a completely different-sounding record.

Tony: Right. Herbie Hancock was on that new version also. We tried as much as we could to get the original sound, but we knew that we had to play it as we play today. I mean, we played those tunes on the original recording one way, and I'm sure if we had recorded it even the next week, it would have been a little different. And so on.

Ben: The music on the *Out To Lunch* album is so delicate in many ways that it almost seems like it was made to be played in a controlled environment like the studio.

Tony: Actually, when we did it live recently at that Blue Note concert, it was pretty strange. It was the first time the music had ever been done live, because the original Eric Dolphy record was just a studio record. We never played it live at that time. I'm sure we could have, and it would have worked out, but it was never done.

Ben: So often today, we rely on recording studio versions of music for lack of live experiences. I think it's a loss for both listeners and musicians. And particularly when we're talking about the difficulties a drummer might encounter while trying to establish him or herself as a leader, live contact seems important. I, for one, hope to see more of you playing live with your band in the near future. Perhaps you'll be less reclusive in the coming months?

Tony: Well, I'll try.

Ben: If not, I'll come and find you again.

Tony: [Laughs.] Okay. You know where I live.

* * *

Keith Jarrett (February, 1987)

A few weeks prior to our conversation, Keith Jarrett had released an album called Spirits, *which featured him playing various percussion instruments and flutes rather than the acoustic piano for which he is so well known. Those who have followed his career remember that even during the '60s, when he performed with Charles Lloyd, he would play wind instruments (such as the melodica) as well as keyboards, so the premise of his new record was not a total surprise. What was surprising, however, was how compelling this "little" percussion record of his was. The album captured something spiritual, as the title implied, and I wanted to discover how the process of making this record compared to his live performances, which often take on the aura of a mass seance, with Keith up on stage appearing to be in an advanced state of possession, literally lifting off the piano bench during the more intense passages, moaning loudly. I met him at the recording studio located near the corner of Broadway and Bleeker streets in Manhattan. As he got off the elevator and walked down the narrow hallway, he was already in mid-sentence. He is somebody who clearly has a lot on his mind.*

Ben: You said as you walked in the door that New York is becoming more of an alien environment for you than ever before.

Keith: Well I think I may just be perceiving it, you know. If we live in a house long enough, we're looking at the same rooms, but then we stop perceiving those rooms. But if a guy comes in that never saw it before, he often might say something like, "Wow! What a beautiful room," and you've been so unaware of that for a while. Well, the reverse I think is happening for me with New York. It's like the things that lent its excitement I find synthetic to any purpose that might move any hearts any further than they are. Or, what it seems to me is, like, a large record store that wants to stock everything that's been recorded. And therefore, they don't have any taste. [Laughs.]

Ben: Moving hearts further than they are. I like that. It's the kind of poetic image that also appears in your writing.

Keith: Well you know, the funny thing about that kind of a statement coming from me is that, the very least reason why I come up with it is poetic. All I'm trying to do is find a way to use words that still connote a little bit of what they did connote, let's say, a long time ago, and put them together. If I said something like, "New York doesn't knock out people." Well of course people would say, "It knocks *me* out." But if you say, "Well, but does your heart, you know, are you struck there?" And they'd probably say, "What do you mean? My heart is a machine and we all know that, and it pumps, we know what it does. What are you talking about?" I'm talking about metaphor, maybe. "What's that?" So, I try to find words that really couldn't mean anything else. But, of course, they still might be hard for people to know what I'm saying.

Ben: It's suggestive of the kind of metaphor that was more common, I think, during the '60s, when people talked about spiritual elements as if they were real.

Keith: Yes, and now, of course, we could say, "the heart of the city." Well, we'd have to take that apart and say, "Do they mean the center of it?" And it probably isn't exactly the center, physically, that they're speaking of. But if you could take away all the things it wasn't, what they'd be trying to say was what anyone would be trying to get to if they said that they were moved, that their heart was touched. But then, when you apply it to the city, that makes the city okay. You know, that's saying, "The city's okay because it has a heart."

Ben: I think there's a deli around the corner called "The Heart of the City."

Keith: Yeah. But meanwhile, I'm not at all sure that people are aware of the earth under the city.

Ben: That imagery plays a big part in your music also. The '60s were not so long ago, although they seem like a long time ago. But, of course, in the middle '60s your work, specifically with Charles Lloyd, cast you in a role that very few jazz players at the time experienced. You became almost a pop celebrity, playing for large pop audiences that were not necessarily listening to you on the level that you were performing.

Keith: Yeah. Well, I shared a lot of the questions that people that came to the Fillmore and those places had. Outside of music, I mean, just the questions, the life-size, universe-size questions. So, I don't know, it didn't feel like I was in the wrong place. But I felt that what we were doing was ineffectual in those places. It definitely was.

Ben: Because of the context of those places, Charles Lloyd at the Fillmore was almost like a high school dance.

Keith: Yeah. But if, say, 600 of those people were in a small room, and we could play for them, I think we could've established a very strong connection that would've made them not even think anymore about whether they were listening to a "jazz band" or whatever. See, because this category thing always comes up, but the simple truth of it is that once a category exists, what's in it isn't potent.

Ben: Define a thing and you can dispense with it.

Keith: Well, even if it is exactly the same thing it was before the category was formed, it isn't potent anymore. And I think the only thing that I've been interested in, all along, are the potentials that are missed in any given scene, you know. The things that are forgotten by a whole audience, in any given hall. In solo playing, that was one of the most exciting things, because if there was something that could come through that hadn't been remembered, you know, something about music, something about the way music *is* that could actually be produced in front of an audience, they would *have* to hear it. They might not hear *what* it was. But they'd have to hear it as a physical thing.

Ben: You mean an actual harmonic thing, or . . .

Keith: I can't really go any further . . .

Ben: OK . . .

Keith: I mean, in a way, it's like I'm taking some sort of pulse as I walk on stage. And, it would be like, not necessarily prescribing this. But usually when something's out of balance, you're missing something, you know. And I think that whole cultures are missing more and more because it's safer not to think. It's safer not to know some things. So the people in cities are proud of their cities, and they think their city's the greatest city in the world, and they love and they advertise their city, and they put bumper stickers on it, because they don't wanna think further than that.

Ben: You talk about taking the pulse of the room when you walk on stage. That's really in some ways just the opposite of what a lot of musicians do. They try to go in there and take over the pulse of the room.

Keith: Yeah, they lay something on 'em . . .

Ben: But listening to your music, I start to see you as a groove player. A different kind of groove player, quite the opposite of today's groove players, more of a mantra groove player.

Keith: Yeah, definitely . . .

Ben: And this is something that you could hear all the way back in the Charles Lloyd days, up to the present, through all your work.

Keith: Well you know, this thing I just mentioned. It's something that, if I'm aware of, like, a tension somewhere, or a too relaxed vibe from something I have already played, these are just clues about what it is that should be played in the rest of the evening, you know. Not that I can get around to it by magic or anything, but if I'm just staying aware of that, I can get in a groove, and the groove might not have anything to do with that. But any groove that gets into *itself* is everything, while it's going on. It isn't just, "Hey, that's a groove and now we'll leave." You can't leave when something's happening like that. So, you know, at least I know that no one was gonna leave [laughs] during the section, and I would enjoy that, those grooves too.

Ben: You once described the feeling of doing this, not exactly this particular piece, as "drowning." I asked you if it's possible to demonstrate your technique briefly and you said to me, "Well, you want me to drown for a little while." I love that. I mean, that made it very clear to me what the process must be like for you.

Keith: Well, put it this way, all through each day, every day, I am aware of that place. It's like a place, a state. And I would say that it's the only state from which to make music of any value to you or anyone else. But, because I know of it, I know it's also a gift. I mean, it isn't as though we'd have to have this state available to us. And I would never have been able to invent it. I consider it a sacred thing, not to be fooled with, or played with, you know. So, the strange thing is that, luckily, if I say I'll do a concert, that concert is already set long in advance. Which means that I'm not "playing" when it gets to be eight o'clock. It is serious at that point. You know. That state is requested of me, because I have set a precedent for being in it, at least for myself. So I don't consider just the fact that I have an eight-thirty show to be playing around with the state. But if somebody said, "Would you improvise a little to show us some of the things you do?" That's playing around, you know. Because, actually, the answer to that is, "No, I can't." The answer I gave you is not exactly right. I should have just said "No, I can't do that." Because I literally couldn't do it. I could say, "This is A on the recorder." I could do a recorder class, you know, or I could say, "This, you know, these are the sounds on a tabla drum," but I wouldn't, if you said, "Okay, now immerse yourself in playing. Show them what you might have done in the *Spirits* recording." Well, the *Spirits* recording, I was gone, you know. I mean, I was completely gone, except during breakfast, lunch and dinner.

Ben: Now that's interesting, because the *Spirits* recording was done in layers, unlike a lot of the things you've done in the past. It wasn't a moment captured on tape, or in some other medium. It was done in layers. It gave you the luxury of considering and reconsidering what you were doing. And, surely, it was a different pool in which to drown, or a different way in which to drown in the pool.

Keith: Actually, although that's all true on the surface, it's completely inaccurate. Okay, while I know I went in and made guesses where the volume levels should be, and while I know I was doing overdubs, I was not taking time to consider anything, and I was not really doing overdubs. These overdubs were as though I had just started to play this piece, and I'd come back, rewind the tape, and I would continue to play this piece, but on another instrument. And since there were no other people in the building, and I was in a kind of a, I wouldn't say trance, but it was like a very, very strong pull that made me fly into the studio to do something, and then quickly rewind the tape, and then change the cassettes, and then go back out. I didn't even have time to change mic positions. The mics were standing in the same place for every instrument, on every track. Ahh, it wasn't any different than doing something solo that's been captured, at the moment. It was as though my metabolism had changed, so I could do a moment in more than a moment.

Ben: Do you do self-hypnosis? Do you do formal meditation? . . .

Keith: No . . .

Ben: Have you done it?

Keith: Not in the way most people would consider that. I mean, I could say very sincerely that before solo concerts, I was doing something, but I would be able to do it with lots of people around, or while I was laughing or . . . You know, it wasn't like "I'm now going to get ready for the concert."

Ben: But it was a getting in touch with a different spot.

Keith: Yeah. But it was almost as though I just gave myself the message that "It's time to begin to . . . " I was just focusing stronger and stronger on something. I don't know what, but, I don't know how to explain it. It wasn't music, it was just the energy. Kind of like a warming. That's the right way to express it. Things started getting warm, you know. And I don't mean like I would be sweating, but I mean, there was a gradual coming of some energy that I needed for the thing.

Ben: You're describing to me something that sounds very much like a technique used to alter a certain brain wave states, or whatever, that can be taught in a technical fashion, and has been taught, and is understandable, I think, to a lot of people today, because a lot of people have . . .

Keith: They've either read about it or done it or had experiences in it.

Ben: But from what you tell me, it suggests it's something you came upon and have been in touch with for some time. And use it as the heart of your music.

Keith: It *is* the music. As a matter of fact, I even have this feeling, and I think it's true, that even in a concert where if I listen to it later, it's bad, I don't like it. And maybe no one liked it. If I was in the state, if I remember that I was in the state at the time of playing, then it doesn't matter to me whether the music sounds the way it does or not. It's like a secondary effect, you know. And that's difficult, being a recording artist, because it's like trying to tell your audience that, "don't believe what's on the records." But that is what I'm saying. But I don't know how it came, except from the need. I mean, the need to get to something.

You know, like, if somebody says, "I would like to get from a to b." And they're in the desert, and they don't have a vehicle. It will of course depend on their health and everything, whether they ever get there, if it's far away. But it will mostly depend on how much they really do want to get there. So the person who wanted to get there the most will have gotten the farthest, even though he may have died too. And that's so simplistic sounding that it bothers me. But it's as simple as that. Some painters have been known to say, you know, people ask them what they do. "I paint. You know. That's what I do. I paint." Well, what are you? "I mean, I'm a painter." The guy going from a to b, someone could've asked him, you know, "What made you the one that got there?" I got there, that's what made me the one that got there. I mean, how could he be able to say, "I had more desire to get there than those other guys." I mean, he wouldn't know that. So that always breaks down. When people say, "How do you do this?" The simple answer to that is, "I do it." And one thing that came up, as, I think, even a side effect of that, was getting into that *state*. Because I never did it intentionally. There wasn't a time when I was sitting around *trying* to get into the state, or sitting around meditating for the concerts, and then later, this thing happened automatically. That wasn't like that.

Ben: As a very young man, this state would be part of the experience of sitting at the piano?

Keith: Possibly, yeah. Possibly. It grew. Everything grew. I mean, I'm speaking about fairly recent history. I'm not speaking about when I was a kid. I don't really know what happened as a kid. I know I felt a strong connection to the piano, but I'm not sure . . . This warmth thing didn't come from . . .

Ben: You're grew up in Allentown, Pennsylvania. As a young boy, this feeling wasn't there. Were you playing piano primarily because that was something to do, and there was nothing else to do?

Keith: No, no. I, if I thought about other incarnations, and if I was the kind of person that was into that, I would say that something made me have to be a musician in this life. And I think I sensed that very, very early. There was no other path for me. So you know, when people think I'm being ultra serious, in what they consider a negative way, if I say something like "It's what I'm supposed to do. I know it's what I'm supposed to do." Ah, that's spiritualism, man. No, no, no! I mean, I didn't know what spiritualism was when I was seven. You know?

Ben: I hear you describe the basis of a technique, a technique that you've developed, and it's drowning. Drowning is the technique . . .

Keith: That's right . . .

Ben: The technique of drowning.

Keith: In fact, so it's becoming more and more, I'm getting to the point where I can actually say this, in the next solo concerts. You know, it's, what I'm saying is the process. It says "A program of solo improvisations." The program is the drowning.

Ben: For example, your recording, *Spirits,* was recorded in May and June of 1985, using some cassette recorders at home. You're playing flutes in the first piece, primarily, and then in the second piece, flute and some drums, and at the end, piano. Was some of it written or was it completely improvised?

Keith: [Laughs.] Ah, right. I might have walked into the studio and had a sudden rhythm feeling, but these were all so simple, it's impossible to even say. I might have had this "eh, ugh, eh, ugh." But to me it was like "Wow! Oh! I don't wanna forget that." So I turned everything on. I go and do that. There were a few things where I would play the piano, and it would be an improvisation. And then I'd go and listen for once to it, to see how the recording was. And then pick up a flute and start to play with it, and turns into a song. But it wasn't a song. But I could have written it down and then done it again.

Ben: How different was this experience than playing with other people?

Keith: It was different than anything I've ever done, or ever will do, I think. Because, I think I was just lucky to be at home at the time. Lucky to be not on tour, lucky to be healthy. And lucky to be able to have all those instruments sitting around for years, not knowing what they were going to be doing. And all those things came together. Plus the fact that my studio isn't all that quiet, depending on what kind of traffic or airplanes are going by. And during this whole recording, nothing came past the road, nothing flew over the building. I didn't think about that then, you know. I'm not even sure I would have heard it if it was happening. But, to me, it's really a miracle that it was done at all. No tape breakages or problems. No machines going crazy. And I had no engineer, so if they were gonna go crazy . . . So no second takes. There's no working on a piece as though "that's not good enough. I think I'd like to play that over again."

Ben: Particularly layering. If you don't like a layer imbedded within there, you're in trouble.

Keith: Yeah. And really, no mixing. I mean, it's a two-track thing. And when I was doing, let's say, the voices on some of the things, I just moved away from the mics if I heard myself too much in the headphones. Or moved to one of them more than the other one. And, already people have commented on some of the depth that they hear in it. It's like kind of a magical mix sometimes. And it is. But it was me, while I was doing it, not while someone was in the control room.

Ben: Well of course, that's the magic of all the music from the '50s and early '60s. That was live mixed. I mean, it captures the space in the room. And you can almost have a sense of the dimensions of the room. This recording, particularly, is amazing for cassettes.

You mentioned going to the room with a little "boom, boom" sound, like a little heart beat feel, and proceeding from there. I said earlier that I see you as a groove player, but in a particular way. And that is, your playing very clearly delineates the difference between rhythm and meter.

Keith: Oh, yeah. I know exactly what you mean. If I had a click track, there would be no *Spirits*.

Ben: Yeah. Exactly right. Not only would there be no *Spirits*, I suspect there wouldn't be 99 percent maybe the stuff that you have recorded . . .

Keith: No, no. Not at all . . .

Ben: You even carry that into the playing of standards. The two volumes that you did with Gary Peacock and Jack DeJohnette are remarkable approaches to the classic jazz repertoire, because this material is so well known and everybody has an inclination to sing along with it. And again, you're using that as the pool to drown in, or the way to drown . . .

Keith: That's right . . .

Ben: You breathe, it's like I hear your breath, the melody is being breathed out by you, through the piano. It's a very breath oriented thing.

Keith: Well, you know, the trio wasn't just an idea of getting together with Jack and Gary and playing standards. There is another level, behind it, that was private, not secret, but it was something that I needed to get through to them, and share with them, before we started to record at all. And it was that we are singing these pieces. We're gonna play only pieces we like, that we mostly know the lyrics to. But we're going to also not try to possess them. You know, it was, at least then, and certainly now, it's a time when, if you're a musician and you have a group, and you wanna record or do performances, the first thing that people wanna hear is your own material. So it's as though the only way to get a job is to write. Well, that means that, just by pure mathematics, there'll be 9,999 bad tunes being written, and maybe one group that's able to write something worthy of being released.

And certainly I've played a large role in what people think of as the possessiveness of music, since here I am improvising any time I want to, two hours of my own music that I'll never play again. But I certainly have the right to call it my own. So I wanted to make the trio reflect the reverse of that, and show that, and this, of course, this isn't all we were interested. We would like to swing and we'd like to be playing what we want to play. But, it was to try to depersonalize even the solos. You know, like if you feel like playing a lot, play a lot, but don't worry about whether it's you sounding like you, or whether it sounds like bebop that somebody else played, or whatever.

And that had an amazing effect on everybody, because it turned out that everyone was waiting for a moment to just be able to sit down and play. Instead of play as Gary Peacock and play as Jack, you know? So, it seems to me that whenever I get the trio together, Jack and Gary, who have to work a lot with other players, and sort of make themselves known in a given situation, don't have to consider that at all in the trio. I mean, everybody already knows the quality of music they're capable of playing, and they just come out, and we sit down and play what we want to play. Which sounds, you know . . .

Ben: Simple enough . . .

Keith: Sounds simple, yeah, but how much of our life did it take to be able to do it that way successfully, in front of lots of people? It's not that simple.

Ben: You refer to the privilege of being able to be somebody who can go out and play for a couple of hours. Your solo work brings in the blues, bebop and there's expressionistic or impressionistic music in there as well. The latter is what's lead you to be associated with so-called "new age" music. And I wonder if that rankles you to be thought of as the father or the grandfather of this "new age" music.

Keith: It does. Although, *rankles*, I don't know if that's the right word. It saddens me to realize that people can draw only straight lines. [Laughs.] You know, it's like musicians will ask me what music influenced you. And if I say, "Well, I've never really been influenced by music. I'm influenced by the spirit behind some music. But I'm not influenced by the notes. The notes don't influence me." What we're talking about here is the same kind of thing. Some of the notes on the solo concerts lend themselves to being translatable into new age music, so people draw their straight line from there to there and say, "Hey, look at that. I've figured that out."

It's completely untrue. Because of all the forms of music that seem to have categories that have popped up recently, that's the one I am least connected with in any way. I mean, I couldn't even imagine, even though minimalism and I are not friends, I can imagine that being something that I might have had some real part in. There are parts of solo concerts that are complete, if you just lopped off what came before and what came after, they're minimalist works. And the thing that started to get to me was then it became a category.

Ben: And it'll be here if you walk away and come back in a year, it could still be . . .

Keith: Well that I know is true. [Laughs.]

Ben: But part of the tension in your music, I think, comes from this constant awareness of a foreground and a background going on simultaneously.

It's not a simple thing, like you say. When you go to play a gig, it's not a simple thing to play the gig and get paid and go home. There's always a situation that involves a tension that you're stepping into. And you seem, like a surfer or a tight-rope walker or whatever, to enjoy very much being on that fault line, where it's about to break.

Keith: But that's where the beauty is. I mean, beauty walks a razor's edge. We've heard Dylan say that. It's the only place. If you wanna look around, you have to be on the edge. Everywhere else you are, you're not able to survey anything. In other words, it's the only mountain peak. And that's one of the sad things about "new age" and the new age world we're in right now. It's that that tension is something that isn't considered good. You know, it's like, people come home from work. They've been tense. They would like to hear something soothing. Okay. So they can either eat something soothing or hear something soothing, or do something soothing. But to me, it's not music. Because music has to be on that edge and has to deal with that tension. Or an artist, I'm not just talking about music now either, if it isn't dealing with that, then the artist is merely reflecting a life situation.

Ben: It's an interesting variation on what you, in the past, have referred to as "progress filibustering." Normally you'd think of the bank of synthesizers as progress filibustering. But this is another kind of progress filibustering. The illusion of simplicity in a world of chaos.

Keith: Yeah. I mean, you know, the noble Indian. I mean, all those warps on the reality of the thing are not reality. If they don't include everything. And part of everything is tension. I mean, we're born into a world where tension is why we're alive.

Ben: I'm sure that the stuff we're talking about now is very difficult for the average jazz fan sitting at home to want to hear.

Keith: Well, but isn't a jazz fan at least used to the tension? You know, a jazz fan seems to me to be at least prepared for that. Whereas, say a subscription ticket purchaser to the "Mostly Mozart" every year, even though Mozart is on the top of my list of composers who I consider monuments to music, you know, I'm not sure that tension thing is going to, you know, they're not gonna want to hear Bartok even. They think of Bartok as avant-garde, you know.

Ben: Another tension that your music points to, if you look back over the work you've done, is the tension between very old and very new, and avant-garde and primitive. The recordings that you did with Dewey Redman, Charlie Haden and Paul Motian in the late '70s suggests this to me. I've been saying all along that your piano playing has breathing in it and all your music has a breathing in it. Here you are playing a wind instrument. When, in the '60s, you were playing with Charles Lloyd, you also picked up a melodica from time to time, and used your breath.

Keith: Yeah, and I had the soprano at that time. Actually a few times Charles and I were playing together. I think there's a recording with us, too.

Ben: It's been part of your work. And there's a particular track, "Konya," clearly says to me that ethnic music is not primitive at all. In a very real way it's contemporary, even avant-garde.

Keith: Well, you know, it's funny you picked that track. I think you're the only person that picked that track on any interview I've done. And I appreciate it because, no one knows this of course, but on that date, we had material to record. But the reason this fit so well to the *Spirits* thing we were talking about before is that Paul Motian had brought in a gong, and was setting up his drums, and he played the gong. I heard the gong, and the gong wrote the piece. So it was very, very much like *Spirits*. It's the most related to that that you could've found in anything I think. Before I heard the gong, nothing about this piece existed. After I heard the gong, I just got a piece of paper out and wrote a few notes down, gave a few to Dewey, gave myself a few and overdubbed a few horns after we did it . . .

Ben: Very similar . . .

Keith: Yeah. And since no one else was really, there wasn't even soloing, so it was really very much like *Spirits*. All Paul had to do was stand there and hit his gong, you know.

Ben: So perhaps it's a way to perform the music from *Spirits* in public?

Keith: I doubt it very much. Actually, I don't doubt that it can be done, I doubt whether I wanna do it. In the same way that there were a few pieces on *Spirits* that sounded so good that I tried more takes of them, and made them more into little productions of those pieces. And everyone got worse. Not that I was playing worse, and the truth of the matter was if I hadn't heard the first one, they would be acceptable. But I had to throw them out. And I have a feeling what would happen is I would ruin my experience of having done *Spirits* if I tried to do anything like it in public, you know. Then it would be a presentation.

Ben: Isn't there an irony here in the recording medium for yourself. I mean, if *doing* it is everything, and participating in the doing, whether you're a listener or a performer, is equally good, then *recording* it, in however clear a fashion, is sort of like trying to capture the sea in a fish net. You can't do it.

Keith: Right, but what's captured is more than I thought. I mean, put it this way. I knew what I was feeling would never be on the record. And that's true with every record that I've made. I mean, that's why artists keep making things. They realize they aren't quite able ever to get what they see or hear to be physical. Okay. So the thing about *Spirits* that is legitimate on record is that it wasn't intended to be a record. And by virtue of it not being intended as a record, I think the music became as close to what it could be on record as it ever can be. In person it could never be like that. There are, you know, distractions. I was alone in the studio, dancing around. Now, I mean, somebody could easily say, "Well, we'd like to see you do that."

Ben: You wouldn't be alone dancing around if somebody else was there to see you...

Keith: I wouldn't be alone dancing around. Right. So it's like we're into physics now, you know. You can't observe a particle without the particle telling you what you're observing on the one hand, and then something else is unobservable.

Ben: The "uncertainty principle." So therefore, in a way, it's just another form of the tension that you ride.

Keith: It's quantum physics, is what it is. [Laughs.] Of course, you know, I mean, out in the woods, going into my studio, I wasn't thinking of quantum physics.

Ben: One final curiosity on my part. And that is, what does music mean? How can the music *mean* something?

Keith: [Long pause.] It can mean something by its intent. It can't mean something that you can tell me it means...

Ben: I don't understand...

Keith: Okay, I guess I could say music means the presence of possibility.

Ben: It suggests a kind of hope then.

Keith: Music means the presence of possibility. In other words, we know there's energy, we know we have energy, and we know different kinds of energy. But those become categories. Those have become categories for us too. If we think of a certain kind of energy, electrical energy, that's a category. But no one knows what electricity is, so how can we make a category out of it? We did. Music suggests the presence of potential that is not collapsed into those categories. But it isn't something you can take home and use. To me, what music should do at its most potent, is it should make a listener question himself. That's what I mean. It's the presence of possibility...

* * *

Branford Marsalis **(September, 1985)**

People tend to group Branford Marsalis together with his younger brother Wynton (as I have done in this very sentence). In fact, the two musicians are as different as night and day. Whereas Wynton's outlook is overtly intellectual, even brooding, Branford tends to be lighter, more offhand with his remarks, even flippant at times. But while he is prone to clown around—especially since he has taken on the role of Jay Leno's sidekick on NBC's Tonight *show—he too possesses a razor-sharp intellect and the ability to cut directly to the heart of the matter. In fact, what is startling is how much substance his apparently casual conversation contains. One could say this quality is also reflected in his music. It has a playfulness that belies the years of careful experimentation that have gone into its execution. The following conversation took place not long after Branford released his first solo record,* Scenes In The City, *while he was on the road with Sting's band and was receiving a lot of criticism from the jazz press for playing pop music.*

Ben: Branford, the first time we met and spoke was 1981 when you were working with Art Blakey's band. Then about four years later, in 1985, we started talking about getting together again. Now another year has gone by, and finally, here we are, on the eve of your concert at Radio City Music Hall with Sting. You've really been busy. What's going on here? Just business as usual?

Branford: Music as usual. Not business as usual, but music as usual.

I've been very fortunate in that the past three years especially, I was lucky enough not to be one of those guys that had to do things he didn't want to do. For some reason, God's blessed me so that I can play different types of music and still fulfil myself musically, so I don't have to do things for the money.

I've never done anything for public acceptance. You know, that will never be the criteria for any move that I make. Sting's probably the only pop guy out there that could have drawn me to do this.

Ben: Why is that?

Branford: Because his music is interesting. He's logical, he has a very logical way that he writes. Very experimental "A" sections with very simple hooks, based on moving bass lines. I love the way he does that, just from hearing his music with The Police over the years. I mean, Marvin Gaye, but he's dead... Stevie [Wonder], but he's not really doing what he used to do with *Innervisions*, you know, those creative year periods. There are a few people that I'd like to play with. You know, Luther Vandross, Aretha Franklin, I'd love to play with them, but as far as conceptual collaboration, Sting is the only guy that comes to mind.

Ben: There's been a lot of talk about Sting using jazz musicians to achieve an end. What are *you* getting out of this experience? What impact is this experience having on your musical conception?

Branford: Well, it's renewed my love for jazz. [Laughs.] You know. I don't know if you really want to call it "hindsight," but a lot of it is hindsight. A lot of things I was doing when I was playing with Wynton and just playing jazz I won't do when I start playing jazz again. Because now that I'm playing this, I have a chance to look back on those things, hear it in a different light. It's hard to see things when you're in the middle of it. When you're away from it, and looking at it, you know, you have a chance to size it up and really see it. Your attitude changes about a lot of things.

I'm probably practicing now more than I was when I was playing jazz on a regular basis. You know the theory that familiarity breeds contempt? I said in a couple of articles that I was bored playing jazz, but that doesn't look right on paper so I have to find another way to say that.

Playing jazz is like being married. And anybody who says they don't get tired of their spouse is telling a fib. And being tired of your spouse doesn't mean that you want to leave them. It doesn't mean you want a divorce. You just need a break.

Ben: Let's confront the rumor about the rift between you and Wynton over your joining Sting's band. How did that get started, and what's the truth?

Branford: The rumor? I don't know how that got started. I mean, those kind of things get started any time you have people as close as Wynton and I. I mean when we first started playing people were saying that Wynton and I were gay, and, you know, you read all this kind of stuff. Who knows how it got started.

It was only logical. If I was a newspaper person, knowing Wynton's stance on pop music, knowing how he feels about pop music and what he thinks about jazz versus pop, and classical versus pop, it would be very easy to just assume that Wynton would be miffed about something like that. And just write it up.

Ben: Wynton was quoted somewhere as saying you had promised him this would be the only time you would do something like this...

Branford: No. I was quoted as saying that. And I was kidding. I said, "Wynton's giving me a little grief," you know what I mean? I said, "Wynton's giving me a little grief over doing this." Which he is. He didn't want to see his band break up. I don't blame him. I mean, he was worried about the band and the music. And my father was mostly interested, not that I was doing this, but if I was going to forsake everything I had worked for. Which would be kind of crazy. He said, "Well, is this what you're going to do with the rest of your life? Are you going to start wearing sequined suits and get your hair curled up and have a couple of lip operations?" And said, "No, man, this is something I want to do."

Because contrary to popular belief, I was weaned on R&B as I was growing up, not jazz. My first musical hero was not Charlie Parker, it was Elton John. And the line went from Elton John to The Beatles to Yes, you know what I mean, rock and roll bands. And by the same token, Aretha Franklin, James Brown, Marvin Gaye, Parliament, Funkadelic, The Barkays, The Ohio Players . . . I was in one of those bands. I lived for that. I lived for the next rehearsal, the next gig. I wrote up all the arrangements for everybody. I was just into that.

So this is like fulfilling a long-time dream. When I went to Berklee [School of Music], I went to Berklee to be the next Quincy Jones. To be the next great producer. You know, I had studied all this music, I had learned all these techniques . . . I didn't know the technical terms for them but I knew how to make it sound right on the record. And I was confident that if I got my arranging chops together, you know, everything else would take care of itself in the long run. And I just got bit by the jazz bug in the middle of it.

Mostly it was seeing Wynton playing with Art Blakey that changed me up. I said, "Damn, look at that. That's great." And I went for it.

But I change my mind a lot. I change all the time. I just put this on the back burner. But that doesn't mean I didn't want to do this anymore.

Ben: What changes has this whole thing made in your career? I mean, what were you about to do when you got the call to join Sting's band?

Branford: Nothing. I was about to just keep playing with Wynton's group, you know. The same thing. Music as usual. And I got the call, and I said, well this is different. A new band, new sound, new music. I didn't want to play with The Police, because when you play with established groups, your musical common sense forces you to go along with what's already been put down. It's an already established sound and you have to adhere to the sound. You're talking about a new group, untested, untried, anything you do, that becomes the sound. You know what I mean? It was too juicy to turn down.

Ben: This crossing, in your experience, between jazz and R&B, that's not unusual at all for a jazz player. Historically, there really wasn't such a big distinction between the two idioms at various times. And then, of course, it became segmented. A lot of people think it's more of a journalist's problem than a musician's problem.

Branford: Well the music is a lot different than it was in the fifties and the forties when jazz was pop and pop was jazz. You know, Bill Haley and Little Richard and all these folks came along, and it began to become obviously different.

And from playing this, I can tell you it's a different sound, playing jazz and playing pop. The requirements are different. The sound of the instrument has to be different. The approach is completely different. I was surprised I caught on to it as quick as I did. Not musically. Musically, it's not that difficult. But emotionally. And conceptually. It's a completely different animal.

You know, it's like me and Charnett [Moffett] were talking about it. It's like the difference between playing acoustic bass and electric bass. And granted that acoustic bass is harder to play, but a lot of jazz cats think all you got to do is pick up an electric bass and start playing and wizz across the bass. You know. But there is definitely an electric bass "sound." There is a meaty, full sound that those guys have. When they hit that bass you can tell that they've been practicing and listening to that and playing that. And you're not going to just put down an acoustic bass, pick up an electric bass and get that sound because you play jazz.

Ben: How does that apply to a soprano saxophone?

Branford: Soprano saxophone is easy, because it's never been really used in pop, so you can pretty much create your own thing. It's much more difficult on tenor, since that sound is an established sound. Which I hate.

Ben: You hate the sound of the tenor?

Branford: The sound of the tenor in rock music. The real thin sound. It wasn't like that twenty years ago. I don't know what made it change. It just changed. It's terrible now.

I like the full, dark sound. A lot of guys say, "Yeah, man, you got that jazz sound." So what was really interesting for me was to take what they call the jazz sound and fuse that into what they call the pop sound, conceptually. So conceptually, I'm playing rock and roll tenor saxophone but my sound doesn't sound like that real nasal, disgusting, frustrating, whining sound that you hear on most of those records.

Ben: Listening to the song "The Children's Crusade" from Sting's record *The Dream of the Blue Turtles* your sound really does stand out. In part because, as you pointed out, you don't hear soprano saxophone on pop music very often. But also because there's a point in that track where it turns loose and the band just shifts gears and takes off, and you are clearly leading the way. And it's so refreshing because it feels like a band playing, not just a "track" being cut.

Branford: That's well put. That's the best way to describe it. It's a band. You know, most records now are production jobs because there are no bands anymore. Hire some studio cats, walk in, they got a click track or a drum beat that's already laid down, you know, and you just play. And it's soulless. People dance to it. It's like listening to Madonna's stuff, you know what I mean? You listen to "Like A Virgin," the drummer plays the same drum beat in the same place every time.

Ben: Well, it's probably a drum machine that's programmed to do that.

Branford: No variation! And it's gonna sell records and people dance to it, but it doesn't have any soul.

Ben: It's got to be frustrating for this band, with Omar Hakim and Kenny Kirkland and Daryl Jones and you to be in the studio cutting tracks like this, as opposed to playing out . . .

Branford: Well, it was probably most frustrating for Omar and Kenny. Because Kenny's used to playing a lot, and now he's just playing chords. He created those parts so it's not as frustrating as just reading notes, but . . .

Ben: I once asked McCoy Tyner if he feels that when he goes out and plays gigs that he has to "cover" a record in the way some musicians do, you know, play it close enough to the document that the audience feels they heard it over "again." And of course he said "No," playing live was a totally different experience each time. I suspect that's also true for Sting's band, which is a departure from standard rock and roll procedure.

Branford: Yeah, we don't sound anything like the record. Nowhere near. It's no comparison. When we go out and play, we play.

Ben: It sounds to me, listening to cuts off the Sting record, that you're functioning almost like Sting's musical conscience. You play commentary to his vocals sometimes, and your sound is placed in a particular way that you're commenting on him. But I mean more than that when I say "conscience." Just the purity of your musical attitude seems to function that way. Is that true?

Branford: I guess. Well, background saxophone is supposed to be just that. It's not that anymore. You don't even hear sax solos behind singers anymore. They don't even do that, because those guys, they don't even listen. They're not accustomed to listening, because the sax player comes in after the singer's done the track, and they play those cliches that work on top. So generally, you don't hear saxophones or acoustic instruments playing behind the singer. They have a little solo spot where they can play. And then it's "Thank you very much. Go Home."

I think that as a result of playing jazz, especially playing with Wynton, you know, it's given me an ability to respond. It's like playing football. When me and Wynton play football, we play football like we play music.

The interaction is immediate. We don't even have to call plays sometimes. He knows, he just knows.

Ben: He goes deep . . .

Branford: It's that kind of thing. I know not to throw him the ball. I know he's setting up a fake. I don't even have to think about it. And sometimes, he psyches me out. That's the way it is, it's like a hit-and-miss thing.

You know, it's the same thing in music. And my role in Wynton's band was to complement Wynton. And I think that's a very wonderful role to be in. I think people don't take that role seriously. You know, being America, being the land of "number ones," everybody wants to be a leader before they follow. Following has made me a very successful career. And I enjoy it, because it's a challenge. To me it's easy to play your own ideas. Because anybody can play their ideas. To me, the challenge is to play somebody else's ideas. Take the ideas from somebody else and play against them, and toy with them, and work around them, and send them back but don't send them back the same way.

That's like the straight man in the comedy routine. When you see them feeding off of each other. But it's spontaneous. And you can tell when they vary from the script, and it just *goes* that way. It takes off. It's that kind of thing.

Ben: You say you want to reinvent the way saxophone is used in pop music. And Sting has said that he's put this band together because he wants to feel some pressure, and he wants you to feel some pressure. Are you feeling pressure?

Branford: Not any more. Now the only time I feel pressure is when it's time for me to start dancing. I feel pressure then. Because I haven't danced in ten years. It's like starting all over for me. But the first month of the gig, yeah I felt pressure because I didn't feel like I was doing the job right. I felt like a jazz musician playing rock and roll.

Ben: I know what you mean by that. Jazz musicians tend to think rock and roll is easy.

Branford: Even on the record. On the record, if I had any wishes, the major wish I would have had was a month of gigs before we did the record. But on the other hand, after hearing the record and hearing what was wrong, I corrected it, and now it's not like that on the gigs.

Ben: Well, let's turn to a record that you did make as a leader, *Scenes In The City*. There's a song on it called "Waiting For Tain," which also features Kenny Kirkland on piano and Charnett Moffett, who you mentioned before, and Jeff Watts on drums. You know, somebody said to me the thing about Branford Marsalis is that you can almost hear him *think* when he plays. And this track is a good example of that. You can almost hear the thought process going on. Is this because it was your first album as a leader, or is it something more typical of your approach?

Branford: That's the way I play. That's why I stop . . . I always stop when I'm playing. I'm always analyzing things. I'm very analytical. I think things out. My music and my playing is based on bebop. And the way that I think I change it up is that as I'm playing those very popular bebop phrases, I hear myself say "Ok, you're playing that again. Are you going to resolve it like you always do?" And I say, "No, let's do something else." "Well, what are we going to do?" "Let's do this." You know what I mean. That's what makes my music different.

And it's very difficult for me to function with a rhythm section that's not happening. Because I rely so much on other people to give me ideas, and I take them and shape them my way and throw them back at them. That's why it was so great playing with Wynton, Jeff and Kenny and Charnett. They throw an idea out. Especially Kenny. And Jeff. They throw ideas out at you. And you take it back, and they throw it back again. And we'll just . . .

Like playing rhythm, five against four. Jeff knows so many varieties of five against four, and I'll play in-between that, and he'll play the in-between and invert it, and then Kenny will play in the middle of it. I mean, it's almost like you have to look at it on a graph. You know, it's like drawing two lines six inches apart and then drawing another line in the middle, in-between those six inches—that's me—and then drawing another line in-between that one and another line on the opposite side—and that's Jeff and Kenny. And it gets thicker and thicker and thicker.

And right when it gets so thick, they just let it go. [Laughs.]

Ben: And that's where time becomes pulse.

Branford: Yeah. Like we don't even think of time in 4/4 in Wynton's band. We think of it as "one."

Ben: Like the title, "Think of One."

Branford: Yeah. [Laughs.] Well, that was Monk's thing. But everything is "one." Like when we're playing those kind of tunes, like "Knozz-Moe-King," or even when we're playing standards, we think of every beat as its own beat. You know, whereas a lot of cats think of "one, two, three, four, one, two, three, four . . ." and they play in four bar phrases. [Sings a four bar phrase.] We don't think like that. We think in "one." Every beat is its own beat. And you keep the changes at the same time. So where you come in can be anywhere. You can start the phrase on the middle of the third beat, you know, the up-beat going into the fourth beat, and keep playing and stop at the second beat. Then wait seven beats and start again.

And it works. You just have to know where you are. [Laughs.]

Ben: You have to sort of be in two places at once; "there," and back watching yourself be "there."

Branford: Yeah, but it makes the music challenging. Rather than playing bebop all day.

Ben: How would you have approached "Waiting For Tain" differently if you had recorded it now as opposed to a year ago, before your experience with Sting?

Branford: I would have recorded it slower. Because ideas flow freer when you go slow. I mean, nobody's reflexes are that quick. Nobody. Charlie Parker had those kind of reflexes. That's about it. Bird did. When it's really fast, that's when it becomes like automatic pilot. You play what you know. But when you play slower tempos, you play things you never thought of before.

My record was groundbreaking for me. A lot of the things I played on that record I don't play anymore. Because now that I've heard them . . . I mean, I do my records for me. I used to get all kinds of suggestions from everybody. You know, like play this on your record, play that, do this for the people, do that for the people. But I mean, if you're going to play jazz, you can't think about the people anyway, because you're not going to sell that many records. So my records are mostly for me. Not even for historical documentation. More for my own personal experiments. And so, as a result, I don't play things that I feel need to be documented, I play things I like. And then when I hear them back on record, I know what's right and what's wrong. It's my own personal growth process.

That's why I don't churn out records, two a year, three a year. Because that's not enough time to think. Not enough time to grow, get old. You know, see the world differently.

Ben: Let's talk about the subject of growth, then, in young players and particularly the subject of jazz education. I know you had a teacher at the Berklee School of Music named Andy Jaffe. In fact, you recently recorded with him on a record called *Manhattan Projections*. How did he fit into your personal growth?

Branford: Andy Jaffe was my favorite teacher in school. Because he was the only teacher that understood. No, there was another guy, Jeff Friedman, who was also an arranger.

But Berklee has its own system of doing things, the Berklee way, the Berklee method. They basically say that when you write things that are theoretically against the Berklee method, then they're incorrect. Even if they sound great. Musically they sound great, but theoretically it's wrong, so it's wrong. Which is not the purpose of music. Music theories are just theories.

Andy was one of those kind of guys, he knew how I was. He knew I was just a lazy, shiftless . . . he understood me, you know what I mean? That was my first class, Mondays, Wednesdays and Thursdays. Nine in the morning. Impossible for me. You know, I graduated from high school so I wouldn't *have to* get up at nine in the morning. So, you know, I'd always miss class. So I'd be late, I'd be in bed. So he would either send this girl in the class named Michelle Mancini, or he would come up himself. You know, he would knock on the door. "Bran, you gotta go to class," you know, he'd send somebody up and say "Come on, man, get dressed, you're late for class." I mean, he never chewed me out about it. And a couple of times I'd miss, I'd say, "Oh man, I'm sorry I missed class." He'd say, "Oh, man, you know this shit anyway. Yeah, you gotta come a couple of times to make it look good, so the other students won't get too pissed off, but why bother . . ."

Ben: But you said he was your favorite teacher. Surely he wasn't your favorite teacher just because he let you slide. There must have been some other element . . .

Branford: No, he was a great teacher. That was part of his teaching process. If I didn't know the material, he wouldn't let me get away. He wouldn't let me slide, you know. I'd see him in the halls, and he'd say, "Okay, we're going over something I don't think you know, so you should be in class today." And believe me, I was in class. Because I respected him, because he respected me. Where another teacher might say, "I run a tight ship. I run a tight ship."

Like I went to Southern University. That, in itself, was just a mind-blowing experience. Because from going to the New Orleans Center for Creative Arts in high school, I'd learned like college junior-level theory and ear training and all this stuff. So I get to Southern as a freshman and it's a black college and the instructor there starts running down to me the whole history of segregation and blah blah blah and, "You see, we must make every student in this school feel like they're equal. We must make the kid from Leesburg, Louisiana, feel like he's no less than the kid from New Orleans. Therefore, even though you know the next three years of this stuff, you're gonna have to sit in this freshman class. And point out whole notes. And a 'C' scale." Which was ridiculous for me to have to sit there and do this, when I could have tested out of that class and taken junior level.

It wasn't about being holier-than-thou, because I'm not one of those condescending folk. I would still be with the freshman class. I wouldn't want to hang with the juniors. I was just lucky, I had it in high school. I was fortunate to go to a high school that takes care of business. Most high schools in America don't, in terms of music. And, I basically had to go on a one-man strike, like not showing up for class, only showing up for the test after having never studied and passing the test with no problem. Which didn't really solve anything, it just made me kind of disliked among the teachers. But the issue should have been why does he have to be in this class in the first place. But they made the issue, "Well he's missing school. You're missing classes that you don't have to take."

And Andy was the kind of guy who would say, "You know this? Go do something you don't know. I'll tell you what. You go learn this Horace Silver tune for me, and come back and tell me why it's hip. Or write me an arrangement on this." I mean, you couldn't ask for a better teacher. He'd write things, he'd say, "Yeah, this ain't the Berklee theory, but it's great anyway." You know what I mean? It was like a godsend to have a teacher like that. Because everybody else in the school is the other way.

Ben: Well, it's interesting to note that on the *Manhattan Projections* album there's also an alto player named Ed Jackson, who I like a lot and who also works with a group called the Twenty-Ninth Street Saxophone Ensemble, a group of players who are known to play on the streets and in the subways of New York City. That's another form of jazz education, and I think there are a lot of great players literally out on the streets of the city.

Branford: That's right.

Ben: Maybe you can learn more out there sometimes than you can in a lot of these classrooms?

Branford: Definitely.

Ben: You have been widely recorded over the last few years as a sideman. You've shown up on records by Dizzy Gillespie, Miles Davis, Art Blakey, and you've been playing a lot more soprano than tenor saxophone. It's becoming your major instrument. I'm reminded of something John Coltrane said about turning to the soprano saxophone because he couldn't "hear" his voice as well on the tenor. When he turned to the higher instrument, his own internal voice became more clear. Is there a similar reason for your use of the instrument, or was it more mundane?

Branford: My reason is much more mundane. I mean, things happen to me so matter-of-factly that it almost sounds cocky when I say it, but it's true. My grandfather bought me a soprano sax. I got it to play a Ronnie Laws solo for a pop band. I used to love Ronnie Laws, and he played soprano. No voices, none of that stuff. I wanted it because I wanted to have it. I had an alto, I wanted a soprano. So my grandfather goes and sends off for a soprano in the mail. And that's the one I play now. It's a Selmer Mark VI, one of the best horns I think they ever made. It plays perfectly in tune. Well, not perfectly. You have to switch your lips around and stuff. And nobody believes I got in the mail.

There was no incentive to play it. I mean a guy told me a story, that he was working for the Chicago Transit Authority, and he heard a John Coltrane record and quit the next day and bought a saxophone. I mean, I wish I could say a story like that, because I think that that's wonderful, but it wasn't the truth.

Ben: The soprano has a reputation for being a very difficult horn to play.

Branford: It never was difficult for me. I played it like I play clarinet. I played clarinet for seven years. So for me, it was ten times easier than a clarinet because you didn't have to cover holes. It wasn't till after I got to New York, till after Wynton's record, that people started saying "You have a wonderful soprano sound." I said "I what?" It just never registered, because I was so obsessed with trying to learn to play the tenor.

I never played the soprano when I was at Berklee. I did a recital, I didn't play it at all in the recital. I played in this funk band, I never played it. It just sat there. I picked it up every now and then. And I picked it up for Wynton's record. I brought it on the road with Art Blakey, I think, for a week. Other than that, it didn't knock me out.

Ben: One thing about the soprano saxophone is that it seems to fall nicely into a lyrical context. There's a track on Wynton's record *Black Codes*, it's called "Aural Oasis," on which you project such a beautiful, relaxed feeling. Part of the secret, I think, is that this album was obviously recorded after the band had done a lot of playing and traveling together.

Branford: For all those detractors we had, those detractors of Wynton's band, who said we sounded like Miles', you know, *Black Codes* was the first album we had done in two years. I mean, *Hot House Flowers* wasn't a quintet record. And we did that in January of 1985. Wynton's band was a brand new band in '82. We put the first record out in '83. We were a bunch of greenhorns. We had just heard a sound that we wanted to pursue.

And because we went and started getting a lot of attention, rather than people being really honest and realizing that we were like a new group, like completely green, you know . . . Wynton didn't really know how to lead a band yet. We didn't know how to follow. I was just starting to play tenor and we didn't have any identities of our own.

We were given no time. We were pushed up there and they said, "These guys suck. They sound like early Miles." And we never got down. I was just amazed at so much criticism. That the critics could actually be so inept. I was amazed at the opinions based on misinformation. You know, people said we sounded like things that we didn't even sound like. They made references off of wrong records. And all this stuff.

But I looked forward to this album [*Black Codes*] all of '84. I said, man, we got to do a record. It's time. Because it was obvious from the way we were sounding, it was time. And we did it. And I'm proud of this one. I mean, I was proud of Wynton on the other records. But this one is a band record . . .

Ben: You know, you talk as if, although you've gone on to other things, you're still in Wynton's band.

Branford: I am, spiritually. I am. I mean, that's my man. That's the best band out there to me, and I'm out of it now.

It was amazing to me to hear so many people say the band sounds "mainstream," as if the only way to have a new sound is to have a complete disregard for the past. Which goes against any historical logic. When you read about the history of anybody who's ever done anything, not just music, it's just based on having a great foundation. A great foundation. And since jazz is so subjective, you know, I can get out there in a pair of underpants and a rubberband and say what I'm doing is innovative, and if five people believe it, then, hell, I got five people. That means it's innovative.

Ben: Especially if you do it in New York.

Branford: Well that's the only place where people will be gullible enough to fall for it actually, New York. [Laughs.] They wouldn't fall for it in Wisconsin.

Ben: Well, if five people do fall for it in New York, and they're the right five people . . .

Branford: Twenty people in Wisconsin . . .

Ben: Right. It's the Emperor's New Clothes all over again. They'd say, "What a tailor that cat has!"

Branford: But this album makes my heart glow. It really does. And I've never bragged before. But I sure as hell will brag now. I'm proud of this one.

Ben: Making a "band record" is so different from making a studio date, like some of these other records you did. For example, recording with Miles. You played some nice soprano on the song "Decoy." What was the recording process like on that track?

Branford: We just played. Miles called me up, he said, "Hey man, can you make it to the studio tonight?" I said, "Yeah." He said, "Solid. Come on." I went in, he looked at me and he pointed his finger. And I played. [Laughs.]

That was it. I mean, we cracked a few jokes, you know. I went in. Ate a shrimp sandwich. Gave him a bite, that kind of thing. And that was the record. I mean what we played, when I heard it, I couldn't believe it was the same record. Because the way I remember it sounding then and the way it came out is two different things.

Ben: Because of all the overdubs they'd done later with synthesizers?

Branford: Yeah, I think so.

Ben: They made arrangements out of parts that were just thrown away initially.

Branford: Yeah, that's what he did. He took certain parts and he made them, he put them into the arrangement. They were all of a sudden *in* the arrangement. I was like, "Man, look at Miles." I think it was significant, because it was the first album he produced on his own.

Ben: Well, it's a kind of half-way-house between the spirit of jazz, captured music, and the way a lot of pop records are made, manufactured music.

Branford: That's right.

Ben: Is that something you would be interested in trying for your own record?

Branford: No.

Ben: What do you have in mind for your next record?

Branford: Acoustic. That's all I know. I mean, I'm listening to a lot of different kinds of music now. I've gotten off into Keith Jarrett a lot. It's conceptual. I love the way he writes. And the way he conceptualizes his different bands for his different records.

Ben: Do you also listen to his *Standards* album?

Branford: I can't get to *Standards*. You see, when you play "out," to me, there's a way to play "out" and make it "in." And a lot of that stuff to me just meanders off. So much so that I can't focus in on it. On *Standards Vol. Two*, though, "Never Let Me Go," that's great. But, I mean, unfortunately I can't get to *Standards One* at all. But like, "My Song," and "Changes," you might hear some of those influences on my next record. [Note: *Royal Garden Blues* was released in late '86.]

Ben: Is there anything specifically that you will take with you into your music from your experience with Sting's band?

Branford: Yeah. For me, the thing I always had trouble with, playing with Wynton's band, is that energy switch. An on and off switch, right? It's like I get so intellectually wrapped up in what I'm doing, the emotional thing doesn't take off. It builds up and builds up. As I got ready to leave Wynton's band, I got better at it. But the music became so inside and so interpersonal that it left the average person in a trail of smoke somewhere, sitting there looking.

Kenny and Wynton had that emotional power thing that they could drop and people could get to it. Whereas my playing was always aloof. As soon as it would get to a point where people would get in, I'd see them getting in and immediately cut it off. I don't know why I used to do that.

But from playing this kind of music, I have now a "get to the point" kind of attitude. Because in this music you have to get to the point. And now I can get to the point real quick. And I'm going to try to use that a lot more when I play. Just get to the point. You know, still have that other stuff, though, because it's fun to watch people get confused when you play.

It may sound mean. I guess it *is* mean. But it's so much fun. [Laughs.] It's like we just get so wrapped up . . . I mean, we don't sit on the stage and trip on that. We don't say "Look at them, they don't know what's happening." Every now and then, maybe, when it's really obvious. Especially when I'm playing with Jeff. We get into a thing, where we got so wrapped up looping around the next guy, we get way over here somewhere. I mean, it's cool. It works itself out. It's just that jazz is experimental music. And we're just doing a lot of experimentation. Sometimes, it leaves the people out. But I hope they understand.

Ben: You're talking about rhythmic jokes.

Branford: Rhythm has always been the most important aspect of music to me. Too many people think "melody, melody, melody . . ." They learn the chord changes and play a million eighth notes. You know, the Coltrane way. [Demonstrates.]

Ben: I always suspected, even listening to bebop, that what made bebop's harmonic and melodic lines happen was the rhythmic concept behind them. Not the notes. The notes were just a way to get there.

Branford: That's what it was. The notes were the same twelve notes that everybody else was using. You know? It's the rhythm. The rhythm changed it up.

Ben: Why is this so hard to teach?

Branford: It's only hard when the school system teaches melody all day. It's hard to talk about rhythm. The School systems try to simplify complex things. It's like scientists trying to explain God, you know what I mean. "Oh, that's easy. Men were apes." But how did the apes get here? "Oh, that was very easy. The Big Bang. They started from amoebas." Well who put the amoebas here? "Oh, that's very easy . . ."

It's like, they say with Charlie Parker, "Oh, that's very easy." They say, "Oh, here's Bird in the third measure of the fourteenth chorus and he plays 'Anchors Away.' " But that doesn't explain anything. Because they weren't there when the sailor walked in the door. And Bird saw the sailor and responded to that.

You talk to Art Blakey. He'll tell you, "Bird, man. I remember one time a woman walked in that Bird just saw and he dug her and he immediately plays 'Where Have I Loved You Before.' " Just immediately. His brain just homed in on that. And then you have all these scholars sitting around and they're trying to find in little books musical reasons as to why he would do that. They think too much. They think about the wrong things. They should just chill out. They should let their instincts take over.

And it's hard to tell students that when, since they were this big, they were told to learn their "two-five patterns" and your "basic fourths" and get the Slonimsky book. I mean, there's no logical application to the Slonimsky scales. You just find where you can use them and you use them.

It's like people say that Ornette Coleman is an intuitive genius because he can't explain. Some things you can't *explain*, you know.

Ben: He's also a media genius to come up with a concept like "harmolodic" and give somebody a tail to chase and not bother him.

Branford: That's what it was, too, a tail to chase.

And it's not just music. You see a fullback, right, like Marcus Allen, in that Superbowl run against the Redskins. He ran sixty-three yards. What was the first stupid thing that comes out of the reporter's mouth? "Marcus, what were you thinking . . ." You know, here's these two big, seven-hundred pound behemoths about to crush your skull and they ask you what you were "thinking." As if you were sitting there saying, "Well, there's no hole here so I merely looked to the right and I said to myself . . ." I mean, by the time you say all that to yourself, you're dead.

Ben: I like the analogy with sports. For a musical group to be a group, it's like a basketball team. You don't have time to look at a diagram. You're going to hit it or you're not.

Branford: That's what it's about. It's reflexes. You have to play with somebody so well that you *know* what they're going to do before they do it. It's like you see the Lakers in motion. And you don't see them saying "Throw the ball back." I mean, you see Magic with the ball and he's going up, and all of a sudden, the ball's back there! And the man is standing there with the ball, and it's like, "how did he know the ball was going to be there?" He's there. That's how he knows.

Some things have to be thought out before. Marcus Allen has conceptualized those moves before he got out on the field. When you're on the field, it's too late.

That's the way I approached driving, when I first learned how to drive a car. I would conceive every possible error. I would conceive, "What happens if this goes wrong, what happens if that goes wrong." And I'd think this over for years. Two or three years. I'd be driving down the road thinking, "What would I do if this car came in front of me? What would I do if that happened?" And I would think out solutions. And at least three times, I've used those solutions. On the spur of the moment, without having to think about it. And I feel if I had never considered it, there would have been accidents.

It's like I put myself in musical situations too, you know? I sing songs and I sing them till I learn them. It took me eight months till I learned how to play "Airegin." And I still haven't got it down quite right. But I can hear the changes now. And then when I play it on my horn, I've already figured it out.

* * *

Rudy Van Gelder (December, 1985)

Recording engineer Rudy Van Gelder never gives interviews. He agreed to talk with me only after I assured him that if he didn't like the way it went, he could keep the tape. Perhaps because he's spent his entire life on the other side of the microphone, he knows all too well the historical importance of pushing the record *button. Rudy is a legend in the recording world, not only because of the thousands of classic jazz sessions he's captured on tape, particularly the early Blue Note records, but also because he's a man who, many fans believe, helped invent the sound of contemporary jazz. His recordings from the early '50s still sound modern today. Rudy is not unaware of his position in the jazz pantheon, and actively guards his "secrets." He will not talk about the kinds of microphones he uses or where he places them, or anything even vaguely related to the technical process of recording music. For many of today's young jazz musicians, walking into his studio is a bit like arriving at the inner chamber of the great pyramid (where the mysteries of the past have unfolded); for many older musicians, it's like coming home.*

Ben: We're talking in the control room of your recording studio here in Englewood Cliffs, New Jersey. I've done interviews from all over, hotel rooms, musicians' apartments, back-stage dressing rooms and, of course, recording studios. But I think this is the first one I've done from the *control room* of the studio.

Rudy: By the way, I'm, I'm on the wrong side of this microphone. This is very strange for me. I just feel very uncomfortable. I'd rather be on the opposite side. This is the first time I've ever done anything like this, so it's a very strange feeling.

Ben: When did you discover that you wanted to be on the "other side" of the microphone? Was there a particular moment when you realized you wanted to be a recording engineer?

Rudy: A particular moment? No, not really. But I remember certain times, yes, that I felt that's what I wanted to do. You know, for a long time I was in another profession.

Ben: You were an optometrist?

Rudy: That's right. That's right. And during the time I was in school studying, occasionally we would visit radio stations, or places other than the environment that I was studying, and I really felt that I wanted to be in that other situation. I really strongly felt that. Maybe because it was in Philadelphia. Maybe something about Philadelphia that makes you feel you're in the wrong place. [Laughs.]

Ben: As it says on W.C. Fields' tombstone, "I'd rather be here than in Philadelphia," right? But it's hard for us to realize, in these days when every twelve- or thirteen-year-old child has more technology strapped on their body than the whole city of Philadelphia had back in the '40s, but records, up through the '50s, were recorded in radio studios. They didn't have recording studios as we do today.

Rudy: That's right. There was actually no record industry as such. It was an off-shoot, from an engineering standpoint, of the radio stations. And the engineers usually worked with companies who were associated in some way with radio. There were a few exceptions to that, but there was no record industry as an independent industry, the way it is today. No, it was totally different. The equipment was different, everything was different.

Ben: And, initially, you were a hobbyist?

Rudy: Yes, that's right. I was a radio ham originally. Also an amateur musician, of course, and those two things sort of came together, and that's how it happened.

Ben: That's probably a real important point, the fact that you weren't coming just from a musical side, or the ham radio side, but you brought the two together.

Rudy: It was, yes, yes. It was. I always felt it was a strange combination, just a strange combination of ways to look at music. On the technical side, at that time, you had to build all your own equipment. There was nothing available that you could go out and buy. So, you had to build amplifiers, recording consoles. There was no manufacturer of consoles. That thing didn't exist. You had to make your own. See, the big companies were doing that, but they had their own staff of engineering people and maintenance people who would do that. That's why there was only two or three companies doing it. And not for sale.

Ben: RCA or . . .

Rudy: That's right. You'd see a conglomeration of knobs and meters and you'd know that was put together by RCA engineers.

Ben: Did you go into those studios when you were very young?

Rudy: Yeah. Occasionally I'd visit, yeah. Even I'd visit a session now and then.

Ben: Did you have a sense that there was another way to do it, when you went in there? I mean, was there a feeling that maybe there was a more musical way to do it?

Rudy: Not at that time. I would now. But not then. But at that time, it was a curiosity as to how they were doing what they were doing. And that's why I would seek out those people and places.

Ben: And, when you were in Philadelphia, were you out recording your musician friends, as a hobby?

Rudy: Oh, absolutely. Like we'd have sessions over the house. People would come and . . .

Ben: What would you record them on?

Rudy: Disc. You know, a little 10-inch, 12-inch turntable, 78 rpm, then 33, with a big transcription turntable. That was before the days of tape. And it was direct to disc. Definitely.

Ben: And, you were building your own amplifiers at that point?

Rudy: Yes, that's what I meant before. In order to do that, you had to build everything yourself. That's right.

Ben: And you practiced as an optometrist?

Rudy: Um hm. Thirteen years I did that. It was in another town near here. Hackensack. About five minutes, ten minutes from here . . .

Ben: This was in the '40s?

Rudy: Very late, very late '40s. Yes. Late '40s. '48, '49, '50. Of course during that time, I was recording as a hobby in my parents home. And I was doing both. I was practicing the optometry, and then in my spare time, recording. Actually it was during that period that I was doing all those early Blue Note things, and Prestige, the Modern Jazz Quartet and Miles. And all those people were coming over, and I was recording them. But at the same time, I had the practice going. 'Course then, the whole time thing reversed, after I spent more time doing the recording than I did the other.

Ben: Recording them in your house?

Rudy: In my parent's house. Yes. Right.

Ben: In your parent's house. I'm sure thousands of people out there, who hold those old Blue Note records in their hands and turn them over, are struck, as I was, by the photos. You'll see a picture of Horace Silver at the piano, and there's this lamp behind him. And then on another album, you'll see a picture of Bud Powell at the piano, and the same lamp is behind him. And there's Monk. And the same lamp. Wait a minute. What's going on here? This same lamp. And you really get a sense that it was all being recorded in somebody's living room.

Rudy: It was. That's right. Of course, the house was built, they built that. It was my father and mother, my parents, built that at the time, as their home. But, they were aware of my interest in the sound, and we had a little control room built right off the living room. This little glass window, overlooking the living room, with a small control room. And it's nice . . .

Ben: And there was a place in the living room where you'd always put the drum kit, and . . .

Rudy: Most of it. Yeah. There was nothing rigid about it. But I remember this one place where I sent Kenny Clarke. Kenny Clarke would always go in that corner. We used to call it "Klook's Corner." That's where he would always set up the drums.

Ben: There's a song called "Klook's Corner."

Rudy: That's right. That's how it came about. Right.

Ben: Because he liked it there.

Rudy: That's right. We got a good sound. It was a good size room, actually. Not huge, but acoustically it sounded nice. Had a nice-sounding room.

Ben: Did you design the room to be a recording studio?

Rudy: No, not then. No. It was, that was within the context of the house. It was a one-floor house. But it was a nice high ceiling in the living room, and had little hallways and little nooks and crannies going off. It was really nice. Nice place to record. I made some good records there.

Ben: You made some wonderful records there. Did you practice optometry in the building as well, or were you coming back . . .

Rudy: No, No. Never. I had an office, a separate office.

Ben: So you'd come back after a day of . . .

Rudy: . . . of doing whatever I was doing and do a session. That's right. Or on Wednesday, when I had off, I would record for Prestige or Savoy, or Blue Note, during the day.

Ben: So fairly early on, you were going four and five days a week for Blue Note Records.

Rudy: Yes. It got busy very quickly.

Ben: When I talk to musicians who were involved in these early recordings, Horace Silver, for example, they say to me, "Well, if you want to know about the Blue Note sound, you've got to talk to Rudy Van Gelder. He'll tell you about the Blue Note sound." But I know from talking to you in the past, you'll tell me that I should talk to Alfred Lyon. That as the owner of the company and the producer of those sessions, what he did was as important as what you were doing.

Rudy: Oh, absolutely. I mean, I think you can't separate. If you're talking about the Blue Note sound, you can't separate what I did from what he did. He was really the motivation for creating that, the opportunity to make that kind of a record. Yes. Not only that, he was the first to do it also.

Ben: Is there some way you can tell me why your Blue Note records didn't sound like anybody else's records? Why did your records sound different?

Rudy: Well, it's not easy to really describe it in words. I have complicated feelings about it. First of all, I really don't wanna be too specific, because I'm still at this. You know, I'm still doing it. And I had certain ideas. But really, it's a question of Alfred presenting me with a problem, and my solution to the problem.

Ben: How was the problem presented?

Rudy: The problem, well, that was . . . you really should have been there. And really, the problem was presented to me by him walking in the door with these musicians, some of whom you mentioned, some of whom I've mentioned. And both of us having an image of what the finished product should sound like. He was unique at that time in that he had an idea; he previsualized or preoralized his records. He knew what he wanted before he came to the studio. He had a good idea what a record should sound like, what he wanted it to sound like. He would then bring these musicians in, and I considered it was my job to make these people sound the way he thought they should sound. Now I wanna say, that's within the framework of the musicians themselves, too. Really, it's the way the musicians themselves felt that they wanted to sound. That's where it really begins. It's not with Alfred, it's not with any other producer.

We're talking about jazz, now. Not the multi-track, overdub, layered kind of situation that you would find today. I'm not talking about that situation. I'm talking about jazz, where it's an expression of a musician's personality and his own sound, and he's recognizable and he's unique, and you can identify him as just as easily as I can recognize your voice or your face when I see you. Alfred had a way of presenting the situation. Here they are, this is the way they sound as individuals, this is the way. And he said, "Now you go ahead, and you do what you have to do to make that thing sound the way we want it to sound." And that's how he would present the problem.

Ben: Now this is interesting because it implies your job was to capture what was there, except it was more than that. Because you invented some sounds, some musicians sounded more "real" on your recordings than they would, say, in a club. It wasn't just captured.

Rudy: Right. I never considered that the goal any more than a good photographer really captures a moment. That's not really it. A great photographer will really create his image, and not just capture a particular situation. There are some people who would disagree with that, but that's the way I feel anyway.

That reminds me of something that happened just the other day. I'm in the process of recording Jimmy Raney, a wonderful guitar player. He came into the control room yesterday and he said, "Rudy," he says, "I really like this studio." He says, "Most of the places I go into, it sounds great in the room, and when it comes into the control room, you're disappointed. Something's wrong. You didn't get my sound." He says, "When I'm here, it always sounds better than it sounds in the room."

Ben: I think some musicians don't know what they sound like until they hear themselves on tape.

Rudy: That's right. I believe that, and there's nothing really bad about that. I mean, it's understandable, a trumpet player who's playing his horn, he's three feet from where the bell is and twenty feet from where the sound is really created. You know, he doesn't know how he sounds, unless he's sitting in the audience listening to another trumpet player . . .

Ben: He still doesn't know how *he* sounds.

Rudy: No, that's right. All he knows is how he sounds on the recording. And that's usually, to his own mind, it's usually different from what he thinks he should sound like. You know, someone who's not a professional, they'll come in and record the way their voice sounds, and then they'll say, "Oh, that doesn't sound like me." It's very common, because people listen from the inside, they don't hear themselves from the outside. Of course, experienced professionals, they know how to compensate for that. But to them, it's always a slight distortion of the way they think they should sound.

Ben: So you have a musician who's playing his instrument, who has an idea of how he wants to sound, then you have yourself, an engineer, who knows how it does sound, and how it could sound, and you have to find some common purpose.

Rudy: That's right. And then, all the tools of my trade, that's what I use in order to do that. And it's really also a question of personalities. Sometimes you have to, depending on the personality of the musician, you have to know how they react to your version of what they sound like. That's kind of a subtle distinction, but, you know . . .

Ben: It would seem to me that you have to be careful about making somebody sound larger than life, when you put it on a record, because you make it permanent in a way.

Rudy: I don't accept that larger-than-life description. I know what you mean, but I just don't like the implication of "larger in life." It implies a really exaggerated perspective, and a distortion of the musician's sound. And that's really not what I try to do.

Ben: I guess what I'm saying is, there are live recordings, where you go to a club, set up some mikes, do a live recording, capture the moment. And then there are studio recordings, and you seem to me, historically, to have been one of the key people in establishing what a studio sound could be.

Rudy: In so far as jazz is concerned, yes. But what about the records I made in the clubs? Aren't they kind of unique too? What about the Birdland recordings with Art Blakey ? What about Coltrane at the Vanguard?

Those are location recordings. So why divide my efforts into studio and remote? Why not combine them?

Ben: Well, because, if you do that, then it's not a question of needing a specific room. I mean, we attribute this room we're in as being kind of a magic space. Even more so, the room that you were in, the house that your parents built . . .

Rudy: Why more so? . . .

Ben: Well, perhaps it's because the early days have a kind of romantic aura about them, and the sound of that room was part of it.

Rudy: Well, it's the musicians and their personalities, who they were and how they played, that made it, not where it was. If they were here, you'd have the same feeling about this place.

Ben: Let's talk for a minute about the feeling that those musicians brought with them when they came into the room. Is your memory specific in terms of what the feeling was then, doing those sessions, night after night?

Rudy: It's not a specific feeling, it's more of a general feeling. I don't have any specific feelings. But I have a recollection that what we were doing was important at the time. We knew we were making good records. The music was important. It was important to the producers that I worked for at the time, and it was important to me. And I felt that it was more important than the politics of the day, or anything else that was going on. What we were doing really had a significance, that it would have a lasting significance. I really had that impression at the time. I've heard stories about, you know, people making records or doing whatever musicians do when they perform, and, you know, people'd say, "Well that was great," and then, you know, in some perspective from a later date, it's looked back upon. And then hearing them say, "Well, I just, I don't even remember what I did." You know. But I really must say that in general, not specifically, I really felt that we were doing something that really counted.

Ben: Let me try a specific recording session and see if there's a recollection you might have of it. How about John Coltrane's *Blue Train* session? I don't remember the date exactly of that session . . .

Rudy: You know, somewhere in my files in the back, I probably have a paid bill which gives you the date and everything if you want to know. It's the only way I can track that down . . .

Ben: No, it's not necessary. I'm just curious about what you *remember* about the session. The players were Lee Morgan, Curtis Fuller, Kenny Drew, Paul Chambers, Philly Joe Jones, John Coltrane. Do you have any recollections of that particular recording date?

Rudy: No, I can't say that I do. No. To me it was not that different from the other ones that I was doing for Alfred at the time. Of course, the musicians, as individuals, I have specific recollections of them. But not on that particular session, no.

Ben: Do you have specific recollections of working, for example, with John Coltrane, or on recording his sound, capturing his sound?

Rudy: Our relationship was over a long period of time. I recorded him when he first came on the scene. And this was in Hackensack. I think that we had recorded some albums for Prestige. And I remember when he first came to town, and I remember how he played, and I remember exactly where he stood in the Hackensack studio. And I remember he didn't have a car at the time. He always wanted a car. He'd just started making enough money to have a car, but he didn't have a drivers license, so he bought the car, and someone else would drive him around. I remember that. That's when he first came.

And then, as time went on, he went with another company, and he had experience with them. And then when the time came for him to depart that company, he knew how he had sounded on that label, and he felt that he wanted me to record him from then on. So then, thereafter, he was back. But during that time I had gone from Hackensack to here, so all those ABC Impulse records were done here. And this is where John wanted to record. And he used to call me and say he'd want to come in, say, Wednesday night at 7:30. And he'd show up with his trio or quartet, or whatever it was, and they would get the music together here. And sometimes the producer wouldn't even be here. It would just be between John and myself. And I would run the master tape and a tape for him to take home. And he wouldn't even do a whole album at one time. He'd do like one tune. He'd teach 'em the figure, whatever it was, and they'd play that for an hour and a half, say between seven and nine o'clock. Then he'd go home, and then that would happen again in another two weeks. And then it would happen often enough that he'd have enough for an album, and that would be the album. And it was really nice. We got along great. And there were no technical discussions. I don't get along with people who talk about db's and highs and lows and equalization, and all that stuff. I never had success with a record producer who would talk to me on those terms. It always gets in the way of the music.

Ben: The process you just described strikes me as being very musical. You know, coming in with the group, working it out at the same time you're capturing it and setting up your microphones.

Rudy: It's to an almost irreducible minimum of interference of technology that way. The only way it could possibly be better is if the musicians could do it themselves. And they can't....

Ben: Why can't they? ...

Rudy: Because it's a conflict in personalities. What you have to be and have to know to do what I do interferes with your musical process.

Ben: But so many musicians today are setting up studios in their homes. And, especially with technology, with the synthesizers and drum machines, they're not even using microphones. They're plugging directly into tape recorders or digital devices . . .

Rudy: You don't need a studio for that. You can do it in somebody's office.

Ben: Exactly.

Rudy: I'm not putting that down. I mean, that's another world from what we've been talking about, you know. There's nothing wrong with what you're saying. That's okay. But we're talking about music as an expression of a person's personality.

Ben: Let's talk just a little bit longer about the magic of the Hackensack studio. I'm curious about the atmosphere of the place. For example, I'm wondering if, because the studio was in your parents' home, and because jazz musicians have such a reputation for being night people, if there weren't some conflicts between your parents' life and the studio?

Rudy: There were some minor conflicts, yes. I mean, in that way, of course, they were very kind to time. They allowed me to do it. They also considered what I was doing important. That was an essential part of that. Because if they didn't, I couldn't have done it. So, understanding that, they allowed me to do what I felt had to be done, without interfering too much in their lives. But when things really got busy, towards the end of the '50s, in 1959, I really had a very strong motivation to get outta there. And I felt that I could do a lot of things that I couldn't do there. I mean, it was a much larger room, designed acoustically the way I felt it should be.

And, oh sure, it was a whole new world that opened up, of different types of sessions, different times of doing it. Remember that, before this place was built, certain types of sessions I had to do as a location recording, as a remote. We had to go into New York. We did a lot of good records there too. There was a place in the city, a big hall, where we did the Jimmy Smith, Stanley Turrentine things. Very nice. Kenny Burrell, lot of good records made in New York as a remote. Of course when I came here, I didn't have to do that anymore. That became just part of the studio operation. It was a great relief to get out of Hackensack.

Ben: Yeah. How did that Hackensack experience affect you, spending that time in your own home, with all these great players?

Rudy: Why, I think it's contributed to my enjoyment of making records today. It's the foundation of what I'm doing now. Everything that happened then was the foundation upon which I built what we're doing now.

Ben: What do you listen to from those days?

Rudy: The Red Garland, Philly Joe things for Prestige. I don't even remember the names of the records, but I just remember that beautiful sound that Red Garland had on the piano. Miles. All those beautiful ballads that Miles did. Can't escape that. He can't escape it either. I remember he always used to come in with a beautiful ballad, every session he did. That was one of the things that was his specialty. He'd have this ballad. You'd never forget that. That was just fantastic. "Surrey With The Fringe On Top." Things like that.

Ben: When you hear that, do you think to yourself, "We got that right."

Rudy: Right. Of course. There's hardly any way I could do that better. That's one of the reasons I'm so enthusiastic about digital now. I really feel that digital is an ideal way to preserve that. It's an ideal storage medium for what I'm doing. But that held up pretty well. Those tapes, even though they're, how many years old now? But, if you want to keep it, keeping it digitally is the right way to do it.

Ben: Those records you mentioned were made several decades ago. Has your philosophy of recording changed drastically?

Rudy: No. It hasn't changed at all. I feel the same way about what I'm trying to do now as I did then. The only thing that's changed is if I were to gage the success of what I do, what percentage have I reached, I would have to say maybe, 85 or 90 percent. At that time, back in the Hackensack days, I was back to maybe 30 or 40 percent of what I felt I could do. I mean, referring to things like the equipment. Maintenance. When you started the session and you plugged in a microphone, whether it worked or not. There's a much higher chance of it working now. Whether the tape machine was doing what everyone thought that it should be. Things are more reliable now than they were then. That gives me a chance to concentrate on the things I should concentrate on.

Ben: Well, specifically, what comes to mind, is that *Blue Trane* record we talked about was done direct to two track . . .

Rudy: Right . . .

Ben: You got your mix when you recorded it.

Rudy: That's right. No one knew any better. No one knew better.

Ben: Some people say they still don't know better.

Rudy: I'll buy that. Well, wait. One thing you did forget. It was mono. I must say that. We weren't dealing with more than just the one track.

Ben: Okay. But the process of recording was integral with the process of playing. If somebody was the soloist and you wanted to hear a little more of a piano solo, then the engineer would give you a little more of the piano, right then.

Rudy: Oh, that's right, that's right. It had to be done. There was no other way to do it. That's right. It was *an event.*

Ben: It was an event. I think everybody was aware of that.

Rudy: That's right. Today, each one of those things is a step in the process.

Ben: So the music is being manufactured now, not captured.

Rudy: Right. If you choose to do it like that. Yes.

Ben: What was your feeling when the multi-track recording first came along?

Rudy: Well, in the beginning, I really resisted it. For a long, long time . . .

Ben: Really?

Rudy: Yeah. Of course multi-track didn't happen at once. It evolved, track by track. First one track, then two track, then three track, then four track. Then eight track, then sixteen track, and with maybe twelve in between. And all the variations in between. That's right. So it really was an evolvement, not a breakthrough. That's why I don't consider it a breakthrough. It wasn't really, it was an evolution. Track by track. And the more tracks you had, the more tracks you used. And the more you used, the less you had to "do it right," from the beginning. And that's the way this record industry is built.

Ben: What was exciting to you when multi-track came along?

Rudy: Well, I looked at it in a different way. It was my philosophy at the time, "Well, this thing is really great." I mean, if you assume that the more microphones you use, the more flexible your recording technique is going to be, then nothing is good enough but 24 tracks. Let's assume that. I thought, "This is terrific. Now I'm gonna have a second chance at this." If I make it, I don't have to be great on each date. I can relax, I can just make sure everything goes right. And then we're gonna mix it later, and I'll have a second chance at everything. If I miss an entrance of a solo, or something like that, I'm going to be able to fix it later.

But it didn't work out like that. Because musicians were just as aware of this as I was. And it ended up that they used it for different purposes. They wanted to overdub. And therefore, once you got into an overdub situation, they had to have earphones. And everyone had to hear what was on the tape. And a generation of musicians developed that relied on that, and expected to be able to use that as a way to make records.

Ben: Earphones. You didn't use earphones in Hackensack?

Rudy: That's right . . .

Ben: People just set up the room and played?

Rudy: Yeah. They played, they arranged themselves in such a way that they could hear each other the best they could. And if a drummer was playing very loud, everybody else knew. So they would do something about it. I mean, there were other problems, but I gave you that as an example.

Ben: That's an interesting point. The use of earphones was a radical departure.

Rudy: Absolutely. Do you know that when they come in and do a session today, it takes me practically no time to set up and get a nice sound, but it takes twice as much time just to get the earphones set?

Ben: Everybody wants a different mix. Everybody wants to hear less bass, more bass. More drums.

Rudy: Right, that's right. Each musician has his own feeling about what he wants to hear. Now that didn't exist in the time period you're discussing.

Ben: So the *event* nature of what you were all doing back then had to do with the fact that people were having to make live adjustments in order to get the music down.

Rudy: Absolutely . . .

Ben:. And these days, we're talking about ways of removing each individual from the live process.

Rudy: That's exactly right. It's almost as if you wanted to think of a way to inhibit creativity in jazz music, in a studio, if you wanted to think of a process to inhibit creativity, I would come up with a multi-track machine. A 24-track recorder that you could overdub on.

Ben: Once you're into that, then you're into the whole concept of earphones, and you're into the concept of doing it again, and you're into the concept of doing it later. "Fixing it in the mix."

Rudy: It's inseparable. It's a machine of mass destruction. [Laughs.] Artistically.

Ben: Well, it's kind of a snake swallowing its tail. A circular problem. Because today, from the creative side, there are a lot of great young players, a lot of brilliant technical players. But we don't have so many stylists as we used to have. People don't sound as distinctive as they used to. Do you think that's part of the same technical problem?

Rudy: I don't know if you can blame the machines for that, entirely. There are other factors. But, maybe you can, if you really dig into this, if you want to. If a young musician feels that that's the way he has to record, he's really in this thing alone.

I mean, what we've been saying is that, in order to make a presentable record, a jazz record, everybody has to play together. And they have to play together at one time. Once you eliminate that necessity, then you describe a situation where you don't have to play together, and the musician doesn't have to listen to other musicians. He can just do his own thing and you can fix it later. Or if the piano's too loud behind the saxophone solo, they'll fix it later. But if you *can't* do it later, then while the saxophone player's playing, or while the piano player is playing, or the two musicians are playing with each other, they *have* to listen to each other. They have to. Otherwise it's not good. It's gonna sound rotten. So maybe it is related.

Ben: And maybe when people listen to each other, they start to develop a distinctive way of doing things. And maybe that's part of where style comes from.

These days, I know you're doing a lot of direct-to-two-track digital recording. Live mixing, rather than fixing it later, much like you used to do back in the '50s. Seems like we've gone a long way to get back to where we started. Is there some irony in that for you?

Rudy: I don't think irony is the right word. To me, it's made working a pleasure. I really enjoy doing what I'm doing now. It's like starting all over again and being excited about things. Little things, like being able to play back a great sound to the group right after they have played it. And they can hear it right then, not worrying about how it's gonna to be later. Everybody knows it's good, before they go home.

Ben: That's the way it used to be.

Rudy: Right. Sure, it's excitement. It's put excitement back. I guess you could call that an irony, but it's given me a new way of looking at recording.

* * *

George Benson (December, 1987)

Everybody knows George Benson. For years, he was the jazz singer that even those who didn't like jazz knew about. Within the jazz community, however, he continued to enjoyed a reputation for being a hard swinging guitar player who came up through Jack McDuff's band and who, coincidentally, sang a little bit. His records have sold in the millions and his style of playing and singing has become part of the greater jazz lexicon. It is now common practice, for example, for guitar players to sing along with their solos, a practice popularized by George. Perhaps more than any other contemporary jazz player, he has experienced the tensions of tremendous commercial success and the strain of fighting to keep his music intact and a viable part of the jazz tradition. We first met years ago, before his first hit record Breezin' *was released, and the circumstance of our first meeting is where the following conversation began.*

Ben: Good to see you George . . .

George: Well, it's my pleasure, Ben. It brings back memories.

Ben: We first met a while ago . . .

George: Yeah, I always say it was a very confusing week for me. People would come downstairs; we were working in these twin nightclubs. You were in the big room in the back. I was working up front at the Jazz Workshop, and people would come in and they'd ask them, "Which room do you wanna be in? Who do you wanna see?" And they'd say, "I wanna see Ben Sidran." And somebody, you know, would confuse it with "Benson." So they ended up, a lot of people, were in your room for my show, and a lot of your people were in, you know, my room. So, it was confusing.

Ben: A lot's happened since then, since you were playing in those little jazz clubs. I mean, it was a small room. You couldn't get more than four people up on that stand, but you sure had a burning band at that time.

George: We used to have some incredibly burnin' rhythm sections. I've had several groups. One of them had Lonnie Smith in it. Another one had a kid from Washington D.C., Charles Covington, a great organist. He's one of the finest organists I played with. And then the one I had with Earl Klugh was one of the last groups I played there with. I featured him because Boston's the guitar town, you know, because of the music schools. So that was some cookin' playing we had going on back there.

Ben: You mentioned Lonnie Smith. I suppose a lot of people who know you and your current music aren't really aware that when you started out, you played with organ players all the time. You were in Jack McDuff's group for a while. And that was the tradition: guitar players traditionally went out with organ players, right?

George: I think that's what really helped the guitar to come to the front, you know, as far as jazz music is concerned, because there was never any real, dynamic guitar playing, except for exceptional guys like Wes Montgomery, and even he came by way of the organ at first. And Kenny Burrell and just a couple of others, but I think the organ gave the guitar a form, you know. It featured the guitar so much. Guys could really test themselves, and night after night they had to come with some interesting solos, so it was a good format for guitar players.

Ben: It was also one of the first electronic formats. Having an electric guitar in an all-acoustic band, that was one thing, but the organ was plugged in too, so together it was kind of the start of the electronic jazz group.

George: That's true. I do remember the dissension that it caused in the industry, because it took jobs away from bass players, because organ players were playing their own bass line and things like that. There was a controversy about it because it kept the number of musicians down. But the trios, they'd have big sound, you know, so it had its advantages.

Ben: I know that when you started out as a young man, you were listening to people like Charlie Christian. Who are some of your other first influences?

George: You're right. Charlie Christian definitely was the first guitar player that I remember hearing. And he set such a precedent, you know. After that, I mean, not everybody sounded good to me. You know, I had a high opinion of what the guitar should sound like. And then I became a fan of people like Kenny Burrell, because he cut some of the very first organ hits with Jimmy Smith. And they were fine records. He and Stanley Turrentine.

And then I fell in love with a guitar player named Grant Green, who was just a tremendous player. I loved him for his lyrical playing, and his sense of rhythm, and the clarity of his guitar. He was very articulate, you know. And that impressed me. But the guy who really made me want to play jazz guitar was a country guitar player called Hank Garland. When I heard him, he reminded me so much of Charlie Christian. But Charlie Christian always played as if he was on fire all the time. You know, everything was urgent with him. And I thought that was what was missing from guitar for many years. And after hearing him, I started going to jam sessions. I was in my late teens then. And I wanted to learn how to play. I had been playing guitar since I was ten, but I never really got serious. It was just an instrument to back my singing up with, you know.

Then I, all of a sudden I wanted to play. And I would take my guitar to jam sessions and all the musicians would walk off the bandstand when they saw me take it out of the case. Because they knew I was not a guitar player. And, they weren't ready to put up with my practicing on their bandstand. So I did have some problems. I think that would be like a normal thing, you know, that would happen even today.

Ben: It is kind of unusual to start out as a part-time player or an accompanist on an instrument and then become a world renowned soloist, I think.

George: Well, I always had good ears, I just didn't have any chops, you know. I didn't execute things very well, and I wasn't knowledgeable with harmony and theory. I didn't know the possibilities. I would always get what I was going after, but I wasn't hearing anything significant, and I couldn't really get in and out of the chord changes the way that jazz musicians were noted for at that time. I think the treatment they gave me at that time made me more determined to play because I wondered what it was I *didn't* have. And I went out and searched for it, you know. I don't think I ever found it, but I found something that works well for me.

Ben: So you're still hearing something you can't get to?

George: Well, I'm hearing new things all the time. I'm always saying, "Why? Why didn't I ever think of that?" You know?

When I came to New York in 1963 to live, I was nineteen years old and I was with Jack McDuff. He brought me to New York. And I was getting ready to travel the country. I went around to different clubs to hear what was going on. And every time I saw someone who was a very noted and great guitar player, I watched them for hours, you know, and then marveled at what they were doing. But I was waiting to see them do something that I could not do. And none of them did that. I said, "Wow!" Except one young guitar player, Pat Martino [laughter]. He was the big shocker for me, when I found out he was only seventeen years old, and I saw what he could accomplish. He was one of the first guitars I saw when I came to New York, and he had no big name. He was like myself. He had just come to New York to work. He was working with the Willis Jackson band. And I walked into the nightclub. It was in the middle of Harlem, and here was a young Sicilian boy with his sunglasses on, standing up reading the music on the floor.

Ben: He must have weighed all of ninety pounds.

George: That's about as much as he weighed. And when they let him take a solo, I mean, he lifted that song up off of the ground and turned it every way but loose. And I said, "Boy, this is an example of what's going on in New York City! I better hurry up and get out of here." But I didn't realize he was really an exception. But all the other players who had big names at that time, I would watch them and I'd say, "Well, there's nothing they're doing that's out of my reach. All I have to do is apply myself."

And so I started trying to. I would steal a few things off of everybody and turn it around and try to make it comfortable for me. And pretty soon it all started coming together.

And even the band leader who had fired me after the first night, I mean he was just waiting to find me another gig. He could hear the difference and he decided to keep me. It was a great challenge for me, I'm going to tell you. But I think the thing that did it for me was when I saw my name in the paper for the first time with the word "guitarist" under it, and that was like, wow man, it was like, it blew my mind: George Benson, guitarist with the Jack McDuff Quartet. Although the reviewer didn't say flattering things about me, it was just seeing my name, you know, printed as "guitarist." Oh man, it had such a nice ring, you know.

Ben: Of course, you've always been linked to this controversy between being a guitar player and being a vocalist. I don't think many people realized that you were a singer long before you were a guitar player. How old were you when you started performing?

George: Well, I was about four years old when I first won a singing contest. And I was seven years old when I took my Ukelele into the streets and started trying to make a living. You know, instead of selling papers like the rest of my friends, I took my Ukelele, and I used to make a fortune. I made as much money in one evening as my mother used to make two weeks working in the hospital. But she didn't know I was making this kind of money and I didn't know what money was, so I would give it away to my friends, you know. Until one morning, she looked under my pillow and she saw this money spilling out. She said, "Where did you get all this money?" I said, "I got it playing music on the corners." And I said, "I make this kind of money every night." And it really shocked her. By the time I was ten, I had a recording contract with RCA Victor and I cut records for RCA Victor as a vocalist. I had the Ukelele, and at nine years old, I switched to the guitar, but they were just back-up instruments. You know, I couldn't play anything on them.

Ben: So at that point you could have just as easily gone out and been a singer and that would've been that.

George: I don't know if I really would have excelled. I had a decent voice when I was a youngster, and I had a top singing group in my area at the time, in Pittsburgh, Pennsylvania. And we covered like three states which came together, Ohio and West Virginia. And we were very popular, but we never sold any records. We did cut one or two records at that time, but they never got big outside of my home town. I don't know if I ever would have done what the guitar put me in a position to do. I developed an audience for my guitar playing who was listening and buying the records, and started buying them in the hundreds of thousands. So I had a hundred thousand people who were listening, and they were playing my records because I had some credentials. And then finally something came up. I mean I had been cutting vocals all the time, but nobody paid any attention to them because I was always labeled "Guitarist George Benson." So, you know, it was almost a fluke, really.

Ben: A lot of great players have come through Jack McDuff's band. What did you get from him, and why did you leave? Were you unhappy playing the blues night after night?

George: Well, I was very happy in Jack McDuff's band, to tell you the truth, although he was a very tough bandleader. I learned things, and so it made it worth the ear beatings I used to get from him, you know. He was a good teacher in the sense that he always stuck with the basics. He was a blues man. He wanted everything to have a blues touch to it. I don't care if it was a ballad, it should be a bluesy ballad. So I learned that from him, and you know, it works, because blues, being so universally understood, it's easier to get across than any other music. It works everywhere. Not in a big way, but it works. Wes Montgomery taught me something else. A pretty woman, everybody loves her, even other women who envy her, respect her beauty. And so beautiful music is also something that people give credence to. They don't necessarily run to the store and buy it, but they have to acknowledge it. And so I try to combine those methods. But that was a value I learned in Jack McDuff's band, the value of playing everything with a little blues touch. You know, adding a bended note here and there, a little cry over there, a little glissando here. It really helped to give me a concept, something to build on.

Ben: Speaking about your concept, the fact that you sing along with the lines you play has become something of a trademark for you. Now when other guitarists do it, they say, "Oh, that's like George Benson."

George: Hey, you know, that's kinda weird, because I think all musicians who don't play a wind instrument do that under their breath anyway. Some of them don't do it very well. Some of them, it just translates into grunts, you know. They make noises because of the intensity of their concentration. It comes out much like a fighter who's, you know, belting out things. He doesn't know what he's doing, but he's doing it anyway. And some people do it in tune, but they don't have the microphone up to their mouth. So you never really hear it. And of course, Slam Stewart, who was a bassist renowned, did it for many years. And there was a kid called "Booloo" from France who did it very well. At the age of thirteen, I think he was. So it's nothing new. But I think because of the success of the albums, and how they really went around the world, it became associated with me, that people, every time they hear it, they think of the *Breezin'* album or George Benson.

Ben: It's one of those things, as you say, that's totally natural for a musician to do, because the connection from your brain to your mouth is the same as the brain to the hands, right? Once you find the note, you find it in all places at once. People who aren't musicians think that you're having to work real hard to do it, but it's probably not something you even have to think about.

George: Yeah, and what's interesting is I find I can do things as a vocalist when the guitar is in my hands that I cannot do, that I wouldn't dare attempt to do, when it's not in my hands. When I'm playing with the guitar, I am automatically, like you said, connected. My brain is giving commands to both of them at the same time, only I'm not paying attention to my voice, right? And it's following that guitar, and the guitar is taking me to high notes. When I hear it back I said, "Man, whatever possessed me to sing something that high?" But that's one advantage that it has. That it pulls each one, pulls on the other, helps the other. Where if I sing out of tune, the note is not out of tune, because it has been tuned electronically, see. And if I sing something wonderful, you know, if I have great phrasing with my voice, then we can turn that up in the mix. So, although I do it all at the same time, I can never do the same thing twice. I've tried and I can't do it. Something always interesting happens, you know, when I do that. And I think that's what people are picking up on. There's a dynamic, there's an intensity that happens between my voice and the guitar that is slightly different.

Ben: You mentioned the influence of Wes Montgomery, somebody who taught you that what is beautiful will always be noticed. Wes Montgomery's career foreshadowed yours a little bit. He was associated with Creed Taylor at one point, when Creed pioneered the format whereby jazz was made more commercial. He had Don Sebesky arranging strings for Wes, and Wes did a series of records that featured shorter tracks, three, four minute tracks, and popular tunes. They did Beatles tunes, or whatever, and took jazz in a direction that it hadn't been taken before.

George: I think so. Creed is very responsible for this concept of the strings, big band arrangements. He was successful with Oliver Nelson, with Jimmy Smith, "Walk On The Wild Side." He helped make Bossa Nova music very famous around the world with these recordings of Gilberto and Charlie Byrd with Stan Getz, those great recordings, you know. So he was very instrumental in putting that concept together, and it worked well.

I think that when he tried to put me in that same category, there was some dissension in the industry. Mainly because Wes Montgomery was a different person. I am not Montgomery, and as much as I learned from him, my intention was never to be a Montgomery. I mean, even if I could have accomplished that, and I don't think I could ever accomplish that. He was a guitarist extraordinare, and he was a hero of most guitar players and a lot of non-guitar players, you know. I think most musicians really had a tremendous respect for him. It was he and John Coltrane, Miles Davis, and a very few others in the world, who had that kind of respect.

So that's a tall order when you try to put someone in the same category with Wes Montgomery. But I have to admit, that without his success . . . well, I think he opened some doors. At least he made people guitar conscious. And they were looking for someone. And I think that door was still open at the time *Breezin'* came out. I had already established some footing in that area, you know, with the pretty guitar thing, or the guitar with the strings and so forth, with the album *White Rabbit*. Which really brought me a great audience. It made people think of me differently. Not just another cookin' or chunkin' jazz guitar player on fire, but someone who could play all kinds of things, very versatile, and classy, you know? Someone who could fit in with the classy concept that Creed Taylor put around an artist.

Ben: Perhaps one thing about it that distinguished the album *Breezin'* from the earlier Creed Taylor attempts to make a "classy" George Benson album was that by that time, you had a kind of a repertory group of players, great funky players, who also were very studio conscious and could give you that authentic feel. The groove on the song "Breezin'" is a lot funkier than anything Creed had done with you. And the guys in your band really help make that happen.

George: That's for certain. Tell you what happened on that particular bit. On that album, four of the six tunes were either first takes or one take only, like "This Masquerade," "Breezin'," I think Ronny Foster's tune "Lady," and my tune, "So This Is Love." They were only recorded once or were the first take. The first thing we recorded for the album was "Affirmation." And it was the very first take. We tried to do it twice after that, and nothing happened like it did on that one take. And Phil Upchurch, we did his tune "Six To Four." But everything on there was live. Jorge Dalto, I think, was responsible for much of the energy that came across and how it felt, 'cause he had a Latin feel underneath, and a very light percussive thing happening that kept the rhythm just floating along. It made it so easy for me. I was like riding on a carpet when I played the guitar. I was sailing, you know.

Ben: Good example of the value of having a bunch of guys you're comfortable with. If you're comfortable with these guys, you can go in there and you can play it like a performance. Instead of having to manufacture the music, you can just capture it.

George: I think that is the key that we did not have any drawbacks when we went in. I was in control. I knew what the band could do, and I used them to what I thought was their fullest. I knew that when I needed a funky solo, all I had to do was point to Ronny Foster and he would play something on the synthesizer like nobody else could in the world. I rank him among the top synthesizer players I've ever heard. I have played with some other great players since then, but I think Ronny still has an edge. His stuff comes purely from the gut, you know, he's not a reader. He can read, but he doesn't prefer to, and he works so much better when you just teach him the song and let him feel it out for himself and you leave him alone. And he's a good writer, too. He and Phil Upchurch both.

I love what Phil did with "Six To Four." And he's the one who suggested I do "Take Five" with a funky feel. And I said, "Man, now why in the world would I want to cut 'Take Five'? There's only one 'Take Five' and that's a classic. I don't mess with no classics, you know." He said, "No man, I'm thinkin', you know, why don't we play it with a little funk underneath." I said, "How can you play it funk in 5/4 time?" And he showed me. So it was really a good challenge for us and it was a lotta fun.

That's another thing about the album *Breezin'*, it was fun. It was a breeze. We went in there and we had four days to do an album. We finished in three days, and on the fourth day—one day I'm gonna put out the recordings that we did on the fourth day—we had nothing to do. We had finished the album. We fixed everything, 'cause there was little tiny things that need fixin', you know.

Ben: Just one of those magic moments, huh?

George: Oh, that's for certain.

Ben: What about the details that went into a song like "Breezin' "? For example that little guitar hook on the front that everybody recognizes. Where did that come from?

George: [Sings the lick.] It's very, very interesting how that happened. The melody of the song "Breezin'" is so straight ahead that it's disinteresting for a jazz player, because it doesn't really create a challenge. When the producer asked me to record it, I said, "Now wait a minute, now." There had been two versions of that, and both of them were hits. I think one was put out by the Hip-Huggers or something, and then it, one was done with Phil Upchurch by Gabor Szabo and Bobby Womack, who wrote the tune. And I said, "Well, the only way I would do this tune again," I said to the producer, "is if you get Bobby Womack to come in and play some rhythm for us." Because I knew he was one of the finest rhythm guitar players in the world. And if he had any new ideas, we could, you know, work with them. And sure enough, he came in, and he said, "You know, I've never liked the way this tune was recorded." I said, "Whadaya mean, man? There are some great versions of this thing." He said, "Yeah, but there's always been a thing I wanted to happen. It didn't happen." I said, "What is it?" He said, [sings the lick]. And that's the thing that is not on the other recordings. I said, "Well let's go for it, man. Let's do that." And that's what we did.

Ben: Again, a magic moment depends on the right people being in the room.

Now prior to this record, you were playing the clubs as many musicians do, and suddenly this record changed everything. How did it change things for you?

George: Well, the first thing, I got such a different response from my audience. You know, all of a sudden, I was a hero. I said, "Wait a minute, now, these are the same people who didn't care anything about us a little while ago. Now all of a sudden they like us, a lot." I said, "Why?" So that's what a hit record does, you know. I always wondered what it would be like to have a hit record. I mean, a *real* hit. And "Breezin'" was every bit of that. I mean, it made, the whole band heroes. The guys in the band would say, "Oh yeah, I work with the George Benson group." And I mean, suddenly they were, you know, they were *in.* And every place I went, eyes were on us, and I felt like I was being put under a magnifying glass all the time, you know? I didn't know whether I really liked that. It became very strenuous. I suddenly began to believe that people expected us to be more than what we were. I said, "Wait a minute. How can I ever live up to their expectations?" And that's what first went to my mind. I said, "Nobody can live up to their expectations, because they raised you up to a god." You know?

And I suddenly became very conscious of what I was playing, whereas before, my guitar and I have always been natural. When I got a guitar in my hand, I mean, it just felt like that's the way it's always been. I can't remember when I didn't have one in my hand. Even when I was just using it to play behind my singing, it was there, you know. But now, all of a sudden, I begin to pay attention to it, where I didn't so much before. I mean, I began to work at something that actually I felt was already natural, and I think that's something that happens to many of us in the business. We begin to examine ourselves. And the public forces you in that direction.

Ben: For better or for worse, or both?

George: I think it can work for you. I think it worked for me in some cases and against me in others. 'Cause there's such a thing as trying too hard. And I don't think a person has to try when they already have it. If you got something that's naturally together, I mean, what are you going to change? If they already like you, then what are you doing, you know? It also caused me to underestimate the guitar. The power that the guitar had for me. See, I think that the guitar is what put me in the position to have an audience in the beginning, and then the vocal thing won some Grammies and took us to places where no other jazz artists had ever been. But I think it can be overplayed. I began to worry about what I was singing. Do people want me to sing? And some people would say, yes, and some people would say, no, you know, so we were in the middle, kinda like caught.

It took me awhile to realize that, "What do you wanna do, George? because, when it's all over, that's what's gonna count." And I think I have a lot more things to say on the guitar, and I'm anxious to say them, to tell you the truth.

Ben: The follow up to *Breezin'*, I thought, interestingly enough, was a live record with a live band. And the hit from that record was a song whose lyrics kinda say what we're saying now. The song was "On Broadway," and the lyrics are "I'm gonna be a star 'cause I can play this here guitar." And that's what you've been saying, it's the guitar that's doin' it for you. That was a great groove and a great night. And I think everybody who heard "On Broadway" at the time said, "I'm going to go out and hear this band, 'cause I wanna be there when he does this."

George: Yeah, that was one of the hardest, toughest things I have ever done in my life. That live record. I think it really put the pressure on me. Because that joint, that small club we recorded in, had such a great vibe and atmosphere. I felt, "Man, I must perform. I've got to do it. Tonight is the night." And all the pressure was on. They had twin twenty-four track recordings going on at the same time, you know, all night. And we had done the song on the first set. We were gonna be there for three nights, and we were doing two shows each night, to make sure that we had enough material to pick from for an album. And I remember that during the first set, the song "On Broadway" was kinda slow, but we had a decent response. And on the second set, I repeated the song and this time, after I counted the time off, I waited until it settled. And then I got into it. So when you hear the recording, you'll notice that the beginning has two distinctly different tempos. I started, then the audience told me where *they* wanted it. They joined in and started clapping and pattin' their hands. Then I knew where the tempo should be. And *then* I started singing. And that's what I think made the difference.

It made me go to places I had never been before. And I won't forget after that night was over. It was a very, very tough evening for me. I mean, I felt I almost died that night. There was so much tension and hypertension going on. I remember going back to the hotel and sitting beside the swimming pool and listening to that song. And I couldn't believe what had happened. Because I don't remember doing any of that. I just remembered the audience and how much fun it was. And when I heard that recording, and it was a great recording done live by Al Schmidt, who is one of the finest engineers ever. He had captured what I thought was the finest thing I will ever do on records, you know, and I was glad that I was alive long enough.

What did happen, which is real interesting, is that the producer did not hear that performance like I heard it. He picked another performance of that song, the first set on that night, Friday night. And, when we went to mix the album, he played for me his version of what he thought was the great one, and I said, "No, man, this is not it. This is not the one. The one I heard is from the second show, Friday night." He said, "George, you know, we erased a lot of tapes, because we felt we were gonna run out of tapes. We were running tapes, so much tape, we had to go back and go over some of what I thought were not so good performances." And I almost bust into tears. And they ran through all the tapes, took another day, and they found it. And he put it on. I said, "Now, let's hear the hit. This is the hit." You know, so he put it on. He say, "Yeah, you're right, this is better." I said, "Wild, man," you know, "this has got everything." We had a dance tempo now, where before it wasn't. It was in between.

Ben: 'Cause the crowd had told you where the time was supposed to be.

George: Oh, the crowd told me where it was at.

Ben: Well, you know, after that record, you put out a lot of records that didn't have much guitar on them. How do you feel about that now? Is there a vocal from that period that you would say, "Well, that's as high, in terms of art, as the best instrumental stuff," or are you really saying to me, "There's nothing as high as a great instrumental performance."

George: Well, what I'm saying is that the guitar is a side of me that is very important and I think it can do things that my voice can never do. First of all, I can play more than one note at a time, harmonically speaking. And then it makes me think in areas where I couldn't even begin to think as a vocalist, you know? And it articulates at a rate of speed that my voice can't keep up with. Wider passages with more accuracy. And just for the sound of the instrument, the feel of the guitar, what it represents to all our lives, it has had an effect on every human being on earth who's ever heard it. So for that, for all those things that it represents, I could never put the guitar down. That's first of all; I'm gonna always play it.

Now, will it get into my albums? I've had trouble with producers who don't think that it's important. That has been my problem, and I've been going along, you see, being congenial. But I think it is time that we put some things on our album with the same concept that we've always had, you know. If we found a great piece, let me have it, let me turn it inside out and see what I can extract from this particular piece. Allow me to mess with it. That's what they used to do. I have problems doing that today. Being left alone.

Ben: You mentioned before that, after the hit, you got to go places where no jazz musicians had gone before. You were like the Starship Enterprise at one point. "To boldly go . . ." But one thing I noticed is that you did continue to come out and, as best you could, play with the cats. You'd show up at the Blue Note or wherever it was, and sit in with the guys. But it must have been difficult, because once you're livin' that life, on that level, you just don't run into the old guys the way you used to, right?

George: That's true for a lot of reasons. They have a concept of you. They feel that you've changed. And a man who goes from rags to riches, so to speak, overnight, he does change, but maybe not to the degree that other people believe. Your friendships can change simply because you are now going places where you didn't go before. And other musicians who have not been there don't feel comfortable there. And they'll see you at a place where you're surrounded by persons who will be on the social ladder differently, and they'll associate you with them, and they'll feel that you're being, you know, uppity, so to speak. High falutin', to use some old terms.

And then the money thing. Money is always a divider. Money separates people, you know, for many reasons. It's the most sought after thing, probably, or at least one of the most sought after things in the world. So when you have money, many people feel that you should share with them. And of course, you do, with some of them. But you cannot do it with all of them, and that is the problem. So money has brought many problems along with the enjoyment of having a lot of money. It brings problems too. So it has changed my relationships with a lot of people over the years. We picked up some friends, and we've lost some. And I think that is a normal thing that happens in any situation where, you know, where your lifestyle, your social position has changed.

Ben: So now, say it's Monday night, Tuesday night, and maybe you feel like going out and sitting in somewhere. But if George Benson shows up with his guitar to sit in, suddenly the show stops, and it's not the same. Is it hard for you to feel a contact with the music the way you used to?

George: Because jazz is a demanding music, I think I will always be able to make music *feel* good. But it also, today's music is bogged down to some degree by a lot of harmony, theory, and concepts which go beyond what we used to do years ago. Jazz used to be very, very simple. If you had a good feeling and you played reasonably well, I mean, you could get over. But today, you better know what B-flat-seven with a raised five [Bb7+5] is, you know. Or flatted fifth, or raised ninth, or whatever. And you better be able to get around those notes and chords reasonably well, in order to have the kind of clout and respect that'll get you in on a jam session. And you have to practice. That is the main thing. You have to practice doing the thing that you must do when you play jazz music. You've gotta get into those tunes, you gotta stay with it. Your chops got to be up.

Now if I worked a couple of weeks singing, and played three songs a night, and sang fifteen, then my guitar chops are down. And, well what I like about jazz people is they don't go down. Their chops are up, you know. So if you're sittin' in with Wynton Marsalis or Dizzy Gillespie, who's been playing music constantly for many, many years, you'd better have some chops. And that's the one area where I suffer. It takes me two or three songs in order to warm up. But on a jam session, you might not get two or three songs. Play one and everybody's ready to get down. You know. So that's been the only problem. But now, when I have played some, rehearsed with the guys, and I go to a jam session, then we burn the house down. As a matter of fact, I become one of the leaders at that. I inspire the guys. "Come on, let's burn it down, you know." And I enjoy that.

Ben: That's an important point, because now you have taken on the statesman role. Because people in the world of jazz refer to your success as a potential for their own success. "Well, George has done it and look at the success he's had," which means, you know, that jazz can prosper and you can prosper too as a jazz player. You are now an instigator by your very presence.

George: I'm glad you mentioned that. I think that's a very important point, and there's another thing that put a little weight on me, because I feel that if I had failed after having the kind of success we had with *Breezin'* that the people in the industry would call it a fluke, and other artists would not get the advantage and know that it *can* happen to them. And that it is not a fluke, that if you make the right moves, and if you pay attention to what you're doing that it can happen. If you have an honesty about your music.

One thing that we have with our songs, no matter what we do, it always sounds like I meant to do it. And that's something that Jack McDuff gave me, too. You know. He said to me one evening, I'll never forgot it, he said, "You know, the people who are listening don't know whether you can play or not, because they can't hear you. You're playing so far back, as if you're afraid. At least if they can hear you, they can make a judgement as to whether you're good or bad." He said, "Man, play it out! Let 'em hear you." You know. And I found by doing that, after getting over the fear of doing it, when I thought I was making very big mistakes, and you know, obvious clunks in the music, they weren't picking up on it, because they didn't know what I *meant* to play. They just know, "Well, he's playing and it's got energy, and it feels good." But they never picked up on the clunkers, or what I played when I thought, "Oh, man, I didn't mean to play that." But it wasn't bad, it just wasn't what I meant to play. So once I found that out, I was gone. I felt everything should be played with *authority*. And that was the word he used, "Play it with authority, like you mean to play it. 'Cause you can't make me believe it if you don't believe it." And so I've been doing it that way ever since.

Ben: Classic jazz advice: if you make a mistake, play it again and play it loud.

George: They'll say, "He meant to do that, man. Listen, he going do it again."

* * *

Wynton Marsalis (January, 1986)

I remember speaking with Wynton Marsalis in 1982, when he was being honored in his hometown of New Orleans. A few years before, he had left New Orleans for New York, where, after a short period of time with Art Blakey's Jazz Messengers, he seemed to burst upon the national scene as a full-blown star, winning Grammy awards in both the jazz and classical categories. This day in 1982, however, we were traveling up the Mississippi River on a large stern-wheel paddleboat along with 3,000 happy fans who had gathered to hear his band play and celebrate "Wynton Marsalis Day," which had just been declared by the mayor of that city. I asked him then if he felt particularly proud to return home to New Orleans with this kind of recognition. Wynton said, "No," that it really didn't mean that much to him. He said that he felt New Orleans never had been much of a jazz city, that it was just portrayed that way in the media, that opportunities to play real music had always been limited there and that most of the people who had come on board the boat probably didn't even know, like or understand his music. They were there, he felt, primarily because the media had told them that they should be there. He said, "Man, if they really listened to this music, it would change their lives." Over the years, Wynton has continued to be outspoken about the lack of awareness of jazz in America and has never succumbed to the hype surrounding his own celebrity, which continues to grow.

Ben: Wynton, you're not just a trumpet player. You're a cause célèbre. For better or for worse, that's a big part of your story. You came to us, of course, a man dedicated to the jazz tradition, but then were vaulted into this other position, that of spokesperson for all of jazz.

Wynton: Right.

Ben: I'm reminded of something Norman Mailer once said about being famous. He said that as soon as he became a celebrity, he could no longer observe people the way he used to because they were always observing him. It changed his ability to work. Has your fame changed your ability to work in this way?

Wynton: I'm not that famous. I can ride the subways. People don't look at me. It's cool.

Ben: Yes, but in another way, when you're on the top, people are always "gunning" for you. They're looking for you.

Wynton: Yeah. It is like that. But unfortunately for us, it's not done with their horns or anything like that. You know what I mean? I would feel good if it was actually about music. If cats would come up on the bandstand and play and just blow the roof off. But now it's just talk and stuff, man, and that's a waste of time.

Ben: A lot of the talk that surrounds your albums, particularly your early albums, invariably speaks about whether your playing is better than those who came before you, that sort of thing, rather than examining exactly what it is you are trying to do.

Wynton: Yeah. Well that's unavoidable. That comes with the territory. And at that point, I really felt fortunate just to be able to make an album, and to be able to play with Ron [Carter], Herbie [Hancock] and Tony [Williams] and my brother [Branford]. I just felt fortunate to be able to play, at that point. So if they cut it down or said it was good, it didn't matter. Because before then, before I started playing with Art Blakey, I didn't even see how it was possible to play jazz. How could you make a living doing that? How could you get a job doing that? How could you learn to do it? Where was the environment to play and develop? I didn't see that environment. So I felt so fortunate just to be in a position to produce my own music and to play, and to provide an environment to play in, that I didn't really care whether they were saying it was as good as with 'Trane recording with Miles. I know it wasn't on that level, but I just felt fortunate to be able to play.

Ben: You and I first met when you were working with Art Blakey. And the way all the musicians treated each other in that band really seemed to elevate the experience beyond the notes. There was a very special feeling in that band.

Wynton: That band opened up a whole other world of understanding for me. Before then, I just used to think you played the scale with the chords, or whatever. My understanding of the music was limited. A lot of that was due, of course, to the environment I grew up in. But a lot of it was just due to misconception. I can honestly say that when I started playing with Art Blakey I didn't understand what you were supposed to be trying to do when you played a solo. I did not understand that. I thought you wanted the audience to clap or something. I hadn't really thought about playing the music or the blues idiom or any of that. I mean, I grew up playing blues, but in the most generic sense. I didn't grow up really playing blues, like blues were played in the '40s, or '30s, or '20s, or even '60s. I grew up just playing blues from the standpoint of "this is a blues form."

Ben: The chords.

Wynton: Yeah, you know, that didn't really describe anything to me. Because by then our popular music of the time was not blues-based. The popular music of the bygone days was blues-based music. And just the whole conception of structuring a solo, and just listening to everybody in the band when you play, I didn't grow up in that age. And I didn't know any of those recordings, like 'Trane's recordings in the '60s, or Miles' recordings in the '60s. Those serious group-interaction recordings. I never listened to Louis Armstrong. I never listened to Ornette Coleman. So at that point, when I first started playing with Art, my knowledge of the music was extremely limited. I feel fortunate that he allowed me to come up on the bandstand and play. I mean, I didn't even know his music. At that point, I didn't even know the music of Art Blakey and the Jazz Messengers. I mean, I knew the music *we* were playing. But I didn't really have intimate knowledge of all of his recordings.

Ben: It sounds like as soon as you got on that band, the world of jazz opened up for you.

Wynton: Definitely. Because I was functioning under the illusion that if you just existed, you could play. You could play just off of the energy. I knew you had to know harmony and theory, but I had studied that in high school. But I didn't understand that you have to have intimate knowledge of the music, in specific terms. Like, if you're a musician, you're supposed to know what's on the records enough to go to the piano and play it, know what the drums are playing, the bass, the function of the horn.

That's my job, to know that. See I hadn't hooked all that up then. I didn't start hooking that up until I was 19 or 20 years old. Right now, I'm still trying to understand certain things.

Ben: Well you've really been scrambling then, because you were thrust onto center stage. And the first thing you said to millions of people at the ceremony where you won your first Grammy Awards was to tip your hat to the tradition and to all the players who came before you. You didn't waste any time making this your cause.

Wynton: That's my job, too. Because the thing about jazz is, it's always "now." Charlie Parker would be great if he came today and played the same exact stuff he played. He would still be a genius. So I have to pay my respects to music. Man, I'm not out here trying to prove that I'm the greatest person to ever play the trumpet. I mean, we know Louis Armstrong, Miles, when he was really playing, Clifford Brown, Fats Navarro, Dizzy, them cats played, man. I'm just trying to learn some of the music.

Ben: The trumpet tradition is a mighty tradition in jazz.

Wynton: It sure is. There's been a lot of cats who really spent hours at the craft. That's the thing. I feel a lot of times our music is tied up in serious folklore. And the musicians add to that a lot. Which was cool for that era. But now that we're in the serious crunch, so far as understanding the aesthetic of our music, we can't be as folkloric as we used to be. We have to understand that. Louis Armstrong, he didn't have more soul than King Oliver. You can't say that Louis had more soul. But he played more trumpet, we know that to be true. So the main thrust now has to be craft. People have got to understand that you *must* learn the craft of the music. The artform has a craft. And it's important for us to maintain the integrity of our form by adhering to the standards that have been.

Like who knows Monk's music? Who takes the time to put on Monk's albums and learn his tunes on the piano and study that logic of his? He didn't just come up with that music, because his name was Monk! I mean, he studied music. I find that even now, in 1986, we still are fighting that same battle.

Ben: Traditionally it seems that our schools considered jazz something you might play, but that "classical" music was something you would learn and study. There was a distinction in how you approached these forms. As you say, you learned to play jazz just because you were here.

Wynton: Well, you cannot learn how to play a type of music in school. What you learn is the craft of whatever it is. In classical music, when you're a classical musician and you recreate some music that someone else wrote, what you're doing is lower on the level of creativity than the composer. So when you learn classical music, mainly you learn your instrument. And if you're a good enough musician, and you can hear music well enough, then you will be able to be truer to the vision of the composer. In classical music, the composer is the important figure. We can't lose sight of that. People run around saying, "I'm a classical musician." You are playing someone's music. It's like being a workman or something. Which is a valuable position, I'm not saying it isn't. But we can't get somebody reading Beethoven's music confused with Beethoven. Or Bartok. Or Stravinsky. The composers are the key.

In jazz, you are the composer and the performer at the same time. So then you not only have the responsibility of virtuosity, you then have the added responsibility of vision. And it's a lot easier to become a virtuoso than it is to have vision. But you might have vision, and if you don't have the virtuosity, then you can't carry forth the vision. See, that's the misconception that I'm constantly having to fight. The belief that if you have the vision then you don't need the virtuosity.

I mean, we can use that analogy of King Oliver and Louis Armstrong over and over again. Many people might have thought of playing something that Bird thought of. Maybe I can sit down in my living room and think of some music like Monk. Or think of playing trumpet in a fashion.

That's in my *mind*. But I can't pick my horn up and do it. And that's what the issue is.

Ben: You seem to disagree with those people who say that part of your greatness is in the fact that you are a classical performer as well as a jazz performer?

Wynton: It's not that big a deal, man. Because I'm not responsible for actually presenting the world from a German point of view. I mean Beethoven's music or Haydn's music has human implications that override its immediate setting, the setting it was created in. What I'm doing is re-creating one part of some music that Haydn wrote. I play the trumpet part. There are thousands of other parts going on.

So basically what's required is just an understanding of the style of the music, which one can get from studying. I understand the form of it. That's not hard. You can get a book and learn that in an hour. Technique comes from just practicing and studying. But I'm not responsible for having a vision in that music. In other words, I couldn't take a pen and write a concerto an equivalent of a Haydn concerto. That would be something.

Ben: But you have a career in that music, if not a vision.

Wynton: I have a career performing music that's a result of other people's vision, yes. Because that's where careers in that field are. That's what people do in that field. But you can't confuse recreating something with creating something. Those are two totally different propositions.

Ben: When you say that it's your job to stand up in front of audiences and tell the musical truth as you know it, does that truth then include this distinction between your role as a Western classical musician and a jazz musician?

Wynton: It is definitely my job. Definitely. Because like I said before, I mean, I believe in practicing, man. I'm not trying to be fraudulent or I'm not trying to get credit for myself. I believe that you practice and you develop throughout your entire life to as high a level as you can get to.

I won't be Bird. That's life. But since I realize right now that I'm not Bird, that doesn't mean that I'm going to change my opinions on music to make myself the greatest musical hero. I'm not going to say, "But Bird, he didn't play classical music." He didn't want to play classical music. He could have played it if he wanted to play it.

Ben: But Bird very much wanted to be respected by the classical establishment, however.

Wynton: He didn't necessarily want to be respected by them. He just felt slighted by the fact that he knew his creations were on a par with any in Western art. And he knew that he wouldn't receive proper credit, that his music would be victimized by misconception. And that really disturbed him. So he would say, "Yeah, I dig Prokofiev," because he wanted people to understand that his music was on as high a level of artistic and aesthetic achievement as their music was. Certainly the degree of virtuosity required is. I'm sure Prokofiev wasn't any more dedicated to his craft than Bird was.

Ben: But the reality of the music business is that we all exist to some extent on other people's terms. That is, you may be a fully realized, creative jazz musician, but to the extent that you exist on somebody else's terms, they will take you seriously. Otherwise, you may be invisible.

Wynton: Well, I don't agree with that. Somebody like Bird, what he was doing didn't depend on anybody. There's nobody playing like Bird now. If they had somebody, we would know who they were. People always try to make you think, like, "Oh, Louis Armstrong. You should have heard so-and-so in Arkansas." That so-and-so in Arkansas did not exist.

Ben: Or we would have heard of him?

Wynton: We would know. Because when people make artistic statements with that type of depth and power, the people in their environment know. That's part of that degree of power. I mean, when Bach was writing music, sure it took 150 years, and Mendelssohn discovered him, but people knew who he was. People in his craft knew he was there. They'd say, "Oh yeah, somebody up there is doing something." When Bird was playing, the musicians knew.

Ben: So what do you tell the thousands of young musicians who today are using your career as a model for their own lives? They see that your success with Western classical music has helped you get exposure in the jazz area. So now they are starting to think that this is the way for them to proceed, that they have to play classical music in order to be accepted as a jazz player.

Wynton: See, that's what's unfortunate. People will look at things that way. I grew up playing classical music. I played with the New Orleans symphony when I was in high school. I took lessons, played with the brass quintet, played with the civic orchestra, played the Haydn trumpet concerto with the orchestra when I was 14, listened to tons of classical records. I went to school for that. I played jazz—my father's a jazz musician. I'm still trying to develop in that idiom. Of course it has been a lot harder for me to understand what jazz music is about than it was for me to understand classical music, from a performance standpoint. Because, like I said before, I am not responsible for providing a vision in classical music.

For people who look at it now that I've received publicity for it and think that's a reason for doing it [classical music], they won't make it. Because when I started off doing it, I did it with the utmost sincerity and desire to learn how to play. Because I had no intentions of even doing a classical record or knowing I would receive publicity for that. I didn't do it as a gimmick. That's not what made me practice all those hours. In a way, I'm disturbed by the fact that everybody thinks that now we'll all do classical recordings. Oblivious to the level. You know, Wynton Marsalis, he plays classical music. Like just anybody can pick up on it now and say, "I play the Haydn trumpet concerto." Or just, "I play jazz and classical." I mean, it's almost like a joke now.

And as a matter of fact, I don't play classical music anymore in performance.

Ben: You'll record it but not perform it in public?

Wynton: I may do some more recordings, but I'm not performing.

Ben: Is it uncomfortable for you to perform it?

Wynton: I don't mind performing it. But that's not what I'm . . . I'm trying to concentrate on learning how to play jazz. And furthering the tradition of our music. And it's going to take a lot of time for me to develop into something that's valid, you know?

Ben: Speaking of the tradition, you often talk of Louis Armstrong. When we consider his classic performances, such as the Hot Five recordings from the '20s, what is the message of that music for today's young players?

Wynton: Well, Louis Armstrong is one of the greatest geniuses in Western music. We know this because his music sounds most like what it means to be American. Which is what art is really about. It tells the truth about whatever group of people that the artist rises up out of. And all the things, like the Declaration of Independence and The Bill of Rights, that we think are corny now because they've been compromised to the point of absurdity, well what's more absurd than Louis Armstrong being denied the benefits of being an American, by and large. He came forth and just told this story in music.

First and foremost, his sound is so clarion and has such majesty and nobility. This is just from a human standpoint, something that we can all understand. Now musically, technically and craft-wise, he possessed the highest level of craft possible. He could hear, he played in tune, had ridiculously ingenious rhythm and time. And he practically invented the conception of an improvised solo with a certain type of structure and form and organization, climax and everything. And what he brought to the trumpet, the majesty in the upper levels, or the use of different timbral effects, or just using different registers for weight, to change the weight of the rhythm . . .

Ben: His rhythmic concept is a key element here?

Wynton: Definitely. And his vocal conception of playing. I mean, we have to understand that before he played like this, people just did not play that way. The trumpet just didn't sound like that. And his conception of freedom, too, in music, let him take the corniest song and turn it into a masterpiece of American art. Because that same pioneer-type spirit of freedom, it's all in his music.

Ben: The Hot Five was a kind of transitional group in Louis Armstrong's career. It was a very relaxed environment for him to play in, but his music seemed to mature at that point.

Wynton: Well it was just a studio group, mainly. But the thing about that music is that jazz music, even when it seems like it's casual, that's not what's happening. Because the form of the tunes are the same, and each person understands their role. That's no more casual than if you sit down with a string quartet, and they give you some music and they say, "Play this music." The music is all written out so you have to play a certain part, but you understand your role.

[In jazz] like the drummer played drums, tuba played tuba, trombone, clarinet, you know everybody understood their role. The music was complete within itself. And Pops played what he was supposed to play. The music had a form that had to be kept. The Hot Five recordings, they're adhering to the form. I mean, people are not just soloing and just going in any key or doing anything they feel like doing. So even though it seems like it's not really structured—I mean they were working on the arrangements in the studio and things like that—when it came time for them to put down the final version, everyone knew what they were supposed to be doing.

It's like if you get five guys together on a basketball court. You know, this analogy can't really work aesthetically, but you might not know what play you're going to call. But you know if you play guard, your function, your job is to do this. The center does this. The forwards do that. So as far as you just being out there in a state of chaos and random searching for things to do, that only happens if you don't know what you're doing.

And Louis Armstrong had some of the best musicians at that time. Of course, you can hear that his rhythmic conception is a lot different than theirs.

Ben: He has a rhythmic freedom that the rest of the players had not yet realized.

Wynton: Yeah, because that's hard.

Ben: The rhythm is the hardest part?

Wynton: Yeah. Every time there's a rhythmic innovation in the music, the music changes. See, that's the problem. That's one thing that happened that was not too good in the '70s. What we considered innovation did not entail rhythmic innovation. Every innovation . . . Charlie Parker, that's a *rhythmic* innovation. Everybody wants to say harmony. He played upper intervals. Louis Armstrong played those same notes, man. There are records with Louis Armstrong playing flat nines, flat fives, flat sixes. Duke Ellington was writing all kind of tunes with all types of harmonies. And if you want cross-idioms, Schonberg was dealing with harmony on another entire level.

Ben: You can't take harmony any further than it had already been taken?

Wynton: No, not harmonically. But harmony is not the key to our music. Harmony is used in motion. And motion is rhythm. And rhythm is the most important aspect. I mean everything is important. But, whenever you find a real valid rhythmic innovation, the music changes. It's like when you hear Elvin [Jones] play. Elvin changed the music. You change the rhythm, you change the music. I mean, maybe somebody did throw an extra note in a chord, but so what? To add some notes into a chord does not innovate American music.

Ben: The idea that rhythm can be carried by any instrument is also important. It is not limited to the so-called rhythm section to make the innovation.

Wynton: Definitely. It's like Stanley Crouch always says, "Each instrument is also a drum." And that's true. Each instrument has rhythmic responsibility akin to the drum. Which is an American invention, the drum set.

Ben: You mentioned Elvin Jones, and by extension, his work with John Coltrane. How would you characterize their musical innovation?

Wynton: Well the one harmonic problem that 'Trane did solve is, you know, whenever you play in double-time, the harmony progresses at half the rate. Like if you have two chord changes in a bar, and you double the time, it feels like a bar for each chord. And what 'Trane would do is stick some notes in between those harmonies. It's just amazing that somebody could be diligent enough to really figure that out and have it be logical. I mean, what he's playing is logical, it's not something that's just random.

And rhythmically, well Elvin, McCoy [Tyner], everybody in that band would just swing on the highest level of serious Negroid implication. I mean it was swinging on the highest possible level. And Jimmy Garrison, there's nothing you can really say about that. That's just what it's supposed to be like.

Plus their music was so spiritual. It has very serious overtones. You know that nobody on the stand was playing around or joking or going through no "me" games. The music was the issue. And Elvin . . . people don't talk about Elvin enough.

Ben: Listening to John Coltrane's recordings during the period when he was first trying to form his own band, you hear some tremendous drummers on the dates, like Art Taylor. But as soon as Elvin showed up, the realization of Coltrane's music arrived. It's like the addition of Elvin precipitated Coltrane's final musical breakthrough.

Wynton: Elvin is so great it will bring tears to your eyes. I mean, damn, somebody play drums like that! Just that he could figure out all that. But Elvin, he's such a smart guy. I mean, I've had the privilege to talk to Elvin, and he is so intelligent. When you meet him and you rap to him, then you can understand how he could have figured that out.

Ben: When you go into the studio to make your own recordings, obviously you are aware of everything that's gone before, not only your own efforts but all the other great recordings that make up the tradition we're talking about. Added to that, you also have the expectations of a large record company, which needs you to keep releasing product from time to time. How do you decide what to record and when to record?

Wynton: Generally, I come out with albums because I want to make them. I don't wait until the company says "Put out a record." I'm thinking about doing records all the time, and it's just a matter of when will I go in and do it. I'm always thinking about trying to do one.

Ben: But do you feel pressured to make "great" records, or do you feel that whenever it's time to document your recent progress, then that's the time to make a new record?

Wynton: I don't feel that I can make really great records because I'm not great. I look at my records as being a charting of my development from this stage. It shows where I am at this time. That's what it means to me. And I'm developing, and I'm working on music and each record will get better. Because I will get better. Because I'm practicing and studying and trying to advance in the idiom. And I will not allow myself to lose sight of what the issue is. And the issue is the music.

Ben: Both Louis Armstrong's Hot Five recordings and John Coltrane's records were group records. It wasn't just Louis Armstrong with a bunch of guys or John Coltrane in a studio with whoever happened to be there. Perhaps the only way that your music can grow is through the development of your own group.

Wynton: Definitely. Because the music is group improvisation. I mean, Bach could improvise. Beethoven could improvise. But he couldn't improvise with everybody else improvising at the same time. That's another conception. You need group improvisation. You need musicians who are better than you, who have a vision. If you can't get musicians like that, you're in trouble.

Ben: Talk a little more about the technical aspects of group improvisation.

Wynton: Well first thing is that everyone has to understand their role. The drums have a function, the bass has a function, piano has a function, the soloist has a function, whether it's a saxophone or a trumpet. Let's look at a band like a car. The drums are like the motor, the bass is the wheels, the piano is the body. And the horn players, or whoever's soloing, are in the driver's seat, guiding it wherever it's going to go.

Now the piano can put any type of body on top of it he wants. The piano can change the whole vibe of the band. He might be comping, playing in the upper register. That's a different sound. He might be playing real thick chords, that's another sound. Or he might not play at all, that's another sound. The drums push the band. The drums don't keep time. The bass keeps the time. The drums add things here and there, put kicks in. Like what Elvin does. But everything sits on the bass. If the bass is not happening, the band can't be happening. Anything else in the band can be sad, but if the bass is sad, you're in trouble. Because the bass is the anchor. You listen to McCoy and Jimmy Garrison. What [Jimmy's] putting down swings so hard and is so soulful that it inspired everybody else to play. And what Elvin is doing is embellishing everything that's going on around him. And the motor and the wheels are all well-oiled and tuned up together.

To me, in any rhythm section music, be it jazz or what they call rock and roll or rhythm and blues, any music that's rhythm-section oriented, the key to where the band is is in the bass and the drums. There've been many harmonies and melodies that are pretty, but the key is the bottom of the band. I listen to popular music, all I hear is the bottom. That's the first thing I'm interested in. And it's important when you have a band that the bottom is happening. Like Tony [Williams] and Ron [Carter]. Ron is the anchor of the band. Most of the action that goes on, Ron starts that. Any great rhythm you think of, the bass is what's happening.

Ben: Your album called *Black Codes* seemed to be something of a breakthrough for you. It was as if your conception and your band had finally come together. Was that the case?

Wynton: Yeah, we were playing together for almost three years by the time we did that record. On my other records I was trying to get a lot of different conceptions. But I have to ground myself now, play more blues and really learn how to play. Because a lot of times, conceptually, if you try things, people don't understand. Like when we did *Think Of One*, we used serious band stop-time and I mean that's a conception. It was alright to use it, but it didn't really help me to learn how to play a certain way.

So now we're just mainly swinging. Playing straight forms. But we put different things in. Like "Black Codes" is just an extended blues. Or we use different grooves, like Cuban-type grooves or New Orleans Pocky-Way, which is a Meter's tune, "Hey Pocky Way." So we're still trying different things, but most of the tunes are just straight-out swing.

Ben: Is this a kind of dilemma for you? You seem to be drawn toward conceptual experimentation, but the solution that you're searching for may not be a conceptual solution.

Wynton: Getting better at expressing yourself, in human terms, just comes with personal development. But the problem I have is that somewhere along the line, somebody has told us that intellect is the opposite of emotion. You know, the easiest thing for me to do is to sit down and not say anything about music except, "I feel it." I mean my little brother can come in here and do that and he knows very little about music. But I won't succumb to that urge to do that because I understand that when people like Coltrane went in the studio, he had something very specific in mind. He didn't just go in with "I have a feeling about some music and now I'm going to document it."

Like Duke Ellington, a ridiculous number of years of great work, that's conception. Those works are based on a conception that works. The solution to gettting better is not to sit down in your house and think of how to express things in human terms. That's not what it's about. But if you don't have the conception . . .

Ben: But it seems harder these days to have a common conception among musicians, which was not uncommon in years past. Coltrane or Ellington didn't have this problem.

Wynton: Right, we don't have that [a common conception]. See, now I have to convince musicians that they should play jazz.

Ben: What do you mean?

Wynton: I mean, I have to convince them to play the music. Because if they weren't playing with me, they probably wouldn't be playing jazz.

Ben: Really?

Wynton: I mean, how're they going to make a living playing jazz? You know what I'm saying. There's no jobs for them to play. Who are they going to play with? So I have to convince the musicians that I see that they should play jazz. 'Trane didn't have to convince Elvin to play. Elvin wanted to play. Miles didn't have to convince Wayne to play no jazz. He was interested in developing in this idiom. He didn't feel like he was doing anybody a favor by playing. Now, the musicians . . . I mean, it's weird, man.

Ben: Something dramatic must be happening, then, if the schools are turning out thousands of musicians every year and young people, thirteen, fourteen years old, are running around with portable recording studios trying to cut demos to get a record deal, and yet with all this interest in the music, you have to convince players to play.

Wynton: What I'm trying to get you to see is that in our music, very few people really have craft knowledge. Very few people can sit down with any Miles Davis album from the '60s and tell you what's on that record. Very few people can do that. They don't have people in colleges . . . they have people who like the music, who listen to it. But, you know, we all can listen to music. What makes you a musician is you know the music. That's why you say "I am a musician." That indicates knowledge of craft. Not that you can feel some music. Because all people can feel that.

That's like if I feel pain and I'm soulful. Like one time I read a review that said, "Marsalis has lost many girlfriends." [Laughs.] Man, I laughed so hard when I read that. I said, "Well, people all over the world are losing girlfriends every day and every night." What does that have to do with anything? That's like a real serious misconception. "Are these guys in pain, are they suffering?" I mean, if you can read, you're going to suffer.

See, the thing is awareness. You know what I mean? Awareness is the key. And what does your girlfriend leaving you have to do with awareness? Maybe your girlfriend left you and you weren't aware that that was a tragic situation. Maybe you were glad.

Ben: Back to the dilemma. The dilemma is how to further the music and how to find your voice, right?

Wynton: Yes. But to me, when I listen to myself, I know I sound like me. It's just that I'm not on the level of what's gone on before me. I know that, too. But that's just a matter of practicing and working, like they had to do. You listen to recordings of Clifford Brown, I mean Clifford Brown plays ten times more trumpet than me or anybody I've heard. But when Clifford Brown came into the music, he was playing a type of music. He wasn't responsible for providing an environment of music. I'm sorry. He just didn't have to do that. And in no way am I trying to take a slam at him, because I've gotten hours of joy and awe from hearing Clifford play. But when Clifford played, he could play "Walking" and "Donna Lee" and, you know, the tunes that he played. That was a way for him to play. And when Miles came up, he could play with Bird, play "All The Things You Are" and "Lazy Bird" and all of these tunes. He didn't come up into the music providing a direction, unless you want to consider "Birth Of The Cool," which is not really a direction for the music, really. It's just something that's been gorillaed into the history of the music. To this day I don't really understand how that happened, and I don't think the people on that even understand how that happened.

Ben: Perhaps it happened because the people who are in charge of history are the people who get it written down first.

Wynton: Yeah, but Miles himself didn't start providing a direction until 1954 or '55. His own direction. He played *inside* of the body of the music, to learn the craft of the music. You see what I'm saying? You have to learn the craft. I mean, if all these great musicians didn't do that, how am I going to come out, and I have to provide an environment *and* learn how to play too, at the same time? Come on, man, I can't do that. I mean, it takes a long time.

And now, I don't have any qualms about being cut down, because really, I shouldn't have received as much publicity as I received. It's just a thing that happened. I'm sure that Miles and Clifford didn't get as much publicity as I got. So I got that much publicity, and with that publicity comes getting cut down, because I shouldn't have gotten all that publicity. I have to accept that. But a lot of times, what's disturbed me is that the hype has overshadowed whatever music is coming out. It's like, "Yeah, you know, they're not doing this or that." But nobody knows what we're doing. Because nobody will think about the music or learn what's on it. They didn't learn what was on Miles's albums. They didn't learn what was on 'Trane's albums. You see what I'm saying. They can't sit down and discuss music that's been out here for twenty-five years.

Another misconception is that they'll say, "Wynton is playing a style that's twenty years old." Well the avant garde people are playing a twenty-five year old style, too. And if you include the European style that they're imitating, that's seventy years old. You know, Sun Ra was doing that in the '50s. So that style is not new. It's not a new style that we've never heard.

Ben: How will you know when you arrive at the place where you want to be?

Wynton: Man, I'll never arrive at that. That's unattainable. The only thing I can try to do is just continue to develop and tell the truth as I see it. And if the truth is that I'm not playing, then I'm not playing. It's a developmental thing. I'm not racing against other people. All I'm trying to do is just develop my potential. And stay true to my vision of this country. And the direction I think music should go. That's what I can do as an artist.

But I can't allow that to impair my vision of reality. Like let's say that at one point I discover that I can't play something. That doesn't mean that I have to say, "Well, I can't play this so it ain't shit; because I can't play it, it ain't nothing." See, what we get now is everybody's opinion. I don't want to have an opinion.

That's something that I hate. What we try to do now is reduce everything, no matter how factual it is, unless it has a serious physical implication, we want to reduce that to an opinion. So that's like people will tell you, "Well, in 1940 the people who were SS officers had a different opinion than the people who were Jewish." So then there's no right or wrong. Everything just gets reduced to what your point of view is. And I'm not saying that everything has to be delineated necessarily into right and wrong. But some things are just in the best interest of humanity and some things are not. And those principles, integrity and stuff like that, cannot be compromised based on what you or I feel is correct.

This is something that I feel is extremely serious and important. And that's what I try to pursue, that conception, in music, and in the way I conduct my life in general.

I mean, you're not trying to give a version of something when you're playing music. You're not saying "This is what I think about something." That's not what you're doing. You're saying "This *is* this." And the way you can identify something is through study and understanding. If you don't understand you can't identify. It's like Louis Armstrong, he understood. And you can hear it when you hear him play. You can say, "Louis Armstrong, he sure did understand a lot of stuff about life."

Ben: Survival then becomes important to the artist, staying around long enough to gain that understanding.

Wynton: Not just survival. Art means something higher than survival. Because survival just means existence. Art means that you structure and order. You're trying to understand and give structure to it.

Ben: Struggle, then?

Wynton: Yeah, struggle to understand what's happening. And what's really important, what really will give substance to human existence.

* * *

Charles Brown (November, 1986)

At one point during the late '40s, Charles Brown was one of the most famous jazz singers in the United States, epitomizing the Los Angeles nightclub artist, cool and nostalgic, defining the jazzman's equivalent of "film noir" style. As piano player/vocalist with Johnny Moore and the Three Blazers, Charles influenced a generation of singers that followed, including, quite obviously, Ray Charles, and through them, the entire world of popular music and rock and roll. But when the Three Blazers broke up, he seemed to disappear from the music scene. Thirty years later, I met him in San Francisco just as he was beginning to come out of retirement, at least locally. We had talked about getting together for a year or so when I heard the news that he was reviving his career. We finally spent a few hours talking about his remarkable history and the whims of the music industry. That afternoon, he played a lot of piano and sang many songs and his style was absolutely intact. Although decades had passed, he still sounded like the young jilted lover when he sang those songs of unrequited love, and his keyboard facility was as strong and as idiosyncratic as ever. Several years after our conversation, Charles was invited by Bonnie Raitt to be the opening act on her international tour, and the world once again heard that unmistakable voice and understood that loneliness was the mother's milk of this music.

Ben: We've been talking about doing this for about a year now. We finally managed to arrange it. But I've been lookin' forward to talking to you for many a year, because your style has always seemed to me to be very influential, and very much at a crucial point in the history of jazz music . . .

Charles: Thank you . . .

Ben: Let's go back. You're from Texas originally.

Charles: Yes, Texas City, Texas, a very small town, a seaport town outside of Galveston.

Ben: And your piano style, if I remember correctly, initially came from an interest in watching the old player pianos, seeing the keys move and being fascinated by the piano rolls of players like Art Tatum and Fats Waller . . .

Charles: Fats Waller. And then some others that I didn't even know about, I really treasured those. But when I heard Art Tatum play in the early days, on the radio, we just had a very small radio at home, and he would come on at a certain time of the day, and I'd say: "Oh, that guy playing that piano." I said, "I wanta play like that, Mama." So she made our choices, my Grandmother who reared me, and she used to like Fats Waller. So whenever Fats Waller would bring out a tune like *Cross Patch* or *Honeysuckle Rose*, she would go buy the sheet music and say, "Well I want you to play *that*." And so when I told her, I said, "Well, Mama, you come and listen to *this* man play the piano." When Art Tatum would come on, I'd said, "That guy's really the greatest, that's the way I wanta learn to play the piano." She said, "Well I don't like him as well as I do Fats Waller 'cause Fats Waller has great bass hands," she says. So I say, "Well, you know, I don't know anything about those type of hands." I said, "But, whatever it is, I like Art Tatum."

Ben: What about the vocal style? Were you caught up by Fat's singing at all?

Charles: No. You know, my family had that style of singing. Years ago my Aunt Dee, 'course she's dead now, she used to sing in the church, and we all took that slurring type of thing. And I used to hear Helen O'Connell with Jimmy Dorsey sing that style, and it came into my style, because I said the way she sings is the way I like to sing, the way my family sings. With that little . . . (sings: "Take me, I'm yours") . . . you know, and, well it came out in me differently, but that's the style that I took over.

Ben: And did you begin your career playing little gigs in High School?

Charles: Yes, when I went to Galveston, Texas, they found that I could play the piano, and the man who was the head of the science department, Mr. James, was a tenor saxophone player himself, and he was doing a lot of gigs, beside teaching school, in Galveston on The Beach, which was West Beach. And for a lot of the white clubs. And at the time I could read well, and they heard that I played well, and so they said, "Well, Charles, come on, be with us, you can make some extra money." And at that time, eighteen dollars a week was a lot of money.

Ben: Yes indeed. And so these jobs were casual jobs, playing the hits of the day?

Charles: Yes, we were playing things, something like *Beer Barrel Polka*, and a lot of the things like, ah . . . Oh, *When the Blue of the Night Meets the Gold of the Day*, or something like that, the songs like Bing Crosby used to sing during that period. And they were all standards at that time. We weren't doing any of our type of tunes but on the side I was learning to play boogie-woogie.

Ben: I mentioned earlier that your style seems to me to be an important example of a time where jazz and blues really were just one thing, not two separate things as they have become today. Is that right?

Charles: That's right. What I think it was, because at the time they named it jazz, but they were doing blues and jazz right together. And Bessie Smith was doing it, we heard a lot of her records during that period. So whatever they named it, we just thought it was the blues. And we heard Mamie Smith, and I listened to a lot of those things, and then when Joe Turner came out with Art Tatum doing this song about "It was early one morning . . ."

Ben: "and I was on my way to school . . ."

Charles: ". . . on my way to school." I really liked that. And I think that was the first blues that Art Tatum said he had ever played on the piano. I was fascinated by the way he played it. So I always wanted to upgrade my type of blues. I said, "If I ever get a chance to record, I wanna do it just a little different." But when we made "Driftin' Blues," we kinda changed the style of blues, because blues, in the early days, were kinda of risque, it was preachin' blues, and we thought it could tell a story. "I'm driftin' like a ship out on the sea, and I don't have anybody to care for me," you know, and that's the way we took that "lonely feeling" step.

Ben: Well, we're getting a little bit ahead of ourselves in your story, because "Driftin' Blues" was recorded after you'd gone to Los Angeles . . .

Charles: Well, I tell you what happened. When I first came to California, I came to Berkeley, as a junior chemist. I had been a junior chemist, I had been a school teacher before . . .

Ben: You had also earned a college degree in Chemistry . . .

Charles: Yes, I did. I went to Pine Bluff, Arkansas, as the first black junior chemist. I passed the civil service examination, but in the meantime, I found some problems that I didn't like, and I thought maybe I had better find me something else, so I volunteered to go into Uncle Sam's service, and I was classed 4-F because of asthma. And I decided that I wouldn't take anything essential to the war. I'd go into music, because I could play.

Then I went to L.A. I was working at the shipyards in Long Beach, well, Terminal Island. And my cousin was working as an electrical engineer, and, on Wednesday nights and Thursday nights, I would go into Los Angeles. We were living in Watts then. And I said, "I'm gonna go to this theater, and see what they're doing there." They had amateur shows down there. And I would go there and I'd see these guys winning twenty-five dollars, and the girls. I said, "Maybe I could win twenty-five dollars." I said, "That would be a lot of money for me." But, I didn't try it until I got a job working as an elevator operator, at the Broadway department store. Then I decided, I said "Well, listen, I'm gonna go over here one night and try this." And I went over there, and I had my things together. I had practiced well. And at that time, there was a boogie-woogie on the "St. Louis Blues" that Earl Hines was playing, and everybody liked that. So I said, "I'm gonna learn to play that." And I did and when I went on the amateur show, I played that, and I got such a great big hand for that. And I told them I was from Texas. There were a lot of Texas people and Louisiana people out in California during that time.

Ben: I know that that talent show lead to your forming the Three Blazers with Johnny Moore.

Charles: Yeah, well I won the amateur contest, and Johnny Moore happened to be sitting in the audience. When he saw me, they had told him, "That would be the guy for you." And he came lookin' for me but that was a time later, after I had moved to Sugar Hill. That was the Sugar Hill where all the black movie stars were living, like Ethel Waters, Hattie McDaniels, and Ben Carter. And he came out looking for me. So he didn't know what house I lived in. So the lady next door, she was a white lady, she told him, "Well, I heard a piano next door. He must be there." So he went and knocked on that door, and the landlord came down and Johnny Moore talked to him and said that he wanted see if Charles Brown was living there, and he told him, yes, he was living there. And he said, well, he wanted to talk to him about a job, with a trio. And so the landlord came upstairs and he got me and brought me downstairs, and he said, "Charles, this is Johnny Moore, and he has a job for you."

Well I had been working at the Lincoln Theater when I won the amateur contest. They gave me one week there with Johnny Otis playing the drums. That's how I met Johnny Otis during that time. And, well, when Johnny Moore came, I quit that job because I didn't like the money they was paying. I had to play with the chorus girls, rehearsal, for the shows in the Lincoln Theater, and I didn't think what they were giving me was enough. And I said, "I've saved up a little money and I'm going find me something better." So when Johnny Moore came along and he says, "Well, would you like to play with our trio?" I says, "Well, how much will it pay?" He says, "Well, if we get this audition and we play out at the Talk of The Town, in Beverly Hills . . ." He said, ". . . there's going to be a lot of trios out there." Said, "We'll get about $600 dollars a week." Which was $200 dollars a piece, which was really more than we had been making, because I'd been in the $42-a-week bracket at that time. And I decided, well I said, "Let me think about it." And so the landlord, after Johnny Moore left, he says, "But Charles, listen." He said, "That may be a good break for you."

Now I didn't sing at the time. I was just singing my little church songs and things, and Johnny Moore, during that little audition, when he was over there talking to me, he said, "Do you sing?" I said, "No, just a few numbers." He said, "Let me hear what you do." So I did "Embraceable You," "Take Me." He said, "Man, that's what we want." I said, "I can't sing." He said, "Oh, yeah." He said, "Yeah, that's what we want. They don't want any ladies in the club because it's not but a few men left because everybody's in the service. That's what we want." He said, "How about let's gettin' together and rehearse, the trio, and see can we pass the audition." And that we did, and we passed the audition. They had about twenty trios out at the The Talk of The Town, in Beverly Hills. And we went out there and Mr. Vandergriff, who owned The Talk of The Town, and he had heard all the other trios. And when he got to us, and we played a little round for him, he said, "I don't wanna hear no more trios." He said, "Johnny Moore, can you open up here next week?" Johnny said, "Yes, sir, Mr. Vandergriff, we can open." And that was the starting of the trio.

Ben: Well, that brings us almost up to the trio cutting the song that would make you famous, "Driftin' Blues," which was released on Aladdin Records out of Los Angeles. That song came out in 1945 and went on to sell over ten million copies. An enormous hit record, the equivalent of selling maybe fifty million today. You were living in Los Angeles. You told me at one point you walked into a club where "Driftin' Blues" was on the jukebox and . . .

Charles: Yes. We used to go to after-hours spots in Los Angeles. And they had one, Johnny Carnish had one, "house" after-hours spot. And they had a nice piano there. Art Tatum, everybody would be waiting until he came out from Hollywood to play the piano, because he'd feel it, and play it. But I was playing before he came in. We had just made that recording, "Driftin' Blues," and the people around Los Angeles had heard it. And they all said, "Charles, that was you singing that. Play 'Driftin' Blues.'" I was on the piano playing "Driftin' Blues," and Art Tatum came in. And evidently he had heard that number. And he put his hand on my shoulder, and he says, "What's your name?" I said, "Charles Brown." He said, "You're not the Charles Brown with Johnny Moore?" I said, "Yeah." He said, "Made 'Driftin' Blues'?" I said, "Yes." He said, "That's the greatest blues I've ever heard in my life."

Ben: What was so different about "Driftin' Blues" at the time? What made it sound so different?

Charles: Well, the earlier blues were preachin' blues, and some of them were risque blues. And this one told a better story, like "I'm driftin," rather than "Big Leg Mama, keep your dress on," you know, whatever. We changed it to a kind of a melancholy type of blues, with a feeling.

Ben: More urban, too, you know, more like Los Angeles. You got a little Hollywood. Just the sound of your voice. You know, a little bit later, people started talking about the "cool school" of west coast jazz, where everything was kinda held back and refined. And your style, and Nat Cole's style, kind of anticipated that.

Charles: Well, you know, at the time, they used to call this the "club blues," West Coast. Because at the time we were playing in night clubs, and we had to set an *atmosphere* for those guys who brought their girlfriends or wives in. We set the atmosphere, and you couldn't be too loud. You had to be mellow and play songs that set the mood for the drinking. Sweet numbers and the little ditties and whatnot. The laughable tunes, and that's what we were doing. So that's the style that I took.

Ben: One of the things you do to set an atmosphere is you set up a particular kind of introduction when you sit down at the piano, don't you?

Charles: Always. You know, right today, when I go to play a concert or some place in New York, and I have musicians, I always start off on the piano to set a nice introduction. To get the feeling. And I think that they kinda get the feeling, and that sets my mood, and we're ready to play.

Ben: You're using some passing chords that are not typical of the blues.

Charles: That's the club. [Laughs.]

Ben: That's the nightclub part. I see what you mean. Alright, so the year is 1945, and you're immediately recognized throughout the country as part of the Three Blazers, Johnny Moore and the Three Blazers. And off you go, selling millions of records and traveling around the country on large packages. Is it true that at one point you even hired Buddy Rich to play some dates with you?

Charles: Yes, Buddy Rich and I were very good friends on those dates. And we played what we called the "Chitlin' Circuit." That was the Apollo Theater, we played the Howard Theater in Washington D.C., we played the Royal Theater in Baltimore, and the Adams Theater in Newton, New Jersey at that time.

Ben: Buddy Rich was playing with his big band, and you were featured with him?

Charles: Right. We had the Johnny Moore show, and Buddy Rich's orchestra. See, that's the way it was listed at the Apollo Theater. There was top billing for the Three Blazers and Buddy Rich, 100 percent each. And we had the Will Mastin trio, Sammy Davis was working for us on that show. 'Cause we were all booked out of William Morris Agency at the time. And we had Jackie "Moms" Mabley. We had Tim Moore, who was with Amos and Andy. We had a wonderful show in those days.

Ben: Jazz was part of the variety package . . .

Charles: Variety, right . . .

Ben: So there you were, somebody who didn't sing having the number one record in the country as a singer.

Charles: Yeah, and the funny thing, Sammy Davis was on the show which was really interesting because Sammy would come out imitating me before we came on, and ask the audience, "Well, who is this?" And he would do this thing, "Are the stars out tonight . . ." You know, and they'd say, "That's Charles Brown, Charles Brown." So, that would be the cue for us to come out.

Ben: I'm curious, how does your success with that vocal style relate to Nat Cole's success and style around that time?

Charles: Well, it's a funny thing. Nat started just a little before we did. And he was very popular around Los Angeles, the 331 Club on 8th street. And everybody was going crazy for trios, at the time. Well I never . . . I heard Nat's record, but I never had a chance to see him perform, you know, in person. But he did use my piano, 'cause Oscar Moore was the brother of Johnny Moore, and they didn't have any place to practice. And I had bought this little piano when I came to Los Angeles for $500. It was just a small upright grand. And Nat and his trio would come over and rehearse on my piano. And we got to be good friends after that.

Ben: A couple of years after this, another remarkable record hit the air waves, that to this day, every year, around Christmas time, is a record that is played a lot. Tell me the story about "Merry Christmas Baby."

Charles: Well, "Merry Christmas Baby" was 1947, and everyone wants to know really who wrote that number. At the time, it was Johnny Moore's Three Blazers, but I was the one who was doing all the little arranging, and the singing. In fact, people thought Johnny Moore, that I was Johnny Moore, because they didn't advertise Charles Brown as being the singer with Johnny Moore. It was Johnny Moore's Three Blazers. And if you look on the record, you could see: "Vocals, Charles Brown." But a lot of people didn't pay that any mind. They said, "Well, if it's Johnny Moore's Three Blazers, Johnny Moore must be singing."

So when I had a chance to write tunes, Lou Baxter came to me, who used to follow us around, and he said, "Charles, I want you to help me, because I need an operation of the throat." He had something wrong with his throat, which we'd say cancer today. And he said, "I need about $500 ." He said, "But I'm sure that if you would do a number of mine, I could get an advance . . ." which they were giving $500 advances. And so he brought me his little satchel, with a lot of songs in it. I looked at them overnight, and I saw a "Merry Christmas Blues." But, the way he had the words, it wasn't effective at all. I said, "I'm gonna say 'Merry Christmas Baby.' And I wrote it according to the way I'd say my words. Because, I was . . . I used to have an impediment of the speech. I didn't say my words good at the time. So I always had to be careful of certain words to say. I chose "Merry Christmas Baby, you sure did treat me nice. You gave me a diamond ring for Christmas . . ." Well, when they gave it to Exclusive Records, Mr. Renee, and we went out on the road, they put Johnny Moore's name on there. And Lou Baxter, rather than Charles Brown. And now, when it made a hit that

Christmas of '47, in Chicago, Johnny Moore's name was already on it. But I was the writer of that. Johnny Moore couldn't even write a song. He just played guitar, that's all. But to this day, a lotta people said "Merry Christmas Baby," you know, it's been over a million seller too, they said Charles Brown, they associate me with "Merry Christmas Baby" ...

And you know who's done that number? They tell me that this album coming out with Bruce Springsteen's "Merry Christmas Baby." But he's trying to do it like Otis Redding did it.

Ben: But the original version of "Merry Christmas Baby "was done in 1947, vocals and piano and celeste, by Charles Brown, with Johnny Moore on guitar and Eddie Williams. Charles, one thing that stands out on that record is the simplicity of the arrangement. Everything is very tasty, very controlled, and very simple.

Charles: Thank you. That's the way that I had the feeling to write for myself. Simple things, but yet effective with your style of singing, you know.

Ben: Particularly because you were accompanying yourself, it forced you to make these little arrangements to kind of enclose your vocals ...

Charles: Yes, I thought so ...

Ben: It also related you more to the jazz school of writing than a lot of the other blues musicians. Its was something that later on Ray Charles paid a lot of attention to. That kind of simple arrangement, to make a jazz feeling to what might be a blues.

Charles: Yes, and fortunately I had the pleasure, when I was the number one rhythm and blues artist, to have Ray Charles on the bill, by himself, along with Floyd Dixon. These guys were both singing just like me. So when I did come out, the people say, "Well, is that Charles Brown?" Well my voice was a little heavier than theirs, just a little difference. Even though we were sounding alike, but I still had a little lowness, 'cause Ray Charles was just a little higher than I am.

Ben: What'd you think about that? I mean, you started earlier by saying you weren't even a singer. You didn't even think of yourself as a singer, and the next thing you know, you're influencing all these people.

Charles: That is the truth. I never even thought about it. But you know, I think that when the people, the majority gathers the feeling from your style, and it seems to be a hit among the majority, then it seems that everybody tends to want to do it that way, because if that's a hit with the people, they wanna do that same thing. And I think that even comes today, like Michael Jackson or whoever makes a big hit, they wanna do the things like he does.

Ben: That's the business part of it, isn't it? If you sit down and order yourself a hamburger, and have a hit record, everybody's gonna go to that same place and order that same hamburger. They figure, maybe it was the hamburger that did it. But talking about the simplicity of your arrangements, leads me to another song. It's called "It Ain't Gonna Be Like That." It was written by a young singer at the time who played some drums, pretty talented guy . . .

Charles: Yes, Mel Torme . . .

Ben: Mel Torme. And he wrote this song, and you did pretty well with it.

Charles: Very well. And you know who brought that song to me? Frankie Laine. Frankie Laine brought the song from Mel Torme to me. And I had to learn it, "It Ain't Gonna Be Like That," and we did it with Oscar Moore.

Ben: But again, you did your own arrangement of it, all the little pieces . . .

Charles: Yes, the little simplicity.

Ben: Charles, the piano solo on that was interesting. A little block chord feel.

Charles: Yes. You know at that time, I think Lionel Hampton, with that fellow that played the piano, what was his name? Oh, I can't think of his name that played the piano. He was doing a lot of little lock chords. It was just coming in to the makin' then, so I got the idea from that.

Ben: This song was recorded right about the time when you left the Three Blazers and went out on your own, as Charles Brown. And as somebody who had been associated with all these hits, it must have been a surprise to find out that Charles Brown wasn't as well known as the Three Blazers.

Charles: So true. The people told me, they said, "Well Charles, since you're not getting the money that you should, why don't you go out on your own? Because everybody thinks you're Johnny Moore anyway, and some of them look on the record and they see Charles Brown. So you could do it on your own, you don't need Johnny Moore." In fact, we had a little run-in about monies, and we were supposed to split the monies, and when it come to find out my share was never gotten, and I'd asked for my share, and I was insulted. And I decided that I would leave. And when I left, I went on my own and organized a group called Charles Brown and the Smarties. And I had to start all over again. I couldn't use the name "Three Blazers" anymore. And that was Charles Brown Trio and the Smarties. I don't know if you have any of those early records but that was the way we went out.

Ben: Charles Brown and the Smarties had some success . . .

Charles: Yeah, we had "Black Night." We had "Trouble Blues."

Ben: Did you stay living in Los Angeles at this time?

Charles: Yes, I was living in Los Angeles. In fact, I stayed in L.A. from 1943 on until my Grandfather passed in '62. Then I went on the road, and I went back to Ohio.

Ben: What changes did you find when you went out on the road as Charles Brown and the Smarties as opposed to the Three Blazers?

Charles: Well, you know, there weren't many changes because a lot of people had heard about, when we did *Get Yourself Another Fool,* that I had left Johnny Moore's Three Blazers and they were all on the alert. And, in fact, we had our first engagement down in Houston, Texas, with Julius White, who was a promoter, and Howard Lewis out of Dallas, Texas, and you couldn't get into those auditoriums at the time. And they were really frequented by a lot of blacks. And we had white spectators, and it was very nice because, at that time, it wasn't any mixing. And we really went over real well. And people began to say "Charles Brown, Charles Brown," and then I went on the road and won the best rhythm and blues artist of that year, 1951.

Ben: When you were in Los Angeles at that time, was there a lot of interaction between the blues artists and the jazz artists? Were some horn players, for example, interested in playing with you?

Charles: Yes. When I was with Johnny Moore, we did a thing at the Elks, and Charlie Parker was in town at the time. I think he had come out of New York for some reason, I don't know. But he had asked Johnny Moore could he play the next engagement with us, which was the Christmas holidays. We had about two nights at the Elks club on Central Avenue. And Johnny Moore told him yes, because he'd been with Jay McShann's band, and we heard about how great he was with "Hootie Blues" and all that. And so Johnny Moore told him yes. So that's the time we played with Charlie Parker.

Ben: This trio played with Charlie Parker?

Charles: Yeah. I mean, he was on the bill. He had the band. We took the intermissions. We had to play at intermission, because it was our show. But the band played for the dancing, and at intermissions we came on and entertained the people. Lot of them didn't dance, lot of them just stand up and look at you. It was really interesting during those days. Just a house full of people. Then when we got off, we had people wanting autographs, and you had to run through all these people, you know, to get back to dressing room.

But jazz was great, because at that time, out there, the fella that did this *'Round Midnight* was playing on Central Avenue . . .

Ben: Dexter Gordon . . .

Charles: Dexter Gordon, we used to go in and watch him play. They had a club there called the Downbeat Club. But in L.A., at that time, jazz was mostly out on Hollywood Boulevard, because they had lot of people at the Suzie Q playing jazz, and they had the New Orleans Jazz Band playing out on Hollywood Boulevard. But we were down in the club sections doing our blues and ballads.

Ben: Well, 'round about 1954 Charles Brown and the Smarties were heard down there doing a song that sounds to me like the jazz people had contributed, and so had you, to some sort of mutual idiom. This is the song "Honeysipper."

Charles: Yeah, "Honeysipper."

Ben: Charles, even that song, which is kind of a novelty song, a cute song, has a tremendous mood to it.

Charles: Thank you. Well, you know, at the time we always tried to capture that feeling of "not too fast," where the fellow and his girlfriend could hold each other, and just barely do the little rocking dances at that time.

Ben: Yeah, the little rockin' dances. Well Ray Charles went on to become a *huge* star around this time. Nat "King" Cole went on to become an *enormous* success around this time. What happened to Charles Brown?

Charles: Well, it's a funny thing that, when I came along, in fact, Atlantic Records wanted me to sign up with them. But now the people that I was with, Aladdin Records, Eddie Mesner and Leo Mesner, didn't want me to leave them. And they didn't want to give me a count of my royalties, and we had a little run-in about it. In fact, I had to go out there and get a copy of my contract from the secretary, which he tried to put me into the jail, because he said that I stole my contract. You don't steal it when they hand it to you. So the lawyer told me to go ask for it. And when I get my contract, to walk out the door with it, 'cause it's part of your contract as much as it is theirs. And we had a court settlement on it. And quite naturally, it caused me to be a no-no for Mr. Mesner. And so they put my records on the shelf. They said, "We not going to play any more Charles Brown records, and we'll get some guys to imitate you." They put into the company people like Floyd Dixon, anybody who was doing my style. And they wouldn't turn me loose.

So when you don't hear about an artist in a year or so, and new records are coming, you're dead. So that's really what happened to me. And then I had to go on my own to try to work in the clubs by myself, to try to just make my money. And quite natural, that threw me way back. And while the other people were taking your style and going right on and making records, I was on the shelf, and they said, "What happened to Charles Brown?" But I was still working, but I was called the "Chitlin' Switch Circuit" and just by myself, trying to hold on.

And then, another case happened to me, with the agency, Billy Shaw agency. When I was working, under Billy Shaw, when my grandfather took sick, I wanted to go home and take care of him, because he was my father, the only one I knew, and he reared me. And they said, "Well, you can't leave, because we have dates booked for you." And when I did, they sued me, and when they sued me, I had to go on the blacklist with the musicians union. And so, when I went on the blacklist, I was blackballed.

So that's funny but it's true. When you're not in the limelight for awhile, people said, "What happened to you?"

Well, in the meantime, I had to do bootlegging. I was kicked out of the union. I couldn't get back in the union, because you had to have a certain amount of money, and you had to do the best you can to try to make money. And that's why you didn't hear me. And so, all the years that I spent trying to hold on, finally, all these people died that had these claims against me. Then the National [Union] told me that I could get back into the union, because I didn't have any claims against me anymore, because they were all dead. Then I got back into the union again, and then started working on my own. Well see, that's 1956 until 1962. I got back into the union in '62. Then, I worked until 1965. Then I was out of the union again, because I had somebody else sue me. Because they claimed they had another case against me. Then I'm blackballed again. I had to go all that time and work as a scab musician, until 1970. And then I got back into the union again, and then I went down to Atlanta, Georgia, 1975, and I signed up with an agency called the . . . I can't think of the last name, but anyway, they sued me because I went to Cleveland on my own, and they claimed that they were supposed to book me. And I had the money myself. I booked myself, because they didn't have anything for me. They sued me, and when they sued me, the union put me out again. Then I had to be a scab musician again. So 1975, '76, '77, '78, '79, '80. In '79 I went to Sweden, which I didn't have to be in the union. Then in 1980 I went to New York. '81, New York, '82, New York, '83, New York, '84, I got back in the union, and I'm now in the union, and starting on a new bag. [Laughs.]

So that's why you didn't hear Charles Brown. But I was still playing my little . . . Well people really wanted me, I played those places, and I was able to make a few dollars.

Ben: Well, in 1987 Charles Brown recorded a new record, in New York City, featuring a well known jazz drummer, Kenny Washington, who recorded with Johnny Griffin, for example.

Charles: We had Billy Butler playing the guitar, and everyone knows him as playing "Honky-Tonk," that great thing with Bill Doggett. And we had Earl May, a great jazz bass player out of New York, and we had Harold Ousley on the tenor. And yours truly, Charles Brown, playing the piano. And all my simple arrangements.

Ben: Simple arrangements and live vocals . . .

Charles: Well, and everyone who heard it, they claim that it's unusual to see a fellow who hasn't been recorded in a long time to make a comeback and sound almost the same like he did before. So it made me feel very good on the first record. And we did another tune on there, which I wanta tell you about, "Save Your Love For Me," that Nancy Wilson did. We just did a variety of things to get started back.

Ben: And the music doesn't sound old-fashioned to my ears at all . . .

Charles: Thank you . . .

Ben: I think possibly it still sounds fresh because what we're hearing is a style of blues playing with a little swing, which has been at the heart of jazz for a long time, certainly since Kansas City, and so it has a timeless quality to it.

Charles: Yes, because we weren't really considered blues artists. We were considered jazz, jazz ballad singers, what we called the club singer, singing ballads. We were a borderline case. You know, we weren't real jazz, and we weren't real blues, we're just in between. So we were "Mr. In-Betweens" which was really wonderful. Because we played a lot of the songs like that, with a little jazz touch to them, you know.

Ben: Looking back at your career, which has had its enormous ups and downs over the last forty years, is there something you'd do differently, if you had to do it over again?

Charles: Well, I think it would be, that I would be more alert about, have more knowledge about my recordings and the things that I had the chance to write. And go in the right direction, you know, to copyright the number, and put it into the copyright office, and get the right contracts, and then have the people sign it, and keep the contracts and know what you gonna get. Because at the time we wrote a lot of numbers and people said, "Just write the numbers," and we didn't know nothing about the value in the later years. And we were out of a lot of songs. And I think that's what's happening today, that they're trying to go back and recap a lot of things that happened in the '50s to the artist who wrote tunes that didn't get credit for them.

Ben: You've outlived a lot of the people who stood in the way, didn't you?

Charles: Yes, isn't that the truth? You know, they were stepping stones, even though they were stumbling blocks in one way, but they became stepping stones because I'm still here and they're gone. And you know, I said that one night in the club and people just fell out and laughed. I said, "You know, they beat me out of a lot of my songs." And I said, "But those people that made all that money, they're gone. I'm still here and everybody just died right up in . . ."

Ben: They took your money but you got your life.

Charles: Yeah, I got my life, I'm still here.

* * *

Dr. John a.k.a. Mac Rebennack (November, 1984)

Perhaps because he is such a colorful figure and so thoroughly identified with his "Dr. John the Night-Tripper" persona, Mac Rebennack is rarely recognized as one of the great wellsprings of contemporary piano playing. His style incorporates elements from virtually every American jazz and blues tradition, from the stride and boogie-woogie players of the '20s and '30s, the beboppers of the '40s and, quite obviously, the rhythm and blues players of the '50s. Further, he has lived through a dramatic period of popular music in New Orleans, where sophisticated urban jazz players joined more primitive rural or street singers to cut some of the biggest commercial records of the twentieth century. This cross-pollination of jazz and blues, which is at the heart of the New Orleans piano experience, and the importance of the human side of dance rhythms, are subjects that Mac Rebennack has turned into a science—a science that may only have its true exposition in his piano playing, but one which he is more than happy to discuss, particularly in the context of his many favorite musicians.

Ben: One of the things that I'd like to talk about with you is the importance of the piano in New Orleans music, particularly as a reservoir of rhythmic innovation.

Mac: Well, like one of the things of the New Orleans piano is the multiple rhythm thing. There are three basic rhythms that would go on within a New Orleans song, like say, á la Professor Longhair. And I think what was unique within the New Orleans thing was that people dance all three ways, slow, fast, or half-fast, as the joke went. But seriously speaking, it made the musicians play within those three realms, alternately, to accompany the dances which formed at some point. What we have today, which is mostly in the recording of today, you hear the cut-time rhythm, or that half-fast thing, implied with the drums. But, originally, all three of those things would be there, maybe one part on the high-hat, one part on the snare, and another part on the bass drum, all played at the same time by the drummer, then, variously, accentuated by the pianist to cushion the drummer.

One of the things, and I don't know that this has been mentioned before, but one of the things that Professor Longhair did, and Little Brother Montgomery's thing of playing in the left hand figures that, I believe, always went with the drums playing the ruffs [the little rolls a drummer does]. So it's cushioning the drummer's part making a bigger range for the drummer to make his ruffs within. And, the ruffs being such a natural thing, it's like part of all parade music.

Ben: Actually, this is a real important point in terms of the evolution of New Orleans piano. A lot of the music that's thought of as piano music today initially was parade music, marching band music translated to the keyboard. And we can hear that "second line" beat in the rhythm sections today. How would you describe the "second line" feeling?

Mac: Well, it's like two beats accented later in the groove, as a big accent, over a long period of a song. You keep, like . . . 1-2, 1-2-3-**4**, 1-2-3-**4**, and at some point . . . 1-2, 1-2-3-4-1-**2**, and that thing is like a cap, or a exclamation point. It's like running into the next chorus to pick the lead instrument up, or the vocalist, or whatever, to create a little more life or jolliness.

Ben: A little jolliness. I like that because it sounds to me like almost a musical transcription of the dances you see in the streets of New Orleans, you know, picking up your knees high and struttin' down the street. It's got an equivalency there.

Mac: I think not only the parade thing, but the Indian thing, and all the various parts that lock in to make this gumbo of sound work, is partly due to the piano and the drums acting as a rhythm ensemble, but also to leaving a space for the bass and the other instruments to *set up* rhythms, rather than to just accompany basically rhythms. It's almost more important to make pick-ups *to* things, to the chord changes, pick-ups *to* the rhythmic fills. That is an integral part of the music, as much as the basic changes are, so a lot of songs have, over the years, become modified to the rhythmic pulses more than they have to the original chord structures or the way the chords lay in the structure. A lot of songs maybe don't land on a "one," but just start everybody hittin' on a "two." It's not felt as a back beat, it's just felt as a funky rhythm.

Today, when you say the word "funky," it's one of the most misunderstood words we have. As everybody has a different idea of what "funk" means. Originally funk, you know, meant stinky . . . that thing. But within our realm of musician, "funk" meant something of playing and leaving a *lot of open space* to get nasty. And what made this thing nasty or dirty or whatever way people wanna connotate this in their mind, is *leaving space* for musicians to play more. And this is something that has come into all forms of jazz. I think maybe Horace Silver might be as funky a guy as you can find, and he's not from New Orleans. And I'd say maybe a record like Lee Morgan's "Sidewinder" might be one of the funkiest records ever made. But it's the idea of the spacing being all inclusive to the actual piece. And not only in the solos, but the whole structure of a song being based around that openness . . .

Ben: Yeah, it's in the concept, it's in the whole rhythmic concept, which gets us to a really interesting point, which is that even when you have a piece by a solo pianist, what you're hearing is an approach that's been developed over years and years of accompanying other musicians and of playing in front of people. So that the act of being a solo pianist is very much a reflection of all the years that you've experienced as a group player. And you develop a style of setting up rhythms in a particular way because, in your head, you're hearing all these other things. You're hearing the drums, you know, whether there's a drummer with you or not.

Mac: And it's also the thing where you know that *dancers* are going to feel this in a certain way. People just enjoying the rhythm, they could be sitting down, they don't have to be dancing physically, they could be dancing in their seats. But it's things like, you know: Um-pa-ta-ta-ta-ta—uh . . . yeah! That makes a certain thing happen. And people'll know to say "Yeah!" after that series of quarter note triplets. That thing has been used within every structure of music, in various ways, just basically setting up a chord progression rhythmically in such a way that nobody's gonna miss that moment. And as jazz progressed to a point where things were not so necessary to be set up, or to be so "obvious," and people knew where the "yeah" went even if you didn't play it, then you came to the point where soloists could play the setup without actually playing the part. It's like a "within" thing; it's felt.

Ben: Perhaps an analogy in the world of art might be "to paint the gesture and not the hand." In a way, what we're talking about is sort of "to play the gesture and not the hand," to play around the fixed rhythmic sign posts, and given various constraints, it either sounds free, or it sounds confusing to some people, or it sounds eccentric.

Let's talk about some of your New Orleans peers. Recently we were listening to the song called "Sweet Home New Orleans," from your album *The Brightest Smile In Town*, and while we were listening you turned to me and said: "You know what that really is, that's a series of Huey Piano Smith turn-arounds."

Mac: That's all it is, just a compilation of a thing I used to hear Huey Smith do very frequently at record dates. It's a I to V turn-around. I turned it into a basic blues kind of a thing, but it's just fooling around with a very predominant thing that if anybody hears Huey Smith, they would hear him do this, consistently in certain types of tunes.

Ben: What about all those upper harmonies that you play? Would Huey Smith play them?

Mac: Actually, Huey Smith was very aware. The first time I ever heard this, um twelve-tone and quarter-tone thing is in a hit record by Smiley Wilson, "I Hear Ya' Knockin'." And Huey played like an altered chord leading into the song.

Ben: I stand corrected.

Mac: And Huey was always fooling with things. He had to be subtle, but he heard these things, and this was sometime back in the '50s and on rock 'n' roll records. I don't think that a lot of people would be familiar that Huey Smith, or somebody like that, would fool around with things like that, but these were in rock 'n' roll records of that era, and a lot of things he did were very modern. Whenever he was given a chance he would sneak things in. Of course most people who heard that would just think it was discordant. And maybe like it just for that, not knowin' it was comin' from a whole-tone row or whatever.

Ben: You know, that's a good point too, because sometimes there's a very fine line between a conscious working with the upper harmonies of a chord, discordancy, and somebody just playing a cluster because it feels good to just put your hand down that way on the piano. This tradition of the "accidental" discovery of advanced techniques is a big part of avant-garde music today, such as the music of Ornette Coleman, and it's interesting to note that many avant garde musicians originally played in r&b bands. That connection has always interested me.

Mac: Yeah, well, Ornette and I used to work with Joe Valentine's band in Baton Rouge. You know, at the time Ornette was with them, he was not appreciated for what he was doing, but on the other hand, he may have turned that band on to something that may have benefited them later on in life without them knowing at the time.

Ben: Well, a lot of what musicians pick up, I think, a lot of the best of it sometimes, they pick up through the floorboards as opposed to through the books. Or as Ron McClure, the bass players, once said to me, "Often, what you stumble on is a lot better than what you're looking for."

Mac: Yeah. I remember Edward Blackwell was a drummer in New Orleans that wasn't hired much because he wouldn't back-beat. But yet, in spite of this, he was used on a lot of sessions because he was such a creative drummer, and had a real gift for putting together home-made rhythms, playing them on home-made drums, and making some unique things happen. And like in the right settings, it was much more valuable to have that than a back-beatin' drummer. But, yet and still, it was a prejudice against Edward because of the not, you know, not hearin' that 2 and 4. And it took a long time for the man to be appreciated, you know...

Ben: And, of course, he did go on to become a key player in Ornette Coleman's band and on the whole cutting-edge scene of jazz. You know one thing that makes New Orleans so special in terms of the music community is that you have players there who draw on all these traditions and carry on the education of kids coming up. Lately, of course, because of the success of his sons Wynton and Branford, we hear a lot about pianist Ellis Marsalis. He taught for years at the New Orleans Center for Creative Arts, which really owed its existence to Ellis.

Mac: Well I first met Ellis when I was a guitarist in New Orleans and he would, you know, be playing on r&b dates, like Red Tyler had arranged a lot of things and I had the good fortune to play with Ellis on them... At the time, I would say he remind me of Wynton Kelly, in that mold of pianist, but he was also a very excellent New Orleans style piano player. But, you know, Wynton Kelly was definitely much more in the be-bop tradition then Ellis could have imagined at the time. But I think that Ellis' association with guys like Alvin Batiste and Willy T. and a lot of the guys that came up from Cannonball and Nat Adderley and their association...

Ben: That's the Florida circuit, the Florida part of the Gulf Coast influence there...

Mac: I think it's the Florida A&M, Southern University connection in some way. There's a real appreciation between those two schools of music, and the musicians that have come out of there, as well as their good teaching that has come out of there. These guys, Wynton and Branford, are wonderful examples of that good teaching, and one of the great openings that I believe that Ellis gave them, being their father, was a greater understanding of the overall picture of the whole reality of the music industry. A lot of guys coming up today could never have that.

Ben: Clearly when you talk to Wynton, he's very quick to point out that all the press and the business success he's had is secondary to playing and to trying to further the music and find a personal voice. One of the things that's also clear is that all of the technique in the world doesn't take the place for developing a style in jazz. As Coltrane once said that: "To me, I recognize a player's contribution when I recognize their voice. To me that *is* the contribution." Which leads me to Thelonious Monk, because Monk was the supreme jazz stylist. And his technique was not abstract at all. It was designed specifically to achieve his goals. You know, his playing was a classic example of rhythm and melody growing out of the same tree. For example, he always held some notes slightly longer than other ones, whereas most pianists will play with kind of an even touch. But he was a master of space and time, wasn't he?

Mac: I think Monk was not only a master pianist but a master composer. He may be, a million years to come, the only composer of our time that may be remembered like a Duke Ellington, or something. Maybe even more, I don't know. I think Monk's compositions went way beyond the scope of "jazz," or any one name. Even his piano playing is beyond words that I have to put on it. But there's an area of Monk's music that is so traditional and beholding to all of the time of music. I mean, I hear the origins of where it all came from within his music. Almost every time I hear Monk play something solo, it's like ragtime all the way through progressive jazz, it's all within each piece, 'cause he's playing butterfly, stride, all of it.

Ben: You know, that's a good point. It ties into what we were saying earlier, because Monk played everything from circus gigs to bebop. I mean, in the course of his career, he played in a lot of different styles, a lot of different circumstances, and that's all come into his composition.

And what's really interesting is how hearing just a minute or two of Monk's playing can totally change your mood. It captures us in a way that has nothing to do with the literal notes, and I think that effect is a direct reflection of his physical technique on the instrument. Because if you listen to Monk's music, you have to stop. You can't just sort of dash on about your business. It slows you down and brings you into his experience.

Mac: I've always been able to put on a Monk record late or night and be able to be in a relaxed mood to sleep or whatever that very few records, maybe John Coltrane playing some ballads, but there's very few musicians that could put you in a mood that's that at peace. I mean, a man has to be a very strong personality to affect the mood that way. And there's not many people that I've ever heard that could have a complete effect on your whole physical being that way.

Ben: I know you've tried in the past to capture Monk; you've recorded a Monk tune from time to time. How do you go about it? Do you try to capture what Monk does?

Mac: I've tried every attack I could think of to make a sound like Monk, or spacing, time, everything, and it does not sound like Monk. I've even had things that I've learned, the whole voicing and everything, struck the chord every kind of way I could, and it does not come out sounding like Monk. And all I would do would be to play a Monk composition, but as far as attempt to play it *like* Monk would be ridiculous.

Ben: You know, that's interesting. A lot of people are doing tributes to Monk these days, and often they try to change the way they play when they do it, to try to slip into Monk's bag. But that's probably the last thing you should do if you're going to play a Monk tune, change how you play.

Mac: Yeah, like I've heard the Dirty Dozen Brass Band, who always play "Blue Monk" or something, and to hear the way they do that, I enjoy that much more than hearing somebody try and *do* Monk. Monk was a one of a kind, and it should be respected for that. I think it's very futile for somebody to try to duplicate . . . It's like, we'll never have another Monk, we'll never have another Art Tatum, and let's appreciate it for itself, so people can go back and listen to the original Monk recordings and not some piano roll, or whatever somebody's trying to do.

Ben: Yeah. Perhaps that's the message of Monk's music: be yourself. And maybe you can get that message whether you're a listener or a player or driving your car or whatever you're doing.

Mac: Yeah, 'cause you can't be anybody better than you can be yourself.

Ben: Let's talk for a moment about another piano style that was also a reservoir of rhythm: boogie-woogie. I know it's primarily a Chicago style, but there's a collection of Albert Ammons and Meade Lux Lewis piano pieces that came out recently on the Mosaic label, and it's very revealing in terms of the diversity of this tradition.

Mac: Well, Albert Ammons had a big influence on Fats Domino and a lot of New Orleans pianists. Even a lot of Texas piano players, guys like Lloyd Glenn, Amos Milburne, a lot of great pianists came right out of the Chicago boogie thing, and I think Albert Ammons was sort of the focal guy of all of that.

Ben: The thing about boogie-woogie that people like to talk about is, suddenly the left hand started carrying the time. This gets back to what we were saying earlier about the the piano being a reservoir for rhythm. Boogie-woogie came out of rent parties, where perhaps there was only enough money to hire *one* guy. If you can only hire one guy, that guy has to do everything.

Mac: I know that Mosaic package you're talking about. I hope this isn't off the wall, but I heard this record at Doc Pomus' the other night, and there's a cut on there where Albert Ammons does that thing we talkin' about, like how the left hand went along with the ruffs on the drums. . . .

Ben: What about the distinction between the two, Albert Ammons, who was really more of a blues player than Meade Lux Lewis, who was maybe a bit more refined . . .

Mac: The whole thing is, he [Meade Lux Lewis] plays so much sixths . . . That whole thing of his, I don't know, it's like something of the '40s era. I guess it was an era before I got into something about it, or whatever. I just never related to it . . .

Ben: Well, I think maybe you're being polite in saying what you don't like about Meade Lux's playing is its politeness. And the way he uses sixths rather than sevenths is an example of that.

Mac: Well, no, it's just something I didn't never care for. It's like I first heard Meade Lux Lewis playing on a Joe Turner record. And I always loved Joe Turner from the first time I heard him do *Piney Brown Blues*, when I was a kid. And from that day on, I must have had every record I could get my hands on by Joe Turner. And I remember a record I got ahold of, not that long ago, and Meade Lux Lewis was the piano player. And it was like the first record I ever heard by Joe Turner, of those great old records, that I didn't like. And I realized it was Meade Lux Lewis, and it was like he played a very cocktail version of the blues to me. That's what it is. I don't know, in my understanding of the sixth chord thing, it doesn't fit in all blues. Maybe in some things . . . To me it falls in an area of, it reminds me of my Auntie, the way she plays a boogie or something. I don't know.

Ben: I love it, we're getting into the finer points of boogie playing now. These are the short strokes . . .

Mac: I don't know. To me, Albert Ammons played the blues and he played boogie, but it was bluesy. And Meade Lux played boogie but maybe it was from a thing that I didn't know about or something. That's all I can say, 'cause it just wasn't never something I got into.

Ben: I appreciate your comments. They're very enlightening, particularly from my point of view as a piano player . . .

Mac: Well I would hate to think that I would turn somebody off to something by something I said . . .

Ben: Finally, on the subject of the reservoir of rhythm, what about the use of drum machines that is so prevalent today? How do rhythm computers figure into what we've been talking about? Because the drum machine is very unforgiving. It's there. It doesn't move. And the New Orleans feeling generally is kind of a snakey thing.

Mac: Yeah! It's circular more than regimentally square. And I think that it's hard to play in and out with the drum machine, which is what makes funk rhythms work . . .

Ben: Talkin' about that space again.

Mac: Yeah. It's like layin' back and then lettin' it develop and adding space by just lettin' the rhythm cushion itself back to "one." Not actually playing with the time but just relaxing to a point where the rhythm feels like it almost dies, and then lettin' it come back to "one." I'm not too partial to the electronic drums in a lot of ways, and there's a lot about that that turns me off to a lot of music today. Especially with the snare syndrum that has come out with it. I think people have lost the hearing of the different sounds of a real snare drum. I wish more people would hear an Art Blakey or something than the Simmons drum that is so popular a sound today.

Ben: Well, we started out talking about how the piano has been for many years the reservoir of rhythm in many different idioms, and about how rhythm can determine the melody, how the melody grows out of rhythm. But here we are, today, where the micro-chip is the reservoir of the rhythm, and it's just a much greater responsibility for the musicians who use it to find a way to let it breathe and open up that space that you were talking about. Because you really can't fight progress or technology . . .

Mac: Yeah, well we can't ever judge things that we haven't understood yet, 'cause, like we was talkin' 'bout earlier, at one point the electric bass and the electric guitar were frowned upon, and later they found uses for 'em. And it's like, in the early days, I remember when the electric Wurlitzer piano first came out, it wasn't until Huey Smith and Ray Charles and a few guys almost used it like a guitar that it found a place in music. And it turned out to be a sound to replace a guitar in a band more than it was an actual piano. So it did find a space to live. But then, along came so many more electronic keyboards, that I think the technicality of it passed up, a lot of times, what was happening with the music. And it's always musicians what makes the instrument not the other way around. So whatever these instruments, no matter where they're at at a particular time, there will be found a use for them. Whether we can appreciate them at any given time or not just depends how the guy has "shed" on it.

Ben: The real problem, then, is how to apply your technique to instruments with such huge capacity to absorb you.

Mac: I know I started out many years ago playing the guitar, and using a lot of electronic gimmickry in the 50s, and I turned full circle because, at some point, I knew I was getting hired to do record dates not because I was a guitarist but because I had the vibratos and echo and stuff, and other guys didn't have this. And it was simply a matter of, "Well if you hire this guy, he's gonna' bring this stuff on a date." And nowadays, it's the same principle, except there's millions of more boxes. There's guys who get hired not because of their musicianship, but because they have all the tricknology of current day guitarism or pianism or whatever the idiom may be. It's more of the electronic side of it than the musical, you know, the musicianship.

* * *

Joe Sample (May, 1987)

Anybody who played jazz/r&b in a bar band during the '70s played the music of Joe Sample and The Crusaders. While the critics of the day argued about whether their music was really "jazz," Joe and the rest of the group were steadily going about the business of reshaping the face of contemporary music. Miles Davis is often cited as the key innovator in merging jazz and rock, but several years before his experiments, The Crusaders wrote the guidebook (or fake-book) to combining jazz and r&b, and did so in a way that supported bebop improvisation without killing the groove. The Crusaders' brand of music immediately became the lingua franca for bands who played in bars and roadhouses all across the country, because it gave musicians a way to stretch out at the same time it gave dancers a reason to get down. Joe, of course, went on about his business, expanding his own musical horizons and making the music happen for hundreds of artists that he has backed up since his arrival in L.A.

Ben: Joe, you're the piano player on so many of my favorite albums, and a lot of them fall under the title of The Crusaders, and before that The Jazz Crusaders.

Joe: Exactly, right. The Jazz Crusaders. That name came about, I believe, the fall of 1960. Let's see, after leaving Texas in '58, we went out to Los Angeles with the almost promise of a recording contract with Contemporary records. And once we were there, in Los Angeles, it seemed as if the whole jazz world had just completely crumbled or whatever. And at that time, we were nineteen years old and like not quite ready. And so, in the meantime, we worked around Southern California as a dance band and we were sorta like the number one or the number two dance band at all of these dance clubs, in the valley, and Long Beach, and also the Hollywood area.

Eventually we ended up in Vegas and after six months in Las Vegas as a show band, we just got, "Uh, uh. This isn't my cup of tea." And then we returned to Los Angeles about October or November of 1960, and we went to the Pacific Jazz studios and we made an audition on tape. And after the third song, Dick Bach came in and he said, "Okay, guys, just calm down and relax now. Hey, you've got a record deal." You know. He said it. The album actually came out in '61 and it was titled *Freedom Sound.*

Ben: You were a dance band. I didn't know that, but it makes a lot of sense in terms of the way the music came down for the next ten or fifteen years from you. When you say you were a dance band, what kind of things were you playing?

Joe: Well, all we were basically doing was the music of my neighborhood, which was rhythm and blues, out of Houston, Texas. In other words, as we were growing up, let's say on the high school campus there, and then eventually over to Texas Southern University, I was earning money on the weekends, as a teenager, in backing up, like, this blues singer, and that blues singer, and we were working all of these little country towns. A lot of times we were going over to Louisiana, and then, you know, let's say up to the Arkansas line and all that. And it was rhythm and blues.

And, you know, I can remember when rock and roll first came out. In fact, our very first gig, other than the high school dances and those kind of things, it was at the dance club that was in downtown Houston. And they booked us in there as the Blackboard Jungle Musical Kids. The movie had come out and I think it was the first time that rock and roll had ever really made a dent anywhere. It was in conjunction, let's say, with the appearance of Presley and . . . what was that guy's name . . .

Ben: Bill Haley?

Joe: Bill Haley and The Comets.

Ben: And that's about '54, '55, right?

Joe: Yeah, right, right. In '54 I was, what, I think I was 15 years old. And so they booked us into this dance club, and we were really playing rhythm and blues, which later, it was actually named rock and roll.

Ben: You were traveling with Wilton Felder on tenor and Wayne Henderson on trombone, and Stix Hooper on drums.

Joe: And then we had an alto player in the band, which was Hubert Laws.

Ben: No kidding . . .

Joe: Okay, so Hubert was in the band, and then we had a bassist, his name was Lala Wilson, and we were just in there playing the rhythm and blues things. And we would have a singer with the band also. And we were doing all of the rhythm and blues favorites of that particular day. Hey, there was Big Joe Turner and "Shake, Rattle And Roll" and all those kind of things. And then we used to copy and imitate the Bill Doggett band and we basically had us a number of blues singers who would come through Houston and they were recording, let's say, at Duke and Peacock records then. I mean, everybody was comin' in. And there was Big Mama

Thornton, and it just went all down the list. And when I was a teenager, I used to go over there and write lead sheets on the songs that Peacock was recording with these blues artists.

Ben: The Texas sound at the time, too, might have been called rhythm and blues, but there were a lot of great jazz players, from Ornette Coleman to James Clay, that came out of that Texas r&b situation. And people like T-Bone Walker were playing jazz, in a way, or blues, so I imagine it was hard to say what was going on, or what to call it.

Joe: You know what happened. It seemed like the major portion of the population then, they hated jazz. And so the musicians would love it, and so you would have to disguise the jazz with back-beats and then that soulful sound of the day. You know, the sound today that I would say that almost all of the saxophonists have, you can go from Sanborn to Brandon Fields . . .

Ben: Even Michael Brecker, that cry . . .

Joe: Michael Brecker, yeah. It's that Texas sound. Right, and all that started out of Texas and it began when, well we were workin' barns, basically. And in those days, there was one microphone, and that was for the singer. And so the saxophone player, he had to cut over the drums, all the roar of the crowd, all the whatever, and they would get those steel mouthpieces, which it was a piercing sound. And they had to soar over the band. And it was one thing about Texas, also. It didn't have any piano players, basically. There were 900,000 saxophonists. Everybody played the saxophone. It was almost like the state, let's say, sound.

Ben: One thing I noticed about you, though. Unlike a lot of players at that time, even on your early Pacific Jazz records, like the one called *Tough Talk,* you're playing a harpsichord on that record. And as you go through the Joe Sample recordings, you play a lot of different kinds of keyboards.

Joe: Well, you know, we were all so adventuresome in those days. We were sort of outlaws. Now the first album we did, it was the *Freedom Sound* album. The second album was the *Looking Ahead* album, and on the *Looking Ahead* album we had this one song, it was titled "The Young Rabbits." Now for some particular reason, this song got on pop stations. It was number five in Chicago. It was a big hit in Miami. And it was a bebop tune. But it seems as if our concept of bebop was quite different from all of the New Yorkers, all the Detroit sound and all that, in that particular day. We always had a factor of rhythm and blues under the music. And it was very, very appealing to listeners. And we had a lot of success as far as fans went, and also as far as selling records.

And also seemed like the critics at the same time looked upon us as not quite a jazz band. And a number of them loved us, because we had something different, and then a number of them didn't like us, because it wasn't in the purist form. And then the thing of going to the clavinet, the harpsichord, the Rhodes, or even the Wurlitzer piano, all those things. I was always interest in trying things like that. It seems like now, in my later years, though, I love the basic piano now. I really don't get into the synthesizers. And it actually seems like today's world of music is a keyboard player's world.

Ben: Yeah, it is. And, you know, you mentioned something. You were the Jazz Crusaders up until around the early '70s and then you became The Crusaders, dropping the "Jazz." As a way of responding to the kind of criticism you were getting from the critics?

Joe: Exactly. We changed the name, I believe it was '69, and it was a lot of thought and lot of courage to do it, because I knew we would get blasted for doing it and all that. But at the same time I recognized that I had six or seven, or 10 or 15 different sides of music in me. And there was the classics, and there was my love for Latin, and there was my love for let's say blues, and also the gospel, and that was basically our music. And up to that point, I had actually been imitating and copying, up to a degree, all of the guys who had created previous styles. And all of a sudden one day, I began to realize, and also the other guys, that we had our own, hey, let's say, style of music. We had our own personal feelings about music, and we knew that it was like partly jazz, it was partly blues, it was partly this, partly that. And at the same time I wanted people to just *listen* to the music and do not prejudge it by saying The Jazz Crusaders. I wanted someone to say, "What is this music?" And then say, "You know, that's jazz, but I like it."

Ben: You mention the influences of Latin music and all these various elements, and they were very much of the group's sound. And part of the sound was also the combination of the tenor saxophone and the trombone, with Wayne and Wilton. Part of the sound, particularly in the early '70s after you signed with Blue Thumb Records, was that kind of "chicken scratch" guitar, and the way Larry Carlton fit in. Another part of it, I think, was the perspective of the bass and the drums on the records, and where the grove was focussed. And part of it, like you say, was this piano style that you'd developed from all these different elements. There was one tune that you recorded back in 1973 that really stuck out. It was called "Put It Where You Want It," and to this day it's a standard in bar bands everywhere.

Joe: Well, you know, at that particular time, it seemed like we had reached a point, and also after working together ever since we were kids, I mean, I began playing with the guys, officially, in '54. And all of a sudden, now, by 1970, we had just gotten to the point where we could sit in a recording studio and just look at each other and call signals, and just do kinds of various things. And we noticed, every time we went in the recording session, we had, I don't know, ten, twelve songs, whatever, and we would begin to play 'em and the decision was to just use the best versions on an album. Then it got to the point where we could not figure out which ones were the best versions. And then we had to make a decision. Is this a single album or a double album? So we did about three doubles in a row, as you say.

Ben: And you had a thing goin' on, not unlike the way the Memphis thing affected R & B music a decade earlier, or the Detroit thing during the 60s. It was identifiable to you and, in a way, it defined the direction for the entire jazz community, even though, as you say, the critics had probably given up on you and had gone off to follow something else. But you were very influential, I think, at the time. Were you aware of that impact you were having?

Joe: You know, I know that I was. Yes. And even nowadays, I get a little bit shocked when I read a lot of the critics. You know the thing I hate? You know, I don't mind the critics saying he doesn't like me and this and that. What really appalls me is to change the history. Is to deny something. And I see things now that are mentioned by certain critics, where they will give us either no mention of a particular kind of style that surfaced, or a minimal mention. And I know that we had a lot to do with all of that. In other words, it was younger bands that came in and created, like, their interpretations of what the Crusaders were doing. And it doesn't sound like us, and it maybe sounds like something new. But I know where the roots came from. And that is the main factor that disturbs me.

I have actually seen, sometimes when, you know, the writers or the critics, they said, "Well, the Crusaders are really not jazz." And then when the fusion writers begin to write about fusion, they say, "Hey, they're really not fusion." You know, we have been sitting in a limbo for years and years and years, which only tells me one thing. I'm original. I don't fit into any categories. Which I love it, and I really don't care if I fit into these categories. Again, I go back to the one factor that disturbs me, and it's that, hey, don't deny me, that I had nothing to do with a lot of these styles, or the Crusaders had nothing to do with these styles. And that really bothers me.

Ben: It's particularly ironic, given the number of acknowledged jazz players today who are flat out playing dance music. The Crusaders and the Jazz Crusaders before them were probably the only precedent we had at that time. And, at the same time this was going on for you, you and the other members of the Crusaders became more involved in the Los Angeles recording studio scene, because people wanted that sound that you had. They wanted the Crusaders rhythm section sound on their records.

Joe: Yes. It came about when, after I'd say seven years of doing the jazz circuit, from this club to that club to this club, it culminated one week in Cleveland, Ohio, when I was in this jazz club. The piano was not a piano, and you couldn't even play it. There was no microphones. Then the guy told us that we had to play for the show, which was something like shake dancing, or some kind of thing. And I made up my mind on that particular night that there had to be a better way. You know, as a pianist, I was not growing. I was only given just terrible pianos. And I actually looked at it as a waste of my time and my life. And at that particular time I was going around, let's say, carrying the banner of jazz, or playing as a jazz musician, and actually standing up. And we were still call it the Jazz Crusaders then, at that time.

And I just got bugged, where I began to realize that, no, I had to have my own thing. I had to have my own way. I had to go learn something else about music. It was an absolute waste of my time to work the clubs. Basically because there was never any good pianos to play. Alright. So we went back to Los Angeles and we made a decision that I wanted to crack the recording nut. I wanted to find out suddenly what was going on with this record company. How did they make that music. And how did they put all of these strings together with the horns. And suddenly my appetite to just get into other forms of music, music I had always loved. I wanted to do it. And I'm talking about pop things, the Motown things, the great things that Gil Evans was doin' with Miles, with the orchestras and all that, and some of the movie soundtracks. You know, I wanted to find out exactly how did they put all of this stuff together.

And eventually I got into it and then the wildest thing was, I wanted to find out how can I get into someone else's music. And you know, I always realized that if I could feel what someone else was feeling, then I could. It's like, I could only grow then. And I knew that was, hey, that was goin' to school for me, and really concentrating. In other words, how was I gonna get into Michael Franks? How was I gonna get into Aretha Franklin? How was I gonna get into Johnny Mathis? or Steely Dan? or Joni Mitchell? It was a ball. Where I would actually sit down and I would listen to people's recordings and I'd say, "Okay, now, when I play with this guy, I can't use this kind of voicing." And I used to say, "Okay, fingers, don't do that, don't you dare do that." And I used to have to practice. In other words, in not learning how to do something, but learning how *not* to do something, right? Hey, those old habits, you have to break down, like, your personal habits and totally free yourself to actually reach like someone else's inner feelings.

Ben: You mentioned the Michael Franks record. *The Art Of Tea* was kind of a magic record for a lot of us when we heard it, both because of the style of singing and, I think primarily, because of the way the tracks felt.

They were so well organized and at the same time so spontaneous. This whole record is full of charming little arrangements. It feels like the arrangements themselves are almost like little solos, the way they're so effortless. Was the session that effortless?

Joe: This particular session was one of the most rewarding sessions I have ever done in my life. Based upon the previous thought I was telling you about, that one of the greatest things I believe any player can do is to get into someone else, musically, this particular session, every single player on that session was that kind of player. And they had that concept of getting into the next guy, exactly what the next guy is feeling.

When Michael came in, he began to play these songs for us. And you know, I really didn't know anything of Michael's previous recordings or anything. It was just, you know, Tommy LiPuma called me up and said, "Look, man, I have this singer and I also have Johnny Guerin and, you know, I have Wilton and then I have Larry Carlton." And he said, "It's gonna be a fabulous session." So I went there saying, "Well, great, Tommy." And then once we got there, there was Michael singing, and he had these songs that, the first time listening to 'em, you could say, "Man, this guy is really an original. What in the world is he playing?" Right? And, you see, everyone had to really sit there and concentrate.

He would play the songs, he had a guitar, and so he was strumming on the guitar, and all of a sudden, each of us, like individually, began to think, "Now how can I take this guy's song and turn it into something that a band would play?" So one by one, each of us begin to come up with a concept, an intro concept, a concept in the verse. A concept in the chorus. And it went on and on and on. And then Tommy would say, "Hey, that sounds great. Let's turn on the tape." And then I would say, "No, no man, hang on for one minute. You know, I have another thought in the chorus." And then Tommy would say, "Hey, it sounds great." And then Wilton would say, "No, no, no. Just hang on for one minute." And then Johnny Guerin would say it, and then Larry Carlton would say it.

And all of a sudden, what you'd had happening were the best of the listeners and the best, I believe, of those musicians who can get into the other musicians, and then into the artist at same time. And all those songs were basically done in one and two takes. And every song. It went on from the first song into the second song. And it went on and on and on and on and we were all just knocked out about it. And in the meantime, we realized, we had come up with a very refreshing sound, that was totally not like anything we had around, basically because it was all inspired by Michael Franks, who had this off-the-wall music. I mean, it was, it was out there. Hey, this guy was unique. He came in with his own style. And that was a thing that I constantly say that turns me on. I love to hear something original and unique. And then at the same time, it's like,

"Okay, now how do I fit in it, and how do I help this guy to do what he would like to do?"

Ben: You did a lot of sessions around this time that had that spirit. Another interesting one was called *Swing Street Cafe* which you did with David T. Walker. It wasn't a big hit or anything, but I really noticed, again, the way everything worked together. On "Rock House," for example, the way the guitar line works against the head and the band kicks. The way the dynamics are used. It's kind of a good-time, roadhouse song, but done in a very sophisticated way. All the songs on this album are like that. It's the legacy of the Crusaders come home to Hollywood.

Joe: That was actually recorded direct to two-track. Basically, it was made to sell in the German and the Japanese market. It was for the audiophile fans. And at that time, the Japanese and the Germans were the leaders of the audiophile movement. And they still are today, I believe. Unfortunately, at the same time, we ran a two-track tape. And so, as the record was being played, it was being mixed. We were in there one day, and we recorded side one. Which, we would play the first track, and we would wait six seconds. Immediately would go into the second song. And then we came back the second day and then we did side two same way. It was no overdubbing. It was like a performance, and I mean a very, very fast performance. It was no waiting around, you know, in between the tracks and all that, because we had to get it all, by 24 minutes, onto that disc. So we had to hurry up to count off the next song on it also.

The album was done, I would say, basically, because our Crusader label came into existence, and I was asked, "Hey Joe, record something." And so I came up with this concept. I came up with the concept for a couple of reasons. I had been working with David T. Walker and also loved the way that David played. And we had the same love of this particular style of music. Now, the other thing was, ever since I was a teenager I used to listen to records, and all of these songs basically were the songs I had grown up, you know, as a kid or a teenager. Now I used to put on these records for hours and hours, and I would listen to them, and the piano was buried in the background. So I decided that this particular piano style was such a wonderful and beautiful style that I wanted to just lay it right out front. So I then called up David and said, "If you can help me with a selection of songs . . ." or whatever. And we had two rehearsals in my living room and then I wrote charts, and then a month later we were in the studio recording.

Ben: Well, the selection of tunes includes "Hallelujah," "Rock House," "Honest I Do," "Next Time You See Me, Things Won't Be The Same," "Woke Up This Morning," "C. C. Ryder," "Honky-Tonk," "After Hours." Classics. Absolute classics. You mentioned the piano style that was traditionally buried on these records. On this record, your piano style is a unique mix of gospel, rock, soul, jazz, but it's not patched together. Doesn't sound like somebody trying to grab from here and grab from there. It's one smooth thing. I can hear almost the inevitability at that point, of Joe Sample becoming a solo artist . . .

Joe: Right, right . . .

Ben: Which up until that point you had not been. Not long ago, you made a solo piano album and you called it *Roles*. An interesting title, because you have played a lot of roles and there's even a quote on the album jacket from Shakespeare, "All the worlds a stage. And all the men and women merely players." And the roles that you take on on this record as a piano player incorporate all the styles we've been talking about. Your love for classical, your love for orchestration, your love for grooves.

Is it possible for us to break down your thing, even a little more clearly? Would there be some way to say, "This is what Joe Sample's piano approach is really about?"

Joe: I really believe it's my classical training. It is my taking my piano lessons when I was six years old. And I can remember, I used to cry, to say, "Mama, please let me have some piano lessons." And they would say, well, "Hey Joe, we don't have any money." So I said, "But I want 'em, I want 'em." Right? And then my oldest brother also played piano. He's dead now, and at that time, he was a professional pianist. And, now this was back in the early '40s. Let's say '44. I was five years old. And so he was in this all Navy band, and they would come through Texas, and there would be these guys sitting in my living room with sailor suits on. A trombonist, a tenor saxophone player, all the various instruments, and I'm just fascinated with it.

At that time that was boogie-woogie, right? There was just boogie-woogie, boogie-woogie. I was born the same day Sugar Chil' Robinson. Sugar Chil' Robinson was a little black kid that used to have on the white shoes, and he used to play with his fists. And he was five years old and he used to play the boogie-woogie. I wanted to do that too, so I would sit at the piano, and I learned how to play all of the boogie-woogie things. But the basic thing that got me molded into the current musician I am today was my training with the classics.

And by training with the classics, I mean, you know, as you read the music, you'll have, you should retard here, or you should speed up there, or you get a little louder here, or you get a little softer there. Or you play this with a lot of sympathy, or you play this very romantic. And they will lay all of these things out on the music. And of course, you know, I played Brahms, Beethoven, Chopin, and all that. And as you are reading all this music, all of these dynamic things are there. So when I'm incorporating the blues, you know, I use that basic training. Even, you know, like dynamics. Get very, very loud, and then suddenly get very, very, very soft. You know, when you're listening to a philharmonic in your car, it keeps you runnin' for the button, right? It gets so soft that it seem like it just vanish off the air. And then all of a sudden you reach there and turn it up and then they hit you with a triple fortissimo and they will break your speakers, right? Well, that's off of my classical training too. And I believe that that is, like, the basic thing.

Hey, let's say the overall concept, which is the guiding thing, is that every two bars, every four bars, every eight bars, there must be something different. I also learned that from Fats Waller. Fats Waller amazed me. It seem like every four bars, he was shifting gears. It was almost like Fats was trained as a classical pianist. He constantly shifted gears. And that's one of the things that if I don't shift gears, then I become bored with myself.

Ben: What about internally, in terms of the way you are approaching a voicing that might be substantially different? Have you worked on that aspect of it?

Joe: Well, voicings I learned a valuable lesson once, when I was in a piano club with Clare Fischer and George Shearing. And it was George Shearing's club. And it existed I'd say from '62 to '63, and then unfortunately he had to let it go, because certain members in the club went into the business side of the club as a political force. But that one year, we were in his organization, I learned a lot from Clare and George Shearing with the techniques of voicing.

I was taught to just take any chord and all of a sudden, just take it through every single key, every single imaginable voicing that I could come up with. Just runnin' through every single key. And Clare Fischer told me, he said, "Joe, you will get to that point, once you run everything through every, every single key," he said, "you will reach that point that you could just throw your hands on the keyboard and play blindly, and you gonna play a chord. You gonna play some type of voicing." And that was something I worked on for years.

And it also, I have another system I came up with. I don't look at chords now. I do not look at, say, this as an E-flat-major-seven [plays]. I actually look at this scale [plays scale]. Now I'm not playing the fourth because it clashes with the third. I will play the flat fourth. So now, you know, I feel that I could play the song by just [plays chordal sounding "Tenderly" for a few measures] and I can still hear the chords. So all I'm basically doing is, for every single chord, you know, I look at the scale. So, if I could do that, and still hear the song, then I figure, "Well, gee, man, I can really have fun now." I can grab a couple of these notes here, and some of those there [plays chord], it still gonna be an E-flat-major-seven *sounding* chord.

You know, in just choosing some of the scale tones, in any way or form, it's up to me then to choose what density I would like. And why I'm choosing it. Am I backing up a singer at this particular moment, where she's really getting ready to belt out, so I have to get under her with a lot of power? Or am I just up here floating around because, hey, that's all the weight I need at that particular moment? So I just choose tones of the scale.

Now if you can get past that, I'll even get into the twelve tones of things. And the twelve tones of things, I think it gets into the courage that, okay, I'm going to play something that's wrong. I know this is supposed to be an E-flat-major-seven, right? But naw, that's just too bland, it's too plain, I just wanna do something with it [plays chords and melody]. Now I'm using the principle of Clare Fischer, just let your fingers hit the keys anywhere, and I'm also using my principle of the scale tones of, like, every single chord.

... I'm also using this third principle, which is, like, be brave and keep moving. You know, you can play like wrong notes. I played so many wrong notes on a recording. Oh man, and I hit it real strong. But I know it will sound like a masterpiece based upon what I do immediately after playing that wrong note. So...

Ben: It could sound adventurous...

Joe: I'm shuckin' and jivin', basically.

Ben: Well, you know, you haven't come that far from the days when you were puttin' it together, back home.

Joe: We are constantly still puttin' it together, right? And that's the thing that makes this musical game so wonderful. You know what the wildest thing is? I can remember when I used to say, "Gee, if I could do that, man, I would have it made." And suddenly you can do it. Then the next thing you say, "Well, but if I can do that," you know, "hey, man, then I would have it made." Then all of a sudden, I've been recording since 1960. I've been playing the piano for forty-two years, and I still feel like that. There's so much more I still don't know about, you know. It just keeps goin' on and on and on and on and on. So you're in that constant state of being a student.

***

Jack DeJohnette (March, 1985)

Because the drum technique of Jack DeJohnette is so extraordinary, it is difficult for many jazz fans and critics alike to accept the fact that he is also a highly competitive jazz pianist. Of course, there is a long tradition of jazz drummers who play piano—Philly Joe Jones and Joe Chambers to name only two—but Jack's piano playing is on another level of competency. I wanted to explore the interaction of these two passions with Jack, but also to discover what conditions generate such originality in concept and execution. And finally, since Jack's drumming is unlike any other percussionist's in terms of touch and feel, and his personal history includes performing experience with so many of the legends of contemporary jazz, he is a perfect candidate to plumb the reasons why the drums have been at the bottom of so much jazz history.

Ben: Jack, you've worked with some of the finest musicians in the world, including Bill Evans and Miles Davis. Let's talk a little about how you got there, how you became a world class musician yourself. I know your first instrument was the piano, and you began your classical training at age four. You grew up in the city of Chicago.

Jack: Well, you know, I was born and raised in Chicago. And in the black neighborhoods of Chicago where we lived, black people were struggling to better their financial and living situations. It was a cultural thing to give your children the violin or piano, or dance, you know. So they decided I would take piano, and so my grandmother knew a friend who lived right around the corner from me, who was a piano teacher. And she had a degree, she was a graduate from the American Conservatory of Music in Chicago. And I started studying piano from her. Her name was Viola Burns. And I studied with her for about ten, eleven years I think. I've almost forgotten half of the classical music that I learned. But I was so good at one time, she really had dreams of puttin' me on the concert stage. She used to give recitals with all the other piano students she had, and she had a good way of teaching us, give us inspiration, competition. You know, we'd all play and we'd get gold stars or silver stars, according to how well we played the pieces. And since I lived around the corner, I had more advantage than most of the students, because I'd go around and walk the dog, and you know, have a little better special treatment.

I should backtrack a bit, because my uncle was a big jazz fan, you know. His name was Roy Wood, and he started out as a jazz teacher. He later wound up being a news broadcaster, commentator, and finally, I think he's retired now, he wound up being the vice-president of the Mutual National Black Network of Broadcasters. And, he used to have all these old Decca records and OKeh records. And before I could read, around four or five years old, we used to have one of those old victrolas. And I used to get all these records with Count Basie, Ella, Tommy Dorsey. And I used to play these records. Crank up the machine and play them. Now, when I think about it, I wasn't even aware that it was necessarily jazz I was listening to. But I played these records, and I'd know which record it was by the color of the label, and how far away the end of the groove was, which side I was playing. So I developed a system where I could just play the records myself and listen to 'em.

And I used to be fascinated with all those records. Not being aware of what I was listening to, but I loved the music. And I guess I fed myself all of that information on my own really. And we used to have one of those short wave radios where we used to listen to European music and the Grand Old Opera, when radio was happening. And classical concerts and popular music. Then, when I got into high school, my piano studies stopped for awhile. And since I couldn't play the piano in the concert band, I tried bass, acoustic bass, for about half a semester. And then I made a switch into the drum department, where I played bass drum, snare drum, in marching band, for the football games.

But then some of the other guys, we got together, and I got interested in the piano again, through rock and roll, by way of Fats Domino, who was playing "Blueberry Hill." I started playing the piano again, playing all the doo-wop records. And I used to sing in some doo-wop groups, you know. And I used to play the piano, the accompaniment to all those parts. And then, we started playing some jazz in the group.

And then, Ahmad Jamal, who's one of my favorite pianists, came out with *Ahmad Jamal At The Pershing*. We used to play with a jazz trio, piano trio, things like "But Not For Me." We would play for some of the functions at high school, so much so that I got kicked out of school, because I was always up in the music room. I was really turned on by music, and eventually I realized I needed to study a little bit more, and got into it a little bit more. I started listening to the records of my uncle. When he became a jazz teacher they start delivering these records and I started playing them. And one of the guys in one of the combos we had left his drums in the basement of my house for about two months.

And I started going down with the set, they were set up. Or I'd go somewhere, and if I saw a jazz trio playing, I watched the drummer. And I picked up from that, and then I went home, started playing with the records, you know, records like Max Roach, Philly Joe Jones, and Miles and Art Blakey and the Jazz Messengers. And, in about a month or so, I developed my independence and everything.

And then I started studying piano on the side with Muhal Richard Abrams. And another friend of mine, Pat Patrick, helped me out. I used to go to these jam sessions and didn't know how to play rhythm changes, you know. I could play blues changes, and I really got embarrassed one time when I got up to play, and everybody yelled at me, "Lay out." You know, and so Pat came up my house. He lived around the corner from me. He started showing me changes. And then one of the things that got me together with the piano was playing these gigs. We played these jobs on the north side, and in Chicago, there was definitely racial barriers there, but black musicians were allowed to go into the north side, the white neighborhoods, and play, you know, because we were entertainers, we were looked on as entertainers.

Ben: We're not talking that long ago either.

Jack: No, not too long ago. And it's still like that in some parts of Chicago. It's really some parts are worse than the South. And, at any rate, we would go, and one of the things that the musicians used to tell me was, "Get a fake book and learn all the standard tunes, because all the bebop tunes are written off of those changes." You know, "Donna Lee," and "How High The Moon." He said, "You'll notice once you learn all your standard tunes, you'll be able to play anything." You know, play 'em in all the keys. And so I started playing gigs where some guy was singing. Some gigs I played where I was singing. I would sing. Play cocktail gigs. And I learn all the show tunes, and that really got me together, and I started a rigorous practice study. I would practice my drums and practice the piano equal time, during the day until I got the drums up to the level of my piano playing. And so, pretty soon, I was playing gigs on both instruments. You know, I might divide it up playing a trio gig on piano one part of the week and playing a blues gig with Leo Blevens and some of the black blues singers around Chicago, playing drums. Playing shuffles and things like that. And, meanwhile, I was up and coming as one of the top younger piano players in Chicago, and I guess there was some piano players that were glad that I stopped playing piano and switched to drums. But I actually never stopped. Because, while I decided intentionally to make a name for myself as a drummer, I had a plan, to develop as a composer and become a band leader and bring the piano back into the spotlight eventually.

Ben: You intentionally set out to establish yourself as a drummer when you came to New York?

Jack: Well, I intentionally set out to establish myself on both instruments, actually. Mainly as a piano player. But I came to New York in the mid '60s and I sat in up at Mintons. I sat in on the piano with Hal Mayburn and Junior Cook and I think Al Foster was playing drums. And I sat in on both instruments. And John Patton happened to be in the house, heard me playing drums and was looking for a drummer. And so I got hired as a drummer. My first gig. So something clicked there. I said, "Well, maybe I can do better on this instrument. And I'll keep developing the piano." I always practiced the piano. I stayed at the "Y" and they had a piano there, so I was always practicing the piano. And when I played drums and played with horn players and piano players, you know, all that information was being filed away. So I've been gettin' harmony lessons and music lessons just sittin' at the drums, because of the piano knowledge. Because the subconscious records almost everything, even when we don't think it is. And so, by playing with people like Herbie and Keith Jarrett and Cedar Walton, just to name a few, and even Ahmad Jamal, I got a chance to play with him once, I realize that I've absorbed a lot of information that I wasn't even aware of. Now I'm beginning to try and apply it to my concept.

Ben: And now you have recorded a piano trio record, *Jack DeJohnette Plays Piano*, with Eddie Gomez and Freddie Waits.

Jack: Yes, I'd really like to get people more acquainted with me as a pianist. I felt good about the program on that record. I did three originals, and some jazz classics. You know, I did "Minority," a Gigi Gryce composition that I heard and was very impressed with on *Everybody Digs Bill Evans*. Came out with Sam Jones, Philly Joe. And Bill's version was really a classic version of that piece. Those voicings of his really opened it up, made it a lot more modern, contemporary. And then I took two Coltrane classics, which were off of the Coltrane *Giant Steps* album. One was "Countdown" which, even now, when you mention that tune to bass players or horn players, they go, "Ow!," because that's a hell of a tune, you know, and it's played very quick. And I understand from what I've read that on that date, with Tommy Flanagan, Paul Chambers and Art Taylor, that 'Trane had spent a year with "Countdown," spent time just playing the changes on the piano, you know. And as you know, 'Trane was always searching for different things to do.

Anyway, on "Countdown," on 'Trane's recording, Tommy Flanagan doesn't take a solo on that composition. And I'm sure that, sight unseen, putting that in front of him, if I were Tommy I wouldn't have played a solo on it either. It's a very difficult composition at the tempo he's playing it at. But 'Trane spent a year with that, from what I understand, playing the voicings on the piano over and over, just the chords, so he'd get that *sound* in his ear. So that he would hear it. And so I decided I would like to record that piece, because I never heard anybody record it, although I know musicians have, or, for theory and harmonic study, can play this piece. But I've never heard anybody really pay homage to it. So I spent a year with this composition, just playing it at all tempos, slow, fast, adhering to those progressions, and trying to play it. When I did finally record it, I recorded it, not purposely, but actually faster than 'Trane played it. And to play at that tempo, I had to play some ideas, complete concrete ideas, you know.

Ben: Let me ask you, what are some of the problems you run into, trying to improvise to changes at such a breakneck tempo? I mean, is it like running through a forest where the trees are suddenly closer together than they were before?

Jack: Well, you have to break it down, play it slow, real slow.

Ben: But when you do get it up to tempo, to play it as fast as you played it, are you thinking your way through all those changes? Are you homing in on tonal centers? How are you approaching it?

Jack: Yeah, I'm thinking about phrasing, you know? The phrasing, and the harmonic, and the rhythmic. Everything, and voice leading at the same time.

Ben: But, I mean, those changes are coming by like this [claps fast time], right? Change, change, change, change.

Jack: Yeah, but I'm not thinking in terms of that. I'm thinking in terms of a like a connected phrase, overlapping bar lines, more than worrying about this change, that change, that change, that change. I'm trying to voice lead a melody, you know, rather than thinking, "here comes the next change, here comes the next change, here comes the next change." And so I'm just thinking of one continuous phrase, which can be broken up, you know, for breath.

Ben: You mentioned that Coltrane spent a year getting the sound of those changes in his head.

Jack: And then adapting them to his horn.

Ben: The *sound* of the changes is what you're talking about.

Jack: The way they moved. The movement. Yeah, so it's like a painter, you know. If you take Picasso. He takes something that we see with our eye, but then transforms it, extends it and builds upon it, so that when you look at it, it's taking on abstract proportions. At first you look at it, it might be repulsive, and then after you look at it again, it begins to make sense. You begin to see what the artist is trying to say, rather than, "That doesn't look like, you know, what your reference is of a guitar or recorder." But, then you say, "Oh I see what he's trying to do." So that's the approach that I'm thinking of. I mean, Picasso was asked about that, "why is the way you draw that guitar so abstract?" And he said, "Well, what I draw is the movement that you don't see, from the person who walks into the room, from the entrance of the room to the chair." He draws that, that movement. So that's included in there. So, like in a photo, where you put a long time lapse, you see that. That becomes abstract. That movement. And it's the same thing with the painter.

Ben: And with the changes. You're also painting the movement through the cycles.

Jack: Right, exactly. Exactly. So that it becomes like one continuous mood, which shifts all the time, you know. On a piece like that, you're aware of the tempo and the time, but I'm not letting that really bother me. I feel really quite relaxed at the tempo. The faster it is, the more relaxed, because at the same time, I'm also slowing it down *underneath*. Thinking of it in terms of half time maybe. You know, not one-two-three-four, one-two-three-four, one-two-three-four. Thinking of it as duple and on top of it. And contributing over that, over a chord in those feels.

Same way with the drums, you know. When you play real fast, you're dupling over a slower tempo, and that way you think, your ideas become more spread out and not so right on top of each other. Not so close, not so crammed. I'm not thinking that I gotta fill everything up. Give yourself room to breathe. So that's the approach I usually take, you know, improvising with the changes or with the drums.

Ben: One of the things that's said about your style of drumming is that it's very musical, or very orchestral, and the phrase "touch" comes up. Certainly in regard to your piano playing as well. Is there some way that your approach to the piano, your touch on the instrument, carries over to your approach on the drums?

Jack: Yeah, well, it was the piano, finally, that taught me that. Actually, the combination of the piano and some of the other drummers who had, I realized, had a distinctive touch on the instrument. Like, Philly Joe had a distinctive touch. Tony Williams has a distinctive touch. Roy Haynes and Elvin, all these drummers have very strong personalities, and that touch that they have on the instrument . . . it turned out to be also the way they tuned the drums. Which, nowadays, a lot of drummers don't necessarily tune their drums, you know, because we're at the age of commercialism and drum machines.

Ben: Tune it with a dial instead of a key. But you said something before about playing the instrument, versus attacking the instrument.

Jack: Right. Ah, that's something you have to learn. I mean, when I first started playing drums, and when Elvin was playing with Coltrane, you know Elvin, that music was so powerful and so intense that a lot of drummers got turned around by the volume at which he played. Up until that time, drummers did not overpower a band the way Elvin did. But it was necessary, and I found that I knew it was necessary, because I had the great fortune, while in Chicago, to play jam sessions when Coltrane was there. And I used to come and watch him and the quartet every night when they played. And it happened to be my fortune one night that Elvin went out and disappeared for the last set. And the club owner said, "'Trane, let Jack go up. He plays the sessions. We need to do the last set." And Coltrane didn't bat an eye. And I went up and played three tunes with him and the quartet. And I realized why Elvin had to play the way he played. Because 'Trane was like a locomotive. He really pulled you. And Elvin had to play that way. I mean, as you hear Elvin now, he plays very tastefully, you know. Without giving up any of his personality and his aggressiveness.

But when drummers heard Elvin play that way, drummers started to feel, "Oh, well, great, I can really open up and play." And as a result, you had quite a few drummers, including myself, not realizing that the drums, unlike a piano or acoustic bass, when you just touch it, it makes the sound. Because you're hitting a cylinder with a head on it. It's amplified. That touch is triple the amplified when you hit it. So, you have to realize that instrument is amplified already, in its natural acoustic sound. And you have to realize that your dynamics depends on what's going on in the music, and who you're playing with. And so Jackie McLean had pulled my coat to that once when I was playing with him and I was playing very loud. And in between sets he said, "Man, you should really, when you can't hear the rest of the solos, you can't hear what I'm playing, then you should bring your volume down." And I thought about it, and I said, "He's right."

But obviously, I mean, even with Miles, there's some things I played with him when I hear some of the tapes that are just like I want to run under a cover and hide, because, you know, there was overplaying. But Miles . . . I was thankful that I had band leaders who understood that and were patient. And eventually, you know, I learned a lot. I learned about that by playing in different circumstances, with trios and quintets. Now I always know how to play in any situation. I can play with Keith Jarrett's trio with Gary Peacock, which we've been doing. With Keith, it's more disciplined in the sense that you're dealing with softer dynamics but not giving up the intensity. And so the art of trio playing for drummers is very . . . it *is* an art doing that, without overpowering the trio. Being a piano player myself, I understood that. And so it gives me a lot of advantages.

Ben: Having worked with so many great piano players, wasn't it a little daunting to pick up the instrument again yourself?

Jack: Right, yeah. As I said before, I had planned somewhere down the line to bring the piano back into the forefront. And you know, it's hard enough just playing one instrument. To go from drums to piano, it involves another set of muscles and another way of thinking. Both instruments involve harmony and textures. But the piano is more complicated because you're dealing with ten fingers, you know. And I had a concept in mind about working with trios. Because a trio format is very difficult to pull off. I mean, you can put together some people and go into a place and have a trio and see how it goes, and I've done a lot of experimentation with music, in a lot of different textures or context. But what I wanted to do now, what I'm involved in now, is really making sure a presentation is tight and is given some thought. And also to have a style. Because one of the things that impressed me about piano trios, like, Bill Evans, he had a distinctive *sound*. Keith's piano trios have a distinct *sound*. Ahmad Jamal, you hear right off. Oscar Peterson, you know, Erroll Garner. There are only so many people who really worked with the piano trio format to develop it to its highest level. And that is something that I wanted to work in, because it's such a challenge, and such a tremendously difficult act to really pull off.

Ben: Since we're talking a little bit about the overlap in your technique as a drummer and a piano player, I notice that when you play piano, you're very much a right-handed, single-line player. You have a tremendous harmonic understanding, but you choose this very understated approach.

Jack: Well, you see, a lot of piano players tend, because the left hand is there, they think they have to use it all the time. You know, you're playing a single line, that in itself, you're weaving harmonically and melodically. At the same time. So when you do use the left hand, it should add something to it, so that it compliments. And when it's used infrequently, I mean, people like Ahmad and Keith, or Bill, or Michel Petrucciani, that left hand, there's an element of surprise. You don't have to play a chord every bar, every beat. Now, I don't necessarily want this album, this first piano album of mine, to represent that's exactly how I would approach everything else, because the left hand is very important. And further down the line, with other recordings, I will venture out more, utilizing the left hand as an independent voice. Soloing with the left hand, comping with the right hand, or two lines contrapuntal together, you know. But, for this particular record, I thought to keep it simplistic. But yet, in the understatement, people who can hear know that there is more to what I'm doing than is actually on the surface. So it's the subtlety, the understatement of knowing when to make runs.

Ben: I was thinking that one of the effects of your being a drummer is that you don't feel obligated to keep the time with your left hand like a lot of piano players do. That's a reaction, keeping the time going, but because of your experience as a drummer, knowing what other pianists do and that the time is there, you're free of that, in a way.

Jack: Yeah, right, right. And so I don't think you have to feel like it's emptier, that you have to play all over the instrument just to show that, yeah, technically you're equipped and you can run this off. I mean, when the time comes to use it, the line and the emotion and the intellect should all merge at once, and then, whatever that is, if it comes out technically dazzling, fine. If it's not done for that reason. If it's done just to express that particular mood or feeling at that moment.

Ben: It sounds to me a lot of what you're doing is the subtext, or the intention, of what you're doing as opposed to literally what you're doing. As we talked about before, painting the gesture rather than the hand. A lot of times you seem to be doing that, playing the gesture. As opposed to being "literal" or "specific" in your playing. I'm curious, when you synthesized your style as a drummer, did you literally take specific licks from your favorite drummers? And who were they?

Jack: Oh, definitely. Ah, well, you know, it goes back. I mean, it started when I was listening to records. I was listening to Baby Dodds and Sid Catlett and those people on the early records when I was a kid. Then I started listening to Max and Philly Joe, Kenny Clarke, Art Blakey, you know, and Art Taylor, then Elvin, Tony, and I started checking out the licks. I checked them out thoroughly. It's like, you know, Tony and everybody else, there's nobody that really escapes that. You play the licks, you find out how they did it. I think most fun is hearing what they play and then working it out your way, because it comes out different when you try to copy it. But it was an understanding of how that person phrased, how it went, and just see what they felt like. Then I'd say, "Okay, that's good. Now I understand it. Now what happens if I do this?" I add my own thing to that. And so I built upon the knowledge of understanding those licks. Because it's so beautiful, you know, building off of classics. That's a formal kind of study. You know, or transcribe some solos, or whatever. Just for the idea of understanding, getting more information. But it shouldn't be getting that information and then just playing that style. Because those people don't play that way anymore. They change, you know. Elvin doesn't play the same way he played when he was with 'Trane. Tony doesn't play that way. I don't. We keep moving on, and it keeps changing. So we always have to remember when you study those styles and licks, you can get in trouble and become dated if you leave them as they were when they were played. But if you take them and you recycle them and make new things out of them, original things, then you move on.

Ben: One of the things that strikes me, listening to this, is that we really come such a long way in such a short time in this music. The way the drums are used, for example, in your recent recordings is so different from the way the drums were used, say, 25 years ago. The whole concept of drums has changed in just 25 years. If you look at the progression of Western classical music, things happened in hundreds of years. But in jazz, we've gone through so much music and covered so much ground in such a short period of time.

Jack: But you know, the reason we went through it faster is because in those days, the only means of transferring this music was by pen and paper, or hearing it, you know, transferred. But through the medium of phonograph records, and broadcasting, everything is so speeded up now. So we get more information faster and we develop faster. We are absorbing information faster at a younger age than we did before.

Ben: There's no question about it, the record business has revolutionized the music. For better or for worse. For better and for worse, I guess.

Jack: Yeah, for better and for worse. But I think it's time now that the musicians start revolutionizing the record business. To turn that around and start gaining control in dictating where this music will go. Because otherwise, it's gonna wind up in a museum somewhere, if we're not careful, you know? You just got to keep pushing, and look at the reasons why it's not as widely accepted as it could be, and how can we do it without necessarily making the music formatted and predictable. Because it's that unpredictable element that makes this music what it is. The spontaneous of it. And we have to be careful of not losing that. Listen to the re-issues and all that. That's beautiful, and there's still a lot to be learned from that. But we have to be careful not to be too nostalgic with the past, and not live in it. We got to look at the present and carry on. There's a lot of work that has to be done. A lot more work. Even harder work now, because we have video and we have all this information being thrown at us all the time. And for our children, it has to be monitored. It has to be really carefully checked out, what's going where. And make sure people understand where this music is coming from. And that's for everybody, not just for hipsters and for intellectual people. But it's for everybody, you know? You have to remember that we play this music for people and not just to be off in some corner, separated from everybody else. It's for the people.

* * *

Denny Zeitlin (July, 1988)

Jazz pianist/psychiatrist Denny Zeitlin must surely claim two of the most exotic career choices extant, and doing the following interview gave me pleasure twice over. Aside from the obvious pleasure of meeting Dr. Zeitlin for the first time, having enjoyed his music for so many years, I had the double pleasure of reading his words again in order to prepare this interview for publication. He is a man for whom passion is the foundation of thought and lucidity is the medium of delivery. Also, having grown up in the vicinity of Chicago myself, I had a great deal of empathy for his story of a young man, pumped with enthusiasm for a music that struck him like a bolt out of the blue, slipping into the nightclubs by any means necessary. Today, Denny Zeitlin seems like a very happy man. In this business, that says an awful lot.

Ben: I've been a fan of yours since the very early '60s when you appeared on the scene, as it appeared, full blown from the forehead of Zeus, playing great on a CBS album with Jeremy Steig. For the people who missed that record then, let's bring 'em up to speed. You're from Chicago.

Denny: Yeah, I grew in a suburb of Chicago, along the north shore of Lake Michigan, called Highland Park. Grew up there, went to high school there. After having had a classical background, but always enjoying improvising and composing as a kid, I fell into jazz in high-school, and lucked out that there was so much jazz activity going on in Chicago in those days. This was early to mid '50s. I played a lot there and then went to University of Illinois and played there. Went to medical school at Johns Hopkins and was lucky again to find players to play with. And that took me up to 1963.

Ben: [Laughs.] That's a pretty good capsule.

Denny: Quick capsule. Then when I was on a fellowship at Columbia, in psychiatry, Paul Winter, who had been an old friend from the Chicago days, grabbed me kicking and screaming to meet his producer John Hammond. I'd had no aspirations to record at all at that point. Actually, I was rather puristic and thought that to record meant your musical ideals would be hopelessly subverted and I didn't even have any concrete plans for a public musical career at all. I was very involved in music, and felt I would always wanna play, but really didn't have that in mind. And sort of just sidled into it. Hammond liked what I was doing and suggested that I get my feet wet recording by doing an album with this incredible new flutist that he was going to record. And that's how the *Flute Fever* album happened. It was in the fall of 1963.

Ben: You really did not have any desire to be a public performer?

Denny: It didn't seem that important to me. I was loving sitting in and playing, and feeling that I was growing and developing, and that's been more important to me than any of the public aspects of music. I do hope I can continue now to record, and to perform and tour. But what is really most crucial is this sense of being a part of music and to be able to have access to it. To be able to go downstairs and, you know, play my Steinway in the studio, and just get into the music. That's what really just is... it's for my soul to do.

Ben: Well that's interesting, because it indicates very early on a diversion between yourself and many people who are in jazz today, which is the whole performance aspect of the music.

Denny: I love to perform, but it's really not as crucial as the activity itself.

Ben: The doing of it...

Denny: Yeah...

Ben: You went real fast through the telling of your Chicago experience. Briefly, who was there at the time? I think maybe Ira Sullivan was...

Denny: Yeah, Ira was I think the major cat on the scene when I started to sneak into these after-hours clubs, when I was fifteen years old and fortunately was tall enough and I had a little I.D. I carried with me, and so I could pass. And it was also in the days when there was virtually no Crow Jim or Jim Crow in Chicago. And if I was the only white cat in the club, it was fine. And I'll forever be grateful to the musicians that took me under their wings and let me play and put up with my fledgling attempts at this music. And Ira, in particular, was just wonderful. I mean, he was a bottomless cauldron of energy and openness. And to get a chance to play with him would just galvanize you as a musician. It was an incredible learning experience. And there were other wonderful players. Bobby Cranshaw, Walter Perkins, Johnny Griffin, Wilbur Campbell, Wilbur Ware. You know, lots of wonderful players. But I do think of Ira right at the top when I think of the spirit of Chicago back in those '50s years.

Ben: Let's talk just for a minute about your transition from a classical musician to a jazz musician, and where those two intersected for you.

Denny: Well, let's see. I really started out as an improviser, at age two or three.

Ben: Do you remember age two or three?

Denny: I have some flashes of crawling up on the lap of whichever parent was playing the piano.

Ben: They were both musicians?

Denny: Of sorts. My father, I say "of sorts" in that he couldn't read a note but had an uncanny ear, a totally idiosyncratic approach to harmony that's almost humorous. The kinds of chords he would play . . . But he always hit the melody notes right. And he loved music. And my mother was a classical pianist, not of concert level, but she played and she was actually my first music teacher. And they were both involved in medicine. So I really had both careers going from both sides from day one. My father is a radiologist who still practices at age ninety. And my mother was a speech pathologist. She doesn't practice now, but they were both deeply involved in music and science. And so she taught me how to read music.

And then I had an odyssey of classical pianists. There was one very important crossroads, I remember, when I was about nine or ten. When my then classical teacher took my parents aside and said "Now is the time you have to take your boy and impress upon him the importance of his classical piano career. Eight hours a day of practicing. He has this future . . ." My parents listened sagely and gravely to his words and then shined him on, because they really realized that that was not my temperament. That I would never be happy with a classical music touring, performing career, no matter how good I might have gotten. 'Cause they understood what would happen. I would learn a piece of classical music. As soon as I understood how it was put together, I had no further interest in it whatsoever. The idea of having a repertoire of classical pieces to reiterate had no magic for me at all.

Which is not to denigrate this particular kind of creativity that classical musicians have, that they infuse into these constant reinterpretations of the same notes, night after night. I couldn't do it. I would be bored to death. And that's just my personality.

So I was an improviser and a composer at heart, really. And so, when I heard jazz, when I was in eighth grade, when my music teacher, with whom I was studying harmony at the time, brought in a ten inch MGM George Shearing album called *You're Hearing George Shearing*, I felt like I was shot out of a cannon. I said, "What in the world is that?" I mean, I think, subliminally, I must have heard some jazz on the radios over the years. I never had paid attention or the time wasn't right, or whatever coalescence of forces that have to be for someone to be truly galvanized, happened at that night when she played this album. And that just really started me off. I got into high school. There were fortunately lots of young jazz musicians wanting to play, form groups. I played Dixieland for my freshman year, but began to listen to bop. And there was a guitar player who had all the Charlie Parker and Bud Powell sides, and I began listening to that. And I was just pulled immediately in that direction.

Ben: You said something that I think might be a key to your parallel careers in psychiatry and music. And that is, classical music interested you to the extent that you could understand how it fit together. You know, your interest in knowing how it fits together and how the process works, I think, might be parallel in both cases.

Denny: Boy that's a good point. I think that's really very much at the heart of it for me. I also have memories of age six or seven, on the playground at school, of having kids come up and talk to me, spontaneously, about themselves, about their lives, about problems. And I was fascinated in just the way you describe. What makes life work? What makes people act and feel the way they do? Why would somebody do something with another kid that seems so patently self-destructive? I mean, that intrigued me even then. So this hunger to understand process, and to understand how things are organized, is very central to my character. I think it's really a good point . . .

Ben: And I think also that we can see jazz as being a parallel experience, not simply for you, but for all of us, in a way, to help understand the world. It has many of the human elements in it, but in a symbol system that can be manipulated almost safely, huh?

Denny: Yes. And it's a continuous unfolding, as is doing psycho-therapy with somebody. It's not, it's not a finished product. I guess in some ways, playing Ravel's "Gaspard de la nuit," as much as I love to hear somebody play it, would have too much of a concretized, finished aspect for me. I wanna have this open-ended process in front of me, and jazz has always meant that to me.

Ben: You know, it's marvelous, because when one listens to a Denny Zeitlin performance, the thing that one comes away with is this sense of unfolding. For me, your playing keeps opening, and that's the experience of it, as opposed to other styles, which are also great but may be more linear or more driving toward a particular point. The point of your playing seems to me to be this "opening."

Denny: I'm glad you hear it that way. That's very much my intent. Maybe an unconscious intent much of the time, but that really speaks to me when I hear you describe it that way.

Ben: Well, let's talk a bit about the music. First of all, before we get too far ahead, the happenstance that occurred through the interjection of John Hammond, when you recorded with Jeremy Steig, a young flute player from New York who had clearly been influenced by Roland Kirk and other people who were starting to vocalize through the instrument. Somebody, we should say, who had suffered a facial injury in a car accident not long before he recorded, and learned a special technique that allowed him to still play.

Denny: Yeah, he had a special device, like a prosthetic device he would shove in his mouth to keep air from escaping from the flaccid side of his face. And he just played his tail off. Man, this cat could really play.

Ben: Your first record date, then, was with Ben Riley on drums and Ben Tucker on bass.

Denny: It was neat. You know, it was literally a blowing date. We just got together, never having played before, and played. It was just, I think, done in a day. But I think there was some nice natural spark that happened that day.

Ben: And you can imagine in 1963 what those of us who heard this record thought, when we heard Denny Zeitlin. Your playing suggested, a little bit, the playing of Lennie Tristano, but not really. George Russell, but not really. Bill Evans, but not really. A lot of parallels were drawn at that time.

Denny: Well, you know, those are all people that were certainly a big part of my musical influences as I was growing up. Bud Powell, I would certainly have to add to the pianistic influences. Billy Taylor was an early and important influence, and by then Coltrane was a big influence on me. And Miles had been a tremendous influence. And then a lot of the modern twentieth-century classical composers were equally important as any of these jazz people I mentioned.

Ben: But you obviously didn't divert your career by being a member of the Jeremy Steig group. It seemed, instead, that you settled into your medical career. You took up your residence in San Francisco rather than go on tour.

Denny: Yes, I was a junior in medical school at Johns Hopkins when that was recorded, and then I did another album for Columbia next, which was my first trio album. Well, I guess the first of four albums I did for Columbia in the mid and late '60s. And during that time I did my internship at San Francisco General Hospital and started and completed my residency in psychiatry, University of California in San Francisco, and then set up a private practice and have been teaching at UC ever since.

Ben: So you were there in San Francisco as it transitions from a kind of quiet, sleepy Italian neighborhood into the Haight-Ashbury. You were there in the midst of that madness, as a musician.

Denny: And as a psychiatrist too. You know, that's a wonderful time to learn. I mean, besides, it's sobering but exciting from a scientific angle, in terms of drug abuse and what was happening with psychedelic drugs. Our hospital was literally three blocks from the center of the Haight-Ashbury, and for several years I was consulting and working on a youth drug abuse study unit, where we had an opportunity to really work in depth with people who were literally blowing their minds. And it was very, very sobering to see what was happening. But it was very exciting, as a learning experience.

Ben: Let's talk briefly about why you think jazz musicians have used and abused drugs, since the beginning it appears, but certainly since the '40s. What are your thoughts on that? Why heroin? Why drugs? Why jazz?

Denny: Complex question. I think though that probably one central aspect of it is that everybody who tries to create has to deal with the issue of noise. External noise is the more obvious sort that we think of, and certainly a musician who has to stand up on a bandstand in a nightclub and fight the Waring blender, the tinkling of glasses, the patrons screaming "Play Melancholy Baby," and everything else that happens in the external world, those distractions are tremendously potentially destructive to any ongoing flow of the music. But I think even more insidious is the kind of internal noise that most of us as creative people have to deal with at one time or another.

In a sense, I think it's an ongoing issue to deal with that internal noise. And that can take a number of forms. Sometimes it can be, for example, somebody who gets up to play, or is about to be involved in a creative activity, who has an internal feeling of, "I have no business being here," or "I haven't really prepared," or "What happens if I play and I flub a few notes," or "There's a tremendously important pianist out there in the audience. What's he gonna think of this voicing," or . . . All these kinds of internal things that can start to percolate, that have to do often with fears of public humiliation, of failure, sometimes of loss of control. At other times it's a more interesting theme of fear or guilt about being successful. Which is interesting.

In my private practice over the years, where I've often had a larger percentage of people involved in creative pursuits perhaps than other psychiatrists, that theme comes up again and again. Where people unconsciously have a tremendous inhibition about allowing themselves to be successful. And then often, historically, what it turns out is that it involves some early familial experiences, whereby they learned or came to believe that their success would be at the expense of somebody else in the family. For example, a very talented saxophone player, and I'll disguise the elements here so that there's no way the person could be identified. Let's call him a saxophone player, comes to my office with the stated complaint that he was tremendously [in] fear of, had a tremendous fear of failure on the bandstand. He thought he was an imposter, he thought he was no good. And he was so almost phobic about performing that his career had ground to a halt.

We began doing intensive psychotherapy. And after a number of months it turned out that that fear of failure theme was really a cover story for a more pervasive underlying guilt over being successful. He was the older of two brothers, and he always felt that he had been favored in the family, and that his younger brother had suffered, and had been somehow shoved off in the corner. Never had a chance to shine. So when he was up on the stand, potentially being able to really play, and he knew on some level that he was more talented than everybody else in the band that he was playing with, and that he could literally blow them away. And when he would talk about that imagery, you could feel the potential destructiveness that had in his fantasy life. That his playing well would blow other people away. Annihilate them. That's what he felt on a symbolic level he was doing to his brother by excelling. And after being able to be able to work this through, in psychotherapy, his career began to really take off, and he went on to make some really major contributions.

Ben: Two things come to mind. One, the idea of internal noise. You know, Charlie Parker once was quoted as saying, "You don't play better on heroin, but you do hear better." Because a lot of the noise drops away. And what you hear is the music.

Denny: Yeah. I think that one of the major reasons why people would take drugs is to quell noise. And to have more access to the purity of the merger state, which to me is a prerequisite for true creativity. Where I think there's a severe backlash for most players, and I'm not talking about legal issues, or ethical issues here, but, I don't wanna say that there might not be people who, literally, given their make-up and their background, would play better on drugs. And there probably are some that do. But I think for most people, the price one pays esthetically for the drug, for getting to that place where you don't have the noise, is a huge price, in that the sense of form typically goes out the window. In that, where there may be a subjective feeling that you're really burning, "It's really happening, man," you know, and it feels wonderful, if one goes back often and listens critically to the tapes of such experiences, you find out that there's a lot of heat but not much light. That often it can end up being what sounds like a form of musical masturbation. That whatever organizing principal a person internally has about the shape of an improvisation, or the compositional inevitability that one often hopes is going to emerge from playing, that doesn't seem to happen as frequently.

Ben: Well that's interesting also. The inevitability of music is really an illusion, isn't it? We do this music. This music is not literally done through us. We do it. A lot of musicians, John Coltrane included, expressed the sentiment that they're merely the vessel and the music passes through them. And to some extent it's true, but . . .

Denny: It's a useful state of mind to have, I think, and I think getting into the merger state helps promote that, that feeling of being one of the people in the audience, almost, listening to the music. And I think that allows us as musicians often to less consciously manipulate the music, which I think gives it a more natural and spontaneous feel. But there's no question: "There ain't nobody else at the keyboard."

Ben: Someone's doin' it. It's so easy sitting here with you, Denny, to get far afield. But of course, the main reason we're here today is because you're a player. You're a player first and foremost to most people. I'm sure your patients would argue otherwise, but to the rest of us, we think of you when we hear your music, as being an original voice. For somebody who is such a gifted acoustic piano player, with such an original voice, I think it was a surprise to many that you became very involved in electronics. Talk about that a bit.

Denny: Well, it happened in, I guess, the mid '60s. It actually was even before I recorded my last acoustic modern jazz trio album for Columbia, which was called *Zeitgiest*. I began to get very restless with what felt like the limitations of the acoustic piano. Was envious of horn players who could sustain notes and bend notes and guitar players who could get distortions. And I'd been listening to rock and roll and the unusual electronic effects people were getting, and I was thinking, "Why, why can't I do some of that?" And I think somewhere inside I'd always wanted to be an orchestra. So I began an odyssey of finding engineers to build me various kinds of components.

As you know, this was well before the days you could go into your corner grocery and come out with a Moog synthesizer under your arm. So I had people build me a ring modulator, build me another piece of gear. And gradually, over a period of several years, I really withdrew from any public performance during this time. I amassed what looked like a 747 cockpit of keyboard instruments. Which initially included things like the Fender Rhodes, the electric piano, the clavinet, the Farfisa organ. And these things would go through endless wires and sound altering equipment and things, and eventually when synthesizers began to appear, I had an ARP up there, you know. And I was trying to integrate, then, everything that I'd had any contact with, musically. Classical music. Avant-garde music, electronic so-called serious music. The elements of rock and roll that I felt jazz musicians were eschewing because they were really so threatened by its popularity, and so angry about it.

Then this tremendous energy and a different feeling of time, and I wanted to be able to get into that and to have a sense of that, and to be able to move from that kind of time to jazz time, where you'd feel the time was way up on top of the beat at the edge of the ride cymbal, and to be able to move back from there to the solar plexus and back again. And that challenge was exciting to me. And there was a couple of very fine musicians in the bay area, George Marsh on drums and Mel Grades on bass, with whom I explored a lot of territory over several years.

We recorded; actually my initial foray into the field was on my own mail order record label, because I couldn't find any established company...

Ben: Double Helix...

Denny: Yeah, this was Double Helix records. Established labels who heard some of our demo tapes, I think genuinely were intrigued by the music, but they said, "Frankly, we have no established conduit to sell this stuff. I don't think either of us would be happy as a commercial venture." So I put this out myself and sold out the first pressing of several thousand copies, and that was enough to interest a local label. And I think this whole electronic period reached its peak for me in a project that again I fell into, just like analogous to the Columbia trip.

Phillip Kaufman, this wonderful movie director, had turned out to be a fan of my music. He'd grown up in Chicago, had heard me play, and heard my albums, and had it in the back of his head that some day he would like me to do a project with him. So he approached me when he was doing the remake of *Invasion Of The Body Snatchers*, in 1977. And at that time he was planning that the score would be a jazz score. And as we began to talk and he was talking with his producer, the score evolved into a twentieth century electronic and symphonic score. And I then had to sell his producer on the idea that I could do it. I had no established credentials in this field at all. And I think if I'd been him, I wouldn't've hired me. But I'm pleased that they gave me a chance and I sort of felt like I'd descended into this strange Hollywood world where this project that I thought would be so musical turned out to be maybe thirty percent music, seventy percent other things. Mathematics. Film technology, interpersonal relationships, military logistics, budget. I mean, it was just incredible.

It was a ten-week thing that took me away from my practice half-time for five of those weeks, and in five of the weeks I simply closed my office. That's the longest I've ever had my office closed before or since. And fortunately I had many months in advance and my patients knew about it, and there were no reverberations of a negative kind. But it was so demanding that I don't know that I'd ever wanna repeat it then. It literally took me off this planet. My life with Josephine, which I feel is the hub of my life, I mean, it was like I would never see her. She would have to scrape me off the piano stool after eighteen hours hunched over my score pad and dump me into the hot tub, and then put me to bed. Night after night, you know.

Ben: What a wonderfully ironic title for a project that literally snatched your body away from your life.

Denny: I might mention something about this score. There is some prepared piano on it, there is writing for a full sixty-piece orchestra, and there's also electronic music and synthesizers. And this film used the first ten-voice Prophet synthesizer that had ever been made, so it was the debut of polyphonic synthesizers, really.

Ben: I'm sure that not only did this experience cure your desire to go to Hollywood, but maybe it hastened your interest in the performing of acoustic music again?

Denny: Well, you're right on it. That's exactly what happened. I was so blown out and yet exhilarated after that project was over, I had a tremendous hunger to get into the total simplicity and purity of acoustic music again. And so the pendulum had swung then all the way back to my earliest roots, and even though I still have my electronic set-up at home, I've done virtually no performing or recording other than acoustic, since 1978. And it seems like all that electronic experience deepened my appreciation and ability to play the acoustic piano in ways that are funny. I can't really articulate, but I think I *hear* better. I hear more of the overtone series. I seem to be able to produce more of the harmonics. There, there is a some kind of increased freedom of moving through the music for me that I wish I could put my finger on. But it just seems to be there, and I'm not complaining, because it seemed to have sort of goosed me along into another level of playing.

Ben: Well, recently, you made an acoustic trio album, working again with Peter Donald, a drummer who you've played with on and off for many years, and bass player Joel DiBartolo. Listening to this record is almost like going full circle from where we were in the '60s.

Denny: Yeah. *Homecoming* is a kind of straight ahead jazz album. I think it does, though, show some of the new musical territory I've been in since the Columbia years in the '60s. And yet, I think people who are familiar with and enjoyed my Columbia albums, will respond to this new release.

Ben: And also, you're playing some compositions that are almost inside jazz standards by other writers. There's a version of the Charlie Mingus tune "Goodbye Pork Pie Hat," which has been done by a lot of people. And your version is not the obvious version, the slow six-eight feel is, again, exploring the unexpected. Hit 'em where they're not.

Denny: Isn't that an amazing tune, Ben? The structure of that tune is, to me, wonderfully elusive. It's always a challenge to play. Because I think he takes you in spots you'd never expect to go on that piece.

Ben: You can approach that song, as many people do, like a straight blues. You can play it with three chords, practically. Or you can really get involved with a lot of substitutions. An interesting story, which I've told before but really applies here, is that I once asked John Handy, the saxophone player who recorded this song with Mingus, about the original chord changes. And John said, "Well I can't tell you the chords, because Mingus never gave us any music. When we recorded that, he sang us our parts." [Denny laughs.] So there you are. Your approach is as correct as any.

Denny: That's a neat story, man.

Ben: What feeling do you have being out here today as a player versus a psychiatrist? Since you spend most of your time practicing medicine, is this something of a diversion for you, and then you go home to be involved in the serious business of being Denny Zeitlin? And, also, do you sense that the industry doesn't take you as seriously as they might, as a player, because you have another career?

Denny: Well, let's see. The first question first. I don't feel like I'm sort of taking a vacation from my real identity, by being down here and playing at Catalina's tonight. But I feel really that each of these activities is as central to me as the other. And I can't imagine not being involved in both careers. I mean, if somebody came along tomorrow and handed me a billion dollars, so that was no issue at all anymore, I wouldn't change the shape of my life one iota. I just really wouldn't want to. So this feels just as wonderful and natural to me as going to my office and, you know, seeing a bunch of patients on any given day. As far as the industry's taking me seriously or not, I think there probably initially was some tendency for people to at least approach the music with an idea that this must be some kind of dilettante. And then they would have to be convinced. And hopefully they were when they listened. There was probably a little bit of that when I first appeared in San Francisco as a doctor, having had a couple albums out already. And some psychiatrists wondering, "Well, how serious is this resident in psychiatry going to be about his medical career?" And they had to get to know me a bit and see my work to learn that I was extremely dedicated. So I think that has tended to pass with the years. But initially I think each field had that take on me.

Ben: My feeling is that, just as those two careers or professions are really a part of a whole, so too many musicians have many sides to them that tend to be dismissed because it doesn't fit into the stereotype of what a jazz player should or should not be. And I think maybe that's part of the torture, or the pleasure, of being a jazz player. From your unique point of view, what can you tell us about the drive to perform jazz? Why do some people choose do this?

Denny: Ehh, boy. Who knows what really ultimately spurs the creative impulse in somebody, whether it's to be a jazz musician or a sculptor, or to be a brilliant entrepreneur, or whatever.

Ben: You think that's all part of the same impulse, and they're just different branches of it?

Denny: Yeah, yeah. I think so. I think we're born with different kinds of predilections, and some of us have a kind of inborn musical talent and predilection for improvisation, which is this very special kind of spontaneous composition. Which seems to be so much at the heart of what jazz is about. I think the need to communicate, the need to be part of something greater than oneself, the need to be able perhaps to reach some eternal values, immutable values in the universe that we experience as often chaotic and full of change. These are probably some of the things. There is, to me, an absolutely transcendent quality about getting into jazz playing, when it's happening, that is so magical and so totally non-verbal that I don't have any words to describe it.

But it is so exhilarating and so ecstatic, I think in the true meaning of that word, where you really get beyond yourself, and you lose the positional boundaries of who you are and you become merged with this marvelous experience. I think players have a hunger for that. If you've tasted that, you wanna get more of it. And it has a lure, and there's the hope that every time you get into that space, that somewhere around the corner, some new aspect of yourself, of your music, of everything that, intellectually and emotionally, you've ever been involved with, with music, will somehow get a chance to just happen. Like a flowering of a plant that will suddenly have a new leaf or a new stem on it. And I think there's a tremendous lure for us as players.

Ben: It sounds like you're describing the impulse that drove so many young people to take LSD in the '60s.

Denny: Yeah. Here's a drug-free way.

* * *

Don Cherry (December, 1986)

His language, like his life, is free flowing, a stream that follows the lay of the land and rushes forward from a natural source. He is full of joy and enthusiasm, and his ideas often run ahead of his speech. Thus a conversation with Don Cherry is not a linear, organized event. It takes many contours, and it describes the journey of a remarkable mind and spirit. Just as his music encompasses the ethnic expression of cultures as far flung as the hills of North Africa and the Watts ghetto of Los Angeles, the New York art scene of the '50s and the free community of the diggers in Sweden during the '70s, Don Cherry has always played his own way, a very personal music. Starting as a trumpet player and then moving to the "pocket trumpet" which he made famous while working with Ornette Coleman's band, Don moved on to flutes, double-reed instruments, African string instruments (such as the "hunter's bow"), and even became a singer in order to set free his musical voice. Don Cherry is a pioneer in the field of "world music," which, ironically, has lead him back to the classical jazz scene in the United States.

Ben: We've gotten to spend some time together this past year, working on radio and television programs together, and it's been revealing for me to get to know you as a person—having lived with your music for many years—because you are as charming, intellectual, and humorous as your music is.

Don: Oh, thank you. Well that is one of the problems that I have in America. I haven't been a part of the media in America, which is something I really want to do more.

Ben: I became aware of you back in the late '50s with your work with Ornette Coleman.

Don: Right, that was a group that we started out in California with Billy Higgins and Ornette and Charlie Haden playing bass. And a lot of the listeners today haven't had a chance to really experience that group because it's mostly played with records. We played up until '61 together. And since then, we've had different meetings and played together on different records.

But when I was first playing with Ornette, I felt, as I feel now, that I was studying with him because he had so much to offer. And he had a lot of persecution and people really put him down because of his music and because of the way he would look. Because in the late fifties, he was one of the first people that I know who had long hair. And he would get a lot of persecution for that.

Where I first heard Ornette was in Watts, where I was raised in Los Angeles. It was at a record shop in Watts. It was like the center of Watts where we all went to hear all the records, and where we would buy reeds and valve oil. It was a musician, Mr. Canard, that had the shop. And they would make congas there and musicians would come from all over because it was really a center. And that's when there were 78 records. And we couldn't buy all the records, but we could go and hang out and listen.

And I remember walking towards [the store] and we were about two blocks away and heard this sound! Me and a friend of mine named George Newman that plays alto saxophone and we were raised together. And we had heard about Ornette because of Janie Cortez, who was his first wife and a very prominent American black poet. She was like George Newman and my guru, where she would lend us records and we would take them home and it would be Charlie Parker or Thelonious Monk or Bud Powell and we would learn the songs and bring the record back and play the song to her. And then she would allow us to borrow another record. And sometimes, we would even play parts of the solos because we all knew the solos. If not play them, we could sing them. So that's where I had heard about Ornette . . .

And I remember when Charlie Parker came to Los Angeles, and I had the privilege of hearing him three times . . . once with Stan Kenton's band and once in concert with him and Chet Baker and Lawrence Marable and Amos Trice, and I think Harper Cosby was playing bass, and then again I heard him at the 5/4 Ballroom . . . and Ornette was to go sit in with him at the Tiffany Club. And Ornette's saxophone wasn't a new saxophone and he had it all taped up with rubber bands and he wanted to borrow a saxophone to go play. So he asked George Newman. Actually Janie did, to let Ornette use the saxophone to go play with Charlie Parker. And when he got to the club, they wouldn't allow him in because of his long hair.

So that never happened. But they did meet. And I was so happy to hear Bird around the period because it was really something to hear. We had been hearing records, but to hear him live like that in person . . . and we were very young. I was like sixteen or seventeen years old at the time.

Ben: The interesting thing is that a few years later when Ornette finally did get recorded, and there was a firestorm of controversy about him, there were some comparisons of him with Bird, in terms of his use of intonation and the way he extended the blues form.

Don: Well you have to understand that Ornette was coming from Texas and Texas has some very strong culture in saxophone playing. Some fantastic saxophone players have come out of Texas. And we were all like the students and listening to Bird. And even when we started playing together, we would have a set, a medley of Charlie Parker songs that we would play. And actually Ornette would not play the same *phrases* as Bird but he knew the concept and would get the sound of the phrases. You know, have a tribute for Bird and still sound like Ornette Coleman.

Ben: Ornette talks at one point in the liner notes to one of his early records about getting "the human sound" and how important that is. And he also talks about rhythm being like breathing, something that rises and falls . . .

Don: And another wonderful thing was around that particular time in Los Angeles, Edward Blackwell was there. And Edward Blackwell and Ornette would play together a lot. And I can feel within the compositions of Ornette that Blackwell's concept was inspiring Ornette for the way that he wrote. And when they played together it was something so special.

And Blackwell at that time had a small set of drums. Like he had a tom tom for his bass drum. It looked like a miniature set of drums. And it was something I couldn't understand, what made his playing so different. I mean, he was from New Orleans, and you know Edward Blackwell used to tap dance in the street, so he had that New Orleans feeling in his playing. But he always made mallets and practice pads and he was always practicing. And he has this independence, which is the real concept that he's playing.

But, when he plays you don't hear a crash . . . it was so clean because of the control that he had developed. Everything he played was very clean and so you had to really play, and swing, in order to play with him. And when he hears the sound, he knows how to make it swing. Or which direction you're going.

And that's what made the group special. We could play the compositions of Ornette and improvise from the compositions and create forms in our improvisation. Not just stick to the standard AABA form, even though maybe the songs were made that way. But the feeling of the composition, and the way it was moving, and the groove, the swing that it had, was what we would pivot off of in our improvisation. So that was the only different thing in the way that we were playing was that we could improvise and create forms. And the rhythm section was "down" enough—they had elephant ears—where what direction you would go, the musical, natural direction, they could follow and accompany. And then they would lay something that you would follow. So it was a give and take.

Ben: How is this related to the concept of "Harmelodic" playing, which is a term Ornette has used to describe his music.

Don: Well, with us playing without a piano . . . on the first record, we played with a piano and Walter Norris was the pianist who is a grand piano player, coming from Tatum and Bud Powell, that source . . . but afterwards, with us playing without a piano, we had to play phrases where the harmony could be heard. And the harmony we're speaking of in relation to chord changes. I mean, Thelonious Monk is another good example of that because his melodies are where you can hear the harmonies in the melody, and you can improvise from Monk's tunes from the melody or from the chords. You know, you have two to work from. But in the harmelodic concept when you improvise you play phrases where you can hear the harmonies too.

And the human side was more of the sound. Because in jazz music, it's the *sound* that swings. I mean, the rhythm is coming from the rhythm section, but the actual *sound* is what really makes it swing. I mean, Lester Young is a good example of that, how he would play the simplest of phrases but his sound had it swinging, you know. You can feel the swing within the sound.

And Ornette would always write the compositions down, which a lot of people didn't know. And he had his own way of notating where he didn't use bar lines. Now he has a clef, a harmelodic clef. There's a treble clef and the bass clef and the figure "8," which is the harmelodic clef. And to really explain it, Ornette is writing a book and it's better for him to explain it.

But I can tell you one story. When we would learn compositions, Ornette and I, and we would learn it in unison, then I would play the composition and he would write a harmony. And his harmony would end up being a melody. So the melody that I'd be playing from the beginning would end up being a harmony. So when we were playing in later years, with Dewey and three pieces, he would write a third part. So Dewey, the third part, would end up being melody and the other two parts would end up being harmony. So when you listen to pieces like "Skies Of America," for example, where he had a whole orchestra and he did that, it's really something. To me, I believe this piece is one of the absolute musical pieces of our times. And that's a good example of how the harmelodic system has developed.

But if musicians really want to learn the harmelodic system, they have to study with Ornette, and the best way is to study Ornette's compositions.

Ben: In harmelodics, then, you improvise off of the intervals and the relationships . . .

Don: To the sound of each note, yeah.

Ben: Each note is the tonic...

Don: And the swing of each note too. Like [sings an Ornette melody]... the movement, you can feel how it's moving. [Sings more.] That's a whole little composition within itself. And you're working in C there, but it's ending in A flat, the last phrase. Where it's starting out in G minor and it goes into C and resolves.

So you can feel the swing in it. And the rhythm section can. Like we would never count a tune off, like say "one, two, three, four" and then go. We'd feel each other and then hit right on it. And then that's the way we could feel the tempo, what it would be. And we could play the compositions in different tempo and they still would have a different kind of swing or different story to tell in relation to it.

And then when we opened up at the Five Spot, every night, Ornette would bring at least two to three tunes that we would play that night. And we would go over them before the gig, play one each set and then play them all together. Or play one as a check at the end of the night.

Ben: When you opened at the Five Spot in New York, it was quite an event. And you played there for several months...

Don: Yes, it was very unusual to play in New York at one club for such a long time. And there was always two groups playing.

Ben: Some people loved what you were doing, they called it "the shape of things to come," which later became a title for an Ornette composition. And there was a lot of excitement about the spiritual basis of the music too. Of course many critics and musicians hated what was happening. Every night must have been something else.

Don: Yes, that's true. At that time, a lot of musicians thought that we were just playing completely free and hadn't really studied. But I think that once the musicians realized that it was notated first and memorized, and we would play compositions that we would practice forward and backward, and we always were studying the law of intervals... and the swing was one of the main important things of the music... and that spiritual side that you speak of is just the honestness. And it's something that we could never explain.

Ben: What was the scene like at the Five Spot? I know a lot of musicians were coming around to check the group out.

Don: Yeah. And a lot of artists. It was mostly the support of the whole art scene. Painters from the Cedar Bar, you know, de Kooning and Bob Thomson and Larry Rivers, LeRoi Jones and poets like Ginsburg. It was just the whole scene, Jackson Pollock and Hans Hoffman was the whole inspiration of the art scene at that time. I can remember Chamberlain, many other names come to mind because everyone came at one time or another. And musicians from Thelonious Monk to Miles Davis and Coltrane came a lot. And Mingus and Phineas Newborn and Max Roach, they would come and sometimes they would sit in. Even Lionel Hampton came one night and sat in.

Something was really happening, and the Jazztet was playing opposite us. Randy Weston was playing opposite us. I mean it kept changing with the different groups and musicians. And then it was a period that because of the cabaret cards, Billy Higgins had to leave and Charlie Haden had to leave. So that's when Scott La Faro came and that's when Edward Blackwell came.

And we had both known Scott La Faro in Los Angeles. Because there was a time when Scott La Faro and Charlie Haden lived in a garage and each one had an apartment on each side. And I used to come there to play, and I'd stand in front of the door, and I could hear both of them practicing. And I didn't know which door to go into. [Laughs.] And the thing about Scotty is that Scotty always played the top, and he was the first bass player I know that used the technique with all his fingers, as a guitar, and plucking. He sounded to me like he was in the cello clef. Where Charlie was the opposite. He played in the bottom. And Charlie had that country-Western gospel sound, coming from the Ozarks, and Scotty was in the classical tradition. He turned me on to a lot of composers, like Kodaly and Stravinsky.

I mean, between Scott La Faro and Steve Lacy, those were two teachers that really turned me on to contemporary classical music. Actually, Ornette and Blackwell and I had all been contacted by the people that were working with Harry Partch. And Harry Partch was a composer who made his own instruments and made his own studio. We went to San Francisco and stayed in his studio and it was the first introduction to Harry Partch and his music. And he never had his music recorded at that time because he felt the technology wasn't ready. And when he would do his pieces, they would be operas, and so it was a certain production, and he would make the instruments also. And that sort of opened it up for ethnic music.

Ben: This whole area you're talking about is that intersection where the avant-garde is synonymous with ethnic music, is synonymous with technology at the cutting edge of musical theory, it's a great musical "stew" . . .

Don: Yeah, of what's happening now in music. You can really feel it. But I remember like me and Ornette went to hear, in the '50s, at UCLA when Stockhausen played a piece. I remember he [Stockhausen] came out and said, well he shouldn't play his music because the architecture wasn't really that good at Royce Hall, but that he had traveled so long he'd do it. And that was one of our first introductions to electronic music.

Ben: You once told me that around this same time you met and played with Miles Davis in Los Angeles.

Don: Yes. Well, you know I had been listening to Miles for years and had been a fan. And one night, I used to have a gig in Hollywood on Sunset at a club called the Renaissance Club, and Billy Higgins and Leroy Vinnegar used to play trio there on Monday nights. And around this time Miles Davis came out with the group with Cannonball, Philly Joe Jones and Paul Chambers and John Coltrane. And they played for two weeks and that particular Monday night they were off. And we were playing at the Renaissance, and I had just gotten the pocket trumpet. And we were in the second set and all of a sudden somebody tapped me on the shoulder. On the bandstand. And I turned around and it was Miles. And he had his hand out, he wanted to try my trumpet. And also, the rhythm section, when Leroy and Billy Higgins get together that's really something cooking, and so he [Miles] played something on my horn. And then I played some and then we both played and so he spent the whole night. And that was when we first really got a chance to meet each other.

And then in later years, when we were in New York, he would come in and he would have the waiter bring a little note up. And he says, "Can I play your horn . . . Miles Davis." And he would come in and sit in with the group with Ornette. And what he liked to play was a song called "When Will The Blues Leave." And it was always great to hear him and be around him. I've always loved Miles' playing and the way he's developed.

Ben: And particularly lately, where he has maintained his sound and moved into the area of electronics, this reminds me of some of the things you were talking about where there is an intersection of the avant-garde with ethnic music and technology.

Don: Yes. He's within the last few years really developed a lot within the technology side. As a trumpet, he's always had it anyway. But he's gone through the technical period, and now I feel what he's doing, he's balanced the two out.

Ben: You also mentioned John Coltrane coming by the Five Spot and I know that Ornette and the scene you were on in New York had a real impact on his playing in the late '50s and early '60s.

Don: Well yes, and I remember that when I first came to New York, I stayed with Steve Lacy. And Steve Lacy is a person that collects books and is very much into the art scene. One of his favorite painters is Dubuffet. And he only played soprano saxophone. He just mastered the soprano saxophone. And we went on the road [with Ornette] for a while and came to Chicago to play, and we came a little earlier because 'Trane was playing. So we came a day early to hear 'Trane before we opened up.

And 'Trane was playing soprano saxophone, that was the first time. So I called New York City on the phone in the club, I think it was the Sutherland Lounge, and I said "Steve, listen to this." And I put the telephone for him to hear, and it was 'Trane playing soprano. And so Steve said, "So that's why John Coltrane asked me what key the soprano saxophone was in, because he was going to get one." And he knew it was 'Trane, you know, over the phone. And that was one of those bright moments of contact with all of us as artists.

And then later we recorded together, 'Trane and I.

Ben: It was a wonderful record called *The Avant-Garde*, with Percy Heath on bass and Edward Blackwell on drums. I remember particularly you did the Ornette Coleman composition "The Blessing."

Don: Yes, and this is something that I just figured out myself. You know 'Trane has written a song called "Naima." And the first phrase of "The Blessing" contains the first phrase of "Naima." So I was thinking that maybe, in some kind of way, he felt how the phrase and the intervals were moving to write "Naima." Even though I know it was inspired, with 'Trane, probably by a more spiritual [moment]. Because his compositions came to him as a message.

And you know, John Coltrane was one of the first musicians that actually said, publicly, that he played his music for the spirit of music. And when he reached a certain enlightenment, it changed the whole scene because of him being a vegetarian and meditating and everything. And everyone became more aware of health and balance and life. And there was a whole period where we all went through that to survive. But he was one of the main persons to really set an example. He didn't speak about it, he just set an example.

Ben: Around this time, you also went to Europe for the first time.

Don: Yes, I went to Europe with Sonny Rollins. And the way that happened was after playing with Ornette, and he made a change in his group. And I had went back to California and I was out there going crazy in Los Angeles. You know, California is the kind of place that if you play like somebody else, it's good. But if you're original, well then you have it real hard. And that's one of the reasons that Ornette really had it hard, you know?

But around the time when I was young out in California, there was musicians like Dexter Gordon and Wardell Gray and Hampton Hawes and Harper Cosby—who was one of my teachers—and the bass player Lawrence Marable.

And then I remember when Max [Roach] came out there with Clifford Brown and I met Clifford and became very close with him, and he really helped me a lot. He always said that to play a trumpet you have to really be in shape like an athlete, and he was always that way. And I remember he used to say "If you're reaching for high notes and you miss them, go back, keep going back, keep going back." And they would play songs like

"Jordu" and "Daahoud," I would call Brownie up the next day and he would give me the chords over the telephone so I could practice them.

Ben: That was back in the early '50s . . .

Don: Right. So actually, being in California at that time was special, because things were really happening. And me coming through that scene, with Wardell and Frank Morgan and going to Jefferson High School and Horace Tapscott was there, and all the musicians were on the scene at that time. I mean, I could sit up and just name names for ever. But you know, it was also the other scene over on the other side, the "Cool" side with Shorty Rogers and Chet Baker. I mean that scene was really alive in Los Angeles.

But when I went back the other time there was nothing really happening in the '60s. And I was going crazy. But Sonny Rollins came out and he had a group with Jim Hall and it a was more quiet, conventional type of group. And after the gig, Sonny felt like playing more so we used to drive and I would take him to different spots in California, by the sea and in the mountains, where we would practice together until the sun would come up. And so he said he would like to send for me in the future, you know, and I thought it would be wonderful, and then he left and went to San Francisco.

Then about two weeks later, he called and told me to come to play with him in San Francisco. And I had been out in California and I was really *out*, you know, I don't think I even had a horn. I was just like "down." So I finally got a horn together and went to San Francisco to play with Sonny Rollins at this club. And I had all these feelings in me and just one night I played, and I was "out." I played too much, or whatever. And the group was very cool. Cause you know Jim plays very good but he was very cool. And I needed the release to be free, because of what I was going through. And so Sonny, that night he paid me for the whole week and said, "Don, I don't think it's going to work out." [Laughs.]

So then I went back to Los Angeles and he said he would send for me. And he went back to New York and a month passed. And he called and he said, "Are you still free?" And I said yes. And he said, "Well, stay on cue." And I waited and waited and waited and finally he called. And the funny thing is that I had got a job at United Airlines, because I had wanted to get back to New York. So I got a job bustin' dishes. And I remember they had a magazine called *Mainliner*. And you know, like I'm going around taking things off the tables and this airline hostess is sitting up reading this magazine and I look at the cover and there's my picture on the cover!

So anyway, the job was too much because it was so far, the airport from where I lived, that by the time I would get there and get back home it was time to go to work again, you know. Because there was no busses.

The busses stopped in the ghetto late at night. So when Sonny sent for me to come, finally—and that's when we came to make this record at the Village Vanguard called *Our Man In Jazz*—when I was leaving Los Angeles on United Airlines, all the people that worked there saw me leaving. And they said, "Where you going? What do you think you're doing?" I said, "I'm going to New York," and they said, "Aw, you better get on back in the kitchen." [Laughs.] And I was getting on the ramp going to the plane, and you could see the kitchen from the ramp, and I waved at everybody. And they were standing there with their mouths open.

And I came to New York and we made this record. And Bob Cranshaw was playing bass and Billy Higgins and Sonny and myself. And no piano. And then that group went to Europe. And that was in '63.

We went to Rome first and stayed there for a week. And Sonny had suits made for everybody, tuxedos, and we took off for every major city in Europe. And that's when I met Albert Ayler.

Now when we were speaking in relation to the whole spiritual side of the music, Albert Ayler was one of those persons that really had—and to the end—there was something that he had to do and his life was dedicated to doing it. And when you heard his sound, it would make you feel you were in the church. It was real what we call gospel sound, but he was a jazz player. And he had been in the army and had got out of the army and gone to Russia. Then he came back and was living in Sweden. And Moki, my wife, they were very good friends. They inspired each other and it was quite a period around that time. Because Cecil Taylor came to Stockholm at that time. And Albert was staying in Stockholm and they played together.

And then afterwards, he came to Copenhagen. And that's when I met him, in Copenhagen. He was waiting on the sideline from the stage after the concert, and he asked me did I want to go to a session at the Montmartre. So I said sure, and so then we went to Montmartre and at this session was Don Byas, Dexter Gordon, I think Niels Henning was playing bass, at that time he was very young. And Albert and myself. So we played a jam, you know, a blues or something, and then they played a medley. And Albert didn't play on the first tune, just me and Dexter and Don and the rhythm section. But then they played a medley of ballads and everybody played a ballad. I think I played something like "I Cover The Waterfront" and then I heard Albert Ayler, his sound come. As I remember it—now me and Billy Higgins, we argue about it 'cause he was there too—and I thought he had played "Moon River" like [sings opening line], but it was like the primal scream. And that's a whole different thing about when the music actually started screaming. But at this particular session, I heard him and chills went up my spine. Billy Higgins says that he played "Summertime," which is a piece that Albert could really play too. But I remember that it was "Moon River."

But anyway, it was just like that same feeling when I first heard Ornette at that record shop and we could hear him two blocks away and Ornette was trying a number four reed. And it was like that same feeling of something that's so familiar, but it's for the first time. And that particular period was important for me because I met Albert, and I met Bud Powell, and I met Johnny Griffin in Stockholm.

I went back to New York after that in '63 and I came back to Europe six months later with John Tchicai and Archie Shepp, Don Moore and J.C. Moses. And then I came back to New York and then went back to Europe again with Albert. I remember Albert and Milford Graves came to my house and asked me if I wanted to go to Europe. And after that Albert came back to New York and I went to North Africa.

And that was my first time of going to another country where it's a different time and a different smell.

Ben: Was that when you encountered what many call "world music" for the first time, as opposed to American music taken to another country or European music?

Don: Yes. And that's a part of what I've been involved in the last few years also.

I mean, in growing up, my parents have American Indian background, so I've always been listening to different American Indian songs and trying to have that feeling in my whole way of life when I was young, making teepees and bow and arrows and my first drum. But going to North Africa was like the first time I was in a country where I lived . . . I went to Jujuka, which is a village *of* music. And there's a painter called Amrah, who lives in Tangiers who's from Jujuka, and he plays music too. And we met in Tangiers and he said, "You play music? You must go to Jujuka."

So when I went up there, it's in the mountains, you can't drive up there, you have to walk. And I remember you have to take sugar to the village and then the man of the store, they have a meeting where they accept it, and the sugar and you, you can stay. And they would have a little hut that you would go up to every night and play. You know, sit up and cut the kif and they would just play music almost all night. And they would be playing those pan or double reed instruments and the flute, which is the "ne," which you play from the top of the cane, of the bamboo.

And this is where I started really being interested and living with the music. And it's an Islamic country so I was really trying to study Islam at that time. Which is an endless study also. But the thing is, some of the older musicians would learn me songs, which has been inspiration for other music that I've done in later years. And later, Ornette has even been there and recorded with the pipes and some other English musician who has been there. I think it was Ginger Baker or something, many years ago.

But it was one of the great experiences in my life. Before that, living in America, I was always raised around people from Mexico so I always played in Latin bands. And then the whole harmony that's happened between the Latin people and black people, which is very important and has been an inspiration in jazz music all the time, with Charlie Parker and Machito and Dizzy Gillespie and George Russell. I studied with George Russell, and with Kenny Dorham, he's another teacher of mine. And Gunther Schuller, and, when we went to the Lenox School of Music, Herb Pomeroy who teaches orchestration at the Berklee School of Music. That was when me and Ornette went to the school in Berklee.

But the experience in North Africa was really strong enough for me to continue, and I became very much interested in playing the flute. And the voice. And after that, I returned to Stockholm. And in Stockholm I really realized from studying more. In Europe, there's many people there from other lands, and many Europeans that travel a lot and study other instruments. And I started, some kind of way in my Karma, finding them and we were finding each other.

Moki and I, we started something called "Organic Music." A movement incorporated. And we would go from city to city and give concerts. And we would spend time working with people in that city and then we'd have a concert that was open to the people of the community. And there would be us and other people that were playing different instruments or doing poetry or dance. And Moki would do the environment, and this was where we started really working on giving performances where we were using the environment. Moki would make tapestries and it was like ecology because she would find different pieces of fabric. And she'd always have a scissors and she would cut pieces of fabric and people would give her things, so the tapestries were not only paintings and environment and color—because Moki's concept is that color is light—but they would also be songs.

Because when I was teaching in Stockholm they would have classes and people teaching dance or Montessori school would all come to these classes. And we would be studying together. And you can't teach anyone how to improvise but you can make a format for people to be able to play, like an empty canvas. That's what I call some of the motifs or the forms. And I was always looking for the basic forms, like from the blues changes, the twelve-bar blues, to eight-bar blues changes, to certain Caribbean forms. And we would work from those forms and we would improvise from them.

So we started traveling around, and we traveled all the way down to France and gave performances and met a lot of the people in Europe that now are established in jazz music and now what we call "world music." And I remember like realizing the different ways of playing the bamboo. Like in Japan they play the shakahachi from the top and the sakina in South America they play from the top. We use the transverse from the side. And I started realizing how the bamboo has little pores. And when you're playing, you're not just playing through the tube but it's to vibrate the pores. And you really can understand that when you see a double-reed instrument like the oboe from different countries, from Slavic countries and the Arabic countries and even in Italy, parts of Italy and Sardinia, they have this double reed. Which is very powerful and electronic. And I even started putting the double reed in the trumpet at certain times because of the possibility of creating the drone.

So all these things we started exploring and studying.

Ben: And you became part of a group that really broke out the concept of "world music."

Don: Yes, there were musicians in Sweden that I was playing with that had studied in Africa. One musician named Ben Berger had studied in India. He studied tabla and merdungam, which is a drum that's played from both sides, where the table is like the same drum cut in half. Tabla is very classical and it's like tap dancing, it's related to the art of tap dancing. Which is a very high culture in America, tap dancing. And I always loved to dance. I felt that my expression in music was either to feel nature and have the picture of nature in my mind and heart and soul, or to express dance and movement with the phrases I would play.

You know, people always ask you, "What do you think about when you play?" and that's what I think about.

And there was Christa Botine who first showed me the Dusonguni, which is the "hunter's guitar" from Mali. It has six strings with a calabash and a skin over the top. And the strings are made from fishing nylons. And then you have a little rattle at the top. And you play different phrases, and it's either like a harp, like a bass, like a guitar or a snare drum, all in one. And Christa Botine, we played together and he learned me the traditional rhythm. And I have a friend that went to Africa, and went to the Mountain of the Moon with the pygmies, and when he was in Mali he had two dusongunis made and had them shipped to me in Sweden. And one day the mailman delivered this big box and so that was the beginning of when I started playing this instrument.

And I went to India to study voice. And you know, in Indian music they have certain tals of different beats, you know sixteen, or six, or seven, or even eleven and a half. But you know, you always have the cycle and you come back to the one. The one is called the "sum." And when you're playing a piece, you never finish at the end. If you have a cycle of sixteen, you never finish at the end of the sixteen, you finish on the one again.

So that to me that was something that was very exciting. In realizing how you play with the "one." And then getting involved in African music it became more clear to me how you come off the "one" or you come to the "one."

And Ornette's music is that way. That's like when I said we never count the song off because we always come off the one. You know, Paul Chambers was a bass player that when he played, there was something about his playing that was different, I felt. And that was because he would always play a little ahead. And that's something that makes the music transcend. It's to be able to know the "one" and how you work with the "one." And then this thing of "tones" and not just "notes." And that gets more into the human feeling.

Ben: It's like the music is always happening and we just have to tune in to it, or as Coltrane said, the music doesn't belong to anybody, it just passes through us all . . .

Don: You know recently I had an experience in Paris of meeting John Lee Hooker. I even played with him. I had my dusonguni back stage and I played it for John Lee Hooker, and right away he just started singing the blues with it. And so it shows how the essence of this instrument from Africa is related to the blues. I mean the real blues. It's really all one music.

* * *

Carla Bley (February, 1985)

Like her music, Carla Bley is totally disarming. She has a great mop of hair that she likes to hide behind when she talks, and you have the sensation that this cat-and-mouse game—from time to time she peeks out from behind the bangs to record your reaction to something she has just said—is just a part of the greater game of contradictions she expresses in her music. She is enigmatic both because she has proven herself to be a successful business woman in a business where very few women take control of the means of their own production, and because her compositions, while they reflect several contemporary idioms, are unquestionably unique to her own style. Her music is alternately thought of as avant-garde and very traditional, and the musicians who have worked with her over the years are very loyal, appearing as her private repertory group as she continues to expand her vision (while hiding behind those bangs). We spoke on a cold New York afternoon.

Ben: Carla, you are a one-woman industry at this point. You have the Watt Record label, the Jazz Composers Orchestra of America, the New Music Distribution Service. You're involved in all the mechanics of the recording industry as well as being an artist and a composer.

Carla: Yeah . . . but I don't really do anything but compose. There's people doing that for me, mainly Mike, my husband [trumpet player Mike Mantler]. He has a bent for it. He likes it.

Ben: When you say you compose, it's a process that conjures up a lot of images. There's the image of somebody sitting there with a quill and parchment scribbling it down, or maybe using a cassette recorder and singing ideas into it, or these days, using sequencers and synthesizers. Where do you fit into this spectrum?

Carla: No, it's quill and parchment.

Ben: One note at a time, huh?

Carla: Yes.

Ben: Your music has a refreshing quality—I realize this is subjective on my part—because it seems so "human"; there's generally a very serious emotional content to it but, quite often, there's also a really humorous aspect.

Carla: Yeah. I can't figure that out at all. I think I catch myself and then have to say something light to make up for saying something heavy.

Ben: Do you see yourself as a "child of the '60s"?

Carla: No! I didn't fit into the '60s at all. I wasn't a hippie. I was writing music.

Ben: At a school, or by yourself?

Carla: I never went to a school in my life. Actually, I was writing music at a farm in Maine, and they did call me a hippie. That's right. And I drove a Volkswagen bus, and I had long hair. I was a hippie in the '60s!

Ben: Aha!

Carla: Yeah, you got it.

Ben: Okay! What did you want to do? What was your goal at that point?

Carla: Ah, I didn't have thoughts or goals or anything.

Ben: You didn't see yourself as a formal composer at that point, or performer?

Carla: I haven't even seen myself yet. I can't be self-conscious. What am I doing and why have I been doing it all these years? Because it's, it's what I like to do, and I like to sit at the desk and figure out how something should sound, and that's what I've always done since I was a little kid. I don't know why.

Ben: Working with sounds?

Carla: Yeah. Hearing them, in my head.

Ben: When you were younger, how did you get them out?

Carla: I put them on pieces of paper, like I do now, with that quill. No, I was writing music, let's go back. I can't remember unless I start at the beginning, but I'll be really quick.

I didn't write music when I was born. I started, I think, when I was about . . . I started, I know I gave a recital when I was three on the piano. But we're from California, and so it wasn't any big deal. I played *Three Blind Mice* on the black notes with my little fists, and actually did it in concert. And before that night, I'd already been touring as a act where I held a little tin cup at church affairs and sang *This Little Light of Mine*, and then I'd pass the tin cup around afterwards, and people would give me money. But I had to give it to the church.

Ben: You were touring with a family group?

Carla: Yeah, my family were religious people, and they, ah, they toured around. It's California, you have to understand the mentality. It's strange.

Ben: Did your formal training begin when you were very young?

Carla: No, I've not had any training that I can think of . . .

Ben: You keep saying that. But how, then, did you learn to put your quill to the parchment, as it were, and write down the sounds you heard in your head? How did you know how to do that?

Carla: I don't know how I . . . Oh, my father. Okay, I really will go through the whole thing. When I was four, I stopped performing, and I actually started writing—I swear to you this is true—and the first piece of music I wrote, my father gave me a blank piece of manuscript and I wrote a million little dots on it. It was almost covered with dots. And my father said to me, "Nope, that's too many notes!" So I took half of them out, and he said okay. I think I still have that piece of paper. And then I wrote an opera when I was five. I'm not kidding you . . .

Ben: Now wait a minute. Did you know what these notes were when you wrote them down?

Carla: Sure, he taught me to play the piano when I was—I won't exaggerate—probably about two.

Ben: And you could read music at four well enough to notate it?

Carla: Oh, yes.

Ben: You say this as if I should not be surprised, but I've never heard anything quite like that.

Carla: Can't you do that? Didn't you do that when you were four?

Ben: No, not at four.

Carla: Oh, I guess it was weird.

Ben: Were you aware at that early age that what you wanted to be was a composer, that this was what you're doing?

Carla: Yes, and I was going to be one until I was about fourteen and I took a vocational test in school. And that came out saying I had no talent whatsoever for music. And I think they said I should be, ah, in the mechanical area. I can't remember the categories. But I know that I excelled in the mechanical area. And then I used to tell *wild* tales to my teacher. I said, well I either want to be, ah, I want to dig for gold, you know, like they used to do here in these hills. Or I want to be a deep sea diver, or, you know, things like that. But I thought, music is not a way to make a living. It isn't. And I'm sure many musicians would agree with me even today. Unless you're very lucky and way on the top of your pack. But I didn't think so, so I thought, well, I'll be a secretary. And I wrote down "secretary" into the space of what I wanted to be. But I misspelled it, and the teacher handed back the paper saying, "Not 'til you learn how to spell it." There was a lot of funny things that happened to me when I was a kid. Or at least, those are the things I remember.

Ben: How old are you now, in the story?

Carla: I'm now fifteen years old. And I was making a living as a musician all this time while I was trying to decide what to be. I was playing weddings and funerals, for the church, on the organ, and I was singing Handel's

Messiah in the choir, the alto parts. I was a little kid. I mean, that was before I was fifteen . . . I got it all wrong, because I was an atheist by the time I was twelve, I think.

Okay, so when I was about eight, I was singing Handel's *Messiah*, and playing organ for weddings and funerals. And no one thought anything about it. I mean, they didn't think I was too small or anything. And so church was everything. And I actually, before I quit church, played one of those Youth For Christ crusades. Ah, I don't think it, was it Billy Graham . . . yes, it *was* Billy Graham, and it was at the Oakland Auditorium, and I played the piano. I played variations on the hymn "Onward Christian Soldiers." And I played it as a tango, and I played it as a dirge, you know, I played it as a waltz, and every possible way to play "Onward Christian Soldiers." And then I dropped out of the church, and took up roller-skating.

Now we're getting to fourteen. I was a roller skater, for two years, and a good one too. I was skating in competitions and everything. But the highest I got was seventh in the state competition. And I liked music a lot, and skating was a way of expressing music then. I used to play; I didn't know anything about really serious classical music. I used to play the film score from *Gone With the Wind* or something, and choreograph a skate dance to it, stuff like that. And we also had a real organ player at the skating rink, and I think that's when I started noticing that there was another side to the organ, from him. A wonderful live organist at the rink every night. And, now, no I'm not in New York yet. I dropped out of school when I was fifteen, and, ah, dropped out of skating at sixteen. Now everything was behind me, and I think I had serious problems for about a year, of not being able to leave the house or not being able to sleep without my shoes on, or, you know, all kinds of incredible, almost mental illness type problems. And, ah, I was really fine as a child, I really was, nothing wrong with me as a child. And then for a couple of years I was almost ill, in my mind.

And then, I left home! And I drove to New York with . . . with . . . with, this is great, with the son of the Concert Master of the Boston Symphony Orchestra, who was also a freak. And we drove across the United States, with a credit card that we had borrowed, and a loaf of bread. And we had no money, and it was really rough. Slept in the car every night. And the reason we did this is because I wanted to go to Cafe Bohemia and hear Miles Davis. And I got there and went right to the Cafe Bohemia, and then my life really started.

That was like a sort of rough transition, and then I found out the kind of music that I liked and what I wanted to do. And I think then I was probably about seventeen. And I couldn't support myself doing hardly anything, since I wasn't trained for anything, although I could have thought of some musical job. So I became a cigarette girl at Birdland. And there I heard all the bands. I heard everybody, and I hardly ever sold any cigarettes. I'd just stand up near the bandstand and someone would say, "Ah, could I have a pack of Lucky's?" and I'd just be lost. I couldn't even sell very well. And I sold rabbits, toy rabbits.

Ben: On the streets?

Carla: No, at Basin Street. On the street? Basin Street. I had a tray around my neck, for customers who wanted a momento of having seen Gene Krupa or something. I sold rabbits in those days.

Ben: Are we in the '60s yet?

Carla: No, I think we're in the late '50s. Hmm. Oh, I don't remember, early '50s maybe. Something like that. And, it was before Birdland closed down. And, now, wait a minute . . .

Ben: This is an extraordinary story, Carla. I'm not quite sure why I haven't heard this before, but I mean, it really is an extraordinary story. And how it leads to somebody being an important jazz composer is probably as big a mystery to you as it is to me at this point.

Carla: It sure is. I really don't understand it at all.

Ben: Maybe that's part of the message. That, if you want to get to here from there, don't ask too many questions.

Carla: That's right. Don't become self-conscious.

Ben: Don't become self-conscious. Right. Which gets me back to my first question, which was "How do you compose"? And you say, well, it's a quill on parchment, but I suspect there are other things as well.

Carla: Well, oh, yes, there is something. The fantasy world. This is a technique that I used, I think, in the last three years, and I no longer use it. I would think of words for a song before I thought of the melody. It wasn't as though I was thinking of words for a song, it was as though I was thinking . . . "I gotta have this *feeling*." It could be anything, like: "I feel horrible, I want to die." Okay. So I would think, well what's the shape of that melody. And the words would dictate the melody. It was really simple. And I thought, well what's the next thing I want to say, and then I thought, well, "But I think I'll stick around." And "But I think I'll stick around" had another melody to it. And then of course the melodies always dictate the harmony. And the rhythm is dictated within the melody during that stage of it, so then you've got it all, just using words. Helped me for three years.

Ben: What made you transit out of that mode of composition?

Carla: Ah, I don't have, I don't have any human emotions at the moment.

Ben: I beg your pardon?

Carla: I don't have human emotions at the moment. Now I have more abstract emotions, musical emotions.

Ben: Could you amplify that in some way? What do you mean by that?

Carla: I don't have anything I want to say in language. I don't feel horrible, I don't want to die, and I don't think I'm going to stick it out. [Laughs.] I don't feel terribly happy either. So when that happens . . .

Ben: Well, aren't those human emotions?

Carla: Right, I don't have any of those right now.

Ben: Are you, and perhaps this is an aside, a practitioner of any spiritual discipline?

Carla: No.

Ben: Ah, let me get out of this place I'm in right now.

Carla: Go on, get out of it.

Ben: The fantasy world, well you may have stepped out of it, but you've also produced the "Carla Bley Audio." The "Carla Bley Audio" is "Carla reacts against videos by making an audio to promote her album *Heavy Heart*." And, a reaction against videos maybe, makes some sense in that videos take away your fantasy world, don't they? I mean, when you stare at somebody else's impression of what music is about, it relieves you of the ability or even the opportunity to explore your own imagination.

Carla: I didn't even think of that. That's true.

Ben: I've always felt that. It's a great imposition on my fantasy world to show me a video.

Carla: Oh, that's really true.

Ben: But in any case, you made an audio which tells *how* to listen to your music, specifically the song "Heavy Heart." How did the fantasy world, as we're speaking of it, generate that track? Did an image really generate that song, or was that after the fact?

Carla: That song is, the real truth is that that song had words first, and the words were: "There's plenty of fish in the sea, no, you're the only fish for me." And I knew that right there I had the song. And then, I knew it was for two people 'cause one person wouldn't say that. And so, I, it had a lot more words than that: "I'll show you one you like just as much . . . No, you're the only one that I could touch." I mean, it just went on and on with these little banal sayings. And they had beautiful melodies to them. And then I think I strayed, after I got into the bridge. I think it didn't fit any longer, but then I had the momentum to finish the song. And then I thought of it when we were recording it too, as, you know, not question and answer, but conversation between two instruments. And Hiram [Bullock] did the guitar part first, and afterwards, I did the synthesizer part, trying to match, you know, the way he was feeling it.

Ben: How do you get your musicians to work? You know, it sounds so organic to me, and very much like the way Charles Mingus was reported to have worked. For example, I know that Mingus, in many instances, specifically wouldn't show his musicians the music, but would sing them the parts he wanted instead. This would make them rely on their ears and their emotions rather than their eyes. Your compositions have that kind of emotional quality to them. Do you do that? I mean, I know you compose with pen and paper. But how do you get your players to emote?

Carla: Well, they emote first, and then I write it down. That's really what it is. I write for the musicians, and I know how they play. And I write so they emote first . . .

Ben: Hence the repertory group that you use on all your albums.

Carla: Yeah, really. Soon as I know about it, I don't like to let them slide through my fingers. I'm really putting them on paper, you know? Putting them on paper. And when someone in the band changes, I have a hard time, because I've got to totally rewrite the part to fit the new guy. They all have different, totally different, characters and sounds, and roles within the band.

Ben: You've brought some musicians out, I think also, ah, the work, for me, that Steve Slagel's done with you, I think is some of his most marvelous playing.

Carla: Oh, good, I'm glad you think that. He's a rough one to work with though, you know. I think the rhythm, the rhythm section guys are easier for me, because I'm sort of part of them, and that's, that's in my realm. And when I get to the horns, I don't know, sometimes the horns are difficult. But I love him, I put up with it.

Ben: He's not the vocalist on that infamous track of yours that had to do with beating his lover or something, was he? What was that track?

Carla: Oh, that's in all my songs. It could have been any song. [Laughs.]

Ben: Yes, what is this undercurrent of violence in your music anyway? Let's talk about this theme of sadomasochism and murder because you don't seem to be that way in person.

Carla: I told you, I came from California.

Ben: Oh, that explains it.

Carla: No, but the serious things are a joke. The worse they are, the more we make fun of them. It's just called irreverence. And that sort of tickles me. I like irreverence. About myself and about other people. I try not to be rude, so I don't talk about world figures or anything, but I'll stop no place if it has to do with me or my friends.

Ben: In a way, that kind of irreverence is very much in the jazz tradition, I think. Phil Woods was talking the other day about being on the bus, traveling with the big bands in the old days and what that was all about. And this constant stream of irreverence was very much a part of it. Of course, there aren't any busses anymore, not many big band road gigs . . .

Carla: Oh, listen, there were busses until last July.

Ben: You were on the bus?

Carla: I've been on the bus 'til last July. There are still busses, and now they have video machines on them, full bars, bunks, showers, and toilets.

Ben: Busses are gettin' better.

Carla: Oh, boy, they are. Yeah, no I don't want to be on the bus anymore. I'm just writing. I quit touring.

Ben: Do you plan to perform less and less? Is that part of your plan for the future?

Carla: I'm going to be playing none and none. Not at all.

Ben: You aren't going to perform?

Carla: No! I don't want to perform. I just want to be alone.

Ben: You don't like performing, obviously.

Carla: No, I don't like it. And it's stupid, 'cause I really can do it good, too. I don't like it. Unless it's real.

Ben: What do you mean?

Carla: Well, it's real the first time you play a piece, and maybe it's real for four more times and then you're just acting. And it's real the first time you talk to an audience, and you can't say the same thing to them. If you say the same thing the second night, it's not real, and they won't think it's interesting, and you won't be able to project it to them. So then you have to think of something else. I hate acting. Of all kinds. And so, I'm not gonna act anymore. I'm going to do things, where I play a piece once, maybe twice. And then when I know it, the band knows it, why do we have to keep playing it?

Ben: At that point will you record it, or will you record it first?

Carla: I'll record it afterwards, ideally. Play it a couple of times and then record it. And then forget about it.

Ben: Can you afford not to perform live?

Carla: That costs me so much money, performing alive. Are you kidding, I'm going to be rich, man. [Laughs.] Ten piece band, nine piece crew, plane tickets, four star hotels. Forget it, I can't afford it anymore.

Ben: I think in a way, that's probably really too bad. I haven't heard many contemporary jazz artists that represent a new kind of cabaret tradition, which is what I hear in some of your music. Particularly the live record that you've made, *I Hate To Sing*. There's a lot of theatrics involved with it. It deals with this kind of black humor that we're talking about. And I've often thought that if jazz could incorporate more of a kind of a Kurt Weil tradition, these elements of theatrics and humor, not that it would become more popular, but that it would make a statement that perhaps it hasn't been able to make.

Carla: Yeah, I don't know, I'm trying to move away from that, the theatrics. But my tendency is towards that too. But last night I went to Sweet Basil's and I heard the World Saxophone Quartet, and they had all that. Ah, I think a lot of good music has that in it.

Ben: You say you're moving away from it, but at the same time, you recently put out a record called *I Hate To Sing* which is full of theatrics and dark humor. What about the song "Murder" from that album? It's like the "Perils of Pauline" or something, with members of the band acting out roles . . .

Carla: Oh, no, now America knows about that side of my personality. It's very embarrassing. I sold that record to Japan, thinking that it would never be heard over here. And all of a sudden, it's everywhere. And it's quite embarrassing. We don't do that anymore. We're very, very polite, we play serious music. We don't sing, and, ah, that's like a stage we went through, and, oh, I'm glad it's over.

Ben: I don't believe any of this Carla. I think these theatrics are very much a part of your personality. But, you know, what's also a part of your personality seems to be this kind of "shade behind the shade behind the shade." There are many levels that you're projecting at once. And somewhere back there, I suspect, is not this neurotic, hesitant personality at all, but a very focused person.

Carla: You're wrong! You know, everything I've told you today is the truth.

Ben: Oh, I'm sure of that. Well, I'm not *sure* of that, but I feel that.

Carla: Good, I just wanted you to know that. And when I say that I'm embarrassed about that record, it's true. Although, deep down, somewhere, I like it. You know. It doesn't mean I'm not embarrassed about it, but there's something about that I think is very positive and fun, and every time I listen to it myself, I just laugh, you know? Not that piece in particular, but like when Dee Sharp sings *I Hate To Sing*, I just laugh every time.

Ben: Why are you embarrassed? Are you serious?

Carla: Of course I am. It's a horrible mistake to let that side of me come out when I'm trying to "go straight." [Laughs.] Set me back five years. God!

Ben: Are you saying you want to erase this part of your musical personality?

Carla: Yes.

Ben: Why?

Carla: Because I think that you're only allowed to do one thing very well in life, because it's so short and there are so many people on the earth. If you stick out at all, and by sticking out, I mean, if the world pays you to be alive, if you're a musician and you don't have to be a waiter, then you have to do one small thing very well. And if you go through too broad of an area, that is really self-indulgent. I don't want anything but to do one thing as good as it can be done. But I don't think I'm there yet. And that's gonna be, after my next record, which is a another tangent, it's gonna be writing for a large group of horns. I haven't decided about the instrumentation exactly yet, but I think it'll be about twenty people.

Ben: The part of your personality that is the humorous part is, in some ways, the part that is easiest for people to get to—maybe for cheap reasons, maybe not for artistic reasons—but they can identify with the comic quality of "I Hate to Sing." The vocals have kind of a fey quality to them; there's a humor underlying a very serious, very real feeling. Like your song "Murder," it's "he's there *now*, what about *me*." They're not past tense songs, they're not songs about feelings you might have had once. They're songs set very much in the present tense. I feel this *now*. And this is an unusual, engaging quality for vocals to have.

Carla: Can I tell you what that song is about? Remember the Met murder? At the Metropolitan, the violinist was killed by the guy who worked in the stage crew? I wrote this song the next day. Sometimes things strike me from the newspaper. And I do a song about them. So, I just wanted you to know how that song was written, 'cause you're trying to understand how I write music and I'm telling you; that all of this is the frivolous part. And it's over. Now I'm going to get down to business and be serious.

Ben: Are you, ah, primarily composing for recorded idioms now? I mean, if you're not going to perform, yourself, and I assume that your troop of players is not going to go out there without you, are you focusing and limiting yourself to recorded works?

Carla: No. I've written one hour of music for a sixteen piece orchestra called the Composers and Improvisers Orchestra. I've been working on that for five straight months. It's going to be performed in Seattle. And it's not gonna be recorded.

Ben: But you won't be performing? You'll be conducting or helping them?

Carla: I'll be conducting. And then, two months after that I go to Switzerland and work with a bunch of Swiss musicians, writing music for them, and arranging their own compositions, and that will not be recorded either.

Ben: I stand corrected, but you're still not performing, and you don't want to perform.

Carla: No! Don't want to!

Ben: Let's talk about another composer, a kind of contemporary of yours in that he's writing in a nontraditional way, using folk elements and a kind of repertory ensemble. I'm thinking of Abdullah Ibrahim. Are you familiar with his record *Ekaya*?

Carla: Wow! That was great. It's a much lighter thing than I've heard him do. I thought, when I first met him, that he had such a weight inside of him, and you could hear it in his music, and when I'd go to listen to him, I'd come away feeling very dark, you know, sad in a way. And he must have come to terms with something. That is so much fun to listen to.

Ben: The way he works with his musicians, according to an article that I've read, indicates that he does it similarly to the Mingus method, where he sits down at a rehearsal and plays a figure and then waits for the musicians to absorb various aspects of it, and to then express their personalities through the melody. So the arrangement will evolve.

Carla: And I've told you I do exactly the opposite.

Ben: Yes, you write for the musicians once you know them. And yet I was going to make the point that to my ears his music feels very similar to the way your music feels. Very spacious, very emotional.

Carla: Well, I envy the way he does it. If he can get the musicians to help him afterwards, I think it's easier, and I would like to explore that. I would like to leave some places open and just tell them, "Well, play this. It sounds like the helpless flapping of wings." And then I'm sure they'd come up with wonderful things. But I just don't have enough trust. I've got to write out the helpless flapping of wings.

Ben: Puts a lot of responsibility on you doesn't it?

Carla: Yeah. It does, but it just shows a lack of trust generally in the world around me. Having to create all that order out of all that chaos all the time. And I think most composers are a lot more relaxed than I am about it. And it's something that I've learned recently, and I'm definitely gonna try incorporating it.

Ben: Just to relax more?

Carla: Yeah. Don't figure it all out, you know? When I go into a situation as the doctor, the people don't have to figure it out. I have to figure it out for them. So if I go into some place, there are gonna be doctors there that are gonna figure it out for me, 'cause jazz musicians are doctors. They're willing to perform their medicine on any piece in the world. And it's amazing how underpaid they are for it. They should get composer's royalties.

Ben: Hearing you talk about the musicians as "music doctors," it's a little surprising that you never opened up the arrangements more . . .

Carla: Why haven't I done it? I never knew until a couple of years ago that that's the way other people did it. The people at this orchestra in Seattle told me "have an hour of music." And I've been writing, constantly, fourteen hours a day, for five months. And I found out just last week that Gil Evans writes basically a huge lead sheet, and maybe makes a little notation next to the top notes, as trumpet, and then lower on maybe he'll put "tuba" next to a line. And the guys just like, sort of, you know, read it off of a lead sheet type of a thing, and add their own personalities. So Gil is saving his time for the creative process and leaving all of that nonsense that I occupy months of my life with to the musicians, who are more than willing to do it for someone they love. And they love him, and maybe they love me by now, you know. Maybe, at the beginning they didn't, but maybe they've learned to love me. Maybe they'll do it for me.

Ben: You're also using the new synthesizer technology. With the MIDI interface, you have the ability to use a computer program to do your scoring off of a keyboard. I mean, you can just play it off of a DX-7 and it goes through the MIDI interface and into your Mac and it comes out orchestrated. It just takes a minute.

Carla: Oh, but you're really cheating yourself when you do it that way. I mean, some of my best ideas come in the copying of parts. My ideas come all the way along, from the very beginning to the very last note on, with the ink on the page. And if they do it with computers that way, they're really robbing themselves of last minute changes and ideas and things. I'm not at all curious about that. But I do have all the machines.

Ben: Parchment and quill.

Carla: Parchment and quill for me. I don't have a green thumb, I have a black thumb.

Ben: Backwards into the future. Speaking of backwards into the future, have you heard the Wynton Marsalis album *Hot House Flowers?* Wynton of course is very dedicated to the jazz tradition, and this is his version of standard tunes with lush orchestrations. I believe he might have been thinking of albums like *Clifford Brown With Strings* when he made it.

Carla: I don't like it. I heard it and I don't like it.

Ben: Why not?

Carla: Well, I bought it immediately because I think he's marvelous, and, I really expected a lot from it. I thought the strings were shabby. Listen to the strings.

Ben: Do you not like string writing as a rule with jazz?

Carla: No, I like string writing, but I like it when it means something sociologically. I think that saxophones and trumpets should consider strings as enemies, not as friends. And I think that Wynton Marsalis was friendly towards his strings, and that was a mistake. I think he liked it. My favorite album with strings was the Charlie Parker album.

Ben: Well that's interesting because a lot of people think that the string writing on that album is excessively corny and, in a way, demeaning to Charlie Parker's playing. It's really the meeting of tremendous opposites, this passionate saxophone and this hoky string writing. And you say that was your favorite?

Carla: I love it. That's because Charlie Parker knew they weren't his friends. Those strings were just doing a record date, you know, and they didn't care about him at all, and that's the way it should be. And he didn't care about them. I think that I like the hoky strings because it's poignant.

Ben: Well it sounds to me like you like the album that Bird made with strings because there's a truth there that refers to a lie that's going on.

Carla: Yes!

Ben: And perhaps you don't like the Wynton record with strings because you feel it's a kind of a lie out front...

Carla: Referring to truth.

Ben: Referring to the truth.

Carla: Yeah.

Ben: Who are some of your favorite "classic" string arrangers?

Carla: I think that Ernie Wilkins is an unsung genius. Why doesn't anybody know his name? I mean, he's just been behind the scenes all of his life, and maybe it's for the best. What a good writer, how tasteful he is.

Ben: I think maybe because he's done a lot of film writing, or whatever, and people tend to dismiss that kind of work. It happened to Benny Golson too and to Oliver Nelson, anybody who's done Hollywood writing. People forget the deeply serious part of who they are and what they do.

Carla: Well, I like the deeply serious quality of selling out. I think that musicians get a beautiful poignant edge to their music when they do sell out. It's great. I love it.

Ben: What about you?

Carla: Me? I'll sell out. What does that mean actually? I'm just using the word lightly. I guess it means the sadness of doing things for money. And the sadness comes out in the music. They just pay me to do what I do. So I don't have that edge yet, I guess.

Ben: I'm enchanted by the concept that there's something very positive and constructive, or at least poignant, as you say, about what happens to people when they sell out. Because as I sit here and talk with you, you seem as far from being an overtly commercial artist as I've ever encountered. Are you drawn to trying that, or wanting to have that experience?

Carla: I'm drawn to tragedy like everyone.

Ben: Do you want to put yourself in the middle of it?

Carla: No, I don't want to do it. I'd just rather watch other people do it. It's pretty painful.

* * *

David Murray (October, 1984)

David Murray is a modern practitioner of the saxophone tradition. He started out playing church music and r&b, and then, bypassing the bebop idiom altogether, landed firmly in what has alternatively been called the avant-garde or, during the '60s, the "new thing" of jazz. He likes to push the physical boundaries of the horn and combine the romanticism of the pre-bebop era, the ballad and swing styles, with the extravagance of the so-called "free" style of playing. By connecting both ends of the jazz spectrum—joining the heightened expressionism that goes back to the very roots of New Orleans jazz with the conscious intellectualism of the contemporary avant-garde—he has helped redefine what "traditional" means in the jazz world. David Murray has been an outspoken and active contributor to the saxophone vocabulary, and continues to enjoy himself immensely while on stage.

Ben: We know you through your solo recordings, your duo, trio, quartet, quintet, big band, all sorts of formats, and, of course, through your participation with The World Saxophone Ensemble, which is perhaps the best known "a cappella" horn group in the world. And while you're thought of as a quintessential New York player, I know you came to New York when you were a young man from the San Francisco area. What was the drawing power for your first trip to New York?

David: I originally came to New York to do a study on the saxophone. I was going to school at Pomona College and Stanley Crouch was teaching there, and William Russell was the head of the music department, and Bobby Bradford was teaching there as well. I came here to do a study from 1958 to the present of the saxophone. 1958 I chose because that was when Ornette Coleman arrived. Studied this newer form of the saxophone, dealing with more of an atonal approach or, quote, avant-garde, just dealing with horn players who played a little different than the established traditional horn sound. And so my objective when I came was to interview people, interview Ornette, interview Cecil Taylor, interview Dewey Redman, people like that, which I did. And I would go to concerts, and I would do a critique of the concert. All of which I compiled into what I hoped would one day become a book.

But when I got to Dewey Redman, he said to me, he said, "Why don't you put down that pen and pick up your horn?" He said, "You know, you really just need to play, and forget all the rest of that." And I took it as, ah . . . I don't know, I took it as he was serious, 'cause I had met him out in California, so I knew he wasn't just saying that, you know. So that's what I did.

Ben: Had you played at college in California?

David: Oh yes, I've been playing all my life. My mother was a great pianist in the Sanctified Church, Catherine Murray, a great influence, and my father was as well, him being a guitarist, and all my brothers played clarinet, and my cousins all played trumpet. Everybody played or sang. So, when I was thirteen or fourteen, I had a fifteen piece review . . .

Ben: Is that right? The David Murray Band?

David: David Murray and the Magic Castilations. Then that group developed into a group they called the Notations of Soul, and I played with them. And Rodney Franklin, who's a pianist, who's become well known, at that time he was my protégé. And we all in the Berkeley area, and we backed up different singing groups and, you know, different people. In fact, during that time, we wrote the song "Love Machine," which The Miracles stole and went on to record. We had a very good band.

Ben: Were you playing outside solos, as well, in the context of an r&b band, or straight r&b?

David: Well I think at that time, my model was Maceo Parker, and I always thought, and I still do today, that everything he does is totally avant-garde. Although he plays in different contexts, with the Funkadelics and, previously, with James Brown. He say: "Maceo, come blow your horn." They used to call me "Murray-o." So there was a connection there. And then, as I got a little older, fifteen to sixteen, I got a little trio together. We used to play with an organ player named Charles Green. We used to play around the Berkeley area, at all the Shakey's Pizza Parlors, you know. We'd be playing stuff like, real corny stuff, but we kinda jazzed it up. Like "Taste of Honey" or something. Next thing you know, we're swinging it. So at that point, I guess I was playing jazz, but we were playing corny songs. But we were jazzing them up, you know.

And then, as my interests grew, and especially as I got more away from the church, because as you know, most kids, when they're between thirteen and fifteen or sixteen, they . . . I know especially me, religion was really prominent in my family. You had to really always go to church all day Sunday. And I always had to go to church four nights a week, especially my family, because we were the music of the church. So we had to be there if nobody else was there. But I learned a lot in that time, you know. In fact I remembered the date I got my first saxophone. I knew I was going to play the saxophone. I mean, I'd always heard the saxophone before I'd played it. I played piano before I played sax. But I always wanted a sax, because we had a trombone, a trumpet and a clarinet in the church, but there was no sax. So, I mean, it was obvious that I was going to play the saxophone. So the first night that I got it, I went to church and played all the songs, like, you know, right off. I have a very good ear, which I think is the key to my success. If I can hear it, I usually can play it.

Ben: You also must have had a natural embouchure to be able to walk in the first day and play some songs.

David: Yeah, yeah, well you know, I kind of messed around with my brother's clarinet a little bit too, you know. I mean, that's probably why it took me so long to pick up the clarinet. I didn't pick the clarinet until I really came to New York. Because my brother was really good on the clarinet. He could have been maybe an Alvin Batiste or something on the clarinet. But he decided to sell Japanese cars. Therein lies . . . But we're all very talented in our family. But nobody really takes it serious, you know. I mean, it's like music is something that you just kind of threw away. It was never really that important.

I remember times . . . This sounds crazy but, you know, California's kind of corny, especially then, but I remember my first arrangement was when I was in the sixth grade. I did an arrangement of "Downtown." You know, [sings a couple of measures]. And it was just for the saxophones, just the saxophone row. So it was all these alto players and tenor players, one bari, soprano player. I arranged this piece, you know. But, I mean, when I was arranging it, I always had to . . . When I was at home, I would either have to play the music that was from the school or the music that was from church. I could never really jazz it up in the house, you know, because my mother was: "What are you doin'! Go back to that other stuff." So they're coming up the driveway and I'm writing down [sings another two measures of "Downtown"] and then, I hear 'em come up in the driveway, and the next thing I know I'm runnin' [sings] "Amazing Grace." [Laughs.]

Ben: You were taking music seriously, though, even though the others weren't.

David: Yeah, I was thinking about the sound, and when we stood up and played it, everybody dug it, and everybody clapped.

Ben: So that was the first incarnation of a World Saxophone Ensemble.

David: Well, I don't know, maybe so.

But I had a lot of good influences from my parents, and from the church, although at the time I didn't think they were that good. We used to have a trio, my brother and my cousin on trumpet, and my brother on clarinet, and myself. We used to go around and just stand up a cappella, and just blow, you know. It was real nice. We got a little reputation during that time too.

Ben: It's interesting to me that you started out in an r&b band, as many of the so-called avant-garde players did, including Ornette Coleman, and then decided to study the history of the horn rather than play professionally, and then finally to have a horn player like Dewey Redman say, "Hey man, put down the notebook and take up the instrument." I mean, this is a very wide circling of the musical territory.

David: Well, I was always playing, I never did stop taking up the instrument. But I think because I had a notepad there, he might have thought that. My intentions when coming to New York were to play, but my passport to New York was to do this study and then I was supposed to bring it back and continue school out there.

Ben: Did you ever go back?

David: I didn't go back. That was the thing that Dewy impressed upon me. That I should pay more intention to my horn and forget the notebook stuff. Although I was practicing very diligently during that time, but maybe he didn't know it.

Ben: What sort of things did you discover in your study of the saxophone tradition?

David: Well, traditionally speaking, I always liked the breathiness of a Ben Webster, and the lyricism of a Lester Young, you know. And I liked the dexterity of Charlie Parker, and I liked the elusiveness of Ornette Coleman, and I liked the spirit possession that I heard in maybe the newer guys that were on the scene or had passed, like Archie Shepp and Albert Ayler and Dewey Redman. I liked a certain spirit that was projected through the newer horn players that I thought had absorbed the tradition. And my whole concept was to try to put it all together. I hadn't heard a musician, up to that point when I came to New York, who had consciously done that, and I think that was kind of my objective, to put that all together, and deal with some of these things. Like Eric Dolphy dealt with when he's dealing with the fourth octave and, sometimes, fifth octave. I thought that maybe I could use that, and use a little bit of Ben Webster's stuff, and maybe a little bit of Lester Young's stuff, and little bit of Ornette, little bit of Albert, little bit of Archie, little bit of everybody. Then maybe it might come out David Murray.

Ben: When you're talking about that fourth octave, I guess we should note that's considered off limits for saxophone players. Some would say there is no fourth octave on the horn, that the horn stops . . .

David: You know they say, on paper, you're supposed to stop like on an "F" on the sax, but that's so low to stop, it doesn't make sense, you know. And in classical music, they don't even put you that high, because traditionally the saxophone is an out-of-tune instrument to begin with. So they very rarely put you higher than that F. But then the G on the saxophone is a very pretty note. I mean, everything is open, you know, except this one finger. So I get off on playing higher. I go to the G# and the A and the B flat, even the C or C#. But, what I usually try to do is, I like to express things. Like sometime I'll express the phrase in the lower octave and then I interpolate to another octave. And then, if I can, I'll keep going and try and interpolate in another octave. You know, like a continuous run.

Those are some of the things I was experiencing when I was writing this thesis. But just to continue a little bit, on the *Morning Song* album I do a version of "Body and Soul," and getting into some of the things I was thinking about before, about Ben Webster and Coleman Hawkins, just that breathiness, you know, when I actually play the head on "Body and Soul" on the record, the way I play it is actually part of Ben Webster's solo. And then I do my own solo. It gives you something to work with rather than just playing it straight down. You know, it makes it more soulful to me, if I could add a few little interpolations to it. Like to me, that's mixing the old with the new. And I'm sure that Ben Webster and Coleman Hawkins did that all the time, too. In fact, to me there's nothing more avant-garde than Ben Webster sucking the spit out of his horn. I mean, to me that's one of the most *out* sounds that I've ever heard. You talk about *out*.

And you know, Bobby Bradford told me he was in a situation with Ben one time. He said, "Hey Ben, can you, ah, suck some of the spit out the horn, you know, so it won't sound so spitty?" Ben says, "Well, what-do-ya mean, spitty? That's my sound!" You know, I mean, he's serious. I could live with that, you know. I like that. Because the man sounds like he sounds, and he's not going to let nobody in the studio tell him how to make him sound. He knows what he sounds like. And a lot of times, musicians get jammed up when they go into the studio. Some of the greatest musicians get real tight when they go into a studio, because they let the studio people dictate to them. The next thing you know they're reduced to being a little boy, and they can't do what they do best, which is lead, and play, and . . .

Ben: Be themselves . . .

David: Yeah, be themselves. So first of all, when I go into a studio, I have to have it understood who's in charge. I take great pride in producing my own records. Giovanni Bonandrini has become the record producer of the year, based on all the records that I produced for him. So I don't get credit for it maybe, in *Down Beat*, and all that, but the finest albums that I've made for his label, I've produced them myself.

Ben: Well, maybe that's a sign of a good producer, letting an artist go ahead and do it . . .

David: That's right! Just go on in your pocketbook and let the musician go and do the music. That's fine. I mean, that's wonderful. I think that's great.

Ben: David, I like the way you're talking about stretching the saxophone tradition back toward the past and out toward the future in one continuous gesture. These are not separate things. Craig Harris, when we were talking about this, said, "There's no old jazz/new jazz; there's just this music," and this music is continually new.

David: It is. I mean, in history, the people who have performed the blues, I mean, you hear all kind of sounds that they call now "avant-garde" sounds, just from listening to old blues albums. And these guys, they would be playing some licks that would be *out*, you know, but they'd be kidding. They'd do something like this . . . [sings an "avant-garde" lick] . . . Then they'd laugh or something. But now we're *serious* when we do that, you know? [Laughs.]

So now sometimes I play the blues and I'll do that, and then I'll laugh, you know, just to kind of let people know that, "Yeah, it really ain't all *that* serious." Like sometimes you go to concerts, you got guys there, they're so serious and they play a note, and they just look at you, and then they stop. Then they play another one, and then they look like its supposed to have been so heavy what they just did. But all they did was just put a little air through the horn. So my whole thing is to do it on a high level of art, and to have some fun. If I can't have fun, get me off the stage. I could be mundane at home, you know. But when I'm on the stage, I want to have fun. I think that's why people probably like to see me, 'cause when I'm playing, I'm having a ball. I don't feel like I'm working, I'm just enjoying myself. It's like in football players, those cats get out there and they get pumped up and they just want to *hit* somebody. They're having fun. They're getting paid a lot of money for it, but, when it comes down to it, they're having fun.

Ben: David, you talk about having fun, and before you mentioned Eric Dolphy as somebody who you modeled your playing after, and his playing always had a tremendous sense of humor about it. I think of your relationship to him particularly on the *David Murray Quartet* record where you play "Jitterbug Waltz," the Fats Waller tune that Eric had recorded. It's obviously a "cute" tune, and you played it a little prettier than Eric did, but the fact that you did it and you even used the bass clarinet, like Dolphy, brings up the comparison.

David: Well, gee, when it comes to the clarinet, just to be mentioned in the same breath as Eric Dolphy is a honor. I'm very shy when it comes to the clarinet, always have been, 'cause my brother was a good clarinet player, like I mentioned before. But clarinet has a natural tendency to go to 3/4. I mean, 3/4 is a great time meter for a bass clarinet especially.

And I play it more like a saxophone than probably most clarinet players do. But guys that were around me, like Ed Blackwell and Billy Higgins, I use them in my bands a lot, and they say, "Why don't you play 'Jitterbug'? You know, Eric used to play it all the time." And I was scared to play it, 'cause, you know, I've never really studied Eric Dolphy consciously. Just listened to his things. Not like I've studied saxophone players like Paul Gonsalves or somebody. I've listened to him, I've maybe picked up a few things, but I've never really slowed the record down, like I did with the saxophone. So I was kinda scared to get into things that Eric did on the bass clarinet. But these guys they kinda pushed me: "Come on, man, play the clarinet more," you know, "play it half the time." Instead of, like, a fifth of the time. "Gimme at least two songs a set on clarinet." And that encouraged me to do it, because, personally I really didn't think I was that good on the clarinet.

I still don't really think I'm that good. In fact, my humility just surfaced when I started playing with the clarinet ensemble, The Clarinet Summit, with Alvin Batiste and John Carter and Jimmy Hamilton. We did one gig in particular, the first time we got together. We rehearsed for three days, twelve hours a day. And I just couldn't believe the dexterity of these musicians. I learned more in that period of time than I've ever learned on the clarinet. And I think that in itself is what gave me a boost to just continue playing it, because they liked what I played.

Ben: What sorts of clarinet things did you pick up from those guys, because obviously they are the masters?

David: Well, I learned some false fingerings, some new fingerings that they showed me. I learned how to maintain my embouchure. I learned how to connect the different octaves of the clarinet. I learned how to play cycles of fourths on the clarinet. I learned how to anchor a group. Like, comparing that group to maybe the World Saxophone Quartet, Hamiet Bluiett's position in the World Saxophone Quartet, he sounds like a bass player at times. And I learned how to do that by playing with the clarinet ensemble, as well as listening to Bluiett. But I really realized how hard his job in the group is when I did that with the clarinet ensemble, because they really had me being a bass player, and I was boom, boom, boom, boom, boop-ba, boom, boo, boo . . . and it was nice, you know, because it opened up a whole new thing for me. Like when I listen to Howard Johnson now, he understands the whole philosophy of the bass, he plays the baritone and the contra-bass clarinet and he understands it from the perspective of a bass player.

Ben: The clarinet as an instrument sort of fell out of favor after the 1930s, when Benny Goodman and Artie Shaw and all the swing bands were replaced by the beboppers, who played saxophones. But it seems that the clarinet is definitely coming back. I know it from Jimmy Hamilton's re-emergence with the Clarinet Summit that you mentioned, particularly after you recorded the *The Clarinet Summit* album. And John Carter's certainly working very hard on it, as is Eddie Daniels. Do you also feel strongly that it's important that we bring this instrument back? That the voice of the clarinet is important to modern music?

David: Definitely. And people are finding out now about all of the closet clarinet players that have been playing saxophone all these years. Like, for instance, Bluiett, people don't talk much about his clarinet playing. But he's a fine clarinet player, as is Anthony Braxton. There are lot of good clarinet players out here.

Ben: As an historian, why do you think the clarinet was more popular in the '30s and became less popular during the past forty years, and why do think it may re-emerge again now?

David: Well, I think it has a lot to do a lot with New Orleans, for one thing, and I think it has a lot to do with Sidney Bechet, for another, because, prior to Sidney Bechet . . . They call Coleman Hawkins the king of the saxophone. But I think maybe Sidney might have been a little bit before that, him being a soprano player. They related to soprano probably more than to the clarinet. And in a way, he kind of just slid the soprano in there. So next thing you know, they thought they were hearing the clarinet, but they were hearing the soprano. And in New Orleans, I think it was probably easier to get a clarinet, plus they had all those metal clarinets during that time . . .

Ben: So you think it's got something to do with the spirit of New Orleans. One thing I'm wondering about, too, is that you get the emergence of people like Benny Goodman and Artie Shaw, the really show-biz-pop kind of jazz stars. And so the other players, maybe perhaps the more serious art players, took up the saxophone for exactly that reason, as a reaction against that.

David: Probably. I'm not sure. But I would say that Sidney Bechet probably had a lot to do with it.

Ben: Talk for a minute, if you would, about the difference between playing with the Clarinet Summit and the World Saxophone Ensemble. They're both similar in that they're without rhythm sections, they're stand-up reed ensembles. But they're obviously very different.

David: With the Clarinet Summit, they're different from any group that's probably ever existed, because of the high level of musicianship of those three other clarinet players. I mean, I've never played with anybody who played so well in tune. Who are such excellent musicians in every way. Who are able to project that instrument. Lot of clarinet players don't have great projection, but all these guys, they really project. The fact that Duke Ellington had Jimmy Hamilton in his band, on and off for what, twenty, twenty-two years, that's amazing in itself. I mean, when Jimmy left the band, that composition was dead. I mean, nobody else was gonna touch it, 'cause that was Jimmy's piece. It was just like Johnny Hodges, when he left the band, that was it. Nobody's gonna fill that void for him in that band. The clarinet ensemble is different. Now I've heard other groups that have taken up a similar type of format, but I think it's the individuals involved that really make it what it is. I've heard four clarinet players with the same instrumentation play and they don't sound the same. They'll have excellent compositions as well, but when they finish playing the compositions, there's nothing else happening. Each person in this group can play by themselves for an hour or two at the drop of any hat, you know. I think that the fact that they're excellent soloists is probably what makes *both* of the groups.

Ben: The World Saxophone Quartet being more of an ensemble then?

David: With the World Saxophone Quartet, we've been together longer, and we've been on long tours. And our sound, really, the first year or so we were together, we were just kinda sounding like four guys playing together that really weren't helping each other out. But now we've all assumed various roles. And I know my function in the group. My function is more like a piano or guitar or something. And Bluiett's function is a lot like a bass. And the two altos function is to play things melodic on the top and do different tricks and things. But the World Saxophone Quartet developed out of touring. We went on a tour for five weeks in Germany, and when we came back, I think we were a different group. And at that point, that's when we really became the World Saxophone Quartet. Before that, we were just four guys, just up there blowing, trying to out-blow each other. We still do that, of course, but now we do it constructively.

Ben: The World Saxophone Quartet has some active composers also . . .

David: Yeah, well you know, Julius Hemphill is one of the top five composers that I've ever heard. We'll get on a plane and he'll have this notepad. By the time we've finished that hour flight, he's passing out parts. And the paper was blank before that. I mean, he's written the whole composition and passing out parts by the time we get off the plane. Okay, now, to me, that's the sign of a genius. I've never seen anybody that talented in that area. So I have a lot of praise for Julius' writing.

Ben: He wrote a song on one of your recent albums called "My First Winter" which features you almost exclusively . . .

David: Well him having such big ears, what he basically did was he just heard my sound and really just copped what he thought was my most exciting areas of the horn. And he wrote that piece right in that horn. The piece was right in the horn. I didn't even have to touch it. It just almost came out automatically. He wrote it so well.

Ben: Toward the end of that piece, when you have a long solo passage, it almost strikes me like musical pointillism. You're moving so fast and you're everywhere; it's not just technique that I'm hearing, it's like you're painting with your horn. Do you think of that sometimes?

David: Yeah, I call that spirit possession. Like a lot of times in the Sanctified Church, people go off, you know, they start dancing and weeping uncontrollably, and doing things that they never thought they would do. I think it's a madness, is what it really is, that I think can be contained, and that's what I'm trying to do in that sequence. I think some of the things I play, like I do some circular breathing on that if I recall, and then I'll come out and like even it off, you know, to make it seem like: "Oh, he wasn't really crazy. He just put a little form to it." I'm not thinking this consciously when I'm playing it, I'm just kinda going with the flow of emotions, you know. And if I were to recapture the feeling that I felt so many times in the church, of people just going completely off, and then when they come back, they come back in such a reverent way, that it's like the spirit was wild, but then it became focused and contained, and then they had control over it. But for a moment, they didn't. The dichotomy of the two is, I think, where some of my specialness is.

Ben: This speed and spirit has long been part of the saxophone tradition, though. For example, Johnny Griffin's playing, especially on some of the things he did with Monk . . .

David: Oh! Yeah, Johnny Griffin's playing is very fluid, greased lightning. Just talking to Johnny is almost the same as hearing him play. He's a very accurate person, very dexterous. Very fluid speaking, and a very, very nice person, and his warmth comes through his music

Ben: You find that in general people talk like they play?

David: Yeah, I do. Most musicians are kinda shy, though, I think. But once they get going, then they pretty much talk the way they play, I think.

Ben: I find Johnny Griffin to be quite a philosopher.

David: Oh, definitely. And you can hear that in his playing. The tradition that he's covering, I mean, he sounds like . . . There were times, you know, when they was trying to figure out who's the fastest saxophone player, him or 'Trane. As far as I'm concerned, Johnny Griffin always had the nod.

Ben: He had the speed.

David: Yeah, he always had the speed over anybody that I could think of. Even now, he is really prolific. I had a chance to sit and listen to him about five nights in a row, once, when we were over in Holland, at a festival. He was doing the house band thing there, and I really got a chance to become good friends with him and to really peep into his musicianship. He's an incredible musician. And his ideas, he's the kind of guy, like a cat, he's never afraid to attack a new idea. He's kind of like

Bird in a way. You know, he'll try anything, and if he messes up he'll laugh at the end of a phrase or something. He's a very nice person.

Ben: Yeah, and speaking of Monk, a lot of his music is available today because people are more and more interested in the full body of this music, and not just what's the latest piece of plastic out there. I think one of the most optimistic signs in jazz today is the success of catalog sales. Records from the past. One day of course, the records that we talked about today by The David Murray Quartet and the World Saxophone Quartet and Clarinet Summit, well, they'll be catalog sales too . . .

David: Yeah, and I just want everyone to know that one of my kids is gonna be a boy, and maybe even if it's a girl, they're gonna be a lawyer, and they're gonna come get every dime. So just remember that, all you people who re-issue all these albums. When I'm dead and gone, I will have someone here.

* * *

Steve Gadd (March, 1989)

Because he's appeared on thousands of today's hit records, Steve Gadd is sometimes overlooked by jazz critics who fear that being the originator of so many popular dance grooves automatically disqualifies a player from being an artistic innovator. On the other hand, Steve almost always places at or near the top of readers' polls, and even after several years of self-imposed retirement due to his determination to get on top of a chemical dependency problem, he continued to lead the pack of modern drummers in fan appreciation. Steve Gadd is not only a musical innovator but a survivor, and his lasting success, as much as his rhythmic approach, has been an inspiration to several generations of younger drummers who have followed him in the jazz business.

Ben: Your contribution to contemporary music, from the mid-'70s to the mid-'80s, has been as significant as that of any composer or arranger, which for a drummer, I think, is extraordinary. Did you have any idea when you were a kid back in Rochester, New York, that you were headed for this kind of notoriety? Did you have any vision of changing the way the music was put together?

Steve: No, I had no idea. I really had no idea. It's amazing the way things just fall into place, you know? I guess I had a dream of playing professionally, and maybe gettin' in the studios, but back then I didn't know if it would ever come true.

Ben: I've heard stories about you performing as a young child, dancing.

Steve: My brother and I used to tap dance. I used to play the drums with a record, you know, my mother would hold a microphone near this little portable record player, and I'd play along with the "Stars and Stripes Forever" or "In The Mood." You know, Glenn Miller's "In The Mood." And then my brother and I would tap dance together, most of the time along with records. We'd go to different hospitals and play for the patients, or, like, youth weeks, where we'd perform at an outside bowl in Rochester. Yeah, I remember that. It was fun.

Ben: You were really young. Six, seven years old.

Steve: Yeah, eight, nine.

Ben: Tap dancing is something Max Roach has talked about as being the basis for a drummer's style. How did it affect your style?

Steve: Well, I don't know if it's the basis, but I mean, I think anything that you do rhythmically, you know, you can apply to the drums, 'cause the drums are a rhythm instrument. And it might have helped with the way I play the bass drum. I'm not saying that it definitely did, but I don't think it could hurt.

Ben: At what point did you get involved in drum corps music?

Steve: I guess when I was about eleven or twelve I started playing in a drum corps. The first corps was sponsored by a volunteer fire department. And so we'd march in a lot of parades. And then there was a junior corps, and then a few years later, I got in the senior corps, which was more . . . they'd go and do competitions on weekends. There were some parades, but it was mostly like these competitions in different cities. And I got into writing drum parts and we had a real good drum section. We didn't, the drum section, didn't only play in the corps together, but we were friends outside too, you know, and we were thinking drums all the time. If we were hanging out watching TV, like, we always had a pair of sticks with us, and I'd be playing on my shoe, and if we had a basketball, we'd be playing on top of the basketball. It was just drums went along with everything. You know what I mean? They were just a part of the 24-hour day.

Ben: What were you listening to musically when you were twelve or thirteen or fourteen?

Steve: My Uncle used to buy me jazz records, like Art Blakey, and Max Roach, Oscar Peterson. I listened to some Dixieland, the Dukes of Dixieland. I listened to Gene Krupa and Buddy Rich. And I was listening to . . . I remember when Elvis Presley became popular. I listened to that. I remember the first time I heard "Don't Be Cruel." I loved it. It had such a nice feel to it. And then on the b-side was "You Ain't Nothin' But a Hound Dog," and then there was Fats Domino, you know, like "I'm Walkin' " and "Blueberry Hill." So a lot of the things that they were playing on the radio I listened to because, as kids, we used to play outside and we'd hook up a radio and plug it in outside, so the music was part of the, you know, it was happening along while we were playing. God, you know, you're taking me back now. It's hard to remember all the stuff I used to listen to. The Platters . . .

Ben: Just looking at your face recalling this, those must have been romantic times for you.

Steve: Oh yeah, well they were. Growing up and, you know, like, hanging out with the kids in the neighborhood and your girlfriend, stuff like that.

Ben: There's a story that Buddy Rich wanted you to travel with him when you were a young kid. Is that the case?

Steve: Ah, no. That wasn't true. I remember . . . Gene Krupa used to come to Rochester with his band, and I used to go sit in with him. And my brother and I used to go tap dance, you know, his band would play and we'd dance. And there was a rumor that when they did *The Gene Krupa Story* he wanted me to play the part of him as a child, but it never developed, it never happened.

Ben: You also studied tap dance at a dance school or something?

Steve: Yeah, my teacher's name was Curly Fisher. My grandmother used to take me for lessons. Take me for drum lessons and take my brother and I for dance lessons.

Ben: Did they want you to be a musician or a performer?

Steve: I don't know if they did. I think they got a lot of enjoyment while I was doin' it as a kid, but I don't know if they really wanted that for me when I got older. I know after I moved . . . I moved out of Rochester when I went into the Army. Well, the first time I moved out was, I went two years to Manhattan School of Music my first two years of college. And then I transfered back to Eastman School of Music and went three years there, which was in Rochester, so I was back home again. But then I left in 1969 to go in the Army and that was really . . . Then I really wasn't back in Rochester for any length of time. From there, when I got out of the Army, I went back to Rochester for a short period, but then I went to New York. And that's where I stayed up until about a year and a half ago. But when I went home, my grandmother was always wishing that, you know, I was doing something in Rochester. They were sorry it sort of took me out of Rochester.

Ben: Did you play in the army also?

Steve: I played in the army field band at Fort Meade, Maryland. For three years. And my first year was in the concert band. And then they put like a studio band together. Which was like a band the size of Buddy's band. And I was in that for my last two years. And we were like the official touring band of the army. So we were on the road about six months out of the year, I think, five or six months, doing tours by bus. I remember, you know, not really liking it that much while I was in it, but looking back, it was good duty. They had good players in this band, they had good writers, and the arrangers were constantly coming up with new material. We had rehearsals every day, so you had to sight read different things. So, I mean, it was really good on a disciplinary level for reading and stuff like that. It really was helpful.

Ben: In '69 of course, a lot of guys were goin' in the army and not coming back. They were goin' to Vietnam.

Steve: Yeah, well, I had a choice of either getting drafted, and taking my chances going to 'Nam, and a lot of my friends went and didn't come back. And I figured, you know, I had a choice. I could either go in on that level or I could try to get in the band. Or I could move some place else and just evade the whole thing. And I guess the simplest thing was to just go in. And I was lucky, 'cause I got in a good band and met some nice people. And it wasn't the best experience while I was going through it, but I look back on it and it wasn't that bad, you know. I had some good times.

Ben: It's interesting to hear you say it was "the simplest thing." I think of your music as being based on that a lot. You know, the simplest thing that you can think of often is the most effective. When you play, what would seem very simple on the surface is often very moving.

Steve: Well, you know, that happened gradually. 'Cause before I came to New York, I was one of these people, when I played it was like the last time I played. You know, I wanted to get *all* my licks in. But you start getting in the studio and you get a chance to hear things back, and a lot of times what would have been exciting live, when it's just in the studio and you get a chance to hear that intensity back, it can be too confusing. You know, it can be too complicated, and when you lose the sense of sight, I think you have to sorta like simplify things, and it makes the music sound stronger when you're just listening to it. You know, when you play live, and people can see you, maybe you can get away with that more, but I learned from hearing things back that lots of times less is more and more effective, and it became a challenge to try and play the minimum that you could play and make it sound full. And if you could, you know, start on that level, you could either stay there and the music would be good, or you could do very little and make it build. And it became a challenge to do that.

Ben: You might have been one of the first of the new breed of studio drummers to grasp that aspect of it. That you were not just playing live in the studio. That you were manufacturing records.

Steve: Well, it didn't come to me all by myself. I mean, I heard other people play who, you know, inspired me along those lines. Like, I remember when I got out of the service I heard Dobie Gray do "Drift Away," and the drummer on that, Kenny Malone was the player, and boy, he sounded so good, the feel was so nice, and everything he played was just perfect for the music, and had its own space. And then I heard, and I don't know if it's true, but I heard that he was in the service as a career, and started his recording career after he got out of the Navy band. And it was so clean, and the thing just fell right in the pocket. And so that was an inspiration to me. And also Rick Moratta, who's a good friend of mine. I heard him play, you know, when I came to New York, and he comes from a place where the groove and the feel was so nice, and with very little effort. It's like you take the simplest thing that you think anyone can do, but when I heard him do it, it was like, "Hold it," I mean, "that's the way to do it!" And so hearing that was also a big inspiration to me.

To know that there was another side of playing other than just playing as much as I could do technically and as fast as I could get around the instrument and as intense as it could be. I mean, you can get another kind of intensity from playing a real simple kind of way, and really, you know, doing everything on purpose. You know, no matter how simple it is, like doing it real intentional. And trying to play the time and make it feel as good as you can, so the other people playing with you *feel good* playing. So it's for them, not as much for yourself, but more for the other people that you're playing with. You know, it wasn't a constant solo. It was like there was a time where you played for other people and then if there was space for you to solo, then you had it. Then you had a chance to get it out of your system. But not continuously through the whole thing.

Ben: Well, in 1975, a piece of music came out and it was a big pop hit and musicians everywhere immediately noticed the drum part. This is Paul Simon's "Fifty Ways to Leave Your Lover." The feel you contributed was kind of a little watershed event, to be honest, for a pop tune. A lot of musicians lit up when they heard your drum figure because of the way you put that floor tom beat on the four, and the way you broke up a simple kind of march rhythm and made it so funky. Were you aware that what you were doing on that date was really so different?

Steve: I don't know about that. I know that I was doing a lot of work in those days. I started to get real busy, and it was a challenge for me to try and not do the same thing on every album that I played on. And it was also inspiring to me to get called to play a variety of different styles of music. It wasn't just pop, but I was doing some jazz things on CTI, and . . . but for "Fifty Ways," Paul was constantly looking for something new. It was like when you went in to do a session with Paul, if you had a set of drums, you had to sort of like do other things to try and come up with something . . . It was almost like it was drums and percussion, you know. On one track I remember taking this rubber pad that you use to warm up with so you don't make a lot of noise, and I turned the snares off and played with mallets on that. It got like a real percussive sound. And then, another time, it was late in the evening, playing with two sticks in each hand. I mean, I was constantly inspired to come up with new things, you know, and he pushed me to do it. It wasn't like I came in with all these ideas, but he was constantly, you know, looking for something different. And like I was playing a lot in the studio, and between takes I would practice, just, different things, just, like, using the left hand and the high hat.

And just, you know when you're behind the instrument that many hours a day, I just tried to think of new things to keep from going crazy, and I was lucky enough to be able to use some of the new things on people's records, and that just happened to be one of them. That was sort of like a little thing that I had been practicing, and I really had never used before, and it worked right for the tune. And we had tried the tune, like, a bunch of different ways, you know, like Paul wasn't really satisfied. I started doing that stuff, and Phil Ramone was the producer. I don't remember exactly how it went down, but it just sort of fell into place and it worked nice. I had no idea that it was going to be that big. And I remember that day that Bruce Springsteen was there too. This was before Bruce was really known. And Hugh McCracken had brought him in. I guess that they were hanging together, and he said: "This guy is gonna be a big star." And sure enough, sure enough, he's one of the biggest, you know. It's amazing.

Ben: It brings to mind that when you're living in the middle of history, it doesn't feel any different than every other day. History feels ordinary from the inside.

Steve: It felt like every day. I mean, I was into my own thing. I was into trying to play this drum thing, and I'm sure Huey introduced me to Bruce, but it was just like, you know, you meet so many people, you know what I mean? But I remember that McCracken said "This guy is going to be gigantic. This guy is tremendous." I'll never forget it.

Ben: At the same time that you were playing all these studio dates, you were playing with jazz groups and jazz musicians and playing everything. And the result of which I think was you were able to really push the boundaries of the pop sessions that you played on. One session that people always like to talk about is the Steely Dan "Aja" track, as being a moment when pop music got extended by virtue of the drums you played. It was with Wayne Shorter on tenor, Chuck Rainey on bass, Larry Carlton, guitar and Joe Sample on piano.

That session, at the time, was kind of legendary. I mean, it was important because pop music suddenly took a turn left. Do you remember that recording session?

Steve: I remember . . . yeah, I do remember it. And it was amazing. The sessions went real smooth. I mean, it was a period in my life where I was doing a lot of different sessions. I think I did a Leo Sayers session that time too. Like, "You Make Me Feel Like Dancing." You know, I was out in LA, and people would hear you were out there and they'd figure, well as long as you were there, let me see if I can get you on an album, get you to play a track. It was just like, everything was happening. You know what I mean? Like it was just great music, great tracks, and the thing about the Steely Dan thing was that, rumor had it that sometimes it wasn't easy to get tracks. They were very meticulous about what they accepted and what they didn't. And I'm not sure if they had been working on "Aja" with other musicians before, or if they'd been working on other tracks, or if they were talking about other albums, you know, like in just the way that it went down. But everyone had their head into like probably it was going to take a long time to get it, if we *ever* would get it. And that day, it just seemed to fall into place. We did the thing, it happened. And it was great. We got the track pretty quick, and it was just one of those magic moments, I guess.

Ben: In the midst of all this activity, you had a band called Stuff. Even today, musicians talk in terms of a Stuff groove. "Let's do it like Stuff would have done it." The work you did back then has become almost like a short hand for a kind of a feel.

Steve: Well, Stuff was a band. It didn't start out as Stuff. It became Stuff. It started out as The Encyclopedia of Soul. And it was Gordon Edwards who actually put the whole thing together. Gordon, who played bass, and Charlie Brown played saxophone, Cornell Dupree played guitar, and there were different keyboard players. I think Jimmy Smith played sometimes, and Richard Tee played. And the first time I did anything with them, we played like this wedding reception out in Brooklyn. And then the band started working at Mikells. And that was when Richard Tee started doing it. And when he couldn't do it, it was Jimmy Smith or sometimes Paul Griffin, and Christopher Parker was the drummer. And they were working, like maybe four nights a week. And I went up and heard them, and they sounded fantastic.

This was at a point in my life when I was living in Woodstock, and I was playing in a band up in Woodstock with Mike Mainieri and Warren Bernhardt and Tony Levin. That's why I had moved to Woodstock. The idea was to get this band off the ground and so I was spending four days in Woodstock, or three days in Woodstock, and four days in the City. One or the other. I'd come in and take as many sessions as I could get in three days. And then I'd go up to Woodstock and we'd rehearse for four days. And it was back and forth. And I went and heard the band at Mikells, and I told Christopher, I think they were working four nights there, four or five nights, I'm not sure. I said "Listen, if you ever can't do it every night, man, I'd be glad to alternate with you, you know." So Christopher said, "Yeah." Because he was busy in the studio, and sometimes it wasn't easy. You know, you worked until four in the morning, and then getting up to do a ten or a nine o'clock session.

And I was in town, so I started splitting up the nights with Christopher. He'd work two nights and I'd work two nights. And then, the band, as we played, the band got real tight. Plus the fact that there was something about the way they all played that I had never experienced, you know? Like the groove, and just the feel and stuff. I mean, I felt I had so much to learn from playing with someone like Tee and playing with Gordon. Because, just as I had approached music on another level, you know, like bebop on another level, these guys approached this music just as intensively, but from a simpler way, a simpler song form. But you know, to be able to make that simple song form get as intense as like, some of the outer stuff I'd ever played, it was . . . you know, they did it. And it was done on a real simple level and a real groove level. And it was a challenge.

And then the band got real good, and we got a record deal. Warner Bros. wanted us to record. And Tommy LiPuma was going to produce the first album. And then Eric Gale got in the band too, so there were two guitar players. So there was Eric, Cornell Dupree, Richard Tee, Gordon Edwards, Chris Parker on some nights, and me on other nights. And when we got the album deal, Gordon wanted everyone to be involved in it, that had participated in getting it to that level. So we went with two drummers. And it worked out good. I had a lot of fun with that band.

Ben: You mentioned the influence of Tommy LiPuma on that record. It's through Tommy that you and I first met, right around late '79, I guess it was, when we made a record called *The Cat in the Hat*. And what I remember specifically about those sessions, I remember one tune that we did just one take of. It was called "Ask Me Now," it was a Monk tune that I had written some lyrics for, and it felt great after one take. And after the take, you jumped up from the drum kit and said: "Okay, that's it." And I said: "Well, I'd like to do it again, because I really could do it better from my point of view." And you looked at me and said: "Everybody knows you can get it right. But nobody cares. What counts is how it *feels*."

Steve: [Embarrassed laughter.]

Ben: It really stayed with me. I've found it to be good advice in the studio.

Steve: Nobody cares if you get it right.

Ben: Yeah. You looked me dead in the eye and told me in no uncertain terms that people care about the feel, not the correctness of what you're doing.

Steve: Well that's what I cared about, anyway. As I get older, I probably believe what I said then [laughs], but I know now, I know more now about how much I don't know. So I'm not sure if nobody cares if you get it right. I'm sure you cared if you got it right, but, you know, back in those days, I was in the studio a lot. And one thing you get to feel is when the thing is magic. And I really believed there were a lot of takes that were magic, and I mean magic on a real musical level, where everyone was listening, and it was sensitive, and it laid right, and no one got in anybody's way, and it was music. And I had been involved in a lot of situations where that magic was just thrown away for perfection. Maybe I was a little outspoken in those days, but I believe in the magic.

I just hated . . . Sometimes you can go over it and go over it, and get one little thing perfect, but you can throw out a lot of magic, you know? Like for one little thing that wasn't right, you can throw away like a beautiful piece of music. And it will never be as beautiful again. It might be perfect, but it might not be as musical as far as I'm concerned. And I know for me, like, if I'm concentrating on only my performance, I can forget there's a whole other group of people that are making up this music with me, and I have to take them into consideration too. I mean, they're out there trying as hard as they can to make it happen, too, and so I think sometimes it's better to let something weird go by on a personal level, for the benefit of the group as a whole. And that's where the music comes from, from the group as a whole, not just from one person. It comes from everybody together. So that's probably what I meant by that.

Ben: It takes a lot of confidence to do that. That album we did came out on Horizon Records and, as we speak, is now something of a collector's item. Most of the songs on *The Cat In the Hat* were first takes, second takes. We really didn't, I don't think, ever get into a third take on the date. One thing that really worked was the arrangement of "Seven Steps to Heaven." We should probably mention that one because it's become so notorious among musicians, particularly drummers. First of all, we were recording bebop standards in a kind of new way, with lyrics and dance grooves. And also because your soloing on that track was phenomenal. It lead up to and through Joe Henderson's tenor solo, and the things you played on the fade sound like a whole Latin percussion session. But it was just you, live at the time, on your kit. I've had to convince drummers that that was a live drum part, Steve; that there were no over-dubs, that that was not a percussion section.

That's an extraordinary drum track. Not just from my point of view, but from every drummer who's heard that. Really. And what's fascinating is, you know, I've gone to Japan to play, and I'll work with Japanese musicians sometimes. And the Japanese musicians are very focused on doing it just like on the record. This track drives them crazy. They're trying to do that.

Steve: Some of them can do it, man. They've got some good players over there.

Ben: They do indeed. What do you think when you hear that?

Steve: That particular track was just to try and do that song after Miles did it . . . with Tony [Williams]. I mean, there's no way to do it any better than that. But we came up with a way to do it different. Which I'm thankful for. Because to try and do it any better than the way they did it would have been impossible, you know. To be very honest, when you said we were going to do that song, I was just, I didn't know what to do, I wasn't sure where to go with it. I'm just glad we were able to put it into a style that worked for me. You know, like into a little groove kind of thing, a Latin thing. And the arrangement was real nice. I'm proud of it. That whole album, I like the whole album. I remember "Ballin' The Jack," we had a ball on that one. And I remember the one about the kids . . .

Ben: Yeah, "Give It To The Kids . . ."

Steve: Yeah, that was one of the albums I used to play a real lot after it came out.

Ben: What's turned around a lot of musicians hearing that is your ability to move from a little funk groove, that little march groove on the front, through the Latin thing, through the bashing thing, back to the groove, into the Latin thing again, to shift all those gears, and to keep your identity in the midst of it. You sound like you're coming from one place, doing all those things.

Steve: Well, I love all those different styles. You know, I came from a place where all I played at one point was straight ahead, and I did it with people where they helped me grow doing it. Like I was able to play like . . . one time we had a band with Chuck Mangione and Chick Corea, when they got off Art Blakey's band. And Joe Ramano and Frank Pullaro, and we were playing six nights a week. And that was one of the first times I had a chance to play with Chick for any length of time, and it really . . . I learned something from it. You know, I learned how to get comfortable playing a certain style of music, and not just be trying to play it, but it became music, you know? And then, at another time in my life, I played with Chick in a Latin band, where I played with Mingo Lewis, who was playing percussion, and he taught me a lot about Latin stuff. And I love it. I mean, I was able to love Latin as much as I love straight ahead, and from hearing the guys playing groove stuff, I was able to love that . . . as much as I loved anything else. And I was lucky enough to have an opportunity to get on that session, where all that kind of playing was called for. It's amazing the way the cards fall into place.

Ben: I remember during those sessions, a lot of the guys on the date were excited about the fact that we were going to play this classic jazz material in a new way. That was what was lighting us all up. We were going to play it, we didn't have to cut "hits." And I think at the time, this was 1979, you were doing so many studio dates, and so many sessions, and so many hit-type tracks, that that was unusual to be able to do these kinds of tunes.

Steve: Yeah, it was. I remember I was playing so many different styles and doing so many sessions that I never felt like I wished I was doing anything else other than what I was doing when I was doing it. Which was nice. Because I always, I had in the back of my mind, I knew that, you know, like if there was a style that I wanted to play that I wasn't playing at that particular moment, like there'd be an opportunity to do it soon, so

I was able to *stay in the moment.* Which is important. I think I have a problem, more of a problem doing that today, you know what I mean? Just, with more time off, and, you know, it's something that I'd like to be able to do more, as a disciplinary thing. I just don't want to do it, because I'm working so much and I'm doing so many different things that that's what's determining me staying in the present. I think it's important to be able to think in the moment. Or else the moment's gone. You know what I mean? If you're worrying about the future or thinking about the past, then you're not living in the present. And the present goes real quick. Like, you know, that second is gone now forever, so it's nice to be in the now.

Ben: That's interesting that all that work you were doing, and you were doing three dates a day, part of the attraction was that it kept you in the moment.

Steve: But to have to stay in the moment by working that hard is pretty crazy.

Ben: We should talk a little bit, also, about the other result of working that hard. Which was substance abuse. And the fact that, after years of living in that particular dream, you have awakened. Why do you think you were able to be taken out by drugs?

Steve: Taken out?

Ben: Taken out. I remember one session, we were waiting for you to show up. You were about an hour late. And somebody said: "Yeah, Steve will show up two hours late, but he'll still be an hour ahead of everybody else." That even if you came in the door late, your reputation was that you were so fast at getting it together anyway, and such a creative force, that you wouldn't slow it down, even then. You were pushing the envelope, you were pushing the boundaries of what you could do, of what was acceptable in the sessions. I think maybe being high was part of that.

Steve: Yeah, I mean I allowed it to happen. I have to be responsible for what happened. No one forced me to do it. I'm still trying to come to grips with "why." You know, your head doesn't clear immediately. I'm sure it had a lot to do with pain I was running away from. Things that I didn't want to deal with. And the whole time that I was using, I see now, is pretty much like a non-growth period. I mean, it was like, a lot of it was like automatic pilot, you know? And so when you stop using, and all the things, whatever they are, they surface gradually. Whatever my fears were, whatever my pain was, it still is. You have to deal with them, sooner or later. I mean, you can only numb 'em for so long, and then you die, or you become a vegetable. I mean, they certainly kill you spiritually. And spirituality is a real important part of life. Knowing that there is a higher power other than yourself takes a tremendous amount of weight off . . . off me.

And so I have to learn how to live. I mean, I survived for a long time, but I'd like to learn how to live. Part of life is like, I mean, there's happiness and there's sadness, and there's pain. I think, knowing how to live, we're able to deal with pain and not just . . . Pain is a natural part of life, I think suffering is a decision we put on ourselves. So you either walk through it, face it and walk through it, and get to the other side, and then you've grown. Or you run away from it, but you can only run for so long. You either die running, or you stop and then all of those things have to be dealt with.

Ben: It's almost as if that at the time you were doing so much, and your phone was ringing so hard, that getting involved with drugs was a back-door way to end it, to make it stop, to make the craziness stop for awhile.

Steve: It might have been. You know, it works in funny ways. It might have been my way. It's like my best thinking got me to where I am today. You know what I mean? [Laughs.] And I'm lucky to be alive. I'm grateful to be alive. I'm not saying it's always easy. But I have a lot of hope. I have faith again. My feeling about playing is, I'm starting to feel like my old feelings towards music and stuff. I got pretty bitter for awhile. And the reasons I thought I was bitter, you know, before, are now, I brought it on myself. Really, I've got so much to be thankful for, I really had nothing to be bitter about. I'm trying to come to grips with that.

Ben: Sometimes success is harder than failure, eh?

Steve: Yeah, and I don't have the answers. It's just one day at a time.

* * *

Donald Fagen (October, 1988)

As one half of the pop group Steely Dan, Donald Fagen comes to the jazz world through the back door, although his great commercial success is in part due to his use of advanced harmonies, great jazz soloists, and his personification of an ultimate hipness. What is particularly interesting, however, is that while his harmonic approach is very modern, defining the post-bebop era and cited by many of today's advanced players as a contributing influence, his literary sensibilities are stylized, recalling a bygone jazz era that is almost "classic," that of the 1950s. Considered by the music establishment as something of an eccentric, he rarely performs live, takes years between completed recording projects, and is often on the minds of today's contemporary jazz producers: they wonder what he's going to do next... so that they can find out what they should do next.

Ben: You have an air of mystique about you, as you know. You're not really out in the public a lot.

Donald: Well I think the mystique was actually born a long time ago, and it probably just has to do with the fact that I don't perform, or at least haven't since Steely Dan came off the road in '74. So it's merely a matter of that, and not any other planned way of life or anything.

Ben: Your music's got a kind of mystique about it too, though, all by itself...

Donald: I hope so...

Ben: And, maybe the fact that you're not touring furthers that, makes it even more mysterious.

Donald: Yeah, well I think when we started, we basically were interested in records. I'm talking about my partner Walter Becker and I. We actually ended up as a touring band by accident, really. And, certainly I became a front man by accident, I know that. We just couldn't find a singer who we felt could convey the attitude we were looking for. And it became obvious that I was probably the one to do it, even though I had very little experience.

Ben: You became a front man by default.

Donald: Oh yeah. I became a front man by default

Ben: Now of course the first Steely Dan record, the first hit, "Do It Again," in 1972, had all the elements that we still associate with the Steely Dan mystique, the kind of mysterious narrative line and characters involved, players.

Donald: Yeah, I think our model for songs was more literary or short story-like than being a model from popular music. So, I guess it had something of theatrical music about it, in that sense, in that it does tell a story.

Ben: The name of the group comes from literary reference of course.

Donald: Right. It's from William Burroughs' novel *Naked Lunch.* From the '50s, or maybe even the late '40s.

Ben: That period, and that style, and that attitude—the mystique I guess that we associate with the '50s, a kind of post-modernism—this romance that you're involved in, there's almost a dream sense about what you're doing. I guess what I'd be interested to know is, what was your life like during that period, during the '50s? How did you come upon your vision of that time and where do you fit into that material?

Donald: Well, I think during the period when most of the Steely Dan records were made we were probably reflecting the present or the recent past, which was in the '60s. In the *Nightfly* record, which was a solo record that I did, that was certainly purposefully about the '50s. Although, you know, I'm sure that our upbringing in the '50s was something you could detect on the Steely Dan records too.

I grew up in Passaic, New Jersey, and then moved to the suburbs. Like a lot of families, my parents moved from the inner city out to the suburbs in the mid-'50s. This was a great shock to me, even when I was a kid. I could see that there was a lot missing about that, the kind of life, that one leads in the suburbs. Especially at that time, which was a very conservative period, and probably the most conservative in recent history, in the country. I think before that, there was never the kind of conformism or kind of repressed type of life that people were living then. And that's what I grew up with. Of course it's the beginning of television. Even as a kid, I could tell that things had changed from when I was a young child. You could tell the world was becoming different. Because of technology and a lot of other factors.

Ben: The kind of lock-step conformism that we can see now in retrospect as having been part of the '50s, at the time was sort of invisible, and people, I think, who recognized it were much more of an underground entity, and clearly jazz players at the time were the voice of the underground entity. Is that how you came upon jazz?

Donald: Yeah, well, luckily, or unluckily, as the case may be—I'm pretty sure it's luckily though—I used to listen to late night radio broadcasts from Manhattan, which I was able to get over in New Jersey across the river. And at that time there were great late night shows playing jazz, which was in a very fruitful period at that time, in the middle, late '50s and early '60s. Mort Fega, Symphony Sid was still on then, and there was a few other shows that you could hear in the evening, or late at night. And when I first heard these shows, when I was about ten, eleven years old, I immediately could see that there was something about jazz . . . Well, first of all I liked the music. But I think I also saw it as a cultural alternative and there was something authentic about it which I detected even at that age. You know, I still love it. I think it holds up, perfectly, and the records that were coming out day by day at that time are now classics. So I think that proves it, really.

Ben: Some of those records really foreshadow your records in their use of orchestration, a kind of very hip modernism. I'm thinking for example about the Oliver Nelson record *Blues and the Abstract Truth.*

Donald: Great record . . .

Ben: A composition like "Stolen Moments" which featured Eric Dolphy on alto sax, Bill Evans on piano, Freddie Hubbard on trumpet. Clearly a record like that had an impact on you, not only as a fan, but a budding musician and a composer.

Donald: Yeah, that record was really appreciated by jazz fans, in that it was using the latest arranging techniques and a lot of dissonance. A bit on the commercial side, I think, as far as just the sound of the arrangements. But it was beautifully made, and the musicians were terrific. Had a great rhythm section. And Eric Dolphy, of course, was way ahead of his time.

Ben: The idea of it sounding commercial to you is interesting, because you're making adventurous, very artistic, commercial music today.

Donald: Yeah, well I think we were influenced by the more commercial jazz, as well as, I guess, what you'd call the more heady or experimental jazz. By experimental, I guess I'm actually talking about more authentic, individual kinds of jazz, like Sonny Rollins or Miles Davis, who I think, really were defying commerciality, and really had no interest in it. At least musically speaking. And rock and roll also influenced us, which was definitely commercial music. I guess when we started writing, there was all kinds of different music around, a sort of music crossing over with other kinds of music. It was just beginning then, and there was something amusing about it to us. The fact that, for instance, we used to try playing Charlie Parker type lines on distorted electric guitars, and things like that; aside from being new sounding to us, it was also very funny. I think a kind of irony about what had happened to popular music, and where it was situated at that time, was one of the things that we used to experiment on.

Ben: Where were you doing these experiments?

Donald: Well, Walter Becker and I met at Bard College. We were both attending school there, from '65 to '69. Walter actually dropped out after the first couple of years. But I met him there and he was interested in doing the same kind of thing I was, which was blending these different genres and so on, and somehow putting together a group that could project that.

Ben: Were you a music student per se or were you a literature student?

Donald: Ah, both. I would switch around. I started out as an English major and then switched to music, which was actually the first time I considered making music a profession. Before that, I was really an amateur player and used to write songs, but wasn't that serious about it. Unfortunately, the head of the music department didn't think that I had the technical expertise, and I was actually thrown out of the music department. At which point I went back into literature and graduated in English.

Ben: What sort of equipment did you bring with you when you decided to be a musician? Had you studied harmony or theory? Had you played in little trios?

Donald: I had a trio in high school, but I was mostly self-taught as a pianist, and off records. I listened to a lot of Red Garland records and a lot of Wynton Kelly performances and just picked it up off records. I had some lessons, and when I got to college, I took harmony and composition and so on, and also spent a summer at Berklee School in Boston. So I had some training, but I started late.

Ben: What about your start as a songwriter, because in a lot of ways, that's really separate from being a player. How did that start? What was your first songwriting like?

Donald: I wrote songs since I was a kid. You know, very primitive songs, of course, when I was really young, but by the time I was in high school, I was writing comic songs and theatrical songs.

Ben: Like Tom Lehrer songs or something?

Donald: That's a good comparison, I think.

Ben: Were you using narrative? Were you developing character in your songs?

Donald: Yeah. I guess it just really came naturally to me. There was no theory behind it. It just was interesting to me to use character and plot and all the things associated with story line in a song.

Ben: Is there a writer or two that you would point toward to explain some of your narrative style?

Donald: I guess there's a lot of theatrical music, the usual standard pop songs, great songwriters like Gershwin and Harold Arlen and so on.

Ben: How about literary writers?

Donald: Well, in high school, Walter and I were both interested in a few writers in common. We both were very big fans of Nabokov, who seemed to both of us to be probably the greatest living writer. And he, I think, was an influence, if it's possible for Nabokov to be an influence on rhythm and blues. Also, those were kind of the days when black humor was burgeoning. That is to say, not black American humor, but sick humor, or cynical humor. Lenny Bruce, we think of as a stand-up comic, was representative of that. But there were writers like Terry Southern and John Barth in those days who were writing more or less in that genre, and Kurt Vonnegut certainly. I think that that kind of extreme irony was interesting to us at that time.

Ben: So how do we get from Bard College to "Do It Again"?

Donald: Well, after college we tried to get a job doing some kind of professional music. It really didn't matter what it was. We had a bunch of songs with us we were trying to sell, really, or use in some way, but we didn't have a band. So we went up to the famous Brill Building, which is on Broadway in New York City, which has long been a place where musicians go to start out songwriting. And a lot of the great standard songwriters were there, and also, in the '50s, the writers who wrote commercial rock and roll were there, Leiber and Stoller, who we were big fans of, who worked with the Coasters and the Drifters in the '50s, and also Carol King. Most of them were no longer active in the Brill Building when we got there, but we looked at it as some sort of edifice that would . . . We pictured all these music publishers with pianos; and that's exactly what it was, really, except not much was going on at that time. There were a few record companies left in the '60s. Buddha Records and Jeff Barry, a couple other writers were there. And we got a job writing pop songs there, and ended up working for the production company of Jay and the Americans, which was a group from the early '60s. And from there, through various contacts, we finally got a job in California as staff writers at ABC Records, in Los Angeles. And we wrote pop songs for them, which were all terrible failures. We were really bad pop song writers, really, but we kept writing these other songs, and eventually we got a band together and made a record.

Ben: Let's talk about your compositional process in general. When you approach a new composition, do you generally start out with chord changes or with a melody line, or do you start with a hook?

Donald: Usually I start off with an idea for lyrics. Then I'll sit down at the piano and some music will come to me which goes with it, or goes against it. Or, you know, just something that somehow will enhance the lyric. Then I'll usually go ahead with the music and write that and then fill in the rest of the lyrics afterwards.

Ben: Of course, the next step is taking it to the studio and making the creature walk.

Donald: Right. I still write on the piano, because I think to some extent, I'm still scared of the technology kind of beating me, you know. I want to use the technology and not really be controlled by it, and I figure if I start writing with the machines, then it'll start to sound like everyone else's records. So I try to get a good musical foundation on the piano first. And then I'll go over to the machines and, basically, use it as an orchestrating tool, really.

Ben: The way you made the Steely Dan records is kind of a mystery, or a legend, depending, within the industry. There have been a lot of stories about songs and sessions that would go on for days before a track would get finished. Let me pick a particular song and ask you how it came to be. Let's just say the song in question is "The Glamour Profession," from the album *Gaucho.* It was recorded in 1980 with Steve Gadd on drums, Anthony Jackson on bass, Steve Khan on guitar, Ralph McDonald, percussion, Michael Brecker on tenor, Tom Scott on lyricon, yourself on piano. "The Glamour Profession" is kind of the favorite song of a lot of musicians now and, in a way, I think, it's one part of the flowering of the Steely Dan writing. How did that song come to be?

Donald: I think we used a different method for every song, depending on what works best. We don't have any separate, general theory of recording. That one, I think we started with the drum track, that is to say we laid down a drum track, and, I can't remember who at the time, I guess it was Steve Gadd.

Ben: He's on the final version, in any case.

Donald: And we then started adding layers on top of that. I think some parts may have been sequenced. That is to say, they were done with computers. Although, when we work with computers, I think, unlike a lot of other people, we try to make them sound as unmechanical as possible, which takes a lot of time. It turns out if you want something to sound human, it takes a lot of very sophisticated programming and trial and error, and so on. So we did that, and eventually we have some kind of track, and then get some players to come in and play over it, just like you would at a normal session.

Ben: How much of that song was prepared in advance?

Donald: When we started, we went in with some kind of a chord chart, and basically depended on the musicians to add parts, and we discussed certain things with them and so on. But, as we went on, our charts became more detailed and on my solo record, for instance, it was really completely charted and most of the details were written in.

Ben: Let's talk about the narrative in "The Glamour Profession."

Donald: Well, I'm doing this from memory, I can't remember exactly what the lyrics are but that song is about a cocaine dealer who finds himself getting some kind of power by selling drugs to celebrities and hanging around with them, being in their scene. I think in the first verse a basketball player meets him in the parking lot and he gives him some, and then there's some various other decadent, monied people that he deals with. The idea of it is the kind of power that someone like that feels. It's sort of the only way that someone on that social level can have power is by being associated with power. And that's basically what the song is about...

Ben: It's about power...

Donald: It's about power, yeah.

Ben: The idea of a hit song being written about power like this is almost unheard of today. I mean, it's an exception. Your music is exceptional in terms of what's going on out there in radio land.

Donald: Well, I think there was a lot more freedom on the radio when we started. There was room for a lot of different kinds of music, and there isn't now. But we were lucky in that there's a certain carry-over and the program directors and the DJs have been really good about that, actually, in realizing, you know, that we were trying to do something a little different, and yet still playing the stuff on the radio. I will say that "Century's End," which is a song I wrote for the *Bright Lights, Big City* soundtrack, did not go on top forty radio. Not so much because the song wasn't liked, but because they just said that today's playlist on top forty was so constricted, or rather, so narrow, that it just didn't fit into the format anymore. So maybe the freedom that we had in the past is not there anymore, to some extent.

Ben: It's almost as if, in the abstract, a great song in the old days, was a great song. Today a great song has to arrive at a particular time for it to live on.

Donald: Well I think today a hit song has to be the same as another hit song.

Ben: Not necessarily another hit song of yours, but another hit song on the radio at the time.

Donald: Yeah, right. Another hit song on the radio. I think technology also has forced music into a certain corner, really. You know, if everyone is using the same computers, most of the records are going to sound the same. Unless you take a little bit more time with it.

Ben: Do you feel that your own music could become more acoustically driven, as opposed to synthesizer driven, in the future?

Donald: Well, I've actually tried that in the past couple years, and I find that what I'm really interested in is electronically simulating acoustical instruments, so that there's some ambiguity about exactly what you're hearing. I can't tell you why, exactly, but I guess, in some sense I feel like I've already dealt with acoustic instruments, that is to say, as a full band. You know, I'm not saying I don't use acoustic instruments, but I like the idea of simulating acoustic instruments with electronic means.

Ben: You've done, actually, one of the most distinctive jobs of establishing a voice on a synthesizer I think that any musician has done in the last ten or fifteen years by using the synthesized harmonica voice. Did you get that from the DX-7?

Donald: Actually, it wasn't the DX. I think they probably got it from me. I guess that sounds somewhat immodest, but the first time I did that was on *Aja* I think, and it was something I programmed into a Prophet.

Ben: But it's become your sound. You've managed to solve one of the universal problems of synthesizer players by coming up with a distinguishable electronic voice, because it's a great problem, if everybody has the same synthesizers, how do you get your own sound?

Donald: Yeah, right. Well, I think that the sound I get actually has a bit more attack than the usual thing you hear. At least I hope so. To solo, I need to feel like I have real contact with the machine in the way that an acoustic player has, and when I hit the key, I like to hear the attack right then. I don't like to wait. And I think some of these other sounds have a kind of delayed attack usually. I don't know if this is interesting to you, but it's interesting to me. And, also it's difficult to find a voice on a synthesizer to solo with because they do fight you. They try to remain machines, and to twist them into being human is difficult.

Ben: You mentioned the soundtrack song, "Century's End," you contributed to the movie *Bright Lights, Big City*. Did you try to respond specifically to the story that the book and the movie told or did you just write a song and hand it over?

Donald: For a while, I had an idea of writing a song that would compare the end of the 19th century in Europe, a kind of sensibility of, say, Paris or Vienna, with the present end of the century. When this movie came along and they needed a song, I could see how it kind of paralleled the story anyway and so I made up my own characters and wrote the song with the late Timothy Mayer, the lyrics. I like the lyrics. I think they came out really well and do present a kind of a nice picture of urban life, as it exists in 1989.

Ben: With a real sense of living on the edge of the future.

Donald: Yeah, you know, the reason I like that book is I think the novel *Bright Lights, Big City,* which has been talked about so much that you can't really separate it from what people think about it these days, but when I originally read it, I thought it had the quality of realness, a piece of life that actually goes on in the city. And, you know, I hope the song does that too.

Ben: A sense of hurtling toward the future, accelerating towards the future.

Donald: Yeah, well, I guess I've written other songs that have that. "I.G.Y.," from *The Nightfly,* has a bit of that, and some of the other songs in *The Nightfly* as well.

Ben: Brings up the song "The New Frontier."

Donald: Right, that's one too.

Ben: "The New Frontier," though, when it treats the subject, has that kind of romantic fog about it. I mean, of course, it's written from the '50s point of view but it talks about London to Paris by train . . .

Donald: Under sea by rail.

Ben: It's a dream vision. It's almost just a step ahead of the Flash Gordon vision of the future, we're having a "summer smoker" underground, in a bomb shelter, you know. It's kind of a romantic adaptation of something that might be terrifying.

Donald: Well, yeah. *The Nightfly*, you know, is more or less autobiographical, sort of presenting my childhood, growing up in the late '50s and early '60s, and of course the fallout shelter was a big item then. This actually was based on a true story that I heard about some kids who, when their parents go away for the weekend, they use the fallout shelter to have a party. It was a perfect party room. It had plenty of stale Twinkies and so on, all the food that you might need, and a lot of beer. And I like the idea of a fallout shelter used for something connected with life rather than something connected with destruction. Of course, the fallout shelters probably would have been useless in the case of living in them anyway, so at least you could have a party.

Ben: What distinctions do you see between your solo work and the Steely Dan work?

Donald: That particular album, *The Nightfly*, was about the era of the late '50s and early '60s, I tried to use forms from that time, and I think that's part of the reason there may have been more jazz harmony and so on is . . . it's just the kind of music I associate with that time. Although, I think I also just have, through the years, learned more about jazz and jazz harmony. Because I wasn't trained young, it's almost an advantage in that, through the years, by studying myself and occasionally taking some lessons and so on, I find new material to use all the time. As far as lyrics, I think the main difference is they're more personal, they're more subjective perhaps, because I was writing about myself really. The sound of the record, I think Walter and I developed that sound together, and at this point I really don't know who contributed what. It's just become a natural way for me to work, using a certain vocabulary of sounds, you know.

Ben: How would you describe that Steely Dan sound? It's become a kind of industry standard.

Donald: It may surprise people but it really wasn't anything planned. I think when we started making records, we had a certain ideal of how a record should sound, but I don't think we knew how it would come out. It always seemed to me that one of the things we were looking for was clarity, making sure you could hear all the instruments. And not too much reverberation or echo to cloud or muddy up the actual sound of the instruments. And if there's any model, I would say a lot of the jazz records Rudy Van Gelder recorded in the late 50s. They have a very dry but live sound which, I guess, Walter and I both loved as kids. By that time, there was a style of recording jazz which was fairly dry and up front. The engineers took a lot of pride in bringing out natural sound. Natural but kind of dead sounding, in the sense that it's different from, say, a classical orchestra recorded in a hall. This would be natural, but studio natural. I think that we may have had that sound in mind.

Ben: When you talk about your work, it seems kind of abstract. You're not saying to me, for example, "Well, you know, I had this need to express myself, and this is the way I had to do it." It's like very purposeful.

Donald: Well, I'm sure I'm probably rewriting the history entirely. You know, in retrospect, you can do that. I guess I'm telescoping a lot of things. When you're involved in it, it's really instinctual. Looking back on it, I can sort of see where certain things were derived.

Ben: Do you think of yourself as an artist?

Donald: Sure. Why not?

Ben: An artist in the tradition of somebody whose work will be studied by the academics?

Donald: I don't know. I don't know if that has anything to do with art anymore. I think because of the world we grew up in, which was very different from the world before, and since American life is based on lack of tradition, and inventing yourself, and all that, you really don't have any models to go by. And, I mean, you can read certain things, and listen to certain music, but in the context of the times, I think that you really end up just making up your own kind of art, and not going by previous models. You know, and I think that's part of the energy of popular art.

Ben: And, as opposed to the art that's in the museums, you're having to do your art in the context of: Will it get on the radio?

Donald: Right. You know, the commercial music and film music, television music, this is what I grew up with, aside from jazz. I wrote an article, I guess a year ago, about Henry Mancini. I occasionally do this column for *Premiere* magazine, which is a film magazine, and I guess, at that time, I was thinking how much I derived from Henry Mancini's music, which generally isn't thought of as any kind of art music. Or it's basically functional music, and designed to ornament or enhance TV shows and films and so on. But he was very original in his way and there's a lot of crossover from jazz. He used a lot of very good jazz musicians on the West Coast and there's both something amusing about it to me, and also very touching about it, you know. And I think at this point, we have to take what was given to us and make something out it. An academic or perhaps a conservative critic of the culture will think it's a big pile of trash. But, nevertheless, this is what we've got, and it really has to do with the way you look at it.

Ben: I know that you're also interested in painting and other forms of art, art that is collected and lives on over centuries. Will this music we're making live on, do you think?

Donald: I don't know. I really don't know. Some music will. I know that the jazz of the late '50s and '60s, I've no doubt that that will live. Because you can really tell by the way it's been regarded since, and it's a truly original modern creation of black Americans mostly, and it'll live forever. I don't know whether the pop music will live. I guess we'll have to wait and see.

* * *

Bobby McFerrin (February, 1985)

I first met Bobby McFerrin on stage at Carnegie Hall, where we were participants in a tribute to jazz singer Eddie Jefferson. Bobby is a fun-loving down-home guy who helped make the rehearsals a joy and the concert extraordinary. Several years later, the enormous success of his record "Don't Worry, Be Happy" hadn't changed that aspect of his presence one bit. Just as that record was a casual expression of a good idea—both musical and philosophical—and not an attempt to abandon an aesthetic path or to "go commercial," it is obvious in what follows that Bobby has for years pursued his own inner voice. And more important, he has always shown a deep respect for and placed a lot of faith in the intelligence of his audience. He's made them a large part of his performances, and, subsequently, of his great success. There's an almost visionary sense in his words as he describes the inevitable rightness of the solo path he's taken. Of equal interest is his obvious bewilderment at being categorized a "jazz" singer.

Ben: We first met in 1980 when you were singing with Jon Hendricks but I don't know too much about how you came to that point. I do know that you grew up in a musical family and that you personally avoided making a commitment to being a musician yourself for quite a while. Why was that?

Bobby: Well, I was raised by musical parents. My father sang with the Metropolitan Opera when I was growing up, when I was in New York City. We came to California in 1958. He was contracted to sing Sidney Poitier's singing voice in "Porgy And Bess," so that brought us out to California. I was about eight years old. And, you know, I was just like regular kids who didn't really know exactly what I wanted to do with myself for a long long time. I don't think that's very unusual. But I guess it wasn't until I was a senior in high school that I made the decision to be a musician because it was the one thing I had been surrounded with all my life.

And then I went through different phases about what kind of musician I wanted to be and the music I wanted to write. But then I was living in Salt Lake City, it was 1977, that I decided to sing. And my first gigs as a singer was in piano bars. And then from local piano bars I moved around the country doing that, ended up in New Orleans in '79 and worked with a great band called The Astral Projects. Great band, great band!

Ben: The Astral Projects?

Bobby: Yeah, they taught me a lot about music. And leading a group. Up until that point, I didn't really know what to do as far as a leader of a group is concerned. And then from there I moved to San Francisco. This was still in 1979. Came upon Jon Hendricks in January of '80 and joined his group a few months after that.

Ben: Now when you say that you decided as a senior in high school you were going to be a singer, in 1977, had you been singing before that point at all?

Bobby: Yeah, but unconsciously. I mean, I sang in church choir, you know, when I was growing up. But I never thought of myself as a singer. And I think that's a really important point, because I never had a vision of myself as a singer. And it wasn't until '77 when I actually started thinking about myself, "Well, maybe I'm a singer . . ." Up until that point, I didn't know. I just wasn't sure.

And I didn't like my voice. I didn't think it was a good voice. And singing didn't excite me in any way.

Ben: Really? And you didn't do it at parties or privately around the house?

Bobby: I probably did, but then it was one of those things where I didn't pay too much attention to it.

Ben: Do you think maybe that's important for your having come up with such a unique style at this point, the fact that it came to you later and you kind of developed it out of whole cloth?

Bobby: That's a possibility. I was probably doing some of these things also without thinking about the value of it, you know. I can remember about 1975 when The Manhattan Transfer had come out with this new album that had "Operator" on it, and "That Cat Is Hot" and stuff like that, and I can remember singing over those changes. But it wasn't any big deal to me then, because I was interested in doing other things. So singing was pretty much a sideline. Friends would tell me that I had a nice voice and, you know, my wife Debbie would say, "You know, you've got a really nice voice," and I sang at our wedding, etc., but it just wasn't me. I just didn't think of it as something that I could make a living at, having such a good time doing it.

Ben: Did your father ever pull you aside and say, for example, "Son, this is the way one gets breath support . . ."?

Bobby: He didn't really do that, but since he was a teacher I would just pick those things up being around the house. So I learned a lot about singing just osmotically because both my parents are singers and teachers. So it meant a lot to them.

Ben: After joining Jon Hendricks' band, you became categorized as a "jazz vocalist," but I know that you don't really think of yourself as a "jazz" singer.

Bobby: You know, the thing that probably ties me in as far as being labeled as a jazz singer is simply because I take vocal solos. This whole thing of being a "scat singer" is tied in with being something that comes from jazz, when historically, you might call some of Bach's coloraturas, you know, scat singing, in a sense. Because he would in some cases write out the notes for these extended wordless solos for the singer to sing. And in some cases, you might say that what I'm doing, in a classical sense, is taking extended cadenzas. So I don't think of myself as a "jazz singer," personally. I get labeled that a lot. *Down Beat* certainly thinks I'm a jazz singer.

Ben: And it's okay to be labeled a jazz singer?

Bobby: It's okay. As long as I'm not seen as only that. But I guess, you know, that's other people's perceptions; they have to deal with it. As long as I don't feel that way I guess it's okay.

Ben: Do you feel strongly about not making specifically jazz material a big part of the program in order to make that kind of statement? For example, you cover James Brown songs and you cover The Beatles. I think of you as kind of an elevated folk musician because you do such a broad range of "people's music."

Bobby: I like to think of it that way. I don't think I'm making any kind of a "statement" when I do a particular type of tune or something, but I'm just drawing from all the music that I was digging when I was growing up. I was digging classical music, I was surrounded by that. And then some of the jazz singers that I heard when I was growing up, my parents used to play Joe Williams and Nat King Cole and Frank Sinatra and Tony Bennett and Dinah Washington and Etta James, Ella Fitzgerald, you know, all the singers. Besides growing up in the sixties with Jimmy Hendricks and Janis Joplin and The Beatles and Cream and Eric Clapton. So all of that, and gospel music and church music and whatever, I synthesized all that when I was growing up.

And I know, as a writer, I was very interested in [Charles] Ives, because he used to take different types of music and superimpose them on top of one another. And I thought, "Wow, that's a really interesting concept." And so, in a concert, in the span of an evening, all that musical terrain is available to me. Especially because I'm doing it by myself and I don't have to write any charts, do any rehearsals. Nothing has to be prepared or unprepared, because I'm doing it by myself, so anything that comes along, anything, even children's tunes, "Ittsy Bittsy Spider," "Twinkle Twinkle Little Star" . . .

And I think it's working because a lot of people, when they see me, in some way I think I might be reflecting them back on themselves. They're saying to themselves, "Well, I'll be damned, you know I do this everyday and now I'm going to get a chance to sing." Because my favorite part of an evening is when the audience joins in and we're singing together.

Ben: I think that is also something significant that separates you from other so-called "jazz singers." Or a lot of jazz musicians. Jazz musicians tend to go on stage with the posture that "I'm doing something that's very obscure and difficult and you can dig me or not but this is me." And you're up there saying, "I'm you, we're all doing this together."

Also another thing that sets you apart from the traditional jazz singer is, as you mention, that you do perform and record completely by yourself. From time to time other jazz singers might have stepped out front, but never has one done what you have. How did you develop the ability to do that?

Bobby: It's still developing. For example, I recently had a wonderful weekend working with a dance troupe. And it was interesting for me because as my style is developing, I've noticed that my body, my entire body, becomes more involved in it. So I was very excited about working with the dancers because I just wanted to see how I'd react with all that movement.

Ben: You provided the music for the dance?

Bobby: I sang while they danced and it was just my voice which was the musical accompaniment. However, sometimes I got the audience involved to accompany some dance pieces, which really came off well. I thought that was wonderful when you've got an audience accompanying a dance. That was great.

Anyway, so I actually got the chance to move around on stage and I find, more and more, that visual movement somehow helps a person to hear a little better. I think sound can be seen. I mean, there are certainly some electronic devices that can show you what a sound looks like. So I think it's the same kind of a thing on stage. As I'm singing, to be moving, I think, in a way, enhances the performance.

Ben: Also, although all singers are rhythmically influenced, you're very much tied into the rhythm. You are doing what the rhythm section normally does when you perform solo.

Bobby: Yeah. You know, you're right, and I discover that more and more. One of the rhythmic devices that I use is playing on my body, my chest, things like that. And I've discovered that a lot of people like that. I think the hardest thing for a lot of solo vocalists, especially when they stick with some of the avant-garde things, is that they don't give the audience enough to tie in with. And rhythm is one of those things. It's like the heartbeat of music and it gives people sort of a floor to walk on. And so the rhythm is very important.

Ben: You once said to me, several years ago, "I don't understand why more people aren't doing what I'm doing. It's so easy." And I walked away from that thinking this is clearly the statement of an individual who has a great gift rather than simply a technique. Because for you, it's effortless. But for the rest of us, it's problematical. Describe what it is that you're doing when you structure your sing solo pieces.

Bobby: Okay. I'm using my chest voice and my head voice. Whenever I'm doing the low notes, I'm pretty much in my chest voice, which is my speaking voice. Whenever I'm up in my high voice, I'm in my falsetto voice. So it's a matter of switching the voices. [Demonstrates.] Chest... head... chest. It's as simple as that, as far as the technique goes.

Ben: And you use that movement between chest and head to set up the rhythm?

Bobby: Right.

Ben: So it's like a bass drum and a hi-hat, or any alternating rhythmic structure.

Bobby: Right. Then put some body against it. [Demonstrates again, slapping his chest in rhythm while alternating chest and head voice.]

Ben: And that's the heart of your technique.

Bobby: That's the heart of it.

Ben: There's also some crazy breathing things going, because I notice you're able to extend phrases much longer than would appear normal and you're never suffering from a lack of oxygen. Is that conscious breathing technique?

Bobby: It's conscious because the breath becomes part of the music. It seems that the only way I can describe it is "learning to breathe musically." Using the breath as part of the music itself. [Demonstrates.]

Ben: The result of all these pieces coming together is a seamless presentation, and when people hear it, they are stunned by what appears to be inexplicable.

Bobby: And it's actually very simple, yes.

It's the same thing as speaking. You're not conscious of breathing when you talk. And the same principle is applied. I'm not conscious of my breathing when I'm singing.

Ben: What are you thinking about when you're singing these elaborate vocal flights? Are you focussed totally on the notes or does your mind wander?

Bobby: Sometimes the mind wanders. But I find that I can't really "think" about anything. What I'm doing is watching it happen as it's happening. That's sounds a bit otherworldly or whatever, but that's really all I have time to do is watch it come out. The moment I start thinking about what I'm doing, then I get lost, my intonation goes right out the window. So I have to be very concentrated on the intonation and the notes. If I'm concentrated on anything, it's keeping things centered.

Ben: So it's like an instrumentalist, say a piano player, who clearly can't think of a musical line as fast as he can play it. So then it becomes a process of getting out of your own way.

Bobby: Exactly, yes, that's it.

Ben: Are you having as much fun performing as you appear to be having?

Bobby: Oh yeah, incredible fun. Here I am making a living having fun.

Ben: And you appear to be coming alive more and more in front of audiences. In the time that I've known you, you appear to be coming out of yourself in a way.

Bobby: Yeah, more and more. That's why this dance experience was very good for me. Because I wanted to come more alive. It's the whole body awareness that I've been trying to get into.

Ben: We've talked a bit about how much pressure you get from the jazz world to be a "jazz singer." How about pressure from the commercial world to be a commercial singer like Al Jarreau, or whoever, to sing "straight"?

Bobby: Oh yeah. I knew after my first album came out and the record company was pretty much dangling this golden carrot in front of my nose and saying "here, take a whiff of this and then you'll really be able to do what you want to do, let's get some money behind you," I never believed that. And I think that's one thing that saved me. I never believed that if I went in this [commercial] direction that I was going to get to do solo things.

And I had a lot of conflict over that for a long time. I was even open minded enough to try. I went down to Los Angeles for a while, for a couple of weeks—that's all I could really take—but I went down there to see, just to see, if it was possible for me to go in that direction. You know, what would it be like to have a lot of money put into an album, etc. But my heart wasn't in it. And I felt that if I went in that direction then I wouldn't be as individual or authentic as I feel that I am. So I decided to do the solo things. And it's worked. It's paid off. And I think the reason is because, first off, I believed in it. I always believed in it. And I think once you believe in something, the power behind that is strong. And people are very much aware of that. I mean, I think they would be able to tell if I was on stage if I was really happy with what I was doing or not.

Ben: Did you want to perform solo all along? Did you know that even, for example, when you were working with Jon Hendricks' group and doing the more traditional jazz material?

Bobby: I started thinking about it a few months after I became a singer. So at first it was pretty much a thought and it stayed pretty much a thought for a long long time. But what would happen, in the course of an evening working with a band, like with Jon, was I would notice that whenever I would do a solo thing, not only did *I* feel good about doing it, but the audience felt good about it also. But I wondered how long they could feel good about it. I mean could I feel good doing a solo concert? This was just one number, you know, five minutes. And it could be unique for five minutes, but could it be unique for ninety minutes?

And I was getting a lot of positive and negative feedback about that. Mostly negative. "No, that's not going to work, people listening to a solo concert for ninety minutes . . ." And I could see the difficulty behind that because it takes an incredible amount of concentration. It's not like when you go to hear an entire band play, because then you can shift your attention on to the bass player, the guitar player, the piano player, the singer, whatever. You know, you've got all this stuff coming at you. In a solo situation, you've got to lean into it. And that's tough. That's like meditation. It's like trying to drive all these thoughts out of your mind, trying to keep your mind steady.

Ben: And from your point of view, you can't "vamp." You can't just let the drummer have it.

Bobby: Yeah, that's right. But I can let the audience have it.

Ben: And you use humor, I think, in a way as a soloist with a band might use the rhythm section sometimes. As a way to catch your emotional breath. And it breaks the tension.

Bobby: [Laughs.] Right. I do enjoy myself, yes.

Ben: So what about working with groups in the future? How do you feel about performing with bands now?

Bobby: Well I enjoy it. I recently worked in New York at the Blue Note with John Scofield and Will Lee and Kenwood Dennard. And we had no rehearsals. We actually got together on the bandstand, you know. So I pretty much took the attitude of a solo concert, the same kind of attitude I have when I walk on stage by myself. I don't know what's going to happen but I'm in charge and whatever goes down, that's it. It works or it doesn't work but I'm going to get through this ninety minutes having as much fun as I possibly can. So I had that same kind of attitude with these musicians. Fortunately, they're incredible musicians with great ears and we just fell into anything. We played anything from Beethoven's "Moonlight Sonata" to Sly and the Family Stone's "Thank You (Falettinme Be Mice Elf [Agin])." Some old rock tunes, some of the modern tunes, and we would just do it, whether I knew the lyrics to it or not, you know?

And I'm finding out more and more that the people, you know they can be dazzled with technique, they can be moved to tears, whatever, but the thing I find refreshing is that if they have a good time, if they think that you are having a joyfully good time with the music, it doesn't matter if you make mistakes or don't know all the words. There's something else that's underneath all the music, anyway. And that's what the essence of true music's all about.

Ben: Which takes us back to Louis Armstrong's forgetting the words to a song and thus becoming the first "scat singer." So this is very much in the jazz tradition.

Bobby: Right. I think it goes back to our childhoods too. You know, like when we're just learning new things. We hear a new song for the first time, we're struggling with the words, we don't know what it is, but we're very excited by this new song. My son's that way. You know, he hears something that he's never heard before, like I might be singing something over and over again, and he stops and he listens and he gradually gets into it more and more. And I think that a lot of that is happening, too, in solo concerts, or any kind of improvisational situation, where everyone is aware that the music is tenuous and fragile. That somehow we all live tenuous, fragile, improvisatory lives anyway, on a day-to-day basis. And they kind of get that message in the music. And I think that's why this is working.

Ben: Because having you do it in front of them takes some of the weight off of them?

Bobby: Yeah. I'm showing them, I'm saying, "Okay, you know how to do this." Like when we do "Twinkle Twinkle Little Star," I say, "Okay, you know this song, so let's sing it together." Or "Ittsy Bittsy Spider." You know the hand movements that go with it, the little spider crawling up the wall and the sun coming out, you know that. And people really enjoy that.

Ben: From an improvising point of view, there are many precedents for an instrumentalist working alone. And from time to time, soloists get together in non-traditional ways, like the World Saxophone Quartet, which works almost as four individual soloists minus the rhythm section. So perhaps you're also heading in a direction where you can redefine what a group is. In other words, maybe your solo career is itself leading you to eventually work with other singers in a new way.

Bobby: I've been thinking about that. That's another idea. You know, I've discovered, not too long ago, that I've got a lot of ideas. I've got so many ideas that I wonder how I'm going to get them all done. But I know that they will happen in their time. I'm just planting seeds, and I take notes, you know, I write things down. I try to keep a journal of ideas and I'm sure at some point working with other singers will come about. Working with dancers is also something I'd love to do more of. I'd love to do more collaborations with visual artists, you know, the visual medium. Working in different environments, for example, say holding some concerts in a giant stairwell, you know. Or, who knows, because of the acoustic environment . . .

When I was in Japan not long ago, I met a sculptor who makes sort of musical sculptures, with water and things. And he said that different parts move and as they touch other parts there's a tone. And I thought, "Wow, what an interesting thing to do, to do a vocal concert with some of his sculptures on stage and sort of interact with them."

The whole thing with solo concerts seemed to be a wild idea in the first place and it's given me "permission" to accept all these other wild ideas I might have, because, who knows, they might work.

Ben: At the same time that you're searching for ways to expand the boundaries of so-called jazz vocals, other singers, mostly from the world of pop music, are trying to just get involved in the idiom. It seems like improvised music is somehow tied into their own sense of longevity. And the problem for many pop artists is they don't often sound like "authentic" jazz singers when they try. They may have great voices, but they still sound nothing at all like jazz singers. Do you have any thoughts on why this is and what makes a jazz singer?

Bobby: What is it about jazz? This is my question. I know what it sounds like. You can put two records on and one would be jazz and one would be rock and it would be very distinguishable. But what is the essence of it? What is the essence of it?

To me, it's simply improvisation, you know, that spontaneity that's *supposed* to be the finger mark of jazz. Sometimes I think that the problem with it is it becomes more and more cerebral. We start thinking about it so much that a lot of people, jazz musicians, myself included, aren't exactly sure. I know when I hear it, but when I'm *doing* it, I'm not sure.

Ben: It reminds me of something Jon Hendricks once said to me. We were in a recording session, this was years ago, and he was teaching me the song "Old Folks." And the engineer happened to roll some tape of the rehearsal. And Jon really liked the result, particularly his vocal performance. So he wanted to put the recording of the rehearsal on the record. I argued against it because there were some really wrong notes on the piano part, because I was just learning the song. But Jon said, "Don't you understand, the mistakes are the only part that's jazz."

Bobby: Right. And that's the same attitude I take every performance. No matter what comes out. It doesn't matter what it is, whether it works or not, whether it's good or bad. It's going through this process. It's like *looking* for this music, you know? And then after ninety minutes is up, or my voice gets tired, whichever comes first, it's over with. And I've done it, it's over with, and I can let go of that moment, as best as I can. I mean, I may be really elated about it or really down about it. But it's happened.

Ben: Which brings up how you prepare yourself, physically, for a concert. It must be a tremendous physical strain on your voice to perform solo night after night.

Bobby: It's amazing. Sometimes I'll really prepare myself for a performance and get to the gig and I don't really feel well. And sometimes I'll just be very lackadaisical about my technique or preparing myself and get to the gigs and I can work for a week or two without feeling any strain at all. So I don't really know. I think the technique comes with just accumulating enough experience with what you're doing. You just learn to work through all the little incongruities that you come across in traveling and performing.

Ben: Someone like Jon Hendricks, who is untrained as a singer, has probably done some serious damage to his voice over the years because he prepares so little and takes so many vocal chances. But even when he misses the notes, his attitude marks him as a superior jazz vocalist. On the other hand, there are many carefully prepared singers out there who sing the notes perfectly but do not convey the message of jazz. Perhaps that's part of the message. A singer with too much "control" projects the "control," whereas the message of jazz has always been that of "giving up control" in some fundamental way and of taking risks. Letting the song sing itself.

Bobby: It's funny. You know, I have a few students and they want to know about improvisation. And I say, "Well, it's a balance between control and surrender." It's like two sides of a highway. And you've got to walk down that yellow line. If you spend too much time on the control side it becomes very deliberate and there's really not that sense of abandonment which goes with being a good jazz singer. Now if you abandon yourself too much without the control, well then what you've got probably is just . . .

Ben: An out-of-work jazz singer . . .

Bobby: [Laughs.] Right, an out-of-work, scatter-brained jazz singer, more than likely. So there's a little bit of both that goes into improvisation.

You know, part of it is people say "Okay, I *want* to be a jazz singer." So they get the standard repertoire, they get jazz musicians together and they audition in jazz clubs. So now they're hypnotized with all the trappings and the ambience of the jazz scene, whatever that is. But what would happen if you took all of that away? And asked the singer to just sing something off the top of their head? To me, that is what I try and get my students to do. I say, "Okay, put your music aside, put your guitar down, or your piano, or whatever, and improvise. Make up a song. Five minutes, I want you to start, sing something for five minutes."

Well then what would you call it? It would be improvisation, which is the essence of jazz. And some singers can do it but most singers can't. I'm not sure what a jazz singer is really, because I'm not sure inside myself . . .

Ben: Perhaps it has something to do with attitude. There's an attitude that rings true and then there's an attitude that the listener has to meet half way.

Bobby: I think that's true. I think I'd have to agree with you. Yeah, attitude. I think it reflects on the times and I think it's all relative. You know, some people might say, "Well, Billie Holiday is a jazz singer." And of course we'd call her a jazz singer, but in her times, jazz music probably was a lot more popular. She could have been called a pop singer, she could have been called a blues singer. Some people say she's a jazz singer because of how she would take a song and throw all these inflections and phrasings which identified her as a jazz singer, but I know, if that's the case, if that's what makes a jazz singer, then I'm aware of a few avant-garde vocalists who would call themselves jazz singers but who couldn't be categorized as a jazz singer. Meredith Monk would be one of them.

Ben: Singers who are stretching the boundaries a bit, like Sheila Jordan or Jay Clayton or Lauren Newton with the Vienna Arts Orchestra, can be very far away from a jazz singer in the traditional sense. Also, it can be difficult for people to hear this kind of singing and so it remains somewhat invisible within the jazz community.

Bobby: You mean hear it intellectually or just that the records aren't around?

Ben: Well, perhaps a bit of both. Because the human voice in some ways is much harder to hear when it's "free" than an instrument.

Bobby: Yeah, that's true, and it's because it's not a tempered instrument like a piano. You know even though I might go hog-wild or helter-skelter all over the keyboard, as difficult as that might be to listen to, it's much harder to listen to a voice which can sing all those semi-tones in between the cracks and the keys or moan and groan for a while. Like Diamonda Galas, whose specialty is that, basically, using sort of a two microphone technique and singing out of some sort of synthesized filter and doing these grunts and groans and screaming or whatever.

It's tough, yeah, because the voice is a lot more demanding. And a lot more emotional. I mean, it picks up on the emotions a lot quicker than another instrument would because it's more immediate. And to be in emotional turmoil for thirty minutes is much harder for the human psyche than listening to the same kind of emotional upheaval on another instrument.

Ben: You can't distance yourself from it.

Bobby: Yeah, right.

Ben: Bobby, you're still so young. Do you have a vision of where this solo performing will lead you?

Bobby: Well, it's still going, and I'm sure it's going to take me wherever it is I want to go to musically. I mean I can't really see the end of it yet, but I do know I'm on the path. It's going to take me someplace.

* * *

Dave Grusin (February, 1987)

Dave Grusin is known as an Academy Award-winning composer of film scores, co-founder of the first all-CD record label (GRP Records), and one of the more perceptive talent scouts in the world of jazz fusion. He is also a fine piano player, although he tends to downplay his keyboard technique, not out of a sense of false modesty so much as an overriding respect for those who came before him and for those who are still "practicing eight hours a day" (as he once did). I first met Dave in the mid '80s while attending the Conference on World Affairs at the University of Colorado, an annual week-long event that has been described as "the leisure of the theory class." We were both panelists at the event, discussing everything from the impact of technology on this music to the implications of the flat five chord, and like everybody else at the conference, I was charmed and enlightened by his presentations on a daily basis. Dave Grusin is somebody who wears his sentimentality on his sleeve but, somehow, the cut is always contemporary and the style is always hip, in a way that speaks of the great traditions rather than what's currently fashionable.

Ben: You keep moving further and further away from civilization. You still work in L.A., where the film business is centered, and your label, GRP, is centered here in New York City, where the record business is, but you, personally, are moving further into the mountains every year.

Dave: Well, I don't believe that it's all happening in either New York or Los Angeles. Or any of the major cities. I mean, I just find these little hotbeds of incredible creative stuff going on all over the place. In jazz, and in other kinds of music too. There's a collection of composers in New Mexico that are serious composers. I mean, really good stuff. And there's a certain amount of recording being done down there. And I love that. I love to know that. So you're probably right about the business. I mean, it's centered here. But certainly in terms of what's happening creatively, I think it's really spread across the country.

Ben: I remember the last time we talked, a couple of years ago, you said how difficult it is to get out and meet new players, and see the world if you're not traveling in a band. And you've tended not to travel, not to perform a lot.

Dave: Yeah, except since we spoke, I've been out for the last two summers for tours with Lee Ritenour and some great musicians, and I've actually had some fun playing live. You know, I think I told you that it's not my favorite thing to do. But when the music is happening and the players are good, and you can hear what you're playing, and your chops are half way up from having done it enough, it really can be a lot of fun. I really understand what that attraction is. Really, for the first time in my life, I really enjoyed doing that.

Ben: Having enough control over the entire environment you're taking with you.

Dave: Yeah. And being relaxed enough, in some context, to be able to deal with the fact that there's an audience sitting out there. Real people. And maybe they're not all gonna kill me, you know?

Ben: Well, part of it too is the fact that when you make these incredibly high-tech recordings, the expectation that people have when they come hear you is very high. They want to hear it like they heard it on the record.

Dave: Yeah, I understand. And that's maybe possible in some pop context. I don't think it's possible for a lot of what we do. And I'm not too worried about it. I think if the intent is there, if it doesn't sound exactly like it does on the record, at least if it sounds great. Maybe it even sounds better in some cases. And maybe the playing is a little more interesting. You know, with whatever freedom there is to stretch in person. And it's something that you think about when you're cranking up to go out and do these tunes that you've recorded. "Oh, how we gonna perform this live?" And that's the last time you think about it, because they suddenly take on lives of their own, and it's a new kind of a new ball game out there.

Ben: And you got a nice little repertory group of players now that you've recorded with.

Dave: Well, yeah. I mean, and it's a little incestuous. I think maybe it'd be good for all of us to stretch. To maybe give it a rest for a while. In fact, Lee Ritenour is out now with a nice band, including Kenny G. And I think Bill Withers is playing it. And Herbie Mann. I mean, it's a whole other kind of a context, and I think it's very good for him to do that.

Ben: Lee is somebody who, like yourself, seems to enjoy taking on the production role, the role of organizer and producer.

Dave: Well, he's very good at it. He's very organized. I thank God he's done it. I mean, because I certainly laid it all on him when we went out in the last two years.

Ben: Your label, GRP, was the first all digital label, devoted to CD's before they were even a gleam in the eye of the record buying public. The recording of "Mountain Dance," I think, was one of early important tracks for this label. When was this?

Dave: '78 I think. It was the first digital thing we did. And we did it live to two-track on Sound Stream. And to my knowledge, it was one of the first jazz recordings on that digital format. It was kinda primitive in those days. I think we had four tracks available, which we didn't use, because nobody knew exactly how to use them. So we just did it like a performance and just recorded it on digital tape. And it's turned out to be, I never thought. I mean, I always liked the tune, but I never thought it would be as well-known as it's become.

I worked on a film once, called *Falling In Love*, and when I showed up to go to work, they had that piece as temporary music on the track of the film. And I said, "Well, that's interesting. That sure doesn't work for me. But, how interesting." They said, "Well we really love that, and we'd love for you to do something like that. We put it in here." You know, they put it in as a guide. And I said, "Well, I'll be happy to try, but I don't think it works." And I tried to do everything else possible and did, and finished the score. And they took it to a preview and they called that night and said, "Do you think it would be possible for us to actually use 'Mountain Dance' in the picture." And so we ended up doing that. We licensed it to them for the film. I'm ambivalent about it. I mean, I'm flattered they thought enough of it, or they thought it worked. On the other hand, I really didn't think it was as functional for the picture as what I had done.

Ben: Brings up the subject of scoring. You've done as much if not more scoring than any performing jazz artist to date.

Dave: Yeah. That's probably true.

Ben: What tips would you give a jazz artist out there who's interested? A lot of jazz musicians are interested in branching out into film writing, and don't know how to go about it. And jazz really is a visual music.

Dave: Well, that's true. You know, I get calls all the time, and letters and inquiries. And they don't know how to go about it, partly because they don't understand what it's all about. A lot of it isn't about music. A lot of it is about the attitude of the production people for whom you're working. You're an element in their big pie. Just as sound effects are, just as dialogue is, just as, you know, timing the film in terms of what it looks like. What the picture actually looks like, the cinematography and so forth.

And we think, we musicians, composers, think, "Oh, they really like this because they really like the music." You know, "They really like what I wrote" or they like this sequence of notes. I mean, you can really narrow it down. And that may not be what they're hearing at all, you know? And you can go through weeks or months of conversations and both thinking you're talkin' about the same thing, and finally it comes out that what they liked maybe was the sound of the guy's cymbal on your record, or the sound of a . . . you know, there was some surprise in it that got them, and not what you thought it was, the whole compositional entity.

So there's a lot of confusion about film scoring. And talking about music is very difficult. I mean, it's even hard for musicians to talk to each other in real specifics about music. A lot of directors feel they know what they need to make their picture work, in terms of specifics. The good directors, the ones I think are good directors in terms of how they work with composers, are the ones who can say to you, "I need in this spot something that upsets me," or "I need something that maybe hints at something that happened back in reel two." Or something that's gonna happen in reel ten. Rather than a director saying, "Look I need a D minor here." Which some of them do . . .

Ben: Really? . . .

Dave: Oh yeah. A lot of directors are musicians of one kind or another and a lot of them fancy themselves good musicians. At least in terms of their own work, their own film. So the preconceptions that they have are sometimes helpful, but a lot of times not totally helpful to a composer who's trying to write something new for them. And the other trap, of course, is that they lay music into their film that's already been done. It's a known entity. And then they tell you that's exactly what they want in their picture. So of course you're not gonna write what they've put in there already. That's somebody else's music. And that's a tough corner to fight your way out of sometimes.

Ben: Brings up the subject that, recently, it appears there is the desire to have hit songs laced throughout the films, songs that are already hits.

Dave: Ahm. Yeah, I was shocked last year. I did a panel for somebody at UCLA in a film class along with a number of other people, but mostly what they call music coordinators, or music supervisors, and record company representatives.

Ben: They're tied together, aren't they?

Dave: Well, I was shocked that it seems that for those kinds of pictures that you're speaking of, ones that want hit songs, the starting point is not with the composers, the starting point is with the record company. If they can make a deal with the record company, or a music supervisor, to supply those songs at X amount of dollars per. And then, usually, they find they need some glue, you know. They can't score the whole thing only with the songs, so then they come to a composer. And I guess I don't know where I've been, but I just kind of was shocked at that revelation. It was a revelation for me. It wasn't a surprise to anybody else. I've been able to kind of avoid that I guess, because I don't get called usually for those kind of films. You know, I'm not really a songwriter, per se, not primarily, and I don't think it's a trend that's growing. Actually I think it maybe peaked.

I think the answer is, wherever there's a buck, if they can really sell enough soundtrack albums, they'll keep doing that. And that may still be going on. But I don't think it's gonna go on indefinitely, and in fact, most of the good directors I know are really interested in the thing that's gonna help their film the most. And that's not always those song scores. Song score might help sell the film, but I like to think that most of the good directors, that really care about their work, that's not their primary interest in film music.

Ben: I was wondering, actually, when you're talking about getting out more the last couple of years and playing, if it was tied into the trend in films to have these canned and pre-packaged scores. If that helped propel you out there and give you a reason to go play more.

Dave: As opposed to staying home and writing? No, I tell you, I sort of average two pictures a year. Sometimes three, and maybe sometimes one. But I think that's been good for me. I'm not a really prolific writer, in terms of jumping from project to project and instantly coming up with something really good. And I learned that about myself maybe ten years ago. And when I moved to New York in 1976, something changed in terms of my perception of what I oughta be doing about film music. And also, I think the fact that I came here, to New York, and got out the sort of rat race that I felt I was in before, where I would take a job because I had just finished one and was available. And that was not, ultimately not a good enough reason to do the project. So that their perception of me changed a little bit, when I came back here. I mean, there was something mysterious about leaving Hollywood for one thing, to them. It wasn't mysterious to me. We had started this record company, and I really spent most of my time here. But, it helped my attitude, I think, about film music, by backing off a little bit.

Ben: You mentioned starting this record company with Larry Rosen. It was significant in a couple of ways. One, because you staked out a little position in the record industry right away, doing quality music, doing quality production. You were covering a particular base that wasn't covered at that moment, and other people were slow to catch on. And by the time they caught on, you were off and running. Similarly, you caught the industry off base with regard to technology. You've always been involved in a certain kind of esthetic and a technology at the the same time . . .

Dave: Yeah.

Ben: How does being involved with technological innovation shape your A&R policy? How does it determine what you put on the record?

Dave: I think the only way it determines what we actually record is it has opened up a whole lot of areas of music, sort of fringe areas close to where we were. And by that I mean a compact disc for instance can handle, I think, 72 minutes of music. When you think that the bulk of our sales now are compact discs and cassettes, not vinyl records, your whole focus changes because now you're dealing with another medium. You're not concerned about keeping the amount of music per side down to where you can really get it hot on the record, you know, you can get enough level when you're mastering. We've always tried to keep it around 20 minutes per side on a vinyl record. Well, those restrictions are totally gone now.

Ben: So it makes a long form even longer.

Dave: It makes a long form longer and, coinciding with the technology, is the sort of change in attitude that people have had in our marketplace, about discovering the alternative to the kind of records that they're used to buying. They can find a GRP kind of fusion element that turns 'em on a little bit, and it's an alternative to the pop stuff that they've been buying. Or Windham Hill, or by any other name. And suddenly, we're no longer talking about needing the whole record, with all the hot tunes on the record being under four minutes, so we can get the airplay.

Because that's not necessarily how we're selling this product anymore. These people are buying it now. The thing that we're really fortunate about, I think, technologically, is that our stuff has always sounded good. And we've tried to be very careful about that. So that we don't offend audiophiles. And we want them to buy this stuff. We wanna expand as far as we can take it in that regard. And when they buy a record, they don't care that the tune is longer than four minutes. Probably better if it's six minutes long. I'm just doing a film theme album now, and it's interesting to note that a lot of main titles that I've done are three minutes or under. So I've extended some of them. I've made 'em into longer form, whether it's adding another 32 bars or another minute and a half to the original. Or combining them with other music from the same film. And I'm gonna have fourteen tracks on this record, where five years ago, when making an analog record, vinyl record, we'd have ten, tops.

Ben: Are you gonna press it on vinyl? . . .

Dave: Yes.

Ben: And you'll leave some of them off?

Dave: Well, we'll have to leave some of them off. I don't think the level will take the whole batch. But our primary market is now CD's, so that's who we're making the product for, essentially.

Ben: You went back and recreated some of your early scores, like *Three Days of the Condor*?

Dave: Yeah, yeah. We went back and tried to . . . it was very interesting. Harvey Mason and Abe Laboriel, Lee Ritenour and four horn players. Chuck Findley and Tom Scott, Ernie Watts and Charlie Loper.

Ben: None of the good guys were available, huh?

Dave: None of the good guys. Well Charlie actually replaced Frank Rosolino, who was on the original. But it was kinda hard to do this again. I mean, I thought it'd be a snap. I had the tape from the original. We all listened to it and said, "Oh, I remember this." And we went back and realized that nobody actually plays exactly the way we did ten years ago!

Ben: Really? The tape stayed the same but you guys moved on . . .

Dave: Just in terms of how we would play, in terms of our own personalities. Harvey came real close to absolutely nailing the original feel. But I was surprised. It was an element that I hadn't reckoned with at all.

Ben: The time has changed. Brings up another of your GRP projects, the digital Duke Ellington recreations. The first time you hear that CD, it's a little bit of a shock to hear Duke's music with that kind of fidelity. A total digital recording.

Dave: You're right, absolutely right. I know. And I don't know if it's a plus or a minus sometimes. We went through, we made a record, a kind of similar retrospective of Glenn Miller's stuff. Well, you never heard the rhythm section with the old Glenn Miller records. That was a horn band. And all of a sudden people weren't really sure if . . .

Ben: That's the way it really went . . .

Dave: Yeah. It didn't sound exactly the same. But it sounds great. I mean, the digital recording sounds wonderful. And in some way, it sounds fresher now. The Ellington things kill me on a number of levels. When you think about the body of work, and we narrowed these tunes down, I think there're maybe fourteen things on this record, and to narrow those down were really hard. Hard to leave out all the other ones that you wanted to do. And to hear those arrangements again, and to hear the thing up close, and for the first time. I mean, when I was a kid, I had no idea how that could possibly be written. That band particularly. That was the most unusual, unique band, in terms of voicings and writing. I mean, for somebody to decide to be a writer based on hearing only the Ellington band, it would be a tough decision. I mean, where do you start?

Ben: It reminds me of a story about Art Tatum's piano style. The story goes that he developed his style in part because, when he was young, he heard a recording made by two pianos, four hands, and he thought it was done by only one person.

Dave: [Laughs uproariously.] Yeah, I can understand that. Well, and the other thing is, growing up hearing Art Tatum it's fairly discouraging if you think you're gonna become a piano player.

Ben: Right. That's about as far as the line draws. But the question of technology and the classics from the past is really interesting. The emergence of compact discs has made available all the catalog from all these labels. Many labels are doing significant business on their catalogs.

Dave: I know, I know. Most that we thought were dead.

Ben: Much of it's jazz.

Dave: Well, that doesn't surprise me. I think it probably surprises a lot of record companies. Jazz has always been this thing, if they were involved in it, it was sort of a peripheral entity. And they had the masters and they don't give stuff up automatically. If they own 'em, they sit on 'em, you know. And suddenly to find a new marketplace. I think it's done a lot, not only for the people who were around then and remember that stuff. I don't think that's the only audience. I talk to kids all the time and their mouths are open about all of this stuff. Because it is new to them. And I try to remember how I felt the first time I heard this music. You know, my dad took me to a Jazz at the Philharmonic concert or something, I couldn't believe it! And it must be a similar experience for whole new generation of people.

Ben: Clearly a different experience today, though, hearing "Take the A Train" off of the GRP Ellington record, as opposed to listening to the Ellington 78rpm, which is where it was taken from. It's larger than life.

Dave: With Branford Marsalis on tenor. Sounding like he was about fifty years old and had been playing with the band for all of his life.

Ben: You know what's amazing about that? Branford is part of a generation of young players who essentially learned to play from records. His experience wasn't hangin' out in sessions like yours probably was, or older players. It was from records, and out of that experience, he's managed to really cop the attitude, the essential attitude of the old style.

Dave: Absolutely. It's not foreign to any of those guys. I mean, I'm just amazed when I hear Branford or Wynton settle into a style like that, that's clearly not a contemporary thing. I don't mean that it's dated but it's been with us for so many years. You know, I heard these kids feel so comfortable with it. And they're not doing a number. They're not trying to do that. They're just comfortable in some kind of method acting situation I guess. It's almost like "Here I am. I'm sitting in the middle of this band, and this is what this band is, and I'm gonna be part of it." And, from everything that comes out of the horn, it's cool from then on.

Ben: You know, there's been a lot of discussion at the educational level about how things have changed for jazz players. Part of it is because there aren't many jam sessions and people don't have a common vocabulary now. Before, if you had a book of standards in front of you, you could go out and play with anybody. Now that's just not true. But on the other hand, the young players have a chameleon-like quality. They can become the real thing.

Dave: I think what you said about growing up, listening to records, and developing a style from this whole spectrum, like the entire history of jazz. Not just one, not just one era. They take the best after a while. You listen to the records, you know what really worked in any given year. And what didn't. And they just kinda concentrate on the best of all of that, and they turn out to be these phenomenal, eclectic players.

Ben: Okay. So as the technology opens up toward the future, it simultaneously throws a spot light on the past as well . . .

Dave: That's right . . .

Ben: Okay. Let's talk about technology. Let's talk about DAT technology, because GRP records, ten years later, is still attempting to push the boundaries. And I know you're getting some heat for championing Digital Audio Tape.

Dave: Well, Digital Audio Tape, DAT, is to the compact disc what regular audio cassettes are to the vinyl LP. In other words, it's a tape format, a little cassette, that looks like a regular cassette that everybody has. It's a little smaller, and there's no actual music on the tape. It's data on the tape. It's a little computer-generated storage medium, is all it is. And, eventually, I suppose everybody will have their Walkman, or whatever, that will play DAT. So what you get is a kind of portable digital music machine that has all the advantages of being as clean as digital music is on a compact disc, and it's tiny. You can take it with you. The heat is coming. We have gotten a lot of heat. We've gotten it from all sides actually. We've gotten it certainly from other record companies who don't understand why we're interested in this stuff. We've gotten it from stores, retailers, who aren't gonna stock it. You know, they're just not gonna stock it. They don't believe in it. We've gotten all kinds of reasons.

I mean, there are, there are hearings now in Washington about the copyrighting infringement potential of having this clean little recording medium that you can now steal from other sources, from radio, from records, from compact discs, and make your own little tapes. It's hard for us the see what the difference is from what's been going on all along anyway, with everybody making their own cassettes. Nobody avoids that. Any music buff that I know, they make their own little programs, you know, from different LP's and so forth. So all this talk of copyrighting infringement, it's going on anyway. We don't see that changing that much. We don't see what the difference is really going to be.

What we really think is that everybody, particularly the major labels particularly, kind of lagged behind in jumping on the CD bandwagon, and now they're on it. Now they're cranking out not only their hit artists, now they're going back in their secondary and tertiary product, catalog product, and putting everything they can on CD, because there're now enough manufacturing plants that we can all get capacity. We can get kind of as much as we need now. Which was not true for the first three years of this. And they want a chance to sell some of this stuff off. And I think the retailers feel the same way. In other words, they've made a significant investment in going to this new medium. Now all of a sudden, there's another new one they've gotta deal with. We can do it essentially because we're small enough to be fluid. We cannot under any circumstances sit there and say, "Well, gee, that's great technology and it works and it's perfect, and the music sounds great on it, but we better not do it." I mean, that's crazy for us to do. We have to be on the forefront because we're not big enough to fight in any other way. If we can be first in this area, and I think that's what'll happen. And then everybody'll come along in two years, three years.

Right now, the biggest handicap is that there are virtually no players in the United States. No hardware. But we see the handwriting on the wall. I mean, when all these major Japanese firms, which is of course where all this stuff emanates from, when they're all cranking up in terms of hardware, and they're serious about it, we know what their programs are, and it's clear that it's gonna be here.

Ben: The image of the future always includes some ultimate form of technology. Where's this leading us? What's the ultimate storage medium? And I guess the other part of that question is, when we finally get to that bright day, what are the record companies like GRP ultimately selling? If all the music is infinitely transferable in pristine form, are you reduced to selling pure information as opposed to pieces of product?

Dave: Well maybe ultimately what you'll sell is a chip, a micro chip. Or maybe all the chips will be in some room, and what you'll buy is the use of it, in your home machine, whatever it is. And you'll just call on the phone and dial in the code and that record will play and you won't have to go anywhere to buy the record. You'll be charged for the call.

Ben: But won't I put it on my own storage medium then and have it?

Dave: Yes, and then you'll put it on your micro chip, you know.

Ben: I guess what I'm thinking, David, is that we're in the business of packaging. That's really what it comes down to. If it was pure information, if all I really wanted was the notes that Branford is playing on "Take the A Train," I could get that. But partly I want to hold the package that you create, that one that fits on the shelf with all my other packages. I think people are basically collectors.

Dave: That's exactly right. And we see the CD, the compact disc, as the '80s version of the collectors item. In other words, people that were record buyers, that were LP buyers, are the logical people to buy these things, because they do sit on your shelf and you can look at them. They're packaged in such a way that they're a little more interesting than a cassette format. The other thing that I see happening is this video disc market.

I don't know enough about it. The reason I'm thinking of it now is just in the last few days we've heard so much about these new formats. There is a disc player that can play the 12-inch disc with video, and the picture resolution is incredible. There's also a compact disc size version of that you can play on the same machine, and a compact audio disc that you can play on the same machine. Potentially the interactive stuff will happen, where you can pick your ending maybe, you know. Or you can pick the music behind whatever the picture is that you're looking at.

Ben: Would you be interested in making a Duke Ellington collection minus the tenor parts for people to play on? [Dave laughs.] A new music minus one?

Dave: A new minus one. Probably not. But maybe that's part of it. That was certainly an example of early interactive home entertainment. Music minus one, I mean it's a real good graphic example. What is the game, the video game, where you can pick the ending to whatever the story is. I have not seen that, but as a concept, I really understand that because I think people are gonna want to get more involved themselves, as participants, rather than remain passive viewers or listeners at home. I think that's where home entertainment is going.

Ben: So technology will bring the artistic process closer to home.

Dave: Yeah. While we were talking before, I was also thinking, the original question about what has technology meant in terms of creativity? I think one of the things is, we've done more acoustic music in the last two years than I think we did in the previous eight years. Just in terms of the original thrust of the project. Because the digital medium really lends itself to nice acoustic stuff. I mean, it's some kind of spatial situation that works wonderfully with acoustic music.

Ben: That's an interesting irony in digital land. Because on the one hand, the technology creates synthesizers that do away with the need for acoustic space, you can plug them right into the digital tape recorder or whatever. But on the other hand, the digital tape recorder really flatters acoustic environments. With digital recording, you'd almost rather hear acoustic instruments.

Dave: That's right. You want ambient stuff that isn't obscured by distortion. I mean, people who are not used to digital sound are frequently disturbed by something. They're not sure what it is. They know it sounds different. And the main difference is the lack of distortion that all analog tape carries with it, just as a concomitance. All analog tape is just two things rubbing against each other. And when they rub, they just make some noise. And we've grown up kind of learning to love that. And when it's taken away from us, sometimes it's disturbing.

* * *

Bob James (January, 1989)

Bob James has had many incarnations in the jazz business. In the early '60s, his piano playing was as far away from the mainstream as possible In fact, his first solo recordings (on the Mercury and ESP labels) were closer to musique concrète *than to jazz. But by the mid '60s, after a stint as accompanist for singer Sarah Vaughan, he quickly became a fixture on the New York studio scene, backing up singers like Dionne Warwick and Roberta Flack, performing with Quincy Jones, and scoring shows for Broadway. By the '70s, after signing on as an arranger with the CTI label, he was well on his way to establishing himself as a producer of hit jazz recordings (for instrumentalists such as Grover Washington and Stanley Turrentine), when suddenly his own solo career took off. Today, he lives within commuting distance from New York City and has returned to his first love, the acoustic piano, by way of the latest digital technology, the sequencers and synthesizers that are part and parcel of today's music industry armament. In addition, he is a vice president of A&R at Warner Brothers Records and the guiding light behind the successful group Fourplay. Bob James has a unique perspective on the jazz business, having seen all sides of this music from his roles as player, producer, and record executive.*

Ben: You started out as a young boy, in rural Missouri, playing the piano to the chickens. I'm being facetious here, of course, but you *have* played a lot of different music—electronic music, avant-garde music, classical music, jazz, popular music—starting as far from the urban centers as possible and arriving at a synthesis of all these elements with great success. At what point did you know where you were headed and how did you get there?

Bob: I knew, I think, very early, that I was gonna be a musician. I started playing the piano so early, and it took so immediately. I started taking lessons when I was four years old, as a result of watching my older sister, who was taking lessons. And I saw what the teacher was having her do, and I was mimicking them, and teacher ended up watching what I was doing, and thought there was something there, so they followed up on it. But, typically, I never liked to practice. And also, as a result of being from a small town, there was not much understanding of what the role of a musician would be, a role model. There were no other real role model musicians that I could relate to. And the standard image of the male was the athlete who eventually became a businessman. And that's about as far as anybody knew how to guide you.

So I always felt like I was fighting for an identity that nobody really had any sympathy for. And, as a result, classical music, which is where I started, was the least understood by my peers. And when I began to listen to jazz, this rebellion, or the lack of formality and the danger aspect of it, or something, was somehow more acceptable, more racy, when I was in high school. And as a result, I got really into that, and fought the whole classical establishment for a long time. And only through the persistence of my mother was I able to stay with an education through college. And I'm very grateful for that, because I think it was helpful in many, many ways.

Ben: You attended the University of Michigan, and while a student there, you participated in the Jazz Festival at Notre Dame. Today there are a lot of jazz competitions; back then, the big one was Notre Dame, where college students from all over came and competed. And you went with your trio, and you competed, and the story is that one of the judges was Quincy Jones, and from there you were catapulted into the music business.

Bob: Yes, that's true, and everybody has their crossroads, their important pivotal times in their lives, and that was definitely a big one for me. And, thinking back on the early thing from when I first started out in a small town, the going away from the establishment, or the rebellion aspect, was part of that process that ended up at Notre Dame, too. Because this trio that I had, with a drummer named Bob Possar and a bass player, Ron Brooks, was involved with performing a lot of avant-garde music in Ann Arbor, Michigan. There just happened to be a very strong group of, what was at that time, very avant-garde classical composers, who were doing lots and lots of things in Ann Arbor. And they liked working with jazz musicians 'cause we could improvise, and most of their scores called upon you to do all kinds of really outrageous things. Stand on your head and shout into the piano, and throw the drums up in the air, and all those kind of things. So, we were so much into that, that the idea of going to a conventional jazz festival was only interesting to us as a way of doing something really outrageous, and really fighting the establishment.

So, when we went down there, and even though we had some chops together, as conventional jazz players, what we really wanted to do was to play some of this weird electronic music and the out stuff. As a small example of that, one of our pieces was written by an Ann Arbor composer named Roger Reynolds. And he had written these big scores that had stems but no notes at the bottom of the stems. And there was no musical staff, but the stems would sort of indicate rhythms that you could play, but you could choose whatever notes that you wanted to add to those stems. And you could choose which instrument you wanted to play them on. His piece was called "Dirvish." And the idea was that we would run around the stage. There were these groups of instruments that we had set up. Some of them were oil drums. Not steel drums of the kind where they've been pounded out and made into notes, but just oil drums that you banged on, and whatever the pitch was, that's what it was. And a variety of exotic instruments. So we ran around the stage, and played the world premiere of Roger Reynolds' "Dervish," much to the total confusion of these judges, with probably the exception of Quincy, who at least had some empathy with what we were doing. I mean he told me later that he thought we were nuts too, just like everybody else did, but I think he liked the idea that we had the guts to do something that unconventional. And it was dramatic. I mean, there were a lot of groups down there. There were probably forty or fifty groups, all playing Count Basie arrangements and Miles Davis tunes, and whatever, and there was so much sameness, possibly, that we definitely stood out. And we were commercial enough, and commercial-minded enough, I guess, to have also included several straight ahead pieces to say to Quincy and the rest of the judges, "We can play this other stuff, too, but we wanna have fun playing the out stuff."

Ben: Coincidentally, right about that time, Quincy had been quoted as saying that he envisioned a time when all music could be one, and you could play Bartok and you could play Charlie Parker and you could play Bo Diddley, and it would all be the same. So I think you struck a sympathetic chord there. I mean, you were in the right place at the right time.

Bob: Yeah, and having the support of somebody with that stature and having them say, "Yes, it's okay." You're not just a strange person that's gonna end up in the back of a lab at some university somewhere doing experimental music that nobody cares about. I'm just astounded with some of the ways that music, popular music, has developed since that time, in the period of 25 years or so, where this electronic stuff that we were dabbling with, filters and tone generators and so forth, eventually evolved into multi-multi-multi-huge business of electronic synthesizers that now dominates the whole pop music world. And at that time it was completely off in the back of the lab, as it were.

Ben: Well, Quincy was a visionary. And he did sign you to a record deal at Mercury Records, where he was a vice-president of A&R. This was around 1963. You made some very "out" music for a couple of years. I remember one album, on the ESP label, you made it around 1965 after you had moved to New York, I believe. It was called *Explosions*, and it was all movements, flashes, motion, darkness, light. Very dramatic music, even though it was completely off the scale for jazz at the time.

Bob: One of the things that we were interested in then was that the accepted practice for improvising in jazz had been either over some standard tune, usually a thirty-two-bar chord structure, or the twelve-bar blues, or whatever the other standard chord patterns that we learned to improvise around. And we felt that there were other ways that one could use structures upon which to build improvisations that may not be as limiting. And so we called upon these two different electronic music composers to give us some electronic pieces of theirs to use as structures. Instead of having chords, we would learn them, knowing that there were these events that would happen during the course of the electronic piece, and that became the shape of the piece, and our improvisations were over the top of that. So we were over-dubbing solos to a pre-existing electronic piece. That was pretty much the concept of.

Ben: Around this time you were also quoted as saying that you were very much involved with the notion that jazz had to be Serious music, capital S. And that what you wanted to do was remove the elements of harmony, tonality, melody and swing from improvisational music. You're laughing now. You're shaking your head in fact, that you said that . . .

Bob: I said that? . . .

Ben: You said it. Well, maybe you didn't, but it was, it had quotation marks and your name after it.

Ben: It's quite possible that I did. It was definitely a time in which there was a tremendous move toward removing the stigma of nightclubs and lower-end-of-the-spectrum treatment for jazz and jazz musicians in order to elevate it to a status of an artform. It was, I guess, to us very important that people take it seriously. And that the move towards getting jazz into the concert hall, a move that I guess, looking back on it now, has a mixed end result. While it is true that it's a quite normal thing now to be able to go to a concert hall and hear jazz being performed, there still is a kind of stiffness about concert halls for any kind of music that is not in a nightclub situation. There is a relaxed and a kind of closer feeling to music, that maybe we don't have as much of that as we used to have, now that the world has become more organized and big business and all those kind of things.

But certainly I went a long way from there, if I did have that attitude then, of thinking that jazz should be more serious, maybe I've come almost full circle from that now. Because I think I like the whole feel the best when some of those pretensions are removed from it. And that gets back to the roots of where I think it started from, which is people dancing and being natural.

Ben: I think if you'd stayed along the path that you were on then, you'd be working in Europe maybe once or twice a year, and that would be the end of it. But you didn't. Interestingly enough, not long after that, you became Sarah Vaughan's accompanist, and at the same time, I think you began doing some arranging in New York studios. What were those experiences like for a young avant-garde rebel? How did you take to it?

Bob: Slowly, maybe. They took to me slowly, too, as a matter of fact. It took quite a few years before there was any kind of regular employment. Even though the Quincy Jones name, as a name-dropping thing, always helped. It got me the job with Sarah as a matter of fact. And then later, after having proved that I could successfully work with her, dropping her name was equally magical amongst the people in our profession. So I found that, like I think probably everybody does in this business, you have to have your calling cards or your way of getting through the door to have people take you seriously. And that was a slow process for me. The most steady work that I got, and I think having the college education and studying orchestration made it possible, was arranging work, and that really allowed me to make a living and allowed me to establish myself so that I was working steadily in New York.

Ben: What about the ability to be flexible too? I mean, I think that it's a kind of invisible talent that people work on or don't work on.

Bob: Yeah, absolutely. And that was what the studio business was all about, then. And the group that I sorta came up with and got to know and watch, the kinds of players who could play on a commercial for toys one day and a recording session with Frank Sinatra the next day, and maybe a symphony session the next day, and a country-and-western session the next day. Those type of players had to first of all have an open attitude about music. They couldn't be too stuck in the kind of trap in which only this one thing is valid and certainly anybody with that kind of attitude would've never survived with studio work. And keeping that open attitude, even though in the back of your mind you may think the stuff is trivial or it's silly, or it's not happening, or whatever, but being willing to take it on that day as a challenge. There is something that I can get out of this country-and-western recording session that is valid musically, if I give my best to it. And the best players, in whatever the idiom, are able to do that. And you find out if you're not a good player in that idiom very quick, because they don't call you anymore. They call the other guy who can really do it. So that openness certainly changed my life drastically.

Ben: We should point out too that this kind of openness, although many people don't like to think about it, was exhibited to some extent by Charlie Parker, who would go and play in country-and-western bands, just for the joy of it. He certainly did not see himself in the narrow bebop definition that people put him in years later. That wasn't him as a person.

Bob: No, absolutely. And his music was so strong and pure, in a different kind of sense of purist, his musical mind was pure, so that it works, no matter where you put it.

Ben: Whatever he played became "his music" in the end. Again, Quincy Jones was a model of this kind of flexibility for you, too. He was also instrumental in bringing you to the attention of Creed Taylor. You played on Quincy's album *Walking In Space* in 1969, which was a model of taste and hipness and, at the time, high technology, and these are the elements that you later went on to develop. Little things, like the minimalism of your piano intro on "Oh Happy Day," they became kind of a signature. You had some great teachers.

Bob: I think another thing that we, those of us who did studio work, gained tremendously from, was like a college education in how to make music. And if you were observant, when you had your opportunity to play on a session, you could learn from the best. And having the opportunity to be hired by Quincy, to come into a session like that, where I look over on my left and there's Ray Brown playing bass, and you look in every direction and there's Toots Thielemans and there's all the people that I had admired, and just for that day maybe. Maybe it's not gonna happen again for another six months, or whatever, but on that day, you're there as not only a person who has to prove himself, to be able to justify being there, but you can also learn. And watching people like Quincy take charge of his music in a recording studio, it left a very deep impression on me. And I'm sure that we can look back after these many years and see the seeds of why I tried to do what I did. Some of it was being an employee. I went on from that session to do a lot of work with Creed Taylor over the next four or five years. And it was that one session that got me all that work, because Quincy wanted to use me on his album. Creed heard the arrangement that I did and heard me playing the piano, and decided that I was somebody that he would like to hire again.

Ben: Talk a little bit about what exactly what you saw Quincy do that day. I'm real curious, because it must have made a real strong impression on you.

Bob: It did, and I thought about it a lot afterwards, as I watched other things that he did, and has gone on to do. And one of the qualities that he has, or talents, or magic, whatever you call it, is the most difficult to reduce into words or into any factual thing, because by that time Quincy was not playing the trumpet anymore. He was very often not doing his own arrangements, and they weren't doing his tunes. So, Quincy, what are you doing here? You know, this is your album, and there was even a temptation on the part of some of us to be resentful of that, who were even working with Quincy, because, "Well, wait a minute, you know. I wrote that arrangement." But if we were really honest about it, we would have to admit that, at least I felt this way, that there was something about what Quincy represented, and his leadership, and his ability to understand when people were doing things at their best, that set him apart from everybody else.

And I could watch—every musician that would come into the room to do a Quincy Jones session was breaking their backs to do their best for him. There were rarely any attitude type of problems that I experienced, like you see with other sessions, where for one reason or another, people are turned off, or they're reading the newspaper, or they're treating somebody's session casually. With Quincy, it became very important to show Quincy what you could do. And everybody felt that way. And as a result, if he had thirty musicians in the room, that are all trying so hard, and giving everything that they've got, this magic would happen. That made us all think, "Okay, well, now we understand. We'll go off and do that when we do our projects." But more often than not, it wouldn't work that way, because it was something that *he* brought to it.

I guess there are a lot of things about it. Very careful choice of musicians to be around. An innate musical sense of when it's really happening, of how, what to have people do. Choices. And I mean, this is just, these are just little things. Overall, I would say that this aura that Quincy created was what impressed me the most. And now he's gone on to such a completely different level. But I would guess that, on those sessions, with Michael Jackson or whatever that he's working on, it's that quality that has shone through for him all these years.

Ben: Interesting. Your first solo Bob James record came out in 1974 on CTI. It was a record that, again, kind of roughed out themes that you carry on in your career as a recording artist, not just as an arranger for other people, but as somebody who suddenly became a commodity himself. I imagine at some point you started to really think seriously, "What kind of commodity am I in this business, and how do I package it, and how do I present it? What do I have to offer that's unlike other people have to offer?" I hear it in your records, and I hear that the elements involved have to do with using classical themes and using disparate techniques. Were you very conscious of that when you went to make *Bob James One*?

Bob: No, I really wasn't then. As a matter of fact, I'm not exaggerating by saying that, when I made that record, I had no thought whatsoever that it would ever go beyond *One*. To me, it was something that I was very happy that Creed Taylor indulged me in, letting me make that record.

I guess the years of working in the studio behind the scenes, as a craftsman, or as somebody who was helping put other people's records together, had gotten me to believe that that was going to be my life. I had reorganized my priorities so much from the Ann Arbor days that I had sort of given up the idea of me as an artist, as the leader. I really liked my role as a sideman. I liked coming in and having it be a Grover Washington album, and that I could be behind the scenes trying to make him sound as good as I could make him sound. It was no problem. And if anything, I felt intimidated about the idea of being stuck out in front of this band, because I was so much more confident, and had all this other experience, while somebody else was out there in front. And, so I made this record, and a number of things happened that were very fortunate. The timing was right, we had done an arrangement of a song called "Feel Like Makin' Love," that Roberta Flack had a humongous hit with. And as a result of the fact that my whole rhythm section was the same that played on her record, both of our versions enjoyed a lot of popularity. I would certainly say that I was piggy-backing on her record.

And suddenly I had this solo career that I really wasn't prepared for. I didn't even really know exactly what or why. I mean, I knew that "Feel Like Makin' Love," I knew there was the reason why that happened, because it was a popular tune. So okay, well maybe that's the so-called formula that I find yet another popular tune, and do that. I also know that, coincidentally, I had done classical themes on record. We had done an arrangement of "Night on Bald Mountain" that got a lot of airplay. I think because it sounded a little different from what was going on out there. It also had an incredible drum track by Steve Gadd, who was at the beginning of his career, which stood out. But I was definitely one of those people who was made an artist by the producer. Creed Taylor had decided now that I was an artist. I didn't go in saying, "Okay, now I want a solo artist career." I just happened to be there. I was his staff arranger, and maybe he didn't have another project booked in the studio that month, and so now it's my time, you know?

But I had to decide what it was I wanted to do after that. How did I want to continue with this? And what am I as an artist? For a long time I had a big problem with that. I still think I have it today. It's hard for me to feature myself on my own records, because I have so much more fun when I'm featuring other people. Now I've got friends like Kirk Whalen who's a great young saxophonist, and I'm so comfortable when I'm comping behind Kirk or writing an arrangement for him, or whatever. And if I'm doing the same thing with Hubert Laws or if I'm doing it for Eric Gale, I know exactly what to do. But, although I'm not trying to sell my piano playing short, once I'm thinking of myself as a pianist, my head immediately turns to Oscar Peterson, or it turns to a hundred other people who I admire. And then I wonder, am I going far enough with actually playing the piano when I make my own albums?

You've got me psychoanalyzing myself, by the way. On microphone, and I'm not so sure that I'm comfortable with that either, but it's something I still think about a lot. How did all of this happen? And now it's fifteen years after that album [*Bob James One*] and I'm still doing it. But the artist identity came about, not in a deliberate way, it came about in a secondary kind of way. And I still think that as an artist, I'm more a combination arranger-keyboard player than I am a keyboard player.

Ben: Ah, fascinating. Because as an acoustic piano player myself, I'm very aware of how you set up the acoustic piano in your tracks, how you make a nice space for it, and how you feature it and give it a lot of weight. You don't minimalize the acoustic instrument.

Bob: I still derive by far the greatest pleasure from playing the acoustic piano. There is never any contest for me. Although there is tremendous power and creative potential from synthesizers and they're still getting better and better, but as a keyboard instrument, the area which remains highly undeveloped in the synthesizer world is the subtlety of action, all of the subtleties of the way the hammers hit the strings and the dampers come up off the strings, all those little fuzzy things that your feet do. And with synthesizers, you put the pedal down and it's either down or up, so the note either sustains or it doesn't sustain. And that's just one example of a whole world of subtlety about playing the acoustic piano that's completely different. So I still find myself wanting to gravitate back to it, even though the timbre of it is very often problematical with the synthesized music. How, if you bring the piano up too much, it's such a resonating, big and powerful instrument, that it tends to muddy up a track that's otherwise clean, and then if you bring the piano down so that you have a strong rhythm track, then the piano sounds puny.

Ben: That's an interesting point. In the world of music, we've really started to create digital space and digital time, and control it and break it down, and quantize it and subdivide it, and in the midst of this, when you interject a purely human element or a purely mechanical element or an acoustic element, you're in a very real way mixing apples and oranges.

Bob: Yeah, but mixing them in, for me, a totally necessary way. Because the more we go away into the world where the machine predominates, the colder it becomes.

Ben: The hungrier you get for the apples, if you got the oranges.

Bob: Yeah, we're humans. We're always gonna be human and we're gonna have human beings listening to this stuff, so that unless we are able to inject that humanity and that creativity and the heart and the warmth, it's gonna be incomplete. And I now find myself working a tremendous amount of time by myself, in a studio that is surrounded by synthesizers. And I work with a computer, and it's been very important to me, and I've paid a lot of dues trying to get to the point where I have some command over working in this idiom. But the thing that's missing, that I find that I continually want to have brought into it, is the injection of other personalities. And even if we were set up with six of us in a room, with six different synthesizer setups, that would be fun for me, because then the other five performers, the other five musicians, would bring their own quirks, their own things about it. But even more realistically, what I like to do now is make sure that I have those other talents in whatever form. That other drummer, that other saxophone player, that other person.

The computer sequencer has now become a major part of my composing life, and most of the compositions that I have done in the last year or two had been demoed into the computer so that all of the elements are there with me when I'm working at home, including the flute and the drums and the percussion, and everything. And what I have tended to do is give my version of what I think that I would ask a drummer or flute player or bass player to do, so that when we go in the studio, I'm not having to try to describe it by word of mouth. I can play my tape and say, "Okay, Alex, this is sort of it. Now you take from there and take it to the next level." And most of the time it's worked pretty well. Sometimes I think that it acts as an inhibitor rather than as a liberator for the musicians, and they feel, I get feedback coming back to me that there is an intimidation: "Well, you've already showed us what you wanted, and now we're a little bit afraid of going to far from that, even though we wouldn't have chosen to do that same thing."

But, selfishly, from the composer's standpoint, I'm able to get much closer to what I think that I wanted, and through the power of manipulation that I have with the computer, I also end up with pieces that are very different from what I would have written just sitting at the piano, writing a rhythm sketch out and taking it into the studio for the other players. It's more complicated in the sense of structure, because I don't worry about it. When it's in the computer, I just do it and if it turns out to be in the key of F-sharp or something, or whatever, I make my transpositions. I'm not thinking, "Gee, I'm gonna end up with a piece of music that's too complicated and the players are not gonna want to have to fight their way through reading this." So now I end up with this piece of music that exists. It's on tape. And instead of having to come in the studio with a chart, I can give them a demo tape. I think it's a really good way of working and there's no question that the composition is very different as a result of that process than it would have been six years ago.

Ben: One of the things that I hear is that there's a little bit more of you in it, somehow, with this new process. I'm not quite sure why, and one would be hesitant to say that relying on the machines is bringing you out. But given the fact that you are an arranger, and given the fact also that you've found a way to interject more of yourself as a player on the newer recordings, I see it as leading you more toward the *you* that's an artist.

Bob: I'm glad, because I'm fighting very hard for that, and I'm feeling it more. For one thing, it's both in the solos, which are improvised, and in the compositions, which are also in some sense improvised. When I turn on the computer recorder, I'm essentially just improvising. And, in the old days, I would improvise and keep repeating some little something or other, some thematic germ, and eventually write it down. And then it has a way of being different from how you improvised it. And sometimes in the writing-down process you lose whatever it was that was fun about that thing that you played. But being able to do it into a recorder, and have it come back at you exactly the way you played it, and then that is your composition, is a fascinating new process, which I really like, and I think that's probably the reason why it is more personal.

Ben: You know, this is interesting. Before, we were talking a little bit about Gil Evans. An observation you made was the importance to an arranger of having a soloist to hang an arrangement on. I mean, as an arranger, you'd like to believe that, in the abstract, it either works or it doesn't work. But truly, the soloist is what makes an arrangement work, and maybe this is a system whereby you can be both.

Bob: Yes, and if I can make that launching pad for myself the way I did it for so many years, and enjoyed doing it for other people, and still do, I can get through my intimidation while I'm still there in the practice room, without anybody watching me through the part of the process that may be clumsy.

I also think that as long as we keep our ears open and our tastes and everything, those of us who are working with these new machines, composing tools, recording tools, there are lots of things that we can take advantage of that we shouldn't feel guilty about. We shouldn't apologize for them or worry about it. We should worry about what comes out: the music. And there's lots of controversy about the purity of improvisation, for example. I've heard many people say that they find it to be offensive that, because of overdubbing, a soloist can go in a studio and do a hundred takes of a jazz solo, and pick the best one out of a hundred. And they say, "Well, this isn't really jazz, because jazz is spontaneous," and so forth. And that's true. It isn't *that type* of jazz. It isn't that piece that comes about as a result of that. It isn't the same piece that would've resulted from everything being done live and in one take.

But if you're a good critic of yourself, as the way I think the best soloists are, you know that if you were playing a whole series of concerts, or if you were playing in a nightclub for a month, there'd be a lot of solos that were a lot worse than a lot of your other solos. And that if you had the opportunity to pick your best solo out of a month's worth of live engagements, and have that be on a record for people to listen to, I think most artists would wanna choose that, rather than choose one that was maybe medium or in the lower end of the spectrum just because it was spontaneous and just because it happened. So, taking that to the next step, the moral dilemma that computers give us, I, for example, with this process that I'm using, can play a solo as many times as I want. I'm not even limited by the kind of 24-track format. In the computer, you play as many solos as you want, store all of them, chose your best one, and then you still can manipulate it. Let's say you like this great solo, except there's one note, and you wanted to choose another note. It's just a matter of going into the edit screen and choosing another note, or maybe play that note a little bit too loud. So you can go into the edit screen and make it a little bit less loud. Now it's even less spontaneous also, because you're mentally thinking about it, but it all boils down to choice. What is the choice? What do you choose to have people end up hearing?

Ben: Well, it comes down to capturing music versus manufacturing music. And even as recently as 1983, you were essentially capturing your arrangements, using different elements, and jamming the horn parts as the fade went out, and that sort of thing. Capturing moments, stringing them out. Now we're manufacturing music and we do seem to be at a critical juncture, because in a very few years, young people will have the wherewithal, at their own homes, to make tapes that will be absolutely on a par with professional recordings. And the investment will be minimal, and in many ways, their investment in the traditional musical skills will be minimal as well, certainly much less than what you prepared for 25 years ago at Michigan. How would you describe the crossroads that we're at?

Bob: It's a major dilemma for music educators. I've had a chance to talk to a few of them, and I have a close association with University of Michigan, where I went to school. And I was very happy to see that they've taken up the challenge, and have now developed a center for electronic music and computer music, and are investing in learning the knowledge of how to shift the role of music education into the twenty-first century. And how we face up as musicians to what the challenges are of this new technology which has arrived. It's there and if we look at it in an exciting way, it must be similar to what it must have been like for Beethoven and Mozart when the symphony orchestra was first established. And when inventors of musical instruments were coming up with a brass instrument with valves that could actually play in tune. That gave the composer an opportunity to write things that they didn't have the opportunity to do before, and as a result great music came out of it. Now we have a whole orchestra of the future in that sense. The rules are completely different.

And that's why it's hard for the educators to make the decision. They don't want to just suddenly say, "We're gonna throw away the conventional techniques of the past, just because they don't apply anymore."

Ben: Earlier today, when we were talking about Gil Evans and the importance of having a hook to hang an arrangement on, we were also talking about how the new technology is really changing, conceptually, what young people bring to the music. An analogy we talked about was telling time: if you have a digital watch, as opposed to an analog watch, you lose the concept of "clockwise" and "counter-clockwise" because there is no sweeping hand. The numbers just show up and there's the time. Which is fine. You've got the time, but if then you go to a device later on in life, and someone says, "Well, just turn it counter-clockwise," that doesn't have any meaning for you. So what do you suppose is the parallel in the music game now, when we've got this new equipment, and whatever key you're in is relative, or the tempo is relative, or all these things are relative? What do you think is the analog to this?

Bob: It's got to be the same problem. Anybody who has a computer synthesizer/sequencer type of setup knows that they no longer need to worry about transposition, which was one of the great theoretical hurdles that young music theory students always had to solve. Because on the computer sequencer you just hit the button that says transpose, and you can make it go to any key without having to do the mental pyrotechnics. The computer does it for you. The same thing with speed.

However, if you rely totally on that, then you have just gone one step further into reducing your own control and power over the machine. And I think maybe that might be a way that we old-timers can convince the young musicians of something that they should be concerned about, which is to have the knowledge, even if you choose to let the machine relieve you of some tedium. If you're doing it as a substitute for knowledge that you don't have, you are not in control of the machine. The machine is in control of you. If you make a transposition because you don't know how to transpose, you're admitting that you don't have control of this and if you let that creep into other areas of your music, suddenly you're making music and you're a musician who's lost control. So you don't have the ability to have the taste to make the necessary decisions. If you don't know *how* to transpose, how could you know *when* to transpose? That would be maybe one way of looking at it.

Ben: Interesting. Having control of the ability to do something is also having control of knowing when to do it. You lose control of time if you lose control of space.

Bob: Because, at least at this stage, our sequencer is still mindlessly doing whatever we tell it to do. So if we tell it to go from the key of C to the key of F, okay. Whether or not that has any emotional power at that particular moment in a composition is not of concern to the sequencer.

It just says, "Okay, you wanted to go to F, I'm gonna take you to F right now. It may sound lousy, it may be a disaster for your composition, but I'm gonna do it for you." And unless you know why you did that, and unless you've gone through the process of studying what key relationships are all about, and musical form and all of the conventional theory that allows you to make an intelligent decision about when and how to transpose, then you can't use the machine in its most powerful way and not just punch the buttons.

Ben: This sounds ominous even beyond the musical sphere.

Bob: Well, there's another danger about electronic computer music. It's that it is extremely time consuming once you get into it. And there's a kind of hypnotic, endless manipulation. It's always there waiting for you to do something. And you can find yourself going way into the middle of the night in a never-ending process.

So the beauty and the simplicity and the non-plugged in aspect of the acoustic piano is, I think, a good antidote for that.

Ben: So is this the beginning of the further adventures of Bob James the solo artist?

Bob: I hope there are some further adventures. I've always felt that it is not our place in the world, if you are the artist that is making the commitment to do something with either your music or your painting or your writing, or whatever you've chosen, it's not our place to decide what it is that we are. In my case, the listener decides what I do. And it's enough for me, just the day-to-day process of doing it. I just, I enjoy the process. I don't particularly enjoy the analysis of it too much. Whether I'm going in the right direction or the wrong direction, or whether I should be doing something else. I haven't really found that that's led anywhere for me. I just keep doing it. Some people say it isn't jazz, some people say it isn't classical, some people say it isn't this or that or whatever else. And I really don't worry about that.

* * *

Index

Entries in boldface indicate interview with that person. Subentries with "and" also refer to specific interviews.

Ben Sidran's career includes working as a performing and recording musician, producer, composer, host of radio and television music programs, music historian, and writer. He received his doctorate in American Studies from Sussex University and is the author of the critically acclaimed *Black Talk*, a sociological study of black music in America (also available from Da Capo Press). Throughout the '80s, he was a mainstay of National Public Radio's jazz coverage, hosting NPR's award-winning performance program "Jazz Alive" from 1981 to 1983, providing commentary and reviews for the nightly news program "All Things Considered" from 1983 to 1985, and producing his own weekly interview program "Sidran On Record" from 1985 through 1990. From 1991 through 1993, he was the host of the VH-1 television network's jazz program "New Visions." He has recorded over fifteen solo albums and has produced albums for such noted artists as Mose Allison, Jon Hendricks, and Diana Ross.

Other titles of interest

IN THE MOMENT
Jazz in the 1980s
Francis Davis
272 pp.
80708-4 $13.95

FACES IN THE CROWD
Musicians, Writers, Actors & Filmmakers
Gary Giddins
288 pp.
80705-X $13.95

ASCENSION
John Coltrane and his Quest
Eric Nisenson
298 pp.
80644-4 $13.95

BEYOND CATEGORY
The Life and Genius of Duke Ellington
John Edward Hasse
Foreword by Wynton Marsalis
480 pp., 119 illus.
80614-2 $15.95

BIRD: The Legend of Charlie Parker
Edited by Robert Reisner
256 pp., 50 photos
80069-1 $13.95

BIRD LIVES!
The High Life and Hard Times of Charlie (Yardbird) Parker
Ross Russell
431 pp., 32 photos
80679-7 $15.95

BLACK BEAUTY, WHITE HEAT
A Pictorial History of Classic Jazz, 1920–1950
Foreword by John Hammond
Frank Driggs and Harris Lewine
360 pp., 1,516 illus.
80672-X $29.95

BLACK TALK
Ben Sidran
228 pp., 16 photos
80184-1 $10.95

CELEBRATING THE DUKE and Louis, Bessie, Billie, Bird, Carmen, Miles, Dizzy & Other Heroes
Ralph J. Gleason
Foreword by Studs Terkel
New introduction by Ira Gitler
302 pp., 9 photos
80645-2 $13.95

CHASIN' THE TRANE
The Music and Mystique of John Coltrane
J. C. Thomas
256 pp., 16 pp. of photos
80043-8 $12.95

DEXTER GORDON
A Musical Biography
Stan Britt
192 pp., 32 photos
80361-5 $12.95

ELLA FITZGERALD
A Biography of the First Lady of Jazz
Stuart Nicholson
368 pp., 29 illus.
80642-8 $15.95

THE ENCYCLOPEDIA OF JAZZ
Leonard Feather
527 pp., over 200 photos
80214-7 $24.95

THE ENCYCLOPEDIA OF JAZZ IN THE 70s
Leonard Feather and Ira Gitler
400 pp., many photos
80290-2 $17.95

THE ENCYCLOPEDIA OF JAZZ IN THE 60s
Leonard Feather
312 pp., 200 photos
80263-5 $16.95

Printed in the United States
61752LVS00004B/27

9 780306 806131